THE EMPLOYMENT LAW LIBRARY FROM WILEY LAW PUBLICATIONS

AMERICANS WITH DISABILITIES ACT HANDBOOK (SECOND EDITION)
Henry H. Perritt, Jr.

AMERICANS WITH DISABILITIES ACT HANDBOOK FORMS AND PROCEDURES (SECOND EDITION)
Henry H. Perritt, Jr.

CIVIL RIGHTS ACT OF 1991: SPECIAL REPORT
Henry H. Perritt, Jr.

COVENANTS NOT TO COMPETE (SECOND EDITION)
Kurt H. Decker

DRAFTING AND REVISING EMPLOYMENT CONTRACTS
Kurt H. Decker and H. Thomas Felix II

DRUG-USE TESTING IN THE WORKPLACE: LAW AND SCIENCE
Kurt M. Dubowski and R. Slaton Tuggle III

EMPLOYEE DISMISSAL LAW: FORMS AND PROCEDURES (SECOND EDITION)
Allen J. Gross

EMPLOYEE DISMISSAL LAW AND PRACTICE (THIRD EDITION)
Henry H. Perritt, Jr.

EMPLOYEE PRIVACY LAW AND PRACTICE
Kurt H. Decker

EMPLOYMENT LAW FORMS DISK LIBRARY
Wiley Law Publications

INDEPENDENT CONTRACTOR STATUS: STATE BY STATE LEGAL GUIDE
Robert W. Wood

LEGAL GUIDE TO INDEPENDENT CONTRACTOR STATUS
Robert W. Wood

1994 WILEY EMPLOYMENT LAW UPDATE
Henry H. Perritt, Jr., Editor

PUBLIC EMPLOYEE DISCHARGE AND DISCIPLINE
Isidore Silver

REMEDIES IN EMPLOYMENT DISCRIMINATION LAW
Robert Belton

REPRESENTING PLAINTIFFS IN TITLE VII ACTIONS
Kent Spriggs

Sexual Harassment in the Workplace: Law and Practice (Second Edition)
Alba Conte

Tax Strategies in Hiring, Retaining, and Terminating Employees
Robert W. Wood

Workplace Torts: Rights and Liabilities
Henry H. Perritt, Jr.

SEXUAL HARASSMENT IN THE WORKPLACE

LAW AND PRACTICE

SECOND EDITION

VOLUME ONE

SUBSCRIPTION NOTICE

This Wiley product is updated on a periodic basis with supplements to reflect important changes in the subject matter. If you purchased this product directly from John Wiley & Sons, Inc., we have already recorded your subscription for this update service.

If, however, you purchased this product from a bookstore and wish to receive (1) the current update at no additional charge, and (2) future updates and revised or related volumes billed separately with a 30-day examination review, please send your name, company name (if applicable), address, and the title of the product to:

Supplement Department
John Wiley & Sons, Inc.
One Wiley Drive
Somerset, NJ 08875
1-800-225-5945

For customers outside the United States, please contact the Wiley office nearest you:

Professional and Reference Division
John Wiley & Sons Canada, Ltd.
22 Worcester Road
Rexdale, ONT M9W 1L1
CANADA
(416) 236-3580
Phone: 1-800-263-1590
Fax: 1-800-675-6599

John Wiley & Sons, Ltd.
Baffins Lane
Chichester
West Sussex, PO19 1UD
UNITED KINGDOM
Phone: (44) (243) 779777

Jacaranda Wiley Ltd.
PRT Division
P.O. Box 174
North Ryde, NSW 2113
AUSTRALIA
PHONE: (02) 805-1100
Fax: (02) 805-1597

John Wiley & Sons (SEA) Pte. Ltd.
37 Jalan Pemimpin
Block B # 05-04
Union Industrial Building
SINGAPORE 2057
Phone: (65) 258-1157

SEXUAL HARASSMENT IN THE WORKPLACE

LAW AND PRACTICE

SECOND EDITION

VOLUME ONE

ALBA CONTE
Portland, Oregon

Wiley Law Publications
JOHN WILEY & SONS, INC.
New York • Chichester • Brisbane • Toronto • Singapore

This text is printed on acid-free paper.

Library of Congress Cataloging-in-Publication Data

ISBN 0-471-01447-8 (v.1)
ISBN 0-471-01448-6 (v.2)
ISBN 0-471-01446-X (set)

Printed in the United States of America

10 9 8 7 6 5 4 3 2

For all the women who finally decided that enough was enough
and Jay

A.C.

PREFACE

In his foreword to "Tailhook 91", the report of the investigation of the events which took place at the 35th Annual Tailhook Symposium, the Inspector General of the Department of Defense summarized the inquiry which would leave the Navy debilitated and a nation reeling—not exactly from shock, but from the realization that sexual harassment is so widespread and insidious that laws alone will do little to eradicate such a cultural institution:

> In this report, . . . [w]e determined that at least 90 indecent assaults took place and a considerable amount of improper and indecent conduct occurred. Although our purpose is not to shock or offend readers or to sensationalize the accounts of the various incidents, there are sections of the report that contain graphic language. After considerable reflection regarding how best to present our findings, we determined that general descriptions and euphemisms failed to convey a full impression of the prevailing atmosphere in which the assaults took place.
>
> * * *
>
> It is important to understand that the events of Tailhook 91 did not occur in a historical vacuum. Similar behavior had occurred at previous conventions. The emerging pattern of some of the activities, such as the gauntlet, began to assume the aura of "tradition." There is even some evidence to suggest that Tailhook 91 was "tame" in comparison to earlier conventions. Although there were some attempts in past years to curb improper behavior, such attempts were ineffective. In fact, many of the younger officers who attended Tailhook 91 felt the excesses that occurred there were condoned by the Navy. This belief is understandable given that the Navy continued to support the Tailhook Association and the annual convention notwithstanding the knowledge on the part of many senior Navy leaders of significant misconduct that had taken place at prior conventions. More disturbingly, the evidence indicates that at least one former high-ranking civilian Navy officer engaged in lewd behavior at a prior Tailhook convention in front of junior officers. However, to be fair to those engaged in nonassaultive activities, such as indecent exposure and drunkenness, the reader must keep in mind that an atmosphere was permitted to develop over a period of years which encouraged officers to act in inappropriate ways.[1]

[1] Department of Defense, Inspector General, *Tailhook 91, Part 2: Events of the 35th Annual Tailhook Symposium* i (February, 1993).

Other nonassaultive conduct included the wearing of T-shirts which stated "Women are Property" and "He-man Women Hater's Club", live strip shows, and the shaving of women's legs and pubic areas.[2] Unfortunately, out of 140 cases stemming from the incident, not one person was court-martialed[3] and the female lieutenant who blew the whistle on the scandal resigned, allegedly because of continued harassment over Tailhook.[4]

Only one year earlier Anita Hill caught the world's attention with her allegations of sexual harassment by Supreme Court nominee Clarence Thomas. Although courts had been grappling with the issue for over 15 years, with coverage limited to legal journals and the occasional popular magazine, it took the Senate confirmation hearings to make sexual harassment household words. Anita Hill's stoic testimony gave a voice to thousands of harassed workers and may inspire others to come forward with stories of their own. But while the senators showed great interest in the substance of a pornographic movie and the decade-long silence of Ms. Hill, there was neither an analysis of the legal standard for sexual harassment, nor an examination of the motivations of the victim or the harasser. The fallout from the Clarence Thomas hearings had barely settled when the reality of sexual harassment once again took hold of the public's attention by the Tailhook revelations. After the Navy incident, Senator Alan Cranston (D-Cal.), calling sexual harassment "one of our deepest military secrets," introduced legislation to provide support and treatment for victims of Tailhook. Subsequently, the Veterans Administration announced that sexual harassment in the military has been so pervasive and has left such deep scars that it planned to offer group therapy to female veterans for the first time.

What is clear is that the Thomas hearings and media attention to the issue of sexual harassment accelerated the passage of the Civil Rights Act of 1991, the product of a two-year struggle between Congress and the White House. This law will have an enormous impact on the employment discrimination bar. It overturns eight Supreme Court rulings and amends five civil rights statutes. The Act will encourage victims of sexual harassment to take advantage of federal remedies by, among other things, providing for compensatory and punitive damages for victims of employment discrimination. It allows a plaintiff to choose a jury trial in cases seeking damages and the payment to a prevailing party of expert witness fees as part of reasonable attorney fees. United States Senate employees and political appointees of the executive branch are now protected by Title VII.

---

2 *Id.* VIII-1 to 4.

3 "Last Tailhook Convention Case Dropped," The Oregonian, February 10, 1994 at A10, Col. 1.

4 J. Taylor, "Lieutenant Who Blew Tailhook Whistle Quits," The Oregonian, February 11, 1994 at A12, Col. 5.

This book reviews the history and state of sexual harassment law, surveys the options available to the sexual harassment claimant, and guides their attorneys through administrative and judicial proceedings. It provides a state-by-state breakdown of relevant common and statutory law and discusses issues unique to the area of sexual harassment. The number of court opinions generated by sexual harassment claims have increased exponentially since the publication of the first edition, and I have tried to incorporate as many of those decisions as possible in an area where common threads are intertwined with disparate facts, and where even judges who are careful to articulate the law in this politically charged realm may reach a conclusion from stereotypical notions of the relationships between men and women. As I noted in the first edition, most sexual harassment victims are women; although men have brought these suits and such actions do fit within the traditional employment discrimination framework, the psychological context that gives rise to the challenged conduct is not gender neutral. Thus, in this book a victim generally will be referred to as "she" and an alleged harasser as "he." This is not to diminish the power of authority, regardless of gender. A female superior has the power to make someone's life just as miserable as would a male superior. However, given physiological and psychological realities and the nature of today's workforce, almost all sexual harassment plaintiffs are women. Hopefully the force of law and societal awareness will not only help curb incidents of sexual harassment but will result in patterns of conduct which will inspire genuine respect among coworkers.

Portland, Oregon
February 1994

ALBA CONTE

ACKNOWLEDGMENTS

I began searching for a publisher for this book in 1984 when sexual harassment in the workplace had already inspired a number of court opinions, but had neither found its way to the Supreme Court nor had given enough workers pause to realize that this was a problem that had to be addressed before women could achieve economic or social parity. In 1988 Mary Hope, a former senior editor at Wiley Law Publications called and asked if I was still interested in such a project. We proceeded with the book and although I was confident that we as a nation had just begun to hear about sexual harassment, little did we know that the issue shortly would be thrust to the forefront of societal consciousness. But Mary had faith in the project even before Clarence Thomas, Bob Packwood, and the Tailhook convention caught America's attention, and I'll thank her for that for the rest of my life. Carol Gross has been my liaison for the second edition, and I thank her for her help and friendly nature. Jay Giliberty was indispensable as my paralegal and assistant.

I would also again like to thank the attorneys who contributed their pleadings and encouragement to both the first and second editions of this book. These include Jane Lang, S. Beville May, Susan Winshall, Charles R. Ashman, Rory Divin, Patricia C. Benassi, Ellen Robinson, A. Richard Gear, Patricia Shiu, Paul Sunderland and others.

Finally, I would like to thank my friend and mentor, the late attorney and author Herbert B. Newberg, whose only flaw was leaving us thirty years too soon.

A.C.

ABOUT THE AUTHOR

Alba Conte graduated summa cum laude from Douglass College of Rutgers University and received her law degree from the University of Pennsylvania Law School, where she received the Alice Paul Award for outstanding contributions to the status of women at the university, and edited several publications about women and the law. She is co-author of *Newberg on Class Actions,* a six-volume treatise now in its third edition, the author of *Attorney Fee Awards, 2d ed.,* a book covering common fund and statutory fees as well as fee sanctions, a contributing author to the 1992 and 1993 editions of *Wiley Employment Law Update* (John Wiley & Sons, Inc.), and the author of several articles.

SUMMARY CONTENTS

DETAILED CONTENTS

Volume 1

SHORT REFERENCE LIST

Short reference	***Full reference***
EEO	Equal Employment Opportunity
EEOC	Equal Employment Opportunity Commission
EEOC Guidelines	EEOC Guidelines on Discrimination Because of Sex, 29 C.F.R. § 1604.11 (1993)
EEOC Policy Guidance	EEOC Policy Guidance on Current Issues of Sexual Harassment
FEP	Fair Employment Practice
§ 1983	42 U.S.C. § 1983 (1988)
Title VII	Title VII of the 1964 Civil Rights Act

CHAPTER 1

SEXUALITY, SOCIAL RELATIONS, AND THE WORKPLACE

§ 1.1 Introduction

In late 1980, the United States Merit Systems Protection Board directed the first broad-scale study of sexual harassment within the federal government.[1] The board is an independent, quasi-judicial agency that decides appeals from personnel actions against federal employees and evaluates the effectiveness of the civil service and other merit systems. The study found that 42 percent of all women and 15 percent of all men surveyed experienced some form of sexual harassment. In 1986, the board conducted a follow-up study to determine if explicit directives to government agencies and increased social attention to the problem had reduced its incidence.[2] The results were startling. Although the respondents showed increased sensitivity to the type of conduct that may be considered sexual harassment, there was no substantial change in the percentage of federal employees who said that they had experienced some form of uninvited and unwanted sexual attention.[3] The level of harassment remained constant despite implementation of Equal Employment

[1] United States Merit Systems Protection Board, Sexual Harassment in the Federal Workplace—Is It a Problem? (1981). The board surveyed 23,000 federal employees.

[2] United States Merit Systems Protection Board, Sexual Harassment in the Federal Government: An Update (1988) [hereinafter Merit Board survey].

[3] *Id.* at 16. Males experiencing sexual harassment dropped from 15% to 14%.

Opportunity Commission (EEOC) guidelines (see **Chapter 2**), a tremendous rise in the number of sexual harassment charges filed with the EEOC,[4] a 1986 Supreme Court decision clarifying the problem (see **Chapter 2**),[5] and federal efforts to combat harassment through training programs and policy statements during the seven-year period between the two surveys. The study found no clear correlation between any agency's estimates of its training efforts, which varied among agencies and was not evenly distributed among all employees, and the reported incidence of sexual harassment. Employees who had worked both in and outside the federal government reported that sexual harassment in the government was no greater a problem than outside this sector. Most respondents indicated awareness of their agency's sexual harassment policies and the available internal complaint procedures.[6]

The survey confirmed the findings of previous research. Of the 9,000 women who voluntarily responded to one of the first surveys on workplace sexual harassment in the mid-1970s, 9 out of 10 women had experienced sexual harassment.[7] *Redbook* magazine, which conducted this study, later joined with *Harvard Business Review* to survey 7,408 managers, 63 percent of whom said there was sexual harassment at their companies.[8] In a survey by the United Nations Ad Hoc Groups on Equal Rights for Women, 51 percent of women interviewed had either suffered or witnessed sexual harassment on the job.[9] A study of women in the traditionally male fields of engineering, science, and management revealed that 75 percent of the respondents had experienced one or more types of harassment.[10]

---

4 Correspondence, Office of the EEOC, Aug. 16, 1988, and Aug. 15, 1989.

5 Meritor Sav. Bank v. Vinson, 477 U.S. 57 (1986).

6 Merit Board survey at 25.

7 C. Safran, *What Men Do to Women on the Job: A Shocking Look at Sexual Harassment,* Redbook, Nov. 1976, at 149.

8 E.G.C. Collins & T.B. Blodgett, *Sexual Harassment: Some See It . . . Some Won't,* 59 Harv. Bus. Rev. 76 (Mar.–Apr. 1981).

9 B.A. Gutek, Sex and the Workplace 46 (1985) (53% of respondents had experienced sexual harassment); *see also* B. Glass, *Workplace Harassment and the Victimization of Women,* 11 Women's Stud. Int'l F. 56 (1988) (45% of 607 women randomly selected in Forsyth County, N.C., had experienced at least one unwanted sexual advance; women's average age was 40.36 years).

10 E. Lafontaine & L. Tredeau, *The Frequency, Sources, and Correlates of Sexual Harassment Among Women in Traditional Male Occupations,* 15 Sex Roles 433, 436 (1986). *See also* B.E. Schneider, *Consciousness About Sexual Harassment Among Heterosexual and Lesbian Women Workers,* 38 J. Soc. Issues 75 (1982); B.A. Gutek & B. Morasch, *Sex-Ratios, Sex-Role Spillover and Sexual Harassment of Women at Work,* 38 J. Soc. Issues 55 (1982). *Cf.* T.C. Fain & D.L. Anderton, *Sexual Harassment, Organizational Context and Diffuse Status,* 17 Sex Roles 291, 303 (1987) (harassment occurred or was reported more frequently in female-prominent groups).

Studies show a significant disparity between the actual rate of sexual harassment and the number of complaints received by human resources professionals. A 1988 *Working Woman* survey of sexual harassment in the Fortune 500 service and manufacturing companies found that few incidents of harassment were reported to employers.[11] The formal complaint rate for a one year period was a scant 1.4 per 1,000 women employees.[12] In a chief executive officer survey by the Portland *Oregonian,* 50 percent of the 202 respondents said they seldom receive sexual harassment complaints and 35 percent indicated that they never have complaints.[13] However, 57 percent were only somewhat knowledgeable about sexual harassment regulations, and only 40 percent had educated their employees on the subject. Of those who did educate their employees, only 17 percent conducted formal training. Although 86 percent of the *Working Woman* respondents believed that mandatory training programs helped prevent sexual harassment, only 58 percent actually offered such training.[14]

A recent study of gender bias in the federal court system found that women lawyers, clients, and employees face bias and harassment ranging from subtle comments to "groping under the conference table."[15] In a survey of more than 230 judges and 3,500 lawyers in the Ninth Circuit, 60 percent of the women lawyers stated that they had been the target of unwanted sexual advances or other forms of harassment by lawyers, clients, judges, or other court personnel.

Finally, the magnitude of the problem is underscored by the steady increase in sexual harassment charges filed with the EEOC since 1980, when the commission published amendments to its Guidelines on Discrimination Because of Sex. In 1980, only 75 complaints were filed with the EEOC.[16] Complaints rose to 7,495 from October 1991 through June 1992, compared with 4,962 during the same period the previous year.[17]

What explains the tenacious grasp sexual harassment has on the workplace? An increased awareness of what constitutes sexual harassment and of the informal and legal avenues of relief may account for affirmative responses from some employees who would not have reported similarly in

---

11 Klein Assocs., 1988 Working Woman Sexual Harassment Survey Executive Report (1988) [hereinafter Working Woman survey].

12 *Id.* at 10.

13 D. Sorenson, *Survey Finds Few Sexual Harassment Cases in Oregon,* The Oregonian, June 25, 1989, at D4, col. 1.

14 Working Woman survey at 15.

15 S. Torry, *60% of Women Attorneys Harassed, Study of Circuit Court System Shows,* The Oregonian, Aug. 5, 1992, at A9, col. 1.

16 Correspondence, Office of the EEOC, Aug. 16, 1988, and Aug. 15, 1989.

17 M. Blackmun, *Hill Inspires U.S. to Fight Harassment on the Job,* The Oregonian, Oct. 10, 1992, at E1, col. 1.

1980, but positive efforts on the part of the federal government to reduce sexual harassment should have more than corrected this disparity. To reconcile these results and those of numerous other studies that show that sexual harassment is still a pervasive force in the workplace, one must examine the relationship of socialization, sex roles, and power.

§ 1.2 Sex Roles and Workplace Relations

Despite legal efforts to improve their status, women have continued to dominate less prestigious and lower paying occupations. For example, in 1972, 99.1 percent of all secretaries were women. In 1990, the percentage decreased to 99 percent. Registered nurses who were women decreased only from 97.6 percent in 1972 to 94.5 percent in 1990.[18] The number of women in skilled trades rose only slightly during the five-year period ending in 1988. The 1.2 million women working as precision production, craft, and repair workers represented only 8.7 percent of such workers in 1988, compared with 8.1 percent in 1983.[19] In the construction trades, only 2 percent were women, about the same as 1983.[20]

Often women are received with hostility in traditionally male jobs,[21] find the climb to higher positions long and lonely, and earn far less than their male colleagues. In 1988, for workers receiving hourly wages, women's median hourly earnings were 74 percent of men's; for full-time wage and salary workers, women's median weekly earnings were 70 percent of men's; and median annual earnings were 66 percent of men's annual earnings.[22] In 1979, a woman lawyer earned 55 cents for every dollar a male lawyer earned; by 1986, the ratio had shrunk by only 8 cents.[23] Table 1-1 presents the disparity seen in all types of jobs:

---

[18] U.S. Dep't of Labor, Bureau of Labor Statistics, *Working Women: A Chartbook*, Bulletin 2385 at 43 (Aug. 1991).

[19] Facts on Working Women, *Women in the Skilled Trades—A Five-Year Review*, No. 90-5 (Women's Bureau, U.S. Dep't of Labor, Jan. 1991).

[20] *Id.*

[21] E. Lafontaine & L. Tredeau, *The Frequency, Sources, and Correlates of Sexual Harassment Among Women in Traditional Male Occupations*, 15 Sex Roles 433 (1986).

[22] Facts on Working Women, *Earning Differences Between Women and Men*, No. 90-3 (Women's Bureau, U.S. Dep't of Labor, Oct. 1990).

[23] Bureau of the Census, U.S. Dep't of Commerce, *Male-Female Differences in Work Experience, Occupation, and Earnings: 1984*, Series P-70, No. 10, at 5 (1987).

Table 1-1

Comparison of Female Jobs by Percentage of Male Median Earnings

Occupation	1983	1989
Accountants	60	72
Bookkeepers	79.1	83.8
Computer programmers	82.7	83.1
Engineers	82.8	85.7
Guards	80.6	86.4
Janitors	81	85.1
Registered nurses	99.5	89.7[24]
Sales reps, except retail	71.1	84.5
Teachers, except college	84.9	85.6[25]

Sexual harassment is a major consequence of gender stratification in the workplace. Studies show that sexist behavior is most likely to occur in organizational cultures that specifically value characteristics traditionally attributed to men, and when power is supported by instrumental and social cliques.[26] According to feminist analysts, sexual harassment is one aspect of a patriarchal system in which values are male-defined, and men possess greater sexual and economic power. As Catherine MacKinnon describes it:

> Sexual harassment, most broadly defined, refers to the unwanted imposition of sexual requirements in the context of a relationship of unequal power. Central to the concept is the use of power derived from one social sphere to lever benefits or impose deprivations in another. The major dynamic is best expressed as the reciprocal enforcement of two inequalities. When one is sexual, the other material, the cumulative sanction is particularly potent.[27]

Harassment may be blatant, as when a supervisor conditions a subordinate's job benefit on compliance with sexual advances. It can also be more subtle, through the creation of a hostile atmosphere that systematically erodes women's spirits and threatens their personal development. The power dynamics are more obvious in the situation when the harasser has actual

---

24 Note that as more men entered this field, women's relative earnings decreased.

25 Facts on Working Women, *Earning Differences Between Women and Men,* No. 90-3 (Women's Bureau, U.S. Dep't of Labor, Oct. 1990). *See also* F.S. Coles, *Forced to Quit: Sexual Harassment Complaints and Agency Response,* 14 Sex Roles 81, 83 (1986) ("women typically work in jobs . . . that are extensions of their female role and men assume sexual receptivity is part of that role").

26 J. Acker, *Hierarchies, Jobs, Bodies: A Theory of Gendered Organizations,* 4 Gender & Soc'y 139–58 (1990).

27 C. MacKinnon, Sexual Harassment of Working Women 1 (1979).

authority to alter a subordinate's job status, but the actions of coworker harassers may fit into this paradigm if viewed as punitive in nature and/or conducted in response to: (1) a perception of male/female relations generally, (2) the integration of women into the labor force or traditionally male jobs, or (3) the rejection by women of "wife and mother" as primary or sole social roles.

Sexual harassment degrades women by reinforcing their historically subservient role in the workplace. Women are taught to downplay their talents, lower their expectations, and feel that recognition is undeserved. Many women do not perceive harassing behavior as such because it is merely an extension of conduct experienced outside the workplace. Even women who do recognize certain conduct as harassment often learn to take it in stride. Nevertheless, each episode of harassment further diminishes a woman's sense of control and increases her frustration, as the conduct occurs regardless of work performance and, often, in spite of repeated complaints. When work performance is impaired, it often can be attributed to the harassment itself. A number of courts have recognized this self-fulfilling prophecy in finding that a defendant's asserted basis for firing an alleged victim of sexual harassment—her poor work performance—was pretextual (see **Chapters 6** and **7**).

Sexual harassment can be compared to other types of victimization that women experience. Some social scientists maintain that rape and sexual harassment are conceptually similar, rape being an extreme on a continuum of male-aggressive/female-passive interaction.[28] They contend that battering, sexual abuse, rape, and date rape all are expressions of power and sexuality in a male-dominated society. Because of this gender stratification, societal response to these crimes has focused on the victim's role in the perpetrator's conduct. Whether the alleged conduct was welcome is a key factor in determining sexual harassment. Women who fear antagonizing a superior may attempt to thwart the harassment in a way that gives the appearance of complicity. Skeptics look for evidence to support the widespread belief that women get what they ask for—noting the complainant's choice of dress, use of sexually oriented language, interactions with men in the office, and relationships outside the office. Studies show that any prior relationship between a victim and her harasser significantly diminishes the perception that sexual harassment occurred.[29] Like battered women, victims of sexual harassment often must overcome the societal presumption that if things were so bad, they would have left their jobs long ago.

---

[28] *See, e.g.*, M.A. Groth, Men Who Rape: The Psychology of the Offender (1978); A. Medea & K. Thompson, Against Rape (1974).

[29] T. Reilly, *The Factorial Survey: An Approach to Defining Sexual Harassment on Campus*, 38 J. Soc. Issues 99–110 (1982). *See also* A. Cohen & B.A. Gutek, *Dimensions of Perception of Social Sexual Behavior in a Work Setting*, 13 Sex Roles 326 (1985).

The implications of this feminist perspective may affect the approach to eradicating sexual harassment. The notion that individual incidents of harassment are aberrations in an otherwise egalitarian environment places sexual harassment in easily identifiable compartments and fails to recognize the enduring imbalance between the sexes that produces subtle, but pernicious, types of harassment, such as calling women *girls* while referring to men as *men.* Being careful to not offend is not the same as changing attitudes. The Merit Board Survey findings support the argument that sexual harassment is a response to the more global problem of male/female relations, and victimization stems from such dysfunction rather than individual incidents of harassment.

§ 1.3 The Victims

No group of women has escaped sexual harassment. One study of charges filed in a county office in the California Fair Employment and Housing Department "challenge[d] the assumption that sexual harassment victims are [predominantly] young."[30] Forty-one of the complainants were under 29 and 33 of the complainants were over 30. The Merit Board survey (see **§ 1.1**) found that women who are single or divorced, are between the ages of 20 and 44, have some college education, have a nontraditional job, or work in a predominantly male environment or for a male supervisor have the greatest chance of being sexually harassed, but that harassment occurs among women and men of all ages, backgrounds, and job categories.[31] Another study showed that certain types of sexual advances were more likely to be aimed at certain groups of women.[32] For example, women who were younger, never

---

30 F.S. Coles, *Forced to Quit: Sexual Harassment Complaints and Agency Response,* 14 Sex Roles 81, 91 (1986).

31 Merit Board survey at 20. Studies also indicate that women with feminist attitudes are more likely to be sexually harassed or to report such harassment.

> This link between sex role attitudes and reporting harassments should not be interpreted to mean that harassment is any less real. Some would argue that most reports of sexual harassment come from feminists who are "oversensitive," and exaggerate an insignificant interaction out of proportion. . . . However, an equally likely explanation is that feminists are simply more aware of the structural causes of harassment; therefore they are less likely to interpret a man's advance as idiosyncratic or personal, and are more likely to report it as harassment. Alternatively, it may be that women who are perceived by men as "libbers" may in fact be subject to more harassment in that these women are seen as threatening and in more acute need of being "put in their place."

B. Glass, *Workplace Harassment and the Victimization of Women,* 11 Women's Stud. Int'l F. 56, 64 (1988).

32 B. Glass, *Workplace Harassment and the Victimization of Women,* 11 Women's Stud. Int'l F. 59 (1988).

married, or divorced were more likely to receive unwelcome looks, gestures, teasing, joking, touching, cornering, and phone calls, and younger, married women were more often pressured for dates.[33] The sexual pursuit of unmarried women "is likely considered more acceptable by males and provides a context in which sexual harassment may be rationalized as normal courtship behavior."[34] Young women are more vulnerable targets because they tend to be less educated, less likely to be married, less likely to be supervisors, and less aware of sexual harassment.[35]

A study focusing on the disparagement and sexual harassment (through sexual advances) of women lawyers in the private and public sectors showed that women in the private sector, particularly in law firms, and particularly those women who were in token positions, were most likely to experience sexual harassment.[36] Although neither age nor marital status had consistent effects when crossed with public or private workplaces, in the private sector, "being young virtually ensured that women would be disparaged, and being married provided protection from unwanted advances."[37] Women who considered themselves careerists rather than feminists reported significantly more sexual harassment. In this study, Professor Rosenberg addressed the curious result that in private firms, older women were as likely to be harassed as younger women were, and noted that one explanation is that harassment is not primarily sexual behavior but a form of aggression aimed at stabilizing gender stratification and thus if this were true the age of the target would be immaterial. Marriage, on the other hand, may provide protection for those women already "taken" by other men who by reason of marriage are seen to have legitimate claims to them as sexual property.

Rosenberg noted that because of the increased number of women in private sector locations and changing societal values, one might have expected less resistance to women than she found in her study, but that more than 10 years ago, researchers posited that increasing numbers of women in law and other professions might be viewed as intruders and a significant threat to men who "then evoke subtle but effective strategies for protecting the boundaries of their domains,"[38] such as discrimination and harassment.

---

[33] *Id. See also* E. Lafontaine & L. Tredeau, *The Frequency, Sources, and Correlates of Sexual Harassment Among Women in Traditional Male Occupations,* 15 Sex Roles 433, 436 (1986) (single and divorced women experienced significantly higher levels of all but the most severe forms of harassment).

[34] T.C. Fain & D.L. Anderton, *Sexual Harassment, Organizational Context and Diffuse Status,* 17 Sex Roles 291, 303 (1987).

[35] *Id.*

[36] J. Rosenberg, *Now That We Are Here: Discrimination, Disparagement, and Harassment at Work and the Experience of Women Lawyers,* 7 Gender & Soc'y 415 (1993).

[37] *Id.* at 428.

[38] *Id.* at 430.

> If aggression is a defensive response to women as intruders, that does not necessarily mean that all women are equally vulnerable. Some women appear to be safer targets than others. A safe-target explanation may apply to women in structurally isolated positions, such as tokens and solo practitioners. But it also may explain why twice as many careerist as opposed to feminist orientations report that they have been harassed. The explanation may lie in the public persona and the messages unintentionally conveyed by women with different professional orientations. . . . [Careerists] behave as if the fiction of the gender neutrality of the lawyer's role is a reality, as if gender is inconsequential to their careers, and as if it does not shape their relationship to men and other women at work. Their willingness to view the class structure of the profession as a meritocracy resulting from open competition without acknowledging the handicaps of being women, may in fact, be inadvertently sending the wrong message to men, making these lawyers more, rather than less, vulnerable to sexual overtures.
>
> In the absence of a moderating organizational climate in which affirmative action is enforced and universal principles for the allocation of rewards applied, men may believe that careerists, anxious to compete and observant of other professional rules authored by men, have too much at stake to publicly expose them, that they will go along with the professional and social norms that encourage tacit compliance and discourage women from reporting harassment.[39]

Research also indicates that women in traditional and nontraditional jobs are harassed in different ways by different types of harassers. The harassment of women in traditional fields often involves the threat of discharge for failing to comply with sexual demands,[40] while women in nontraditional jobs were more likely to experience a hostile work environment.[41]

§ 1.4 The Response

During a recent two year period, over 36,000 federal employees quit their jobs, were fired, were transferred, or were reassigned because of sexual harassment.[42] The Merit Board (see **§ 1.1**) found that although most federal employees are aware of formal remedies for handling sexual harassment complaints, only 5 percent of both female and male victims took advantage of them. Most found their attempts nonproductive.[43] In fact, victims were just

---

39 *Id.* 429–30.

40 F.S. Coles, *Forced to Quit: Sexual Harassment Complaints and Agency Response,* 14 Sex Roles 81–95 (1986).

41 B.A. Gutek & A.G. Cohen, *Sex Ratios, Sex Role Spillover, and Sex at Work: A Comparison of Men's and Women's Experiences,* 40 Hum. Rel. 97–115 (1987).

42 United States Merit Protection Board (1987).

43 Merit Board survey at 25–27.

as likely to change jobs as a result of the sexual harassment as they were to take formal action. Among women employees, 52 percent of victims did nothing about the harassment, 43 percent avoided the harasser, 44 percent asked the harasser to stop, 20 percent made a joke of the behavior, 14 percent threatened to tell or told others, 15 percent reported the behavior to management, 4 percent went along with the behavior, 2 percent transferred, disciplined, or gave a poor performance rating to the harasser, and 10 percent did something else.[44]

In *Robinson v. Jacksonville Shipyards, Inc.,*[45] the court made findings of fact regarding women's response to sexually harassing behavior, based on the opinion of an expert in the sexual harassment area:

> [W]omen respond to sexually harassing behavior in a variety of ways. The coping strategy a woman selects depends on her personal style, the type of incident, and her expectation that the situation is susceptible to resolution. . . . Typical coping methods include: (1) denying the impact of the event, blocking it out; (2) avoiding the workplace or the harasser, for instance, by taking sick leave or otherwise being absent; (3) telling the harasser to stop; (4) engaging in joking or other banter in the language of the workplace in order to defuse the situation; and (5) threatening to make or actually making an informal or formal complaint.[46]

Avoiding a harasser is much easier than confronting a harasser. A recent U.S. Navy study reported that 51 percent of women officers and 68 percent of enlisted women used this approach.[47] Ignoring sexual harassment, especially the more subtle types, may lead to continued or worse harassment.[48] Coping strategies are not always effective. Unfortunately, the ultimate form of avoidance is resignation, and ultimately, this is the choice many women make.[49]

Why have victims of sexual harassment been so reluctant to complain? There are a number of reasons. First, sexual harassment, like other forms of sexual abuse, is often humiliating. An admission of harassment might suggest that the complainant did something to invite the conduct. Second, workers often feel that complaints are futile. Charges of sexual harassment are

---

44 *Id.* at 24 (a number of those surveyed took more than one action).

45 760 F. Supp 1486 (M.D. Fla. 1991).

46 *Id.* at 1506.

47 A.L. Culbertson, Assessment of Sexual Harassment in the Navy: Results of the 1989 Navy-wide Survey, TR-92-11 (Navy Personnel Research and Development Center, San Diego, CA).

48 J. Cleveland & M. Kerst, *Sexual Harassment and Perceptions of Power: An Under-Articulated Relationship,* 42 J. Vocational Behav. 49, 59 (1993).

49 B. Gutek & M. Koss, *Changed Women and Changed Organizations: Consequences of and Coping with Sexual Harassment,* 42 J. Vocational Behav. 42, 38 (1993).

often ignored or downplayed.[50] The Merit Board survey noted that the length of time for disposition could be a factor. Agencies reported that it took an average of 482 days to process a sexual harassment charge.[51] Third, a complainant often faces hostility, increased harassment, or other forms of retaliation, including discharge.[52] A complainant who is not fired may be ignored, be called a whore or lesbian, or have her work sabotaged. She is often driven to resigning.[53] The sexual harassment victim in *Bundy v. Jackson,*[54] received a double blow, when a supervisor responded to her complaint with the suggestion that "any man in his right mind would want to rape you."[55]

The complainant may feel betrayed by male coworkers who did not participate in the harassment but who did not perceive the conduct as improper or illegal, and by women coworkers who may have empathized in private but feared coming forward. Incidents often are interpreted or reinterpreted as horseplay or joking around by coworkers, rather than sexual harassment, for fear of retribution.

Ignoring the conduct does not make it go away. Seventy-one percent of the female federal employees who did nothing about their sexual harassment reported that ignoring the problem did not help. Only 16 percent of the women who went along with the behavior found that it improved their situation. Most effective was direct confrontation, but only 61 percent of the women who asked or told their harassers to stop reported improved conditions, and only 55 percent of those who threatened to tell or who told others of the harassment succeeded in stopping the conduct. Victims of sexual harassment in the U.S. Navy found that when they complained to their harassers, in most cases, the conduct ceased.[56] Avoiding the perpetrator worked for 45 percent of the harassed women. Victims of harassment who fail to complain to proper authorities may have difficulty establishing a prima facie case of sexual harassment if they subsequently choose to pursue legal remedies (see **Chapter 7**).

---

50 Filing a charge with the government, however, may be more promising. In the study of charges filed in a county office of the California Fair Employment and Housing Department, 42 of the 88 cases were settled by the agency in less than three months. Only 21 cases were withdrawn or denied by the agency, and 18 complainants chose to go on to court action; F.S. Coles, *Forced to Quit: Sexual Harassment Complaints and Agency Response,* 14 Sex Roles 81 (1986).

51 Merit Board survey at 35.

52 Retaliatory discharge is a common response to complaints of sexual harassment although retaliation is illegal under Title VII of the 1964 Civil Rights Act. See **Chs. 3** and **6.**

53 Victims of sexual harassment who quit their jobs often bring charges of constructive discharge along with sexual harassment claims. See **Chs. 3, 6,** and **9.**

54 641 F.2d 934 (D.C. Cir. 1981).

55 *Id.* at 940.

56 J. Cleveland & M. Kerst, *Sexual Harassment and Perceptions of Power: An Under-Articulated Relationship,* 42 J. Vocational Behav. 49, 59 (1993).

§ 1.5 The Effects

Sexual harassment has debilitating consequences. Most obvious is the immediate economic impact on the victim whose job status has been altered. A Working Women Institute study found that 24 percent of sexual harassment victims were fired for complaining of the conduct.[57] Another 42 percent left jobs when they were being harassed, either because they could not stop the harassment or because they were retaliated against for their complaints. Few women can afford the consequences they can expect: loss of income and seniority, a disrupted work history, a blot on their employment record, lack of references, difficulties in obtaining workers' compensation or unemployment benefits, family dysfunction, and loss of self-esteem, creativity, and productivity. The impact of sexual harassment on a woman's job performance is not as clear as the impact on her physiological and psychological states. Less evident at first, yet more far-reaching, is the emotional toll of sexual harassment. State and federal courts have repeatedly recognized the psychological impact of harassment. State common law claims of intentional infliction of emotional distress often accompany suits under Title VII of the 1964 Civil Rights Act. Sexual harassment victims often suffer a range of stress-related symptoms and illnesses from headaches, nausea, and insomnia, to posttraumatic stress disorder. In *Stockett v. Tolin,*[58] a female employee in a film industry training program was subjected to a hostile environment when a managing agent harassed her physically and verbally for over a year. Among other things, the defendant put his arms around the plaintiff from behind, pressed his body up against her and said that he'd love to eat her all up, repeatedly pressed down on her shoulders while she sat in a chair so that she could not get up, then squeezed her breasts, walked into the women's room while the plaintiff was changing her clothes, twice stuck his tongue in her ear and told her that he wanted to have sex with her, repeatedly cornered her and ran his hands over her nipples, saying "You like that, don't you?," constantly grabbed her buttocks, and finally told the plaintiff: "Fuck me or you're fired." The plaintiff subsequently resigned. The court found that the plaintiff did not in any way encourage the advances; on the contrary, she repeatedly pushed the defendant away and told him to stop, avoided him, and tried never to be alone with him. The plaintiff's account of a pervasively hostile work environment was corroborated by the testimony of many other female employees at the defendant companies. The plaintiff had been warned that the defendant liked "young girls" and she warned others. The plaintiff suffered severe emotional distress as a result of the harassment, including sleep disturbances, depression, loss of energy, general anxiety, a sense of

---

[57] Working Women's Institute, The Impact of Sexual Harassment on the Job: A Profile of the Experiences of 92 Women, Research Series Rep. No. 3 (1979).

[58] 791 F. Supp. 1536 (S.D. Fla. 1992).

uncertainty, anger, and an inability to trust men. The plaintiff presented expert testimony by a clinical psychologist regarding both the psychological effects of her experience and why she tolerated the sexual advances. The expert testified that:

> Sexual harassment is an example of a process known as victimization that ranges from the consequences of rape to family violence to spouse abuse to sexist slurs and low grade mistreatment of others. In less violent, more chronic situations, such as those that he opined occurred in this case, a person slowly evolves a sense of helplessness in coping with the situation. This results in anxiety, depression, feelings of personal incompetence, loss of a sense of self confidence and worth, and the inability to develop strategies for handling the treatment.[59]

See **Chapter 9** for additional information on emotional and psychological injuries.[60]

In *Robinson v. Jacksonville Shipyards, Inc.,*[61] the court made findings of fact based on the testimony of an expert on sexual harassment, the former director of the Working Women's Institute:

> Victims of sexual harassment suffer stress effects from the harassment. Stress as a result of sexual harassment is recognized as a specific, diagnosable problem by the American Psychiatric Association. . . . Among the stress effects suffered is "work performance stress," which include distraction from tasks, dread of work, and an inability to work. . . . Another form is "emotional stress," which covers a range of responses, including anger, fear of physical safety, anxiety, depression, guilt, humiliation, and embarrassment. . . . Physical stress also results from sexual harassment; it may manifest itself as sleeping problems, headaches, weight changes, and other physical ailments. . . . A study by the Working Women's Institute found that ninety-six percent of sexual harassment victims experienced emotional stress, forty-five percent suffered work performance stress, and thirty-five percent were inflicted with physical stress problems.

---

[59] *Id.* at 1549.

[60] *See also Sexual Discrimination in the Workplace, 1981: Hearings Before the Senate Comm. on Labor and Human Resources,* 97th Cong., 1st Sess. 518 (1981) (increased stress was most common manifestation of emotional and psychological injury suffered). Women also experienced "feelings of powerlessness, fear, anger, nervousness, decreased job satisfaction and diminished ambition." *Id.* at 524. A study by the Working Women's Institute found that 90% of sexual harassment victims experienced feelings of anger, fear, and nervousness; 63% suffered from nausea, headaches, and fatigue; and 75% indicated that their job performance was affected by the harassment. Working Women's Institute, The Impact of Sexual Harassment on the Job: A Profile of the Experiences of 92 Women, Research Series Rep. No. 3 (1979).

[61] 760 F. Supp. 1486 (M.D. Fla. 1991).

> Sexual harassment has a cumulative, eroding effect on the victim's well-being. . . . When women feel a need to maintain vigilance against the next incident of harassment, the stress is increased tremendously. . . . When women feel that their individual complaints will not change the work environment materially, the ensuing sense of despair further compounds the stress.[62]

Sociological research indicates that sexual harassment is related to high rates of depression among women and often results in symptoms characteristic of posttraumatic stress disorder.[63] In *Laughinghouse v. Risser*,[64] the physical harm requirement for emotional distress damages in a negligent retention suit against the employer was satisfied by evidence that the employee suffered life-threatening hives, high blood pressure, angina, fatigue, depression, and posttraumatic stress disorder as a result of her supervisor's harassment.

Harassed employees who decide to pursue legal remedies face the additional trauma and financial burden of litigation. The potential for compensatory and punitive damages in Title VII suits may ease this problem by providing an incentive for attorneys to accept such cases on a contingency basis or to advance costs to plaintiffs.

The impact of sexual harassment on the employer is profound as well. According to the Merit Board (see § **1.1**), sexual harassment incidents cost the federal government an estimated $267 million from May 1985 through May 1987. This figure is drawn from conservative estimates of the costs of job turnover, sick leave, and individual and group work productivity loss. Approximately 36,647 employees left their positions during the two-year period because of sexual harassment. An average of 13 percent of both male and female sexual harassment victims took sick leave after being harassed.[65] The *Working Woman* survey (see § **1.1**) estimated the cost of sexual harassment for a typical Fortune 500 service or manufacturing company of 23,784 employees to be $6,719,593, or $282.53 per employee per year, excluding costs of litigation. Preventive efforts would cost only $8.41 per employee.[66]

---

62 *Id.* at 1506–07. *See also* Hansel v. Public Serv. Co., 778 F. Supp. 1126 (D. Colo. 1991) (the plaintiff suffered a nervous breakdown as a result of sexual harassment); Morris v. American Nat'l Can Corp., 730 F. Supp. 1489 (E.D. Mo. 1989), *modified* 941 F.2d 710 (8th Cir. 1991) (plaintiff saw several doctors for "nervousness," sleeplessness, blotches or welts on her legs and back, and occasional inability to breathe or difficulty in breathing; conclusions of corporate defendant's doctor supported plaintiff's contention that stress and tension at work as a result of harassment and threat of harassment were source of her health problems).

63 B. Gutek & M. Koss, *Changed Women and Changed Organizations: Consequences of and Coping with Sexual Harassment,* 42 J. Vocational Behav. 28, 33 (1993).

64 786 F. Supp. 920 (D. Kan. 1992).

65 Merit Board survey at 40.

66 Working Woman survey at 25.

CHAPTER 2

HISTORY OF SEXUAL HARASSMENT LAW

§ 2.1 Title VII and EEOC Guidelines

Title VII of the Civil Rights Act of 1964[1] provides in part:

> It shall be an unlawful employment practice for an employer (1) to fail or refuse to hire or to discharge any individual, or otherwise to discriminate against any individual with respect to [her or] his compensation, terms, conditions, or privileges of employment, because of such individual's . . . sex . . .; or (2) to limit, segregate, or classify [her or] his employees or applicants for employment in any way which would deprive or tend to deprive any individual of employment opportunities or otherwise adversely affect [her or] his status as an employee, because of such individual's . . . sex.[2]

Title VII was passed to provide equal opportunity through the removal of artificial barriers to employment.[3] To accomplish the congressional purpose of giving an effective voice to victims of employment discrimination, § 704 of Title VII also prohibits employers from retaliating against employees who initiate complaints.[4] In 1972, Congress extended the protections of Title VII to federal employees.[5] Judicial interpretation of the prohibition against sex discrimination has been largely a self-guided process, with little legislative history available to assist the courts. In fact, addition of the provision prohibiting sex discrimination apparently was a last-minute attempt to defeat Title VII's passage.[6] However, the 1972 amendments to Title VII indicate a clear congressional intent to eliminate sex discrimination.[7]

---

1 Pub. L. No. 88-352, §§ 701-718, 78 Stat. 241 (codified in 42 U.S.C. § 2000e to 2000e-17).

2 Title VII of the 1964 Civil Rights Act, § 703(a), 42 U.S.C. § 2000e-2(a).

3 Griggs v. Duke Power Co., 401 U.S. 424 (1971).

4 Title VII of the 1964 Civil Rights Act, § 704, 42 U.S.C. § 2000e-3(a).

5 *Id.* § 717, 42 U.S.C. § 2000e-16(a).

6 110 Cong. Rec. 2577–82, 2851 (1964) (the word "sex" was added by floor amendment by Rep. Smith, an opponent of Title VII, on Feb. 8, 1964).

7 Equal Employment Opportunity Act of 1972, Pub. L. No. 92-261, 86 Stat. 103 (codified at 42 U.S.C. § 2000e).

Courts have interpreted Title VII broadly.[8] In *Sprogis v. United Airlines, Inc.*, the Seventh Circuit stated that "Congress intended to strike at the entire spectrum of disparate treatment of men and women resulting from sex stereotypes."[9] Ten years after the enactment of Title VII, sexual harassment claims became an important part of the discrimination spectrum.

Initially, federal courts held that no cause of action existed under Title VII for sexually harassing conduct. Unwilling to deem the "personal proclivit[ies]"[10] of supervisors employment discrimination, the courts rendered decisions that lacked consistency and sometimes conviction as judges waded through novel issues without the benefit of legislative history or statutory guidance, and advanced a number of reasons why sexual harassment was not sex discrimination under Title VII (see § **2.2**).

A more enlightened approach surfaced in the circuit courts, when several decisions were overturned on appeal after *Williams v. Saxbe.*[11] In that case, a district court held for the first time that sexual harassment was discriminatory treatment within the meaning of Title VII.

Although *Williams* marked a turning point for sexual harassment law, disparity in judicial construction lingered. Most courts required a showing of the loss of a tangible job benefit.[12] Other courts required plaintiffs to allege that the sexual misconduct was an employer-condoned policy or practice.[13]

---

[8] *See* Rogers v. EEOC, 454 F.2d 234, 238 (5th Cir. 1971), *cert. denied,* 406 U.S. 957 (1972): "Congress chose neither to enumerate specific discriminatory practices, nor to elucidate in extenso the parameter of such nefarious activities."

[9] 444 F.2d 1194 (7th Cir. 1971).

[10] Corne v. Bausch & Lomb, Inc., 390 F. Supp. 161, 163 (D. Ariz. 1975), *vacated on procedural grounds,* 562 F.2d 55 (9th Cir. 1977).

[11] 413 F. Supp. 654 (D.D.C. 1976).

[12] First Circuit: Fisher v. Flynn, 598 F.2d 663, 665 (1st Cir. 1979).

Third Circuit: Tomkins v. Public Serv. Elec. & Gas Co., 422 F. Supp. 553 (D.N.J. 1976), *rev'd,* 568 F.2d 1044, 1048–49 (3d Cir. 1977).

Fourth Circuit: Garber v. Saxon Business Prods., 14 Empl. Prac. Dec. (CCH) ¶ 7586 (E.D. Va. 1976), *rev'd,* 552 F.2d 1032 (4th Cir. 1977).

Sixth Circuit: Munford v. James T. Barnes & Co., 441 F. Supp. 459 (E.D. Mich. 1977).

Ninth Circuit: Miller v. Bank of Am., 418 F. Supp. 233 (N.D. Cal. 1976), *rev'd,* 600 F.2d 211 (9th Cir. 1979).

Tenth Circuit: Heelan v. Johns-Manville Corp., 451 F. Supp. 1382, 1388 (D. Colo. 1978).

District of Columbia Circuit: Barnes v. Costle, 561 F.2d 983, 992 (D.C. Cir. 1977); Williams v. Saxbe, 413 F. Supp. 654, 657 (D.D.C. 1976), *rev'd on other grounds sub nom.* Williams v. Bell, 587 F.2d 1240 (D.C. Cir. 1978), *remanded for trial de novo sub nom.* Williams v. Civiletti, 487 F. Supp. 1387 (D.D.C. 1980).

[13] Fourth Circuit: Garber v. Saxon Business Prods., 552 F.2d 1032 (4th Cir. 1977).

Ninth Circuit: *But see* Macey v. World Airways, 14 Fair Empl. Prac. Cas. (BNA) 1426 (N.D. Cal. 1977) (although defendant had an antidiscrimination policy, it was

Some required an employee to exhaust the employer's administrative grievance process before bringing a Title VII action, whether or not the process was likely to be effective.[14] Plaintiffs had to show actual, rather than constructive, discharge.[15]

Although all federal courts eventually recognized sexual harassment as a form of sex discrimination under Title VII, confusion surrounding the issue prompted the Equal Employment Opportunity Commission (EEOC) to develop a framework for analyzing sexual harassment claims[16] (see **§ 2.8**). The EEOC is a bipartisan commission with primary responsibility for the administration and enforcement of all federal laws prohibiting discrimination in employment. Congress granted the EEOC the power to issue regulations in the Civil Rights Act of 1964.[17] Such regulations are nonbinding administrative interpretations of the Civil Rights Act,[18] but "constitute a body of experience and informed judgment to which courts and litigants may properly resort for guidance."[19] The commission promulgated the guidelines when "[a]ctivity in the courts indicated that both public and private employers were in need of help in understanding and defining their liability for acts of sexual harassment in the workplace."[20]

The EEOC guidelines followed well-established Title VII precedent in the areas of racial, religious, and national origin discrimination. Regardless of whether they knew of the conduct,[21] employers were held vicariously

---

"abundantly clear" that hostility of some mechanics toward having a woman on a flight line caused supervisor to participate in course of harassment leading to her discharge).

Tenth Circuit: Heelan v. Johns-Manville Corp., 451 F. Supp. 1382, 1389 (D. Colo. 1978).

District of Columbia Circuit: Williams v. Saxbe, 413 F. Supp. 654, 660 (D.D.C. 1976), *rev'd on other grounds sub nom.* Williams v. Bell, 587 F.2d 1240 (D.C. Cir. 1978), *remanded for trial de novo sub nom.* Williams v. Civiletti, 487 F. Supp. 1387 (D.D.C. 1980). *But see* Barnes v. Costle, 561 F.2d 983, 993 n.75 (D.C. Cir. 1977) ("a single instance of discrimination may form the basis of a private suit" (quoting King v. Laborers Int'l Union, 443 F.2d 273, 278 (6th Cir. 1971) (racial discrimination in employment))).

14 Heelan v. Johns-Manville Corp., 451 F. Supp. 1382 (D. Colo. 1978); Munford v. James T. Barnes & Co., 441 F. Supp. 459, 466 (E.D. Mich. 1977).

15 Corne v. Bausch & Lomb, Inc., 390 F. Supp. 161 (D. Ariz. 1975). *See also* Clark v. World Airways, 24 Fair Empl. Prac. Cas. (BNA) 305 (D.D.C. 1980). *Cf.* Young v. Southwestern Sav. & Loan Ass'n, 509 F.2d 140 (5th Cir. 1974) (religion); Compston v. Borden, Inc., 424 F. Supp. 157, 160–61 (S.D. Ohio 1976) (religion).

16 EEOC Guidelines on Discrimination Because of Sex, 29 C.F.R. § 1604.11 (1993).

17 Pub. L. No. 88-352, § 713, 78 Stat. 265 (1964) (codified at 42 U.S.C. § 2000e-12).

18 Griggs v. Duke Power Co., 401 U.S. 424, 433–34 (1971).

19 Meritor Sav. Bank v. Vinson, 477 U.S. 57, 65 (1986) (quoting General Elec. Co. v. Gilbert, 429 U.S. 125, 141–42 (1976)).

20 J.C. Smith Jr., *Prologue to the EEOC Guidelines,* 10 Cap. U.L. Rev. 471, 472 (1981).

21 Young v. Southwestern Sav. & Loan Ass'n, 509 F.2d 140, 144 (5th Cir. 1974); Lucero v. Beth Israel Hosp. & Geriatric Ctr., 479 F. Supp. 452 (D. Colo. 1979) (religion);

liable for their supervisors' discriminatory acts. Under Title VII, harassment may occur in several ways. The conduct may directly affect a job benefit,[22] or a discriminatory work environment may exist.[23] The EEOC and courts have found consistently that Title VII grants an employee the right to a working environment free of racial intimidation:

> [I]t is my belief that employees' psychological as well as economic fringes are statutorily entitled to protection from employer abuse and that the phrase "terms, conditions, or privileges of employment" in **§ 703** is an expansive concept which sweeps within its protective ambit the practice of creating a working environment heavily charged with ethnic or racial discrimination.[24]

Constructive discharge also has formed the basis of Title VII claims[25] (see **Chapter 3**).

The guidelines confirmed the viability of the sexual harassment claim and extended the doctrine to include coworkers, nonemployees, and supervisors, as well as environmental harassment and *quid pro quo,* or tangible benefit harassment (see **§§ 2.9** through **2.12**). Although the guidelines

---

Calcote v. Texas Educ. Found., 458 F. Supp. 231, 237 (W.D. Tex. 1976), *aff'd,* 578 F.2d 95 (5th Cir. 1978); Compston v. Borden, Inc., 424 F. Supp. 157, 160–61 (S.D. Ohio 1971).

22 *See, e.g.,* Gray v. Greyhound Lines, 545 F.2d 169, 176 (D.C. Cir. 1976) (discriminatory route, equipment assignment, and discipline); Slack v. Havens, 522 F.2d 1091, 1092 (9th Cir. 1975) (black but not white employees asked to clean department); United States v. United States Steel Corp., 371 F. Supp. 1045, 1054 (M.D. Fla. 1973), *modified on other grounds*, 520 F.2d 1043 (5th Cir. 1975) (discriminatory temporary assignments and refusal to train blacks); Trivett v. Tri-States Container Corp., 368 F. Supp. 137 (E.D. Tenn. 1973) (requiring women employees to remain at posts while men "clock out").

23 *See, e.g.,* Gray v. Greyhound Lines, 545 F.2d 169, 176 (D.C. Cir. 1976).

24 Rogers v. EEOC, 454 F.2d 234, 238 (5th Cir. 1971), *cert denied,* 406 U.S. 957 (1972). *See also* EEOC v. Murphy Motor Freight Lines, 488 F. Supp. 381, 384 (D. Minn. 1980); Lucero v. Beth Israel Hosp. & Geriatric Ctr., 479 F. Supp. 452 (D. Colo. 1979) (religion); United States v. City of Buffalo, 457 F. Supp. 612, 631 (W.D.N.Y. 1978); Calcote v. Texas Educ. Found., 458 F. Supp. 231, 237 (W.D. Tex. 1976), *aff'd,* 578 F.2d 95 (5th Cir. 1978); Compston v. Borden, Inc., 424 F. Supp. 157, 160–61 (S.D. Ohio 1976) (religious views); United States v. Lee Way Motor Freight, 7 Fair Empl. Prac. Cas. (BNA) 710, 748 (W.D. Okla. 1973) (referring to black employees in derogatory manner); EEOC Dec. No. 74-05, 6 Fair Empl. Prac. Cas. (BNA) 834 (1973) (ethnic "kidding" of Spanish-surnamed employee); [1973] EEOC Dec. (CCH) ¶ 6347 (1972) (supervisor's preaching caused plaintiff employee to resign); [1973] EEOC Dec. (CCH) ¶ 6193 (1970) (blacks routinely called "niggers").

25 *See e.g.,* Young v. Southwestern Sav. & Loan Ass'n, 509 F.2d 140 (5th Cir. 1974) (atheist required to attend business meeting beginning with religious convocation and who subsequently quit was constructively discharged; liability imposed although plaintiff's supervisor lacked actual authority to discharge her; supervisor's apparent authority sufficed.) *Accord* Calcote v. Texas Educ. Found., 458 F. Supp. 231, 237 (W.D. Tex. 1976), *aff'd,* 578 F.2d 95 (5th Cir. 1978).

opened the door to more sexual harassment litigation, not all courts accepted its provisos. In particular, courts continued to apply varying standards of liability to sexual harassment cases.

§ 2.2 *Quid Pro Quo* and Hostile Environment Harassment

Although sexual harassment encompasses a broad range of conduct, it usually falls into one of two general categories.[26] The first is tangible benefit or *quid pro quo* harassment. This is the most obvious type of harassment; it involves the exchange of employment benefits by a supervisor or employer for sexual favors from a subordinate employee. The second form consists of conduct that rises to the level of a hostile or offensive working environment. In this type of case, no deal is sought or struck; the day-to-day working environment has been polluted with verbal or physical abuses. The two types of harassment are often intertwined. Failure to comply with sexual demands may give rise to a hostile environment as well as a *quid pro quo* harassment claim, and a hostile environment may affect an employee's job status if she is fired for complaining or if it causes her constructive discharge.[27] To be actionable, sexual harassment must be unwelcome.[28] Although both types of harassment violate Title VII, and both are often alleged in sexual harassment complaints,[29] each contains unique elements.

---

[26] Katz v. Dole, 709 F.2d 251 (4th Cir. 1983).

[27] EEOC, Policy Guidance on Current Issues of Sexual Harassment, N-915.035 (Oct. 25, 1988) at 2–3.

[28] Meritor Sav. Bank v. Vinson, 477 U.S. 57, 68 (1986).

[29] Second Circuit: Koster v. Chase Manhattan Bank, 46 Fair Empl. Prac. Cas. (BNA) 1436 (S.D.N.Y. 1988); Christoforou v. Ryder Truck Rental, 668 F. Supp. 294, 301 (S.D.N.Y. 1987); Neville v. Taft Broadcasting Co., 42 Fair Empl. Prac. Cas. (BNA) 1314 (W.D.N.Y. 1987).

Fourth Circuit: Hopkins v. Shoe Show of Va., Inc., 678 F. Supp. 1241 (S.D. W. Va. 1988).

Fifth Circuit: Jones v. Flagship Int'l, 793 F.2d 714 (5th Cir. 1986), *cert denied,* 479 U.S. 1065 (1987); Benton v. Kroger Co., 640 F. Supp. 1317 (S.D. Tex. 1986).

Sixth Circuit: Highlander v. K.F.C. Nat'l Management Co., 805 F.2d 644 (6th Cir. 1986); Shrout v. Black Clawson Co., 46 Fair Empl. Prac. Cas. (BNA) 1339 (S.D. Ohio 1988); Pease v. Alford Photo Indus., 667 F. Supp. 1188 (W.D. Tenn. 1987).

Seventh Circuit: Dockter v. Rudolf Wolff Futures, Inc., 684 F. Supp. 532 (N.D. Ill. 1988), *aff'd,* 913 F.2d 456 (7th Cir. 1990).

Ninth Circuit: Ambrose v. United States Steel Corp., 39 Fair Empl. Prac. Cas. (BNA) 30 (N.D. Cal. 1985).

Tenth Circuit: Hicks v. Gates Rubber Co., 833 F.2d 1406 (10th Cir. 1987), *aff'g district court's finding of no hostile environment,* 928 F.2d 966 (10th Cir. 1991).

Eleventh Circuit: Sparks v. Pilot Freight Carriers, 830 F.2d 1554 (11th Cir. 1987).

Quid pro quo harassment typically involves a situation in which a supervisor demands sexual consideration in exchange for employment benefits.[30] A tangible economic loss may include termination,[31] transfer,[32] delay or denial of job benefits,[33] or adverse performance appraisals.[34] The loss may occur in one of several ways: benefits may be withheld from an employee until she submits to sexual demands, an employer or supervisor may retaliate against an employee who has refused sexual advances by firing her or altering or withholding tangible job benefits, or an employee may submit to the advance and still not receive the job benefit.[35] Applicants for employment also have been refused work for failing to

---

30 Henson v. City of Dundee, 682 F.2d 897 (11th Cir. 1982).

31 Third Circuit: Tomkins v. Public Serv. Elec. & Gas Co., 568 F.2d 1044 (3d Cir. 1977) (continued employment conditioned upon submission to sexual advances); Stringer v. Pennsylvania Dep't of Community Affairs, Bureau of Human Resources, 446 F. Supp. 704 (M.D. Pa. 1978).

Sixth Circuit: Boyd v. James S. Hayes Living Health Care Agency, 671 F. Supp. 1155 (W.D. Tenn. 1987); Pease v. Alford Photo Indus., 667 F. Supp. 1188 (W.D. Tenn. 1987); Munford v. James T. Barnes & Co., 441 F. Supp. 459 (E.D. Mich. 1977). *Cf.* Highlander v. K.F.C. Nat'l Management Co., 805 F.2d 644 (6th Cir. 1986).

Tenth Circuit: Heelan v. Johns-Manville Corp., 451 F. Supp. 1382 (D. Colo. 1978).

District of Columbia Circuit: Williams v. Saxbe, 413 F. Supp. 654, 657 (D.D.C. 1976), *rev'd on other grounds sub nom.* Williams v. Bell, 587 F.2d 1240 (D.C. Cir. 1978), *remanded for trial de novo sub nom.* Williams v. Civiletti, 487 F. Supp. 1387 (D.D.C. 1980).

32 Broderick v. Ruder, 685 F. Supp. 1269 (D.D.C. 1988).

33 First Circuit: *Cf.* Morley v. New Eng. Tel. Co., 47 Fair Empl. Prac. Cas. (BNA) 917, 924 (D. Mass. 1987) (employee who had personality conflict with supervisor and demonstrated that she was discriminatorily denied promotion was not sexually harassed when only two statements by supervisor could be considered to have sexual overtones).

Eleventh Circuit: Sparks v. Pilot Freight Carriers, 830 F.2d 1554 (11th Cir. 1987); Sowers v. Kemira, Inc., 46 Fair Empl. Prac. Cas. (BNA) 1825 (S.D. Ga. 1988) (promotion and salary increases delayed).

34 Shrout v. Black Clawson Co., 46 Fair Empl. Prac. Cas. (BNA) 1339 (S.D. Ohio 1988) (performance evaluation and salary review withheld).

35 Second Circuit: Koster v. Chase Manhattan Bank, 46 Fair Empl. Prac. Cas. (BNA) 1436, 1447 (S.D.N.Y. 1988); Neville v. Taft Broadcasting Co., 42 Fair Empl.. Prac. Cas. (BNA) 1314 (W.D.N.Y. 1987).

Third Circuit: Craig v. Y&Y Snacks, 721 F.2d 77 (3d Cir. 1983) (plaintiff fired when she rebuffed supervisor's advances).

Fourth Circuit: Hopkins v. Shoe Show of Va., 678 F. Supp. 1241 (S.D. W. Va. 1988).

Sixth Circuit: Shrout v. Black Clawson Co., 46 Fair Empl. Prac. Cas. (BNA) 1339 (S.D. Ohio 1988) (performance evaluation and salary review withheld); Boyd v. James S. Hayes Living Health Care Agency, 671 F. Supp. 1155, 1165 (W.D. Tenn. 1987) (ample evidence demonstrated that plaintiff's refusal to submit to sexual advances resulted in her discipline and discharge); Pease v. Alford Photo Indus., 667 F. Supp. 1188, 1201 (W.D. Tenn. 1987) (when plaintiff complained of harassment, employer sent her on a "journey to termination").

acquiesce to sexual demands.[36] Romantic relationships gone sour have also led to charges of *quid pro quo* sexual harassment when the supervisor retaliated against the employee for terminating the relationship.[37] In situations short of termination, an employer may alter the plaintiff's job status to give the supervisor a basis for criticizing her work.[38]

Courts also have recognized that psychological well-being is included within Title VII's "terms, conditions, or privileges of employment."[39] In enacting Title VII, Congress did not explain what constitutes a condition of employment. Hostile environment claims challenge workplace practices, rather than tangible job benefits, and consist of "verbal or physical conduct of a sexual nature" that unreasonably interferes with one's work or creates an "intimidating, hostile or offensive working environment."[40] This type of harassment is both more pervasive and more elusive. While *quid pro quo* sexual harassment can only be committed by someone with authority to change the employee's job status, employers, supervisors, coworkers, customers, or clients can create a hostile work environment (see **Chapter 3**).

§ 2.3 Early Cases

Early federal sexual harassment cases were unsuccessful in the lower courts. Most early sexual harassment cases involved tangible benefit or *quid pro quo* harassment of a factually similar nature. Most plaintiffs were fired for allegedly resisting sexual advances by their superiors. However, in *Corne v. Bausch & Lomb,*[41] the first reported sexual harassment case under Title VII,[42] the plaintiffs alleged that they were forced to resign their positions because their supervisor's verbal and physical sexual advances

---

Ninth Circuit: Collins v. City of San Diego, 841 F.2d 337 (9th Cir. 1988); Ambrose v. United States Steel Corp., 39 Fair Empl. Prac. Cas. (BNA) 30 (N.D. Cal. 1985) (plaintiff terminated for resisting sexual advances).

District of Columbia Circuit: Barnes v. Costle, 561 F.2d 983 (D.C. Cir. 1977) (victim's job abolished for refusing sexual advances); Williams v. Civiletti, 487 F. Supp. 1387 (D.D.C. 1980) (plaintiff discharged for refusing to submit to advances).

36 Rinkel v. Associated Pipeline Contractors, 17 Fair Empl. Prac. Cas. (BNA) 224 (D. Alaska 1978).

37 Boddy v. Dean, 821 F.2d 346, 348 (6th Cir. 1987).

38 Boyd v. James S. Hayes Living Health Care Agency, 671 F. Supp. 1155, 1166 (W.D. Tenn. 1987).

39 Rogers v. EEOC, 454 F.2d 234 (5th Cir. 1971), *cert denied,* 406 U.S. 957 (1972).

40 29 C.F.R. § 1604.11(a) (1988).

41 390 F. Supp. 161, 163 (D. Ariz. 1975), *vacated on procedural grounds,* 562 F.2d 55 (9th Cir. 1977).

42 Another sexual harassment case, Barnes v. Train, 13 Fair Empl. Prac. Cas. (BNA) 123 (D.D.C. 1974), *rev'd sub nom.* Barnes v. Costle, 561 F.2d 983 (D.C. Cir. 1977), was decided in 1974 but not reported for several years.

had made their jobs intolerable, and that other women who complied with the supervisor's demands enjoyed enhanced employment status. The court dismissed the action on the basis that the plaintiffs had failed to state a claim under Title VII, noting that discriminatory conduct in other Title VII sex discrimination cases arose out of company policies rather than the "personal proclivity, peculiarity or mannerism" of a supervisor.[43] By his alleged sexual advances, the court said that the supervisor "was satisfying a personal urge," which "had no relationship to the nature of the employment." The court stated that the conduct could not be considered "company-directed policy which deprived women of employment opportunities" and that there was "nothing in the Act which could reasonably be construed to have it apply to 'verbal and physical sexual advances' by another employee, even though he be in a supervisory capacity, when such complained of acts or conduct had no relationship to the nature of the employment."[44]

The court failed to reconcile its position with Title VII precedent, which generally held employers liable for the discriminatory acts of supervisors,[45] or with Title VII language in § 2000e(b) treating an employer's agents as employers for purposes of liability; nor did the court apply an agency law analysis under which an employer is liable for the acts of its agents.[46] Instead, Judge Frey displayed a cynicism that would be expressed by a number of courts:

> [A]n outgrowth of holding such activity to be actionable under Title VII would be a potential federal lawsuit every time an employee made amorous or sexually-oriented advances toward another. The only sure way an employer could avoid such charges would be to have employees who were asexual.[47]

Thus, it was unclear whether an employer's sexual conduct was ever sex discrimination or if it was necessary to show a nexus between a tangible employment benefit and the alleged harassment.

---

43 Corne v. Bausch & Lomb, 390 F. Supp. 161, 163 (D. Ariz. 1975). *See also* Ludington v. Sambo's Restaurants, Inc., 474 F. Supp. 480, 482 (E.D. Wis. 1979) (plaintiffs subjected to "obscene and vulgar suggestions and physical conduct" by manager were not protected by Title VII when they did not allege that their termination as result of sexual harassment was in any way approved by employer).

44 Corne v. Bausch & Lomb, 390 F. Supp. 161, 163 (D. Ariz. 1975).

45 Flowers v. Crouch-Walker Corp., 552 F.2d 1277 (7th Cir. 1977) (discriminatory discharge); Ostopowicz v. Johnson Bronze Co., 369 F. Supp. 522 (W.D. Pa. 1973), *modified,* 541 F.2d 394 (3d Cir. 1976), *cert denied,* 429 U.S. 1041 (1977) (subjective employment tests; supervisor's recommendations); Tidwell v. American Oil Co., 332 F. Supp. 424 (D. Utah 1971) (discharge). *Cf.* Croker v. Boeing Co. (Vertol Div.), 437 F. Supp. 1138, 1191 (E.D. Pa. 1977) ("employer cannot be liable for the unauthorized conduct of its employees even if those employees are front line supervisors").

46 Restatement (Second) of Agency § 2(2) (1958).

47 Corne v. Bausch & Lomb, 390 F. Supp. 161, 163–64 (D. Ariz. 1975).

In early cases alleging termination in retaliation for resisting sexual advances, courts required a plaintiff to show the loss of a tangible job benefit[48] as a result of an employer-condoned policy or practice[49]and the employer's knowledge of the supervisor's conduct.[50] These courts were reluctant to impose liability for sexual harassment absent misconduct by the employer himself,[51] and found employer liability only if the employer

---

48 First Circuit: Fisher v. Flynn, 598 F.2d 663 (1st Cir. 1979).

Third Circuit: Tomkins v. Public Serv. Elec. & Gas Co., 568 F.2d 1044 (3d Cir. 1977).

Fourth Circuit: Garber v. Saxon Business Prods., 552 F.2d 1032 (4th Cir. 1977).

Sixth Circuit: Munford v. James T. Barnes & Co., 441 F. Supp. 459 (E.D. Mich. 1977).

Seventh Circuit: Ludington v. Sambo's Restaurants, 474 F. Supp. 480 (E.D. Wis. 1979).

Ninth Circuit: Miller v. Bank of Am., 600 F.2d 211 (9th Cir. 1979).

Tenth Circuit: Scott v. City of Overland Park, 595 F. Supp. 520 (D. Kan. 1984) (failure by plaintiff to use the word "retaliation" in her complaint was not fatal to her charge when it was clear she was allegedly denied training in retaliation for contacting EEOC); Heelan v. Johns-Manville Corp., 451 F. Supp. 1382, 1388 (D. Colo. 1978).

District of Columbia Circuit: Barnes v. Costle, 561 F.2d 983, 992 (D.C. Cir. 1977); Williams v. Saxbe, 413 F. Supp. 654 (D.D.C. 1976), *rev'd on other grounds sub nom.* Williams v. Bell, 587 F.2d 1240 (D.C. Cir. 1978), *remanded for trial de novo sub nom.* Williams v. Civiletti, 487 F. Supp. 1387 (D.D.C. 1980).

49 Fourth Circuit: Garber v. Saxon Business Prods., 552 F.2d 1032 (4th Cir. 1977).

Tenth Circuit: Neeley v. American Fidelity Assurance Co., 17 Fair Empl. Prac. Cas. (BNA) 482 (W.D. Okla. 1978). *But see* Heelan v. Johns-Manville Corp., 451 F. Supp. 1382, 1389 (D. Colo. 1978) (plaintiff did not have to prove "policy or practice of the employer endorsing sexual harassment").

Eleventh Circuit: Price v. John F. Lawhorn Furniture Co., 24 Fair Empl. Prac. Cas. (BNA) 1506 (N.D. Ala. 1978).

District of Columbia Circuit: Williams v. Saxbe, 413 F. Supp. 654, 660 n. 8 (D.D.C. 1976), *rev'd on other grounds sub nom.* Williams v. Bell, 587 F.2d 1240 (D.C. Cir. 1978), *remanded for trial de novo sub nom.* Williams v. Civiletti, 487 F. Supp. 1387 (D.D.C. 1980) (allegation that supervisor's conduct was policy or practice imposed upon plaintiff was "an essential allegation for presenting a cause of action").

50 Third Circuit: Tomkins v. Public Serv. Elec. & Gas Co., 568 F.2d 1044 (3d Cir. 1977).

Fourth Circuit: Garber v. Saxon Business Prods., 552 F.2d 1032 (4th Cir. 1977).

Sixth Circuit: Munford v. James T. Barnes & Co., 441 F. Supp. 459 (E.D. Mich. 1977).

Tenth Circuit: Neeley v. American Fidelity Assurance Co., 17 Fair Empl. Prac. Cas. (BNA) 482 (W.D. Okla. 1978).

Eleventh Circuit: Price v. John F. Lawhorn Furniture Co., 24 Fair Empl. Prac. Cas. (BNA) 1506 (N.D. Ala. 1978).

District of Columbia Circuit: Vinson v. Taylor, 23 Fair Empl. Prac. Cas. (BNA) 37 (D.D.C. Feb. 26, 1980), *rev'd,* 753 F.2d 141 (D.C. Cir. 1985), *aff'd in part, rev'd in part sub nom.* Meritor Sav. Bank v. Vinson, 477 U.S. 57 (1986).

51 Tomkins v. Public Serv. Elec. & Gas Co., 568 F.2d 1044 (3d Cir. 1977); Barnes v. Costle, 561 F.2d 983 (D.C. Cir. 1977); Heelan v. Johns-Manville Corp., 451 F. Supp. 1382 (D. Colo. 1978).

knew of the misconduct and failed to take corrective action. Courts addressed the unique elements of sexual harassment by ignoring Title VII precedent and drawing from *Corne* to conclude that the challenged conduct was a product of interpersonal strife not subject to federal law. These courts failed to provide any guidance as to what constituted sexual harassment under Title VII, and instead, offered somewhat specious rationales to deny recovery. For example, in *Barnes v. Costle*[52] the District of Columbia Circuit held that Title VII is violated when an employee's job is abolished for failure to comply with a supervisor's sexual advances. In a concurring opinion, Judge MacKinnon agreed with the majority on this point, but rejected a holding that an employer should be held vicariously liable for the tortious acts of its employees. He suggested that sexual harassment is more troublesome than other types of employment discrimination because women may welcome sexual advances as a normal part of social relations.

§ 2.4 *Williams v. Saxbe*

In *Williams v. Saxbe,*[53] a district court again considered whether retaliation against an employee for refusing a supervisor's sexual advances was sex discrimination under Title VII. The plaintiff alleged that after she refused his sexual advances, her supervisor harassed, humiliated, and ultimately fired her. The court found a cause of action under Title VII because "the conduct of the plaintiff's supervisor created an artificial barrier to employment which was placed before one gender and not the other, despite the fact that both genders were similarly situated."[54] The court rejected the defendant's contention that the supervisor discriminated not against women, but only against people who refused to submit to his sexual demands. The defendant argued that the application of Title VII should not be based on the sexual preference of the employer.

The court also reiterated *Corne's* finding that a supervisor's conduct must constitute an employer policy or practice for a cause of action to lie. However, in response to the defendant's argument that the supervisor's conduct was not a policy but a personal encounter, the court stated:

> [W]hether this case presents a policy or practice of imposing a condition of sexual submission on the female employees of the CRS or whether this was a non-employment related personal encounter requires a factual determination. It is sufficient for purposes of the motion to dismiss that the plaintiff has alleged it was the former in this case. For, if this was a policy or practice of

---

52 561 F.2d 983, 1001 (D.C. Cir. 1977).

53 413 F. Supp. 654 (D.D.C. 1976).

54 *Id.* at 657–58.

plaintiff's supervisor, then it was the agency's policy or practice, which is prohibited by Title VII.[55]

§ 2.5 Federal Circuit Court Recognition of Sexual Harassment

Within a year of the decision in *Williams*, circuit courts tentatively began to accept the notion that sexual harassment constituted sex discrimination. In *Barnes v. Train*,[56] a case decided at the trial court level before *Williams*, the district court held without elaboration that a female employee who had been belittled, harassed, and whose job ultimately was abolished had been harassed not because she was female, but because she refused to have an affair with her supervisor. The court stated, "This is a controversy underpinned by the subtleties of an inharmonious personal relationship. Regardless of how inexcusable the conduct of plaintiff's supervisor might have been, it does not evidence an arbitrary barrier to continued employment based on plaintiff's sex."[57]

The court of appeals reversed the decision, finding nothing in the case "to support the notion that employment conditions summoning sexual relations are somehow exempted from the coverage of Title VII," which explicitly proscribes discrimination "because of sex."[58] The court concluded that the plaintiff had in fact been sexually harassed in violation of Title VII:

> But for her womanhood, . . . her participation in sexual activity would never have been solicited. To say, then, that she was victimized in her employment simply because she declined the invitation is to ignore the asserted fact that she was invited only because she was a woman subordinate to the inviter in the hierarchy of agency personnel. Put another way, she became the target of her supervisor's sexual desires because she was a woman and was asked to bow to his demands as the price for holding her job. The circumstance imparting high visibility to the role of gender in the affair is that no male employee was susceptible to such an approach by appellant's supervisor. Thus gender cannot be eliminated from the formulation which appellant advocates, and that formulation advances a prima facie case of sex discrimination within the purview of Title VII.[59]

---

[55] *Id.* at 660–61.

[56] 13 Fair Empl. Prac. Cas. (BNA) 123 (D.D.C. 1974), *rev'd sub nom.* Barnes v. Costle, 561 F.2d 983 (D.C. Cir. 1977).

[57] *Id.* at 124.

[58] Barnes v. Costle, 561 F.2d 983, 994 (D.C. Cir. 1977).

[59] *Id.* at 990 (footnotes omitted).

The court drew from the legislative history of the 1972 amendments to the Civil Rights Act[60] and Title VII precedent[61] to conclude that the alleged conduct was discrimination based on sex.[62] Because the plaintiff's job retention was conditioned upon her submission to sexual advances, the court found that the plaintiff's terms of employment differed significantly from those for male employees.[63] The court applied a literal Title VII analysis of liability, taking issue with the district court's reference to the parties' relationship as an "inharmonious personal" one, and noting that a plaintiff need not demonstrate a "pattern" of offensive conduct:

> Were we satisfied that this characterization was but a part of the reasoning underlying the court's ruling that the discrimination was not sex-based, we would have no need to address it further. The fact is, however, that we are uncertain as to the reach of the court's observation, and concerned about implications to which it is susceptible.
>
> If the court meant that the conduct attributed to appellant's supervisor fell outside Title VII because it was a personal escapade rather than an agency project, no support for a summary judgment could be derived therefrom. Generally speaking, an employer is charged with Title VII violations occasioned by discriminatory practices of supervisory personnel. We realize that should a supervisor contravene employer policy without the employer's knowledge and the consequences are rectified when discovered, the employer may be relieved from responsibility under Title VII. But, so far as we are aware, the agency involved here is not in position to claim exoneration on that theory.
>
> If, on the other hand, the court was saying that there was no actionable discrimination because only one employee was victimized, we would strongly disagree. A sex-founded impediment to equal opportunity succumbs to Title VII even though less than all employees of the claimant's gender are affected.[64]

Though *Barnes* was subsequently cited in support of a strict vicarious liability rule,[65] its breadth was somewhat limited by the fact that the employer was aware of the harassment and failed to take corrective

---

[60] Pub. L. No. 92-261, 86 Stat. 103 (1972), 42 U.S.C. §§ 2000e–2000e(17) (1982).

[61] Barnes v. Costle, 561 F.2d 983, 991 (citing Phillips v. Martin Marietta Corp., 400 U.S. 542, 544 (1971)); Willingham v. Macon Tel. Publishing Co., 507 F.2d 1084, 1089 (5th Cir. 1975) (en banc); Sprogis v. United Airlines, Inc., 444 F.2d 1194, 1198 (7th Cir.), *cert denied,* 404 U.S. 991 (1971).

[62] Barnes v. Costle, 561 F.2d 983, 995.

[63] *Id.* at 990.

[64] *Id.* at 992–93.

[65] Miller v. Bank of Am., 600 F.2d 211, 213 (9th Cir. 1979); Neidhardt v. D.H. Holmes, 21 Fair Empl. Prac. Cas. (BNA) 452, 467 (E.D. La. 1979); Munford v. James T. Barnes & Co., 441 F. Supp. 459, 466 (E.D. Mich. 1977) (construing Barnes as imposing per se

action.[66] The court of appeals noted in dicta that an employer might not be liable if the supervisor violated company policy without the employer's knowledge and if the employer took appropriate action after learning of the harassment.[67] Subsequently, some courts cited *Barnes* in holding that employer knowledge is a prerequisite to liability.[68]

Another plaintiff faced the choice between submitting to sexual advances or suffering adverse job consequences in *Tomkins v. Public Service Electric & Gas Co.*[69] During lunch with her supervisor, the plaintiff was informed that she would have to consent to sexual relations with the supervisor to enjoy a "satisfactory working relationship" with him.[70] When she attempted to leave the restaurant, she was physically restrained for several hours and threatened. When she returned to work, the plaintiff requested and was promised a transfer. When one was not available, she was forced to accept a lower position and was ultimately discharged. Her complaints were never investigated. The district court found that "sexual harassment and sexually motivated assault do not constitute sex discrimination under Title VII":

> Title VII was enacted in order to remove those artificial barriers to full employment which are based on unjust and long-encrusted prejudice. . . . It is not intended to provide a federal tort remedy for what amounts to physical attack motivated by sexual desire on the part of a supervisor and which happened to occur in a corporate corridor rather than a back alley. . . . While sexual desire animated the parties, or at least one of them, the gender of each is incidental to the claim of abuse. Similarly, the pleadings in this case aver that the supervisor's advances were spurned. Had they been accepted, however, and plaintiff thereby preferred, could co-workers be heard to complain in

---

vicarious liability, court would not apply this rule but stated that employer has affirmative obligation to investigate sexual harassment complaints and take appropriate action); Vinson v. Taylor, 23 Fair Empl. Prac. Cas. (BNA) 37, 41–42 (D.D.C. 1980), *rev'd,* 753 F.2d 141 (D.C. Cir. 1985), *aff'd in part, rev'd in part sub nom.* Meritor Sav. Bank v. Vinson, 477 U.S. 57 (1986).

66 Barnes v. Costle, 561 F.2d 983, 985, n.11 (D.C. Cir. 1977).

67 *Id.* at 993. In his concurrence, Judge MacKinnon argued that these dicta should be the rule of the case, and he would have required that agents of the employer other than the harassing supervisor knew of the harassment but allowed retaliation or hindered investigation of a complaint. This assertion was also inconsistent with Title VII language and precedent.

68 Neidhardt v. D.H. Holmes, 21 Fair Empl. Prac. Cas. (BNA) 452, 470 (E.D. La. 1979); Heelan v. Johns-Manville Corp., 451 F. Supp. 1382, 1388 (D. Colo. 1978); Vinson v. Taylor, 23 Fair Empl. Prac. Cas. (BNA) 37, 41–42 (D.D.C. 1980), *rev'd,* 753 F.2d 141 (D.C. Cir. 1985), *aff'd in part, rev'd in part sub nom.* Meritor Sav. Bank v. Vinson, 477 U.S. 57 (1986).

69 422 F. Supp. 553 (D.N.J. 1976), *rev'd,* 568 F.2d 1044 (3d Cir. 1977).

70 568 F.2d at 1045.

> federal court as well? It is clear that such a claim is simply without the scope of the Act. The abuse of authority by supervisors of either sex for personal purposes is an unhappy and recurrent feature of our social experience. Such conduct is frequently illegal under the penal statutes of the relevant jurisdiction. Such conduct might well give rise to a civil action in tort. It is not, however, sex discrimination within the meaning of Title VII even when the purpose is sexual.[71]

The court also voiced the ubiquitous concerns over the "natural" relations between the sexes and the potential flood of litigation:

> [N]atural sexual attraction can be subtle. If the plaintiff's view were to prevail, no superior could, prudently, attempt to open a social dialogue with any subordinate of either sex. An invitation to dinner could become an invitation to a federal lawsuit if a once harmonious relationship turned sour at some later time. And if an inebriated approach by a supervisor at a Christmas party could form the basis of a federal lawsuit for sex discrimination if a promotion or raise is later denied to the subordinate, we would need 4,000 federal judges instead of some 400.[72]

The court of appeals reversed, finding that because the employee's "status as a female was the motivating factor in the supervisor's conditioning her continued employment on compliance with his sexual demands," *quid pro quo* sexual harassment had occurred.[73]

> We conclude that Title VII is violated when a supervisor, with the actual or constructive knowledge of the employer, makes sexual advances or demands toward a subordinate employee and conditions that employee's job status—evaluation, continued employment, promotion, or other aspects of career development—on a favorable response to those advances or demands, and the employer does not take prompt and appropriate remedial action after acquiring such knowledge.
>
> We do not agree with the district court that finding a Title VII violation on these facts will result in an unmanageable number of suits and a difficulty in differentiating between spurious and meritorious claims. The congressional mandate that the federal courts provide relief is strong; it must not be thwarted by concern for judicial economy. More significantly, however, this decision in no way relieves the plaintiff of the burden of proving the facts alleged to establish the required elements of a Title VII violation. Although any theory of liability may be used in vexatious or bad faith suits, we are confident that traditional judicial mechanisms will separate the valid from the invalid complaints.[74]

---

[71] 422 F. Supp. at 556.

[72] *Id.* at 557.

[73] 568 F.2d 1044, 1047–49 (3d Cir. 1977).

[74] *Id.* at 1048–49.

In the *Tomkins* case, the court established a two-part analysis for sexual harassment claims: "first, that a term or condition of employment has been imposed, and second, that it has been imposed by the employer, either directly or vicariously in a sexually discriminatory fashion."[75] The court easily found that the supervisor's demands "amounted to a condition of employment, an additional duty, or burden."[76] Drawing from *Barnes*,[77] the court concluded that the plaintiff had become a target of her superior's sexual desires because of her sex. The court distinguished *Corne,* in which the plaintiff did not allege that acquiescence to the sexual advances was made a condition of employment. *Tomkins* had clearly established the connection between the demands and acceptance of the demands as a condition of employment.

Both *Tomkins* and *Barnes* held that to prove that sexually harassing conduct is discriminatory, a plaintiff need only show that the harassment would not have occurred but for the plaintiff's sex. A plaintiff need not show that comparable male employees were treated differently.[78] As the court noted in *Tomkins,* "[i]t is only necessary to show that gender is a substantial factor in the discrimination, and that if the plaintiff "had been a man she would not have been treated in the same manner.'"[79]

The issue of liability was not so clear, however. Although the court in *Barnes* had stated that "generally speaking, an employer is chargeable with Title VII violations occasioned by discriminatory practices of supervisory personnel,"[80] courts required the plaintiff to show that the employer had actual or constructive knowledge of the offensive conduct,[81] despite analogous Title VII and common law precedent to the contrary. The Ninth Circuit challenged this approach in *Miller v. Bank of America.*[82]

§ 2.6 *Miller v. Bank of America*

The Ninth Circuit was the first court to impose vicarious liability without regard for employer knowledge in *Miller v. Bank of America.*[83] The plaintiff

---

75 *Id.* at 1048.

76 *Id.* at 1047.

77 561 F.2d 983 (D.C. Cir. 1977).

78 *See, e.g.,* Phillips v. Martin Marietta Corp., 400 U.S. 542 (1971); Kyriazi v. Western Elec. Co., 461 F. Supp. 894 (D.N.J. 1978), *modified,* 473 F. Supp. 786 (D.N.J. 1979), *aff'd,* 647 F.2d 388 (3d Cir. 1981).

79 Tomkins v. Public Serv. Elec. & Gas Co., 568 F.2d 1044, 1047 n.4 (3d Cir. 1977) (citing Skelton v. Balzano, 424 F. Supp. 1231, 1235 (D.D.C. 1976)).

80 Barnes v. Costle, 561 F.2d 983, 993 (D.C. Cir. 1977).

81 *Id.* at 995; Tomkins v. Public Serv. Elec. & Gas Co., 568 F.2d 1044, 1048–49.

82 600 F.2d 211 (9th Cir. 1979).

83 418 F. Supp. 233 (N.D. Cal. 1976), *rev'd,* 600 F.2d 211 (9th Cir. 1979).

alleged that she was offered a better position in exchange for sexual compliance and was fired when she refused. The district court dismissed the complaint on the basis that company policy did not "impose[] or permit[] a consistent, as distinguished from isolated, sex-based discrimination claim on a definable employee group."[84] Unlike the defendant in *Corne*, the Bank of America claimed that it had a companywide policy condemning the alleged conduct. The district court accepted the defendant's argument that the existence of the policy redeemed the employer when the plaintiff neither complained nor requested an investigation, and thus the "isolated and unauthorized sex misconduct of one employee to another" was not attributable to the employer.[85] Although the court acknowledged that "there may be situations in which a sex discrimination action can be maintained for an employer's active, or tacit approval, of a personnel policy requiring sex favors as a condition of employment," it, too, was concerned about the potential for unchecked litigation, conceivably based on "flirtations of the smallest order."[86]

The Ninth Circuit reversed, holding that even though the supervisor's conduct allegedly violated bank policy, the bank was liable for the alleged tortious conduct under the theory of respondeat superior:

> Title VII and § 1981 define wrongs that are a type of tort, for which an employer may be liable. There is nothing in either act which even hints at a congressional intention that the employer is not to be liable if one of its employees, acting in the course of [her or] his employment, commits the tort. Such a rule would create an enormous loophole in the statutes . . . We conclude that respondeat superior does apply here, where the action complained of was that of a supervisor, authorized to hire, fire, discipline or promote, or at least to participate in or recommend such actions, even though what the supervisor is said to have done violates company policy.[87]

The court also rejected the bank's contention that the plaintiff could have obtained redress through the personnel department but did not do so, and thus should not have been allowed to sue. The court "decline[d] to read an exhaustion of company remedies requirement into Title VII."[88]

---

[84] *Id.* at 236.

[85] *Id.* at 234.

[86] *Id.* at 236.

[87] 600 F.2d 211, 213 (9th Cir. 1979).

[88] *Id.* at 214.

§ 2.7 Inconsistencies after *Miller*

The courts continued to treat liability issues inconsistently after *Miller.* A district court of the same circuit declined to adopt the *Miller* court's reasoning, holding in *Vinson v. Taylor*[89] that an employer should not be found vicariously liable without knowledge of the alleged harassment. The plaintiff alleged that she submitted to her supervisor's sexual advances because she feared termination. She brought a discrimination action against the supervisor when she was fired for allegedly taking an indefinite sick leave. The court rejected the plaintiff's argument that notice of the harassment to the offending supervisor constituted notice to the employer bank: "It seems reasonable that an employer should not be liable in these unusual cases of sexual harassment where notice to the employer must depend upon the actual perpetrator and when there is nothing else to place the employer on notice."[90] Although the U.S. Supreme Court ultimately decided this issue in *Meritor Savings Bank v. Vinson,*[91] it remains somewhat cloudy (see **§ 2.14**).

The District Court of the District of Columbia continued to restrict employer liability in *Clark v. World Airways,*[92] a hostile environment case in which the plaintiff asserted a Title VII sexual harassment claim and a tort claim for sexual assault. Because the plaintiff was neither fired nor forced to submit to sexual advances as a condition of continued employment, the court found that her Title VII claim was not actionable. It rejected the plaintiff's argument, drawn from interim EEOC guidelines,[93] that the supervisor's actions violated Title VII because they created a hostile and discriminatory work environment. Even though a jury found the defendant's conduct to constitute assault, the court declined to conclude that such behavior "had the effect of substantially interfering with plaintiff's work performance or creating an offensive work environment."[94] This view would soon wane somewhat with the publication of EEOC's final guidelines on sexual harassment, dividing sexual harassment law into two distinct lines of reasoning.

---

89 23 Fair Empl. Prac. Cas. (BNA) 37, 38 (D.D.C. 1980), *rev'd,* 753 F.2d 141 (D.C. Cir. 1985), *aff'd in part, rev'd in part sub nom.* Meritor Sav. Bank v. Vinson, 477 U.S. 57 (1986).

90 Vinson v. Taylor, 23 Fair Empl. Prac. Cas. (BNA) 37, 42 (D.D.C. 1980), *rev'd,* 753 F.2d 141 (D.C. Cir. 1985).

91 477 U.S. 57 (1986).

92 24 Fair Empl. Prac. Cas. (BNA) 305 (D.D.C. Oct. 24, 1980).

93 29 C.F.R. § 1601.11 (April 3, 1980).

94 24 Fair Empl. Prac. Cas. (BNA) at 308 n.11 (citing 45 Fed. Reg. 25,025 (interim guidelines)).

§ 2.8 EEOC Guidelines

Affirming its longheld position that sexual harassment in employment violates Title VII of the 1964 Civil Rights Act,[95] the EEOC published final guidelines on sexual harassment on November 10, 1980.[96] These guidelines are aimed at sexual harassment that causes "concrete economic detriment to the plaintiff" and results in "creating an unproductive or an offensive working environment."[97] Although sexual harassment law was being shaped by the courts long before the EEOC published its guidelines, their issuance encouraged victims to come forward. In 1980, the EEOC recorded 75 sexual harassment complaints. The following year, the number of complaints climbed to 3,812. By 1987, the yearly number of complaints had risen to 6,775.[98]

Although EEOC guidelines generally are interpretive and do not have the force of law,[99] the U.S. Supreme Court has said that they are "entitled to great deference."[100] The portion of the Guidelines on Discrimination Because of Sex that deals with sexual harassment specifically states:

> § 1604.11 Sexual Harassment.
>
> (a) Harassment on the basis of sex is a violation of § 703 of Title VII. Unwelcome sexual advances, requests for sexual favors, and other verbal or physical conduct of a sexual nature constitute sexual harassment when (1) submission to such conduct is made either explicitly or implicitly a term or condition of an individual's employment, (2) submission to or rejection of such conduct by an individual is used as the basis for employment decisions affecting such individual, or (3) such conduct has the purpose or effect of unreasonably interfering with an individual's work performance or creating an intimidating, hostile, or offensive working environment.
>
> (b) In determining whether alleged conduct constitutes sexual harassment, the Commission will look at the record as a whole and at the totality of the circumstances, such as the nature of the sexual advances and the context in which the alleged incidents occurred. The determination of the legality of a particular action will be made from the facts, on a case by case basis.

---

95 Pub. L. No. 88-352, § 701-16, 78 Stat. 253-66 (1964) (codified at 42 U.S.C. § 2000e-2 (1982)).

96 29 C.F.R. § 1604.11 (1988). *See* 45 Fed. Reg. 25,024 (1980) (Principles in guidelines also apply to discrimination on basis of race, color, religion, or national origin); 29 C.F.R. § 1604.11(a) n.1 (1988). Final EEOC guidelines are almost identical to interim guidelines published at 45 Fed. Reg. 74,677 (1980), with substitution of "unreasonably" for "necessary" in subsection (a)(3) and addition of subsection (e) regarding conduct of nonemployees.

97 Preamble to guidelines, 29 C.F.R. § 1604.11 (1988).

98 Correspondence, Office of EEOC, Aug. 16, 1988.

99 Albermarle Paper Co. v. Moody, 422 U.S. 405, 431 (1975).

100 Griggs v. Duke Power Co., 401 U.S. 424, 433–34 (1971).

(c) Applying general Title VII principles, an employer, employment agency, joint apprenticeship committee or labor organization [hereinafter referred to as "employer"] is responsible for its acts and those of its agents and supervisory employees with respect to sexual harassment regardless of whether the specific acts complained of were authorized or even forbidden by the employer and regardless of whether the employer knew or should have known of their occurrence. The Commission will examine the circumstances of the particular employment relationship and the job functions performed by the individual in determining whether an individual acts in either a supervisory or agency capacity.

(d) With respect to conduct between fellow employees, an employer is responsible for acts of sexual harassment in the workplace where the employer (or its agents or supervisory employees) knows or should have known of the conduct, unless it can show that it took immediate and appropriate corrective action.

(e) An employer may also be responsible for the acts of non-employees, with respect to sexual harassment of employees in the workplace, where the employer (or its agents or supervisory employees) knows or should have known of the conduct and fails to take appropriate corrective action. In reviewing these cases the Commission will consider the extent of the employer's control and any other legal responsibility which the employer may have with respect to the conduct of such non-employees.

(f) Prevention is the best tool for the elimination of sexual harassment. An employer should take all steps necessary to prevent sexual harassment from occurring, expressing strong disapproval, developing appropriate sanctions, informing employees of their right to raise and how to raise the issue of harassment under Title VII, and developing methods to sensitize all concerned.

(g) Other related practices: Where employment opportunities or benefits are granted because of an individual's submission to the employer's sexual advances or requests for sexual favors, the employer may be held liable for unlawful sex discrimination against other persons who were qualified for but denied that employment opportunity or benefit.

The guidelines define sexual harassment broadly and require that a totality of the circumstances be considered to determine whether particular conduct constitutes sexual harassment. The U.S. Supreme Court endorsed this approach in *Meritor Savings Bank v. Vinson*[101] (see § **2.14**). The guidelines outline two types of employer liability: (1) vicarious liability for harassment by agents or supervisors, and (2) direct liability for harassment by coworkers or nonemployees when the employer (or its agents or supervisors) knew or should have known of the conduct. An employer may defeat direct liability by demonstrating that it took "immediate and appropriate corrective action" upon learning of the harassment.

---

[101] 477 U.S. 57 (1986).

Vicarious liability in the context of a hostile environment action was rejected in *Meritor*, which held that employers are not automatically liable for sexual harassment by their supervisors.[102] The solicitor general's amicus curiae brief for the United States and the EEOC retreated from the guidelines' position regarding employer liability, and the U.S. Supreme Court embraced this modified stand. The Court's *Meritor* opinion clearly established the place of sexual harassment in sex discrimination law, but failed to articulate clear standards for determining employer liability and employee responsibility. The EEOC issued a policy statement in 1988 clarifying these liability issues (see **Chapter 3**).

§ 2.9 Hostile Work Environment

The EEOC guidelines condemn offensive sexual conduct regardless of whether a tangible job benefit is at stake. The guidelines hold an employer absolutely liable for the acts of its agents and supervisors, regardless of whether the sexual harassment was forbidden by the employer or whether the employer knew or should have known of the occurrence. Although the absence of a knowledge requirement distinguished the guidelines from most judicial construction at the time they were published, they were based on sound precedent. The scheme for employer liability agrees with other Title VII cases in the areas of racial, ethnic, and religious harassment. Since 1969, the EEOC has construed § 703(a)(1) of Title VII[103] prohibiting discrimination in "conditions of employment" to require an employer to maintain a workplace free of racial, ethnic, or religious discrimination.[104] Courts have unhesitantly held employers liable under Title VII when racial

---

102 *Id.* at 72.

103 42 U.S.C. § 2000e-2(a)(1).

104 EEOC Dec. No. 74-05, 6 Fair Empl. Prac. Cas. (BNA) 834 (1973) (ethnic "kidding" of Spanish-surnamed employee); EEOC Dec. No. 72-1114, 4 Fair Empl. Prac. Cas. (BNA) 842 (1972) (supervisor's preaching caused plaintiff employee to resign). The EEOC found a variety of conduct to violate Title VII, including use of "girl" to refer to adult women. EEOC Dec. No. 72-0679, 4 Fair Empl. Prac. Cas. (BNA) 441 (1971); EEOC Dec. No. 74-05, 6 Fair Empl. Prac. Cas. (BNA) 834 (1973) (telling derogatory ethnic or racial jokes); EEOC Dec. No. 72-1561, 4 Fair Empl. Prac. Cas. (BNA) 852 (1972); EEOC Dec. No. 71-1442, 3 Fair Empl. Prac. Cas. (BNA) 493 (1971); EEOC Dec. No. 70-683, 2 Fair Empl. Prac. Cas. (BNA) 606 (1970); EEOC Dec. No. CL 68-12-431EU, 2 Fair Empl. Prac. Cas. (BNA) 295 (1969); EEOC Dec. No. 72-0957, 4 Fair Empl. Prac. Cas. (BNA) 837 (1972) (use of word "nigger"); EEOC Dec. No. 72-0779, 4 Fair Empl. Prac. Cas. (BNA) 317 (1971); 1973] EEOC Dec. (CCH) ¶ 6193 (Dec. 24, 1970); EEOC Dec. No. 71-909, 3 Fair Empl. Prac. Cas. (BNA) 269 (1970).

The EEOC and courts recognized that psychological harm is caused by the perpetuation of demeaning stereotypes that reinforce one's perception of inferiority in social position. *See, e.g.*, Griggs v. Duke Power Co., 401 U.S. 424 (1971) (requirement of

or ethnic harassment has created psychologically debilitating environments.[105] The notion that conditions included the working environment was first asserted in *Rogers v. EEOC,*[106] a Fifth Circuit opinion that formed the theoretical basis for the U.S. Supreme Court decision in *Meritor* (see **§ 2.14**) by holding that Title VII protects an employee's working environment. Judge Goldberg noted that:

> Congress chose neither to enumerate specific discriminatory practices, nor to elucidate in extenso the parameter of such nefarious activities. Rather, it pursued the path of wisdom by being unconstrictive, knowing that constant change is the order of our day and that the seemingly reasonable practices of

---

high school diploma or passage of intelligence test for employment affected blacks disproportionately); Phillips v. Martin Marietta Corp., 400 U.S. 542 (1971) (refusal to hire women with preschool-age children); Sprogis v. United Airlines, 444 F.2d 1194 (7th Cir. 1971) (requirements that female flight attendants be single); EEOC Dec. No. 72-0679, 4 Fair Empl. Prac. Cas. (BNA) 441 (1971) (calling black female employees "girls"); 1973] Empl. Prac. Dec. (CCH) ¶ 6251 (1971) (requiring black employees to use exaggerated courtesy titles when addressing white supervisors); 1973] EEOC Dec. (CCH) ¶ 6161 (1971) (referring to black employees by first names while using "Mr." or "Mrs." for white employees).

105 *See, e.g.,* Ways v. City of Lincoln, 871 F.2d 750 (8th Cir. 1989) (city police officer of black and native American descent was subjected to racially hostile work environment); DeGrace v. Rumsfeld, 614 F.2d 796 (1st Cir. 1980) (employer liable under Title VII when supervisors allowed racial harassment by coworkers); Cariddi v. Kansas City Chiefs Football Club, 568 F.2d 87 (8th Cir. 1977) (derogatory ethnic slurs could be so excessive and opprobrious as to constitute unlawful employment action under Title VII); Firefighters Inst. for Racial Equality v. City of St. Louis, 549 F.2d 506, 515 (8th Cir.), *cert denied,* 434 U.S. 819 (1977) (city could not allow on-duty fire fighters who used city cooking facilities to exclude blacks from informal "supper club" eating arrangements); Gray v. Greyhound Lines, 545 F.2d 169, 176 (D.C. Cir. 1976) (discriminatory hiring policies that affect plaintiff's psychological well-being can fall under Title VII); Rogers v. EEOC, 454 F.2d 234 (5th Cir. 1971), *cert denied,* 406 U.S. 957 (1972) (working environment heavily charged with discrimination may constitute unlawful practice under Title VII); EEOC v. Murphy Motor Freight Lines, 488 F. Supp. 381, 384 (D. Minn. 1980) (employer was liable under Title VII when he knew or should have known of numerous instances of harassment); Lucero v. Beth Israel Hosp. & Geriatric Ctr., 479 F. Supp. 452 (D. Colo. 1979) (religion); United States v. City of Buffalo, 457 F. Supp. 612, 631 (W.D.N.Y. 1978) (repeated racial slurs and harassment created work environment charged with discrimination); Calcote v. Texas Educ. Found., 458 F. Supp. 231, 237 (W.D. Tex. 1976), *aff'd,* 578 F.2d 95 (5th Cir. 1978); Friend v. Leidinger, 446 F. Supp. 361, 383 (E.D. Va. 1977), *aff'd,* 588 F.2d 61 (4th Cir. 1978); Croker v. Boeing Co. (Vertol Div.), 437 F. Supp. 1138 (E.D. Pa. 1977) (employer liable for harassment when employee's supervisor made comments regarding dress and used racially demeaning language); Compston v. Borden, Inc., 424 F. Supp. 157, 160–61 (S.D. Ohio 1971) (barrage of antisemitic verbal abuse by supervisor was discriminatory); United States v. Lee Way Motor Freight, 7 Fair Empl. Prac. Case. (BNA) 710, 748 (W.D. Okla. 1973); Murry v. American Standard, Inc., 373 F. Supp. 716 (E.D. La.), *aff'd,* 488 F.2d 529 (5th Cir. 1973) (calling only the one black employee "boy" was discriminatory).

106 454 F.2d 234 (5th Cir. 1971), *cert denied,* 406 U.S. 957 (1972).

> the present can easily become the injustices of the morrow. Time was when employment discrimination tended to be viewed as a series of isolated and distinguishable events, manifesting itself, for example, in an employer's practices of hiring, firing, and promoting. But today employment discrimination is a far more complex and pervasive phenomenon, as the nuances and subtleties of discriminatory employment practices are no longer confined to bread and butter issues. . . .
>
> We must be acutely conscious of the fact that Title VII of the Civil Rights Act of 1964 should be accorded a liberal interpretation in order to effectuate the purpose of Congress to eliminate the inconvenience, unfairness and humiliation of ethnic discrimination. . . . Furthermore, I regard this broad-gauged innovation legislation as a charter of principles which are to be elucidated and explicated by experience, time, and expertise. . . . [E]mployees' psychological as well as economic fringes are statutorily entitled to protection from employer abuse, and that the phrase "conditions, terms, and privileges of employment" in § 703 is an expansive concept which sweeps within its protective ambit the practice of creating a working environment heavily charged with ethnic or racial discrimination.[107]

Nevertheless, courts were reluctant to apply the same standard to sexual harassment cases.[108] Some rejected the hostile environment concept outright and required the loss of a tangible job benefit to state a sexual harassment claim under Title VII.[109] Other courts, however, recognized the severe emotional and psychological effects of sexual harassment and extended Title VII protection to include the work environment.

The first case to reject implicitly the tangible loss requirement and apply the EEOC guidelines was *Brown v. City of Guthrie,*[110] in which the district

[107] *Id.* at 238.

[108] *See, e.g.,* Neeley v. American Fidelity Assurance Co., 17 Fair Empl. Prac. Cas. (BNA) 482 (W.D. Okla. 1978). Although five women testified that defendant supervisor had harassed them during a five-year period by making sexual remarks and jokes, exhibiting pictures of sexual activities, and touching them sexually, and the women had complained to no avail to both the supervisor and the public relations director of the company, the court found no liability on the grounds that the conduct was "personal" and made without employer's sanction or knowledge. *Id.* at 485. Language in the opinion indicates that the judge believed the harasser intended no harm, and thus no harm was done. The supervisor merely "affectionately touched the shoulders of some of the female employees . . . never intending to be offensive or otherwise abusive. . . ." *Id.* at 482. *See also* Bundy v. Jackson, 19 Fair Empl. Prac. Cas. (BNA) 828 (D.D.C. 1979), *rev'd,* 641 F.2d 934 (D.C. Cir. 1981) (district court found harassment "a standard operating procedure, a fact of life, a normal condition of employment . . . a game played by male superiors"). *Id.* at 831.

[109] Clark v. World Airways, 24 Fair Empl. Prac. Cas. (BNA) 305 (D.D.C. 1980).

[110] 22 Fair Empl. Prac. Cas. (BNA) 1627 (W.D. Okla. 1980). Other courts suggested that hostile work environment was discriminatory under Title VII without specifically identifying it as such. *See, e.g.,* Macey v. World Airways, 14 Fair Empl. Prac. Cas. (BNA) 1426 (N.D. Cal. 1977). The court found a Title VII violation when hostility from male

court found that verbal sexual advances to a female police dispatcher from her shift commander created an impermissible condition of employment that forced her to resign. The plaintiff had demonstrated that she complained to the highest officer in her company and he had disregarded her complaints. Although the court acknowledged that the extent of employer liability in such cases remained unclear, it found that the plaintiff had met her burden of proof "even under the more stringent test" of employer liability.[111] The court noted that an isolated incident was insufficient to support a finding of sexual harassment in violation of Title VII.[112]

In 1981, the District of Columbia Circuit rendered a landmark sexual harassment opinion in *Bundy v. Jackson.*[113] The court held that the victim of sexual harassment need not lose a tangible job benefit nor be forced to resign to obtain protection from Title VII. The plaintiff had charged that several supervisors made continual sexual advances and propositions, questioned her about her sexual proclivities, ignored her complaints, criticized her work performance, and blocked her bid for promotion. Reversing the district court's decision, the court of appeals drew precedent from racial, religious, and national origin cases to conclude that a discriminatory work environment violates Title VII:

> The relevance of these "discriminatory environment" cases to sexual harassment is beyond serious dispute. Racial or ethnic discrimination against a company's minority clients may reflect no intent to discriminate directly against the company's minority employees, but in poisoning the atmosphere of employment it violates Title VII. Racial slurs, though intentional and

---

coworkers toward a female radio and electronics mechanic caused her supervisor "to become a participant in a course of harassment ultimately leading to her discriminatory discharge." *Id.* at 1428.

[111] Brown v. City of Guthrie, 22 Fair Empl. Prac. Cas. (BNA) 1627, 1633 (W.D. Okla. 1980).

[112] *Id.* at 1632–33. *See* also DeGrace v. Rumsfeld, 614 F.2d 796, 804–05 (1st Cir. 1980) (Title VII was violated when coworkers frequently sent racially threatening letters to plaintiff); Cariddi v. Kansas City Chiefs Football Club, 568 F.2d 87, 88 (8th Cir. 1977) (racial comments as part of one casual conversation did not violate Title VII); EEOC v. Murphy Motor Freight Lines, 488 F. Supp. 381, 384 (D. Minn. 1980) (more than a few isolated incidents of racial harassment necessary to violate Title VII); Winfrey v. Metropolitan Util. Dist., 467 F. Supp. 56, 60 (D. Neb. 1979) (calling black man "boy" in one isolated conversation did not violate Title VII); Friend v. Leidinger, 446 F. Supp. 361, 382–83 (E.D. Va. 1977), *aff'd,* 588 F.2d 61 (4th Cir. 1978) (isolated racial slurs and harassment in violation of employer policy did not fall under Title VII); Croker v. Boeing Co. (Vertol Div.), 437 F. Supp. 1138, 1191 (E.D. Pa. 1977) (plaintiff must demonstrate more than isolated, "accidental," or sporadic discriminatory acts); Fekete v. United States Steel Corp., 353 F. Supp. 1177, 1186 (W.D. Pa. 1973) (employer who took steps to prevent and control few isolated incidents of harassment over a five-year period was not liable under Title VII).

[113] 641 F.2d 934 (D.C. Cir. 1981).

> directed at individuals, may still be just verbal insults, yet they too may create Title VII liability. How then can sexual harassment, which injects the most demeaning sexual stereotypes into the general work environment and which always represents an intentional assault on an individual's innermost privacy, not be illegal?[114]

The court noted that without this rule, an employer could legally condone the perpetuation of an offensive environment simply by taking no employment action against a noncompliant employee.

> The employer can thus implicitly and effectively make the employee's endurance of sexual intimidation a "condition" of her employment. The woman then faces a "cruel trilemma." She can endure the harassment. She can attempt to oppose it, with little hope of success, either legal or practical, but with every prospect of making the job even less tolerable for her. Or she can leave her job, with little hope of legal relief and the likely prospect of another job where she will face harassment anew.[115]

Although expansive, the decision in *Bundy* suggested that a liability determination could depend on employer knowledge of the alleged harassment. Supervisors on several levels were aware of Bundy's complaints of harassment, yet they ignored them and participated in the conduct. The court cited *Barnes* dicta that an employer might not be liable for sexual harassment by its supervisors if the supervisors contravened company policy without the employer's knowledge and the employer took appropriate action immediately[116] (see **§ 2.15**).

In 1982, the Eleventh Circuit provided an analytical framework for hostile environment sexual harassment determinations in *Henson v. City of Dundee.*[117] The plaintiff alleged that she resigned under duress after working as a police dispatcher because the chief of police had subjected her to sexual harassment, creating a hostile and offensive working environment. She also asserted that she had been threatened with discharge if she did not yield to the chief's sexual advances and was prevented from attending the police academy because she refused to comply with his demands. The court held that under certain circumstances, "the creation of an offensive or hostile work environment due to sexual harassment can violate Title VII irrespective of whether the plaintiff suffers tangible job detriment."[118]

> Sexual harassment which creates a hostile or offensive environment for members of one sex is every bit the arbitrary barrier to sexual equality at the

---

[114] *Id.*

[115] *Id.* at 946.

[116] *Id.* at 943.

[117] 682 F.2d 897 (11th Cir. 1982).

[118] *Id.* at 899–901.

> workplace that racial harassment is to racial equality. Surely, a requirement that a man or woman run a gauntlet of sexual abuse in return for the privilege of being allowed to work and make a living can be as demeaning and disconcerting as the harshest of racial epithets. A pattern of sexual harassment inflicted upon an employee because of her sex is a pattern of behavior that inflicts disparate treatment upon a member of one sex with respect to terms, conditions, or privileges of employment. There is no requirement that an employee subjected to such disparate treatment prove in addition that she has suffered tangible job detriment.[119]

The court modified the traditional prima facie elements (see **Chapter 6**) to require:

1. The employee was a member of a protected group.
2. The employee was subjected to unwelcome sexual advances.
3. The harassment was based on sex.
4. The harassment affected a "term, condition, or privilege" of employment.
5. The harassment was either actively or constructively known by the employer who failed to take prompt remedial action.[120]

The court offered a basis for the difference in liability between *quid pro quo* and hostile environment actions:

> The environment in which an employee works can be rendered offensive in an equal degree by the acts of supervisors, coworkers, or even strangers to the workplace. The capacity of any person to create a hostile or offensive environment is not necessarily enhanced or diminished by any degree of authority which the employer confers upon that individual. When a supervisor gratuitously insults an employee, he generally does so for his own reasons and by his own means. He thus acts outside the actual or apparent scope of the authority he possesses as a supervisor. His conduct cannot automatically be imputed to the employer any more than can the conduct of an ordinary employee.
>
> The typical case of quid pro quo sexual harassment is fundamentally different. In such a case, the supervisor relies upon his apparent or actual authority to extort sexual consideration from an employee. Therein lies the quid pro quo. In that case the supervisor uses the means furnished to him by the employer to accomplish the prohibited purpose. He acts within the scope of his actual or apparent authority to "hire, fire, discipline or promote." Because the supervisor is acting within at least the apparent scope of the authority entrusted to him by the employer when he makes employment decisions, his conduct can fairly be imputed to the source of his authority.[121]

---

[119] *Id.* at 902. *See* also Morgan v. Hertz Corp, 542 F. Supp. 123, 128 (W.D. Tenn. 1981), *aff'd,* 725 F.2d 1070 (6th Cir. 1984) (sexually offensive comments to female employees constituted sexual harassment).

[120] Henson v. City of Dundee, 682 F.2d 897, 903–05 (11th Cir. 1982).

[121] *Id.* at 910 (footnotes omitted).

§ 2.10 —Refining Proof Requirements

At the time the hostile environment doctrine was developed, most courts were holding employers vicariously liable for sexual harassment by supervisors in *quid pro quo* harassment situations, citing the supervisors' position of authority. However, despite the fact that the EEOC guidelines did not distinguish between the two types of sexual harassment for purposes of liability, the knowledge requirement continued to appear in analyses of hostile environment cases. In *Katz v. Dole,*[122] the Fourth Circuit concluded that a workplace that was "pervaded with sexual slur, insult and innuendo" and harassment in the form of "extremely vulgar and offensive sexually related epithets addressed to and employed about" the plaintiff by supervisors as well as coworkers was sexually hostile and in violation of Title VII.[123] The court further refined the analytical framework of *Henson v. City of Dundee:*[124]

> Although such a claim of sexual harassment might be analyzed under the familiar Title VII disparate treatment formula, we think that a somewhat different order of proof is appropriate. . . . In the usual case involving allegations of disparate treatment, once the plaintiff establishes that he or she was disadvantaged in fact by some employment decision or practice, the crux of the matter is the question of motive: was there an intent to discriminate along legally impermissible lines such as race or gender? In cases involving claims of sexual harassment, on the other hand, the sexual advance almost always will represent "an intentional assault on an individual's innermost privacy." Bundy, 641 F.2d at 945. Therefore, once the plaintiff in such a case proves that harassment took place, the most difficult legal question typically will concern the responsibility of the employer for the harassment. Except in situations when a proprietor, partner, or corporate officer personally participates in the harassing behavior, the plaintiff will have the additional responsibility of demonstrating the propriety of holding the employer liable under some theory of respondeat superior. We believe that in a "condition of work" case the plaintiff must demonstrate that the employer had actual or constructive knowledge of the existence of a sexually hostile working environment and took no prompt and adequate remedial action. . . . The plaintiff may do this by proving that complaints were lodged with the employer or that the harassment was so pervasive that employer awareness may be inferred. Thus, we posit a two-step analysis. First, the plaintiff must make a prima facie showing that sexually harassing actions took place, and if this is done, the employer may rebut the showing either directly, by proving that the events did not take place, or indirectly, by showing that they were isolated or trivial. Second, the plaintiff must

---

[122] 709 F.2d 251 (4th Cir. 1983).

[123] *Id.* at 254.

[124] Henson v. City of Dundee, 682 F.2d 897 (11th Cir. 1982).

> show that the employer knew or should have known of the harassment, and took no effectual action to correct the situation. This showing can also be rebutted by the employer directly, or by pointing to prompt remedial action reasonably calculated to end the harassment. Title VII is not a clean language act, and it does not require employers to extirpate all signs of centuries-old prejudice. But to avoid liability under Title VII, an employer on notice of sexual harassment must do more than indicate the existence of an official policy against such harassment. Where, as here, the employer's supervisory personnel manifested unmistakable acquiescence in or approval of the harassment, the burden on the employer seeking to avoid liability is especially heavy.[125]

In *Craig v. Y&Y Snacks,*[126] the Third Circuit rejected the defendant's contention that *Tomkins* (see **§ 2.5**) required an employer to have actual or constructive knowledge of the alleged sexual harassment at the time the advance was made, finding that actual knowledge at the time of the employment decision sufficed. However, the court further to indicated that employment decisions by a supervisor may be imputed to the employer "as long as the distinction between purely personal conduct and conduct having direct employment circumstances set forth in *Tomkins* is observed."[127] *Tomkins,* decided in 1977, did not recognize hostile environment sexual harassment and distinguished "complaints alleging sexual advances of an individual or personal nature" from "those alleging direct employment consequences flowing from the advances."[128] Thus, the implications of the *Craig* court are unclear. The suggestion that conduct creating a hostile environment is of a "purely personal" nature, as well as the notion expressed in *Henson* that supervisor hostility is generally outside the scope of employment, contradict the language and substance of the EEOC guidelines and other judicial construction of the hostile environment theory.

§ 2.11 —Expansion of Employer Liability

The most expansive opinion generated by the hostile environment cases came from the Third Circuit in *Vinson v. Taylor.*[129] The court held that an employer was absolutely liable for sexual harassment by supervisors, whether the employer knew or should have known of the misconduct. The court concluded that a supervisor was an agent of the employer under Title VII, even if the supervisor lacked the authority to hire, fire, or promote:

---

125 Katz v. Dole, 709 F.2d 251, 254–56 (footnotes omitted) (4th Cir. 1983).

126 721 F.2d 77 (3d Cir. 1983).

127 *Id.* at 80–81.

128 Tomkins v. Public Serv. Elec. & Gas Co., 568 F.2d 1044, 1048 (3d Cir. 1977).

129 753 F.2d 141 (D.C. Cir. 1985), *aff'd in part, rev'd in part sub nom.* Meritor Sav. Bank v. Vinson, 477 U.S. 57 (1986).

We agree [with the EEOC guidelines] that treatment of supervisory personnel as "agents" is in conformity with "general Title VII principles." Our cases have established, as the cornerstone of present analysis, that sexual harassment is a violation of Title VII. Neither the statutory language nor its legislative history suggests that, as a trespass on Title VII, it should be treated any differently from transgressions arising out of racial or religious discrimination. And the caselaw in these latter areas establishes beyond cavil that "an employer is chargeable with Title VII violations occasioned by discriminatory practices of supervisory personnel."

We have no difficulty in concluding that an employer may be held accountable for discrimination accomplished through sexual harassment by any supervisory employee with authority to hire, to promote or to fire. An employer's delegation of this much authority vests in the supervisor such extreme power over the victimized employee that the supervisor's stature as an "agent" of the employer cannot be doubted. We do not believe, however, that vicarious responsibility is limited to discrimination by supervisors so richly endowed.

The mere existence—or even the appearance—of a significant degree of influence in vital job decisions gives any supervisor the opportunity to impose upon employees. That opportunity is not dependent solely upon the supervisor's authority to make personnel decisions; the ability to direct employees in their work, to evaluate their performances and to recommend personnel actions carries attendant power to coerce, intimidate and harass. For this reason, we think that employers must answer for sexual harassment of any subordinate by any supervisory superior.

In so holding, we consider only the statutory language and interpretations authoritatively placed upon it. We do not resort to common-law doctrine of respondeat superior.

* * *

More particularly, limitations imposed by the doctrine of respondeat superior have no place in enforcement of the congressional will underlying Title VII. Confining liability, as the common law would, to situations in which a supervisor acted within the scope of his authority conceivably could lead to the ludicrous result that employers would become accountable only if they explicitly require or consciously allow their supervisors to molest women employees. While modern courts seem more inclined to treat intentional misconduct on the job as arising out of and in the course of the employment, and thus as providing a basis for liability under a somewhat expanded theory of respondeat superior, there simply is no need to so confine either the analysis or the solution where Title VII applies.

To hold that an employer cannot be reached for Title VII violations unknown to him is, too, to open the door to circumvention of Title VII by the simple expedient of looking the other way, even as signs of discriminatory practice begin to gather on the horizon.

* * *

> Employer responsiveness to on-the-job discrimination at the supervisory level is an essential aspect of the remedial scheme embodied in Title VII. It is the employer alone who is able promptly and effectively to halt discriminatory practices by supervisory personnel, and only the employer can provide reinstatement, backpay or other remedial relief contemplated by the Act. Much of the promise of Title VII will become empty if victims of unlawful discrimination cannot secure redress from the only source capable of providing it.
>
> A requirement of knowledge by the employer of Title VII transgressions by supervisory personnel would effectively eliminate vicarious Title VII responsibility altogether. It would reserve Title VII liability for only those employers who fail to redress known violations—a direct, not a substitutional, theory of attribution. This would be a retreat from the level of protection Title VII has consistently and designedly afforded, and take a backward step we refuse to endorse.[130]

The *Vinson* court's approach to employer liability broadened the disparity in liability analyses between *quid pro quo* and hostile environment cases. The implications of the decision may have prompted the U.S. Supreme Court to review *Vinson* and render its first opinion on sexual harassment (see § **2.14**).

§ 2.12 Coworker and Nonemployee Harassment

Pursuant to §§ (d) and (e) of the EEOC guidelines, courts extended Title VII protections to coworker and nonemployee harassment when an employer knew or should have known of the harassment and failed to rectify the situation. Coworker conduct constituted sexual harassment in *Kyriazi v. Western Electric Co.,*[131] when male employees made "loud remarks" about the plaintiff's marital status, wagered about her virginity, and drew a cartoon designed "to humiliate her as a woman."[132] The court found that although three male supervisors were aware of the conduct, they failed to take any action to control it, and thus the employer was liable under Title VII. The court also exercised pendent jurisdiction of the plaintiff's state claims and found all the defendants, including the supervisors and coworkers, guilty of malicious interference with the plaintiff's employment contract. In a separate opinion, the court assessed punitive damages against the coworkers and supervisors as well as the employer,

---

[130] *Id.* at 149–52 (D.C. Cir. 1985) (footnotes omitted).

[131] 461 F. Supp. 894 (D.N.J. 1978).

[132] *Id.* at 934.

noting that "[w]hile it is hardly this Court's role to penalize n ness, when a party's deliberate conduct is so extreme that it inte. interferes with another's ability to practice a profession or earn a hood, the wrongdoer must be punished and deterred."[133]

The Minnesota Supreme Court rendered a much-cited decision reg ing hostile environment harassment in *Continental Can Co. v. Minnesota.*[134] The court held that verbal sexual advances, sexually derogatory statements, and sexually motivated physical contact with a female employee by male coworkers violated the Minnesota Human Rights Act.[135] Continental Can had failed to respond to the plaintiff's complaints to her supervisor, and when she complained to the plant manager, Continental did not initiate a formal investigation for more than two weeks. A week later, company officials informed employees at a plant meeting that verbal or physical harassment would not be tolerated. When the plaintiff refused to return to work because the company would not ensure her safety, she was terminated. A hearing examiner for the Minnesota Department of Human Rights concluded that the employer had discriminated on the basis of sex, and awarded back pay. On appeal to the state district court, the hearing examiner's decision was reversed and the complaint dismissed with prejudice. The department appealed the decision to the state supreme court, which found a violation of the Human Rights Act. Citing analogous racial discrimination cases[136] and the EEOC guidelines, the court noted that a violation of the Act is clearer "when promotion or retention of employment is conditioned on dispensation of sexual favors."[137] However, the court recognized the power of an offensively charged atmosphere and held that the Act prohibits hostile environment harassment when the employer knows or

---

[133] Kyriazi v. Western Elec. Co., 476 F. Supp. 335, 340 (D.N.J. 1979).

First Circuit: Hosemann v. Technical Materials, Inc., 554 F. Supp. 659 (D.R.I. 1982) (antifemale comments by coworker did not constitute sexual harassment when record did not show that conduct substantially interfered with plaintiff's work performance; plaintiff had stated she would have been happy to return to her position).

Second Circuit: *Cf.* Kramer-Navarro v. Postal Serv., 586 F. Supp. 677, 684 (S.D.N.Y. 1984) (plaintiff did not suffer sexual harassment at hands of male coworkers when record indicated that plaintiff had "by her hostile and belligerent attitude, succeeded in alienating her coworkers and provoking arguments at every turn").

[134] 297 N.W. 2d 241 (Minn. 1980).

[135] Minn. Stat. Ann. § 363.03(1) (West 1991 & Supp. 1993).

[136] Friend v. Leidinger, 446 F. Supp. 361 (E.D. Va. 1977), *aff'd,* 588 F.2d 61 (4th Cir. 1978); Howard v. National Cash Register Co., 388 F. Supp. 603 (S.D. Ohio 1975). Other cases involving coworker harassment include EEOC v. Murphy Motor Freight Lines, 488 F. Supp. 381, 384 (D. Minn. 1980); DeGrace v. Rumsfeld, 614 F.2d 796 (1st Cir. 1980) (employer liable under Title VII when supervisors allowed racial harassment by coworkers); Bell v. St. Regis Paper Co., 425 F. Supp. 1126, 1137 (N.D. Ohio 1976).

[137] Continental Can Co. v. Minnesota, 297 N.W.2d 241, 248.

should have known of harassment by nonsupervisory employees and fails to take timely and appropriate action. It said that "[r]epeated, unwarranted and unwelcome verbal and physical conduct of a sexual nature, requests for sexual favors and sexually derogatory remarks clearly may impact on the conditions of employment."[138]

---

[138] *Id.* at 249. *See* also Second Circuit: Taylor v. Faculty-Student Ass'n. of State Univ. College, Inc., 40 Fair Empl. Prac. Cas. (BNA) 1292, 1294 (W.D.N.Y. 1986) (although employer asserted it was not liable for obscene remarks made by male coworkers of plaintiff dining hall worker when it took immediate remedial action, employer was not entitled to summary judgment because it was unclear when defendant became aware of plaintiff's allegations).

Third Circuit: Freedman v. American Standard, 41 Fair Empl. Prac. Cas. (BNA) 471, 476 (D.N.J. 1986) (discharged female pilot who received obscene message from coworkers, was treated rudely by other pilots on two occasions and coolly by one pilot when she refused his sexual proposition, and was required to clean up plane interior after other employees had gone home was not sexually harassed when incidents were isolated and not brought to attention of her supervisor; plaintiff was discharged because three times she failed to pass required basic flight checks); Ukarish v. Magnesium Elektron, 31 Fair Empl. Prac. Cas. (BNA) 1315 (D.N.J. 1983). Sexually oriented "banter" between plaintiff and male coworker was not sexual harassment despite credible diary entries by plaintiff indicating exchanges were offensive when male employee did not single out plaintiff as target; plaintiff did not complain to higher management, and middle manager to whom she complained responded promptly. There was no indication the conduct had significant impact on plaintiff's job.

Fifth Circuit: Durant v. Owens-Illinois Glass Co., 517 F. Supp. 710 (E.D. La. 1980), *aff'd,* 656 F.2d 89 (5th Cir. 1981) (two incidents of verbal harassment by coworker, who was later reprimanded, did not constitute sexual harassment).

Sixth Circuit: Martin v. Norbar, Inc., 537 F. Supp. 1260, 1262 (S.D. Ohio 1982) An employer was not granted summary judgment in action by female employee alleging that employer's refusal to take corrective action after plaintiff complained of sexual harassment by coworker made submission to sexual harassment a term or condition of employment. Employer contended it had no duty to reassign plaintiff on basis of one complaint and in face of coworker's denial, and that failure to grant motion for summary judgment "would be tantamount to holding that an employer must treat all allegations of sexual harassment as true, regardless of the circumstances."

Seventh Circuit: Scott v. Sears, Roebuck & Co., 605 F. Supp. 1047 (N.D. Ill. 1985), *aff'd,* 798 F.2d 210 (7th Cir. 1986) (plaintiff car mechanic who never complained to superior of alleged sexual harassment by coworkers and who offered no evidence that employer knew of harassment could not hold defendant liable for sexual harassment; challenged conduct also fell short of severity and pervasiveness necessary to establish actionable hostile environment); Zabkowicz v. West Bend Co., 589 F. Supp. 780, 784 (E.D. Wis. 1984) (hostile environment was found when coworkers subjected plaintiff to abusive language and exposure, called her "slut," "bitch," and "fucking cunt," grabbed her crotch, and displayed sexual offensive drawings, some of which included plaintiff, and no disciplinary action was ever taken).

Eighth Circuit: Barrett v. Omaha Nat'l Bank, 726 F.2d 424, 427 (8th Cir. 1984) (district court properly concluded that defendant took immediate and appropriate corrective action in response to plaintiff's complaint that on the way to and during a two-day conference, a coworker talked about sexual activity and touched her in offensive way;

Courts also applied Title VII to situations in which employees were sexually harassed by nonemployees, such as customers or passersby. For example, a sexually provocative dress code could violate Title VII when it was imposed as a condition of employment. In *Marentette v. Michigan Host, Inc.,*[139] the plaintiff alleged that the uniforms she was required to wear subjected her to verbal and physical harassment as well as insults and taunts from customers.[140] In *EEOC v. Sage Realty Corp.,*[141] the court held that it was discriminatory to require a female lobby attendant to wear a "short, revealing and sexually provocative" bicentennial uniform. By doing so, the court said, "[the] defendants made her acquiesce in sexual harassment by the public, and perhaps by building tenants, a prerequisite of her employment as a lobby attendant."[142]

§ 2.13 Decisions after EEOC Guidelines

By the time the EEOC guidelines were published and only several years after a string of decisions had rejected the viability of sexual harassment claims, case law had firmly established that sexual advances constituted sex discrimination under the law. All courts concurred that, at the very least, *quid pro quo* harassment violated Title VII,[143] but agreement often stopped

---

within four days of complaint, employer informed offending coworker and other worker who failed to intervene that their conduct would not be tolerated).

Eleventh Circuit: Wimberly v. Shoney's, Inc., 39 Fair Empl. Prac. Cas. (BNA) 444, 453 (S.D. Ga. 1985). (Five former employees failed to establish that supervisors and coworkers created hostile environment in violation of Title VII when alleged incidents were "random, sometimes meaningless, encounters." One plaintiff did establish that she was verbally and physically sexually harassed, but court did not decide whether acts amounted to creation of hostile environment when none of plaintiffs complained to higher management (because they feared retaliation) and harassment claims were not so pervasive as to impute knowledge to employer.

139 506 F. Supp. 909 (E.D. Mich. 1980).

140 The case was dismissed as moot when injunctive relief was no longer necessary and plaintiff did not request back pay for a one-day suspension.

141 507 F. Supp. 599 (S.D.N.Y. 1981).

142 *Id.* at 609–10 (*Sage* case was not purely a sexual harassment action; the court based its holding in part on unequal dress requirements).

143 Third Circuit: Horn v. Duke Homes, Inc., 755 F.2d 599, 605 (3d Cir. 1983) ("Because of her sex . . . Horn was disadvantaged by pressure to submit to an additional, humiliating condition of employment that served no legitimate purpose of the employer. Her right to refuse this condition was protected by Title VII."); Craig v. Y&Y Snacks, 721 F.2d 77 (3d Cir. 1983) (*quid pro quo* harassment found); Tomkins v. Public Serv. Elec. & Gas Co., 568 F.2d 1044 (3d Cir. 1977); Blessing v. Lancaster County, 609 F. Supp. 485 (E.D. Pa. 1985) (cause of action stated).

Fifth Circuit: Simmons v. Lyons, 746 F.2d 265 (5th Cir. 1984) (*quid pro quo* harassment claim survived summary judgment motion); Capaci v. Katz & Besthoff, Inc., 525

there. Overall, the EEOC guidelines provided an effective framework for analyzing sexual harassment claims, and the current state of the law reflects deference to most of the guidelines' provisions. As noted in §§ **2.9** through **2.12,** the guidelines encouraged judicial recognition of hostile environment, coworker, and nonworker harassment. Homosexual harassment also was found to fall within Title VII.[144] Constructive discharge[145]

F. Supp. 317 (N.D. La. 1981), *modified on other grounds,* 711 F.2d 647 (5th Cir. 1983) (cause of action stated).

Eighth Circuit: Mays v. Williamson & Sons, 591 F. Supp. 1518 (E.D. Ark. 1984), *aff'd,* 775 F.2d 258 (8th Cir. 1985) (prima facie showing of *quid pro quo* sexual harassment); Meyers v. I.T.T. Diversified Credit Corp., 527 F. Supp. 1064 (E.D. Mo. 1981) (plaintiff demonstrated she was discharged and suffered disparate treatment because she refused to acquiesce to supervisor's sexual advances).

Eleventh Circuit: Phillips v. Smalley Maintenance Servs. Corp., 711 F.2d 1524 (11th Cir. 1983) (former employee established she was terminated for refusing sexual advances); Cummings v. Walsh Constr. Co., 561 F. Supp. 872 (S.D. Ga. 1983) (plaintiff stated claim of *quid pro quo* sexual harassment); Carter v. Dialysis Clinic, Inc., 28 Fair Empl. Prac. Cas. (BNA) 268 (N.D. Ga. 1981) (stated claim of *quid pro quo* harassment).

No *quid pro quo* harassment was found in the following cases:

Second Circuit: Ramsey v. Olin Corp., 39 Fair Empl. Prac. Cas. (BNA) 959 (S.D.N.Y. 1984).

Third Circuit: Anderson v. University Health Ctr., 623 F. Supp. 795 (W.D. Pa. 1985); Reichman v. Bureau of Affirmative Action, 536 F. Supp. 1149 (M.D. Pa. 1982).

Fourth Circuit: Yourse v. Miller, 38 Fair Empl. Prac. Cas. (BNA) 287 (M.D.N.C. 1982).

Sixth Circuit: Hill v. BASF Wyandotte Corp., 27 Fair Empl. Prac. Cas. (BNA) 66 (E.D. Mich. 1981).

Seventh Circuit: Kwiatkowski v. Postal Serv., 39 Fair Empl. Prac. Cas. (BNA) 1740 (N.D. Ill. 1985); Burns v. Terre Haute Regional Hosp., 581 F. Supp. 1301 (S.D. Ind. 1983).

Ninth Circuit: Cordes v. County of Yavapai, 17 Fair Empl. Prac. Cas. (BNA) 1224 (D. Ariz. 1978).

Tenth Circuit: Davis v. Bristol Lab., 26 Fair Empl. Prac. Cas. (BNA) 1351 (W.D. Okla. 1981).

Eleventh Circuit: Wimberly v. Shoney's, Inc., 39 Fair Empl. Prac. Cas. (BNA) 444, 453–54 (S.D. Ga. 1985) (testimony did not support claims of five plaintiffs that they were victims of *quid pro quo* sexual harassment); Hall v. F.O. Thacker Contracting Co., 24 Fair Empl. Prac. Cas. (BNA) 1499 (N.D. Ga. 1980).

District of Columbia Circuit: Bouchet v. National Urban League, 33 Fair Empl. Prac. Cas. (BNA) 536 (D.D.C. 1982), *aff'd,* 730 F.2d 799 (D.C. Cir. 1984).

Federal Circuit: Downes v. Federal Aviation Admin., 775 F.2d 288 (Fed. Cir. 1985).

144 Joyner v. AAA Cooper Trans., 597 F. Supp. 537 (M.D. Ala. 1983), *aff'd,* 749 F.2d 732 (11th Cir. 1984). *See also* Wright v. Methodist Youth Servs., 511 F. Supp. 307 (N.D. Ill. 1981); Barlow v. Northwestern Memorial Hosp., 30 Fair Empl. Prac. Cas. (BNA) 223 (N.D. Ill. 1980).

145 Second Circuit: Kramer-Navarro v. Postal Serv., 586 F. Supp. 677, 684 (S.D.N.Y. 1984) (plaintiff postal worker was not constructively discharged because of sexual

and retaliation[146] claims became common elements of sexual harassment suits. Although Title VII claims were by far the most common, constitutional[147]

---

harassment by coworkers when record indicated "plaintiff had, by her hostile and belligerent attitude, succeeded in alienating coworkers and provoking arguments at every turn").

Third Circuit: Toscano v. Nimmo, 32 Fair Empl. Prac. Cas. (BNA) 1401 (D. Del. 1983) (although court found that plaintiff had been sexually harassed and had been subjected to unlawful retaliation for complaints of harassment, it did not find that plaintiff's transfer to lesser grade level constituted constructive demotion).

Sixth Circuit: Vermett v. Hough, 627 F. Supp. 587 (W.D. Mich. 1986) (constructive discharge claim could not stand); Lynch v. Dean, 39 Fair Empl. Prac. Cas. (BNA) 338 (M.D. Tenn. 1985); Robson v. Eva's Mkt., 538 F. Supp. 857, 859 (N.D. Ohio 1982).

Eighth Circuit: Barrett v. Omaha Nat'l Bank, 726 F.2d 424 (8th Cir. 1984) (constructive discharge not established); Gan v. Kepro Circuit Sys., 28 Fair Empl. Prac. Cas. (BNA) 639, 641 (E.D. Mo. 1982).

Eleventh Circuit: Henson v. City of Dundee, 682 F.2d 897 (11th Cir. 1982) (former police dispatcher resigned not because of sexual harassment, but because man with whom she was having affair was forced to resign); Wimberly v. Shoney's, Inc., 39 Fair Empl. Prac. Cas. (BNA) 444 (S.D. Ga. 1985).

146 Second Circuit: Cobb v. Dufresne-Henry, Inc., 603 F. Supp. 1048 (D. Vt. 1985) (plaintiff discharged for lying, not for complaining about allegedly sexist poster at work).

Third Circuit: Toscano v. Nimmo, 32 Fair Emp. Prac. Cas. (BNA) 1401 (D. Del. 1983) (plaintiff, who complained of discrimination, subjected to retaliatory harassment by supervisor).

Sixth Circuit: Vermett v. Hough, 627 F. Supp. 587 (W.D. Mich. 1986) (plaintiff presented no evidence that defendant retaliated against her for filing EEOC charge); Sand v. Johnson, 33 Fair Empl. Prac. Cas. (BNA) 716 (E.D. Mich. 1982) (plaintiff fired because of constant tardiness, not alleged harassment).

Eighth Circuit: Barrett v. Omaha Nat'l Bank, 726 F.2d 424, 428 (8th Cir. 1984) (alleged retaliatory actions not causally connected to sexual harassment complaint); Harrison v. Reed Rubber Co., 603 F. Supp. 1457 (E.D. Mo. 1985); Mays v. Williamson & Sons, 591 F. Supp. 1518 (E.D. Ark. 1984), *aff'd,* 775 F.2d 258 (8th Cir. 1985).

Ninth Circuit: EEOC v. Judson Steel Co., 33 Fair Empl. Prac. Cas. (BNA) 1286 (N.D. Cal. 1982) (plaintiffs established claim of unlawful retaliation by showing they were suspended almost immediately after lodging charges with EEOC and reasons for suspension were essentially without merit).

Tenth Circuit: Arnold v. City of Seminole, 614 F. Supp. 853 (E.D. Okla. 1985) (city retaliated against plaintiff female police officer for filing discrimination action); Scott v. City of Overland Park, 595 F. Supp. 520 (D. Kan. 1984) (plaintiff stated retaliation claim despite failure to use term "retaliation" in her charge; allegedly denied training because of sex and because she contacted EEOC).

District of Columbia Circuit: Jaspers v. Alexander, 15 Fair Empl. Prac. Cas. (BNA) 1234 (D.D.C. 1977) (plaintiff failed to show she was harassed because of her sex or in retaliation for having filed EEOC complaint or pursuing Title VII rights).

147 Third Circuit: Gobla v. Crestwood Sch. Dist., 609 F. Supp. 972 (M.D. Pa. 1985) (§ 1983); Blessing v. Lancaster County, 609 F. Supp. 485 (E.D. Pa. 1985) (§ 1983); Skadegaard v. Farrell, 33 Fair Empl. Prac. Cas. (BNA) 1528 (D.N.J. 1984) (§ 1983).

and pendent state[148] claims were heard with increasing frequency, and the number of state court actions climbed as well (see **Chapters 9** and **10**).

But although the number of claims was increasing and more courts were recognizing the invidious nature of sexual harassment, many issues remained unsettled. Most significant was the uneven treatment of hostile environment claims. Most courts acknowledged the viability of such actions,[149] but some rejected the hostile environment theory outright or

---

Fifth Circuit: Simmons v. Lyons, 746 F.2d 265 (5th Cir. 1984).

Sixth Circuit: Estate of Scott v. deLeon, 603 F. Supp. 1328, 1332 (E.D. Mich. 1985).

Seventh Circuit: Trigg v. Fort Wayne Community Sch., 766 F.2d 299 (7th Cir. 1985) (equal protection, privacy); Huebschen v. Department of Health & Social Servs., 716 F.2d 1167, 32 Fair Empl. Prac. Cas. (BNA) 1582 (7th Cir. 1983) (§ 1983); Woerner v. Brzeczek, 519 F. Supp. 517 (N.D. Ill. 1981) (§ 1983).

Tenth Circuit: Scott v. City of Overland Park, 595 F. Supp. 520 (D. Kan. 1984) (§ 1983 and Title VII).

148 Third Circuit: Wolk v. Saks Fifth Ave., 728 F.2d 221 (3d Cir. 1984) (Pa. Human Relations Act); Robson v. Eva's Market, 538 F. Supp. 857, 859 (N.D. Ohio 1982) (tort claims); Stringer v. Pennsylvania Dep't of Community Affairs, 446 F. Supp. 704 (M.D. Pa. 1978) (tort claims).

Fourth Circuit: Frykberg v. State Farm Mut. Auto. Ins. Co., 557 F. Supp. 517 (W.D.N.C. 1983) (intentional infliction of emotional distress).

Seventh Circuit: Zywicki v. Versa Technology, Inc., 31 Fair Empl. Prac. Cas. (BNA) 1348 (E.D. Wis. 1983) (wrongful discharge).

Eighth Circuit: Harrison v. Reed Rubber Co., 603 F. Supp. 1457, 37 Fair Empl. Prac. Cas. (BNA) 1544 (E.D. Mo. 1984) (assault and battery, intentional infliction of emotional distress).

Eleventh Circuit: Bell v. Crackin Good Bakers, Inc., 777 F.2d 1497 (11th Cir. 1985) (intentional infliction of emotional distress); Phillips v. Smalley Maintenance Servs. Corp., 711 F.2d 1524 (11th Cir. 1983) (common law battery and state invasion of privacy law); Wimberly v. Shoney's, Inc., 39 Fair Empl. Prac. Cas. (BNA) 444 (S.D. Ga. 1985) (tort claims); Cummings v. Walsh Const. Co., 561 F. Supp. 872 (S.D. Ga. 1983) (tort, invasion of privacy claims); Forde v. Royal's, Inc., 537 F. Supp. 1173, 31 Fair Empl. Prac. Cas. (BNA) 213 (S.D. Fla. 1982), *aff'd,* 705 F.2d 445 (11th Cir. 1983) (breach of contract, intentional infliction of emotional distress).

District of Columbia Circuit: Coleman v. American Broadcasting Co., 38 Fair Empl. Prac. Cas. (BNA) 65 (D.D.C. 1985) (tort); Epps v. Ripley, 30 Fair Empl. Prac. Cas. (BNA) 1632 (D.D.C. 1982) (tort); Stewart v. Thomas, 538 F. Supp. 891 (D.D.C. 1982) (assault, battery, intentional infliction of emotional distress); Rogers v. Loews L'Enfant Plaza Hotel, 526 F. Supp. 523 (D.D.C. 1981) (intrusion, assault and battery, intentional infliction of emotional distress).

149 Second Circuit: Hosemann v. Technical Materials, Inc., 554 F. Supp. 659, 666 (D.R.I. 1982).

Third Circuit: Bellissimo v. Westinghouse Elec. Corp., 764 F.2d 175 (3d Cir. 1985), *cert denied,* 475 U.S. 1035 (1986); Smith v. Acme Spinning Co., 40 Fair Empl. Prac. Cas. (BNA) 1104 (W.D.N.C. 1986); Reichman v. Bureau of Affirmative Action, 536 F. Supp. 1149 (M.D. Pa. 1982).

Fourth Circuit: Katz v. Dole, 709 F.2d 251 (4th Cir. 1983).

through omission,[150] some applied a strict liability standard in treating supervisor sexual harassment pursuant to agency law and the EEOC guidelines,[151]

Sixth Circuit: Coley v. Consolidated Rail Corp., 561 F. Supp. 645 (E.D. Mich. 1982); Robson v. Eva's Mkt., 538 F. Supp. 857 (N.D. Ohio 1982).

Eighth Circuit: Polk v. Yellow Freight Sys., 801 F.2d 190 (6th Cir. 1986); Harrison v. Reed Rubber Co., 603 F. Supp. 1457 (E.D. Mo. 1985); Walter v. KFGO Radio, 518 F. Supp. 1309 (D.N.D. 1981).

Tenth Circuit: Arnold v. City of Seminole, 614 F. Supp. 853 (E.D. Okla. 1985); Brown v. City of Guthrie, 22 Fair Empl. Prac. Cas. (BNA) 1627 (W.D. Okla. 1980).

Eleventh Circuit: Henson v. City of Dundee, 682 F.2d 897 (11th Cir. 1982); Hayden v. Cox Enters., 534 F. Supp. 1166 (N.D. Ga. 1982).

150 Third Circuit: Sheekey v. Nelson, 40 Fair Empl. Prac. Cas. (BNA) 1216 (D.N.J. 1986) (plaintiff must show that job status is conditioned upon favorable response to sexual advances).

Fourth Circuit: Ross v. Communications Satellite Corp., 34 Fair Empl. Prac. Cas. (BNA) 260 (D. Md. 1984) (nothing in record indicated that acquiescence to sexual advances by coworker was condition of employment); Yourse v. Miller, 38 Fair Empl. Prac. Cas. (BNA) 287 (M.D.N.C. 1982) (plaintiff did not demonstrate that submission to sexual "references" was term or condition of employment).

Seventh Circuit: Kwiatkowski v. Postal Serv., 39 Fair Empl. Prac. Cas. (BNA) 1740 (N.D. Ill. 1985) (plaintiff failed to show that alleged harassment affected "term, condition or privilege" of employment).

Eight Circuit: Meyers v. I.T.T. Diversified Credit Corp., 527 F. Supp. 1064 (E.D. Mo. 1981) (described only elements of *quid pro quo* harassment).

Tenth Circuit: Davis v. Bristol Lab., 26 Fair Empl. Prac. Cas. (BNA) 1351 (W.D. Okla. 1981) (to present prima facie case of sexual harassment plaintiff must plead and prove that submission to sexual advances of supervisor was term or condition of employment).

151 Third Circuit: Horn v. Duke Homes, Inc., 755 F.2d 599, 605 (3d Cir. 1983) ("sex discrimination can best be eradicated by enforcing a strict liability rule that ensures compensation for victims and creates an incentive for the employer to take the strongest possible affirmative measures to prevent the hiring and retention of sexist supervisors").
Seventh Circuit: Horbaczewsky v. Spider Staging Sales Co., 621 F. Supp. 749, 750 (N.D. Ill. 1985) (adopting reasoning in Horn v. Duke Homes, Inc., 755 F.2d 599 (3d Cir. 1983)).

Ninth Circuit: Ambrose v. United States Steel Corp., 39 Fair Empl. Prac. Cas. (BNA) 30, 35 (N.D. Cal. 1985) (alleged harasser's "position as supervisor and his perceived status as an up-and-coming authority at U.S. Steel gave him the power to intimidate and harass"). *See* Jeppsen v. Wunnicke, 611 F. Supp. 78, 37 Fair Empl. Prac. Cas. (BNA) 994, 997 (D. Alaska 1985):

> The . . . employee who stays on the job the longest and puts up with the most offensive sexual harassment is more likely than not going to be the employee who is the most dependent on retaining the job. . . [and] the one most reticent to complain. . . . Requiring knowledge on the part of the employer in a hostile work environment case might very well provide the court with an easy tool to use in deciding many cases, but this court fears that such a requirement holds the potential for grave injustice as well as subversion of the purpose of Title VII.

and others applied the knowledge requirement the EEOC reserved for coworker and nonworker harassment situations.[152] Most courts chose this last approach with little discussion, finding that employer liability must be predicated upon employer knowledge and inaction.[153] At the same time,

---

EEOC v. Judson Steel Co., 33 Fair Empl. Prac. Cas. (BNA) 1286 (N.D. Cal. 1982) (even though employer knew of harassing conduct, it might have been liable anyway under respondeat superior).

Tenth Circuit: Arnold v. City of Seminole, 614 F. Supp. 853 (E.D. Okla. 1985) (quoting EEOC guidelines).

District of Columbia Circuit: Vinson v. Taylor, 753 F.2d 141, 146 (D.C. Cir. 1985), *aff'd in part, rev'd in part sub nom.* Meritor Sav. Bank v. Vinson, 477 U.S. 57 (1986).

152 Third Circuit: Craig v. Y&Y Snacks, 721 F.2d 77 (3d Cir. 1983); Sheekey v. Nelson, 40 Fair Empl. Prac. Cas. (BNA) 1216 (D.N.J. 1986).

Fourth Circuit: Katz v. Dole, 709 F.2d 251 (4th Cir. 1983); Smith v. Acme Spinning Co., 40 Fair Empl. Prac. Cas. (BNA) 1104 (W.D.N.C. 1986).

Sixth Circuit: Davis v. Western-Southern Life Ins. Co., 34 Fair Empl. Prac. Cas. (BNA) 97 (N.D. Ohio 1984) (defendant employer was not liable even though plaintiff demonstrated that supervisor created hostile environment because she never complained to supervisors); Ferguson v. E.I. Du Pont de Nemours & Co., 560 F. Supp. 1172 (D. Del. 1983).

Eighth Circuit: Moylan v. Maries County, 792 F.2d 746 (8th Cir. 1986); Harrison v. Reed Rubber Co., 603 F. Supp. 1457 (E.D. Mo. 1985); Mays v. Williamson & Sons, 591 F. Supp. 1518 (E.D. Ark. 1984), *aff'd,* 775 F.2d 258 (8th Cir. 1985); Meyers v. I.T.T. Diversified Credit Corp., 527 F. Supp. 1064 (E.D. Mo. 1981).

Ninth Circuit: EEOC v. Judson Steel Co., 33 Fair Empl. Prac. Cas. (BNA) 1286 (N.D. Cal. 1982) (hostile environment found when supervisor with authority to make employment decisions harassed women bricklayers; higher management failed to take corrective action).

153 A hostile environment was found in the following cases:

Fourth Circuit: Katz v. Dole, 709 F.2d 251, 254 (4th Cir. 1983) (prima facie case) (workplace was "pervaded with sexual slur, insult and innuendo").

Fifth Circuit: Lamb v. Drilco, 32 Fair Empl. Prac. Cas. (BNA) 105 (S.D. Tex. 1983) (supervisor made verbal and physical advances and made sexually abusive calls to plaintiff at home).

Sixth Circuit: Coley v. Consolidated Rail Corp., 561 F. Supp. 645 (E.D. Mich. 1982) (supervisor consistently made sexually explicit and demeaning remarks to plaintiff, including references to size of her breasts, and kept track of her menstrual periods); Morgan v. Hertz Corp., 542 F. Supp. 123, 128 (W.D. Tenn. 1981), *aff'd,* 725 F.2d 1070 (6th Cir. 1984) (company had history of management's tolerating vulgar language directed toward women employees).

Seventh Circuit: Zabkowicz v. West Bend Co., 589 F. Supp. 780, 784 (E.D. Wis. 1984) (coworkers subjected plaintiff to abusive language, grabbed her crotch, and displayed sexually offensive drawings, some of which included her).

Eighth Circuit: Harrison v. Reed Rubber Co., 603 F. Supp. 1457 (E.D. Mo. 1985) (supervisor frequently inquired about plaintiff's home life and asked her to leave her husband, initiated physical contact, and remained in plaintiff's work area more than necessary); Mays v. Williamson & Sons, 591 F. Supp. 1518 (E.D. Ark. 1984), *aff'd,*

courts generally held that vicarious liability was appropriate in *quid pro quo* cases.[154]

Despite the EEOC framework, no clear definition of unwelcome sexual advances emerged. Complex facts, the subjective nature of the claims,[155]

---

775 F.2d 258 (8th Cir. 1985) (supervisor made verbal and physical advances to plaintiff, peered over stall when plaintiff was in bathroom, and jerked and threatened her).

Ninth Circuit: Priest v. Rotary, 634 F. Supp. 571 (N.D. Cal. 1986) (employer kissed, rubbed up against, trapped, touched, unzipped uniform of, and exposed himself to plaintiff); EEOC v. Judson Steel Co., 33 Fair Empl. Prac. Cas. (BNA) 1286 (N.D. Cal. 1982) (working environment "fraught with sex bias" in which supervisor made statements to other male employees that he had tried to and intended to get rid of female employees violated Title VII).

Tenth Circuit: Arnold v. City of Seminole, 614 F. Supp. 853 (E.D. Okla. 1985) (supervisor informed woman police officer that he did not believe in women officers, and made derogatory statements about her, pornographic cartoons and photographs with plaintiff's name were placed in public view, and "bitch" was written by her name on work schedule); Brown v. City of Guthrie, 22 Fair Empl. Prac. Cas. (BNA) 1627 (W.D. Okla. 1980) (verbal advances to police dispatcher).

A hostile environment was not found in these cases:

Second Circuit: Collins v. Pfizer, Inc., 39 Fair Empl. Prac. Cas. (BNA) 1316 (D. Conn. 1985).

Third Circuit: Reichman v. Bureau of Affirmative Action, 536 F. Supp. 1149 (M.D. Pa. 1982).

Fourth Circuit: Smith v. Acme Spinning Co., 40 Fair Empl. Prac. Cas. (BNA) 1104 (W.D.N.C. 1986).

Sixth Circuit: Davis v. Western-Southern Life Ins. Co., 34 Fair Empl. Prac. Cas. (BNA) 97 (N.D. Ohio 1984); Sand v. Johnson, 33 Fair Empl. Prac. Cas. (BNA) 716 (E.D. Mich. 1982).

Eighth Circuit: Craik v. Minnesota State Univ. Bd., 731 F.2d 465 (8th Cir. 1984).

Eleventh Circuit: Wimberly v. Shoney's, Inc., 39 Fair Empl. Prac. Cas. (BNA) 444 (S.D. Ga. 1985).

District of Columbia Circuit: Evans v. Mail Handlers, 32 Fair Empl. Prac. Cas. (BNA) 634 (D.D.C. 1983).

Federal Circuit: Downes v. Federal Aviation Admin., 775 F.2d 288 (Fed. Cir. 1985).

154 Third Circuit: Toscano v. Nimmo, 32 Fair Empl. Prac. Cas. (BNA) 1401, 1407 (D. Del. 1983) (knowledge of alleged harassment is not prerequisite to liability when supervisor makes decision to promote someone based on discriminatory criterion); Ferguson v. E.I. Du Pont de Nemours & Co., 560 F. Supp. 1172, 1198–99 n.62 (D. Del. 1983).

Seventh Circuit: Horn v. Duke Homes, Inc., 755 F.2d 599, 604 (3d Cir. 1983).

Ninth Circuit: Miller v. Bank of Am., 600 F.2d 211, 213 (9th Cir. 1979).

Eleventh Circuit: Henson v. City of Dundee, 682 F.2d 897, 910 (11th Cir. 1982); Cummings v. Walsh Constr. Co., 561 F. Supp. 872 (S.D. Ga. 1983).

District of Columbia Circuit: Bundy v. Jackson, 641 F.2d 934, 947 (D.C. Cir. 1981).

155 *Cf.* Sand v. Johnson, 33 Fair Empl. Prac. Cas. (BNA) 716 (E.D. Mich. 1982). Plaintiff testified that her supervisor took her to dinner 15 to 20 times after working overtime during her first year of work, during which he touched her regularly and asked her questions about her social life, and he attempted to embrace and kiss her another time

and the minimal precedent available for analysis made the task difficult.[156] Moreover, conflicting testimony and the absence of witnesses often forced courts to reduce their analyses to credibility determinations.[157] Testimony by other women employees regarding the offensive conduct, or lack thereof, was particularly helpful in hostile environment cases.[158] The importance of the sexual nature of the challenged conduct was underscored by some courts[159] and played down by others.[160] Some courts found

---

and gave her gifts. Nevertheless, the court found that the plaintiff's inconsistent statements and psychiatric testimony regarding plaintiff's emotional problems, which made her "hypersensitive to conduct by men," rendered her reliability as a witness tenuous. *Id.* at 720. Moreover, the plaintiff never complained of sexual harassment until after her discharge, did not suffer retaliation, was chronically tardy, and was helped in finding a new job. *Cf. also* EEOC v. Olin Corp., 24 Fair Empl. Prac. Cas. (BNA) 1646 (W.D.N.C. 1980) (conduct subject to interpretation).

156 Between 1980 and 1985, 24,000 sexual harassment charges were filed with the EEOC, but only about 150 federal court opinions were rendered.

157 First Circuit: Norton v. Vartanian, 31 Fair Empl. Prac. Cas. (BNA) 1259, 1260 (D. Mass. 1983).

Fourth Circuit: Grier v. Casey, 643 F. Supp. 298, 310 (W.D.N.C. 1986).

Sixth Circuit: Hill v. BASF Wyandotte Corp., 27 Fair Empl. Prac. Cas. (BNA) 66 (E.D. Mich. 1981).

Eleventh Circuit: Hall v. F.O. Thacker Contracting Co., 24 Fair Emp. Prac. Cas. (BNA) 1499 (N.D. Ga. 1980).

158 Third Circuit: Reichman v. Bureau of Affirmative Action, 536 F. Supp. 1149 (M.D. Pa. 1982) (other female employees testified to absence of harassment).

Eighth Circuit: Mays v. Williamson & Sons, 591 F. Supp. 1518 (E.D. Ark. 1984), *aff'd,*, 775 F.2d 258 (8th Cir. 1985) (other harassed employees testified).

Ninth Circuit: Ambrose v. United States Steel Corp., 39 Fair Empl. Prac. Cas. (BNA) 30 (N.D. Cal. 1985).

District of Columbia Circuit: Vinson v. Taylor, 753 F.2d 141, 146 n.40 (D.C. Cir. 1985), *aff'd in part, rev'd in part sub nom.* Meritor Sav. Bank v. Vinson, 477 U.S. 57 (1986) ("Such evidence could be critical to a plaintiff's claim").

Federal Circuit: Downes v. Federal Aviation Admin., 775 F.2d 288 (Fed. Cir. 1985) (all other female employees signed petition in support of alleged harasser).

159 Turley v. Union Carbide Corp., 618 F. Supp. 1438 (S.D.W. Va. 1985) (plaintiff who alleged that supervisor picked on her "all the time" and treated her differently than male employees stated a cause of action for sex discrimination but not sexual harassment, when she was not subjected to harassment of a sexual nature; the distinction was important because in a sexual harassment case, unlike a disparate treatment action, the analysis does not focus on a discriminatory motive).

160 Sixth Circuit: Rimedio v. Revlon, Inc., 528 F. Supp. 1380 (S.D. Ohio 1982).

Eleventh Circuit: Bell v. Crackin Good Bakers, Inc., 777 F.2d 1497, 1503 (11th Cir. 1985) (hostile environment in violation of Title VII can be made up of "threatening, bellicose, demeaning, hostile or offensive conduct by a supervisor in the workplace because of the sex of the victim of such conduct").

District of Columbia Circuit: McKinney v. Dole, 765 F.2d 1129 (D.C. Cir. 1985) (district court improperly granted the defendant's motion for summary judgment when

certain conduct to be sexual and offensive but declined to find that it interfered with the plaintiff's work.[161]

The fact of whether the plaintiff complained of the alleged offensive conduct was consistently used to measure its impact on the plaintiff's work environment, and was at least partially determinative in many cases.[162]

---

a substantial issue of material fact existed regarding whether a supervisor's use of physical force against the plaintiff was sexually motivated).

> Clearly . . . if a supervisor consistently uses physical force toward an employee because of that employee's sex, the use of such force may, if pervasive enough, form an illegal "condition of employment." So too a pattern of mixed sexual advances and physical force may be illegally discriminatory if based on the employee's sex. Consistently disparate treatment, however, need not take the form of actual physical assault and/or battery in the classic sense. A pattern of threatened force or verbal abuse, if based on the employee's sex, may be illegally discriminatory. In fact, any disparate treatment, even if not facially objectionable, may violate Title VII.

Id. at 1139.

[161] Second Circuit: Hosemann v. Technical Materials, Inc., 554 F. Supp. 659 (D. R.I. 1982) (verbal sexual conduct by coworker was not discrimination).

Third Circuit: Ukarish v. Magnesium Elektron, 31 Fair Empl. Prac. Cas. (BNA) 1315, 1321 (D.N.J. 1983) (sexually oriented "banter" between plaintiff and male coworker was not sexual harassment).

Fourth Circuit: Ross v. Communications Satellite Corp., 34 Fair Empl. Prac. Cas. (BNA) 260 (D. Md. 1984) (verbal sexual conduct alone was not sexual harassment).

Eighth Circuit: Walter v. KFGO Radio, 518 F. Supp. 1309 (D.N.D. 1981) (no hostile environment was found when plaintiff did not demonstrate that offensive touching of her buttocks and breasts interfered with her work).

[162] Fourth Circuit: EEOC v. Olin Corp, 24 Fair Empl. Prac. Cas. (BNA) 1646 (W.D.N.C. 1980) (verbal and other conduct were subject to more than one interpretation and thus did not constitute sexual harassment; plaintiff never reported conduct to company officials or filed an EEOC charge).

Sixth Circuit: Vermett v. Hough, 627 F. Supp. 587 (W.D. Mich. 1986) (when plaintiff complained of harassment, alleged offender was counseled, reprimanded, and given a damaging performance evaluation); Scott v. City of Overland Park, 595 F. Supp. 520 (D. Kan. 1984) (defendant's motion for summary judgment was denied when there existed genuine factual issue as to whether the supervisors violated equal protection clause); Coley v. Consolidated Rail Corp., 561 F. Supp. 645 (E.D. Mich. 1982) (hostile environment harassment was found when plaintiff complained and employer did not respond); Sand v. Johnson, 33 Fair Empl. Prac. Cas. (BNA) 716 (E.D. Mich. 1982) (plaintiff never complained of sexual harassment until after she was discharged).

Seventh Circuit: Scott v. Sears, Roebuck & Co., 605 F. Supp. 1047 (N.D. Ill. 1985), *aff'd,* 798 F.2d 210 (7th Cir. 1986) (plaintiff car mechanic who never complained to superior of alleged harassment by person who trained her as brake mechanic but who possessed no power to hire, fire, or promote her could not attribute to employer actual or constructive knowledge); Zabkowicz v. West Bend Co., 589 F. Supp. 780, 784 (E.D. Wis. 1984) (plaintiff complained many times to supervisors about coworker harassment and brought offensive drawings to them about 50 times); Burns v. Terre Haute Regional Hosp., 581 F. Supp. 1301 (S.D. Ind. 1983) (plaintiff did not complain of harassment).

Although compliance in *quid pro quo* situations was found to be irrelevant to a finding that sexual harassment occurred,[163] such evidence was used to vitiate a claim of hostile environment harassment.[164] The fact that other employees did not mind or even participated in the challenged conduct did not necessarily dilute a sexual harassment charge.[165] Decisions often turned on the frequency or repetitive nature of the challenged conduct;[166] plaintiffs

---

Ninth Circuit: EEOC v. Judson Steel Co., 33 Fair Empl. Prac. Cas. (BNA) 1286 (N.D. Cal. 1982) (defendant employer was liable to two female bricklayers who had complained of sexual harassment to higher management, who failed to take any corrective action); Collins v. City of L.A., 18 Fair Empl. Prac. Cas. (BNA) 594 (C.D. Cal. 1978) (plaintiff did not complain and indicated she had been happy in her job and wanted to return to work).

Eleventh Circuit: Bell v. Crackin Good Bakers, Inc., 777 F.2d 1497, 1503 (11th Cir. 1985) (ample evidence existed that plaintiff had complained of supervisor's conduct and that no remedial action had been taken; it was error for the district court to grant defendant's motion for summary judgment when evidence was sufficient to establish prima facie case of sex discrimination); Wimberly v. Shoney's, Inc., 39 Fair Empl. Prac. Cas. (BNA) 444 (S.D. Ga. 1985) (no complaints).

163 Cummings v. Walsh Constr. Co., 561 F. Supp. 872 (S.D. Ga. 1983) (plaintiff submitted to sexual advances by supervisor at first because she was intimidated by him and he had promised that he would no longer bother her, but later she rebuffed his advances).

164 Second Circuit: Halpert v. Wertheim & Co., 27 Fair Empl. Prac. Cas. (BNA) 21 (S.D.N.Y. 1980) (plaintiff used "coarse" language).

Third Circuit: Ukarish v. Magnesium Elektron, 31 Fair Empl. Prac. Cas. (BNA) 1315, 1321 (D.N.J. 1983) (sexually oriented "banter" between plaintiff and male coworker was not sexual harassment); Reichman v. Bureau of Affirmative Action, 536 F. Supp. 1149 (M.D. Pa. 1982) (plaintiff could not sustain sexual harassment claim when her flirtatious and provocative manner and repeated dinner invitations to her supervisor persuaded the court that no unwelcome sexual advances were made by the supervisor, who allegedly attempted to kiss her; plaintiff did not establish that the conduct created an offensive atmosphere or that she was required to submit to sexual advances as a term or condition of employment).

Eight Circuit: Gan v. Kepro Circuit Sys., 28 Fair Empl. Prac. Cas. (BNA) 639 (E.D. Mo. 1982) (plaintiff contributed to and encouraged conduct).

District of Columbia Circuit: *Cf.* Evans v. Mail Handlers, 32 Fair Empl. Prac. Cas. (BNA) 634, 637 (D.D.C. 1983) (plaintiff failed to show that she was subjected to unwelcome sexual advances when she and alleged harasser had carried on a consensual sexual relationship and plaintiff "did not consider the conduct of the defendant] to be offensive or intimidating until the relationship began to deteriorate").

165 Sixth Circuit: Morgan v. Hertz Corp., 542 F. Supp. 123, 128 (W.D. Tenn. 1981), *aff'd,* 725 F.2d 1070 (6th Cir. 1984) (despite participation by other female employees in challenged conduct, vulgar and indecent language constituted sexual harassment when plaintiffs and many other women found the comments offensive).

Ninth Circuit: Priest v. Rotary, 634 F. Supp. 571, 579 (N.D. Cal. 1986) (although evidence showed some employees did not object to challenged conduct, it did not prove that the conduct was objectively inoffensive).

166 EEOC v. Judson Steel Co., 33 Fair Empl. Prac. Cas. (BNA) 1286, 1295 (N.D. Cal. 1982) (plaintiff's working environment was "fraught with sex bias, causing the women

who asserted isolated incidents usually did not make a showing of sexual harassment.[167] Prompt remedial action usually relieved an employer of liability.[168] The mere existence of a grievance procedure or a policy against discrimination or sexual harassment, however, did not relieve

---

serious physical and emotional distress, thus violating their right to work in a nondiscriminatory environment").

[167] Fourth Circuit: Smith v. Acme Spinning Co., 40 Fair Empl. Prac. Cas. (BNA) 1104 (W.D.N.C. 1986) (evidence of three isolated incidents of harassment over three-year period was not sufficient to impute knowledge to employer, who investigated when he did receive complaint and was prepared to remedy the problems).

Sixth Circuit: Vermett v. Hough, 627 F. Supp. 587, 607 (W.D. Mich. 1986) (sexual harassment did not occur when court found that only one of alleged incidents actually occurred, and that even this act was not meant to be of a sexual nature); Estate of Scott v. deLeon, 603 F. Supp. 1328 (E.D. Mich. 1985) (in equal protection clause action, defendant's motion for summary judgment was denied when record created a genuine issue as to whether defendants knowingly acquiesced in or deliberately disregarded alleged sexual harassment); Lynch v. Dean, 39 Fair Empl. Prac. Cas. (BNA) 338 (M.D. Tenn. 1985) ("isolated and ambiguous" comment by supervisor that he would help plaintiff "warm her ass up" failed to rise to level of discrimination).

Eighth Circuit: Craik v. Minnesota State Univ. Bd., 731 F.2d 465 (8th Cir. 1984) (50 incidents over 10 years did not create an oppressive working environment).

Eleventh Circuit: Wimberly v. Shoney's, Inc., 39 Fair Empl. Prac. Cas. (BNA) 444 (S.D. Ga. 1985) (random encounters).

Federal Circuit: Downes v. Federal Aviation Admin., 775 F.2d 288 (Fed. Cir. 1985) (five incidents over three years did not indicate hostile environment).

[168] Second Circuit: Taylor v. Faculty-Student Ass'n of State Univ. College, 40 Fair Empl. Prac. Cas. (BNA) 1292 (W.D.N.Y. 1986) (although defendant employer asserted it was not liable for three obscene remarks made by male coworkers of plaintiff dining hall worker because it took immediate remedial action, defendant was not entitled to summary judgment because evidence was ambiguous regarding when defendant became aware of plaintiff's allegations); Hosemann v. Technical Materials, Inc., 554 F. Supp. 659 (D. R.I. 1982) (employer showed concern and alleviated problem of coworker's harassment by transferring plaintiff).

Third Circuit: Bellissimo v. Westinghouse Elec. Corp., 764 F.2d 175 (3d Cir. 1985), *cert denied,* 475 U.S. 1035 (1986) (no employer response to complaints); Freedman v. American Standard, 41 Fair Empl. Prac. Cas. (BNA) 471, 476 (D.N.J. 1986) (discharged female pilot was not sexually harassed because offensive incidents were isolated and were not brought to attention of her supervisor; plaintiff was discharged because she failed three times to pass required basic flight checks); Toscano v. Nimmo, 32 Fair Empl. Prac. Cas. (BNA) 1401 (D. Del. 1983) (harassing supervisor's superiors "not only failed to take prompt and appropriate remedial action when advised of what he had done, but took action which could fairly be construed as condoning and ratifying that conduct." *Id.* at 1407).

Fourth Circuit: Smith v. Acme Spinning Co., 40 Fair Empl. Prac. Cas. (BNA) 1104 (W.D.N.C. 1986) (evidence of three isolated incidents of harassment over three-year period was not sufficient to impute knowledge to employer, who investigated when he did receive complaint and was prepared to remedy the problems); Yourse v. Miller, 38 Fair Empl. Prac. Cas. (BNA) 287 (M.D.N.C. 1982).

Fifth Circuit: Lamb v. Drilco, 32 Fair Empl. Prac. Cas. (BNA) 105 (S.D. Tex. 1983) (in response to plaintiff's complaint that supervisor made verbal and physical sexual advances toward her despite her requests to stop, the department's general supervisor promised to speak with plaintiff's supervisor but did not); Capaci v. Katz & Besthoff, Inc., 525 F. Supp. 317 (N.D. La. 1981), *modified on other grounds*, 711 F.2d 647 (5th Cir. 1983) (when plaintiff reported touching incident by store manager to store supervisor, store supervisor adequately responded by confronting store manager and warning that company would not tolerate such conduct); Durant v. Owens-Illinois Glass Co., 517 F. Supp. 710 (E.D. La. 1980), *aff'd*, 656 F.2d 89 (5th Cir. 1981) (two incidents of verbal harassment by coworker who was reprimanded after incidents did not constitute sexual harassment).

Sixth Circuit: Vermett v. Hough, 627 F. Supp. 587 (W.D. Mich. 1986) (when plaintiff complained of harassment, alleged offender was counseled, reprimanded, and given damaging performance evaluation); Estate of Scott v. deLeon, 603 F. Supp. 1328 (E.D. Mich. 1985) (defendant's motion for summary judgment was denied when question existed as to whether defendants acquiesced in or deliberately disregarded sexually harassing conduct by supervisor); Coley v. Consolidated Rail Corp., 561 F. Supp. 645 (E.D. Mich 1982) (no employer response); Robson v. Eva's Mkt., 538 F. Supp. 857, 859 (N.D. Ohio 1982) (no response); Martin v. Norbar, Inc., 537 F. Supp. 1260, 1262 (S.D. Ohio 1982) (employer contended it had no duty to reassign plaintiff on basis of one complaint against coworker and in the face of coworker's denial, and protested court's failure to grant motion for summary judgment as "tantamount to holding that an employer must treat all allegations of sexual harassment as true, regardless of the circumstances").

Seventh Circuit: Bohen v. City of E. Chicago, 622 F. Supp. 1234 (N.D. Ind. 1985), *aff'd in part, rev'd in part,* 799 F.2d 1180 (7th Cir. 1986) (no response); Scott v. Sears, Roebuck & Co., 605 F. Supp. 1047 (N.D. Ill. 1985), *aff'd,* 798 F.2d 210 (7th Cir. 1986) (when employee did not complain of coworkers' harassment and did not allege employer knew, employer's conduct fell short of severity and pervasiveness necessary to establish actionable hostile environment); Zabkowicz v. West Bend Co., 589 F. Supp. 780, 784 (E.D. Wis. 1984) (hostile environment was found when coworkers subjected plaintiff to abusive language and displayed sexually offensive drawings, and no disciplinary action was taken).

Eighth Circuit: Barrett v. Omaha Nat'l Bank, 726 F.2d 424, 427 (8th Cir. 1984) (district court properly concluded that defendant took immediate and appropriate corrective action in response to plaintiff's complaint that on the way to and during a two-day conference, a coworker talked about sexual activity and touched her in an offensive way; within four days of complaint, employer informed offending coworker and other worker who failed to intervene that their conduct would not be tolerated); Harrison v. Reed Rubber Co., 603 F. Supp. 1457 (E.D. Mo. 1985) (merely telling supervisor to limit time with plaintiff was inadequate response to plaintiff's sexual harassment claims); Mays v. Williamson & Sons, 591 F. Supp. 1518 (E.D. Ark. 1984), *aff'd,* 775 F.2d 258 (8th Cir. 1985) (employer response inadequate); Meyers v. I.T.T. Diversified Credit Corp., 527 F. Supp. 1064 (E.D. Mo. 1981) (no rectification).

Ninth Circuit: EEOC v. Judson Steel Co., 33 Fair Empl. Prac. Cas. (BNA) 1286 (N.D. Cal. 1982) (aware of plaintiffs' complaints, higher management failed to take corrective action).

Eleventh Circuit: Bell v. Crackin Good Bakers, Inc., 777 F.2d 1497, 1503 (11th Cir. 1985) (ample evidence existed that plaintiff had complained of supervisor's conduct and that no remedial action had been taken; it was error for district court to grant defendant's motion for summary judgment when evidence was sufficient to establish prima facie case of sex discrimination).

the employer of liability without an analysis of the procedure or policy's efficacy.[169]

Under § 1604-11(g) of the EEOC guidelines, employees who are passed over for employment opportunities or benefits because another employee has submitted to an employer or supervisor's request for sexual favors may have a cause of action under Title VII. This provision added yet another dimension to sexual harassment law and sparked controversy among commentators.[170] However, it was unclear whether third parties could recover under Title VII for discriminatory treatment based on a romantic relationship between a supervisor and another employee.[171]

District of Columbia Circuit: Gold v. Gallaudet College, 630 F. Supp. 1176 (D.D.C. 1986) (employer responded immediately).

169 Katz v. Dole, 709 F.2d 251, 256 (4th Cir. 1983) (to avoid liability under Title VII, "an employer on notice of sexual harassment must do more than indicate the existence of an official policy against such harassment"); Cummings v. Walsh Constr. Co., 561 F. Supp. 872, 878 (S.D. Ga. 1983) ("The fact that an employer may have a policy prohibiting sexual harassment is of little significance if prompt remedial action is not taken"; employer may be liable for the conduct of a supervisor on a respondeat superior basis, even though company policy is violated, when the supervisor possesses the power to hire and fire or to participate in such decisions).

170 *See, e.g.,* J.W. Waks & M.G. Starr, *Sexual Harassment in the Workplace: The Scope of Employer Liability,* 7 Employee Rel. L.J. 369, 382 (1981-82) ("by adopting subsection (g), the EEOC may have laid the groundwork for a flurry of claims that will more likely hinder than advance the quest for equal employment opportunities for women"); J.C. Leventer, *Sexual Harassment and Title VII: EEOC Guidelines, Conditions Litigation, and the United States Supreme Court,* 10 Cap. U.L. Rev. 481, 485 (1981) (provision assumes that women "sleep their way to the top").

171 Second Circuit: *Cf.* Malarkey v. Texaco, Inc., 559 F. Supp. 117 (S.D.N.Y. 1982), *aff'd,* 704 F.2d 674 (2d Cir. 1983) (plaintiff failed to state Title VII cause of action when she asserted that younger women were viewed by management as more attractive than older women, and that plaintiff was as qualified as younger women who were promoted in her stead; "nowhere does plaintiff allege that she has at any time been in competition with a male"; Sand v. Johnson, 33 Fair Empl. Prac. Cas. (BNA) 716 (E.D. Mich. 1982) ("sensitive" plaintiff).

Third Circuit: Anderson v. University Health Ctr., 623 F. Supp. 795 (W.D. Pa. 1985) (evidence of romantic relationship between supervisor and another female employee is irrelevant absent showing that another worker was favored, promoted, or replaced plaintiff); Toscano v. Nimmo, 32 Fair Empl. Prac. Cas. (BNA) 1401 (D. Del. 1983) (Veteran's Administration was liable under Title VII when chief of its administrative division conditioned his selection of chief medical administration assistant on receipt of sexual favors, thereby denying promotion to woman who did not have an affair with him).

District of Columbia Circuit: King v. Palmer, 778 F.2d 878 (D.C. Cir. 1985) (district court improperly held that plaintiff who was denied a promotion failed to offer direct proof that sexual relationship between the person promoted and the supervisor had been consummated).

By the time the U.S. Supreme Court decided to review *Meritor Savings Bank v. Vinson,*[172] sexual harassment law was ripe for refinement, particularly in the area of employer liability for supervisor conduct in the hostile environment context. However, despite a landmark ruling regarding the viability of hostile environment sexual harassment claims generally, the Court declined to rule on liability, except to suggest that vicarious liability may not be appropriate in hostile environment cases.

§ 2.14 *Meritor Savings Bank v. Vinson*

The Supreme Court finally addressed the highly charged issue of sexual harassment on June 19, 1986, in the *Meritor Savings Bank v. Vinson* case[173] and rendered an opinion both lauded and criticized by commentators.[174] In an opinion by Justice Rehnquist,[175] the Court unanimously held that "without question" sexual harassment is a form of sex discrimination and that hostile environment as well as *quid pro quo* harassment violate Title VII (see **§ 2.16**). Unresolved questions regarding scope, employer liability, and evidentiary issues remain, however, to concern employers, employees, supervisors, unions, personnel staffs, and employment attorneys. Nevertheless, in this decision, the U.S. Supreme Court took an important step towards legitimizing this elusive area of law for complainants and

---

172 477 U.S. 57 (1986).

173 *Id.*

174 *See, e.g.,* D. Bennett-Alexander, *The Supreme Court Finally Speaks on the Issue of Sexual Harassment—What Did It Say?,* 10 Women's Rights Law Rep. 65 (1987); B. Zalucki, *Defining the Hostile Work Environment Claim of Sexual Harassment under Title VII,* 11 W. New Eng. L. Rev. 143 (1989); Note, *Between the Boss and a Hard Place: A Consideration of Meritor Savings Bank FSB v. Vinson and the Law of Sexual Harassment,* 67 B.U. L. Rev. 445 (1987); Note, *Employer Liability under Title VII for Sexual Harassment after Meritor Savings Bank v. Vinson,* 878 Colum. L. Rev. 1258 (1987); Note, *Meritor Savings Bank v. Vinson: Title VII Liability for Sexual Harassment,* 17 Golden Gate U. L. Rev. 379 (1987); Note, *Meritor Savings Bank v. Vinson: Sexual Harassment at Work,* 10 Harv. Women's L.J. 203 (1987); Note, *Meritor Savings Bank v. Vinson: Finally a Supreme Court Ruling on Sexual Harassment: For What It's Worth,* 38 Mercer L. Rev. 733 (1987); Note, *A Right with Questionable Bite: the Future of "Abusive or Hostile Work Environment" Sexual Harassment as a Cause of Action for Women in a Gender-Biased Society and Legal System,* 23 New Eng. L. Rev. 133 (1988).

175 Joined by Burger, C.J., and White, Powell, Stevens, and O'Connor, J.J. Justice Marshall, joined by Justices Brennan, Blackmun, and Stevens, wrote a concurring opinion in which he agreed with the majority's holding regarding the illegality of hostile environment harassment but disputed the standard of liability to be applied. Justice Stevens joined both the majority and the concurrence because he did not *see* any inconsistency between the two opinions.

putting employers and harassers on notice that unwelcome sexual conduct will not be tolerated in the workplace.

Although the facts in *Meritor* revealed particularly egregious conduct, the three federal courts hearing this case reached their conclusions in three different ways. Such disparity in reasoning reflects the judicial ambivalence that continues to surround this subject.

§ 2.15 —Federal Court Holdings

Mechelle Vinson was hired in 1974 as a teller-trainee by Sidney Taylor, a vice-president of Meritor Savings Bank. During her four years under Taylor's supervision, Vinson received merit-based promotions to teller, head teller, and assistant branch manager.[176] In 1978, Vinson took an indefinite sick leave. Two months later, she was discharged for excessive use of that leave.

After taking sick leave but before her termination, Vinson brought an action against the bank and her supervisor, charging that during her four years at the bank, she had constantly been sexually harassed by Taylor in violation of Title VII.[177] She stated that although Taylor treated her in a "fatherly" way and made no sexual advances during her probationary period, he started making repeated sexual advances shortly thereafter. After first refusing, she submitted to sexual relations because she feared dismissal. In addition to 40 or 50 instances of sexual intercourse, Vinson testified that Taylor fondled her breasts and buttocks in front of other employees, followed her into the women's room when she was there alone, exposed himself to her, and raped her on several occasions. After one such incident, she sought a doctor's care. Vinson also testified that Taylor touched and fondled other female bank employees[178] and that she never reported the harassment to any of his supervisors or used the bank's complaint procedure because she was afraid of Taylor; he had allegedly threatened her life and

---

[176] It was undisputed that the promotions were based on merit. Employers seldom refute a claim that an employee has been promoted on the basis of merit; to do so might suggest that it would be possible to succeed in the employer's business on something other than merit.

[177] Vinson v. Taylor, 23 Fair Empl. Prac. Cas. (BNA) 37, 38 (D.D.C. Feb. 26, 1980).

[178] *Id.* at 39. The district court allowed Vinson to call witnesses in support of this allegation because it related to the bank's notice of Taylor's conduct, but declined to allow "wholesale evidence of a pattern and practice relating to sexual advances to other female employees." *Id.* at 38–39, n.1. The court of appeals found this ruling unjustly restrictive. 753 F.2d 141, 146 (D.C. Cir. 1985). Evidence of this sort could demonstrate that the alleged behavior was not an isolated incident and that a women might have a Title VII claim if required to work in an offensive environment, even if she herself was never the object of harassment.

threatened to have her raped. No other employee had filed an internal complaint either, which was not surprising, because employees were required to submit grievances to their immediate supervisor. Vinson sought an injunction, compensatory and punitive damages, and attorneys' fees.

Taylor denied all Vinson's allegations of sexual activity, contending that Vinson made her accusations in response to a business-related dispute regarding whom Vinson would train as head teller while Taylor took a vacation.[179] The bank also denied Vinson's allegations and maintained that any sexual harassment by Taylor was unknown to the bank and engaged in without its consent and approval.

The district court denied Vinson's pleas for relief, finding that the relationship between Vinson and Taylor was a voluntary one and that the bank would not have been liable anyway, given its express policy against discrimination and its ignorance of the alleged behavior. The court found that notice to Taylor did not amount to notice to the bank when Vinson did not complain to anyone else about the harassment, there was no evidence that Taylor conspired with other supervisors to harass Vinson, and the bank had a policy regarding equal treatment of employees. The court said, "[I]t seems reasonable that an employer should not be liable in these unusual cases of sexual harassment where notice to the employer must depend upon the actual perpetrator and when there is nothing else to place the employer on notice."[180]

The Court of Appeals for the District of Columbia reversed and remanded the case,[181] finding that the district court had failed to consider whether the defendants had created a hostile or abusive work environment in violation of Title VII.[182] The court was unclear on the district court's finding that the relationship between Vinson and Taylor was voluntary and

---

179 23 Fair Empl. Prac. Cas. (BNA) at 39. Taylor and the bank also alleged that the district court did not have jurisdiction to hear the case because Vinson had filed her Title VII claim before filing a complaint with the EEOC. *Id.* Vinson did receive a right-to-sue letter, however, and the district court found that she was properly before the court.

180 *Id.* at 42.

181 Vinson v. Taylor, 753 F.2d 141 (D.C. Cir. 1985). The court of appeals denied a suggestion for rehearing en banc, 760 F.2d 1330 (D.C. Cir. 1985), but three Reagan appointees, Bork, Scalia, and Starr, filed a dissenting opinion suggesting not only that the case should be reheard but that the opinion should be reversed. The dissent maintained that to prohibit the use of evidence showing that the claimant solicited the alleged sexual advances and that the relationship between the complainant and the supervisor was a voluntary one was authorized by neither Title VII nor the Federal Rules of Evidence and deprived the supervisor and employer of any available defenses. The dissent also argued that previous case law required the employer's actual or imputed knowledge. Judge Bork criticized generally the extension of employment discrimination law to include sexual harassment, stating that "Title VII was passed to outlaw discriminatory behavior and not simply behavior of which we strongly disapprove." *Id.* at 1333 n.7.

182 Vinson v. Taylor, 753 F.2d at 145. The court relied on its earlier holding in Bundy v. Jackson, 641 F.2d 934 (D.C. Cir. 1981), decided after the trial in *Meritor,* which advanced the theory of hostile environment harassment.

unrelated to Vinson's employment. The court noted that a finding of whether the relationship was voluntary did not preclude remand when her acquiescence would be immaterial if evidence otherwise showed that Taylor made Vinson's tolerance of the alleged sexual harassment a condition of employment.[183] In addition, the court said that the "voluminous" testimony regarding Vinson's dress and personal fantasies "had no place in this litigation" and should not have been used, if it was, to support a finding of voluntary status.[184] The court noted that *Bundy v. Jackson,*[185] the first case to address hostile environment sexual harassment, did not require a woman to "waive her Title VII rights by her sartorial or whimsical proclivities."[186]

Finally, the court of appeals held that an employer is strictly liable for sexual harassment by supervisors, whether the employer knew or should have known about the misconduct. The court stated that a supervisor is an agent of his or her employer for purposes of Title VII, regardless of whether the supervisor has the authority to hire, fire, or promote:

> The mere existence—or even the appearance—of a significant degree of influence in vital job decisions gives any supervisor the opportunity to impose on employees. That opportunity is not dependent solely upon the supervisor's authority to make personnel decisions; the ability to direct employees in their work, to evaluate their performances and to recommend personnel actions carries attendant power to coerce, intimidate and harass.[187]

The court noted that its decision on liability was based on the statutory intent and judicial construction of Title VII, rather than on the common law theory of respondeat superior,[188] as the limitations imposed by that doctrine "have no place in the enforcement of the congressional will underlying Title VII."[189]

---

[183] 753 F.2d 141, 146. The court also held that in a hostile environment case, the alleged victim may introduce evidence of harassment of other employees to demonstrate a hostile environment.

[184] *Id.* at 146 n.36.

[185] 641 F.2d 934 (D.C. Cir. 1981).

[186] Vinson v. Taylor, 753 F.2d 141, 146 n.36.

[187] *Id.* at 150. The court of appeals drew support from the EEOC guidelines, which state that an employer "is responsible for its acts and those of its agents and supervisory employees with respect to sexual harassment regardless of whether the specific acts complained of were authorized or even forbidden by the employer and regardless of whether the employer knew or should have known of their occurrence." EEOC guidelines, 29 C.F.R. § 1604.11(c) *quoted in* Vinson v. Taylor, 753 F.2d 141, 149.

[188] *Cf.* Miller v. Bank of Am., 600 F.2d 211, 213 (9th Cir. 1979) (under doctrine of respondeat superior, employer is responsible for tort of her or his employee if employee was aided in accomplishing the tort by existence of the agency relationship). *See also* Restatement (Second) of Agency, § 219(2)(d) (1958).

[189] Vinson v. Taylor, 753 F.2d 141, 151.

> Confining liability, as the common law would, to situations in which a supervisor acted within the scope of his authority conceivably could lead to the ludicrous result that employers would become accountable only if they explicitly require or consciously allow their supervisors to molest women employees. While modern courts seem more inclined to treat intentional misconduct on the job as arising out of and in the course of employment, and thus as providing a basis for liability under a somewhat expanded theory of respondeat superior, there simply is no need to so confine either the analysis or the solution where Title VII applies.[190]

The U.S. Supreme Court affirmed the court of appeal's holding that hostile environment sexual harassment is a violation of Title VII.[191] The Court also held that the complainant's voluntary participation in sexual conduct is not an absolute defense to a sexual harassment suit under Title VII, but it is relevant to a determination of whether harassment has occurred. Finally, despite its reluctance to issue a definitive rule regarding employer liability, the Court rejected the strict liability analysis of the court of appeals. The Court stated that Congress intended courts to look to agency principles to determine liability.

§ 2.16 —Hostile Environment and Title VII

The Supreme Court in *Meritor* confirmed that a plaintiff may establish a violation of Title VII by proving that discrimination based on sex has created a hostile or abusive work environment, but that such conduct must be "sufficiently severe or pervasive" as to affect a term, condition, or privilege of employment.[192] Finding the EEOC guidelines instructive, but not controlling,[193] Justice Rehnquist noted that the guidelines appropriately draw on a body of case law that characterizes Title VII as a device to ensure an employee's "right to work in an environment free from discriminatory

---

190 *Id.*

191 Meritor Sav. Bank v. Vinson, 477 U.S. 57, 66 (1986).

192 Meritor Sav. Bank v. Vinson, 477 U.S. 57, 67 (1986). The court did not address circuit court dissent's remark that classifying sexual harassment as sex discrimination would create a "doctrinal difficulty" because of hypothetical potential for indiscriminate harassment by a bisexual supervisor. ("After *Meritor,* there is no mistaking the acceptability of the EEOC definition (and verbiage) found at § 1604.11(a).") *See also* Scott v. Sears, Roebuck & Co., 605 F. Supp. 1047 (N.D. Ill. 1985), *aff'd,* 798 F.2d 210 (7th Cir. 1986).

193 Meritor Sav. Bank v. Vinson, 477 U.S. 57, 65. Because the EEOC does not have the statutory authority to issue regulations, guideline standards can acquire the force of law only through adoption by the Supreme Court or through a Title VII amendment that would enable the EEOC to promulgate binding regulations. *See* General Elec. Co. v. Gilbert, 429 U.S. 125 (1976).

intimidation, ridicule, and insult,"[194] whether the harassment is based on race,[195] religion,[196] or national origin.[197] He said that nothing in Title VII suggests that "a hostile environment based on discriminatory sexual harassment should not be likewise prohibited."[198] Vinson's allegations included not only pervasive harassment but "criminal conduct of the most serious nature," and thus the Court found they were "plainly sufficient" to state a claim for hostile environment harassment.[199] Because conduct creating a hostile environment can vary in substance and severity, a determination of whether such an environment existed must be made on a case-by-case basis.

Recognition of the hostile environment theory was based on sound legislative and judicial authority. Title VII does not limit recourse to those who have suffered economic and tangible discrimination, and the EEOC guidelines emerged from substantial judicial and EEOC precedent that held that under Title VII employees have the right to work in an environment free from discriminatory hostility (see **§§ 2.8** through **2.13**). The Court reasoned that the requirement that "a man or woman run a gauntlet of sexual abuse in return for the privilege of being allowed to work and make a living can be as demeaning and disconcerting as the harshest of

---

194 Meritor Sav. Bank v. Vincent, 477 U.S. 57, 65 (1986).

195 Patterson v. McLean Credit Union, 491 U.S. 164 (1989), the U. S. Supreme Court reaffirmed its earlier pronouncement in *Meritor* that the elements and burden of proof placed upon a plaintiff in both a racially and sexually charged harassment action arising within a hostile work environment are identical. *See also* Risinger v. Ohio Bureau of Workers' Comp., 883 F.2d 475 (6th Cir. 1989).

See also Firefighters Inst. for Racial Equality v. City of St. Louis, 549 F.2d 506, 514–15 (8th Cir.), *cert denied,* 434 U.S. 819 (1977) (firefighter supper clubs which refused membership to black firefighters violated Title VII); Gray v. Greyhound Lines, 545 F.2d 169, 176 (D.C. Cir. 1976) ("atmosphere of discrimination" implicated by black bus drivers' claims that company's discriminatory hiring practices resulted in unfair disciplinary and route assignment procedures); EEOC v. Murphy Motor Freight Lines, 488 F. Supp. 381, 384 (D. Minn. 1980) (racist comments constitute harassment).

196 Compston v. Borden, Inc., 424 F. Supp. 157, 158, 160-61 (S.D. Ohio 1976) (derogatory religious epithets made Jewish employee's work atmosphere "miserable" in violation of Title VII).

197 *See, e.g.,* Rogers v. EEOC, 454 F.2d 234, 238 (5th Cir. 1971), *cert denied,* 406 U.S. 957 (1972). *Cf.* Cariddi v. Kansas City Chiefs Football Club, 568 F.2d 87, 88 (8th Cir. 1977) (derogatory ethnic comments made by supervisor of Italian-American were "part of casual conversation" and did not rise to the level of a Title VII violation).

198 Meritor Sav. Bank v. Vinson, 477 U.S. 57, 66. Justice Rehnquist noted that the sex discrimination provisions of Title VII are not supported by extensive legislative history. Several years before Congress passed Title VII, there had been efforts to pass legislation prohibiting sex discrimination in private employment, but it surely would have been defeated if the provisions had not been part of racial and ethnic discrimination legislation.

199 *Id.* at 67.

racial epithets."[200] Moreover, most appellate courts had accepted the hostile environment theory in the area of sexual harassment as well as other forms of discrimination under Title VII (see §§ **2.9** through **2.12**). Finally, requiring a victim of sexual harassment to demonstrate the loss of a tangible economic benefit would undermine the purpose of Title VII, which was to prevent discrimination against an employee with respect to "terms, conditions or privileges of employment."[201]

§ 2.17 —Complainant's Voluntary Participation

Although the U.S. Supreme Court affirmed the court of appeal's conclusion in *Meritor* that a hostile working environment violates Title VII, its reasoning varied substantially from that of the circuit court. It held that the court of appeals erred in concluding that testimony regarding Vinson's provocative dress and publicly expressed fantasies had no place in the litigation.[202] The Court rejected the bank's contention that it could not be held liable for the alleged sexual conduct because Vinson participated in the acts voluntarily, concluding that the district court had improperly focused on Vinson's compliance with the alleged conduct. The correct inquiry was whether Vinson "by her conduct indicated that the alleged sexual advances were unwelcome, not whether her actual participation . . . was voluntary," and that evidence such as dress and fantasies was obviously relevant in determining whether sexual harassment occurred.[203] The Court also found support for this conclusion in § 1604.11(b) of the EEOC guidelines, which requires that the record as a whole and the totality of the circumstances be considered in determining sexual harassment. So, although voluntary participation is not an absolute defense to a claim of sexual harassment, it is a factor in deciding whether sexual advances were unwelcome.

Because Taylor maintained that the alleged sexual incidents never occurred, not that Vinson welcomed his advances, the Court could have declined to consider whether Vinson's fantasies and clothing supported a finding that Taylor's advances were welcome.[204] By admitting such evidence, courts turn the plaintiff into the accused and shift the focus from the conduct of the harasser to the nature of the harassed. While employers still should be able to argue that the plaintiff welcomed sexual advances, such a

---

200 *Id.* (quoting Henson v. City of Dundee, 682 F.2d 897, 902 (11th Cir. 1982)).

201 *Id.* at 63 (quoting 42 U.S.C. § 2000e-2(a)(1) (1982)).

202 Meritor Sav. Bank v. Vinson, 477 U.S. 57, 69 (1986).

203 *Id.* at 68–69.

204 *Id.* at 72. The court had noted that the district court failed to resolve particular fact issues such as whether Taylor made any sexual advances toward Vinson at all, "let alone whether those advances were unwelcome."

showing should be made without introducing highly charged and subjective evidence. Courts may now feel compelled to consider this type of evidence whether or not it considers it appropriate to do so. For example, in *Jones v. Wesco,*[205] the Eight Circuit stated that "[a] court must consider any provocative speech or dress of the plaintiff in a sexual harassment case," and observed from the record that the plaintiff "wore non-provocative clothing." Such consideration seemed unnecessary in light of the court's acceptance of the alleged facts:

> From the beginning of her tenure with Wesco, Ms. Jones was barraged with repeated sexual advances, requests for sexual favors, and other verbal or physical contact of a sexual nature. For instance, Ben Rose would come up behind Ms. Jones and rub his hands up and down the sides of her body, touching her breasts. He would pinch her, pat her on the bottom and kiss her on the top of the head. At one point, Rose even put his hand on her outside thigh.
>
> His oral comments included a statement that someday her breasts would be his. On one occasion, Ben Rose entered the kitchen area in the Wesco suite and informed Ms. Jones that he thought it was a good idea that Ms. Jones spend more time in the kitchen area where it was cool because he could see her nipples much better in the cool temperature.
>
> On at least three occasions, Mr. Rose requested Ms. Jones to accompany him to unoccupied apartment buildings ostensibly for advice involving the building or redecoration of the apartments. Each time, Ben Rose put his arm around Ms. Jones before she could extricate herself from the situation. On one of these occasions, Ben Rose also kissed her on the lips before she could pull away.
>
> On each of the above occasions, Ms. Jones would either push Ben Rose away, remove herself from the room, or inform Rose that she was only interested in a business relationship. Doing so halted Rose's advances, but only temporarily. His uninvited attentions recommenced with the next available opportunity.[206]

In *Weiss v. Amoco Oil Co.,*[207] a wrongful termination action by a male employee fired for sexual harassment, the plaintiff sought to engage in discovery concerning the alleged victim's sexual history. According to the plaintiff the alleged victim had cards pinned up at her work station that were of a sexual nature, sent another male employee a birthday card that showed the torso of an adult female wearing a bikini, made sexual jokes with other employees, and discussed her sexual activities while at work. The court held that the alleged victim, a nonparty witness, failed to meet her burden of showing that information concerning her sexual history was

---

205 846 F.2d 1154 (8th Cir. 1988).

206 *Id.* at 1155 (footnote omitted).

207 142 F.R.D. 311 (S.D. Iowa 1992).

irrelevant and not reasonably calculated to lead to discovery of admissible evidence. The court cited *Meritor* and *Mitchell v. Hutchings,*[208] in which the court noted that evidence of sexual conduct that is remote in time or place to the plaintiffs' working environment is irrelevant:

> Unlike the factual situation in *Mitchell,* Weiss is not seeking discovery of Streebin's sexual history "remote in time or place" to Streebin's employment with Amoco, or to discovery her sexual conduct which is unknown to him. Rather, Weiss seeks to "depose Ms. Streebin regarding her sexual conduct with other employees of Defendant during her employment with Defendant and which Plaintiff had knowledge . . ." Weiss's discovery request is exactly tailored to be in keeping with the *Mitchell* decision.
>
> The court cannot say, as a matter of law, that the discovery sought by Weiss from Streebin will be irrelevant to the issues generated in this litigation. Such discovery is relevant in divining what conduct or actions Weiss thought were welcome, and in determining whether Streebin found Weiss's conduct unwelcome. This discovery may also prove relevant in explaining the context of Weiss's words and actions toward Streebin.
>
> * * *
>
> Finally, the material sought is relevant in assessing the thoroughness of Amoco's investigation into Streebin's complaint of sexual harassment. Weiss alleged that he and Streebin were social friends who dated occasionally, and that Streebin dated other fellow employees. Weiss alleges that a thorough investigation into Streebin's complaint against him would have disclosed these facts; facts which would be necessary in any analysis of Streebin's sexual harassment complaint against Weiss.[209]

§ 2.18 —Employer Liability and Agency Principles

The U.S. Supreme Court in *Meritor* declined to issue a definitive rule on employer liability, noting that the record was insufficient to decide the issue,[210] but it concluded that the court of appeals erroneously applied a strict liability standard to employers whose supervisors have created a

---

[208] 116 F.R.D. 481 (D. Utah 1987).

[209] 142 F.R.D. 311, 316–17 (footnote omitted).

[210] Meritor Sav. Bank v. Vinson, 477 U.S. 57, 72 (1986). The court found the record inadequate because (1) there was no finding that Taylor had made any sexual advances toward Vinson, (2) if advances were made, there was nothing in the record to indicate whether the advances were unwelcome, and (3) the record did not indicate whether the harassment was so pervasive that the employer must have been aware of it.

hostile environment.[211] Rejecting the views of both the EEOC guidelines and the court of appeals, the Court stated that it was "wrong to entirely disregard agency principles[212] and impose strict liability on employers for the acts of their supervisors, regardless of the circumstances of the particular case."[213] The Court felt that in defining employer under Title VII to include any *agent* of the employer, Congress intended to limit the scope of employer liability.[214]

Unlike *quid pro quo* sexual harassment cases, in which a supervisor has actual or apparent authority to affect the employee's job status, the creation of a sexually hostile environment is less clear cut in terms of whether a supervisor is acting within the scope of his or her employment. In *quid pro quo* cases, employers are strictly liable because agency principles impute notice of supervisory harassment to the employer.[215] In a typical hostile environment action, the harassers may be coworkers[216] who do not act as the employer's agents, and thus the employer should not be liable without notice and an opportunity to remedy the situation.[217] In a

---

211 *Id.* at 70 (quoting brief for United States and EEOC as amici curiae at 22). Justice Rehnquist noted the EEOC position that strict liability should be applied in quid pro quo harassment situations: "where a supervisor exercises authority actually delegated to him by his employer, by making or threatening to make decisions affecting the employment status of his subordinates, such actions are properly imputed to the employer whose delegation of authority empowered the supervisor to undertake them."

212 *See* Restatement (Second) of Agency §§ 219–237 (1958). It is not clear to what extent agency principles will be applied to hostile environment cases. The Court did state that the "common law principles may not be transferable in all their particulars to Title VII." *Id.* at 72. The concurring opinion criticized the majority for not following the EEOC guidelines, which recommend that employers be held strictly liable in hostile environment as well as *quid pro quo* cases. *Id.* at 74–78. (Marshall, J, concurring). Justice Stevens found no inconsistency between Rehnquist and Marshall's opinions and concurred in both.

213 Meritor Sav. Bank v. Vinson, 477 U.S. 57, 73.

214 *Id.* at 72.

215 *Id.* at 70.

216 U.S. Merit Systems Protection Board Office of Merit Review and Studies, Sexual Harassment in the Federal Workplace: Is it a Problem? 59–60 (1981).

217 *Cf.* Kotcher v. Rosa & Sullivan Appliance, 957 F.2d 59 (2d Cir. 1992). A manager who regularly commented that his sales would be more substantial if he had same bodily "equipment" as the female employee plaintiff, and who often pretended to masturbate and ejaculate at her behind her back, created a hostile work environment. Despite the plaintiff's complaints, the court concluded that the district court declined to impute liability to defendant company. Although the actions of a supervisor at a sufficiently high level in the hierarchy would necessarily be imputed to the company, here the district court could reasonably have found that the company, whose main office was in another city, did not have constructive notice of the challenged conduct. The case was remanded to consider whether the plaintiff had been subjected to retaliation after complaining to management about sexual harassment.

case like *Meritor*, however, in which a supervisor created the hostile environment, the U.S. Supreme Court's position is less convincing. The power enjoyed by supervisors over employees would seem to leave no room for a liability distinction between *quid pro quo* and hostile environment cases. The legal relationship between an employer and a supervisor should be such that an employer is on notice of liability for all of its supervisors' actions. In his concurrence, Justice Marshall argued that there is no justification for a distinction between liability in *quid pro quo* and hostile environment cases,[218] and indicated that he would have adopted the liability standard suggested by the EEOC guidelines:

> A supervisor's responsibilities do not begin and end with the power to hire, fire, and discipline employees, or with the power to recommend such actions. Rather, a supervisor is charged with the day-to-day supervision of the work environment and with ensuring a safe, productive workplace. There is no reason why abuse of the latter authority should have different consequences than abuse of the former. In both cases it is the authority vested in the supervisor by the employer that enables him to commit the wrong: it is precisely because the supervisor is understood to be clothed with the employer's authority that he is able to impose unwelcome sexual conduct on subordinates. There is therefore no justification for a special rule to be applied only in hostile environment cases, that sexual harassment does not create employer liability until the employee suffering the discrimination notifies other supervisors. No such requirement appears in the statute, and no such requirement can coherently be drawn from the law of agency.[219]

In its amicus brief, however, the EEOC indicated that a different rule should apply in hostile environment cases because the supervisor "is not exercising, or threatening to exercise, actual or apparent authority to make personnel decisions affecting the victim"[220] (see **§ 2.19**).

Though the majority rejected the notion of strict liability in hostile environment cases, it recognized that agency principles "may not be transferable in all the particulars to Title VII" and appeared to reject an absolute requirement of notice as well, stating that "absence of notice to an employer does not necessarily insulate that employer from liability."[221]

---

218 Meritor Sav. Bank v. Vinson, 477 U.S. 77 (1986).

219 *Id.* at 76–77 (some courts have imposed strict liability on employers when the harassing supervisor participates in the decision-making process that forms the basis of the alleged discrimination); *see, e.g.,* Hamilton v. Rodgers, 791 F.2d 439 (5th Cir. 1986); Jones v. Metropolitan Denver Sewage Disposal Dist., 537 F. Supp. 966 (D. Colo. 1982).

220 Brief for United States and EEOC as amici curiae, Meritor Sav. Bank v. Vinson, No. 84-1979 (Dec. 11, 1985) at 24.

221 Meritor Sav. Bank v. Vinson, 477 U.S. 57, 72. *See also* Hicks v. Gates Rubber Co., 833 F.2d 1406 (10th Cir. 1987) (rejecting lack of notice as an absolute defense).

Nor does the existence of a grievance procedure and a policy against discrimination preclude a finding of liability.[222]

§ 2.19 EEOC Retreats

The brief by the solicitor general for the United States and the EEOC as *amici curiae* in *Meritor* represented a political metamorphosis that was somewhat difficult to reconcile with the EEOC guidelines' original prescription. "While . . . claims of sexual harassment may state a cause of action under Title VII . . . such claims, particularly when they fall in the 'hostile environment' category, are distinct in Title VII jurisprudence, both in their theoretical formulation and in the practical problems that

---

See also Dias v. Sky Chefs, 919 F.2d 1370 (9th Cir. 1990), *vacated on other grounds,* 111 S. Ct. 2791, *on remand,* 948 F.2d 532 (9th Cir. 1991), *cert. denied,* 112 S. Ct. 1294 (1992). The court rejected defendant's argument that the company should not be held responsible for the sexual harassment of a female employee by the general manager because any sexual harassment committed was the sole responsibility of the alleged harasser. The defendant admitted that the general manager was the agent of the company and asserted that his motivation with respect to the plaintiff was to obtain improved work performance.

> The jury reasonably could have concluded that Nathalia the supervisor] viewed Dias' resistance to sexual harassment as undercutting his approach to furthering discipline and productivity among women employees. The jury reasonably could have concluded that Nathalia's treatment of Dias, including her discharge, was thus in furtherance of his administrative responsibilities and within the scope of his employment, despite the fact that his approach was misguided and contrary to public policy.

Id. at 1376. Nichols v. Frank, 732 F. Supp. 1085 (D. Or. 1990) Hearing-impaired postal worker who alleged that her supervisor repeatedly required her to go from the work floor to a private locked office where he forced her to perform sexual acts stated claims for *quid pro quo* and hostile environment sexual harassment. The court rejected the defendant's contention that the action should be dismissed because the plaintiff failed to allege that the Postal Service knew or should have known of the alleged harassment when in her complaint, the plaintiff alleged that her supervisor had the authority to give her permission to take leave and and he generally directed her work:

> The cases regarding hostile environment harassment generally treat the issue of employer liability as a question of fact and emphasize that various circumstances may be considered in determining employer liability, such as the duties and authority of the supervisor, and the existence and efficacy of anti-discrimination policies and grievance procedures. . . .

Id. at 1090. Moreover, the plaintiff's allegations supported a claim for *quid pro quo* harassment as well, so that even if the Ninth Circuit would not impose strict liability in the context of hostile environment harassment, the action would stand.

222 Meritor Sav. Bank v. Vinson, 477 U.S. at 72–73. Robinson v. Jacksonville Shipyards, Inc., 760 F. Supp. 1486 (M.D. Fla. 1991) (grievance procedure inadequate).

they pose."[223] The EEOC went on to compare sexual harassment with sexual attraction. "Sexual attraction is a fact of life, and it may often play a role in the day-to-day social exchange between employees in the workplace."[224] The commission concluded that "while racial slurs are intrinsically offensive and presumptively unwelcome, sexual advances and innuendo are ambiguous," and contrasted racial prejudice with "the naturalness, the pervasiveness, and what might be called the legal neutrality of sexual attraction."[225] Under Title VII, however, sexual advances that are unwelcome constitute sexual harassment. Once it has been demonstrated that the sexual conduct is not welcome, there remains no ambiguity regarding the mutuality of the conduct; sexual attraction does not enter the analysis.

The EEOC under the Reagan and Bush administrations would hold employers vicariously liable for *quid pro quo* harassment only; the employer would have to have actual notice of the harassment in hostile environment cases unless the victim had no reasonable means to complain to higher management.[226] The EEOC feared that allowing vicarious liability in hostile environment cases would be counterproductive because employers would be discouraged from hiring women and forced to regulate employee relationships. It therefore recommended that knowledge of the sexual harassment be imputed to the employer only when the employer has structured its grievance procedure so that it is ineffective for the employee to complain.[227] The commission's fears appear to have been unfounded. Refusing to hire women is a violation of Title VII, and the employer would not have to regulate employee relationships any more than necessary in the *quid pro quo* harassment situations. If anything, a hostile environment would be easier for an employer to ascertain than threats by a supervisor toward particular female employees.

The U.S. Supreme Court in *Meritor* drew extensively from the EEOC brief,[228] noting its inconsistency with the earlier guidelines but apparently accepting the commission's assertion that its proposal was merely an "elaboration" of the guidelines' agency discussion.[229] But inconsistencies appeared within the brief itself. The EEOC stated both that an employer is liable only for those acts of its agents that are "within the scope of the

223 Brief for United States and EEOC as amicus curiae, Meritor Sav. Bank v. Vinson, No. 84-1979 (Dec. 11, 1985) at 12–13.

224 *Id.* at 13.

225 *Id.* at 26.

226 *Id.* at 27.

227 *Id.* at 26–27.

228 Meritor Sav. Bank v. Vinson, 477 U.S. 57, 70–71 (1986).

229 Brief for United States and EEOC as amici curiae at 27, Meritor Sav. Bank v. Vinson, No. 84-1979 (Dec. 11, 1985).

agents' employment" and that "sexually harassing conduct almost by definition is outside the scope of any employee's job description."[230]

The U.S. Supreme Court failed to explain how the principles of agency law were to be applied to hostile environment harassment. Under agency law, a master is held vicariously liable for the harmful conduct of its servants.[231] Vicarious liability controls unauthorized acts that both do and do not further the master's business and also covers the unintentional torts of servants, even though the acts may be outside the scope of employment.[232] Under the theory of respondeat superior, a master is liable for servants' torts committed within the scope of employment, and the conduct must be "of the same general nature as . . . or incidental to the conduct authorized."[233] The imposition of vicarious liability in the sexual harassment context turns on the perceived authority of the supervisor in question. A broad view envelops the day-to-day management functions of supervisory personnel as well as particular authority to make personnel decisions, while a narrow view would limit liability to situations involving specific employment decisions. The knowledge standard proposed and apparently accepted by the U.S. Supreme Court requires actual or constructive knowledge by the employer, which renders the scope of employment issue irrelevant.

It is inappropriate to isolate supervisory employees' capacity to make decisions regarding the employment status of other employees from the context of an ongoing work environment. Drawing a legal line at the tangible job benefit simply because it is tangible ignores the common effects of both types of harassment and the policy considerations underlying Title VII. The more elusive power of supervisory personnel comes from the potential for making work-related decisions and necessarily precedes conduct affecting tangible benefits. Conceptual difficulties should not vitiate liability when the standards for sexual harassment are met.

§ 2.20 The Civil Rights Act of 1991

On November 21, 1991, President Bush signed the Civil Rights Act of 1991, ending a two-year political battle. The Act went into effect on the date of enactment, November 21, 1991. The Act overturns eight U.S. Supreme Court decisions, and addresses topics such as compensatory and punitive damages, jury trials, disparate impact cases, business necessity, expert witness fees, challenges to settlements, mixed motive cases and

---

230 *Id.* at 22, 26.

231 *See* W. Prosser & R. Keeton, Prosser and Keeton on the Law of Torts § 69 (5th ed. 1984).

232 *Id.* § 70; Restatement (Second) of Agency § 219(2) (1958).

233 Restatement (Second) of Agency § 229(1).

interest and filing time in suits against the federal government. The Act amends Title VII of the Civil Rights Act of 1964, § 1981 of the Civil Rights Act of 1866, the Attorney's Fees Awards Act of 1976, the Age Discrimination in Employment Act of 1967, and the Americans With Disabilities Act of 1990. The Act will have a significant impact on sexual harassment cases by providing damage awards in federal court as well as expert witness fees and jury trials. The Act will be particularly beneficial to sexual harassment plaintiffs who live in states where damages for such conduct are not available under state law.

§ 2.21 —Compensatory and Punitive Damages

Under prior law, damages were available only to victims of intentional racial or ethnic discrimination. Section 102 of the Civil Rights Act of 1991 will correct the inadequate remedial provisions of Title VII by extending compensatory and punitive damages to victims of employment discrimination based on sex, religion, and disability, as well as race, under Title VII, the ADA, and Section 501 of the Rehabilitation Act of 1973.

Compensatory damages are available from private employers and federal, state, and local governments. Punitive damages, however, may only be recovered from private employers when the employer acted "with malice or with reckless indifference to" the rights of the victim. Under the new law, damages will be capped at $50,000 for employers of 100 or fewer employees, $100,000 for employers with 101 to 200 employees, $200,000 for employers with 201 to 500 employees, and $300,000 for employers of over 500 employees. For victims of sexual harassment, this is a monumental change in the federal discrimination laws. Up to now, sexual harassment plaintiffs who sought monetary relief for their injuries had to resort to state court or pendent state law claims and their concomitant standards. A major deterrent to the litigation of sexual harassment claims has been the financial investment necessary to obtain elusive remedies. Reinstatement is often not an option, as the victim of sexual harassment may be unwilling to return to a hostile environment or has found other employment during what can be years of litigation. An injunction provides only prospective relief, and back pay may be offset by subsequent earnings in a new job. Now victims of sexual harassment will be able to recover compensatory damages for medical bills or psychiatric treatment necessary as a result of the harassment.

Compensatory damages include "future pecuniary losses, emotional pain, suffering, inconvenience, mental anguish, loss of enjoyment of life, and other nonpecuniary losses."[234] Punitive damages may be recovered

---

234 Rehabilitation Act of 1973 § 102(b)(3), 105 Stat. 1073.

when the plaintiff can demonstrate that the employer acted "with malice or with reckless indifference" to the individual's federally protected rights.[235] The damages caps, which do not apply to claims of discrimination based on race, are likely to be challenged in court.

The number of state court actions or pendent state claims for damages may diminish as a result of an enhanced federal law. In *Bristow v. Drake Street,*[236] the court declined to award compensatory damages to a female employee who was sexually harassed when a jury awarded her $30,000 for intentional infliction of emotional distress. Awarding compensatory damages would have issued duplicative judgments.

§ 2.22 —Expert Witness Fees

Section 113 of the new Civil Rights Act reverses the U.S. Supreme Court's decision in *West Virginia University Hospitals, Inc v .Casey,*[237] in which the Court held that expert witness fees were not part of the reasonable attorney fees awarded under the Civil Rights Attorney's Fees Awards Act or Title VII, and thus recovery for such fees was limited to $30.00 per day. New Subsection (c) of the Fees Act and amended § 2000e-5(k) of Title VII now include expert witness fees as part of attorney fees. Experts play an important role in sexual harassment cases. In *Robinson v, Jacksonville Shipyards, Inc.,*[238] as well as a number of other cases,[239] the court relied on the testimony of expert witnesses on sexual harassment and sexual stereotyping to conclude that pin-ups of nude and partially nude women, demeaning sexual remarks and other harassment created a hostile working environment. Under the Act, prevailing parties should be able to recover fees for expert consultation throughout the course of litigation, as the Act provides for expert fees, not only expert witnesses fees. In *West Virginia University Hospitals,Inc.,* the court pointed to the differences between federal statutes that provide fees for expert witnesses and those that cover expert fees generally.[240]

---

235 Rehabilitation Act of 1973 § 102(b)(1), 105 Stat. 1073.

236 57 Fair Empl. Prac. Cas. (BNA) 1367 (N.D. Ill. 1992).

237 499 U.S. 83 (1991).

238 760 F. Supp. 1486 (M.D. Fla. 1991).

239 See **Ch. 6.**

240 111 S. Ct. 1138, 1141–43.

§ 2.23 —Jury Trials

Jury trials have seldom been allowed under Title VII. Under the 1991 Act, any party to a discrimination action may now demand a jury trial when compensatory or punitive damages are sought. In addition, the court may not inform the jury about the cap on damages.

§ 2.24 —Government Employees

Title III of the new Act extends Title VII, the ADA, and Section 501 of the Rehabilitation Act to Senate employees and executive branch appointees. Although punitive damages are prohibited, prevailing employees may be awarded compensatory damages, attorney fees, and other remedies. The president and senators must reimburse the United States Treasury within 60 days for any compensation by the government to victims of discrimination. Complaint resolution will be handled by the Office of Senate Fair Employment Practices and either party can request judicial review by the U.S. Court of Appeals for the Federal Circuit. House of Representative and legislative branch agencies employees are covered by Title VII.

§ 2.25 —Mixed Motive Cases

The U.S. Supreme Court decision in *Price Waterhouse v. Hopkins*[241] held that a defendant employer in a discrimination action could win by showing that it would have made the same employment decision based on nondiscriminatory grounds. Section 107 of the Civil Rights Act, which adds subsection (m) to § 703 of Title VII, states that a plaintiff can establish an unlawful employment practice by demonstrating that one of the prohibited factors motivated an employment action, even if the employment decision was also motivated by lawful considerations. A court may not award damages or require reinstatement, hiring, or promotion if the employer proves that it would have acted the same absent the discriminatory motive. Injunctive and declaratory relief, as well as attorney fees and costs, may be awarded.

§ 2.26 —Business Necessity

The Civil Rights Act of 1991 adds subsection (k) to § 103 of Title VII, stating that in a disparate impact case, an employment practice is unlawful

---

241 490 U.S. 228 (1989).

if the employer cannot demonstrate that the challenged practice is job related for the position in question and consistent with business necessity. An employer need not show business necessity if it can prove that the challenged employment practice did not cause a disparate impact. But a showing that a practice was required by business necessity is not a defense to intentional discrimination. A plaintiff may also establish disparate impact if it can be proven that a less discriminatory practice was available but not adopted. Each challenged act must be proven separately unless it can be shown that the elements of the decision-making process were not capable of separation for analysis.

§ 2.27 —Filing Time and Interest in Cases Against the Federal Government

The Civil Rights Act of 1991 amends § 717 of Title VII, authorizing actions against the federal government. Section 114 of the Act increases the time for filing suit against the federal government from 30 to 90 days after the receipt of a right to sue letter, as in nonfederal cases. Section 114 also extends the payment of interest for delay in payment of fee awards to actions against the federal government, reversing *Library of Congress v. Shaw.*[242]

§ 2.28 Technical Assistance by the EEOC

Under an amendment to Title VII's Section 705, the EEOC must establish a Technical Assistance Training Institute to assist covered entities in compliance with federal employment discrimination laws. However, employers may not assert the failure to receive assistance as a defense to discrimination charges. The EEOC must also provide educational and outreach activities to persons who historically have suffered discrimination.

§ 2.29 The Glass Ceiling Act

The Glass Ceiling Act of 1991, Title II of the Civil Rights Act, provides for the establishment of a commission to study artificial barriers to the advancement of women and minorities in the workplace and to make recommendations with respect to these findings. A medal is to be awarded annually to businesses that have made significant efforts to promote equal opportunities for women and minorities.

---

242 478 U.S. 310 (1986).

§ 2.30 Retroactivity

Although former President Bush and the Justice Department indicated that federal agencies should construe the Civil Rights Act of 1991 to not apply to cases pending at the time of enactment, the legislative history of the Act is inconclusive regarding retroactivity, and courts have been in conflict over the issue. A number of district courts have applied the Act retroactively in sexual harassment cases.[243] A number of such courts have

---

243 First Circuit: Bonilla v. Liquilux Gas Corp., 812 F. Supp. 286 (D.P.R. 1993) (Civil Rights Act of 1991 would be applied retroactively when no manifest injustice would result); Marrero-Rivera v. Department of Justice, 800 F. Supp. 1024 (D.P.R. 1992) (CRA applied retroactively because damages remedies and jury trial provisions were procedural and remedial, not substantive, and no manifest injustice would result); Mojica v. Gannett Co., 779 F. Supp. 94 (N.D. Ill. 1991) (there was a presumption of retroactivity because language and legislative history did not fairly indicate that the Act was to be applied prospectively only; in addition, increased potential for damages was not likely to have affected alleged discriminatory conduct and thus application of the Act would not cause any manifest injustice.

Second Circuit: Bridges v. Eastman Kodak Co., 800 F. Supp. 1172 (S.D.N.Y. 1992) (Civil Rights Act of 1991 would be applied retroactively).

Third Circuit: Sample v. Keystone Carbon Co., 786 F. Supp. 527 (W.D. Pa. 1992) (CRA applied retroactively to a sexual harassment claim pending at the time the at was signed into law).

Fourth Circuit: Jaekel v. Equifax Mktg. Decision Sys., Inc., 797 F. Supp. 486 (E.D. Va. 1992) (CRA would be applied retroactively to conduct occurring before the Act's effective date when complaint was filed after the Act's effective date).

Cf. Pagana-Fay v. Washington Suburban Sanitary Comm'n, 797 F. Supp. 462 (D. Md. 1992) (CRA provision for jury trial did not apply retroactively); McCormick v. Consolidation Coal Co., 786 F. Supp. 563 (N.D. W. Va. 1992) (CRA did not apply retroactively).

Fifth Circuit: *Cf.* Landgraf v. USI Film Prods., 968 F.2d 427 (5th Cir. 1992)(CRA of 1991 not applied retroactively).

Seventh Circuit: Kennedy v. Fritsch, 796 F. Supp. 306 (N.D. Ill. 1992) (CRA applied prospectively to trial court proceedings as of the filing date of the suit, not at actual time of trial); Aldana v. Raphael Contractors, Inc., 785 F. Supp. 1328 (N.D. Ind. 1992) (the retroactive application of the Civil Rights Act of 1991 would not result in manifest injustice in sexual harassment action; defendants had notice with respect to alleged conduct and its potential liability for compensatory and punitive damages when plaintiff originally sought damages pursuant to state law claims); Bristow v. Drake Str., 57 Fair Empl. Prac. Cas. (BNA) 1367 (N.D. Ill. 1992).

Cf. Zakutansky v. Bionetics Corp., 806 F. Supp. 1362 (N.D. Ill. 1992) (CRA did not apply retroactively to cases filed after the Act's effective date when charged conduct preceded that date).

Eighth Circuit: *Cf.* Davis v. Tri-State Mack Distribs., 981 F.2d 340 (8th Cir. 1992) (Civil Rights Act of 1991 improperly applied retroactively to provide recovery of expert witness fees); Parton v. GTE N., Inc., 971 F.2d 150 (8th Cir. 1992) (damages provision of the Civil Rights Act of 1991 did not apply retroactively to sexual harassment claim that accrued, was tried and was pending on appeal before effective date of the statute);

based their decisions on a conclusion that the application of the Act would not result in a manifest injustice to the defendant. In *Guess v. City of Portage,*[244] the retroactive application of the Act provided for a jury trial and the possibility of compensatory damages in a Title VII action by a police department employee alleging sexual harassment. The application of the Act would not result in a manifest injustice to the city: "The City never had a vested or unconditional right to discrimination against individuals in the workplace and always was required to follow federal and state law in formulating its employment policies." Though confronted with an increased potential for damages, its conduct, if the allegations are true, was improper under both the old and the new law."[245]

§ 2.31 *Harris v. Forklift Systems, Inc.*

In *Harris v. Forklift Systems, Inc.,*[246] the plaintiff alleged that she was constructively discharged from her manager position because of a sexually hostile environment created by the company president. The trial court found that although plaintiff "was the object of a continuing pattern of sex-based derogatory conduct from Hardy," including sexual innuendos about clothing worn by plaintiff and other female employees, throwing things on ground in front of the plaintiff and other female employees and asking them to pick them up, asking the plaintiff and other female employees to retrieve coins from his front pockets, stating to the plaintiff

---

Ninth Circuit: Canada v. Boyd Group, Inc., 809 F. Supp. 771 (D. Nev. 1992) (applying the Act retroactively); Coulter v. Newmont Gold Co., 799 F. Supp. 1071 (D. Nev. 1992) (Reed, Jr., J.) (wrongful discharge for violation of public policy claims dismissed when federal Civil Rights Act of 1991, applied retroactively, was available to recover damages).

Kent v. Howard, 62 Fair Empl. Prac. Cas. (BNA) 945 (S.D. Cal. 1992). The CRA applied retroactively to allow for a jury trial for compensatory damages because rights to jury trial and compensatory damages are remedial and procedural in nature, no manifest injustice would result, the action involved the role of federal law in deciding an issue of great pubic concern, a defendant does not have an unconditional right to limit the remedy available to a plaintiff, and the defendant did not demonstrate that allowing a jury trial and compensatory damages would unfairly impose new and unanticipated obligations on either party.

Tenth Circuit: *Cf.* Hansel v. Public Serv. Co., 778 F. Supp. 1126 (D. Colo. 1991) (Act could not be applied retroactively when congressional intent was not clear).

Eleventh Circuit: Baynes v. AT&T Technologies, Inc., 976 F.2d 1370 (11th Cir. 1992) (Civil Rights Act of 1991 could not be applied retroactively in a case in which judgment was entered before the Act's effective date).

[244] 58 Fair Empl. Prac. Cas. (BNA) 250 (N.D. Ind. 1992).

[245] *Id.* at 253.

[246] 61 Fair Empl. Prac. Cas. (BNA) 240 (M.D. Tenn. 1991).

"Let's go to the Holiday Inn and negotiate your raise," "You're a woman, what do you know," "You're a dumb ass woman," and "We need a man as the rental manager," the plaintiff was not able to prove that the president's conduct was so severe as to create a hostile work environment.

> I believe that Hardy is a vulgar man and demeans the female employees at his work place. Many clerical employees tolerate his behavior and, in fact, view it as the norm and as joking. Plaintiff presented no testimony from other female Forklift employees indicating that they found Hardy's behavior to be offensive or that a hostile work environment existed. This does not mean, however, that plaintiff, a managerial employee, took it the same way.
>
> * * *
>
> I believe that this is a close case, but that Charles Hardy's comments cannot be characterized as much more than annoying and insensitive. The other women working at Forklift considered Hardy a joker. Most of Hardy's wisecracks about females' clothes and anatomy were merely inane and adolescent, such as the running joke that large breasted women are that way because they eat a lot of corn. Hardy's coin dropping and coin-in-the-pocket tricks also fall into this category. I appreciate that plaintiff, as a managerial employee, was more sensitive to these comments than clerical employees, who it appears were conditioned to accept denigrating treatment.[247]

The court did not believe that the plaintiff was subjectively so offended that she suffered injury, when she repeatedly testified that she loved her job, she and her husband socialized with Hardy and his wife, and she herself drank beer and socialized with Hardy and her coworkers.

> Plaintiff herself cursed and joked and appeared to her co-workers to fit in quite well with the work environment. The channels of communication were open between plaintiff and Hardy, but plaintiff was not inspired to broach the issue with him until she had been working at Forklift for over two years.[248]

The circuit court affirmed the dismissal of the sexual harassment claim,[249] and the U.S. Supreme Court granted certiorari on March 1, 1993, to decide the issue of whether the plaintiff in a sexual harassment action must prove severe psychological injury upon a determination that she was offended by conduct that would have offended a reasonable victim in her position. On November 10, 1993, in a unanimous opinion, the Supreme

---

247 *Id* at 243, 244–45.

248 *Id* at 245.

249 976 F.2d 733 (6th Cir. 1992).

Court rejected the standard adopted by the lower courts and held that psychological harm is one factor among many that the courts may weigh in a sexual harassment case.[250] Federal law prohibiting discrimination "comes into play before the harassing conduct leads to a nervous breakdown."[251] Writing for the Court, Justice O'Connor stated that Title VII as applied to sexual harassment is violated when, for any of a variety of reasons, "the environment would be perceived, and is perceived, as hostile or abusive" and that "no single factor is required."[252]

> As we made clear in *Meritor Savings Bank v. Vinson,* . . . [Title VII's] language "is not limited to 'economic' or 'tangible' discrimination. The phrase 'terms, conditions, or privileges of employment' evinces a Congressional intent 'to strike at the entire spectrum of disparate treatment of men and women' in employment," which includes requiring people to work in a discriminatorily hostile or abusive environment. When the workplace is permeated with "discriminatory intimidation, ridicule, and insult," that is "sufficiently severe or pervasive to alter the conditions of the victim's employment and create an abusive working environment," Title VII is violated.
>
> This standard, which we reaffirm today, takes a middle path between making actionable any conduct that is merely offensive and requiring the conduct to cause a tangible psychological injury. As we pointed out in *Meritor,* "mere utterance of an . . . epithet which engenders offensive feelings in an employee," . . . does not sufficiently affect the conditions of employment to implicate Title VII. Conduct that is not severe or pervasive enough to create an objectively hostile or abusive work environment, an environment that a reasonable person would find hostile or abusive, is beyond Title VII's purview. Likewise, if the victim does not subjectively perceive the environment to be abusive, the conduct has not actually altered the conditions of the victim's employment, and there is no Title VII violation.
>
> But Title VII comes into play before the harassing conduct leads to a nervous breakdown. A discriminatorily abusive work environment, even one that does not seriously affect employees' psychological well-being, can and often will detract from employees' job performance, discourage employees from remaining on the job, or keep them from advancing in their careers. Moreover, even without regard to these tangible effects, the very fact that the discriminatory conduct was so severe or pervasive that it created a work environment abusive to employees because of their race, gender, religion, or national origin offends Title VII's broad rule of workplace equality. The appalling conduct alleged in *Meritor,* and the reference in that case to environments "'so heavily polluted with discrimination as to destroy completely the emotional and psychological stability of minority group workers,'"

[250] Harris v. Forklift Systems, Inc., 114 S. Ct. 367 (1993).

[251] *Id.* at 370.

[252] *Id.* at 371.

merely present some especially egregious examples of harassment. They do not mark the boundary of what is actionable.

We therefore believe the District Court erred in relying on whether the conduct "seriously affect(ed) plaintiff's psychological well-being" or led her to "suffe(r) injury." Such an inquiry may needlessly focus the factfinder's attention on concrete psychological harm, an element Title VII does not require. Certainly Title VII bars conduct that would seriously affect a reasonable person's psychological well-being, but the statute is not limited to such conduct. So long as the environment would reasonably be perceived, and is perceived, as hostile or abusive, . . . there is no need for it also to be psychologically injurious.

This is not, and by its nature cannot be, a mathematically precise test. We need not answer today all the potential questions it raises, nor specifically address the E.E.O.C.'s new regulations on this subject. . . . But we can say that whether an environment is "hostile" or "abusive" can be determined only by looking at all the circumstances. These may include the frequency of the discriminatory conduct; its severity; whether it is physically threatening or humiliating, or a mere offensive utterance; and whether it unreasonably interferes with an employee's work performance. The effect on the employee's psychological well-being is, of course, relevant to determining whether the plaintiff actually found the environment abusive. But while psychological harm, like any other relevant factor, may be taken into account, no single factor is required.[253]

Justice Ginsburg concurred, stating that Title VII's critical issue is whether members of one sex are exposed to disadvantageous terms or conditions of employment to which members of the other sex are not exposed, and that as the EEOC as amici curiae emphasized, "the adjudicator's inquiry should center, dominantly, on whether the discriminatory conduct has unreasonably interfered with the plaintiff's work performance,"[254] and that to show such interference, the plaintiff need not prove that her or his tangible productivity has declined as a result of the harassment but only that the harassment so altered working conditions as to make it more difficult to do the job.[255]

Justice Scalia concurred as well, noting that although he knew of no alternative to the course taken by the Court, he was concerned that the term "abusive" did not seem to be a very clear standard and that clarity was not increased by adding the adverb "objectively" or by appealing to a "reasonable person's" notion of what the "vague" word means:

253 *Id.* at 370–71.

254 *Id.* at 372.

255 Harris v. Forklift Systems, Inc., 114 S. Ct. 372 (1993).

Today's opinion does list a number of factors that contribute to abusiveness, . . . but since it neither says how much of each is necessary (an impossible task) nor identifies any single factor as determinative, it thereby adds little certitude. As a practical matter, today's holding lets virtually unguided juries decide whether sex-related conduct engaged in (or permitted by) an employer is egregious enough to warrant an award of damages. One might say that what constitutes "negligence" (a traditional jury question) is not much more clear and certain than what constitutes "abusiveness." Perhaps so. But the class of plaintiffs seeking to recover for negligence is limited to those who have suffered harm, whereas under this statute "abusiveness" is to be the test of whether legal harm has been suffered, opening more expansive vistas of litigation.

Be that as it may, I know of no alternative to the course the court today has taken. One of the factors mentioned in the Court's nonexhaustive list—whether the conduct unreasonably interferes with an employee's work performance—would, if it were made an absolute test, provide greater guidance to juries and employers. But I see no basis for such a limitation in the language of the statute. Accepting *Meritor's* interpretation of the term "conditions of employment" as the law, the test is not whether work has been impaired, but whether working conditions have been discriminatorily altered. I know of no test more faithful to the inherently vague statutory language than the one the Court today adopts.[256]

---

[256] *Id.*

CHAPTER 3

ELEMENTS OF SEXUAL HARASSMENT CLAIMS

§ 3.1 Introduction

Although several years of case law had established the general viability of the sexual harassment claim under Title VII of the 1964 Civil Rights Act, courts held conflicting views regarding what conduct actually constituted sexual harassment, and to what extent an employer was responsible for the sexual activities of employees (see **Chapter 2**). In response, the Equal Employment Opportunity Commission (EEOC) set out to create a framework for sexual harassment claims in its Guidelines on Discrimination Because of Sex.[1] The guidelines clarified a number of issues, but the commission's broad definitions invited a range of judicial construction, particularly in the area of hostile environment harassment (see **Chapter 2**). The U.S. Supreme Court addressed some of the unsettled issues, but left several doors open in *Meritor Savings Bank v. Vinson,*[2] and the unanswered questions were further complicated by the EEOC's substantive retreat during the Reagan administration (see **Chapter 2**).

This chapter discusses the effects of the U.S. Supreme Court decision in *Meritor* and sets out a tripartite analysis of the elements of sexual harassment: the parties, the act, and the effect of the harassment. Because the guidelines[3] and the U.S. Supreme Court recommend a totality of the circumstances approach to sexual harassment determinations,[4] it is somewhat difficult to meaningfully examine individual elements of a sexual harassment claim. It is useful, however, to look at single factors to help create viable parameters of such a claim.

After the guidelines were published, courts began to expand the variety of sexual harassment situations that violated Title VII (see **Chapter 2**). In confirming the propriety of the hostile environment sexual harassment claim, the U.S. Supreme Court decision in *Meritor* invited further expansion, and has set the tone for the way in which Title VII sexual harassment

---

[1] EEOC Guidelines on Discrimination Because of Sex, 45 Fed. Reg. 74,677 (1980), *codified in* 29 C.F.R. § 1604.11 (1993) [hereinafter EEOC Guidelines].

[2] 477 U.S. 57 (1986).

[3] EEOC Guidelines, 29 C.F.R. § 1604.11(b).

[4] Meritor Sav. Bank v. Vinson, 477 U.S. 57, 69 (1986).

claims should be addressed by the courts, employers, and harassment victims.

EFFECTS OF *MERITOR* DECISION

§ 3.2 Implications for Employees

The decision in *Meritor* was generally employee oriented. The Court confirmed the theory of hostile environment sexual harassment as a viable sex discrimination claim under Title VII. Vinson prevailed despite her failure to report her harasser's conduct, her refusal of a transfer, her participation in the sexual activity, and the existence of a company grievance procedure and policy against discrimination. The physical violence perpetuated against Vinson undoubtedly made the case more attractive for the U.S. Supreme Court to review, but the other factors rendered her action far from a perfect sexual harassment case, and thus the U.S. Supreme Court holding should encourage the prosecution of legitimate sexual harassment claims. Judicial concern regarding a potential flood of cases has not been realized. The broad goals of Title VII should not be compromised by the fear that someone might try to benefit unjustly from the law. Sanctions are available to discourage frivolous suits.[5]

Employee participation in the challenged conduct also has been deemed irrelevant in determining whether sexual harassment has occurred, an important factor for harassment victims who blame themselves for encouraging unwelcome conduct and thus believe they have no cause of action. However, the significance of Meritor's holding was diluted somewhat by the Court's admission of evidence about whether the conduct was unwelcome. While the term *welcomeness* suggests a focus on the woman's perspective, the Court stated that "[t]he correct inquiry is whether [Vinson] by her conduct indicated that the alleged sexual advances were unwelcome."[6] Thus, at issue are the employee's actions, rather than her state of mind. Therefore, the employee's compliance with the harassing conduct

---

[5] A variety of sanctions is available. Rule 11 of the Federal Rules of Civil Procedure governs the maintenance of frivolous and meritless litigation, and sanctions under this rule may be assessed against counsel and/or the client. 28 U.S.C. § 1927 imposes liability for misconduct on attorneys who multiply proceedings "unreasonably and vexatiously." Sanctions for frivolous appeals also may be assessed under Rule 38 of the Federal Rules of Appellate Procedure. *See, e.g.,* Jackson-Colley v. Army Corp. of Eng's, 655 F. Supp. 122 (E.D. Mich. 1987) (plaintiff who brought sexual harassment action that was neither well-grounded in fact nor supported by law was ordered to pay defendant's actual costs and attorney's fees, and counsel was fined $500).

[6] Meritor Sav. Bank v. Vinson, 477 U.S. 57, 68 (1986) (emphasis added).

would seem to give credence to her opponent's position, despite the court's admonition against using voluntariness as an absolute defense. The tangential relationship of testimony regarding a female employee's clothing or sexual fantasies is troubling and could deny recovery to a compliant victim who fails to demonstrate that her participation in the sexual activity did not make the harasser's conduct welcome. Moreover, the less severe the conduct—for example, verbal rather than physical abuse—the more difficult it will be to show that compliance did not legally invalidate the harassment. Although most courts apply a reasonable person standard to determine whether conduct is actionable in sexual harassment cases,[7] some courts assess the challenged conduct from the perspective of the reasonable woman employee.[8] Even in an abusive environment, however, the employee's limited participation in the challenged conduct may cause a court to conclude that she was not offended by it.[9] Most courts, however, have not been swayed by this type of testimony, particularly when the alleged harasser's conduct was egregious.[10] For example, in *Gilardi v.*

---

[7] Second Circuit: Koster v. Chase Manhattan Bank, 46 Fair Empl. Prac. Cas. (BNA) 1436 (S.D.N.Y. 1988).

Fifth Circuit: Bennett v. Corroon & Black Corp., 845 F.2d 104 (5th Cir. 1988), *cert. denied,* 489 U.S. 1020 (1989); Dornhecker v. Malibu Grand Prix Corp., 828 F.2d 307 (5th Cir. 1987).

Sixth Circuit: Rabidue v. Osceola Ref. Co., 805 F.2d 611 (6th Cir. 1986), *cert. denied,* 481 U.S. 1041 (1987); Shrout v. Black Clawson Co., 689 F. Supp. 774 (S.D. Ohio 1988).

[8] Sixth Circuit: Yates v. Avco Corp., 819 F.2d 630 (6th Cir. 1987); Vermett v. Hough, 627 F. Supp. 587 (W.D. Mich. 1986). *Cf.* Rabidue v. Osceola Ref. Co., 805 F.2d 611, 626 (6th Cir. 1986), *cert. denied*, 481 U.S. 1041 (1987) (Keith, J. dissenting).

Eleventh Circuit: Robinson v. Jacksonville Shipyards, Inc., 118 F.R.D. 525 (M.D. Fla. 1988).

EEOC Dec. No. 84-1 [1983], EEOC Dec. (CCH) ¶ 6839, 33 Fair Empl. Prac. Cas. (BNA) 1887 (Nov. 28, 1983).

[9] Third Circuit: Ukarish v. Magnesium Elektron, 31 Fair Empl. Prac. Cas. (BNA) 1315, 1319 (D.N.J. 1983).

Fifth Circuit: Loftin-Boggs v. City of Meridian, 633 F. Supp. 1323, 1226–27 (S.D. Miss. 1986), *aff'd*, 824 F.2d 971 (5th Cir. 1987).

Eighth Circuit: Gan v. Kepro Circuit Sys., 28 Fair Empl. Prac. Cas. (BNA) 639 (E.D. Mo. 1982).

EEOC Dec. No. 84-1 [1983], EEOC Dec. (CCH) ¶ 6839, 33 Fair Empl. Prac. Cas. (BNA) 1887 (1983).

[10] Supreme Court: Vinson v. Taylor, 23 Fair Empl. Prac. Cas. (BNA) 37, 38 (D.D.C. 1980), *rev'd,* 753 F.2d 141 (D.C. Cir. 1985), *aff'd in part, rev'd in part sub nom.* Meritor Sav. Bank v. Vinson, 477 U.S. 57 (1986).

Fourth Circuit: Swentek v. USAIR, Inc., 830 F.2d 552 (4th Cir. 1987) (plaintiff did not welcome defendant's lewd conduct despite plaintiff's use of "foul" language); Katz v. Dole, 709 F.2d 251 (4th Cir. 1983) (plaintiff's use of sexual nickname did not excuse coworkers' unfriendly obscenities).

Schroeder,[11] sexual harassment was found despite the plaintiff's frequent social interaction with a supervisor who repeatedly made suggestive remarks and touched her at work. The plaintiff played strip poker with the supervisor, discussed group and "kinky" sex, and once took quaaludes he gave her before he raped her, forced her to perform fellatio, and placed her in bed with him and his wife. After this incident, the supervisor's wife encouraged him to fire the plaintiff.[12]

Although the U.S. Supreme Court stated in *Meritor* that notice does not necessarily shield the employer from liability, courts have stressed the importance of notice and have used the failure to inform the employer of sexual harassment as an important factor in finding against the employee (see §§ **3.5** and **3.6**).

§ 3.3 Implications for Employers

Meritor has placed employers on notice regarding potential liability for their supervisors' conduct. Although the Court did not render a clear ruling on liability, employers must be prepared to promptly investigate claims of sexual harassment. Employers may feel more concerned about the development of romantic relationships between supervisors and their subordinates and may want to discourage this behavior in the workplace. It is also unclear how much notice is necessary and what types of grievance procedures are adequate. Immediacy of response has been determinative in a number of cases (see **Chapter 7**). The U.S. Supreme Court's ruling on the admission of evidence regarding the complainant's behavior will allow employers to refute charges of sexual harassment (see **Chapter 6**).

§ 3.4 Public Policy Implications

The recognition that women often must work in a sexually hostile environment and that such an atmosphere constitutes sex discrimination under the law is replete with implications. Most important is judicial recognition

---

Seventh Circuit: Moffett v. Gene B. Glick Co., 621 F. Supp. 244, 267–68 (N.D. Ind. 1985) (victim of racial harassment need not be "a saint in a den of sinners").

The EEOC has taken the position that a party who participates in sexual conduct at the workplace will be deemed to have welcomed harassing conduct unless she clearly indicates otherwise to the harasser. EEOC Dec. No. 84-1 [1983] EEOC Dec. (CCH) ¶ 6839, 33 Fair Empl. Prac. Cas. (BNA) 1887 (1983).

[11] 833 F.2d 1226 (7th Cir. 1987).

[12] *Id.* at 1228–29.

that acquiescence or participation by the victim does not neutralize the indignity of sexual harassment. Despite the admission of evidence regarding the complainant's own conduct, courts facing sexual harassment issues since *Meritor* have seemed more concerned with the severity of the harassing conduct than the plaintiff's behavior. Although the U.S. Supreme Court noted that absence of notice does not insulate employers from liability, subsequent courts have been reluctant to pin liability on an employer who was not apprised, actually or constructively, of the harassment by the victim. This restraint may reflect a general reluctance to monitor employee relationships and fear that the subjective nature of interpersonal conduct may lead to abuse of the law without the protection of notice.

§ 3.5 1988 EEOC Policy Guidance on Current Issues of Sexual Harassment

On October 25, 1988, the EEOC issued a lengthy Policy Guidance on Current Issues of Sexual Harassment to help define sexual harassment and various issues of employer liability left unsettled by *Meritor*.[13] Drawing from the Restatement (Second) of Agency and the large body of case law that has developed since the U.S. Supreme Court's opinion, the commission clung to the distinctions it supported in *Meritor*, but endorsed several theories that may impose liability on employers despite their lack of knowledge. Essentially, the EEOC said that both employer and employee must share responsibility for a harassment-free environment. Although the mere existence of a company policy against harassment will not shield an employer from responsibility for harassment by its supervisors, an employee's failure to utilize an effective grievance procedure will divest an employer of liability.[14]

The commission agreed that employers always should be held directly responsible for acts of *quid pro quo* harassment. However, it interpreted *Meritor* as requiring a careful examination of hostile environment claims to determine whether the employer knew or should have known about the harassing conduct and was thus directly liable, or whether the harassing supervisor was acting in an agency capacity or within the scope of employment,[15] which would impute liability to the employer.

The commission suggested that an employer would be directly liable for sexual harassment by supervisors if the employer had actual or constructive knowledge of the conduct and failed to take immediate and corrective

[13] EEOC Policy Guidance on Current Issues of Sexual Harassment, N-915.035 (Oct. 25, 1988) [hereinafter EEOC Policy Guidance], reprinted in **App. G.**

[14] *Id.* § D(2)(c).

[15] *Id.* § D(2)(c)(1).

action. Actual knowledge may be acquired through first-hand observations, an internal complaint to other supervisors or managers, or a discrimination charge. Evidence of the pervasiveness of the conduct may create an inference of knowledge or establish constructive knowledge.[16]

The actions of supervisors acting in an agency capacity may be imputed to the employer if they are "generally viewed as being within the scope of employment" or if they fall under an exception to the scope-of-employment rule.[17] The commission noted that although "[i]t will rarely be the case that an employer will have authorized a supervisor to engage in sexual harassment,"[18] the employer's failure to stop the harassment once he becomes aware of it brings the supervisor's actions within the scope of employment. An employer also is liable for a supervisor's conduct if the conduct represents the exercise of apparent authority or authority that third parties reasonably believe the supervisor to possess by virtue of the employer's conduct:

> The Commission believes that in the absence of a strong, widely disseminated, and consistently enforced employer policy against sexual harassment, and an effective complaint procedure, employees could reasonably believe that a harassing supervisor's actions will be ignored, tolerated, or even condoned by upper management. This apparent authority of supervisors arises from their power over their employees, including the power to make or substantially influence hiring, firing, promotion and compensation decisions. A supervisor's capacity to create a hostile environment is enhanced by the degree of authority conferred on him by the employer, and he may rely upon apparent authority to force an employee to endure a harassing environment for fear of retaliation. If the employer has not provided an effective avenue to complain, then the supervisor has unchecked, final control over the victim and it is reasonable to impute his abuse of this power to the employer. The Commission generally will find an employer liable for "hostile environment" sexual harassment by a supervisor when the employer failed to establish an explicit policy against sexual harassment and did not have a reasonably available avenue by which victims of sexual harassment could complain to someone with authority to investigate and remedy the problem.[19]

The commission noted that the existence of a policy against sexual harassment and an effective grievance procedure does not protect the employer who receives actual or constructive notice of harassing conduct and fails to remedy the situation.

---

[16] *Id.* § D(2)(b).

[17] EEOC Policy Guidance §§ D(2)(c), D(2)(c)(1).

[18] *Id.* § D(2)(c)(1).

[19] *Id.* § D(2)(c)(2).

An employer also may be liable for a supervisor's sexual harassment when the employer intentionally or carelessly causes an employee to believe mistakenly that the supervisor is acting for the employer or knows of the error and fails to correct it. An employer who does not properly respond to past incidents of sexual harassment may be liable under this theory, as employees may reasonably believe that any future incidents are authorized and will be tolerated.[20]

Liability under a theory of negligence or recklessness may be imposed if the employer had actual or constructive knowledge of the sexual harassment but failed to take remedial action. The commission noted that an employer cannot avoid liability by delegating to another party a duty imposed by statute.[21]

§ 3.6 1990 EEOC Policy Guidance on Sexual Harassment

The EEOC revised its sexual harassment policy guide slightly in 1990 in light of recent court decisions[22] (see **Appendix H**). The new statement updated its precedence, provided case law for some previously unsupported statements, and added the following guidance:

1. While an employee's failure to utilize an effective grievance procedure will not shield an employer from liability for *quid pro quo* harassment, such failure may defeat a claim of constructive discharge.[23]
2. Employers will usually be deemed to know of sexual harassment that is openly practiced in the workplace or well-known among employees, *especially when there is more than one harasser or victim.*[24]

The Commission noted that it had now addressed the issue of favoritism in its Policy Guidance on Employer Liability Under Title VII for Sexual Favoritism, dated January 1990 (see **Appendix I**).

---

20 *Id.*

21 EEOC Policy Guidance § D(2)(c)(3), *citing* Restatement (Second) of Agency § 492 (1958).

22 EEOC Policy Guidance on Sexual Harassment (Mar. 9, 1990).

23 *Id.* § C(5) n.26.

24 *Id.* § D(2)(b).

EFFECTS OF *HARRIS* DECISION

§ 3.7 Implications for Employees

In *Harris v. Forklift Systems, Inc.,*[25] the U.S. Supreme Court announced a broad definition of workplace sexual harassment that will allow victims of harassment to win lawsuits without having to prove that they suffered psychological injury from the alleged conduct. This means that a victim of sexual harassment does not have to open herself up to psychological examination when alleging a hostile environment, and shifts the focus from the response of the victim to the conduct of the alleged harasser. Victims of sexual harassment who had been reluctant to bring actions against their employers for fear of having to delve into their psychological pasts may be encouraged to seek recourse for their injuries. The psychological impact of sexual harassment may still be introduced when seeking an award of damages.

Another important aspect of the opinion deals with the impact of sexual harassment on job performance. An employee does not need to show that she was unable to perform her job as a result of the alleged harassment. Nor need a plaintiff demonstrate any tangible effects of the offensive conduct.

The language in *Meritor* was general and gave trial courts little guidance, thus resulting in a range of requirements among the circuits. *Harris* indicates that *Meritor* should be applied broadly; rather then focusing on a particular factor, the courts should look at all circumstances to determine whether a work environment is hostile.

Employees must remember, however, that this decision does not affect the obligation to timely respond to offensive conduct by contacting management or supervisory personnel, if possible. Notice to employers is a significant part of an analysis of a hostile environment.

In *Harris* the Court stated that the challenged conduct must be such that a reasonable person would find it hostile or abusive, but this point was not emphasized in relation to the "reasonable woman" standard, as this issue was not before the Court, and it remains to be seen whether courts will continue to use the reasonable woman standard in their analyses. Using a gender-neutral standard may allow some courts to deem as harassment conduct that may not be offensive to men but that may severely affect the working conditions of women. Some courts may find the distinction to be semantic, as the concept of reasonable person in like circumstances may imply the reasonable woman.

---

25 114 S. Ct. 367 (1993).

§ 3.8 Implications for Employers

The decision in *Harris* sends a clear message to employers that sexual harassment will not be tolerated by the courts, and that it is the employer's responsibility to train its employees to avoid sexual harassment. As a result of this case, more cases are likely to go to a jury, and employers, especially larger ones, may be liable for significant amounts of monetary damages. It is important for employers to take the necessary preventative measures to not only avoid liability, but to present a convincing record should it have to defend itself against such accusations. To present a strong defense, employers must be able to show that they have sexual harassment policies with effective grievance procedures, and that they always respond to complaints promptly and attempt to eradicate the offensive conduct.

The decision in *Harris* does not imply that coworkers cannot enjoy friendly relationships. An employee still has an obligation to report offensive conduct if she cannot get the alleged harassment to stop.

§ 3.9 Public Policy Considerations

In *Harris*, the court took sexual harassment analysis to a new level by acknowledging the more subtle aspects of discrimination. It showed that sexual harassment may involve more than the rape and repeated abuse that took place in *Meritor* by holding that a woman need not suffer a nervous breakdown or prove a decline in work productivity to win a sexual harassment case. The decision in *Harris* implicitly approves rulings that hold that a range of conduct that involves no touching, such as the posting of pornography and derogatory comments about women in general, may create a hostile environment. The case was an important one because a ruling for the defendant would have made it extremely difficult for a victim to prove sexual harassment without a barrage of expert witnesses from both sides competing for credibility. Whether or not a case could be made for psychological injury, the cost of proving the case would have been quite a deterrent.

The U.S. Supreme Court's opinion shut the door on arguments that particular conduct was not egregious enough because the plaintiff did not show injury, without considering all the circumstances of the case. The case confirms the notion that sexually harassing conduct is inherently wrong.

ELEMENTS OF A SEXUAL HARASSMENT CLAIM

§ 3.10 The Harasser

When an alleged harasser is the president, director, or majority shareholder of a company, there can be no doubt that actual knowledge of the conduct can be imputed to a corporate defendant to find liability for sexual harassment.[26] Under Title VII, however, the term employer includes agents of the complainant's employer,[27] thus complicating liability issues. The EEOC guidelines state that according to general Title VII principles, an employer, employment agency, joint apprenticeship committee, or labor organization is responsible for its acts and the acts of its agents and supervisors.[28] The EEOC will examine the circumstances of a particular employment relationship and the job functions the individual performs to determine whether a person has acted in a supervisory or agency capacity.[29]

The scope of employer liability in sexual harassment cases is unsettled. In *Kauffman v. Allied Signal,*[30] the U.S. Supreme Court refused to review a decision by the *Sixth Circuit* holding that the proper standard for determining employer liability for a supervisor's actions is whether the supervisor's conduct was forseeable and within the scope of employment.[31]

§ 3.11 —Supervisors

In cases involving *quid pro quo* sexual harassment, courts look at the supervisor's capacity to make personnel decisions (see **Chapter 2**). The supervisory capacity of an employee may be elusive and difficult for the

---

26 Ross v. Twenty-Four Collection, Inc., 681 F. Supp. 1547, 1551 (S.D. Fla. 1988), *aff'd,* 875 F.2d 873 (11th Cir. 1989).

27 42 U.S.C. § 2000e(b).

28 EEOC Guidelines, 29 C.F.R. § 1604.11(c).

29 Swentek v. USAIR, Inc., 830 F.2d 552, 558 (4th Cir. 1987) (usual indicia of an agency relationship were not present between pilot and flight attendant when pilots and flight attendants were attached to different administrative departments within the company and performed under different supervisory chains of command. "USAIR did delegate responsibility to [the pilot] for the safety of his passengers and crew on the aircraft, but Swentek does not allege actionable harassment perpetuated in the exercise of that responsibility. . . . The relationship described here is more one of bickering between coworkers." Plaintiff also failed to establish coworker harassment because company adequately responded to her complaints).

30 Kauffman v. Allied Signal Co., 970 F.2d 178 (6th Cir. 1992), *cert. denied,* 113 S. Ct. 831 (1992).

31 See § 3.11.

harassed employee to ascertain. A supervisor need not have direct authority to carry out a personnel decision; the capacity to make recommendations for or otherwise have influence regarding positions may be sufficient.[32] In *Huitt v. Marher Street Hotel Corp.*,[33] the court noted that even when an alleged harassing supervisor does not carry out an adverse employment action, a causal nexus between the harassment and the action may still be inferred if he participated in making a decision to take such an action. This is particularly so when, as in this case, the alleged harasser and the person who purportedly fired the plaintiff were dating at the time.

A hostile working environment can be created without such authority and by coworkers and nonemployees as well as supervisors. A supervisor who harasses an employee who is or later becomes the subordinate of another supervisor may still possess authority to control the employee's job destiny through his relationship with the employee's supervisor.[34] Because *Meritor* held that employers are not strictly liable for the conduct of their employee supervisors[35] (see **Chapter 2**), notice of the sexual harassment to upper management, when possible, may be determinative.[36]

---

32 Second Circuit: *Cf.* Koster v. Chase Manhattan Bank, 46 Fair Empl. Prac. Cas. (BNA) 1436, 1447 (S.D.N.Y. 1988) (plaintiff presented no evidence that her supervisor recommended termination).

Ninth Circuit: Miller v. Bank of Am., 600 F.2d 211, 213 (9th Cir. 1979); Ambrose v. United States Steel Corp., 39 Fair Empl. Prac. Cas. (BNA) 30 (N.D. Cal. 1985) (employer who lacked knowledge of harassment was held liable when supervisor had recommended termination).

Tenth Circuit: Schroeder v. Schock, 42 Fair Empl. Prac. Cas. (BNA) 1112, 1115 (D. Kan. 1986) ("It is enough if the supervisor has the authority to participate in such a decision").

Eleventh Circuit: Sowers v. Kemira Inc., 46 Fair Empl. Prac. Cas. (BNA) 1825 (S.D. Ga. 1988) (although plaintiff's supervisor was not the ultimate decisionmaker, he had a great deal of influence on plaintiff's awaited promotion and raise).

33 62 Fair Empl. Prac. Cas. (BNA) 538 (D. Kan. 1993).

34 Sparks v. Pilot Freight Carriers, 830 F.2d 1554 (11th Cir. 1987) (district court improperly granted summary judgment on plaintiff's *quid pro quo* harassment claim when plaintiff testified that her supervisor had threatened to have her fired if she did not accede to his demands; supervisor had influenced terminal manager to reprimand plaintiff based on fictitious problems).

35 Meritor Sav. Bank v. Vinson, 477 U.S. at 73.

36 The plaintiffs in these cases finding no discrimination did not notify their employers of the alleged sexual harassment:

First Circuit: Del Valle Fontanez v. Aponte, 660 F. Supp. 145 (D.P.R. 1987).

Fourth Circuit: Jackson v. Kimel, 992 F.2d 1318 (4th Cir. 1993). Slate v. Kingsdown, 46 Fair Empl. Prac. Cas. (BNA) 1495 (M.D.N.C. 1987).

Fifth Circuit: Valdez v. Church's Fried Chicken, 683 F. Supp. 596 (W.D. Tex. 1988); Benton v. Kroger Co., 640 F. Supp. 1317 (S.D. Tex. 1986).

§ 3.12 —Coworkers

The harassment of one worker by a coworker does not violate Title VII unless the act of discrimination is attributable to the employer.[37] Under § 1604.11(d) of the EEOC guidelines, an employer is responsible for the conduct of fellow employees when the employer or its agents or supervisors knew or should have known of the conduct, unless it can be shown that immediate and appropriate corrective action was taken.[38] Corrective

---

Seventh Circuit: Dockter v. Rudolf Wolff Futures, Inc., 684 F. Supp. 532, 539 (N.D. Ill. 1988), *aff'd,* 913 F.2d 456 (7th Cir. 1990); Scott v. Sears Roebuck & Co., 605 F. Supp. 1047 (N.D. Ill. 1985), *aff'd,* 798 F.2d 210 (7th Cir. 1986); Wahab v. Portal Pub, 47 Fair Empl. Prac. Cas. (BNA) 579 (7th Cir. 1988).

Eighth Circuit: Christoforou v. Ryder Truck Rental, 668 F. Supp. 294 (S.D.N.Y. 1987); Neville v. Taft Broadcasting Co., 42 Fair Empl. Prac. Cas. (BNA) 1314 (W.D.N.Y. 1987).

Ninth Circuit: Jordan v. Clark, 847 F.2d 1368 (9th Cir. 1988) *cert. denied,* 488 U.S. 1006 (1989).

[37] EEOC Guidelines, 29 C.F.R. § 1604.11(a) (1988).

Zabkowicz v. West Bend Co., 589 F. Supp. 780 (E.D. Wis. 1984), *aff'd,* 789 F.2d 540, 546 (7th Cir. 1986) (employees may not sue nonsupervisory coworkers for discriminatory acts under Title VII).

Accord Busse v. Gelco Express Corp., 678 F. Supp. 1398 (E.D. Wis. 1988); Guyette v. Stauffer Chem. Co., 518 F. Supp. 521 (D.N.J. 1981).

See also Flowers v. Rego, 691 F. Supp. 177 (E.D. Ark. 1988) (discharged female employee who brought action against car dealership and coworker charging, among other things, that she was discharged in retaliation for her complaints of sexual harassment by defendant coworker, never filed EEOC charge).

[38] Second Circuit: Blesedell v. Mobil Oil Co., 708 F. Supp. 1408 (S.D.N.Y. 1989).

Fourth Circuit: Wall v. AT&T Technologies, 754 F. Supp. 1084 (M.D.N.C. 1990). An employer may be liable for sexual harassment by coworkers:

> The proper inquiry on the liability should not be limited to the interaction between the employee and those who may act on behalf of a defendant, *i.e.* company management. Rather, those actors who may bind an employer in terms of imputed liability includes a broader range of individuals. . . . Anyone can contribute to a sexually hostile environment.

Id. at 1096. Even if greater management participation in the discriminatory incidents was required for imputed liability, the instant case would survive defendant's summary judgment motion when plaintiff alleged management support for coworker activities and evidence manifested the defendant's awareness of the sexual harassment problem.

Swentek v. USAIR, Inc., 830 F.2d 552, 558 (4th Cir. 1987) (employer confronted alleged harasser, questioned him, and interviewed other employees in an effort to seek corroboration of plaintiff's complaint).

Fifth Circuit: Waltman v. International Paper Co., 875 F.2d 468 (5th Cir. 1989) (when supervisor told employee to stop making sexual comments over public address system but did not reprimand employee or make note of incident in employee's file, there was a factual issue as to whether defendant should have taken further measures to

action includes implementing measures to remedy any possible confrontations between the plaintiff and offending coworkers.[39] When a supervisor has been advised of alleged coworker misconduct, or the harassment is pervasive and the supervisor does not respond, the employer is deemed to have constructive knowledge of the alleged harassment.[40] Coworker harassment includes situations involving individual coworkers[41] as well as a "conspiracy" by a group of male coworkers against the sole or few women employees.[42] Several suits have been brought by women who are

---

end harassment); Dornhecker v. Malibu Grand Prix Corp., 828 F.2d 307 (5th Cir. 1987) (employer's response to claims of sexual harassment by coworker was sufficiently prompt when in less than 12 hours after plaintiff complained, she was assured she would not have to work with coworker after current project ended in 1+1/2 days; plaintiff was not propositioned, forced to respond to coworker, or placed in threatening situation).

Sixth Circuit: Faris v. Henry Vogt Mach. Co., 813 F.2d 786, 687 (6th Cir. 1987) (employer implemented measures to prevent confrontations between plaintiff and coworkers); Coley v. Consolidated Rail Corp., 561 F. Supp. 645 (E.D. Mich. 1982).

Eighth Circuit: Barrett v. Omaha Nat'l Bank, 726 F.2d 424 (8th Cir. 1984) (within four days of employee's complaint of sexual harassment, defendant informed alleged harassers that their conduct would not be tolerated and they would be fired for further misconduct).

District of Columbia Circuit: Robinson v. Thornburgh, 54 Fair Empl. Prac. Cas. (BNA) 324 (D.D.C. 1990). A former employee of the U.S. Marshal's Service did not demonstrate that she was sexually harassed when her allegations consisted of being asked out on dates by two fellow male employees. She admitted that she did not feel compelled to date them, she did not report the incidents to her supervisor, did not list these incidents as evidence of being sexually harassed when asked at her pretrial deposition. At the time of her employment the plaintiff had been advised by her superiors that she was not expected to date fellow employees, and that in fact it would be in her interest to decline such invitations.

39 Faris v. Henry Vogt Mach. Co., 813 F.2d 786, 787 (6th Cir. 1987).

40 Eighth Circuit: Hall v. Gus Constr. Co., 842 F.2d 1010 (8th Cir. 1988). Female traffic controllers for construction company were subject to hostile working environment when coworkers referred to them as "fucking flag girls" and "herpes," wrote "cavern cunt" and "blond bitch" in the dust on their cars, repeatedly asked them if they "wanted to fuck" and engage in oral sex, touched their thighs and breasts, picked them up so others could touch them, urinated in their gas tanks and water bottles, exposed themselves, "mooned" the women, flashed obscene pictures, and observed the women urinating in a ditch through surveying equipment. Supervisor knew about the conduct but did nothing.

Eleventh Circuit: Huddleston v. Roger Dean Chevrolet, Inc., 845 F.2d 900 (11th Cir. 1988) (employer car dealership had notice when salesperson who was harassed by coworkers and sales manager complained to general manager).

41 Swentek v. USAIR, Inc., 830 F.2d 552, 558 (4th Cir. 1987); Intlekofer v. Turnage, 973 F.2d 774 (9th Cir. 1992).

42 Fourth Circuit: Llewellyn v. Celanese Corp., 693 F. Supp. 369 (W.D.N.C. 1988). Woman truck driver was victim of unwanted sexual propositions, sexual touching, exposure to nude male coworkers and threats of violence by coworkers and at least one customer, had her truck sabotaged, and had a snake placed in her cab. Following incidents of harassment, plaintiff would receive anonymous threats over her truck CB to

particularly vulnerable to this type of harassment, such as those who enter traditionally male areas of employment such as air traffic control,[43] truck driving,[44] police work,[45] mines,[46] car sales,[47] car repair,[48] corrections,[49] construction,[50] firefighting,[51] sales,[52] and plumbing,[53] and those holding traditionally

---

keep her from filing or going through with complaints and was finally forced to take medical leave because of resulting psychological disorders.

Eighth Circuit: Hall v. Gus Constr. Co., 842 F.2d 1010 (8th Cir. 1988).

Tenth Circuit: Hansel v. Public Serv. Co., 778 F. Supp. 1126 (D. Colo. 1991) (plaintiff worked as an auxiliary tender (machine operator) in the operations department of defendant power plant as one of only two female employees, and plaintiff was often the only woman working in the plant during her shift).

Eleventh Circuit: Huddleston v. Roger Dean Chevrolet, Inc., 845 F.2d 900 (11th Cir. 1988).

43 Katz v. Dole, 709 F.2d 251 (4th Cir. 1983).

44 Llewellyn v. Celanese Corp., 693 F. Supp. 369 (W.D.N.C. 1988).

45 Andrews v. City of Philadelphia, 895 F.2d 1469 (3d Cir. 1990); Barcume v. City of Flint, 819 F. Supp. 631 (E.D. Mich. 1993); Watts v. New York City Police Dep't, 724 F. Supp. 99 (S.D.N.Y. 1989); Haehn v. City of Hoisington, 702 F. Supp 1526 (D. Kan. 1988); Sapp v. City of Warner Robins, 655 F. Supp. 1043 (M.D. Ga. 1987); Headley v. City of Grand Island, No. CV83-L-760 (D. Neb. Jan. 16, 1985); Pennsylvania State Police v. Unemployment Bd., 53 Fair Empl. Prac. Cas. (BNA) 1157 (Pa. Comm. Ct. 1990) (state police officers).

46 Lord v. Kerr-McGee Coal Co., 809 F. Supp. 87 (D. Wy. 1992); Jenson v. Eveleth Taconite Co., 139 F.R.D. 657 (D. Minn. 1991).

47 Huddleston v. Roger Dean Chevrolet, Inc., 845 F.2d 900 (11th Cir. 1988).

48 Scott v. Sears Roebuck & Co., 605 F. Supp. 1047 (N.D. Ill. 1985), *aff'd,* 798 F.2d 210 (7th Cir. 1986).

49 Minteer v. Auger, 844 F.2d 569 (8th Cir. 1988) (sexual remarks by coworkers did not rise to level of severity necessary under *Meritor*); Handley v. Phillips, 715 F. Supp 657 195 (M.D. Pa. 1989) (prison guard); Bennett v. New York City Dep't of Corrections, 705 F. Supp. 979, 986 (S.D.N.Y. 1989) (female corrections officer's claim that she was subjected to unwelcome sexual advances, coarse sexual humor about herself and others, sexual graffiti relating to her, and an unconsented sexual touching in violation of Title VII survived summary judgment motion; court noted that although conditions at prison are harsh and sometimes brutal, "that does not mean that anything goes, particularly among those who are charged with maintaining the discipline of the staff").

50 Hall v. Gus Constr. Co., 842 F.2d 1010 (8th Cir. 1988).

51 Berkman v. City of N.Y., 580 F. Supp. 226, 230–32, 240 (E.D.N.Y. 1983), *aff'd,* 755 F.2d 913 (2d Cir. 1985) (unimpeded hazing of women firefighters by other male employees, graffiti and cartoons making blatant sexual mockeries of plaintiffs, placing of prophylactic devices and wet vibrators in one of plaintiff's beds, stealing work instruments, breaking their equipment, excluding them from meals, and touching buttocks, breasts, waist, and hair on various occasions constituted sexual harassment).

52 Silverstein v. Metroplex Communications, Inc., 678 F. Supp. 863 (S.D. Fla. 1988) (sales manager for radio station; no hostile environment established).

53 First Circuit: Contardo v. Merrill Lynch, 756 F. Supp. 414 (D. Mass. 1990) (stockbroker); Hallquist v. Max Fish Plumbing & Heating Co., 46 Fair Empl. Prac. Cas. (BNA)

female jobs in male-dominated settings, such as fire or police departments[54] or the lumber industry.[55] Coworker harassment usually

---

1855 (D. Mass. 1987). While the fact that plaintiff plumber was the subject of gender-related jokes and occasional teasing was relevant to the question of whether the defendant's explanation for her termination was credible, it alone was insufficient to establish a claim under the hostile environment theory. "It is often difficult to draw the line between a hostile work environment and an environment subject to the ordinary trials and tribulations of the workplace" *Id.* at 1860. Evidence showed that in addition to the jokes, plaintiff was closely supervised and "babied" "in a manner that demeaned her demonstrable plumbing skills," and that after she was laid off, the employer "continued to maintain and add to his plumbing force."

Second Circuit: Danna v. New York Tel. Co., 752 F. Supp. 594 (S.D.N.Y. 1990) (telephone installation service technician).

Third Circuit: Kinnally v. Bell of Penn., 748 F. Supp. 1136 (E.D. Pa. 1990) (engineer); Reynolds v. Atlantic City Convention Ctr., 53 Fair Empl. Prac. Cas. (BNA) 1852 (D.N.J. 1990) ("journeyman" electrician).

Eighth Circuit: Morris v. American Nat'l Can Corp., 730 F. Supp. 1489 (E.D. Mo. 1989), *modified on other grounds,* 941 F.2d 710 (8th Cir. 1991) (machinist/moldmaker).

Ninth Circuit: Ellison v. Brady, 924 F.2d 872 (9th Cir. 1991) (internal revenue agent); Wangler v. Hawaiian Elec. Co., 742 F. Supp. 1458 (D. Haw. 1990) (chemist); Sheehan v. United States, 896 F.2d 1168 (9th Cir. 1990) (army civilian employee).

Tenth Circuit: Hansel v. Public Serv. Co., 778 F. Supp. 1126 (D. Colo. 1991) (machine operator); Graham v. American Airlines, 53 Fair Emp. Prac. Cas. (BNA) 1390 (N.D. Okla. 1989) (airplane mechanic).

54 Bohen v. City of E. Chicago, 799 F.2d 1180, 1188 (7th Cir. 1986) (plaintiff dispatcher for fire department was victim of sex discrimination under equal protection clause when head dispatcher touched her offensively and repeatedly, a captain made a veiled threat of rape, conversation in the fire station was filled with "lurid sexual descriptions," and officers spread rumors regarding her sexuality).

55 Waltman v. International Paper Co., 875 F.2d 468 (5th Cir. 1989).

See also Parton v. GTE N., Inc., 971 F.2d 150 (8th Cir. 1992). A female who worked in the installation and repair department of GTE brought an action charging discriminatory discharge and sexual harassment, alleging that her department was hostile to women employees. Evidence of such harassment included sexually suggestive gestures and comments, posting and distributing lewd cartoons, and assigning of undesirable work to plaintiff and other women when available male employees were not so assigned. The incidents occurred over the course of years, but plaintiff never filed a sexual harassment complaint while she was an employee or made such allegations to union officials or at the union grievance hearing preceding her discharge. Evidence also showed that plaintiff had a record of poor performance, and the lower court concluded that the employer's legitimate reasons for Parton's discharge were not proven to be pretextual by a preponderance of the evidence. The court of appeals rejected plaintiff's contention that this was a mixed-motive case and that the trial court could not find that she was subjected to a sexually hostile environment, as it did, without also concluding that Parton's gender was a factor in her termination. There was no direct evidence that GTE was motivated to terminate plaintiff for gender-based reasons, and thus this was not a mixed-motive case.

involves hostile environment sexual harassment,[56] and a single incident usually will not violate Title VII unless it is extremely egregious (see **Chapter 6**). In the absence of a conspiracy, several courts have found isolated incidents by a number of different coworkers not to constitute sexual harassment, despite the fact that such conduct may be pervasive.[57] An employee who sexually harasses a female employee while lacking true authority to make employment decisions, but who later obtains the power to make those decisions, may have constructive supervisory authority, and his conduct may form the basis for a sexual harassment claim.[58]

Victims of harassment by coworkers should notify supervisors or other management personnel of unwelcome conduct to ensure notice to the employer. Courts usually have declined to find sexual harassment when the alleged conduct was unreported.[59] Nonsupervisory personnel cannot be sued directly under Title VII, but may be liable under state law.[60]

Cf. Goble v. St. Anthony Medical Ctr., 57 Fair Empl. Prac. Cas. (BNA) 187 (N.D. Ill. 1990). Plaintiff female employee did not state a claim for intentional infliction of emotional distress in an action alleging that a female coworker (Ryan) had made romantic overtures toward plaintiff and had spread rumors about plaintiff among defendant's staff when the only evidence suggesting defendant's participation in Ryan's harassment of plaintiff was encouraging Ryan to file a grievance against plaintiff. "Such conduct is, at best, a facilitation of the remedial procedures Defendant made available to its employees, and at worst a means of placating employee Ryan." *Id.* at 188.

56 Minteer v. Auger, 844 F.2d 569 (8th Cir. 1988).

57 Waltman v. International Paper Co., 47 Fair Empl. Prac. Cas. (BNA) 671 (W.D. La. 1988), *rev'd,* 875 F.2d 468 (5th Cir. 1989); Minteer v. Auger, 844 F.2d 569, 571 (8th Cir. 1988) (sexual remarks by coworkers did not rise to level of severity necessary under *Meritor*).

58 Simmons v. Lyon, 746 F.2d 265 (5th Cir. 1984).

59 Third Circuit: Freedman v. American Standard, 41 Fair Empl. Prac. Cas. (BNA) 471 (D.N.J. 1986); Robinson v. E.I. du Pont de Nemours & Co., 33 Fair Empl. Prac. Cas. (BNA) 880 (D. Del. 1979).

Sixth Circuit: Hollis v. Fleetguard, Inc., 668 F. Supp. 631 (M.D. Tenn. 1987) (plaintiff waited three to four months to respond).

Seventh Circuit: Scott v. Sears Roebuck & Co., 605 F. Supp. 1047 (D. Ill. 1985), *aff'd,* 798 F.2d 210 (7th Cir. 1986).

Eleventh Circuit: Silverstein v. Metroplex Communications, Inc., 678 F. Supp. 863 (S.D. Fla. 1988) (plaintiff failed to report alleged harassment despite opportunity to do so).

60 Busse v. Gelco Express Corp., 678 F. Supp. 1398, 1403 (E.D. Wis. 1988).

§ 3.13 —Nonemployees

Sexual harassment by nonemployees usually involves the conduct of clients or customers,[61] that is sometimes encouraged by employers' requirements that female employees wear revealing apparel or act in a provocative manner to stimulate business.[62] The EEOC guidelines state that, as in cases of harassment by coworkers, the employer may be responsible for the conduct of nonemployees if the employer, its agents, or supervisors knew or should have known of the conduct, unless immediate and appropriate corrective action was taken. The EEOC will consider the extent of the employer's control and any other legal responsibility the employer may have with respect to the conduct of such parties.[63]

§ 3.14 The Harassment

The difference between female and male perceptions of what constitutes sexual harassment and the importance of context in determining undesirable behavior have made it difficult to establish precise definitions for the term sexual harassment. The EEOC defines *sexual harassment* as "[u]nwelcome sexual advances, requests for sexual favors, and other verbal or physical conduct of a sexual nature."[64] The U.S. Supreme Court approved this definition in *Meritor*.[65] The Working Women's Institute defines *sexual harassment in employment* as:

---

61 Llewellyn v. Celanese Corp., 693 F. Supp. 369 (W.D.N.C. 1988). Plaintiff truck driver was victim of unwanted sexual propositions, sexual touching, exposure to nude male coworkers and threats of violence by coworkers and at least one customer, had her truck sabotaged, and had a snake placed in her cab. Harassment included touching of her breast by male supervisor at customer's plant, to which safety director at her company responded, "The customer is always right".

62 Second Circuit: EEOC v. Sage Realty Corp., 507 F. Supp. 599 (S.D.N.Y. 1981) (lobby attendant was required to wear revealing "bicentennial" outfit).

Fourth Circuit: EEOC v. Newtown Inn Assocs., 647 F. Supp. 957, 958 (E.D. Va. 1986). Cocktail waitresses were required to project an air of sexual availability pursuant to marketing scheme called "confetti concept," through use of provocative thematic outfits, flirting, and dancing both alone and with customers in a sexually provocative manner. Waitresses were subsequently subjected to unwelcome sexual proposals and physical and verbal sexual abuse.

Sixth Circuit: Marentette v. Michigan Host, Inc., 506 F. Supp. 909 (E.D. Mich. 1980) (sexually provocative dress code may violate Title VII).

63 EEOC Guidelines, 29 C.F.R. § 1604.11(e) (1993).

64 EEOC Guidelines, 29 C.F.R. § 1604.11(a).

65 Meritor Sav. Bank v. Vinson, 477 U.S. 57 (1986).

> any attention of a sexual nature in the context of the work situation which has the effect of making a woman uncomfortable on the job, impeding her ability to do her work or interfering with her employment opportunities. It can be manifested by looks, touches, jokes, innuendos, gestures, epithets or direct propositions. At one extreme it is the direct demand for sexual compliance coupled with the threat of firing the woman if she refuses. At the other, it is being forced to work in an environment in which, through various means, such as sexual slurs and/or the public display of derogatory images of woman or the requirement that she dress in sexually revealing clothing, a woman is subjected to stress or made to feel humiliated because of her sex. Sexual harassment is behavior which becomes coercive because it occurs in the employment context, thus threatening both a woman's job satisfaction and security.[66]

The federal courts have defined sexual harassment using the language of Title VII: conduct which affects the "terms, conditions or privileges of employment."[67] A broad range of conduct has been found to fall within the parameters established by the EEOC and the courts.

§ 3.15 —Sexual Advances

Unwelcome sexual advances can give rise to a sexual harassment claim under Title VII. Although the EEOC guidelines do not define the term, suggesting instead that violations will be determined on a case-by-case basis,[68] sexual advances generally are viewed as invitations to participate in sexual activity and may form the basis of either a *quid pro quo* or hostile environment sexual harassment claim. A sexual advance or request for sexual favors might consist of a request to spend the night,[69] have an affair,[70] go skinny dipping,[71] move into an apartment together,[72] go out for a drink or a date despite repeated refusals,[73] "make out,"[74] or, in one way or another,

---

66 Working Women's Institute, Sexual Harassment on the Job: Questions and Answers (1980).

67 42 U.S.C. § 2000e-2(a). *See also* Katz v. Dole, 709 F.2d 251, 256 (4th Cir. 1983); Henson v. City of Dundee, 682 F.2d 897, 903–905 (11th Cir. 1982).

68 EEOC Guidelines, 29 C.F.R. § 1604.11(b).

69 Sixth Circuit: Munford v. James T. Barnes & Co., 441 F. Supp. 459 (E.D. Mich. 1977).

Eleventh Circuit: Ross v. Twenty-Four Collection, Inc., 681 F. Supp. 1547, 1549 (S.D. Fla. 1988), *aff'd,* 875 F.2d 873 (11th Cir. 1989).

70 Bundy v. Jackson, 641 F.2d 934 (D.C. Cir. 1981).

71 Sowers v. Kemira, Inc., 46 Fair Empl. Prac. Cas. (BNA) 1825 (S.D. Ga. 1988).

72 Tenth Circuit: Heelan v. Johns-Manville Corp., 451 F. Supp. 1382, 1387 (D. Colo. 1978).

73 Carosella v. United States Postal Serv., 816 F.2d 638 (Fed. Cir. 1987); Kalinauskas v. Wong, 808 F. Supp. 1469 (D. Nev. 1992).

74 Sowers v. Kemira, Inc., 46 Fair Empl. Prac. Cas. (BNA) 1825, 1829 (S.D. Ga. 1988).

have sex.[75] Sexual advances may be tied to existing or prospective job benefits,[76] and the cause of action need not accrue at the time of the unwelcome sexual advance.[77] An unwelcome advance (see **§ 3.18**) made by an employee who later acquires decision-making authority and wields that authority in a discriminatory manner may later give rise to a sexual harassment claim.[78] This prospect should encourage employers to make personnel decisions carefully and allow requested transfers by affected parties when feasible.

A plaintiff must establish that certain conduct was in fact based on sex[79] and not business-related activity (see **Chapter 7**). Such an advance need not occur in the office to establish a sexual harassment violation.[80]

---

75 Sixth Circuit: Munford v. James T. Barnes & Co., 441 F. Supp. 459 (E.D. Mich. 1977) (supervisor told plaintiff she would have to accompany him on a business trip and have sex with him).

Seventh Circuit: Bohen v. City of E. Chicago, 799 F.2d 1180, 1183 (7th Cir. 1986) ("constant invitation to engage in deviant sexual conduct").

Eleventh Circuit: Sowers v. Kemira, Inc., 46 Fair Empl. Prac. Cas. (BNA) 1825 (S.D. Ga. 1988) (defendant wanted to have sex in the company storeroom).

District of Columbia Circuit: Vinson v. Taylor, 23 Fair Empl. Prac. Cas. (BNA) 37, 38 (D.D.C. 1980), *rev'd,* 753 F.2d 141 (D.C. Cir. 1985), *aff'd in part, rev'd in part sub nom.* Meritor Sav. Bank v. Vinson, 477 U.S. 57 (1986).

76 Tomkins v. Public Serv. Elec. & Gas Co., 568 F.2d 1044 (3d Cir. 1977).

77 Blessing v. Lancaster County, 609 F. Supp. 485 (E.D. Pa. 1985).

78 Simmons v. Lyon, 746 F.2d 265 (5th Cir. 1984) (plaintiffs alleged that sheriff-elect conditioned their reappointment on submission to sexual advances).

79 Jones v. Flagship Int'l, 793 F.2d 714, 728 (5th Cir. 1986), *cert. denied,* 479 U.S. 1065 (1987); Henson v. City of Dundee, 682 F.2d 897 (11th Cir. 1982). *See also* Sheehan v. Purolator, Inc., 839 F.2d 99 (2d Cir. 1988), *cert. denied,* 488 U.S. 891 (1988) (district court rejected claim of sexual harassment when supervisor's temper was manifested toward men and women, even his superiors); Jackson-Colley v. Army Corps of Eng'rs, 655 F. Supp. 122, 127 (E.D. Mich. 1987).

80 Sixth Circuit: Boyd v. James S. Hayes Living Health Care Agency, 671 F. Supp. 1155 (W.D. Tenn. 1987) (plaintiff was harassed in hotel room at conference).

Seventh Circuit: Gilardi v. Schroeder, 833 F.2d 1226 (7th Cir. 1987) (supervisor drugged plaintiff at his home and had sex with her).

Tenth Circuit: Haehn v. City of Hoisington, 702 F. Supp. 1526 (D. Kan. 1988). Female former employee raised sufficient questions of fact as to whether alleged sexual harassment that occurred after work hours had an evidentiary nexus to her work environment, and plaintiff submitted evidence of at least eight incidents sufficiently pervasive and severe as to alter a condition of her employment; Schroeder v. Schock, 42 Fair Empl. Prac. Cas. (BNA) 1112, 1114 (D. Kan. 1986) (harassment occurred after hours in restaurant parking lot).

§ 3.16 —Same Sex Advances

Although Title VII does not proscribe discrimination based on sexual orientation,[81] the sexual harassment of persons of the same sex is also a violation of Title VII.[82] There has been very little litigation in this area,[83] and

---

[81] Williamson v. A.G. Edwards and Sons, Inc., 876 F. 2069 (8th Cir. 1989), *cert. denied,* 493 U.S. 1089 (1990).

[82] First Circuit: Morgan v. Massachusetts Gen. Hosp., 712 F. Supp. 242, 257 (D. Mass. 1989) (allegations that coworker would stand behind plaintiff and allow plaintiff to bump into him while plaintiff was mopping, would "hang around plaintiff a lot," and would stand next to plaintiff in the men's room and "peep" at plaintiff's "privates" were not sufficiently severe and pervasive to be actionable under Title VII), *modified,* 901 F.2d 186 (1st Cir. 1990) (allegations of homosexual advances did not involve conduct that serves as basis for Title VII).

Seventh Circuit: Wright v. Methodist Youth Servs., Inc., 511 F. Supp. 307 (N.D. Ill. 1981); Barlow v. Northwestern Memorial Hosp., 30 Fair Empl. Prac. Cas. (BNA) 223 (N.D. Ill. 1980) (female former employee who alleged that she was demoted because she resisted a female supervisor's sexual advances and that the employer failed to act on her complaints stated a claim of sex discrimination).

Eleventh Circuit: Joyner v. AAA Cooper Trans., 597 F. Supp. 537 (M.D. Ala. 1983), *aff'd,* 749 F.2d 732 (11th Cir. 1984) (male plaintiff harassed by another man established a prima facie case of discriminatory job environment).

[83] *See also* Fifth Circuit: Polly v. Houston Lighting & Power Co., 825 F. Supp. 135 (S.D. Tex. 1993). An employee did not state a claim for hostile environment sexual harassment when he failed to raise a fact issue regarding whether he would have been treated differently by his coworkers if he had not been male. When asked why he thought his coworkers harassed him, the plaintiff responded that it was because he would not join in on their "dirty" conversations, he had disapproved of the use of profanity at work, and that coworkers were jealous that certain welders including the plaintiff, had been hired.

Michigan: Barbour v. Department of Social Services, 198 Mich. App. 183, 497 N.W.2d 216 (Mich. Ct. App. 1993). In an action by a department of social services employee, alleging that he was subjected to various forms of verbal and nonverbal harassment in efforts to get him to "come out of the closet . . . and to engage in homosexual sex", the lower court improperly granted summary judgment for the department. *Id.* 217. Although harassment or discrimination based upon a person's sexual orientation is not proscribed by the Michigan Civil Rights Act, alleged specific homosexual advances towards an employee by his supervisor were actionable.

Utah: Stokes v. Board of Review of the Industrial Commission of Utah, 832 P.2d 56 (Utah Ct. App. 1992) (Greenwood, J.). The Industrial Commission properly denied workers' compensation to an employee who alleged that she had been sexually harassed by her female supervisor, when evidence supported the conclusion that the harassment did not occur and that disciplinary procedures stemming from activities that violated company policies, such as allowing employees in her department to watch a movie video and to take extended lunch periods to do Christmas shopping, were appropriate. Stokes's supervisor spoke with her about the incidents and placed her on "verbal warning". Several months later, she received a series of unfavorable evaluations relating to productivity and the falsification of reports and started suffering chest pains. During

it is unclear whether a cause of action would lie for bisexual advances.[84]

An important legal distinction in such cases has to do with whether the challenged conduct is based on gender or sexual orientation. In *Barbour v. Department of Social Services*,[85] an action alleging that a male employee was subjected to various forms of verbal and nonverbal harassment in efforts to get him to "come out of the closet . . . and to engage in homosexual sex," the lower court improperly granted summary judgment for the department. Although harassment or discrimination based upon a person's sexual orientation is not proscribed by the Michigan Civil Rights Act, alleged specific homosexual advances towards an employee by his supervisor were actionable.

In *Goluszek v. Smith*,[86] a male employee failed to state a claim of sexual harassment by fellow male employees in a male-dominated environment. Shortly after the plaintiff started working at the company, coworkers descended upon him: they badgered him about having no wife or girlfriend, remarked that he needed to get married and "get some of that soft pink smelly stuff that's between the legs of a woman," suggested that he go out with a female coworker because she "fucks," asked if he had gotten any "pussy" or had oral sex, showed him pictures of nude women, accused him of being gay or bisexual, poked him in the buttocks with a stick, and repeatedly tried to knock him off his ladder. The plaintiff ultimately was discharged for lateness and unexcused absence. The court concluded that the defendant's conduct was not the type of behavior Congress intended to sanction through Title VII:

> The goal of Title VII is equal employment opportunity. . . . That goal is accomplished in part by imposing an affirmative duty on employers to

---

this period she reported the sexual harassment. "Specifically, Stokes claimed that her supervisor kissed her 'passionately' when Stokes gave her a ride to the airport, attempted to seduce her on a weekend trip the two took to Wendover, and repeatedly invited Stokes to spend the night at her house." *Id.* 57. She was eventually terminated because her doctors said that she could no longer work, and was diagnosed as having post traumatic stress disorder. The court of appeals affirmed the finding that the sexual harassment never occurred, as there was no corroborating evidence and the defendant introduced cab receipts showing that Stokes's supervisor took a cab to the airport on the day Stokes claimed to have driven her and been kissed by her at the airport and that Stokes's perceptions of and reactions to disciplinary procedures were abnormal.

84 *Cf.* Bradford v. Sloan Paper Co., 383 F. Supp. 1157, 1161 (N.D. Ala. 1974) (Title VII was not violated when supervisor was equally offensive to members of both races); *Accord* Barnes v. Costle, 561 F.2d at 978, 990 n.55 (D.C. Cir. 1977); Williams v. Saxbe, 413 F. Supp. 654, 659 n.6 (D.D.C. 1976), *rev'd on other grounds sub nom.* Williams v. Bell, 587 F.2d 1240 (D.C. Cir. 1978), *remanded for trial de novo sub nom.,* Williams v. Civiletti, 487 F. Supp. 1387 (D.D.C. 1980).

85 198 Mich. App. 183, 497 N.W.2d 216 (1993) (per curiam).

86 697 F. Supp. 1452 (N.D. Ill. 1988).

> maintain a working environment free of discriminatory intimidation. . . . The discrimination Congress was concerned about when it enacted Title VII is one stemming from an imbalance of power and an abuse of that imbalance by the powerful which results in discrimination against a discrete and vulnerable group. . . . Title VII does not make all forms of harassment actionable, nor does it even make all forms of verbal harassment with sexual overtones actionable. . . . Actionable sexual-harassment fosters a sense of degradation in the victim by attacking their sexuality. . . . In effect, the offender is saying by words or actions that the victim is inferior because of the victim's sex. . . .
>
> During the times relevant to his claim, Goluszek was a male in a male-dominated environment. In fact, with the exception of the reference to a female employee in the letter, each and every one of the figures in this story was a male. The argument that Goluszek worked in an environment that treated males as inferior consequently is not supported by the record. In fact, Goluszek may have been harassed "because" he is a male, but that harassment was not of a kind which created an anti-male environment in the workplace. . . . A wooden application of the verbal formulations created by the courts would salvage Goluszek's sexual-harassment claims. The court, however, chooses instead to adopt a reading of Title VII consistent with the underlying concerns of Congress.[87]

Perhaps the court was correct in concluding that the plaintiff failed to establish that his coworkers created an antimale environment, but the offensive conduct alleged was just the type of behavior that hinders Title VII's goal of equal opportunity for women. This type of conduct differs qualitatively from other types of discrimination. The power imbalance the court addressed results from the conduct itself, not the fact that it is pointed at particular individuals. Such conduct harms both men and women by perpetuating stereotypes, draining productivity, and interfering with professional relationships. The outcome of this case might have been different had Goluszek's posture been one of an injured third party alleging the existence of a hostile antiwoman environment and retaliation for refusing to participate in this conduct.

Under the hostile work environment theory, an employee has a right to work in an environment free of discrimination, and may sue for a violation

---

[87] *Id.* at 1456.

Cf. Hannah v. Philadelphia Coca-Cola Bottling Co., 56 Fair Empl. Prac. Cas. (BNA) 1325 (E.D. Pa. 1991). A heterosexual male employee who worked in heterosexual male environment was not a member of any protected class for whom the hostile environment theory is reserved. While a reasonable man would have been offended by coarse language used by a supervisor (who told plaintiff to stick a coke bottle up his ass), this was an isolated incident and insufficient to establish a hostile work environment. An employer has to be protected from the "hypersensitive" employee, and one would be hypersensitive to find that isolated use of vulgarities constituted a hostile environment.

of that right even if the employee is not a member of the targeted group.[88] The Equal Employment Opportunity Commission (EEOC) also interprets Title VII to afford standing to anyone protesting any form of alleged discrimination.[89] Dicta in *Meritor*[90] support the proposition that "Title VII affords employees the right to work in an environment free from discriminatory intimidation, ridicule, and insult."[91] The denigration of women through the use of sexual slurs and innuendo diminishes the collective integrity of the workplace regardless of whether a woman complains. Nor does the absence of women from a particular work environment or their small numbers give male employees license to perpetuate stereotypes and maintain an environment where women are implicitly uninvited. Although it espoused the contrary, the court in *Goluszek* did appear to succumb to "wooden applications" of discrimination law in its failure either to compensate the plaintiff or even suggest alternative grounds for relief. Allegations of an antiwoman environment by a male plaintiff may cause judicial analysis to take on a different look, as courts are forced to analyze sexual harassment within a framework they have thus far approached with hesitation—one that does not necessarily count the number of "touching" incidents, psychotic episodes, or smiles passed between parties, but one that looks at the alleged conduct for its misogynous messages.

§ 3.17 —Actions by Male Victims

Several reported opinions involve sexual harassment charges by male victims against female alleged harassers.[92] In *Anderson v. SUNY,*[93] a male former employee did not prove a prima facie case of *quid pro quo* sexual harassment when he presented no evidence that his female supervisor

---

88 Rogers v. EEOC, 454 F.2d 234 (5th Cir. 1971), *cert. denied,* 406 U.S. 957 (1972). *See also* Stewart v. Hannon, 675 F.2d 846 (7th Cir. 1982); EEOC v. T.I.M.E.—D.C. Freight, 659 F.2d 690 (5th Cir. 1981); EEOC v. Mississippi College, 626 F.2d 477 (5th Cir. 1980), *cert. denied,* 453 U.S. 912 (1981); EEOC v. Bailey Co., 563 F.2d 439 (6th Cir. 1977), *cert. denied,* 435 U.S. 915 (1978).

89 EEOC v. Rinella & Rinella, 401 F. Supp. 175 (N.D. Ill. 1975); [1973] EEOC Dec. (CCH) ¶ 6314 (1970); [1973] EEOC Dec. (CCH) ¶ 6193 (1970); [1973] EEOC Dec. (CCH) ¶ 6026 (1969).

90 Meritor Sav. Bank v. Vinson, 477 U.S. 57 (1986).

91 *Id.* at 65.

92 Kuhn v. Mellon Bank, N.A., No. 87-2767 (W.D. Pa. June 19, 1989). In a sexual harassment action by a male plaintiff, his claim for intentional infliction of emotional distress was dismissed because an employee may not recover damages in an action at law against her or his employer for such injuries even though they may be intentionally caused by the employer.

93 Anderson v. SUNY, 61 Fair Empl. Prac. Cas. (BNA) 890 (N.D.N.Y. 1993).

made advances or that the negative evaluations she placed in his file were a result of his rejection of advances and there was no adverse employment action taken as a result of the evaluations.

Male employees have brought other actions as well. In *Pacheco v. Hercules, Inc.*,[94] a male former employee could not pursue a claim for intentional infliction of emotional distress against his employer for allegedly failing to control a female coworker's allegedly offensive sexual language and conduct when the plaintiff's response to the conduct was, according to the plaintiff's treating psychiatrist, "excessive and unusual,"[95] and the plaintiff's injuries were not forseeable and the employer had no knowledge of the plaintiff's propensity for such an injury.

§ 3.18 —Welcomeness of the Sexual Advance

Sexual advances must be unwelcome to be unlawful.[96] Courts have held that to prove sexual advances were unwelcome, the plaintiff must show that the conduct was undesirable or offensive, and that it was not solicited or invited.[97] In *Burns v. McGregor Electronic Indus.*,[98] the court of appeals reversed and remanded a judgment in favor of the defendant employer in an action by a female employee alleging sexual harassment by propositions, sexual comments, display of pornographic materials, lewd gestures,

---

94 Pacheco v. Hercules, Inc., 61 Fair Empl. Prac. Cas. (BNA) 825 (D. Utah 1993).

95 *Id.* at 827–28.

96 EEOC Guidelines, 29 C.F.R. § 1604.11(a) (1988); EEOC Policy Guidance on Current Issues of Sexual Harassment, N-915.035 (Oct. 25, 1988) A at 6; Meritor Sav. Bank v. Vinson, 477 U.S. 57, 68 (1986).

97 Moylan v. Maries County, 792 F.2d 746 (8th Cir. 1986). *See also* Jones v. Wesco, 846 F.2d 1154 (8th Cir. 1988) (after sexual advance, plaintiff would push supervisor away, remove herself from the room, or inform supervisor that she was interested only in business relationship); Tozzi v. Joliet Junior College, 57 Fair Empl. Prac. Cas. (BNA) 269 (N.D. Ill. 1989), *aff'd,* 943 F.2d 54 (7th Cir. 1991). Remarks by department chair to female instructor who was denied contract renewal, including that he would not reschedule her class because of space constraints, which plaintiff later interpreted as a suggestion that her request would be granted if she opened up her "personal space" to him, that he had "needs" in response to her inquiry regarding other positions in the department and that she could change her "approach" to rectify low student ratings did not constitute sexual harassment when the comments were "mild double entendres at worst," and the conduct was not unwelcome because plaintiff did not regard the comments as sexual at the time they were made.

Sardigal v. St. Louis Nat'l Stockyards Co., 42 Fair Empl. Prac. Cas. (BNA) 497 (S.D. Ill. 1986) (allegations of rape by coworker were not credible when plaintiff spent time with defendant after alleged incident, visited him at his apartment, and invited him to her home).

98 955 F.2d 559 (8th Cir. 1992).

touching, and threats. The plaintiff had worked for the defendant during three separate periods and alleged harassment during all of them. During her second period of employment, a supervisor allegedly circulated a petition to have the plaintiff fired because nude photographs of her, taken by her father, appeared in two motorcycle magazines. The district court found that there was "no doubt" that a supervisor made unwelcome sexual advances toward the plaintiff during the first two periods she was employed but that "[i]n view of [Burns'] willingness to display her nude body to the public in *Easyriders* publications, crude magazines at best, her testimony that she was offended by sexually directed comments and *Penthouse* or *Playboy* pictures is not credible" and that in light of the totality of the circumstances, she had failed to prove by a preponderance of credible evidence that sexual harassment was sufficiently severe or pervasive to alter the conditions of her employment and create an abusive work environment.[99] The court of appeals found that the district court's findings that a person who would appear nude in a national magazine could not be offended by the behavior that took place, and that the plaintiff had exaggerated the severity and pervasiveness of the harassment, and its effect on her were at odds with its finding that the alleged sexual advances were unwelcome. However, the court did not dismiss the relevancy of the nude photographs:

> Evidence regarding a plaintiff's sexually provocative speech or dress is relevant "in determining whether he or she found particular sexual advances unwelcome." [*Meritor,* 477 U.S.] at 69. Thus, in making the determination as to whether the conduct directed at Burns was unwelcome, the nude photo evidence, though relating to an activitiy engaged in by Burns outside of the work place, may be relevant to explain the context of some of the comments and actions directed by [her supervisor] and coworkers to Burns. . . .
>
> * * *
>
> We believe that a reasonable person would consider the conduct of Oslac and Burns' supervisors to be sufficiently severe or pervasive to alter the conditions of employment and create an abusive work environment. . . . Burns testified that she was offended by the pictures in the pornographic magazines because they depicted couples engaged in various acts of sexual intercourse. She testified that she found Oslac's sexual advances and [coworkers'] comments humiliating and degrading. Burns continually complained to different supervisors, and she quit three separate times when she could no longer tolerate the conduct. The question is whether Burns has shown she is an "affected individual," that is, whether she was at least as

---

[99] *Id.* at 562–63.

affected as the reasonable person under like circumstances. On remand, the district court must determine whether Burns was affected as that hypothetical "reasonable person."[100]

The court noted that there was no evidence in the record that the plaintiff solicited any of the challenged conduct, and that although the gossip, lewd talk, and the petition occurred after the nude photographs of the plaintiff appeared, the alleged harassment by plaintiff's supervisor occurred both before and after the plaintiff appeared in the magazines. Thus, the incidents incited by the photographs would have to be considered separately from the supervisor's conduct, but the district court should take all of the conduct into account as part of the totality of the circumstances in determining whether the plaintiff found the conduct unwelcome. On remand,[101] the district court held that although the employee demonstrated that the harassment was unwelcome, she did not show that it was offensive to her. The court of appeals reversed,[102] holding that the trial court erred in requiring proof that the conduct at issue was unwelcome and offensive:

> The trial court made explicit findings that the conduct was not invited or solicited despite her posing naked for a magazine distributed nationally. The court believed, however, that because of her outside conduct, including her "interest in having her nude pictures appear in a magazine containing much lewd and crude sexually explicit material," the uninvited sexual advances of her employer were not "in and of itself offensive to her." The court explained that Burns "would not have been offended if someone she was attracted to did or said the same thing."
>
> We hold that such a view is unsupported in law. If the court intended this as a standard or rationale for a standard, it is clearly in error. This rationale would allow a complete stranger to pursue sexual behavior at work that a female would accept from her husband or boyfriend. This standard would allow a male employee to kiss or fondle a female worker at the workplace. None of the plaintiff's conduct, which the court found relevant to bar her action, was work related. Burns did not tell sexual stories or engage in sexual gestures at work. She did not initiate sexual talk or solicit sexual encounters with coemployees. Under the trial court's rationale, if a woman taught part-time sexual education at a high school or college, a court would be compelled to find that sexual language, even though uninvited when directed at her in the work place, would not offend her as it might someone else who was not as accustomed to public usage of the terms.
>
> * * *

---

[100] *Id.* at 565, 566.

[101] Burns v. McGregor Electronic, Ind., 807 F. Supp. 506 (N.D. Iowa 1992).

[102] Burns v. McGregor Electronic, Ind., 989 F.2d 959 (8th Cir. 1993).

> We need not remand for reconsideration since we find that it is undisputed that the trial court has determined that the respondent's conduct was unwelcomed by the plaintiff and was such that a hypothetical reasonable woman would consider the conduct sufficiently severe or pervasive to alter the conditions of employment and create an abusive work environment. The evidence that plaintiff had engaged in posing for nude pictures in *Easyriders* magazine, although relevant to the totality of the events that ensued, cannot constitute a defense to her claim of a hostile work environment at the work place when, as here, the trial court has determined that it did not constitute an invitation to engage in sexual discourse.[103]

Similarly, in *Cronin v. United States Service Stations, Inc.*,[104] an action by a female convenience store manager who alleged that she was harassed by a subordinate, the court rejected the defendants' contention that the plaintiff was abused at home by her boyfriend and thus could not have viewed the harassment at work as unwelcome:

> This argument is entirely without merit. That Cronin may have been abused at home in no way means that Cronin deserved abuse at work, that she "welcomed" Webster's abuse, or that she could not possibly be affected by Webster's actions because she was used to such abuse. In this case, the main issues for the court are determining what occurred at work and whether Cronin and Webster acted reasonably at work. Cronin's experiences at home have no general bearing on whether Cronin was subjected to sexual harassment at work. Abuse of a plaintiff in other settings, such as at home, should not be routinely admitted in cases charging sexual harassment in the work place. Indeed, a court should be careful not to allow one party to a lawsuit to pry so far into the personal and private life of the other party that the litigation itself becomes a tool of abuse and harassment and this victimizes the latter party in the very manner that Title VII seeks to prohibit. Therefore, absent a showing of a particularized relevance and need to delve into the deeply private sexual life of a party, a court should not allow it. The defendants did not make such a showing in this case.[105]

Demonstrating that a particular sexual advance was unwelcome is particularly difficult. The response of the harassed employee may range from overt rejection to complete acquiescence, depending on factors such as how much she needs the job, her socialized perception of her role as a woman and place in the workforce, and fear of retribution (see **Chapter 1**). A complainant does not waive legal protections by participating in the alleged sexual activity;[106] nor need she confront her harasser directly, as

---

[103] *Id.* at 963–64.

[104] 809 F. Supp. 922 (M.D. Ala. 1992).

[105] *Id.* at 932.

[106] Swentek v. USAIR, Inc., 830 F.2d 552, 557 (4th Cir. 1987).

See also Weiss v. Amoco Oil Co., 142 F.R.D. 311 (S.D. Iowa 1992) (action by alleged harasser). In a wrongful termination action by a male employee fired for sexual harassment, plaintiff sought to engage in discovery concerning the alleged victim's sexual history. According to plaintiff, the alleged victim had cards pinned up at her work station that were of a sexual nature, sent another male employee a birthday card that showed the torso of an adult female wearing a bikini, made sexual jokes with other employees and discussed her sexual activities while at work. The court held that the alleged victim, a non-party witness, failed to meet her burden of showing that information concerning her sexual history was irrelevant and not reasonably calculated to lead to discovery of admissible evidence. The court cited *Meritor* and *Mitchell v. Hutchings,* 116 F.R.D. 481 (D. Utah 1987), in which the court noted that evidence of sexual conduct that is remote in time or place to the plaintiffs' working environment is irrelevant:

> Unlike the factual situation in *Mitchell*, Weiss is not seeking discovery of Streebin's sexual history "remote in time or place" to Streebin's employment with Amoco, or to discover her sexual conduct which is unknown to him. Rather, Weiss seeks to "depose Ms. Streebin regarding her sexual conduct with other employees of Defendant during her employment with Defendant and which Plaintiff had knowledge . . ." Weiss's Brief at 1. Weiss's discovery request is exactly tailored to be in keeping with the *Mitchell* decision.
>
> The court cannot say, as a matter of law, that the discovery sought by Weiss from Streebin will be irrelevant to the issues generated in this litigation. Such discovery is relevant in divining what conduct or actions Weiss thought were welcome, and in determining whether Streebin found Weiss's conduct unwelcome. This discovery may also prove relevant in explaining the context of Weiss's words and actions toward Streebin.
>
> * * *
>
> Finally, the material sought is relevant in assessing the thoroughness of Amoco's investigation into Streebin's complaint of sexual harassment. Weiss alleged that he and Streebin were social friends who dated occasionally, and that Streebin dated other fellow employees. Weiss alleges that a thorough investigation into Streebin's complaint against him would have disclosed these facts; facts which would be necessary in any analysis of Streebin's sexual harassment complaint against Weiss.

Id. at 316–17 (footnote omitted).

First Circuit: Showalter v. Allison Reed Group, Inc., 767 F. Supp. 1205 (D.R.I. 1991). Male employees were subjected to sexual harassment when their supervisor forced them to engage in various sexual activities with his secretary by threatening them with discharge if they did not acquiesce. Though neither employee complained to anyone, both participated because they feared losing their jobs and the employer did not have a formal grievance procedure. The fact that both plaintiffs contributed to the sexual innuendo prevalent at the workplace did not vitiate their claims of sexual harassment.

Fourth Circuit: Katz v. Dole, 709 F.2d 251, 254 n.3 (4th Cir. 1983) (it was improper of trial judge to suggest that plaintiff's past conduct meant that she welcomed the harasser's behavior).

Ninth Circuit: Wangler v. Hawaiian Elec. Co., 742 F. Supp. 1458 (D. Haw. 1990) For summary judgment, unrefuted evidence that plaintiff actively participated in a relationship with defendant and welcomed his attention by, among other things, baking him

long as her conduct indicates that the advance is unwelcome.[107] Although an inquiry may not focus upon the woman's compliance, (see **§ 3.2**) determinations of whether sexual advances were unwelcome may turn on credibility issues (see **Chapter 6**). Defendants may attempt to dilute the plaintiff's credibility by introducing evidence regarding her dress and behavior (see **§ 3.2**), but the plaintiff should argue that the unfair prejudice arising from such evidence would outweigh its probative value. Nonetheless, some courts have determined that sexual advances were not unwelcome when the plaintiff participated in sexual conduct or initiated social contact.[108] The plaintiff's position may be strengthened by showing

---

birthday cakes, giving him a picture of herself in a belly dancing costume, and signed cards with "Love, Andrea," did not conclusively establish that plaintiff welcomed the alleged advances. Plaintiff clearly stated that defendant forced himself upon her and also submitted a letter written to her by defendant wherein he stated that their "relationship was never mutual. You looked to me for paternal love, whereas I desparately wanted you for my Lolita." *Id.* at 1463.

Tenth Circuit: Zowayyed v. Lowen Co., 735 F. Supp. 1497 (D. Kan. 1990) Defendant employer was not entitled to summary judgment in a sexual harassment case involving the company president when the employer's assertion that plaintiff welcomed the president's advances was based mainly on the supervisor's testimony that plaintiff joked and bragged about the advances and plaintiff testified that she found the advances to be a source of significant mental pain and anguish, stating that whatever joking occurred was intended only facetiously, and not literally, and were merely a means of relieving the tension created by the sexual advances.

EEOC Policy Guidance, N-915.035 (Oct. 25, 1988) A at 9.

107 EEOC Policy Guidance N-915.035 (Oct. 25, 1988) A at 7 n.8.

108 First Circuit: Lipsett v. Rive-Mora, 669 F. Supp. 1188 (D.P.R. 1987), *rev'd on other grounds,* 864 F.2d 881 (1st Cir. 1988) (plaintiff who "smiled back" at defendant's "flirtations" did not demonstrate that the comments were unwelcome).

Third Circuit: Reichman v. Bureau of Affirmative Action, 536 F. Supp. 1149 (M.D. Pa. 1982) (employee acted flirtatiously, moved her body in a "provocative" manner, and repeatedly invited her supervisor home for dinner).

Sixth Circuit: Highlander v. K.F.C. Nat'l Management Co., 805 F.2d 644 (6th Cir. 1986) (plaintiff suggested having "business drink" to discuss her promotability, to which her supervisor responded with suggestion that they continue their conversation at motel across the street).

Rose v. Figgie Int'l, 56 Fair Empl. Prac. Cas. (BNA) 41 (W.D. Mich. 1990). An employee who alleged that her supervisor sexually harassed her for over 15 years until her resignation was not subjected to a hostile environment when she testified that no challenged conduct had occurred for at least a year or two before her resignation, she never complained to her supervisor about his conduct, there was no evidence that his alleged hostility affected her career, and she could not allege any direct sexual advances.

Eighth Circuit: *Cf.* Morris v. American Nat'l Can Corp., 730 F. Supp. 1489 (E.D. Mo. 1989), *modified on other grounds,* 941 F.2d 710 (8th Cir. 1991). Plaintiff's use of profane language and the greasing of other employees' equipment did not vitiate a finding of sexual harassment. Such conduct could be part of plaintiff's efforts to fit in to the

that she made a "contemporaneous complaint or protest" following the harassment, even when the harassment forces an employee to resign.[109] A complaint is *contemporaneous* if it is made while the harassment is ongoing or shortly after it has ceased. The employer has a duty to investigate and to take remedial action, including offering reinstatement, if it finds the allegations to be true.[110]

---

environment, and did not justify the harassing conduct plaintiff endured. It was important that no witnesses opined there was a relationship between what plaintiff did and the materials she received.

Gan v. Kepro Circuit Sys. 28 Fair Empl. Prac. Cas. (BNA) 639 (E.D. Mo. 1982) (plaintiff initiated sexually suggestive physical conduct and had sexually explicit conversations with other employees).

Eleventh Circuit: Weinsheimer v. Rockwell Intl. Corp., 754 F. Supp. 1559 (M.D. Fla. 1990), *aff'd,* 949 F.2d 1162 (11th Cir. 1991). A female quality control inspector failed to demonstrate that the conduct of coworkers was unwelcome despite defendant employer's concession that the workplace was characterized by an atmosphere of vulgarity and sexual innuendo. One coworker allegedly verbally harassed the plaintiff by asking her several times a week to "suck him," "give him head," or give him "some of that stuff," *Id.* at 1561, grabbed her breast and crotch, held a knife to her throat, threatened to "bang her head into the ground," and passed gas and belched in her presence. Another employee allegedly exposed his penis and placed it in plaintiff's hand while she was working and looking away, and another patted plaintiff on the rear and requested an "ice-cube job." *Id.* The court, however, concluded that the clear weight of the testimony indicated that the challenged conduct was not unwelcome when such banter was engaged in by generally all employees, male and female alike, and evidence strongly demonstrated that plaintiff was among the most "prevalent and graphic participants" in this conduct. *Id.* at 1563–64. "Such evidence of Weinsheimer's proven, active contribution to the sexually explicit environment of the back shop belies her contention that much of what occurred there was unwelcome." *Id.* at 1564. In addition, each supervisor stated that they did not consider plaintiff's discussions with them as complaints regarding sexual harassment, but as conversations about general morale, and supervisory and disciplinary problems in the shop:

> Even for an incident as graphic as Edmondson's alleged placing of his penis in plaintiff's hand, the testimony established that Weinsheimer did not report this to management until months later, and then only by an offhand reference during informal conversation in a back stairwell with her supervisor, Mr. Arevalos. Similarly, regarding the knife incident, Weinsheimer in her deposition initially stated that she believed Stoner was kidding and that he did not intend to hurt her. This incident was also reported to management only after a lapse of some months.

Id.

109 EEOC Policy Guidance, N-915.035 (Oct. 25, 1988) A at 6–7.

Third Circuit: Reynolds v. Atlantic City Convention Ctr., 53 Fair Empl. Prac. Cas. (BNA) 1852 (D.N.J. 1990) (plaintiff did not complain of harassment).

District of Columbia Circuit: Robinson v. Thornburgh, 54 Fair Empl. Prac. Cas. (BNA) 324 (D.D.C. 1990) (plaintiff never informed her supervisor of the events that she alleged created a hostile environment).

110 EEOC Policy Guidance at 7 n.6.

A sexual advance is unwelcome as soon as the harassed employee refuses the advance, regardless of whether previous advances were welcome.[111] Analogous to a date rape situation in which a woman has agreed to a certain amount of social interaction but is forced to cross her established limits, a charge of sexual harassment should not be undermined by evidence that previous advances were welcome once the victim clearly has indicated that the advances must stop.[112] However, if the harassment continues, the victim's failure to complain to higher management or the EEOC, though not dispositive, may be evidence that the challenged conduct was welcome or "unrelated to work."[113] If the harassing supervisor's

---

111 Shrout v. Black Clawson Co., 689 F. Supp. 774 (S.D. Ohio 1988) (employee who terminated relationship with her supervisor brought successful sexual harassment action when supervisor attempted to force plaintiff to submit to sexual advances by withholding plaintiff's performance evaluations and salary reviews).

Second Circuit: Babcock v. Frank, 729 F. Supp. 279 (S.D.N.Y. 1990). The fact that the plaintiff had had a consensual sexual relationship with the alleged harasser did not bar her from challenging conduct that occurred after the relationship ended:

> The allegations that Babcock's supervisor Musso implored her to love him again and that he couldn't stand seeing her without being intimate with her, when coupled with his contemporaneous threat to destroy her career at the USPS and his subsequent issuance of a disciplinary letter against her, are more than sufficient to raise an inference in a reasonable person that Musso intended to use—and did use—his supervisorial authority to blackmail Babcock into again accepting his sexual advances. Those allegations comprise a claim of *quid pro quo* sexual harassment. Babcock, after ending her relationship with Musso, "had the right, like any other worker, to be free from a sexually abusive environment, and to reject her employer's sexual advances without threat of punishment." *Keppler [v. Hindsdale Township H.S. Dist. 86,* 715 F. Supp. 862 (N.D.Ill. 1989)]. . . at 869. Nothing in *DeCintio* or *Heubschen* compels dismissal of Babcock's claim on grounds that she previously had engaged in a consensual relationship with Musso.

Id. at 288. The court subsequently dismissed the complaint in *Babcock v. Frank*, 59 Fair Empl. Prac. Cas. (BNA) 410 (S.D.N.Y. 1992), finding that plaintiff did not suffer a tangible job detriment as a result of her rejection of Musso's sexual advances. "Moreover, the postal service acted promptly and appropriately when it learned of Musso's threat to harm plaintiff's career for refusing his advances, which it completely and unambiguously repudiated." *Id.* at 415.

112 EEOC Dec. No. 84-1 [1983] EEOC Dec. (CCH) ¶ 6839, 33 Fair Empl. Prac. Cas. (BNA) 1887 (Nov. 28, 1983) (when female employee had participated in sexual conduct by telling off-color jokes and failed to tell employer/owner that the conduct had become offensive to her, the employer's conduct was not unwelcomed). Courts look at whether complainant's conduct was consistent with her assertion that the sexual conduct was unwelcome. EEOC Policy Guidance, N-915.035 (Oct. 25, 1988) A at 8.

113 EEOC Policy Guidance, N-915.035 (Oct. 25, 1988) A at 10.

Scheider v. NBC News Bureaus, 56 Fair Emp. Prac. Cas. (BNA) 1602 (S.D. Fla. 1991) (no sexual harassment found when plaintiff never complained about the incidents she now claimed consitituted the hostile environment until after she filed sex discrimination charges).

conduct is sufficiently pervasive and work-related, the employer may be placed on notice that the conduct constitutes harassment.[114]

§ 3.19 —Verbal or Physical Conduct

A plaintiff can demonstrate discriminatory sexual harassment by showing that the employer subjected her to unwelcome verbal or physical conduct of a sexual nature and that the conduct affected a term, condition, or privilege of employment.[115] Exactly what constitutes verbal or physical conduct sufficient to raise a sexual harassment claim under Title VII depends on the circumstances and may be more difficult to discern than cases in which sexual advances are involved. Verbal conduct constituting prima facie sexual harassment includes making sexual slurs,[116]

---

[114] EEOC Policy Guidance, N-915.035 (Oct. 25, 1988) A at 10 n.12.

[115] EEOC Guidelines, 29 C.F.R. § 1604.11(a) (1988).

[116] Second Circuit: Barbetta v. Chemlawn Servs. Corp., 669 F. Supp. 569 (W.D.N.Y. 1987) (offensive sexual comments made to and about plaintiff by her supervisors).

Third Circuit: Kyriazi v. Western Elec. Co., 461 F. Supp. 894 (D.N.J. 1978), *modified,* 473 F. Supp. 786 (D.N.J. 1979), *aff'd,* 647 F.2d 388 (3d Cir. 1981).

Fourth Circuit: Katz v. Dole, 709 F.2d 251 (4th Cir. 1983).

Sixth Circuit: Mitchell v. OsAir, Inc., 629 F. Supp. 636 (N.D. Ohio 1986), *appeal dismissed,* 816 F.2d 681 (6th Cir. 1987); Morgan v. Hertz Corp., 542 F. Supp. 123, 128 (W.D. Tenn. 1981), *aff'd,* 725 F.2d 1070 (6th Cir. 1984) (vulgar and indecent language was aimed specifically at female employees).

Cf. Rabidue v. Osceola Ref. Co., 805 F.2d 611, 622 (6th Cir. 1986), *cert. denied,* 481 U.S. 1041 (1987) (although slurs were "annoying," they "were not so startling as to have affected seriously the psyches of plaintiff or other female employees").

Eighth Circuit: Jew v. University of Iowa, 749 F. Supp. 946 (S.D. Iowa 1990) (pattern of verbal conduct in the form of rumors alleging a sexual relationship between plaintiff university professor and head of her department, accusing her of using her sex as a tool for gaining favor, sexually denigrated plaintiff and damaged her reputation, thus creating a hostile environment); Hall v. Gus Constr. Co., 842 F.2d 1010 (8th Cir. 1988) (women flaggers incessantly referred to as "fucking flag girls," woman with skin condition called "herpes," "cavern cunt," and "blonde bitch" written in dust on woman's car door); Continental Can Co. v. Minnesota, 297 N.W.2d 241 (Minn. 1980).

Ninth Circuit: Wangler v. Hawaiian Elec. Co., 742 F. Supp. 1458 (D. Haw. 1990) (plaintiff alleged that one defendant, responsible for training plaintiff, was hostile and referred to her as "the broad" and the other forced himself upon her and wrote a letter wherein he stated that their "relationship was never mutual. You looked to me for paternal love, whereas I desparately wanted you for my Lolita." *Id.* at 1463); Priest v. Rotary, 634 F. Supp. 571, 582 (N.D. Cal. 1986).

Tenth Circuit: Brown v. City of Guthrie, 22 Fair Empl. Prac. Cas. (BNA) 1627, 1629 (W.D. Okla. 1980).

Eleventh Circuit: Huddleston v. Roger Dean Chevrolet, Inc., 845 F.2d 900 (11th Cir. 1988) (plaintiff called "bitch" and "whore"); Henson v. City of Dundee, 682 F.2d 897

propositions,[117] or persistent comments about a woman's body,[118] telling "off-color" jokes,[119] asking intimate or embarrassing questions,[120] making

(11th Cir. 1982); Ross v. Twenty-Four Collection, Inc., 681 F. Supp. 1547, 1549 (S.D. Fla. 1988), *aff'd,* 875 F.2d 873 (11th Cir. 1989).

District of Columbia Circuit: Bundy v. Jackson, 641 F.2d 934 (D.C. Cir. 1981); Barnes v. Costle, 561 F.2d 983, 978 (D.C. Cir. 1977); Clark v. World Airways, 24 Fair Empl. Prac. Cas. (BNA) 305 (D.D.C. 1980).

Pennsylvania: Pennsylvania State Police v. Unemployment Bd., 53 Fair Empl. Prac. Cas. (BNA) 1157 (Pa. Comm. Ct. 1990) (state trooper repeatedly told officer coworkers that he was "going to fuck" them).

117 Third Circuit: Horn v. Duke Homes, Inc., 755 F.2d 599 (3d Cir. 1983); Craig v. Y&Y Snacks, Inc., 721 F.2d 77 (3d Cir. 1983); Tomkins v. Public Serv. Elec. & Gas Co., 568 F.2d 1044 (3d Cir. 1977).

Sixth Circuit: Yates v. Avco Corp., 819 F.2d 630 (6th Cir. 1987); Anderson v. Hewlett-Packard Corp., 694 F. Supp. 1294 (N.D. Ohio 1988); Robson v. Eva's Market, 538 F. Supp. 857, 859 (N.D. Ohio 1982) (propositions, physical assault, and harm to plaintiff).

Eighth Circuit: Hall v. Gus Constr. Co., 842 F.2d 1010 (8th Cir. 1988); Walter v. KFGO Radio, 518 F. Supp. 1309 (D.N.D. 1981).

Tenth Circuit: Brown v. City of Guthrie, 22 Fair Empl. Prac. Cas. (BNA) 1627 (W.D. Okla. 1980).

District of Columbia Circuit: Bundy v. Jackson, 641 F.2d 934 (D.C. Cir. 1981); Barnes v. Costle, 561 F.2d 983 (D.C. Cir. 1977).

118 Fourth Circuit: Wall v. AT&T Technologies, 754 F. Supp. 1084 (M.D.N.C. 1990) Plaintiff employee alleged facts sufficient to support a determination of severe or pervasive harassment. A reasonable trier of fact could find that activities of coworkers "polluted" the working environment to the point that they violated Title VII by rating women as they passed their desks and making comments referring to their hips and breasts and lascivious invitations to engage in sexual relations. Complaints were ineffective when EEO specialist first told her to solve the problem herself and then told her to ignore the situation, and complaints to the department chief were also left unremedied.

Sixth Circuit: Yates v. Avco Corp., 819 F.2d 630 (6th Cir. 1987); Anderson v. Hewlett-Packard Corp., 694 F. Supp. 1294 (N.D. Ohio 1988).

Seventh Circuit: Hrabak v. Marquip, Inc., 798 F. Supp. 550 (W.D. Wis. 1992).

Eighth Circuit: Jones v. Wesco, 846 F.2d 1154 (8th Cir. 1988).

Ninth Circuit: Dias v. Sky Chefs, 919 F.2d 1370 (9th Cir. 1990), *vacated on other grounds,* 111 S.C. 2791 (1991), *on remand,* 948 F.2d 532 (9th Cir 1991), *cert denied,* 112 S. Ct. 1294 (1992) (sexual harassment by the general manager of defendant corporation allegedly took the form of daily comments on the breasts, buttocks, and physical appearance of individual female employees, suggestions to women that they show him a good time and treat him as well as the women employees in the office from which he had been transferred, and staff meetings at which he established job standards for women that included the wearing of dresses or skirts, and nylons and heels specifically so that he could admire women employees' legs). Atwood v. Biondi Mitsubishi, 61 Fair Empl. Prac. Cas. (BNA) 1357 (W.D. Pa 1993) (conduct including taking bets on the color of female employees' underwear and bras and comments suggesting that female employees had sex with a male employee was not "merely juvenile" behavior); Canada v. Boyd Group, Inc., 809 F. Supp. 771 (D. Nev. 1992) (supervisor commented on how good the plaintiff looked in her uniform).

harassing telephone calls,[121] requesting to shower together,[122] calling a woman by an intimate nickname,[123] boasting of sexual conquests,[124] and making disparaging antifeminist comments,[125] homophobic remarks,[126] or threats.[127] Wrongful physical conduct includes fondling, jostling, touching, massaging, rubbing, coddling,[128] pulling down a woman's pants to expose

---

Minnesota: Wirig v. Kinney Shoe Corp., 54 Fair Empl. Prac. Cas. (BNA) 352 (Minn. 1990). Actionable conduct by a coworker included comments about plaintiff's body, offensive sexual names, discussions about what he would like to do to her sexually, kissing, pinching, patting, and putting his arm around her.

119 Ninth Circuit: Canada v. Boyd Group, Inc., 809 F. Supp. 771 (D. Nev. 1992).

120 Sixth Circuit: Yates v. Avco Corp., 819 F.2d 630 (6th Cir. 1987).

Seventh Circuit: Gilardi v. Schroeder, 833 F.2d 1226 (7th Cir. 1987).

Ninth Circuit: Ambrose v. United States Steel Corp., 39 Fair Empl. Prac. Cas. (BNA) 30 (N.D. Cal. 1985) (plaintiff asked views on oral sex and affairs).

Eleventh Circuit: Sowers v. Kemira, Inc., 46 Fair Empl. Prac. Cas. (BNA) 1825 (S.D. Ga. 1988) (questions regarding adequacy of sexual relationship with husband).

121 First Circuit: Hosemann v. Technical Materials, Inc., 554 F. Supp. 659 (D.R.I. 1982) (daily calls by employer to absent female employee in an effort to determine her work return date was not sexual harassment).

Fifth Circuit: Ross v. Double Diamond, Inc., 672 F. Supp. 261 (N.D. Tex. 1987); Lamb v. Drilco, 32 Fair Empl. Prac. Cas. (BNA) 105 (S.D. Tex. 1983) (propositions, physical advances, and harassing phone calls).

Seventh Circuit: Juarez v. Ameritech Mobile Communications, 746 F. Supp. 798 (N.D. Ill. 1990), *aff'd,* 957 F.2d 317 (7th Cir. 1992) (supervisor made sexually suggestive comments directly and over the phone).

122 Ross v. Twenty-Four Collection, Inc., 681 F. Supp. 1547, 1550 (S.D. Fla. 1988), *aff'd,* 875 F.2d 873 (11th Cir. 1989).

123 Volk v. Coler, 638 F. Supp. 1555, 1558–59 (C.D. Ill. 1986), *aff'd in part, rev'd in part,* 845 F.2d 1422 (7th Cir. 1988).

124 Gilardi v. Schroeder, 833 F.2d 1226 (7th Cir. 1987).

125 Volk v. Coler, 638 F. Supp. 1555, 1558–59 (C.D. Ill. 1986), *aff'd in part, rev'd in part,* 845 F.2d 1422 (7th Cir. 1988) (defendant referred to social work practices as "women's lib bullshit"); Delgado v. Lehman, 665 F. Supp. 460, 468 (E.D. Va. 1987) (defendant called women "babes" and used the term "woman" in derogatory manner).

126 Volk v. Coler, 638 F. Supp. 1555, 1558–59 (C.D. Ill. 1986), *aff'd in part, rev'd in part,* 845 F.2d 1422 (7th Cir. 1988).

127 Third Circuit: Craig v. Y&Y Snacks, Inc., 721 F.2d 77, 79 (3d Cir. 1983) (plaintiff's supervisor threatened to "get even" for resisting advances).

Sixth Circuit: Anderson v. Hewlett-Packard Corp., 694 F. Supp. 1294 (N.D. Ohio 1988).

Seventh Circuit: Bohen v. City of E. Chicago, 799 F.2d 1180, 1188 (7th Cir. 1986) (fire department captain made veiled threat of rape to female dispatcher).

128 Second Circuit: Barbetta v. Chemlawn Servs. Corp., 669 F. Supp. 569 (W.D.N.Y. 1987); Carrero v. New York City Hous. Auth., 668 F. Supp. 196, 198 (S.D.N.Y. 1987).

Fifth Circuit: Ross v. Double Diamond, Inc., 672 F. Supp. 261 (N.D. Tex. 1987).

Sixth Circuit: Pease v. Alford Photo Indus., Inc., 667 F. Supp. 1188 (W.D. Tenn.

her buttocks,[129] forceably placing a foot in a woman's crotch,[130] kissing,[131] assault,[132] and even rape.[133] Offensive conduct also has included looking up

1987) (touching arm, shoulder, neck, rubbing hair, hugging, fondling breast); Shrout v. Black Clawson Co., 689 F. Supp. 774 (S.D. Ohio 1988); Anderson v. Hewlett-Packard Corp., 694 F. Supp. 1294 (N.D. Ohio 1988); Continental Can Co. v. Minnesota, 22 Fair Empl. Prac. Cas. (BNA) 1808 (Minn. 1980).

Seventh Circuit: Gilardi v. Schroeder, 833 F.2d 1226 (7th Cir. 1987); Volk v. Coler, 638 F. Supp. 1555, 1558–59 (C.D. Ill. 1986), *aff'd in part, rev'd in part,* 845 F.2d 1422 (7th Cir. 1988); Bohen v. City of E. Chicago, 799 F.2d 1180 (7th Cir. 1986). *Cf.* Dockter v. Rudolf Wolff Futures, Inc., 684 F. Supp. 532, 533 (N.D. Ill. 1988), *aff'd,* 913 F.2d 456 (7th Cir. 1990); (one "misguided act" of touching plaintiff's breast did not constitute sexual harassment).

Eighth Circuit: Hall v. Gus Constr. Co., 842 F.2d 1010 (8th Cir. 1988); Jones v. Wesco, 846 F.2d 1154 (8th Cir. 1988) (touching breasts, pinching, patting, kissing); Moylan v. Maries County, 792 F.2d 746 (8th Cir. 1986). *Cf.* Walter v. KFGO Radio, 518 F. Supp. 1309 (D.N.D. 1981) (supervisor's alleged conduct, including patting employee's bottom, touching her breasts, and trying to have an affair with her while both attended a job-related conference did not establish a prima facie case of discrimination).

Ninth Circuit: Canada v. Boyd Group, Inc., 809 F. Supp. 771 (D. Nev. 1992) (supervisor rubbed the front of his body against the back of the plaintiff's body); Priest v. Rotary, 634 F. Supp. 571, 582 (N.D. Cal. 1986) (supervisor rubbed body against that of woman employee); Ambrose v. United States Steel Corp., 39 Fair Empl. Prac. Cas. (BNA) 30 (N.D. Cal. 1985).

Eleventh Circuit: Ross v. Twenty-Four Collection, Inc., 681 F. Supp. 1547, 1550 (S.D. Fla. 1988), *aff'd,* 875 F.2d 873 (11th Cir. 1989) (defendant attempted to massage plaintiff and force her to lie down in bed with him).

Federal Circuit: Carosella v. United States Postal Serv., 816 F.2d 638 (Fed. Cir. 1987) (offensive touching).

Pennsylvania: Pennsylvania State Police v. Unemployment Bd., 53 Fair Empl. Prac. Cas. (BNA) 1157 (Pa. Comm. Ct. 1990) (touching breasts).

129 Dombeck v. Milwaukee Valve Co., 823 F. Supp. 1475 (W.D. Wis. 1993).

130 *Id.*

131 Second Circuit: Carrero v. New York City Hous. Auth., 668 F. Supp. 196, 198 (S.D.N.Y. 1987).

Ninth Circuit: Priest v. Rotary, 634 F. Supp. 571, 582 (N.D. Cal. 1986).

Eleventh Circuit: Ross v. Twenty-Four Collection, Inc., 681 F. Supp. 1547 (S.D. Fla. 1988), *aff'd,* 875 F.2d 873 (11th Cir. 1989).

Minnesota: Wirig v. Kinney Shoe Corp., 54 Fair Empl. Prac. Cas. (BNA) 352 (Minn. 1990).

132 Sixth Circuit: Robson v. Eva's Market, 538 F. Supp. 857, 859 (N.D. Ohio 1982) (proposition, physical assault, and harm to plaintiff).

Eleventh Circuit: Huddleston v. Roger Dean Chevrolet, Inc., 845 F.2d 900 (11th Cir. 1988) (grabbing and yanking arm).

133 Supreme Court: Vinson v. Taylor, 23 Fair Empl. Prac. Cas. (BNA) 37, 38 (D.D.C. 1980), *rev'd,* 753 F.2d 141 (D.C. Cir. 1985), *aff'd in part, rev'd in part sub nom.* Meritor Sav. Bank v. Vinson, 477 U.S. 57 (1986).

women's skirts and down their blouses,[134] attempting to get into bed with the employee,[135] making arrangements to be alone with a woman employee for making sexual advances,[136] taking unwelcome photographs,[137] "expelling gas" in front of plaintiff's clients,[138] dropping trousers,[139] entering restrooms unannounced, indecent exposure,[140] trapping or restraining a woman,[141] and urinating in view of or in an employee's water bottle and gas

---

Seventh Circuit: Gilardi v. Schroeder, 833 F.2d 1226 (7th Cir. 1987).

Eighth Circuit: Moylan v. Maries County, 792 F.2d 746 (8th Cir. 1986).

[134] Shrout v. Black Clawson Co., 689 F. Supp. 774 (S.D. Ohio 1988).

[135] Ross v. Twenty-Four Collection, Inc., 681 F. Supp. 1547, 1550 (S.D. Fla. 1988), *aff'd,* 875 F.2d 873 (11th Cir. 1989).

[136] Eighth Circuit: Jones v. Wesco, 846 F.2d 1154 (8th Cir. 1988).

Ninth Circuit: Priest v. Rotary, 634 F. Supp. 571, 581 (N.D. Cal. 1986).

[137] Ross v. Double Diamond, Inc., 672 F. Supp. 261 (N.D. Tex. 1987).

[138] Huddleston v. Roger Dean Chevrolet, Inc., 845 F.2d 900 (11th Cir. 1988).

Stockett v. Tolin, 791 F. Supp. 1536 (S.D. Fla. 1992). A female employee in a film industry training program was subjected to a hostile environment when managing agent harassed her physically and verbally for over a year. Among other things, defendant put his arms around plaintiff from behind, pressed his body up against her and said that he'd love to eat her all up, repeatedly pressed down on her shoulders while she sat in a chair so that she couldn't get up, and squeezed her breasts, walked into the women's room while the plaintiff was changing her clothes, twice stuck his tongue in her ear and told her that he wanted to have sex with her, repeatedly cornered her and ran his hands over her nipples, saying "You like that, don't you?", constantly grabbed her buttocks, and finally told plaintiff: "Fuck me or you're fired". The plaintiff subsequently resigned. The court found that plaintiff did not in any way encourage the advances; on the contrary, she repeatedly pushed defendant away and told him to stop, avoided him, and tried to never be alone with him. The plaintiff's account of a pervasively hostile work environment was corroborated by testimony of many other female employees at the defendant companies. The plaintiff had been warned that defendant liked "young girls" and she warned others. The plaintiff suffered severe emotional distress as a result of the harassment, including sleep disturbances, depression, and loss of energy, general anxiety, a sense of uncertainty, anger, and an inability to trust men.

[139] Carrero v. New York City Hous. Auth., 668 F. Supp. 196, 198 (S.D.N.Y. 1987).

[140] Vinson v. Taylor, 23 Fair Empl. Prac. Cas. (BNA) 37, 38 (D.D.C. 1980), *rev'd,* 753 F.2d 141 (D.C. Cir. 1985), *aff'd in part, rev'd in part sub nom.* Meritor Sav. Bank v. Vinson, 477 U.S. 57 (1986).

Eighth Circuit: Hall v. Gus Constr. Co., 842 F.2d 1010 (8th Cir. 1988) ("mooning").

Ninth Circuit: Priest v. Rotary, 634 F. Supp. 571 (N.D. Cal. 1986).

[141] Sixth Circuit: Boyd v. James S. Hayes Living Health Care Agency, 671 F. Supp. 1155, 1558–59 (W.D. Tenn. 1987) (supervisor insisted that plaintiff visit his hotel room at a conference, then turned on pornographic video and tried to prevent plaintiff's departure).

Eighth Circuit: Moylan v. Maries County, 792 F.2d 746 (8th Cir. 1986) (defendant trapped plaintiff on couch in office).

Ninth Circuit: Priest v. Rotary, 634 F. Supp. 571 (N.D. Cal. 1986) (restaurant owner trapped plaintiff in hallway between his body and that of another male employee, preventing her from being able to move away).

tank.[142] The physical work environment also can be found offensive when sexually explicit photographs,[143] literature,[144] cartoons,[145] or calendars[146] are conspicuously displayed, offensive graffiti is pervasive or ignored,[147] or

---

142 Hall v. Gus Constr. Co., 842 F.2d 1010 (8th Cir. 1988).

143 Eighth Circuit: Hall v. Gus Constr. Co., 842 F.2d 1010 (8th Cir. 1988).

Tenth Circuit: Arnold v. City of Seminole, 614 F. Supp. 853 (E.D. Okla. 1985); Brown v. City of Guthrie, 22 Fair Empl. Prac. Cas. (BNA) 1627, 1629 (W.D. Okla. 1980) (propositions, lewd comments, and pervasive display of centerfolds).

Eleventh Circuit: Eleventh Circuit: Robinson v. Jacksonville Shipyards, Inc., 760 F. Supp. 1486 (M.D. Fla. 1991).

144 Second Circuit: Barbetta v. Chemlawn Servs. Corp., 669 F. Supp. 569 (W.D.N.Y. 1987).

Sixth Circuit: Shrout v. Black Clawson Co., 689 F. Supp. 774 (S.D. Ohio 1988); Mitchell v. OsAir, Inc., 629 F. Supp. 636 (N.D. Ohio 1986), *appeal dismissed,* 816 F.2d 681 (6th Cir. 1987).

Eleventh Circuit: Ross v. Twenty-Four Collection, Inc., 681 F. Supp. 1547, 1551 (S.D. Fla. 1988), *aff'd,* 875 F.2d 873 (11th Cir. 1989) (defendant gave plaintiff pornographic magazine and left article on her desk regarding "seminar" on "extracurricular marital affairs without guilt").

145 Fifth Circuit: Bennett v. Corroon & Black Corp., 845 F.2d 104 (5th Cir. 1988), *cert. denied,* 489 U.S. 1020 (1989).

Seventh Circuit: Gilardi v. Schroeder, 833 F.2d 1226 (7th Cir. 1987) (office notepads with drawing of couple having sex).

Tenth Circuit: Arnold v. City of Seminole, 614 F. Supp. 853 (E.D. Okla. 1985).

Cf. Williams v. Kansas Gas and Elec. Co., 805 F. Supp. 890 (D. Kan. 1992). A female employee did not state a claim for hostile environment caused by sexist and racist cartoons when she found the cartoons in a supervisor's desk during work-related duties but was not required to look at them.

146 Barbetta v. Chemlawn Servs. Corp., 669 F. Supp. 569 (W.D.N.Y. 1987).

Eleventh Circuit: Robinson v. Jacksonville Shipyards, Inc., 760 F. Supp. 1486 (M.D. Fla. 1991).

147 Porta v. Rollins Envtl. Servs., Inc., 654 F. Supp. 1275 (D.N.J. 1987), *aff'd,* 845 F.2d 1014 (3d Cir. 1988) (crude graffiti left on office refrigerator for a week until plaintiff asked janitor to remove it);

Second Circuit: Danna v. New York Tel. Co., 752 F. Supp. 594 (S.D.N.Y. 1990) Plaintiff telephone company employee proved that she was subjected to a hostile work environment in violation of Title VII. The plaintiff, a service technician in a male-dominated realm, complained of "incidents that were overtly sexual in nature at the Telco work place" *Id.* at 608:

(1) In response to a question regarding where she could find a certain key, a supervisor allegedly informed her that what she needed was "a good fuck in the ass". *Id.*

(2) Lewd graffiti directed specifically at Danna were scribbled on the walls of the terminal rooms in JFK airport used by Telco's employees, including "Fran Danna you ungrateful cunt you suck," "Sit on Danna's face," depicting a picture of a face with a penis in the mouth, and "Just when you thought it was safe to go into the airport again . . . Fran Danna II," showing an act of anal sex.

employees are required to wear revealing uniforms or act in a "provocative" manner to attract business.[148]

Some courts have indicated that some verbal or physical conduct may not be sexual harassment in violation of Title VII if it is not directed toward one sex,[149] such as in a case in which an employee persistently uses

---

Id. This graffiti were on the terminal walls for at least two years. Although plaintiff admitted that she also had written grafitti on the terminal walls, she only did so in response to graffiti written about her and never wrote derogatory remarks or used profanity. Although plaintiff's supervisors were aware of the graffiti, and with the exception of one incident when an employee was authorized to spray paint over certain graffiti directed at Danna, they did nothing to have it removed, and plaintiff was allegedly told that the supervisor did not think he could do very much about it, and that she would be better off not making a stink about it, because coworkers would do it even more.

Bennett v. New York City Dep't of Corrections,705 F. Supp. 979 (S.D.N.Y. 1989) (graffiti was promptly painted over, but plaintiff correction officer stated claim of hostile environment when graffiti was one of a number of incidents).

Fifth Circuit: Waltman v. International Paper Co., 875 F.2d 468 (5th Cir. 1989) (female employee's evidence of individual acts of harassment coupled with evidence of sexual graffiti throughout workplace could support finding that acts of harassment were sufficiently recurrent to create continuously hostile environment);

148 Second Circuit: EEOC v. Sage Realty Corp., 507 F. Supp. 599 (S.D.N.Y. 1981) (lobby attendant of an office building was required to wear revealing "bicentennial" outfit in violation of Title VII); Barbetta v. Chemlawn Servs. Corp., 669 F. Supp. 569 (W.D.N.Y. 1987) (female employees were required to wear skirts or dresses on certain occasions because visiting supervisor liked to look at legs).

Fourth Circuit: EEOC v. Newtown Inn Assocs., 647 F. Supp. 957 (E.D. Va. 1986) (cocktail waitresses were required to wear thematic revealing outfits and act in "provocative" manner to attract business).

Sixth Circuit: Marentette v. Michigan Host, Inc., 506 F. Supp. 909 (E.D. Mich. 1980) (sexually provocative dress code may violate Title VII).

Ninth Circuit: Ninth Circuit: *Cf.* Dias v. Sky Chefs, 919 F.2d 1370 (9th Cir. 1990), *vacated on other grounds,* 111 S. Ct. 2791 (9th Cir. 1990), *on remand,* 948 F.2d 532 (9th Cir. 1991), *cert denied,* 112 S. Ct. 1294 (1992) (general manager established job standards for women that included wearing dresses, or skirts, and nylons and heels specifically so that he could admire women employees' legs); Priest v. Rotary, 634 F. Supp. 571, 581 (N.D. Cal. 1986) (plaintiff established prima facie violation of Title VII by demonstrating that defendant removed her from her full-time, permanent employment as cocktail waitress because she refused to wear sexually suggestive dress).

149 Sheehan v. Purolator, Inc., 839 F.2d 99 (2d Cir. 1988), *cert. denied,* 488 U.S. 891 (district court rejected claim of sexual harassment when supervisor's temper was manifested toward men and women, even his superiors); Hillding v. McDonnell Douglas, 59 Fair Empl. Prac. Cas. (BNA) 869 (D. Ariz. 1992). A female former employee who alleged that her supervisor engaged in conduct including gambling, drunkenness, watching and following employees during work, riding go-carts, spitting sunflower seeds, and "burping and farting contests" did not prove that any of the conduct was directed at plaintiff because of her gender, but in fact produced evidence showing that the conduct was performed by both men and women and was directed at both men and women. The court noted that although the Ninth Circuit had not yet addressed the issue

vulgar expletives in the workplace without directing them at anyone in particular.[150] This assertion is problematic, requiring application of a reasonable employer standard that makes the employer's intent relevant. From that perspective, very little conduct would constitute sexual harassment, given disparate notions by men and women as to what behavior is

---

of whether harassment must be overtly sexual to be prohibited by Title VII, many other circuits have determined that it need not.

Scheider v. NBC News Bureaus, 56 Fair Emp. Prac. Cas. (BNA) 1602 (S.D. Fla. 1991) (female employee was not subjected to sexual harassment when her supervisor yelled at her in front of other employees when she admitted that the supervisor shouted at all employees of both sexes).

See also Walker v. Sullair Corp., 736 F. Supp. 94 (W.D.N.C. 1990), *aff'd in part, rev'd in part,* 946 F.2d 888 (4th Cir. 1991). In an action alleging sexual harassment by a supervisor with whom plaintiff had previously maintained a sexual relationship, the court concluded that the alleged harassment of employees was conducted on a "sex neutral" basis, and thus did not create a hostile work environment. The plaintiff presented evidence that the supervisor did begin to monitor plaintiff's activities more closely after her remarriage:

> Walker has offered no proof of an unwelcome touching or fondling. There is also no evidence of a workplace "pervaded with sexual slur, insult and innuendo." *Katz v. Dole,* 709 F.2d at 254. Rather, the conduct alleged included close monitoring of the attendance of the plaintiff, monitoring of personal phone calls, public reprimands for poor job performance and various other non-sexual harassment. In fact, the testimony which was offered at trial on this subject tended to show that the sexual banter and remarks made at the Pure Aire Office in Charlotte were often *initiated* by the plaintiff herself.

Id. at 100. The court made findings regarding the number of coworkers with whom plaintiff had had sexual relations, her open discussions about her sex life and fantasies, her sexually suggestive phone conversations, her use of vulgar or offensive language in the workplace, and bringing lingerie in to work.

Cf. Campbell v. Board of Regents, 770 F. Supp. 1479 (D. Kan. 1991). Upon motion for summary judgment by defendants in an action by a female employee alleging that her supervisor crowded her in her office space, made knee to knee contact with her that made her feel uncomfortable, threatened repeatedly to slap her on the butt and did slap her, and told her he would slap her again. The court rejected the defendants' argument that none of the alleged conduct had to do with the fact plaintiff was female:

> The court cannot agree. Wherever else such conduct might be acceptable, a slap on the buttocks in the office setting has yet to replace the hand shake, and the court is confident that such conduct, when directed from a man towards a woman, occurs precisely and only because of the parties' respective gender.

Id. at 1486; Jackson-Colley v. Army Corps of Eng'rs, 655 F. Supp. 1222, 1227 (E.D. Mich. 1987) (court found that defendant's "gawking" was actually an eye problem, his groin scratching stemmed from medical condition, and his excessive use of vulgar language was aimed at all employees, not just women; "gifts" of styrofoam cup, note pad with productivity encouragement slogans, and souvenir of crude oil did not imply that defendant sought "to curry favor." *Id.* at 127).

150 Halpert v. Wertheim & Co., 27 Fair Empl. Prac. Cas. (BNA) 21 (S.D.N.Y. 1980).

offensive and intimidating. Courts are reluctant to find sexual harassment when although the challenged workplace conduct is offensive, both men and women participate in the conduct, even when women are the targets generally of the vulgarity. For example, in *Weinsheimer v. Rockwell Int'l Corp.*,[151] the court concluded that a female quality control inspector failed to demonstrate that the conduct of coworkers was unwelcome despite the defendant employer's concession that the workplace was characterized by an atmosphere of vulgarity and sexual innuendo. One coworker allegedly verbally harassed the plaintiff by asking her several times a week to "suck him", "give him head," or give him "some of that stuff,"[152] grabbed her breast and crotch, held a knife to her throat, threatened to "bang her head into the ground," and passed gas and belched in her presence. Another employee allegedly exposed his penis and placed it in the plaintiff's hand while she was working and looking away, and another patted the plaintiff on the rear and requested an "ice-cube job":[153]

> Title VII bars unwelcome harassment based upon sex. It would seem to be stretching the language and aims of the statute were it to now apply *per se* to any argument between coworkers of opposite sex that involves vulgarities or sexual comments. Rockwell's back shop had two marked characteristics, those of frequent contentiousness and vulgarity. The simple combination of these two traits should not, without more, equal a Title VII violation.[154]

The court also found that the challenged verbal harassment did not rise to the level of "sufficiently severe" required by Title VII when they were apparently commonplace and routine in the shop. But in *Chiapuzio v. BLT Operating Corp.*,[155] in which a male supervisor subjected both men and women to incessant series of sexually abusive remarks, the majority of which referred to the fact that the supervisor could do a better job of making love with the plaintiff wife than could the plaintiff husband, the court did find a hostile environment. Another couple was also subjected to a constant series of sexually abusive remarks, often in front of other

---

151 754 F. Supp. 1559 (M.D. Fla. 1990), *aff'd*, 949 F.2d 1162 (11th Cir. 1991).

152 *Id.* at 1561.

153 *Id.*

154 *Id.* at 832. *See also* Bowen v. Department of Human Services, 606 A.2d 1051 (Me. 1992) (Collins, J.). A former employee of the Department of Human Services could not establish a hostile environment under the state human rights act based on the constant use of vulgar language at work when she did not show that the language was used in her presence or was directed at her because she was a woman. The court discussed an "offensive nickname," "sexually suggestive" jokes, and "vulgar language" without specifics, noting only that a reasonable man would have also found the behavior offensive.

155 62 Fair Empl. Prac. Cas. (BNA) 707 (D. Wyo. 1993).

employees. The plaintiffs generally alleged that the supervisor and his superior were good friends, and that complaining of the harassment would be futile; when one husband did complain, he was fired. The court concluded that the plaintiffs stated a claim for hostile environment sexual harassment, rejecting the defendant's contention that because the supervisor harassed both male and female employees, he could not have discriminated against the plaintiffs on the basis of sex. When a harasser violated both men and women, it is possible that each individual who is harassed is being treated badly because of gender.

> The principal flaw in the defendant's argument is that it assumes that if a harasser harasses both genders equally, it necessarily follows that the harasser did not harass the employees "but for" their gender. Indeed, a critical difference between the theoretical bisexual harasser and Bell is that Bell intended to demean and, therefore, harm [the husband plaintiffs] because each was male. . . . Bell often made his remarks in front of the plaintiffs, their respective spouses, and other employees. The remarks typically concerned Bell's sexual prowess and included graphic descriptions of sexual acts Bell desired to perform with various female employees. . . Thus, the nature of Bell's remarks indicates that he harassed the plaintiffs because of their gender and constitute exactly the type of harassment contemplated to fall within the purview of Title VII.
>
> . . . [I]f this Court dismissed the instant case because Bell harassed the plaintiffs equally, the plaintiffs subsequently could file individual lawsuits against BLT. In each individual suit, evidence of the general work atmosphere, as well as evidence of specific hostility directed toward an individual plaintiff would be admissible. . . . An odd and inefficient result would obtained if the plaintiffs were unable to bring one lawsuit as a group, but could successfully bring individual suits against this defendant.[156]

Although *Meritor*[157] primarily involved sexual advances, the Court also addressed the verbal and physical conduct alleged. Thus, it appears that the Court did not distinguish between the different types of harassing behavior in determining whether the sexual conduct was welcome. The EEOC, however, now distinguishes between verbal and physical conduct:

> The Commission will presume that the unwelcome, intentional touching of a charging party's intimate body areas is sufficiently offensive to alter the conditions of her working environment and constitute a violation of Title VII. More so than in the case of verbal advances or remarks, a single unwelcome physical advance can seriously poison the victim's working environment. If a supervisor sexually touches an employee, the Commission

156 *Id.* at 710.

157 Meritor Sav. Bank v. Vinson, 477 U.S. 57 (1986).

> normally would find a violation. In such situations, it is the employer's burden to demonstrate that the unwelcome conduct was not sufficiently severe to create a hostile work environment.[158]

Nonintimate physical contact exacerbates the hostility of an environment plagued with offensive verbal conduct. When the alleged harassment consists solely of verbal conduct, the commission suggests that courts look at (1) whether the alleged harasser singled out the charging party, (2) whether the charging party participated in the conduct, (3) whether the remarks were hostile and abusive, and (4) the relationship between the charging party and the alleged harasser(s).[159]

Offensive verbal or physical conduct need not be overtly sexual to be deemed sexual harassment.[160] Before 1985, courts held that the conduct

---

[158] EEOC Policy Guidance, N-915.035 (Oct. 25, 1988) C(2) at 16.

[159] *Id.* C(3) at 16.

[160] *Id.* C(4) at 18.

Third Circuit: Reynolds v. Atlantic City Convention Center, 53 Fair Empl. Prac. Cas. (BNA) 1852 (D.N.J. 1990). A female "journeyman" electrician alleged that she was harassed constantly with verbal abuse and obscene gestures during her last two years at the convention center. In addition, plaintiff alleged a variety of other incidents of harassment as grounds for her claim of sexual harassment:

1. Strong resistance and even refusal by some male coworkers to work for plaintiff when she was "subforeman".
2. Men threatened to quit, and some did, rather than work for her.
3. One client exhibitor requested that the two women electricians be prevented from being on the floor during the Miss America Pageant and the work was given to a coworker.
4. Male employees stood around laughing while plaintiff and female coworker attempted to unload heavy boxes.
5. In response to questions regarding disability benefits, the ship steward told plaintiff that the men had not complained and the women should quit if they did not like the lack of benefits.

The court noted that while these acts did not "reflect a strong spirit of cooperation between the male and female electricians at the defendant Convention Center" (*Id.* at 1867), it refused to deem them within the EEOC regulation's proscription or other verbal or physical conduct of a sexual nature".

Fourth Circuit: Delgado v. Lehman, 665 F. Supp. 460 (E.D. Va. 1987).

Eighth Circuit: Morris v. American Nat'l Can Corp., 730 F. Supp. 1489 (E.D. Mo. 1989), *modified on other grounds,* 941 F.2d 710 (8th Cir. 1991). The court rejected defendant's contention that some of the materials received by plaintiff and some of the conduct directed toward her were not sexual in nature, applying a totality of the circumstances test, when the most offending conduct was clearly sexual in nature and the destruction of plaintiff's property more likely than not was generated by the same animus that generated the note "This is what you should be doing instead of a man's job." Defendants did not suggest that any male employee was subjected to a campaign of harassment comparable to that of plaintiff. Although the harassment plaintiff experienced in the weeks before her sick leave may not have been overtly sexual, it was part of a continuing campaign of

giving rise to a sexual harassment claim had to be clearly sexual in nature.[161] In 1985, the District of Columbia Circuit in *McKinney v. Dole*[162] addressed the question of whether a physically aggressive but not explicitly sexual act by a male supervisor against a female employee could constitute part of a "prohibited pattern of sexual discrimination":[163]

> We have never held that sexual harassment or other unequal treatment of an employee or group of employees that occurs because of the sex of an employee must, to be illegal under Title VII, take the form of sexual advances or of other incidents with clearly sexual overtones. And we decline to do so now. Rather, we hold that any harassment or other unequal treatment of an employee or group of employees that would not occur but for the sex of the employee or employees may, if sufficiently patterned or pervasive, comprise an illegal condition of employment under Title VII.
>
> * * *
>
> Clearly, then, if a supervisor consistently uses physical force toward an employee because of the employee's sex, the use of such force may, if pervasive enough, form an illegal "condition of employment." So, too, a pattern of mixed sexual advances and physical force may be illegally discriminatory if based on the employee's sex.[164]

---

clearly sexual harassment that dated back at least two and one-half years, and that was directed at her because she is a woman.

Thompson v. Arkansas Transp. Dep't, 691 F. Supp. 1201 (E.D. Ark. 1988).

Tenth Circuit: Hicks v. Gates Rubber Co., 833 F.2d 1406 (10th Cir. 1987), *aff'g district court's finding of no hostile environment,* 928 F.2d 966 (10th Cir. 1991); Laughinghouse v. Risser, 754 F. Supp. 836 (D. Kan. 1990) (offensive acts need not be clearly sexual in nature when acts would not have occurred but for the fact that plaintiff was a woman).

Eleventh Circuit: Cronin v. United States Serv. Stations, Inc., 809 F. Supp. 922 (M.D. Ala. 1992) (conduct of a nonsexual nature that ridicules women or treats them as inferior can constitute sexual harassment).

District of Columbia Circuit: McKinney v. Dole, 765 F.2d 1129 (D.C. Cir. 1985).

161 Downes v. Federal Aviation Admin., 775 F.2d 288, 290 (Fed. Cir. 1985); Jones v. Flagship Int'l, 793 F.2d 714, 720 n.5 (5th Cir. 1986), *cert. denied*, 479 U.S. 1065 (1987).

162 McKinney v. Dole, 765 F.2d 1129 (D.C. Cir. 1985).

163 *Id.* at 1131.

164 *Id.* at 1138, 1139 (footnotes omitted). *See also* Delgado v. Lehman, 665 F. Supp. 460, 468 (E.D. Va. 1987) ("Sexual harassment need not take the form of overt sexual advances or suggestions, but may consist of such things as verbal abuse of women if it is sufficiently patterned to comprise a condition and is apparently caused by the sex of the harassed employee").

The Tenth Circuit drew from the reasoning in *McKinney* for *Hicks v. Gates Rubber Co.,*[165] in which it held that evidence of threats of physical violence and incidents of verbal abuse could be considered in determining whether the plaintiff had established a claim of a hostile work environment.[166] It is clear that hostility toward women because they are women can be manifested in nonsexual ways.[167] Although courts may be more receptive to charges of nonsexual conduct if brought with sexual conduct claims,[168] nonsexual conduct alone may give rise to a sexual harassment claim. For example, the forcible restraint of a woman employee by her male supervisor who grabbed and twisted her arm was sexual harassment, despite the absence of sexual conduct.[169] The conduct of a supervisor who exhibited a "virulent" antifemale bias in unjustifiably "investigating" a woman employee created a hostile working environment.[170] In *Muench v. Township of Haddon,*[171] a female dispatcher did not have to prove overt sexual conduct in the workplace to establish sexual harassment by a police officer coworker who had been against hiring the plaintiff because she was a woman, believing that the job was for a man, and who refused to answer plaintiff's questions during training, ridiculed her in front of coworkers and over the police radio when other dispatchers could hear him, smeared the dispatcher's window with his fingers and occasionally kissed it, filled plaintiff's work area with cigar smoke after she told him she was allergic to smoke, and made sexual comments:

> In our view, whether the offending conduct is in the form of sexual advances or intimidation and hostility toward a woman solely because she is a woman, the result is the same. Sexual harassment, whatever form it takes, imposes a sense of degradation, closes or discourages employment opportunity for women (or men) and essentially deprives them of "self-respecting employment" . . . Interpreting the [state antidiscrimination law] as prohibiting pervasive and hostile nonsexual harassment best serves the Act's underlying goal of eradicating discrimination in the work place.[172]

---

165 833 F.2d 1406 (10th Cir. 1987).

166 *Id.* at 1415.

167 *See, e.g.,* Delgado v. Lehman, 665 F. Supp. 460 (E.D. Va. 1987) (defendant supervisor, "who was trying to protect his turf and who viewed women as threats," would go out of his way to demean plaintiff, was less polite to women in conversations than to men, acting as if women were not present, but allowing men to speak without interrupting them).

168 Courts seem to find incidents involving touching particularly egregious. *See, e.g.,* Ross v. Double Diamond, Inc., 672 F. Supp. 261 (N.D. Tex. 1987).

169 McKinney v. Dole, 765 F.2d 1129 (D.C. Cir. 1985).

170 Thompson v. Arkansas Transp. Dep't, 691 F. Supp. 1201, 1204 (E.D. Ark. 1988).

171 255 N.J. Super. 288, 605 A.2d 242 (N.J. Super. Ct. 1992).

172 *Id.* at 247.

Rebuffed sexual advances may turn into verbal and other nonsexual abuse.[173]

§ 3.20 Effect of the Harassment: *Harris v. Forklift Systems, Inc.*

Often it is difficult to measure the impact of sexual harassment. While some women suffer obvious physical and emotional injuries, a hostile environment does not always have immediate consequences. In *Harris v. Forklift Systems, Inc.,*[174] the U.S. Supreme Court resolved the conflict among the circuits regarding whether Title VII requires that harassing conduct seriously affect an employee's psychological well-being or lead the plaintiff to suffer injury. In a unanimous ruling, the Court held that while psychological harm, like any other relevant factor, may be taken into account in a determination of hostile environment, no single factor is required. "So long as the environment would reasonably be perceived, and is perceived, as hostile or abusive, . . . there is no need for it also to be psychologically injurious.[175] Whether an environment is hostile or abusive can be determined only by looking at all the circumstances, and these may include the frequency and severity of the alleged conduct, whether it is physically threatening or humiliating or whether it unreasonably interferes with the employee's work performance.[176]

TYPES OF CLAIMS

§ 3.21 Quid Pro Quo Harassment

Quid pro quo sexual harassment cases are analytically similar to traditional Title VII sex discrimination suits. As in the typical disparate treatment case, the plaintiff must demonstrate that she was otherwise qualified to receive the relevant job benefit, and that the job benefit was actually withheld or altered. Underlying sexual harassment and other sexual discrimination claims is the requirement that, but for the sex of the complainant, the offending conduct would not have occurred[177] (see **Chapter 6**).

---

173 Hopkins v. Shoe Show of Va., Inc., 678 F. Supp. 1241 (S.D.W. Va. 1988) (no harassment found).

174 114 S. Ct. 367 (1993).

175 114 S. Ct. at 371.

176 *Id.*

177 Boyd v. James S. Hayes Living Health Care Agency, 671 F. Supp. 1155, 1165 (W.D. Tenn. 1987).

In *quid pro quo* actions, almost all lower federal courts have held employers strictly liable for the sexual harassment of an employee by a supervisor, based on the agency doctrine of *respondeat superior*.[178] An employer is generally liable for the torts committed by its employees who are acting within the scope of their employment (see **Chapter 2**). The doctrine breaks down in this context when sexual harassment occurs outside the scope of employment. The dynamics and potential for coercion remain outside the workplace or without delegated functions, and courts have found employer liability in such situations.[179] Employers should be encouraged to carefully hire and supervise employees and should be responsible for bearing the cost of remedying and eradicating employment discrimination (see **Chapter 11**). The fact that an employer has a policy prohibiting sexual harassment cannot insulate an employer from liability in *quid pro quo* cases, particularly when the complainant must report any grievances to her supervisor, the alleged offender, to invoke internal procedures.[180]

Evidence of sexual advances made to other employees may be admitted on the issue of motive, intent, or plan in making the sexual advances toward the plaintiff.[181]

---

178 Sixth Circuit: Shrout v. Black Clawson Co., 689 F. Supp. 774 (S.D. Ohio 1988).

Tenth Circuit: Sparks v. Pilot Freight Carriers, 830 F.2d 1554, 1564 n.22 (11th Cir. 1987); Davis v. Utah P & L Co., 53 Fair Empl. Prac. Cas. (BNA) 1047 (D. Utah 1990). The defendant supervisor's summary judgment motion was denied when there were disputed material facts regarding whether plaintiff's termination was linked to her refusing to succumb to alleged sexual advances by a supervisor.

Eleventh Circuit: Sowers v. Kemira, Inc., 46 Fair Empl. Prac. Cas. (BNA) 1825 (S.D. Ga. 1988).

179 Hall v. Gus Constr. Co., 842 F.2d 1011 (8th Cir. 1988); Ross v. Twenty-Four Collection, Inc., 681 F. Supp. 1547 (S.D. Fla. 1988), *aff'd,* 875 F.2d 873 (11th Cir. 1989).

180 Meritor Sav. Bank v. Vinson, 477 U.S. 57, 72–73 (1986); Sowers v. Kemira, Inc., 46 Fair Empl. Prac. Cas. (BNA) 1825 (S.D. Ga. 1988). *See also* Keziah v. W.M. Brown & Son, 683 F. Supp. 542 (W.D.N.C. 1988), *modified on other grounds,* 888 F.2d 322 (4th Cir. 1989) (hostile environment case).

181 Sowers v. Kemira, Inc., 46 Fair Empl. Prac. Cas. (BNA) 1825 (S.D. Ga. 1988).

Campbell v. Board of Regents, 770 F. Supp. 1479 (D. Kan. 1991). Although testimony regarding an alleged harasser's sexual harassment of a former secretary could not have contributed to the hostility plaintiff received in her office, such allegations were relevant to the credibility of defendant's denial of plaintiff's allegations.

Cf. Halasi-Schmick v. City of Shawnee, 759 F. Supp. 747 (D. Kan. 1991). A female fire inspector/code enforcement officer who alleged that the fire chief referred to her as a dumb blonde, a supervisor told another employee that she was having an affair with a coworker, the city manager told another employee that she was a bitter woman and that she was subjected to different treatment on account of her gender were insufficient to show a hostile environment. The court found that plaintiff could not rely on hearsay about incidents involving the nine other female employees of the city in opposing the defendants' motion for summary judgment.

§ 3.22 Hostile Environment Harassment

A hostile environment claim challenges workplace practices rather than tangible job benefits, and consists of "verbal or physical conduct of a sexual nature" that unreasonably interferes with the employee's work or creates an "intimidating, hostile or offensive working environment."[182] This type of harassment is both more pervasive and more elusive. It fills the air with a tense combination of lust and contempt. Although *quid pro quo* sexual harassment can only be committed by someone with authority to change the employee's job status, employers, supervisors, co-workers, customers, or clients can create a hostile work environment (see **§§ 3.10–3.13**).

A victim of a hostile environment either seeks an injunction against the abusive conditions or leaves her job and then charges constructive discharge (see **§ 3.27**). A plaintiff can demonstrate either that the sexual harassment was pervasive enough to create a hostile work environment or that the perpetrator(s) altered her working conditions by sexually harassing her.[183] An employer or his agent also can alter working conditions by, for example, denigrating the employee in front of other workers,[184] constantly picking on her,[185] monitoring the plaintiff's work more closely than others,[186] threatening her job security,[187] or giving the employee different work assignments[188] or less desirable physical facilities.[189] Behavior that

---

[182] 29 C.F.R. § 1604.11(a) (1988).

[183] Compston v. Borden, Inc., 424 F. Supp. 157 (S.D. Ohio 1976) (different working conditions because of race).

[184] Huddleston v. Roger Dean Chevrolet, Inc., 845 F.2d 900 (11th Cir. 1988); Compston v. Borden, Inc., 424 F. Supp. 157 (S.D. Ohio 1976).

[185] Thompson v. Arkansas Transp. Dep't, 691 F. Supp. 1201, 1203 (E.D. Ark. 1988) (when the new chair of the transportation commission had a "virulent" antifemale bias, a law enforcement officer for the department was subjected to an "investigation" that was nothing more than a smokescreen to discharge her); Compston v. Borden, Inc., 424 F. Supp. 157 (S.D. Ohio 1976). *Cf.* Miller v. Aluminum Co. of Am., 679 F. Supp. 495, 502 (W.D. Pa. 1988), *aff'd,* 856 F.2d 184 (3d Cir. 1988) ("Snubs and unjust criticisms of one's work are not poisonous enough to create an actionable hostile work environment. . . . Hostile behavior that does not bespeak an unlawful motive cannot support a hostile work environment claim").

[186] *Cf.* Seligson v. Massachusetts Inst. of Tech., 677 F. Supp. 648 (D. Mass. 1987) (testimony that defendant treated all employees similarly was credited).

[187] Sparks v. Pilot Freight Carriers, 830 F.2d 1554 (11th Cir. 1987). *See also* Ross v. Twenty-Four Collection, Inc., 681 F. Supp. 1547, 1550 (S.D. Fla. 1988), *aff'd,* 875 F.2d 873 (11th Cir. 1989) (after many sexual advances, defendant told plaintiff she would be fired if she did not accompany him on a trip).

[188] Mitchell v. OsAir, Inc., 629 F. Supp. 636, 643 (N.D. Ohio 1986), *appeal dismissed,* 816 F.2d 681 (6th Cir. 1987).

[189] Harrington v. Vandalia-Butler Bd. of Educ., 585 F.2d 192, 194 n.3 (6th Cir. 1978), *cert. denied,* 441 U.S. 932 (1979) (different physical facilities because of sex).

constitutes a hostile work environment includes repeated requests for sexual favors,[190] demeaning sexual inquiries and vulgarities,[191] offensive language, and other verbal or physical conduct of a sexual or degrading nature.[192]

---

190 Henson v. City of Dundee, 682 F.2d 897 (11th Cir. 1982); Bundy v. Jackson, 641 F.2d 934 (D.C. Cir. 1981); Ross v. Twenty-Four Collection, Inc., 681 F. Supp. 1547 (S.D. Fla. 1988), *aff'd,* 875 F.2d 873 (11th Cir. 1989); Carrero v. New York City Hous. Auth., 668 F. Supp. 196, 201–02 (S.D.N.Y. 1987); Coley v. Consolidated Rail Corp., 561 F. Supp. 645 (E.D. Mich. 1982).

191 Katz v. Dole, 709 F.2d 251 (4th Cir. 1983); Henson v. City of Dundee, 682 F.2d 897 (11th Cir. 1982); Bundy v. Jackson, 641 F.2d 934 (D.C. Cir. 1981).

192 Second Circuit: Danna v. New York Tel. Co., 752 F. Supp. 594 (S.D.N.Y. 1990). When graffiti and vulgar comments written on walls intimidated and demeaned plaintiff to the point that they were at least a partial cause for her seeking a demotion rather than risking further harassment, plaintiff's failure to "clearly adduce specific harm" did not extinguish the defendant's liability when, with one exception, the graffiti remained on the walls for at least two years and plaintiff was advised to not make "a stink about it." *Id.* at 1650.

Barbetta v. Chemlawn Servs. Corp., 669 F. Supp. 569 (W.D.N.Y. 1987) (evidence of pornography in workplace, vulgar comments by employees and supervisors, requirement that female employees wear skirts or dresses on certain occasions because visiting supervisor liked to look at legs, and unwanted physical contact amounted to hostile environment).

Fourth Circuit: Spencer v. General Elec. Co., 697 F. Supp. 204 (E.D. Va. 1988), *aff'd,* 894 F.2d 651 (4th Cir. 1990) (plaintiff demonstrated the existence of a hostile working environment, alleging that her supervisor engaged in horseplay of a sexual nature with his female subordinates almost on a daily basis, including sitting on their laps, touching them in an intimate manner, making lewd comments, talking about the sexual ability of his tongue, the length of his penis, and his sex life, throwing pennies down women's shirts, making sexual comments about female staff members, and exclaiming that women "have shit for brains," and should be "barefoot and pregnant").

Sixth Circuit: Anderson v. Hewlett-Packard Corp., 694 F. Supp. 1294, 1298–1299 (N.D. Ohio 1988) (defendant made frequent sexual remarks and phone calls to invite himself over and became nasty when rebuffed).

Shrout v. Black Clawson Co., 689 F. Supp. 774 (S.D. Ohio 1988) (defendant touched plaintiff intimately, made frequent sexual remarks, left sexual materials on her desk, splashed water on her, and looked down her blouse and up her skirt).

Seventh Circuit: Dombeck v. Milwaukee Valve Co., 823 F. Supp. 1475 (W.D. Wis. 1993). The jury could reasonably find that alleged sexual harassment, including allegations that the alleged harasser used sexual language, forcefully placed his foot in plaintiff's crotch and wiggled it, pulled the waistband on her pants and exposed her underpants on at least two occasions and slapped her buttocks, created a hostile environment and that the employer knew or should have known of the harassment but did nothing to rectify the problem. An award of $25,000 in compensatory damages was proper but punitive damages in the amount of $75,000 were vacated as there was no basis for any such award.

Zabkowicz v. West Bend Co., 589 F. Supp. 780 (E.D. Wis. 1984).

Eighth Circuit: Jones v. Wesco, 846 F.2d 1154 (8th Cir. 1988) (touching breasts, pinching, patting, kissing); Barrett v. Omaha Nat'l Bank, 726 F.2d 424 (8th Cir. 1984); Schiele v. Charles Vogel Mfg. Co., Inc., 787 F. Supp. 1541 (D. Minn. 1992). A former

In response to steady harassment, tolerance becomes a way to get through the day. Failure to report incidents of harassment, however, may

---

employee established a prima facie case of hostile environment sexual harassment under Title VII, alleging that her employer repeatedly subjected her to unwelcome physical contact and verbal communications of an intimidating, abusive, and sexual nature, such as delivering her a note that read "chocolate chip cookies are great but my favorite is Pussy—I don't mean cats either." *Id.* at 1545 n.1.

Ninth Circuit: Canada v. Boyd Group, Inc., 809 F. Supp. 771 (D. Nev. 1992). A female employee alleged that over a two or three week period her supervisor engaged in conduct including: two incidents of telling "off-color" jokes from which plaintiff walked away, comments on how good plaintiff looked in her uniform, smiling and looking at plaintiff a great deal, one incident in which the supervisor leaned or rubbed the front of his body on the back of plaintiff's body and placed his hand on her shoulder, another incident in which he placed his hand on her shoulder and made one phone call to her home. Soon after these incidents, plaintiff requested a shift change, and over the next five weeks their relationship was strained and she was eventually fired. The court held that plaintiff stated a claim for hostile environment sexual harassment when the answer to the question of whether a reasonable woman who had worked with the supervisor would consider his conduct severe and/or frequent enough to create an abusive working environment was not sufficiently clear to warrant a grant of summary judgment to the defendant. "[W]hile frequency and severity of conduct are important factors to consider when assessing whether a hostile environment was created, ultimately it is the effect or consequences of conduct on the working environment that must be evaluated." *Id.* at 776.

Eleventh Circuit: Huddleston v. Roger Dean Chevrolet, Inc., 845 F.2d 900 (11th Cir. 1988); Phillips v. Smalley Maintenance Servs. Corp., 711 F.2d 1524 (11th Cir. 1983).

A hostile environment was not found in the following cases, despite the existence of repeated advances or other sexual conduct:

Second Circuit: Trotta v. Mobile Oil Corp., 788 F. Supp. 1336 (S.D.N.Y. 1992). A former employee who alleged that defendant corporation allowed sexually offensive conduct at mandatory business meetings and related social functions and that such conduct included the presence of female strippers and women clad in leather astride motorcycles, sexually suggestive gifts, and the projection of a slide of her backside at a company outing and that such conduct caused her to leave the company, failed to show that the conditions of her employment were altered or that she was subjected to a hostile work environment, or that the alleged incidents were sufficiently severe or pervasive to create a hostile work environment.

Sixth Circuit: Jackson-Colley v. Army Corps of Eng'rs, 655 F. Supp. 1222 (E.D. Mich. 1987) (court found that defendant's "gawking" was actually an eye problem, his groin scratching stemmed from a medical condition, and his excessive use of vulgar language was aimed at all employees, not just women).

Seventh Circuit: Scott v. Sears Roebuck & Co., 605 F. Supp. 1047 (N.D. Ill. 1985), *aff'd,* 798 F.2d 210 (7th Cir. 1986) (requests for rubdowns, invitations to go for drinks after job hours, sexual propositions, obscene comments, winking, and being slapped on the buttocks did not constitute harassment).

Eighth Circuit: Staton v. Maries County, 868 F.2d 996 (8th Cir. 1989). Evidence established that alleged sexual harassment, which included numerous sexual advances and a rape, may have been invited and did not significantly affect conditions of employment.

suggest to the court that the conduct was not so severe or pervasive as to alter the plaintiff's condition of employment.[193] Some courts also have held

---

District court found that although the act of intercourse affected plaintiff's psychological well-being, she was able to work a regular shift for 10 days after the incident, and there was no testimony that she was distressed or unable to perform her duties.

Ninth Circuit: Intlekofer v. Turnage, 973 F.2d 773 (9th Cir. 1992). The United States Veterans Administration did not take prompt and appropriate remedial action in response to continued complaints by a female employee of sexual harassment by a coworker when it failed to take more severe disciplinary action against the alleged harasser after learning that the harassment had not stopped. Although the VA had investigated plaintiff's complaints regarding inappropriate touching, suggestions, threats, the drawing of a dildo on plaintiff's locker, and held continuous counseling sessions with the alleged harasser, it was apparent that these measures were ineffective. The court noted that under *Ellison v. Brady,* 924 F.2d 872 (9th Cir. 1991), an employer must take some form of disciplinary action if it knows of should have known of the harassment:

> Of course, I acknowledge that "discipline" can take many forms, and I do not attempt to confine the employer to options specifically mentioned in this opinion. The important point is that the appropriateness of the remedy depends on the seriousness of the offense, the employer's ability to stop the harassment, the likelihood that the remedy will end the harassment, and "the remedy's ability to persuade potential harassers to refrain from unlawful conduct." [*Ellison,* 924 F.2d at 882]
>
> Intlekofer argues that counseling can never be considered "disciplinary," and that therefore the VA failed to satisfy its duty under *Ellison.* Although *Ellison* stated that "Title VII requires more than a mere request to refrain from the discriminatory conduct," counseling sessions are not necessarily insufficient. [*Id.*] Indeed, an oral rebuke may be very effective in stopping the unlawful conduct. At the first sign of sexual harassment, an oral warning in the context of a counseling session may be an appropriate disciplinary measure if the employer expresses strong disapproval, demands that the unwelcome conduct cease, and threatens more severe disciplinary action in the event that the conduct does not cease. I approve of the remedy in a case such as this where the harassing conduct is not extremely serious and the employer cannot elicit a detailed description concerning the occurrence from the victim. I stress, however, that counseling is sufficient only as a first resort. If the harassment continues, limiting discipline to further counseling is inappropriate. Instead, the employer must impose more severe measures in order to ensure that the behavior terminates. Again, the extent of the discipline depends on the seriousness of the conduct.

Id. at 779–80.

193 First Circuit: Lipsett v. Rive-Mora, 669 F. Supp. 1188 (D.P.R. 1987), *rev'd on other grounds,* 864 F.2d 881 (1st Cir. 1988); Del Valle Fontanez v. Aponte, 660 F. Supp. 145 (D.P.R. 1987).

Second Circuit: Koster v. Chase Manhattan Bank, 46 Fair Empl. Prac. Cas. (BNA) 1436, 1447 (S.D.N.Y. 1988).

Third Circuit: Freedman v. American Standard, 41 Fair Empl. Prac. Cas. (BNA) 471 (D.N.J. 1986).

Fourth Circuit: Slate v. Kingsdown, 46 Fair Empl. Prac. Cas. (BNA) 1495 (M.D.N.C. 1987).

that "treatment based on romantic attraction rather than on a desire to discriminate because of gender" does not violate Title VII.[194] This approach necessitates a finding that the romantic attraction was mutual and is irreconcilable with a reasonable woman standard unless the conduct was welcome. In *Drinkwater v. Union Carbide Corp.,*[195] the plaintiff could not sustain a claim of sexual harassment based on her supervisor's relationship with her subordinate when she only made remote references to the relationship's effect on the workplace environment. The court noted that a third-party romance may in some circumstances be part of a hostile working environment:

> Such an atmosphere might have discriminated against plaintiff if sexual discourse displaced standard business procedure in a way that prevented plaintiff from working in an environment in which she could be evaluated

---

Fifth Circuit: Benton v. Kroger Co., 640 F. Supp. 1317 (S.D. Tex. 1986). *Cf.* Valdez v. Church's Fried Chicken, 683 F. Supp. 596 (W.D. Tex. 1988).

Sixth Circuit: Highlander v. K.F.C. Nat'l Management Co., 805 F.2d 644 (6th Cir. 1986) (plaintiff took a long time to report harassment).

Seventh Circuit: Wahab v. Portal Publications, 47 Fair Empl. Prac. Cas. (BNA) 579 (7th Cir. 1988); Dockter v. Rudolf Wolff Futures, Inc., 684 F. Supp. 532 (N.D. Ill. 1988), *aff'd,* 913 F.2d 456 (7th Cir. 1990); Scott v. Sears Roebuck & Co., 605 F. Supp. 1047 (N.D. Ill. 1985), *aff'd,* 798 F.2d 210 (7th Cir. 1986).

Ninth Circuit: Jordan v. Clark, 847 F.2d 1368 (9th Cir. 1988), *cert. denied,* 488 U.S. 1006 (1989).

Eleventh Circuit: Silverstein v. Metroplex Communications, Inc., 678 F. Supp. 863 (S.D. Fla. 1988).

194 Lipsett v. Rive-Mora, 669 F. Supp. 1188, 1203 (D.P.R. 1987), *rev'd on other grounds,* 864 F.2d 881 (1st Cir. 1988). *See also* De Cintio v. Westchester County Medical Ctr, 807 F.2d 304 (2d Cir. 1986), *cert. denied,* 484 U.S. 825 (1987).

Third Circuit: Handley v. Phillips, 715 F. Supp. 757 (M.D. Pa. 1989). In a sexual harassment action by a former prison guard, allegations that plaintiff was subjected to unwelcome verbal and physical advances over an extended period of time, that her rejection of this conduct adversely affected her position at the prison and created a hostile work environment, and that the prison board were aware of the conduct and condoned it presented a claim ripe for adjudication. However, a specific allegation as to dissimilar treatment from defendant's alleged desire to promote another female to whom he was romantically linked was not the basis for a Title VII claim.

Ninth Circuit: Candelore v. Clark County Sanitation Dist., 752 F. Supp. 956 (D. Nev. 1990), *aff'd,* 975 F.2d 588 (9th Cir 1992). An older female employee did not state a claim for *quid pro quo* sexual harassment in an action charging that a younger female employee who allegedly had a sexual relationship with supervisors was treated better than she and others in the office who did not have such relationships when she presented no evidence of any unwelcome sexual conduct directed at anyone. "[P]referential treatment of a paramour, while perhaps unfair, is not discrimination on the basis of sex in violation of Title VII or, in this case, the Equal Protection Clause of the Constitution." 752 F. Supp. at 961.

195 904 F.2d 853 (3d Cir. 1990).

> on grounds other than her sexuality. . . . However, there is no evidence that [the supervisor and subordinate] flaunted the romantic nature of their relationship, nor is there evidence that these kinds of relationships were prevalent at UC. . . .
>
> Plaintiff apparently wants us to assume that the atmosphere was sexually charged or that Kahwaty was making implicit sexual demands on her. We decline to make such assumptions. A sexual relationship between a supervisor and a co-employee could adversely affect the workplace without creating a hostile sexual environment. A supervisor could show favoritism that, although unfair and unprofessional, would not necessarily instill the workplace with oppressive sexual accentuation. The boss could treat everyone but his or her paramour badly and all of the subordinates, save the paramour, might be affected the same way.[196]

Whether the sexual conduct complained of is sufficiently pervasive to create a hostile or offensive work environment must be determined by a totality of the circumstances.[197] "The gravamen of any sexual harassment claim is that the alleged sexual advances were 'unwelcome.'"[198] The plaintiff must show she was actually offended by the conduct and suffered some injury from it.[199]

The unwelcome, intentional touching of "intimate body areas" may be sufficiently offensive to constitute a violation of Title VII.[200]

---

196 *Id.* at 862.

197 EEOC Guidelines, 29 C.F.R. § 1604.11(b) (1988); Meritor Sav. Bank v. Vinson, 477 U.S. 57, 69 (1986); Highlander v. K.F.C. Nat'l Management Co., 805 F.2d 644 (6th Cir. 1986).

198 Meritor Sav. Bank v. Vinson, 477 U.S. at 68.

Second Circuit: *Cf.* Koster v. Chase Manhattan Bank, 46 Fair Empl. Prac. Cas. (BNA) 1436, 1447 (S.D.N.Y. 1988) (affair was welcome).

Sixth Circuit: Highlander v. K.F.C. Nat'l Management Co., 805 F.2d 644, 650 (6th Cir. 1986).

199 Second Circuit: Koster v. Chase Manhattan Bank, 46 Fair Empl. Prac. Cas. (BNA) 1436, 1447 (S.D.N.Y. 1988). No hostile environment harassment was found when "not a scintilla of evidence was proffered that even hinted the affair with defendant Ross was unwelcome. In fact, plaintiff's own witnesses support the conclusion plaintiff welcomed the relationship with defendant Ross".

Sixth Circuit: Highlander v. K.F.C. Nat'l Management Co., 805 F.2d 644 (6th Cir. 1986); Rabidue v. Osceola Ref. Co., 805 F.2d 611, 620 (6th Cir. 1986), *cert. denied,* 481 U.S. 1041 (1987).

Seventh Circuit: Reed v. Shepard, 939 F.2d 484 (7th Cir. 1991). The district court properly concluded that a discharged civilian jailer was not the victim of sexual harassment when evidence demonstrated that plantiff tolerated and contributed to sexually suggestive jokes and activities and admitted that the alleged harassment did not adversely affect her ability to do her job; Scott v. Sears Roebuck & Co., 605 F. Supp. 1047 (N.D. Ill. 1985), *aff'd,* 798 F.2d 210, 212 (7th Cir. 1986) (plaintiff considered alleged harasser to be "basically nice" and a friend).

200 EEOC Policy Guidance, N-915.035 (Oct. 25, 1988) C(2) at 16.

Incidents of sexual harassment directed at employees other than the plaintiff may be used to establish a hostile work environment,[201] and

---

201 Second Circuit: Watts v. New York City Police Dep't, 724 F. Supp. 99 (S.D.N.Y. 1989) Plaintiff former probationary officer alleged that one of her instructors grabbed her breast during practice and in reaction to her protestations, the instructor told her she would fail her test, threatened to "kick the shit out of her" if she did not bend down further while she was loading and unloading her gun, and refused to have her gun serviced, even though it was later found to be broken, claiming that the problem was that plaintiff couldn't shoot. The next day, a coworker twice pulled plaintiff up against his body, told her he wanted to feel her body, and that her body felt good; during the second incident, plaintiff had to strike the coworker with a box of ammunition to get away. As a result of this conduct, plaintiff suffered severe and persistent headaches and stomach aches and took sick leave for one week. Upon her return, she filed a sexual harassment complaint and was subsequently subjected to further harassment in the form of verbal attacks and ostracization by her coworkers and supervisors until her resignation a week later. Plaintiff stated a claim for hostile environment sexual harassment when plaintiff pleaded she was the victim of several incidents of physical and verbal harassment occurring in a concentrated rather than sporadic manner, and the complaint also alleges that other female employees of the NYPD experienced sexual harassment and sexual abuse in the Police Academy work environment. "For these reasons, this is not a case presenting a single, isolated instance of physical harassment." *Id.* at 106 n.5.

Fourth Circuit: Delgado v. Lehman, 665 F. Supp. 460 (E.D. Va. 1987).

Fifth Circuit: *Cf.* Jones v. Flagship Int'l, 793 F.2d 714, 721 n.7 (5th Cir. 1986), *cert. denied,* 479 U.S. 1065 (1987).

Sixth Circuit: Pease v. Alford Photo Indus., 667 F. Supp. 1188 (W.D. Tenn. 1987) (seven women testified to harassment by company president).

Ninth Circuit: Dias v. Sky Chefs, 919 F.2d 1370 (9th Cir. 1990), *vacated on other grounds,* 111 S. Ct. 2791, *on remand,* 948 F.2d 532 (1991), *cert denied,* 112 S. Ct. 1294 (1992). Admitted testimony on discussions of sexual harassment not directly protested by plaintiff was relevant both to show defendant's awareness of and failure to rectify the harassment, and to show the basis for and significance of the protests that plaintiff did in fact make. The lower court did not abuse its discretion in admitting such testimony without first establishing that she knew of incidents, when the court did permit her attorney on some occasions to establish her knowledge of specific incidents of harassment after witnesses were questioned about them rather than before, by way of a foundation. *Cf.* Hanson v. American Express, 53 Fair Empl. Prac. Cas. (BNA) 1193 (D. Utah 1986). Although plaintiff alleged that several other female employees had been sexually harassed by a supervisor, this allegation carried little weight when she introduced no evidence other than her own affidavit to support her assertion and in fact the record demonstrated that two of those women testified that they had not been sexually harassed.

Tenth Circuit: *Cf.* Campbell v. Board of Regents, 770 F. Supp. 1479 (D. Kan. 1991). Although testimony regarding an alleged harasser's sexual harassment of a former secretary could not have contributed to the hostility plaintiff received in her office, such allegations were relevant to the credibility of defendant's denial of plaintiff's allegations.

Hicks v. Gates Rubber Co., 833 F.2d 1406, 1415 (10th Cir. 1987):

> The . . . question is whether incidents of sexual harassment directed at employees other than the plaintiff can be used as proof of the plaintiff's claim of a hostile work environment. The answer seems clear: one of the critical inquiries in a hostile

alleged offensive conduct need not be purely sexual[202] (see § **3.22**). Black women face unique patterns of harassment. In *Hicks,*[203] for example, the Tenth Circuit held that although the employer's work environment was not openly hostile to blacks, evidence of racial treatment could be combined with that of sexual harassment to establish a hostile work environment toward a black woman employee. The court stated, "[A]n employer who singles out black females for less favorable treatment does not defeat plaintiff's case by showing that white females or black males are not so unfavorably treated."[204]

In *Ross v. Double Diamond, Inc.,*[205] the district court for the Northern District of Texas discussed four factors a trial court should consider in determining whether a hostile environment exists:

> First, a court should consider the nature of the unwelcome sexual acts or words. Generally, unwelcome physical touching is more offensive than unwelcome verbal abuse. However, this is only a generalization and in specific situations the type of language used may be more offensive than a type of physical touching. Second, a court should consider the frequency of the offensive encounters. It is less likely that a hostile work environment exists when, for instance, the offensive encounters occur once every week. Third, the Court should consider the total number of days over which all of the offensive meetings occur. Lastly, the court should consider the context in which the sexually harassing conduct occurred. The Court emphasizes that none of these factors should be given more weight than the others. In addition, the nonexistence of one of these factors does not, in and of itself, prevent a Title VII claim. . . . [T]he trier of fact must consider the "totality of the circumstances."[206]

---

environment claim must be the environment. Evidence of a general work atmosphere therefore—as well as evidence of specific hostility directed toward the plaintiff—is an important factor in evaluating the claim.

District of Columbia Circuit: Vinson v. Taylor, 753 F.2d 141, 146 n.40 (D.C. Cir. 1985), *aff'd in part, rev'd in part sub nom.* Meritor Sav. Bank v. Vinson, 477 U.S. 57 (1986) ("Such evidence could be critical to a plaintiff's case, for a claim of harassment cannot be established without a showing of more than isolated indicia of a discriminatory environment."); Broderick v. Ruder, 685 F. Supp. 1269, 1277 (D.D.C. 1988).

202 Hicks v. Gates Rubber Co., 833 F.2d 1406 (10th Cir. 1987), *aff'g district court's finding of no hostile environment,* 928 F.2d 966 (10th Cir. 1991). *Cf.* Scott v. Sears Roebuck & Co., 605 F. Supp. 1047 (N.D. Ill. 1985), *aff'd,* 798 F.2d 210, 212 (7th Cir. 1986) (supervisor never touched plaintiff or asked her to have sex).

203 Hicks v. Gates Rubber Co., 833 F.2d 1406 (10th Cir. 1987).

204 Graham v. Bendix Corp., 585 F. Supp. 1036, 1047 (N.D. Ind. 1984). *See also* Mitchell v. OsAir, Inc., 629 F. Supp. 636, 638 (N.D. Ohio 1986), *appeal dismissed,* 816 F.2d 681 (6th Cir. 1987) ("relentless barrage of sexual innuendos and racial slurs" constituted "working environment fraught with harassment").

205 672 F. Supp. 261 (N.D. Tex. 1987) (racial and sexual harassment created hostile atmosphere).

206 *Id.* at 270–71.

The court noted that a short duration of sexual harassment does not obviate a Title VII claim if the harassment is frequent and/or intensely offensive:

> The United States only recently has recognized the widespread nature of sexual harassment in the workplace. . . . In conjunction with this recognition, the courts have begun to give a broader scope to the areas of sexual harassment which fall under Title VII. This court submits that it would be inconsistent with this new awakening to allege that a human being who has been intensely sexually harassed at the workplace does not have a claim under Title VII because the human being did not stay on the job for a longer period of time and subject himself or herself to further degradation.[207]

§ 3.23 Hostile Environment Cases after *Meritor*

Since the U.S. Supreme Court decision in *Meritor*, courts have embraced the concept of hostile environment sexual harassment, but are sometimes still reluctant "to draw the line between a hostile work environment and an environment subject to the ordinary trials and tribulations of the workplace.[208] In addition, some courts have placed undue emphasis on the plaintiff's physical appearance and nonsexual manner or the absence of touching or actual propositions.[209] In *Scotts v. Sears*

---

207 *Id.* at 271. *See also* Vermett v. Hough, 627 F. Supp. 587, 606 (W.D. Mich. 1986).

208 Hallquist v. Max Fish Plumbing & Heating Co., 46 Fair Empl. Prac. Cas. (BNA) 1855, 1860 (D. Mass. 1987). Although the fact that plaintiff plumber was the subject of gender-related jokes and occasional teasing was relevant to whether defendant's explanation for her termination was credible, it alone was insufficient to establish a claim under the hostile environment theory. Evidence showed that in addition to the jokes, plaintiff was closely supervised and "babied" "in a manner that demeaned her demonstrable plumbing skills," and that after she was laid off, the employer "continued to maintain, and add to, his plumbing force." The court noted that the sexual harassment alleged in *Meritor* "reached a level that was significantly more obvious and intrusive, and extended over a longer period of time, than the harassment alleged against this defendant." *Id.*

Reynolds v. Atlantic City Convention Ctr., 53 Fair Empl. Prac. Cas. (BNA) 1852 (D.N.J. 1990). In determining that no sexual harassment had occurred in a workplace it acknowledged was pervaded by a "lexicon of obscenity," the court emphasized that the obscenities were rarely aimed at any female employees in particular. In support of this conclusion, the court noted that a male coworker testified as to whether any of the men had referred to the women as "cunt" or "douche bags": "I've heard it . . . . When the men were together, yes. Never to the girls." *Id.* at 1856.

209 Fifth Circuit: Benton v. Kroger Co., 640 F. Supp. 1317, 1319 (S.D. Tex. 1986) (court noted that plaintiff had been a bartender and cocktail waitress and that she was an "assertive" woman).

Seventh Circuit: Scott v. Sears Roebuck & Co., 605 F. Supp. 1047 (N.D. Ill. 1985), *aff'd,* 798 F.2d 210 (7th Cir. 1986); Dockter v. Rudolf Wolff Futures, Inc., 684 F. Supp.

Roebuck & Co.,[210] a female mechanic alleged that the senior mechanic assigned to give her on-the-job training on brake repair repeatedly propositioned her, winked at her, offered her rubdowns, and would respond to her requests for assistance with the question, "What will I get for it?"[211] Coworkers also allegedly slapped her on the buttocks and made sexual comments to her. The Seventh Circuit Court of Appeals confirmed the district court's finding of no hostile environment, noting as significant that the defendant never withheld advice from the plaintiff for refusing to "give something" in return, the plaintiff considered the defendant to be a friend and "basically nice," and when asked to evaluate the plaintiff's performance, the defendant responded favorably. It appears that the court applied a *quid pro quo* standard to a hostile environment case, thereby diminishing the value of the threat and the power of objectification.

The legal standard announced in *Meritor* has not been construed narrowly, and the severity of the conduct therein, such as repeated rape, should not be a gauge for offensive conduct. As the U.S. Supreme Court and the EEOC guidelines stress, each determination of sexual harassment should be based on an analysis of all the circumstances.[212] The qualified guidelines advanced in *Ross*[213] provide a flexible framework for hostile environment determinations. The court found that "the work performance and psychological well-being of a reasonable individual would be seriously affected if confronted with the kind of abuse to which [the plaintiff] was subjected,"[214] even though the offensive encounters lasted for only two days, at the end of that the plaintiff was fired. The plaintiff had been subjected to sexual propositions that started her first hour on the job. Her supervisor also asked her to lift her skirt so he could photograph her and to pant over the phone, he pulled her onto his lap, and a coworker put a camera on the floor and took a picture up her dress. In considering the context, the court noted that all the harassment took place on the premises, no other females who testified that they had been subject to unwelcome touching felt it was in jest or brought on by their actions, and the managers who committed the acts were at least 15 to 20 years older than the employees. Another plaintiff who had allegedly been subjected to only one sexual comment and had been segregated from other male employees

---

532, 533 (N.D. Ill. 1988), *aff'd*, 913 F.2d 456 (7th Cir. 1990); (plaintiff was described as an "attractive" female).

210 Scott v. Sears Roebuck & Co., 605 F. Supp. 1047 (N.D. Ill. 1985), *aff'd*, 798 F.2d 210 (7th Cir. 1986).

211 Scott v. Sears Roebuck & Co., 798 F.2d at 211.

212 Meritor Sav. Bank v. Vinson, 477 U.S. 57, 69 (1986); EEOC Guidelines, 29 C.F.R. § 1604.11(b) (1988).

213 Ross v. Double Diamond, Inc., 672 F. Supp. 261 (N.D. Tex. 1987).

214 *Id.* at 273.

in sales training failed to allege conduct that arose to the level of actionable harassment.[215]

Discrepancies appear even between panels of the same circuit. In *Rabidue v. Osceola Refining Co.,*[216] the Sixth Circuit, in an opinion by Judge Krupanski, regressed somewhat from the expanding notions of what constitutes a hostile environment in violation of Title VII. Plaintiff Vivienne Rabidue was discharged after working at a refinery for six years for job-related problems including her "irascible and opinionated personality and her inability to work harmoniously with co-workers and customers."[217] Characterizing the plaintiff, the only woman in a salaried management position, as a "capable, independent, ambitious, aggressive, intractable, and opinionated individual," the court affirmed the district court's conclusion that the plaintiff had failed to prove she was the victim of hostile environment sexual harassment, despite findings that the plaintiff's supervisor "was an extremely vulgar and crude individual who customarily made obscene comments about women generally, and, on occasion, directed such obscenities to the plaintiff."[218] The supervisor routinely referred to women as "cunt," "whore," "pussy," and "tits," and remarked that the plaintiff was a "bitch" and a "fat ass" who needed "a good lay."[219] In addition, other male employees displayed pictures of nude or scantily clad women in their offices and/or work areas, to which plaintiff and other women were exposed. In response to complaints about the supervisor, management unsuccessfully tried to curb his behavior. The court adopted a reasonable person standard and stated that:

> A proper assessment or evaluation of an employment environment that gives rise to a sexual harassment claim would invite consideration of such objective and subjective factors as the nature of the alleged harassment, the background and experience of the plaintiff, her coworkers, and supervisors, the totality of the physical environment of the plaintiff's work area, the lexicon of obscenity that pervaded the environment of the workplace both before and after the plaintiff's introduction into its environs, coupled with the reasonable expectation of the plaintiff upon voluntarily entering that environment. Thus, the presence of actionable sexual harassment would be different depending upon the personality of the plaintiff and the prevailing work environment and must be considered and evaluated upon an ad hoc basis.[220]

---

215 *Id.* at 271–73.

216 Rabidue v. Osceola Ref. Co., 805 F.2d 611, 620 (6th Cir. 1986), *cert. denied,* 481 U.S. 1041 (1987).

217 *Id.* at 615.

218 *Id.* The district court opinion is published at 584 F. Supp. 419 (E.D. Mich. 1984).

219 Rabidue v. Osceola Ref. Co., 805 F.2d at 624.

220 *Id.* at 620.

The court concluded that the supervisor's obscenities "although annoying, were not so startling as to have affected seriously the psyches of the plaintiff or other female employees."[221] The court also quoted the "aptly stated" message of the district court:

> Indeed, it cannot seriously be disputed that in some work environments, humor and language are rough hewn and vulgar. Sexual jokes, sexual conversations and girlie magazines may abound. Title VII was not meant to—or can—change this. It must never be forgotten that Title VII is the federal court mainstay in the struggle for equal employment opportunity for the female workers of America. But it is quite different to claim that Title VII was designed to bring about a magical transformation in the social mores of American workers.[222]

In a lengthy dissent, Judge Keith criticized the court's tolerance of the defendant's rampant antifemale conduct. He noted that in addition to the obvious abuse by plaintiff's supervisor and the daily exposure by women to a misogynous environment, the defendant excluded the plaintiff from activities necessary to perform her duties and progress in her career, such as taking clients to lunch, free lunches, free gasoline, a telephone charge card, and entertainment privileges, and her authority was repeatedly undermined. Although the plaintiff did possess undesirable personality traits, they were clearly no worse than those of her supervisor:

> In my view, Title VII's precise purpose is to prevent such behavior and attitudes from poisoning the work environment of classes clearly protected under the Act. To condone the majority's notion of the "prevailing workplace" I would also have to agree that if an employer maintains an anti-Semitic workforce and tolerates a workplace in which "kike" jokes, displays of Nazi literature and anti-Jewish conversation "may abound," a Jewish employee assumes the risk of working there, and a court must consider such a work environment as "prevailing." I cannot. As I see it, job-relatedness is the only additional factor which legitimately bears on the inquiry of plaintiff's reasonableness in finding her work environment offensive. In other words, the only additional question I would find relevant is whether the behavior complained of is required to perform the work. . . . As I believe no woman should be subjected to an environment where her sexual dignity and reasonable sensibilities are visually, verbally or physically assaulted as a matter of prevailing male prerogative, I dissent.[223]

The dissent also criticized the majority's application of the reasonable person standard, which "fails to account for the wide divergence between

---

221 *Id.* at 622.

222 *Id.* at 620.

223 *Id.* at 620–21.

most women's views of appropriate sexual conduct and those of men. The judge said he would have instead applied a reasonable victim standard "which simultaneously allows courts to consider salient sociological differences as well as shield employers from the neurotic complainant." Unless such a standard is adopted, "the defendants as well as the court are permitted to sustain ingrained notions of reasonable behavior fashioned by the offenders, in this case, men.[224]

> Nor can I agree with the majority's notion that the effect of pin-up posters and misogynous language in the workplace can have only a minimal effect on female employees and should not be deemed hostile or offensive "when considered in the context of a society that condones and publicly features and commercially exploits open displays of written and pictorial erotica at the newsstands, on prime-time television, at the cinema, and in other public places.". . . "Society" in this scenario must primarily refer to the unenlightened; I hardly believe reasonable women condone the pervasive degradation and exploitation of female sexuality perpetuated in American culture. In fact, pervasive societal approval thereof and of other stereotypes stifles female potential and instills the debased sense of self worth which accompanies stigmatization. The presence of pin-ups and misogynous language in the workplace can only evoke and confirm the debilitating norms by which women are primarily and contemptuously valued as objects of male sexual fantasy. That some men would condone and wish to perpetuate such behavior is not surprising. However, the relevant inquiry at hand is what the reasonable woman would find offensive, not society, which at one point also condoned slavery.[225]

In *Reynolds v. Atlantic City Convention Center*,[226] a female journeyman electrician alleged that she was harassed constantly with verbal abuse and obscene gestures during her last two years at the convention center. In evaluating the severity and pervasiveness of the alleged sexual harassment on a summary judgment motion, the court used the reasonable person standard in *Rabidue*. Although the court acknowledged that the workplace environment was one pervaded by a "lexicon of obscenity," it used this reality to support a finding that the alleged acts of sexual harassment were not sufficiently severe and persistent to affect seriously the psychological well being of a reasonable employee. It also gave weight to plaintiff's testimony that she could recall only two occasions when she was called an obscene name to her face, and that no participation by Convention Center management was alleged.

---

224 *Id.* at 625–26.

225 *Id.*

226 53 Fair Empl. Prac. Cas. (BNA) 1852 (D.N.J. 1990).

In *Yates v. Avco Corp.*,[227] a different Sixth Circuit panel affirmed a finding that a hostile environment violating Title VII was perpetuated by a supervisor who "bombarded" the plaintiff with unwelcome invitations for drinks and meals, discussed personal matters such as the lack of a sexual relationship with his wife, made lewd references to parts of plaintiff's body, and insisted on coming to the plaintiff's apartment on several occasions. The employer was held to be liable for the supervisor's acts when evidence showed that the company's published procedures regarding sexual harassment were not effective. The district court properly found that the company knew or should have known that the supervisor was sexually harassing the plaintiff and other females. The harassing conduct in this case was similar to, if not less severe, than that in *Rabidue*, when the palatability of the plaintiff may have been determinative. In *Yates*, the court applied the reasonable woman standard to determine whether the plaintiff had been constructively discharged, citing the dissent in *Rabidue*.[228]

In *Williams-Hill v. Donovan*,[229] the District Court of the Middle District of Florida found that although the plaintiff, an equal opportunity specialist, had been subjected to a "reprehensible working environment" in which racist, sexist, and ethnic jokes were prevalent, the court held the conflict between the parties to be a result of personality problems. The court noted that *Rabidue* presented facts "far more serious" than those in the present case.[230]

Other courts disagreed with the reasoning in *Rabidue*. For instance, in *Barbetta v. Chemlawn Services Corp.*,[231] the District Court for the Southern District of New York took issue with the conclusion in *Rabidue* that pornography in the workplace does not provide a basis for a female employee's claim of hostile work environment, and adopted the position of the dissent:

> [T]he alleged incidents of sexual harassment were often directed exclusively at female employees and they were shown to be more offensive to female

---

227 819 F.2d 630 (6th Cir. 1987).

228 *Id.* at 637 n.2. The reasonable woman standard has also been applied by the following courts:

Sixth Circuit: Vermett v. Hough, 627 F. Supp. 587 (W.D. Mich. 1986).

Ninth Circuit: Ellison v. Brady, 924 F.2d 872 (9th Cir. 1991).

Eleventh Circuit: Robinson v. Jacksonville Shipyards, Inc., 760 F. Supp. 1486 (M.D. Fla. 1991); Robinson v. Jacksonville Shipyards, Inc., 118 F.R.D. 525 (M.D. Fla. 1988).

EEOC Dec. No. 84-1 [1983] EEOC Dec. (CCH) ¶ 6839, 33 Fair Empl. Prac. Cas. (BNA) 1887 (Nov. 28, 1983).

229 43 Fair Empl. Prac. Cas. (BNA) 253 (M.D. Fla. 1987).

230 *Id.* at 257–58.

231 669 F. Supp. 569 (W.D.N.Y. 1987).

> employees than to their male counterparts. The slide show and the "Uncle Buck" calendar featured pictures of nude or partially naked women—not men. The proliferation of such material may be found to create an atmosphere in which women are viewed as men's sexual playthings rather than as their equal co-workers.[232]

The Middle District of Florida also questioned the applicability of the *Rabidue* court's reasoning in *Robinson v. Jacksonville Shipyards, Inc.,*[233] in which it said: "To the extent that *Rabidue* holds that some forms of abusive, anti-female behavior must be tolerated in the work environment because that behavior is prominent in society at large, . . . the case conflicts with established law in this Circuit."[234] In a later opinion, in *Robinson,*[235] in which the court held that pinups of nude and partially nude women, sexually demeaning remarks by male workers, and general harassment such as the posting of a "Men Only" sign created a hostile environment, the court again rejected the *Rabidue* standard:

> The "social context" argument cannot be squared with Title VII's promise to open the workplace to women. When the pre-existing state of the work environment receives weight in evaluating its hostility to women, only those women who are willing to and can accept the level of abuse inherent in a given workplace—a place that may have historically been all male or historically excluded women intentionally—will apply to and continue to work there. It is absurd to believe that Title VII opened the doors of such places in form and closed them in substance. A pre-existing atmosphere that deters women from entering or continuing in a profession or job is no less destructive to and offensive to workplace equality than a sign declaring "Men Only." . . .
>
> The Rabidue analysis violated the most basic tenet of the hostile work environment cause of action, the necessity of examining the totality of the circumstances. Excluding some forms of offensive conduct as a matter of law is not consistent with the factually oriented approach dictated by *Vinson, Henson,* and their progeny. The expert testimony in this case places the many instances of offensive behavior into a context that permits evaluation of the environment as a whole. The Court cannot ignore the expert testimony, or the Court's own perception of the work environment evaluated as a whole; it would have to do so in order to adopt the *Rabidue* conclusion that a sexually charged environment has only a "de minimus effect" on the psychological well-being of a reasonable woman who works in the skilled crafts at JSI.[236]

---

232 *Id.* at 573 (footnote omitted). See also *Id.* at 573 n.2.

233 118 F.R.D. 525 (M.D. Fla. 1988).

234 *Id.* at 530.

235 760 F. Supp. 1486 (M.D. Fla. 1991).

236 *Id.* at 1526–27.

The factual circumstances in *Pease v. Alford Photo Industries, Inc.*,[237] probably represent the most pervasive yet judicially underrated type of harassment situation. The defendant employer, the owner of a photo processing company, admitted touching a number of women employees in various ways but claimed that such touching was nonsexual and stemmed from his "warm, friendly and affectionate" nature. He insisted that he only touched women he knew well; never a "new girl," and that "what the world needs is a lot more touching and hugging."[238] What the preponderance of evidence showed, however, was that:

> Mr. Alford indulged in a sexually harassing pattern and course of conduct toward Mrs. Pease and other females who were at the time employees of Alford's. That pattern and course of conduct consisted of touching, rubbing, fondling, stroking of hair, neck, shoulders, buttocks, grabbing of the upper inner thigh and other parts of the bodies of female employees on the premises of the work place during working hours. The preponderance of the evidence is that this sexually harassing conduct by Mr. Alford was unwelcomed, unwanted, unconsented to and humiliating to Mrs. Pease and similarly situated female employees.[239]

The plaintiff alleged that the defendant touched her five different times, and seven women gave supporting testimony regarding similar experiences. Although the defendant also presented a number of witnesses to testify on his behalf, the court rejected the defense's implication that the alleged victims were "minimum wage people" whose credibility was questionable:

> The Court finds this testimony reprehensible. The Court closely observed the manner and demeanor of each woman testifying. The seven women testifying on behalf of Mrs. Pease had no personal interest in the case other than triumph of the law protecting women from unwelcomed sexual harassment in the work place. The harassment complained of was based on sex. The charged sexual harassment did have the effect of unreasonably interfering with Mrs. Pease's work performance. It did create an intimidating, hostile and offensive work environment. Subjecting female employees to such a pattern and course of sexually harassing conduct would obviously affect their psychological well-being. No reasonable person could find otherwise. The totality of circumstances demonstrated by the evidence in this record leads to only one inescapable conclusion: Mr. Alford engaged in a pattern and course of sexually harassing conduct toward his female employees that was unwelcomed by them, and his conduct violated the laws of the United States and the state of Tennessee. While this conduct may have been a source of fantasy and amusement to Mr. Alford, it was unwelcome and humiliating to his

---

[237] 667 F. Supp. 1188 (W.D. Tenn. 1987).

[238] *Id.* at 1190.

[239] *Id.* at 1191.

> female employees. Apparently, Mr. Alford thought he was at liberty to sexually harass female employees with impunity, so long as, he testified, he did not ask them to go to bed with him. The whole body of evidence in this case shows that Mr. Alford never crossed the threshold, set in his mind, of asking any female employees to go to bed or go out with him. This circumstance, the Court finds, indicates Mr. Alford acted intentionally and deliberately.[240]

The U.S. Supreme Court recently rejected the reasoning of *Rabidue* in *Harris v. Forklift Systems, Inc.*,[241] in which the Court held that psychological injury is only one factor that may be considered in determining whether alleged conduct has created a hostile or abusive environment. *See* **Ch. 2.**

More subtle forms of sexual harassment were addressed in *Robinson*,[242] in which a female welder successfully asserted sexual harassment claims stemming from the extensive, pervasive posting of pictures depicting nude women, and sexual conduct by male coworkers. The court relied primarily on the testimony of an expert on sexual stereotyping and another on sexual harassment to conclude, based on the totality of the circumstances, including the rejection by plaintiff of the conduct and the failure by management to respond to complaints, that a *reasonable woman* would have found that the working environment at the shipyard was abusive. The testimony of the experts provided a "reliable basis upon which to conclude that the cumulative, corrosive effect of this work environment over time affect[ed] the psychological well-being of a reasonable woman placed in these conditions."[243] This type of comprehensive application of the totality of circumstances test looks not to the number of times the defendant touched the plaintiff or the plaintiff complained about the behavior, but at a pattern of conduct that affects a harassment victim both directly and as it reverberates through the work environment. It is this type of sexual harassment case that courts will have to confront in increasing numbers as the subliminal nature of such conduct receives more exposure because it affects everyone in the workplace, and as victims play a larger role in shaping the legal contours of sex discrimination laws.

§ 3.24 The Reasonable Woman Standard

Robinson v. Jacksonville Shipyards, Inc. (see **§ 3.23**) was the first case to delve into the issue of whether sexually harassing conduct should be

---

240 *Id.* at 1202.

241 Harris v. Forklift Systems, Inc., 114 S. Ct. 367 (1993).

242 760 F. Supp. 1486 (M.D. Fla. 1991).

243 *Id.* at 1524–25.

measured by its impact on a reasonable woman, rather than a reasonable person or victim. The Ninth Circuit advanced the reasonable woman standard in *Ellison v. Brady,*[244] to determine whether conduct is sufficiently pervasive to alter the conditions of employment and create a hostile working environment. A female revenue agent for the IRS had alleged that a male coworker's amorous attention frightened her, and even though he was subsequently transferred, he successfully secured his return to her office and wrote her another love letter. Rejecting the standards set in *Rabidue* and *Scott*, the court held that it is the harasser's conduct that must be pervasive or severe, not the alteration in the conditions of employment:

> Although an isolated epithet by itself fails to support a cause of action for a hostile environment, Title VII's protection of employees comes into play long before the point where victims of sexual harassment require psychiatric assistance. . . . [W]e believe that in evaluating the severity and pervasiveness of sexual harassment, we should focus on the perspective of the victim. . . . If we only examined whether a reasonable person would engage in allegedly harassing conduct, we would run the risk of reinforcing the prevailing level of discrimination. Harassers could continue to harass merely because a particular discriminatory practice was common, and victims of harassment would have no remedy.
>
> We therefore prefer to analyze harassment from the victim's perspective. A complete understanding of the victim's view requires, among other things, an analysis of the different perspectives of men and women. Conduct that many men consider unobjectionable may offend many women. . . .
>
> We realize that there is a broad range of viewpoints among women as a group, but we believe many women share common concerns which men do not necessarily share. For example, because women are disproportionately victims of rape and sexual assault, women have a stronger incentive to be concerned with sexual behavior. Women who are victims of mild forms of sexual harassment may understandably worry whether a harasser's conduct is merely a prelude to violent sexual assault. Men, who are rarely victims of sexual assault, may view sexual conduct in a vacuum without a full appreciation of the social setting or the underlying threat of violence that a woman may perceive.
>
> In order to shield employers from having to accommodate the idiosyncratic concerns of the rare hyper-sensitive employee, we hold that a female plaintiff states a prima facie case of hostile environment sexual harassment when she alleges conduct that a reasonable woman would consider sufficiently severe or pervasive to alter the conditions of employment and to create an abusive working environment. . . .
>
> We adopt the perspective of a reasonable woman primarily because we believe that a sex-blind reasonable person standard tends to be male-biased and tends to systematically ignore the experiences of women. The reasonable

---

[244] 924 F.2d 872 (9th Cir. 1991).

> woman standard does not establish a higher level of protection for women than men. . . . Instead, a gender-conscious examination of sexual harassment enables women to participate in the workplace on an equal footing with men. By acknowledging and not trivializing the effects of sexual harassment on reasonable women, courts can work towards ensuring that neither men nor women will have to "run a gauntlet of sexual abuse in return for the privilege of being allowed to work and make a living." *Henson v. Dundee,* 682 F.2d 897, 902 (11th Cir. 1982).[245]

The court noted that under the standard adopted in this case, conduct may be deemed sexual harassment even when harassers do not realize that their conduct creates a hostile working environment. Thus, well-intentioned compliments could form the basis of a sex discrimination action if a reasonable victim of the same sex as the plaintiff would consider the comments sufficiently severe or pervasive to alter a condition of employment and create an abusive working environment.

In *Andrews v. City of Philadelphia,*[246] in which the plaintiff police officers alleged a hostile work environment created by abusive language, sexually explicit pictures at the workplace, the destruction of the plaintiffs' private property and work product, physical injury, and anonymous telephone calls at home, the court of appeals reversed the trial court's ruling against the plaintiffs and held that to prove a hostile environment, a plaintiff must demonstrate that "the discrimination would detrimentally affect a reasonable person of the same sex in that position . . . . The objective standard protects the employer from the 'hypersensitive' employee, but still serves the goal of equal opportunity by removing the walls of discrimination that deprive women of self-respecting employment."[247] The court noted that men and women have different perspectives on obscene language and pornography: "Although men may find these actions harmless and innocent, it is highly possible that women may feel otherwise."[248]

In *Austin v. State of Hawaii,*[249] the district court cited *Ellison* with approval in ruling in favor of the plaintiff English professor in an action alleging sexual harassment by the male chair of the English department:

> He referred to her in ways which reasonable women consider to be typical of males who consider women inferior. . . . The perspective of a reasonable woman is justified because "a sex-blind reasonable person standard tends to

245 *Id.* at 878–79 (footnotes omitted). *See also* Stingley v. State of Ariz., 796 F. Supp. 424 (D. Ariz. 1992) (court applied a reasonable person of the same gender, race, or color standard).

246 895 F.2d 1469 (3d Cir. 1990).

247 *Id.* at 1482–83.

248 *Id.* at 1486.

249 759 F. Supp. 612 (D. Hawaii 1991).

> be male-biased and tends to systematically ignore the experiences of women.". . .Would he have said the same things in the same way about a man?[250]

In *Jenson v. Eveleth Taconite Co.*[251] the court certified a class of women employees alleging sex discrimination including sexual harassment, noting that the common question of law was not how an individual class member reacted, but whether a reasonable woman would find the work environment hostile.[252]

Several state courts have also applied the reasonable woman standard.[253] In *Lehmann v. Toys 'R' Us, Inc.*,[254] the New Jersey Supreme Court carefully considered the basis for such a test:

> In evaluating whether the harassment alleged was sufficiently severe or pervasive to alter the conditions of employment and to create a hostile or intimidating work environment for a female plaintiff, the finder of fact shall consider the question from the perspective of a reasonable woman. If the plaintiff is male, the perspective used shall be that of a reasonable man. We choose an objective and gender-specific perspective for a number of reasons.
>
> We choose an objective standard, first, because . . . the LAD is not primarily a tort scheme but rather is aimed at eradicating discriminatory conduct. An objective reasonableness standard better focuses the court's attention on the nature and legality of the conduct rather than on the reaction of the individual plaintiff, which is more relevant to damages.
>
> Secondly, an objective standard provides flexibility. . . . [M]uch conduct that would have been considered acceptable twenty or thirty years ago would be considered sexual harassment today. As community standards evolve, the standard of what a reasonable woman would consider harassment will also evolve.
>
> However, incorporating community standards through the use of a reasonableness standard brings dangers against which courts must guard. We emphasize that the LAD is *remedial* legislation. Its very purpose is to change existing standards of conduct. Thus, the reasonableness requirement must not be used to hold that the prevailing level of discrimination is "per se" reasonable, or that a reasonable woman would expect sexual harassment

---

250 *Id.* at 628. *See also* Smolsky v. Consolidated Rail Corp., 780 F. Supp. 283 (E.D. Pa. 1991), *reh'g denied,* 785 F. Supp. 71 (E.D. Pa 1992).

251 139 F.R.D. 657 (D. Minn. 1991).

252 *Id.* at 665.

253 Lehmann v. Toys 'R' Us, Inc., 133 N.J. 587, 626 A.2d 445, 455 (N.J. 1993) (plaintiff in a hostile work environment sexual harassment case established the requisite harm if she showed that her working conditions were affected by the harassment to the point at which a reasonable woman would consider the working environment hostile).

254 133 N.J. 587, 626 A.2d 445 (N.J. 1993).

on entering a historically male-dominated workplace. The LAD is designed to remediate conditions of hostility and discrimination, not to preserve and immunize pre-existing hostile work environments.

Thirdly, we choose an objective rather than a subjective viewpoint because the purpose of the LAD is to elminate real discrimination and harassment. . . . A hypersensitive employee might have an idiosyncratic response to conduct that is not, objectively viewed, harassing. Allegations of nonharassing conduct do not state a claim, even if the idiosyncratic plaintiff perceives her workplace to be hostile, because the complained-of conduct, objectively viewed, is not harassment, and the workplace, objectively viewed, is not hostile.

Conversely, an extraordinarily tough and resilient plaintiff might face harassing conduct that was, objectively viewed, sufficiently severe or pervasive to make the working environment hostile or intimidating, but because of her toughness, she might not personally find the workplace hostile or intimidating. Under our objective standard, such a plaintiff would state a claim even if she personally did not experience the workplace as hostile or intimidating. Sexual harassment is illegal even if the victim is strong enough not to be injured. Because such tough employees are perhaps the most likely to be strong enough to challenge harassers, the remedial purposes of the LAD are furthered by permitting claims of emotionally resilient plaintiffs without regard to subjective injury.

* * *

We turn now to our reasons for choosing a gender-specific standard. We believe that in order to fairly evaluate claims of sexual harassment, courts and finders of fact must recognize and respect the differences between male and female perspectives on sexual harassment.

* * *

Two societal realities may underlie the difference in male and female perspectives. First, women live in a world in which the possibility of sexual violence is ever-present. Given that background, women may find sexual conduct in an inappropriate setting threatening. . . .

Second, in many areas of the workforce, women still represent a minority and are relatively recent entrants into the field. Because of their predominantly junior and minority status, for some women it is more difficult than it is for men to win credibility and respect from employers, coworkers, and clients or customers. That can make women's position in the workplace marginal or precarious from the start. Sexual harassment operates to further discredit the female employee by treating her as a sexual object rather than as a credible coworker. That can both undermine the woman's self-confidence and interfere with her ability to be perceived by others as a capable worker with the potential to advance and succeed. . . .

> Because of women's different status in the workplace, conduct that may be "just a joke" for men may have far more serious implications for women.[255]

In *Radtke v. Everett,*[256] however, in which the plaintiff alleged that her employer forcibly held her down, caressed and attempted to kiss her, the U.S. Supreme Court addressed the elements of a prima facie case of a hostile work environment under the Michigan Civil Rights Act and held that the reasonable woman standard violates the legislative intent of the Act:

> Plaintiff. . . maintains that the reasonableness standard should be gender-conscious. Hence, plaintiff urges the application of a "reasonable woman" standard when the plaintiff is female or a "reasonable man" standard when the plaintiff is a male. The Court of Appeals agreed. . . .
>
> Other courts concur. . . . Moreover, some commentators vigorously criticize the reasonable person standard as both male-biased and a prop to support male domination of society.
>
> However, with all respect, we conclude that a gender-conscious standard must be rejected. As noted, the language and purpose of the Michigan Civil Rights Act require that an objective standard be utilized. At the time of the act's adoption, standards of conduct were only defined by the reasonable person. Indeed, Anglo-American jurisprudence had utilized the reasonable person standard and its predecessor, the reasonable man standard, for well over a century before the adoption of the act. . . . If the Legislature intended a departure from that standard, it certainly would have explicitly mandated that alteration. . . .
>
> Moreover, the reasonable person standard should be utilized because it is sufficiently flexible to incorporate gender differences. . . .
>
> * * *
>
> Furthermore, the reasonable person standard examines the totality of the circumstances to ensure a fair result. . . . Hence, the reasonable person standard is sufficiently flexible to incorporate gender as one factor, without destroying the vital stability provided by uniform standards of conduct.
>
> The gender-conscious standard as formulated by plaintiff and the Court of Appeals, on the other hand, places undue emphasis on gender and the particular plaintiff while it inappropriately deemphasizes society's need for uniform standards of conduct. Hence, a gender-conscious standard eliminates community standards and replaces them with standards formulated by a subset of the community. An acceptance of a gender-conscious standard and the logic undergirding it would inexorably lead to the fragmentation of legal standards to the detriment of society. After all, the diversity that is

---

[255] *Id.* at 457–59.

[256] 442 Mich 368, 501 N.W.2d 155 (Mich. 1993).

> Michigan—a multitude of ethnic groups, national origins, religions, races, cultures, as well as divergencies in wealth and education—would demand as many standards. Yet one standard of conduct has always regulated this diverse population, and to hold otherwise would weave great discord and unnecessary confusion into the law.
>
> Furthermore, a gender-conscious standard is clearly contrary to the gender-neutral principles underpinning the Michigan Civil Rights Act. Although well intended, a gender-conscious standard could reintrench the very sexist attitudes it is attempting to counter. The belief that women are entitled to a separate legal standard merely reinforces, and perhaps originates from, the stereotypic notion that first justified subordinating women in the workplace. Courts utilizing the reasonable woman standard pour into the standard stereotypic assumptions of women which infer women are sensitive, fragile, and in need of a more protective standard. Such paternalism degrades women and is repugnant to the very ideals of equality that the act is intended to protect. . . .[257]

§ 3.25 Quid Pro Quo and Third-Party Employees

Otherwise qualified employees who lose employment opportunities because job benefits went to those who submitted to sexual harassment may have discrimination claims under Title VII.[258] Both men and women may be entitled to bring such a claim. In *Broderick v. Ruder*,[259] a female attorney who refused to participate in workplace sexual conduct successfully challenged a work environment in which compliance with sexual advances brought career advancement and other employment benefits to other employees.

A qualified male may lose a potential job benefit on the basis of sex, or a qualified woman who was not approached sexually by a supervisor may lose a job benefit to a less qualified woman who submitted unwillingly to sexual advances.[260] Although romantic relationships between a supervisor and an employee sometimes result in the woman subordinate's enjoying certain unique job benefits, some courts have held that such preferential treatment is not gender-based discrimination.[261] When such romantic

---

[257] *Id.* at 163–67 (footnote omitted).

[258] EEOC Guidelines, 29 C.F.R. § 1604.11(g) (1988).

[259] 685 F. Supp. 1269, 1278 (D.D.C. 1988).

[260] EEOC Guidelines, 29 C.F.R. § 1604.11(g) (1988).

[261] Second Circuit: De Cintio v. Westchester County Medical Ctr., 807 F.2d 304 (2d Cir. 1986), *cert. denied,* 484 U.S. 825 (1987) (promotion criteria that could be met only by a woman with whom employer was having a romantic relationship did not violate Title VII with respect to male applicants for the promotion when no other applicant, male or female, would have been considered for the position, and there was no claim of unwelcome sexual conduct by the successful applicant).

involvement and its job-related implications are a matter of common knowledge, however, the work atmosphere may be tainted in violation of Title VII, and thus a hostile environment claim may be appropriate.[262] Employers might be wise to discourage intimate relationships in the workplace, particularly between supervisors and subordinates.

§ 3.26 Hostile Environment and Third-Party Employees

A hostile work environment is most likely experienced by other employees besides the complainant. "Even a woman who was never herself the object of harassment might have a Title VII claim if she were forced to work in an atmosphere where such harassment was pervasive."[263] This approach is supported by racial discrimination precedent.[264] As noted in **§ 3.2**, this type of harassment includes situations in which male supervisors have romantic relationships with female subordinates and afford them job benefits to the detriment of other employees. In *Broderick*[265] an attorney for the Securities and Exchange Commission was awarded

---

Third Circuit: Polk v. Pollard, 52 Fair Emp. Prac. Cas. (BNA) 538 (3d Cir.1989). A female former employee was not subjected to sexual harassment when the only connection sex had in her discharge was the alleged sexual relationship between the person who fired her and his sexual partner, who allegedly asked him to fire plaintiff. "Another employee of the male gender could have been discharged in the same situation." *Id.* at 540. Miller v. Aluminum Co. of Am., 679 F. Supp. 495, 501 (W.D. Pa. 1988), *aff'd,* 856 F.2d 184 (3d Cir. 1988) ("Male employees in Ms. Miller's workplace shared with her the same disadvantage relative to Ms. Hollihan: none could claim the special place in [the defendant's] heart that Ms. Hollihan occupied. Favoritism and unfair treatment, unless based on a prohibited classification, do not violate Title VII"); Toscano v. Nimmo, 570 F. Supp. 1197 (D. Del. 1983).

Ninth Circuit: *Cf.* Priest v. Rotary, 634 F. Supp. 571, 581–82 (N.D. Cal. 1986) (plaintiff waitress established violation of Title VII when she showed that defendant's consensual sexual partner was given preferential treatment in job assignments and was allowed to continue working despite continual substandard work performance, rudeness to customers, and violation of lounge policy).

District of Columbia Circuit: *Cf.* King v. Palmer, 778 F.2d 878, 880 (D.C. Cir. 1985) (allegations that sexual relationship between supervisor and coworker subjected plaintiff to discriminatory work environment and denied her promotion stated claim for sex discrimination).

262 Broderick v. Ruder, 685 F. Supp. 1269, 1278 (D.D.C. 1988).

263 *See* Vinson v. Taylor, 23 Fair Empl. Prac. Cas. (BNA) 37, 38 (D.D.C. 1980), *rev'd,* 753 F.2d 141 (D.C. Cir. 1985), *aff'd in part, rev'd in part sub nom.* Meritor Sav. Bank v. Vinson, 477 U.S. 57 (1986). *See also* Hicks v. Gates Rubber Co., 833 F.2d 1406, 1416 (10th Cir. 1987), *aff'g district court's finding of no hostile environment,* 928 F.2d 966 (1991).

264 Rogers v. EEOC, 454 F.2d 234 (5th Cir. 1971), *cert. denied,* 406 U.S. 957 (1972).

265 Broderick v. Ruder, 685 F. Supp. 1269, 1274 (D.D.C. 1988).

$120,000 in back pay and interest and previously denied promotions for proving that her office supervisors created a hostile work environment by engaging in sexually offensive conduct. Such conduct included rewarding employees who complied with sexual advances with promotions and other employment benefits to the detriment of Broderick, who had refused such requests.[266] Despite the fact that few of the alleged incidents of harassment had been directed at Broderick herself, the environment "poisoned any possibility of plaintiff's having the proper professional respect for her supervisors and, without any question, affected her motivation and her performance of her job responsibilities."[267] Although Broderick had complained to higher management, no one was ever disciplined for conduct that was common knowledge, and management made no serious effort to enforce guidelines prohibiting sex discrimination.[268]

Broderick clearly established a violation of Title VII through her testimony and that of coworkers. Not only were her working conditions "poisoned" to the extent that she suffered psychologically, but she was denied tangible work benefits as a result of her supervisors' flagrant sexual conduct. The hybrid nature of Catherine Broderick's hostile environment claim, that included allegations that employment benefits were bestowed upon compliant employees to Broderick's detriment, gave the case the *quid pro quo* element that courts have embraced. However, it is unclear how far the courts will take Title VII.

Preferential treatment undermines employees' motivation and work performance and deprives them of job opportunities.[269] Some courts have argued that because both women and men are in the same position with respect to lost employment opportunities, such conduct cannot form the basis of a sex discrimination charge.[270] While it is true that both women and men may suffer the loss of similar benefits, the bases for their respective charges differ. Because the qualified man is an unlikely candidate for an office romance with a presumably heterosexual male supervisor, he relinquishes a job opportunity to the less qualified but involved woman on the basis of his sex, and thus he may bring an employment discrimination action. The qualified woman who loses job benefits to a less qualified but involved woman or who is exposed to male supervisors having affairs with subordinates and showering them with attention is undermined. She is made to feel that, among other things, merit and hard work by women

---

266 *Id.;* Burleigh & Goldberg, *Breaking the Silence: Sexual Harassment in Law Firms,* 75 A.B.A.J. 44, 51 (Aug., 1989).

267 Broderick v. Ruder, 685 F. Supp. 1269, 1273 (D.D.C. 1988).

268 *Id.* at 1276.

269 *Id.* at 1278.

270 Miller v. Aluminum Co. of Am., 679 F. Supp. 495, 502 (W.D. Pa.), *aff'd,* 856 F.2d 184 (3d Cir. 1988).

are irrelevant, women get ahead by sleeping with their superiors, sexual objectification is a byproduct of employment, and women have no control over their professional destinies short of submitting to sexual advances. This sense of loss of control may be enhanced when the plaintiff is also subjected to sexual advances[271] or fears physical violence. Clearly, these elements comprise a hostile work environment in violation of Title VII.

An employee who protests the sexual harassment of other employees may bring a retaliation action if adverse personnel actions are taken in response to such complaints.[272] For such a claim to survive judicial scrutiny, the plaintiff must give the employer a fair opportunity to remedy the situation[273] (see **§ 3.27**).

§ 3.27 Constructive Discharge

An employee is constructively discharged when the employer deliberately makes that employee's working conditions so onerous that a reasonable person would find them intolerable.[274] In *EEOC v. Gurnee Inn*

---

[271] *See, e.g.,* Broderick v. Ruder, 685 F. Supp. 1269 (D.D.C. 1988) (hostile environment was found when plaintiff was forced to work in atmosphere in which she and other female employees were harassed by supervisors who bestowed preferential treatment upon those who submitted to sexual advances).

[272] Jones v. Lyng, 669 F. Supp. 1108 (D.D.C. 1986) (male employee charged retaliation for opposing and disclosing sexual harassment of female employees). *Cf.* Jones v. Flagship Int'l, 793 F.2d 714 (5th Cir. 1986), *cert. denied,* 479 U.S. 1065 (1987) (district court properly determined that a former equal employment opportunity manager who encouraged other employees to file discrimination charges and who sought to maintain a class action clearly engaged in protected activity when she filed a discrimination charge with the EEOC; her subsequent suspension and termination were adverse employment actions, but the causal link between the two was not established).

[273] Dornhecker v. Malibu Grand Prix Corp., 828 F.2d 307 (5th Cir. 1987).

[274] Second Circuit: Watts v. New York City Police Dep't, 724 F. Supp. 99 (S.D.N.Y. 1989) Plaintiff failed to state a claim for constructive discharge when her allegations did not demonstrate that the NYPD intended that her working environment be so intolerable that it sought to force her to resign. While plaintiff adequately pleaded other facts that showed that in certain respects defendant failed to respond to her complaints of abuse, and if proven, "could establish that NYPD acted negligently and unreasonably in fulfilling its obligations to dispel hostility in the workplace, and might even allow a factfinder to conclude that a person subjected to the harassment Watts faced would reasonably feel compelled to resign." *Id.* at 109. However, the allegations did not suffice to raise an inference that the defendant acted deliberately or refrained from acting to make plaintiff's working environment so intolerable as to force her resignation or that defendant otherwise sought to induce her to leave.

Barbetta v. Chemlawn Servs. Corp., 669 F. Supp. 569 (W.D.N.Y. 1987) (evidence of pornography in the workplace, vulgar comments by employees and supervisors,

Corp.,[275] for example, the decision of a female employee to quit her job amounted to a constructive discharge when in addition to rebuffing a supervisor's advances, she was forced to observe sexual conduct in her workplace and watch employees who tolerated it receive better treatment

---

requirement that female employees wear skirts or dresses on certain occasions because a visiting supervisor liked to look at legs, and unwanted physical contact was sufficient to defeat a motion for summary judgment under the standard for constructive discharge).

Fourth Circuit: Llewellyn v. Celanese Corp., 693 F. Supp. 369, 381 (W.D.N.C. 1988) ("No one should be required in order to keep a job to endure the sexual harassment and threats of violence she experienced").

Fifth Circuit: Dornhecker v. Malibu Grand Prix Corp., 828 F.2d 307, 310 (5th Cir. 1987); Benton v. Kroger Co., 640 F. Supp. 1317, 1322 (S.D. Tex. 1986).

Sixth Circuit: Held v. Gulf Oil Co., 684 F.2d 427, 432 (6th Cir. 1982); Pease v. Alford Photo Indus., 667 F. Supp. 1188 (W.D. Tenn. 1987) (four or five touching incidents supported by testimony of other female employees who had similar experiences); Vermett v. Hough, 627 F. Supp. 587 (W.D. Mich. 1986); Coley v. Consolidated Rail Corp., 561 F. Supp. 645, 647 (E.D. Mich. 1982) (plaintiff was constructively discharged when she refused to return to work because of her supervisor's constant sexually explicit and demeaning remarks, including "references to the size of her 'boobs,' keeping track of her menstrual periods on his office calendar and making remarks about her moods in relation thereto, and repeated inquiries as to when she was going to do something nice for him").

Seventh Circuit: Busch v. Pizza Hut, 52 Fair Emp. Prac. Cas. (BNA) 407 (N.D. Ill. 1989) The defendant was not entitled to summary judgment in an action alleging that plaintiff was constructively discharged because of sexual harassment despite its contention that plaintiff did not allege any harassment after she was transferred to another store, and that thus her resignation three months later could not have stemmed from harassment when plaintiff alleged in the complaint and in her affidavit that the transfer was a retaliatory transfer and the affidavit stated that the harassment continued at the new store.

EEOC v. Gurnee Inn Corp., 48 Fair Empl. Prac. Cas. (BNA) 871 (N.D. Ill. 1988), *aff'd*, 914 F.2d 815 (7th Cir. 1990).

Eighth Circuit: Hall v. Gus Constr. Co., 842 F.2d 1010 (8th Cir. 1988) (female traffic controllers were constructively discharged when coworkers referred to them as "fucking flag girls" and "herpes," wrote "cavern cunt" and "blond bitch" in the dust on their cars, repeatedly asked them if they "wanted to fuck" and to engage in oral sex, touched their thighs and breasts, picked them up so others could touch them, urinated in their gas tanks and water bottles, exposed themselves, flashed obscene pictures, and observed the women urinating in a ditch through surveying equipment; the women's supervisor knew about the conduct but did nothing).

Morris v. American Nat'l Can Corp., 730 F. Supp. 1489 (E.D. Mo. 1989), *modified on other grounds*, 941 F.2d 710 (8th Cir. 1991) (plaintiff was constructively discharged).

Tenth Circuit: Downum v. City of Wichita, 675 F. Supp. 1566, 1569 (D. Kan. 1986) (plaintiff dispatcher was not constructively discharged when it was undisputed that she did not quit but was terminated for violation of sick leave policy and defendants did nothing that would have compelled a reasonable person to resign).

by the supervisor. She was unable to help her subordinates avoid the supervisor's advances because management refused to take action.

Sexual harassment may force a person to quit her job, giving rise to a separate constructive discharge claim in addition to claims of sexual harassment,[276] although someone who leaves a position need not prove constructive discharge to obtain relief for sexual harassment under Title VII.[277] Intent may be inferred from circumstantial evidence, including a failure to act in the face of known intolerable conditions.[278] Either type of harassment, *quid pro quo*[278] or hostile environment,[280] may form the basis for a constructive discharge claim. Constructive discharge will not be established, however, merely by demonstrating that sexual harassment occurred.[281] Nor will constructive discharge be established if the incidents

---

Eleventh Circuit: Ross v. Twenty-Four Collection, Inc., 691 F. Supp. 1547, 1551 (S.D. Fla. 1988), *aff'd,* 875 F.2d 873 (11th Cir. 1989) (plaintiff forced to endure repeated verbal and physical advances and threats that led to a medical leave and then resignation and, upon her return, faced the same conduct was constructively discharged).

Allegations that the employer acted deliberately to force the plaintiff to quit her job cannot be conclusory. Hopkins v. Shoe Show of Va., Inc., 678 F. Supp. 1241 (S.D.W. Va. 1988) (such conclusory allegations did not survive a motion for summary judgment on the issue of constructive discharge).

[275] 48 Fair Empl. Prac. Cas. (BNA) 871 (N.D. Ill. 1988).

[276] Llewellyn v. Celanese Corp., 693 F. Supp. 369, 381 (W.D.N.C. 1988).

[277] Huddleston v. Roger Dean Chevrolet, Inc., 845 F.2d 900 (11th Cir. 1988) (plaintiff who made out a prima facie case of sexual harassment was entitled to relief despite the fact that she ultimately quit for other reasons).

[278] Llewellyn v. Celanese Corp., 693 F. Supp. 369, 381 (W.D.N.C. 1988), *quoting* Bristow v. Daily Press, 770 F.2d 1251, 1255 (4th Cir. 1985), *cert. denied,* 475 U.S. 1082 (1986), *quoting* Holsey v. Armour & Co., 743 F.2d 199, 209 (4th Cir. 1984), *cert. denied,* 470 U.S. 1028 (1985). *See also* Coley v. Consolidated Rail Corp., 561 F. Supp. 645, 651 (E.D. Mich. 1982).

[279] Pease v. Alford Photo Indus., 667 F. Supp. 1188 (W.D. Tenn. 1987) (plaintiff fired after defendant employer's wife warned her against making accusations of sexual harassment against her husband); Coley v. Consolidated Rail Corp., 561 F. Supp. 645 (E.D. Mich. 1982).

[280] *See also* Yates v. Avco Corp., 819 F.2d 630 (6th Cir. 1987); Pease v. Alford Photo Indus., 667 F. Supp. 1188 (W.D. Tenn. 1987); Collins v. City of San Diego, 841 F.2d 337 (9th Cir. 1988); Hall v. Gus Constr. Co., 842 F.2d 1010 (8th Cir. 1988).

[281] Yates v. Avco Corp., 819 F.2d 630, 637 (6th Cir. 1987) (plaintiff secretary who resigned when she returned to work after sick leave to find alleged harasser at an adjacent desk was not constructively discharged; employer did not intend for parties to see each other and plaintiff refused to listen when her employer called to explain the mix-up); Pease v. Alford Photo Indus., 667 F. Supp. 1188, 1202–1203 (W.D. Tenn. 1987) (when sexual harassment "was an everyday fact" at the workplace, *Id.* at 1203, aggravating factors existed that supported a finding of constructive discharge); Coley v. Consolidated Rail Corp., 561 F. Supp. 645 (E.D. Mich. 1982); Robson v. Eva's Market, 538 F. Supp. 857, 859 (N.D. Ohio 1982).

of harassment are too remote in time from the resignation.[282] Constructive discharge also will not be found if resignation occurred for reasons other than alleged sexual harassment,[283] or if the employer did not receive actual or constructive notice of the alleged harassment[284] or was not given sufficient time to remedy the situation.[285] The Sixth Circuit has required some inquiry into the employer's intent and the reasonably forseeable impact of its conduct on the employee.[286] A reasonable woman standard should be applied to determine whether the harassed employee quit because of sexual harassment.[287] In *Radtke*[288] the Michigan Court of Appeals held that the constructive discharge claim of a female veterinary technician who was caressed and kissed by her supervisor during a break and who subsequently ended her employment and sought counseling should have survived summary judgment. A single incident of sexual harassment could be sufficiently severe under some circumstances to support a finding that a reasonable woman's employment was substantially affected or that a hostile environment was created. In some cases, the mere presence of a

---

282 Harmon v. Higgins, 188 W.Va. 709, 426 S.E.2d 344 (W.Va. Sup. Ct. App. 1992). In a sexual harassment action by a beauty college instructor against the owner of the college, the instructor's claim of constructive discharge for sexual harassment was barred by the two-year statute of limitations for personal injuries when there was no connection between job reassignment that had prompted her quitting, which occurred during the limitations period, and the alleged sexual harassment, which had ended more than two years before plaintiff filed suit.

283 Huddleston v. Roger Dean Chevrolet, Inc., 845 F.2d 900 (11th Cir. 1988) (plaintiff's resignation notice stated that she feared for her own and her daughter's safety following a threatening incident involving the purchase of an ice cream truck for her daughter and did not mention the sexual harassment; plaintiff's "principal antagonists" had left the dealership several months before her resignation); Henson v. City of Dundee, 682 F.2d 897 (11th Cir. 1982); EEOC Dec. No. 84-1 [1983] EEOC Dec. (CCH) ¶ 6839, 33 Fair Empl. Prac. Cas. (BNA) 1887 (1983).

284 Hall v. Gus Constr. Co., 842 F.2d 1010 (8th Cir. 1988).

285 *Cf.* Dornhecker v. Malibu Grand Prix Corp., 828 F.2d 307, 309 (5th Cir. 1987) (employer investigated and responded to claims of sexual harassment by coworker within 12 hours).

286 *See also* Vermett v. Hough, 627 F. Supp. 587 (W.D. Mich. 1986) ("The employer need not intend to induce the employee to resign. Rather, the employer must intend that the working conditions imposed upon the employee be such that a reasonable person would terminate her employment"); Yates v. Avco Corp., 819 F.2d 630, 637 (6th Cir. 1987).

Fourth Circuit: Llewellyn v. Celanese Corp., 693 F. Supp. 369, 381 (W.D.N.C. 1988) (failure of supervisors to take adequate remedial action "evidences an intent to force [the plaintiff] to quit").

287 Yates v. Avco Corp., 819 F.2d 630, 637, 637 n.2 (6th Cir. 1987); Barbetta v. Chemlawn Servs. Corp., 669 F. Supp. 569, 572 (W.D.N.Y. 1987) (evidence of a hostile working environment that a reasonable woman in plaintiff's position eventually would have found intolerable sufficient to defeat motion for summary judgment).

288 56 Fair Empl. Prac. Cas. (BNA) 923 (Mich. Ct. App. 1991).

harasser may create a hostile environment. The proper perspective to view the offensive conduct from was that of a reasonable woman:

> We believe that a standard which views harassing conduct from the "reasonable person" perspective has the tendency to be male-biased and runs the risk of reinforcing the prevailing level of discrimination which the state Civil Rights Act and Title VII were designed to eliminate. In such a case, harassers could continue to discriminate merely because such harassment was the norm at the workplace. . . . We believe that the adoption of the reasonable person standard, coupled with the consideration of the level of "obscenity" that pervaded the workplace before and after plaintiff's arrival, strips the provisions of the state Civil Rights Act of their effect. In essence, the principles in *Rabidue* prevent the state Civil Rights Act from achieving its purpose of eliminating sexual harassment from the workplace and ensuring employees the right to work in an environment free from discriminatory intimidation, ridicule, and insult.
>
> Accordingly, we adopt the "reasonable woman" perspective. This standard, which ensures a gender-conscious review of sexual harassment, will help enable women to participate in the work force on an equal footing with men, and prevent the trivializing of the effects of sexual harassment that has previously occurred under the gender-neutral "reasonable person" standard. . . .
>
> By adopting a gender-conscious standard that views the harassment from the victim's perspective, it is important to analyze and understand the different perspectives of men and women. . . . For example, because of their historical vulnerability in the work force, woman are more likely to regard a verbal or physical sexual encounter as a coercive and degrading reminder that the woman involved is viewed more as an object of sexual desire than as a credible coworker deserving of respect. Such treatment can prevent women from feeling, and others from perceiving them, as equal in the workplace.[289]

Most courts have applied a reasonable person standard,[290] and the reasonable person "in the plaintiff's position" test may imply a reasonable woman standard.

Coworkers and nonemployees as well as supervisors may create conditions giving rise to a constructive discharge claim (see **§ 3.27**). The failure by supervisors to take immediate remedial action after notice of harassment by coworkers may constitute constructive discharge.[291]

---

289 *Id.* at 926–27.

290 *See, e.g.*, Lipsett v. Rive-Mora, 864 F.2d 881 (1st Cir. 1988); Dornhecker v. Malibu Grand Prix Corp., 828 F.2d 307 (5th Cir. 1987); Ross v. Double Diamond, Inc., 672 F. Supp. 261, 278 (N.D. Tex. 1987).

291 *Cf.* Dornhecker v. Malibu Grand Prix Corp., 828 F.2d 307, 309 (5th Cir. 1987) (employer's response to claims of sexual harassment by coworker came in less than 12 hours).

An employee need not quit her job to raise a claim of constructive discharge.[292] For example, forced medical leave without pay may be deemed a constructive discharge for purposes of back pay liability.[293] Nor does an employee have to resign immediately after the harassing conduct has occurred to plead constructive discharge.[294]

Constructive discharge has been reviewed as both a question of fact under the clearly erroneous standard[295] and as a question of law under the de novo standard.[296]

§ 3.28 Retaliation

Title VII prohibits discrimination against an employee who has either opposed an employment practice made unlawful under Title VII, made a charge, or participated in any manner in an investigation, procedure, or hearing under Title VII.[297] To determine whether an action is protected by Title VII, the court must consider whether the employee's conduct was reasonable in light of the circumstances.[298] The trial court also should balance the employer's right to run a business with the employees' right to express their grievances.[299]

---

292 Llewellyn v. Celanese Corp., 693 F. Supp. 369, 381 (W.D.N.C. 1988) (plaintiff truck driver who was the victim of unwanted sexual propositions, sexual touching, exposure to nude male coworkers, and threats of violence by coworkers and at least one customer, had her truck sabotaged, and had a snake placed in her cab was constructively discharged for back pay liability when her working conditions forced her to take a medical leave without pay). *Cf.* Downum v. City of Wichita, 675 F. Supp. 1566, 1569 (D. Kan. 1986) (plaintiff dispatcher was not constructively discharged when it was undisputed that she did not quit but was terminated for violation of sick leave policy and defendants did nothing that would have compelled a reasonable person in plaintiff's position to resign). *Cf.* Ross v. Double Diamond, Inc., 672 F. Supp. 261 (N.D. Tex. 1987) (plaintiffs did not make out a claim for constructive discharge when they failed to prove that the plaintiffs actually resigned).

293 Llewellyn v. Celanese Corp., 693 F. Supp. 369, 381 (W.D.N.C. 1988).

294 Barbetta v. Chemlawn Servs. Corp., 669 F. Supp. 569 (W.D.N.Y. 1987); Smith v. Bath Iron Works Corp, 943 F.2d 164 (1st Cir. 1991) (a female employee who did not resign until six months after the last act of harassment was not constructively discharged).

295 Huddleston v. Roger Dean Chevrolet, Inc., 845 F.2d 900 (11th Cir. 1988); Ross v. Twenty-Four Collection, Inc., 681 F. Supp. 1547, 1551 (S.D. Fla. 1988).

296 Yates v. Avco Corp., 819 F.2d 630 (6th Cir. 1987).

297 Title VII, 42 U.S.C. § 2000e-3(a). Sections 704 through 717 apply to federal employees (42 U.S.C. § 2000e-16). Chandler v. Roudebush, 425 U.S. 840 (1976).

298 Jones v. Flagship Int'l, 793 F.2d 714, 720 n.5 (5th Cir. 1986), *cert. denied,* 479 U.S. 1065 (1987); Ross v. Double Diamond, Inc., 672 F. Supp. 261 (N.D. Tex. 1987).

299 Jones v. Flagship Int'l, 793 F.2d 714 (5th Cir. 1986), *cert. denied,* 479 U.S. 1065 (1987).

Sexual harassment complaints often include claims of retaliation, and such claims may succeed despite a finding that no violation of Title VII has occurred.[300] A prima facie case of retaliation is established by proof that (1) the plaintiff engaged in statutorily protected opposition or participation; (2) an adverse employment action occurred; and (3) there was causal link between the opposition or participation and the adverse employment action.[301]

The opposition clause of Title VII protects a variety of forms of expression. In addition to the filing of charges,[302] protected activities include resisting advances,[303] registering internal complaints regarding sexual

---

300 First Circuit: Morley v. New England Tel. Co., 47 Fair Empl. Prac. Cas. (BNA) 917, 924 (D. Mass. 1987) (two statements with sexual overtones did not constitute sexual harassment, but defendant did retaliate against plaintiff for filing EEOC charge).

Third Circuit: Porta v. Rollins Envtl. Servs., Inc., 654 F. Supp. 1275, 1284 (D.N.J. 1987) *aff'd,* 845 F.2d 1014 (3d Cir. 1988) (plaintiff's refusal to work a certain shift because alleged harasser would be there "may not be found to lack statutory protection as a matter of law").

Sixth Circuit: Boyd v. James S. Hayes Living Health Care Agency, 671 F. Supp. 1155, 1168 (W.D. Tenn. 1987).

Seventh Circuit: Goluszek v. Smith, 697 F. Supp. 1452 (N.D. Ill. 1988).

The activity may be protected even if the original discrimination claim may have been false and malicious. Proulx v. Citibank NA, 659 F. Supp. 972 (S.D.N.Y. 1987). Some courts have held that resisting advances is not protected unless the advances are found to be an unlawful employment practice under Title VII. Jordan v. Clark, 847 F.2d 1368 (9th Cir. 1988), *cert. denied,* 488 U.S. 1006 (1989); Boyd v. James S. Hayes Living Health Care Agency, 671 F. Supp. 1155 (W.D. Tenn. 1987).

301 Third Circuit: Miller v. Aluminum Co. of Am., 679 F. Supp. 495 (W.D. Pa. 1988), *aff'd,* 856 F.2d 184 (3d Cir.); Ferguson v. E.I. du Pont de Nemours & Co., 560 F. Supp. 1172 (D. Del. 1983).

Fourth Circuit: Strickland v. Sears Roebuck & Co., 46 Fair Empl. Prac. Cas. (BNA) 1024 (E.D. Va. 1987), *aff'd,* 846 F.2d 74 (4th Cir. 1988).

Fifth Circuit: Jones v. Flagship Int'l, 793 F.2d 714, 728 (5th Cir. 1986), *cert. denied,* 479 U.S. 1065 (1987); Ross v. Double Diamond, Inc., 672 F. Supp. 261 (N.D. Tex. 1987).

Sixth Circuit: Yates v. Avco Corp., 819 F.2d 630 (6th Cir. 1987).

Ninth Circuit: Jordan v. Clark, 847 F.2d 1368 (9th Cir. 1988), *cert. denied,* 488 U.S. 1006 (1989).

Tenth Circuit: Sahs v. Amarillo Equity Investors, 702 F. Supp. 256 (D. Colo. 1988).

302 Third Circuit: Miller v. Aluminum Co. of Am., 679 F. Supp. 495 (W.D. Pa. 1988), *aff'd,* 856 F.2d 184 (3d Cir.).

Fourth Circuit: Strickland v. Sears Roebuck & Co., 46 Fair Empl. Prac. Cas. (BNA) 1024 (E.D. Va. 1987), *aff'd,* 846 F.2d 74 (4th Cir. 1988).

Ninth Circuit: Jordan v. Clark, 847 F.2d 1368, 1376–77 (9th Cir. 1988), *cert. denied,* 488 U.S. 1006 (1989) (federal employment/administrative proceedings).

District of Columbia Circuit: Broderick v. Ruder, 685 F. Supp. 1269 (D.D.C. 1988).

303 Boyd v. James S. Hayes Living Health Care Agency, 671 F. Supp. 1155, 1167 (W.D. Tenn. 1987) (rejecting conduct found to be sexual harassment was protected activity).

harassment,[304] testifying on behalf of or supporting the claims of another employee,[305] picketing,[306] or, when appropriate, notifying law enforcement authorities.[307]

Dismissal is the most common form of retaliatory action.[308] Other adverse employment actions may include demotion, transfer, negative evaluation, and verbal misconduct.[309] However, temporary transfers or demotions that

---

304 Sixth Circuit: Hollis v. Fleetguard, Inc., 668 F. Supp. 631, 635 (M.D. Tenn. 1987).

District of Columbia Circuit: Broderick v. Ruder, 685 F. Supp. 1269 (D.D.C. 1988).

305 Jones v. Lyng, 669 F. Supp. 1108 (D.D.C 1986) (male employee charged retaliation for opposing and disclosing sexual harassment of female employees). *Cf.* Jones v. Flagship Int'l, 793 F.2d 714, 720 n.5 (5th Cir. 1986), *cert. denied,* 479 U.S. 1065 (1987) (former equal employment opportunity manager who encouraged other employees to file discrimination charges and who sought to maintain a class action clearly engaged in protected activity when she filed a discrimination charge with the EEOC).

Cf. Castillo Morales v. Best Fin. Co., 652 F. Supp. 412 (D.P.R.), *aff'd,* 831 F.2d 280 (1st Cir. 1987) (complaint of male employee who advised coworker to complain about sexual harassment did not state how, when, or if the employer found out about this advice, and thus he failed to plead with sufficient clarity what constituted protected activity).

306 Delahunty v. Cahoon, 66 Wash. App. 829, 832 P.2d 1378 (1992). In an action by truck stop waitresses alleging sexual harassment and retaliation, plaintiffs established that defendant owners violated the statute prohibiting retaliation against a person opposing a discriminatory practice with evidence that employers replaced waitresses who refused to subject themselves to continued sexual harassment; owners taunted waitresses on a picket line and one owner intimidated the waitresses by threatening that they would never work in the area again.

307 Ross v. Double Diamond, Inc., 672 F. Supp. 261, 275 (N.D. Tex. 1987) (reasonable for plaintiffs to complain to sheriff about treatment by top management person at company and after phone threats).

308 Fifth Circuit: Jones v. Flagship Int'l, 793 F.2d 714, 720 n.5 (5th Cir. 1986), *cert. denied,* 479 U.S. 1065 (1987).

Sixth Circuit: Ross v. Double Diamond, Inc., 672 F. Supp. 261 (N.D. Tex. 1987); Hollis v. Fleetguard, Inc., 668 F. Supp. 631, 635 (M.D. Tenn. 1987); Boyd v. James S. Hayes Living Health Care Agency, 671 F. Supp. 1155, 1167–1168 (W.D. Tenn. 1987).

Tenth Circuit: Sahs v. Amarillo Equity Investors, 702 F. Supp. 256 (D. Colo. 1988).

309 Third Circuit: *Cf.* Miller v. Aluminum Co. of Am., 679 F. Supp. 495, 505 (W.D. Pa. 1988), *aff'd,* 856 F.2d 184 (3d Cir.) ("snubbing" does not amount to unlawful retaliation).

Fifth Circuit: Ross v. Double Diamond, Inc., 672 F. Supp. 261 (N.D. Tex. 1987) (plaintiff was threatened).

District of Columbia Circuit: Broderick v. Ruder, 685 F. Supp. 1269 (D.D.C. 1988) (employer delayed plaintiff's promotion without explanation, reprimanded her, threatened her with termination, gave her adverse performance appraisals, and transferred her); Jones v. Lyng, 669 F. Supp. 1108, 1121 (D.D.C 1986) (removal of job responsibility, unsatisfactory performance rating, and transfer were adverse employment actions).

reduce an employee's duties and responsibilities but maintain her salary and benefits may not constitute adverse employment actions.[310]

The causal link element requires only that the plaintiff establish that the protected activity and the adverse action "were not wholly unrelated."[311] "Essential to a causal link is evidence that the employer was aware that the plaintiff had engaged in the protected activity."[312] This link may be established when only a short period of time has passed between the protected

---

[310] First Circuit: *Cf.* Seligson v. Massachusetts Inst. of Tech., 677 F. Supp. 648, 656 (D. Mass. 1987) (defendant's decision to continue to pay plaintiff her salary for five weeks after relinquishing her responsibilities was motivated by concerns over deteriorating relationships in the office and not by her charge with the EEOC).

Third Circuit: Miller v. Aluminum Co. of Am., 679 F. Supp. 495, 504 (W.D. Pa. 1988), *aff'd,* 856 F.2d 184 (3d Cir.) (early layoff was not an adverse employment action when plaintiff received full salary and benefits until her scheduled termination date); Ferguson v. E.I. du Pont de Nemours & Co., 560 F. Supp. 1172, 1200 (D. Del. 1983).

Sixth Circuit: Yates v. Avco Corp., 819 F.2d 630, 638 (6th Cir. 1987).

[311] Petrosky v. Washington-Greene County Branch Pa. Assoc. for the Blind, 663 F. Supp. 821, 825 (W.D. Pa. 1987) (defendant established that plaintiff had been difficult to deal with before she filed sexual harassment charges).

See also First Circuit: Seligson v. Massachusetts Inst. of Tech., 677 F. Supp. 648, 656 (D. Mass. 1987) (defendant was not aware of the pending sexual harassment charge when it gave plaintiff notice of the date by which she had to leave; "[p]laintiff cannot protect herself from the inevitable by filing a charge and then claiming her termination was retaliatory").

Sixth Circuit: Fuchilla v. Prockop, 682 F. Supp. 247 (D.N.J. 1987) (plaintiff presented no support for allegation of retaliation and defendant showed by reference to its policies regarding medical leaves of absence that plaintiff was fired because she failed to take an available position after expiration of leave); Hollis v. Fleetguard, Inc., 668 F. Supp. 631, 638–639 (M.D. Tenn. 1987).

Tenth Circuit: Zowayyed v. Lowen Co., 735 F. Supp. 1497 (D. Kan. 1990). A retaliation claim survived a summary judgment motion when under the facts presented to the court, there was a distinct possibility that plaintiff's termination resulted directly from her complaints of sexual harassment.

[312] Miller v. Aluminum Co. of Am., 679 F. Supp. 495, 504 (W.D. Pa. 1988), *aff'd,* 856 F.2d 184 (3d Cir.).

See also First Circuit: Castillo Morales v. Best Fin. Co., 652 F. Supp. 412, 415 (D.P.R. 1987), *aff'd,* 831 F.2d 280 (1st Cir.).

Third Circuit: Fuchilla v. Prockop, 682 F. Supp. 247, 263 (D.N.J. 1987); Ferguson v. E.I. du Pont de Nemours & Co., 560 F. Supp. 1172, 1200 (D. Del. 1983).

Sixth Circuit: Hollis v. Fleetguard, Inc., 668 F. Supp. 631, 638 (M.D. Tenn. 1987); Vermett v. Hough, 627 F. Supp. 587, 607 (W.D. Mich. 1986) (even if defendants had known about EEOC charge, there was "absolutely no evidence" that this knowledge was a factor in plaintiff's treatment).

District of Columbia Circuit: Broderick v. Ruder, 685 F. Supp. 1269 (D.D.C. 1988).

activity and the adverse personnel action,[313] and by circumstantial evidence. For example, the plaintiff may have received favorable evaluations before engaging in the protected activity but negative evaluations afterward.[314]

An employee may not use her right to oppose unlawful activity to undermine legitimate interests of the employer. In *Jones v. Flagship International*,[315] the court of appeals affirmed the district court's decision that a former equal employment opportunity manager who encouraged other employees to file discrimination charges and who sought to maintain a class action clearly engaged in protected activity when she filed a discrimination charge with the EEOC. Her subsequent suspension and termination were adverse employment actions, but she failed to establish the causal link between the two. The district court found that the defendant suspended the plaintiff to avoid the "conflict of interest inherent in Jones' representation of Flagship before the agency to whom she made the complaint" and because she planned to initiate a class action suit against the company. The court considered the evidence of Jones' solicitation of other employees to sue or join the class suit:

> In assuming her position as Flagship's manager of EEO programs, Jones neither abandoned her right to be free from discriminatory practices nor excluded herself from the protections of § 704(a). In filing a charge against Flagship on the ground that the company had discriminated against her in terms of pay and sexual harassment, Jones was exercising a protected right under Title VII, as the district court found. . . . However, we are also aware that although eliminating discriminatory employment practices is the goal of Title VII, cooperation and voluntary compliance are the preferred methods of promoting that goal. . . . An employee has a strong interest in having an

---

313 Boyd v. James S. Hayes Living Health Care Agency, 671 F. Supp. 1155 (W.D. Tenn. 1987) (plaintiff was discharged within a few weeks of initial opposition and a few days of public denouncement of supervisor at a staff meeting).

See also Sixth Circuit: *Cf.* Hollis v. Fleetguard, Inc., 668 F. Supp. 631, 638 (M.D. Tenn. 1987) (plaintiff did not establish causal link when she was fired more than three months after her complaints about sexual harassment and almost four months after a negative work counseling session during which she was told to improve job performance).

Ninth Circuit: Jordan v. Clark, 847 F.2d 1368 (9th Cir. 1988), *cert. denied*, 488 U.S. 1006 (1989).

District of Columbia Circuit: Broderick v. Ruder, 685 F. Supp. 1269 (D.D.C. 1988); Jones v. Lyng, 669 F. Supp. 1108, 1121 (D.D.C 1986). *Cf.* Benton v. Kroger Co., 640 F. Supp. 1317, 1321 (S.D. Tex. 1986) (no link established when last incident of harassment took place a month before termination).

314 Morley v. New England Tel. Co., 47 Fair Empl. Prac. Cas. (BNA) 917, 924 (D. Mass. 1987) (defendant retaliated against plaintiff who filed sex discrimination claim by rating her not promotable for performance year).

315 793 F.2d 714 (5th Cir. 1986), *cert. denied,* 479 U.S. 1065 (1987).

> opportunity to settle equal employment disputes through conference, conciliation and persuasion before an aggrieved employee resorts to a lawsuit. . . .
>
> * * *
>
> Jones' action[s] not only rendered her ineffective in the position for which she was employed, but critically harmed Flagship's posture in the defense of discrimination suits brought against the company. Moreover, Jones' right to express her grievances and promote her own welfare did not depend on others joining in her suit. We conclude, therefore, that under the . . . "balancing test" Jones' conduct in soliciting or inviting others to join in her discrimination claim, coupled with her expressed intent to serve at the vanguard of a class action suit, was not protected under § 704(a) and provided Flagship with a nondiscriminatory basis upon which to suspend and discharge Jones.[316]

As in disparate treatment cases, the plaintiff meets the initial burden by establishing facts sufficient to permit an inference of retaliatory motive (see **Chapter 6**). Once this burden is met, the defendant must articulate a legitimate, nondiscriminatory reason for the personnel action.[317] "In a sexual harassment case involving the claim of hostile work environment, the burden on the defendant employer is markedly heavier."[318] The employer must show by clear and convincing evidence that the plaintiff would not have been treated differently if she had not opposed the harassment.[319] The reason for this different rule in sexual harassment cases is that "once a plaintiff establishes that she was harassed . . . it is hard to see how an employer can justify [the] harassment."[320] The plaintiff will prevail if she then demonstrates by a preponderance of the evidence that the proffered reason was but a pretext for retaliation or by persuading the court that the desire to retaliate more likely motivated the employer.[321]

---

[316] *Id.* at 726, 728 (footnote omitted).

[317] Texas Dep't of Community Affairs v. Burdine, 450 U.S. 248, 252 (1981); McDonnell Douglas Corp. v. Green, 411 U.S. 792, 802–05 (1973). *See also* Jones v. Lyng, 669 F. Supp. 1108, 1122 (D.D.C 1986) (employer demonstrated that plaintiff had history of performance inadequacies and was insubordinate, disloyal, and disruptive).

[318] Broderick v. Ruder, 685 F. Supp. 1269, 1278 (D.D.C. 1988).

[319] Bundy v. Jackson, 641 F.2d 934, 952–53 (D.C. Cir. 1981).

[320] Moffett v. Gene B. Glick Co., 621 F. Supp. 244, 270 (N.D. Ind. 1985).

[321] Strickland v. Sears Roebuck & Co., 693 F. Supp. 403 (E.D. Va. 1987), *aff'd without opinion* 846 F.2d 74 (4th Cir. 1988) (poor sales performance); Ross v. Double Diamond, Inc., 672 F. Supp. 261 (N.D. Tex. 1987); Boyd v. James S. Hayes Living Health Care Agency, 671 F. Supp. 1155 (W.D. Tenn. 1987) (defendant's asserted reason for termination, poor job performance, was pretexual in light of strong evidence that termination was retaliatory).

A retaliation determination is reviewable under the clearly erroneous standard.[322]

Alleged harassers who have been dismissed from their jobs also have brought retaliation actions against their employers (see **Chapter 11**).

---

322 Jordan v. Clark, 847 F.2d 1368 (9th Cir. 1988), *cert. denied,* 488 U.S. 1006 (1989).

CHAPTER 4

PREPARING THE SEXUAL HARASSMENT CASE

§ 4.1 Introduction

Before accepting a sexual harassment case, an attorney must review all the legal remedies available and the relevant filing requirements to determine the procedural viability of such an action and the potential for recovery. Although most federal sexual harassment actions are brought under Title VII of the 1964 Civil Rights Act (see **Chapters 2** and **3**), many state employees have brought sexual harassment suits under 42 U.S.C. § 1983 as well (see **Chapter 8**), and state claims (see **Chapters 9** and **10**) are often combined with federal claims under the pendent jurisdiction of the federal courts.[1] Remedies unavailable under Title VII may be recovered through state law claims. Counsel, therefore, should attempt to assert as many plausible causes of action as feasible to maximize the possibility of recovery. Attorneys' fees for time expended on state law claims may be recovered in federal court if the theories stem from the same common core of facts[2] (see **Chapter 11**).

§ 4.2 Client Representation

Client representation may begin at any time during the administrative or judicial process. Employment discrimination statutes and Equal Employment Opportunity Commission (EEOC) regulations have been broadly construed to accommodate the pro se complainant. The appearance of counsel may prompt the court to raise its standards for compliance with statutory requirements, but representation by counsel also may precipitate settlement and result in a larger recovery for the plaintiff. Attorneys who enter cases after the administrative process has started must be prepared to cure jurisdictional defects or otherwise amend pleadings to include all possible parties and claims.

The client interview takes on special meaning in the emotional arena of sexual harassment. From the information the client supplies, an attorney must make a preliminary determination of the case's legal viability. The client's demeanor also may give clues about what direction litigation should take. Sexual harassment victims who seek legal advice may realize that they have been wronged, but in their hearts believe, like rape victims often do, that they somehow invited the abuse or could have stopped it. As a result, the client may be defensive or unable to recount events objectively. Counsel should encourage the client to tell her story unemotionally, without embellishment or judgments that the employer defendant could contradict later.

Counsel should inform the client of the procedural requirements involved, the plausible theories, the length of time the case may take, the

---

[1] *See, e.g.,* United Mine Workers v. Gibbs, 383 U.S. 715 (1966). Sexual harassment claims may be cognizable under other federal statutes as well, such as the Jones Act, 46 U.S.C. app. § 688. Wilson v. Zapata Off-Shore Co., 939 F.2d 260 (5th Cir. 1991). Assertions by a female oil rig worker of "tortious physical contact" and significant physical injury in the form of weight loss, vomiting, and diarrhea were sufficient to create a claim for harassment cognizable under the Jones Act.

[2] *See, e.g.,* Abell v. Potomac Ins. Co., 858 F.2d 1104 (5th Cir. 1988); Wagenmann v. Adams, 829 F.2d 196 (1st Cir. 1987); Aubin v. Fudala, 821 F.2d 45 (1st Cir. 1987); Seaway Drive-in, Inc. v. Township of Clay, 791 F.2d 447 (6th Cir.), *cert. denied,* 479 U.S. 884 (1986).

implications of a trial and protracted litigation, the settlement possibilities, and available fee arrangements. Counsel must be aware of the extreme stress inherent in sexual harassment cases and treat the client with sensitivity.

§ 4.3 Interview Checklist

This checklist outlines the facts that counsel should attempt to learn during the client interview. It also contains information that counsel should give to a potential client. Each point will be discussed in detail in §§ **4.4** through **4.8.**

1. Client's education and work background
    - ____ (a) Degrees and training
    - ____ (b) Types of jobs
    - ____ (c) Length of jobs
    - ____ (d) Work-related problems in previous jobs
    - ____ (e) How jobs ended
2. Client's personal background
    - ____ (a) Marital history
    - ____ (b) Children and extent of care client must provide
    - ____ (c) Social contacts with harassing coworkers and supervisors
    - ____ (d) Social contacts with nonharassing coworkers and supervisors
    - ____ (e) Medical and psychiatric issues
        - ____ Preexisting
        - ____ Brought on by harassment
        - ____ Continuing
3. Offending employer
    - ____ (a) Existence of nondiscrimination policy
        - ____ Implementation procedures
        - ____ Copy provided by client
        - ____ Need to request in discovery
    - ____ (b) Existence of policy against sexual harassment in particular
        - ____ Implementation procedures
        - ____ Copy provided by client
        - ____ Need to request in discovery
    - ____ (c) History of sexual harassment complaints against the employer

____ (d) Employment atmosphere, dress code
____ (e) Satisfaction of jurisdictional requirements
____ (f) Choice of defendants, depending on remedy selected

4. Client's position
____ (a) Type of job
____ (b) Qualifications and duties
____ Copy of job description provided by client
____ Need to request in discovery
____ (c) Is job covered by labor contract
____ Copy of contract provided by client
____ Need to request in discovery
____ (d) Work-related problems with management
____ (e) Performance evaluations
____ Copies provided by client
____ Need to request in discovery

5. Nature of sex discrimination claim
____ (a) *Quid pro quo* harassment
____ (b) Hostile environment harassment
____ (c) Continuing violation
____ (d) Constructive discharge
____ (e) Retaliation

6. Proof issues
____ (a) Showing that a job benefit was denied or altered
____ (b) Showing that a hostile environment affected the terms or conditions of employment
____ (c) Existence of witnesses
____ (d) Documentation of harassment incidents
____ Client's diary
____ Any formal, written complaints
____ (e) Complaints to management personnel

7. Litigation status
____ (a) Attempts made to resolve conflict
____ Copies of relevant written complaints (if required), correspondence
____ (b) Papers filed
____ Dates
____ Copies provided by client
____ (c) Amendments to be made

8. Nature of damages
   ____ (a) Title VII
   ____ (b) Section 1983
   ____ (c) State law
9. Possible employer defenses
   ____ (a) Reasons employer gave for job status change
      ____ Documentation provided by client
      ____ Need to request in discovery
   ____ (b) Existence of legitimate bases for those reasons
10. Implications of trial
11. Settlement possibilities
12. Fee arrangements

§ 4.4 —Client's Background

The defendant may attempt to establish that the plaintiff was terminated or subjected to another adverse employment action because she was poorly qualified. Counsel must establish that the employer knew of the plaintiff's qualifications when she was hired and/or that her qualifications met the requirements for the position. The employer also may try to introduce evidence of previous terminations from other employment or the existence of short-lived jobs to challenge the plaintiff's credibility. Counsel may attempt to block the introduction of this type of evidence but should be prepared to distinguish, if possible, other employment situations.

Although the plaintiff's marital status and social graces have not been explicitly found to be determinative in sexual harassment cases, courts have seemed interested in whether the plaintiff was married or single, passive or aggressive, "one of the guys," or hostile toward men. An employer may argue that the plaintiff's child care responsibilities affected her work performance, warranting termination, or that the plaintiff carried on voluntary social relationships with alleged harassers outside the work context. Counsel should try to elicit facts that demonstrate, if possible, that any change in work performance occurred following the alleged harassment, and that despite any social relationships with the alleged harassers, the plaintiff was subjected to unwelcome work-related sexual conduct.

The client may be particularly unwilling to discuss a sexual relationship with another employee who did not participate in the harassment, especially when the relationship was or is clandestine. Both counsel and client must be prepared to respond to the issue if asserted by the defendant. The complainant cannot count on the sexual partner or confidants to maintain secrecy in the face of possible coercion by the defendant. The client must be advised that intimate details of her relationships may be revealed at trial despite counsel's attempts to exclude this evidence. Pursuant to *Meritor Savings Bank v. Vinson,*[3] the defendant also may try to introduce evidence regarding the complainant's conduct and dress. Even off-handed comments to coworkers may surface as evidence that the challenged sexual conduct was not unwelcome. Medical or psychiatric records also may be introduced if the physical or mental condition of the complainant is at issue. Such often is the case in state tort or federal employment discrimination actions seeking damages under pendent state claims of infliction of emotional distress. Under *Harris v. Forklift Systems, Inc.,*[4] however, a victim of sexual harassment need not prove psychological injury to win a sexual harassment suit. Counsel should consider this possibility in assessing potential remedies.

§ 4.5 —Employer Information

A nondiscrimination policy does not protect an employer from liability. A defendant may try to assert, however, that the plaintiff did not follow the policy's grievance procedures. Failure to complain of the alleged harassment may be a determining factor unless, for example, the company would not have responded anyway, or the complaint had to be made to the alleged harasser. If the client states that she did not complain of the harassment because she feared retribution, counsel must try to ascertain if other employees effectively used the grievance procedure or were discouraged from doing so.

The client should provide counsel with a job description and a history of her work performance for the defendant, including written or oral performance ratings, recognition through awards or promotion, written or oral reprimands, or demotion. Counsel should encourage the client to distinguish carefully between conduct inspired by retaliatory motives and that resulting from legitimate business concerns. For example, if a plaintiff had been reprimanded for lateness before the sexual harassment occurred, and she was subsequently demoted, the earlier reprimands would not bolster a retaliation claim. A defendant may attempt to use those legitimate reprimands to show that the plaintiff was demoted for chronic lateness, rather than noncompliance with sexual demands.

---

[3] 477 U.S. 57 (1986).

[4] Harris v. Forklift Systems, Inc., 114 S. Ct. 367 (1993).

§ 4.6 —Nature and Proof of Claim

If the client has stated that a job benefit was denied or altered because she refused to accede to a sexual proposition or demand, she may have a claim for *quid pro quo* sexual harassment (see **Chapter 2**). Because this is the more obvious type of sexual harassment, the client may not be aware that other related conduct also may constitute hostile environment sexual harassment. The sexual banter common in many work places often is accepted as inevitable even when it is extremely offensive. Counsel should assure the client that participation in the challenged conduct does not necessarily negate a sexual harassment claim. The client also should know, however, that the defendant will introduce evidence of that participation to show that she did not find the conduct offensive. When possible, counsel should try to advance theories of both *quid pro quo* and hostile environment sexual harassment. If the client has quit her job as a result of the harassment, the client should show that the conduct made her work environment intolerable.

The client should provide a list of possible witnesses who may testify on either her behalf or that of the employer. The plaintiff's witnesses may testify either that they saw the individual defendant harass the plaintiff or that they themselves also were victims of the harassment.

The client should attest to the denial of a specific job benefit to support a *quid pro quo* harassment claim. Repeated threats of termination, demotion, or transfer may make up a hostile environment or constructive discharge claim, but the plaintiff must demonstrate that the alleged harasser altered the terms or conditions of her employment through threats. While some courts have found that unwelcome sexual hostility inherently affects the terms or conditions of employment, others have required evidence of more specific consequences of the abuse, such as medical or psychological ailments (see **Chapters 2** and **3**).

The documentation of incidents of harassment and complaints to management personnel may play a critical role in a sexual harassment case. If the client has not kept a record or diary of the events, counsel should help her reconstruct the chain of events as soon as possible. The client should keep a copy of the time line with her at all times to make modifications or additions as events are recalled.

If the client has been terminated or demoted or quit her job because of sexual harassment, she may be entitled to back pay or reinstatement under Title VII. Damages may be available under § 1983 or state common law contractor tort theories, such as intentional infliction of emotional distress. Counsel should assess the length of time before trial and determine whether preliminary injunctive relief is necessary.

§ 4.7 —Employer's Defenses

The client should be asked if there are any documented reasons for her termination, demotion, or transfer, and the validity of these bases. If there seems to be valid reasons for an employment decision, but also evidence of harassment, counsel must elicit as much supporting information as possible and determine whether the case is viable. Sexual harassment cases are seldom decided by motions for summary judgment because of the credibility issues involved, and thus considerable expense may be incurred before an ambiguous, strongly contested case is resolved.

The client must be prepared to face a hostile employer, the employer's attorney, coworkers who cannot afford to take her side, discovery of very personal aspects of her life, and protracted litigation. The defendant may try to characterize the plaintiff as a sexually uninhibited and vengeful person. Because most sexual harassment cases are settled at an early stage, most clients will not have to face cross-examination. However, it remains a possibility, and the discovery process alone may be painful. A client should be reassured that the defendant's approach is typical litigation strategy and should be viewed in that context. Role playing is extremely helpful in these types of cases because it sharpens response skills and reduces the chance that the client will be thrown off guard by a particularly personal question.

§ 4.8 —Settlement and Fees

The possibility of settlement may be difficult to determine at the client interview stage. However, counsel may have a sense of the potential for recovery and should tell the client the factors that must be weighed in determining a reasonable settlement.

Several types of attorneys' fee arrangements are common in employment discrimination actions. In Title VII and § 1983 actions, prevailing plaintiffs are presumptively entitled by statute to an award of attorneys' fees payable by the unsuccessful defendant (see **Chapters 6** and **8**). Counsel and client may enter into a contingency fee agreement based on any monetary recovery or based on whatever fees the court may award. Counsel also may charge the client a straight hourly rate. However, that arrangement may quickly deplete most clients' resources.

§ 4.9 Remedies Available

There are many bases for relief for the sexual harassment victim:

1. Title VII of the 1964 Civil Rights Act (see § **4.10**)
2. 42 U.S.C. § 1983 (see § **4.11**)
3. 42 U.S.C. § 1985(3) (see § **4.12**)
4. Title IX of the 1964 Civil Rights Act (see § **4.13**)
5. Racketeer Influenced and Corrupt Organizations Act (RICO), 18 U.S.C. §§ 1961–1968 (see § **4.14**)
6. State fair employment practice laws (see § **4.15**)
7. State equal rights amendments (see § **4.16**)
8. Pendent state claims (see § **4.17**)
9. State common law actions (see § **4.18**)
   —Assault
   —Battery
   —Intentional infliction of emotional distress
   —Tortious interference with contractual relationships
   —Invasion of privacy

To decide which remedy or remedies would be appropriate in a particular sexual harassment case, counsel must consider a number of factors that would affect the choice of action:

1. Nature of employer
   —Federal government or nonfederal government employer
   —Size of company
2. Administrative requirements
   —Time limitations
   —Discovery issues
3. Burden of proof required by statutes
   —Showing of intentional discrimination required by § 1983
4. Possibility of jury trial
   —Available under Title VII for claims seeking damages under certain circumstances
5. Evidentiary issues
   —Implications of state law pendent claims
6. Damages sought
   —Monetary damages in addition to back or front pay may be available under state law and under Title VII under certain circumstances
7. Attorneys' fee issues
   —Attorneys' fee awards are available to prevailing plaintiffs under Title VII but may not be under state laws

These factors are discussed in the context of each available remedy in §§ **4.10** through **4.18.**

§ 4.10 —Title VII

Most courts have allowed nonfederal employment discrimination complainants to bring suit under other statutes in addition to or instead of Title VII.[5] However, some courts have held that § 1983 (see **§ 4.11**) does not create a right of action separate from Title VII.[6] Title VII provides federal employees with "an exclusive, preemptive administrative and judicial scheme for the redress of federal employment discrimination."[7] The existence of other federal employment-related statutory remedies, such as the Federal Employees Compensation Act,[8] does not preclude a federal employee from asserting a Title VII claim.[9] The requirements of Title VII are covered in detail in **Chapters 5** and **6.**

Nonfederal and federal employees may bring actions under Title VII individually or on behalf of a class. The EEOC is authorized to bring suit on behalf of nonfederal employees only. The U.S. Attorney General may bring suit against a government, governmental agency, or political subdivision.[10] Suits may be brought against private employers with 15 or more employees,[11] state and local governments,[12] employment agencies,[13] labor organizations, or unions.[14] State and local government officials may be sued only in their official capacities. Although civilian employees of the armed forces are covered by Title VII, military personnel or applicants for military services are not.[15] In actions by federal employees, only the head of the agency or unit may be named as the defendant.[16]

---

5 *See, e.g.,* Dwyer v. Smith, 867 F.2d 184 (4th Cir. 1989); Keller v. Prince George's County, 827 F.2d 952 (4th Cir. 1987). *See also* Johnson v. Harris County Flood Control Dist., 869 F.2d 1565, 1573 (5th Cir. 1989) (when a public employee's conduct violates both Title VII and a separate constitutional or statutory right, an injured employee may pursue a remedy under § 1983 as well as under Title VII).

6 Foster v. Wyrick, 823 F.2d 218, 221 (8th Cir. 1987).

7 Brown v. General Servs. Admin., 425 U.S. 820, 828–29 (1976).

8 5 U.S.C. §§ 8101–8193.

9 *See* Miller v. Bolger, 802 F.2d 660 (3d Cir. 1986).

10 42 U.S.C. § 2000e-6.

11 42 U.S.C. § 2000(b).

12 42 U.S.C. § 2000e(a).

13 42 U.S.C. § 2000e-2(d).

14 42 U.S.C. § 2000e-2(d).

15 Johnson v. Alexander, 572 F.2d 1219, 1223–24 (8th Cir.), *cert. denied,* 439 U.S. 986 (1978).

16 42 U.S.C. § 2000e-16(c) (1982).

Subject to exceptions, a plaintiff in a Title VII action must exhaust state administrative remedies before filing suit in federal court (see **Chapter 5**).

Title VII also prohibits retaliation against a person who has asserted Title VII protections. An independent action or claim under the retaliation provision of Title VII may be brought even if the underlying discrimination complaint was not or will not be successful.[17] Federal employees may bring retaliation actions, even though the language of the amendment extending Title VII coverage to federal employees does not create such a cause of action.[18] Under the Civil Rights Act of 1991, a jury trial is available under Title VII for damages under certain circumstances. Other remedies under Title VII are equitable and include reinstatement, back pay, front pay, restoration of benefits, and attorneys' fees.

§ 4.11 —Section 1983

Section 1983 has formed the basis for many sexual harassment claims, both alone and in conjunction with a Title VII claim. Liability under § 1983 requires a showing that the defendant's actions deprived the plaintiff of the rights, privileges, or immunities granted by the Constitution and that the defendant acted under color of state law.[19] In contrast to Title VII, "§ 1983 is not a statute with any substantive content but merely the conduit through which individuals may obtain redress for violations to rights protected by the federal constitution or by federal law."[20] Section 1983 may not be used to sustain an action for violation to Title VII only, however.[21] Similarly, a plaintiff may not bring a § 1983 action based on Title VII against a defendant who could not be sued directly under Title VII.[22]

---

[17] Davis v. State Univ., 802 F.2d 638, 642 (2d Cir. 1986); Kellner v. General Refractories Co., 631 F. Supp. 939 (N.D. Ind. 1986); Downey v. Isaac, 622 F. Supp. 1125, 1132 (D.D.C. 1985), *aff'd,* 794 F.2d 753 (D.C. Cir. 1986). *Cf.* Jurado v. Eleven-Fifty Corp., 813 F.2d 1406, 1411 (7th Cir. 1987) (plaintiff must have reasonable belief in validity of underlying claim).

[18] Hale v. Marsh, 808 F.2d 616 (7th Cir. 1986).

[19] Gomez v. Toledo, 446 U.S. 635, 640 (1980).

[20] Lipsett v. Rive-Mora, 669 F. Supp. 1188, 1195 (D.P.R. 1987), *rev'd on other grounds,* 864 F.2d 881 (1st Cir. 1988) (sexual harassment); Chapman v. Houston Welfare Rights Org., 441 U.S. 600, 616–18 (1979).

[21] Lipsett v. Rive-Mora, 669 F. Supp. 1188, 1195 (D.P.R. 1987), *rev'd on other grounds,* 864 F.2d 881 (1st Cir. 1988). "The reason for this is obvious. If violations to Title VII were allowed to proceed through 1983 actions, the statutory and administrative design enacted by Congress for Title VII actions would be easily circumvented." Here, the plaintiff never filed an administrative proceeding with the EEOC nor met any of the Title VII statutory requirements.

[22] Huebschen v. Department of Health & Social Servs., 716 F.2d 1167 (7th Cir. 1983) (sexual harassment).

Any affected person may sue under § 1983, and any person who acts under color of state law may be sued. The *person* who acts under color of state law has been broadly construed, and includes cities, counties, and other local governmental entities.[23] Private persons may be liable under § 1983 if the nexus between the action and the state is close enough to satisfy the state action requirement of the Fourteenth Amendment.[24] Section 1983 covers federal officials' actions done under color of state law,[25] but not actions done under color of federal law.[26]

The Eleventh Amendment bars a suit against the state[27] unless the state expressly waives sovereign immunity[28] or injunctive relief is sought.[29]

Supervisors are not vicariously liable for the § 1983 violations of their subordinates[30] unless the supervisor knew or should have known of the misconduct and could have prevented future harm but did not.[31] Furthermore, municipalities and other local government entities may not be sued for the acts of their employees unless the unconstitutional conduct stems from governmental "custom" or a "policy statement, ordinance, regulation, or decision officially adopted and promulgated by the body's officers,"[32] and the government entity has notice of the custom or policy.[33]

A plaintiff need not exhaust state administrative procedures before bringing a § 1983 action,[34] but if the plaintiff has sought a state administrative review, the findings of fact are binding in the federal action.[35]

---

23 *See* Lake County Estates v. Tahoe Regional Planning Agency, 440 U.S. 391, 405 n.29 (1979); Monell v. Department of Social Servs., 436 U.S. 658 (1978).

24 Adickes v. S.H. Kress & Co., 398 U.S. 144, 152 (1970); Dennis v. Sparks, 449 U.S. 24, 27–29 (1980).

25 Francis-Sobel v. University of Me., 597 F.2d 15 (1st Cir.), *cert. denied,* 444 U.S. 949 (1979).

26 Stonecipher v. Bray, 653 F.2d 398 (9th Cir. 1981), *cert. denied,* 454 U.S. 1145 (1982); Gillespie v. Civiletti, 629 F.2d 637 (9th Cir. 1980); Hubbert v. United States Parole Comm'n, 585 F.2d 857 (7th Cir. 1978) (per curiam); Smith v. United States Civil Serv. Comm'n, 520 F.2d 731 (7th Cir. 1975).

27 Quern v. Jordan, 440 U.S. 332 (1979); Edelman v. Jordan, 415 U.S. 651 (1974).

28 Florida Dep't of Health & Rehabilitative Servs. v. Florida Nursing Home Ass'n, 450 U.S. 147 (1981); Fitzpatrick v. Bitzer, 427 U.S. 445 (1976).

29 *Ex parte* Young, 209 U.S. 123 (1908).

30 Monell v. Department of Social Servs., 436 U.S. 658 (1978).

31 *See, e.g.,* McClelland v. Facteau, 610 F.2d 693, 697 (10th Cir. 1979); Wulf v. City of Wichita, 644 F. Supp. 1211, 1226 (D. Kan. 1986).

32 Monell v. Department of Social Servs., 436 U.S. 658, 690–91 (1978).

33 Spell v. McDaniel, 824 F.2d 1380, 1387 (4th Cir. 1987), *cert. denied,* 484 U.S. 1027 (1988); Garza v. City of Omaha, 814 F.2d 553 (8th Cir. 1987).

34 Patsy v. Board of Regents, 457 U.S. 496 (1982).

35 University of Tenn. v. Elliott, 478 U.S. 788, 798–99 (1986).

Although the U.S. Supreme Court held in *Monroe v. Pape*[36] that a § 1983 plaintiff need not exhaust state judicial remedies before filing a federal lawsuit, such exhaustion may be required in certain circumstances, such as when unsettled state law issues exist.[37] Courts also have refused to hear § 1983 actions until pending state actions have been resolved[38] when a state court has the authority to adjudicate the merits of the federal claim.[39] In that case, the plaintiff may be bound by res judicata on the issues litigated in the state court. The U.S. Supreme Court also has suggested that the mere availability of state judicial relief may preclude § 1983 actions.[40]

Section 1983 contains no statute of limitations, and thus the analogous state statute of limitations governing personal injury actions[41] is controlling unless "inconsistent" with federal law.[42] Section 1983 actions in states with more than one statute of limitations are governed by residual or general personal injury statutes rather than the statute of limitations for enumerated intentional torts.[43]

A plaintiff in a § 1983 action for damages is entitled to a jury trial. No such entitlement exists when the plaintiff seeks only equitable relief. If both damages and equitable relief are sought, a jury decides the damages claim initially, and the court alone hears the claim for equitable relief.[44]

The plaintiff asserting a § 1983 claim must prove its elements by a preponderance of the evidence. In proving a violation of equal protection under the Fourteenth Amendment, the plaintiff must demonstrate intentional discrimination based on a class characteristic.[45]

A prevailing plaintiff suing for violations of § 1983 may recover a court award of attorneys' fees under 42 U.S.C. § 1988, the Civil Rights Attorney's Fees Awards Act, payable by the losing defendant.

---

36 365 U.S. 167 (1961).

37 England v. Louisiana State Bd. of Medical Examiners, 375 U.S. 411 (1964); Railroad Comm'n v. Pullman Co., 312 U.S. 496 (1941).

38 Gresham Park Community Org. v. Howell, 652 F.2d 1227 (5th Cir. 1981); Lamb Enters. v. Kiroff, 549 F.2d 1052 (6th Cir. 1976), *cert. denied,* 431 U.S. 968 (1977).

39 Middlesex County Ethics Comm. v. Garden State Bar Ass'n, 457 U.S. 423 (1982); Monaghan v. Deakins, 798 F.2d 632, 636 (3d Cir. 1986), *cert. denied,* 484 U.S. 193 (1988).

40 Hudson v. Palmer, 468 U.S. 517 (1984); Parratt v. Taylor, 451 U.S. 527 (1981); Ingraham v. Wright, 430 U.S. 651 (1977). Although these were criminal justice cases, the principle has been applied to the deprivation of other property interests. Yates v. Jamison, 782 F.2d 1182 (4th Cir. 1986).

41 Wilson v. Garcia, 471 U.S. 261 (1985).

42 Burnett v. Grattan, 468 U.S. 42, 53 (1984); Board of Regents v. Tomanio, 446 U.S. 478, 485 (1980).

43 Owens v. Okure, 488 U.S. 235 (1989).

44 Dairy Queen, Inc. v. Wood, 369 U.S. 469 (1962).

45 Batson v. Kentucky, 476 U.S. 79 (1986).

§ 4.12 —Section 1985(3)

Section 1985(3) of 42 U.S.C. provides that if two or more people conspire to deprive another person of equal protection, the victim of the conspiracy may recover damages against any one or more of the conspirators. To succeed in a § 1985(3) claim, a sexual harassment plaintiff must demonstrate that a conspiracy existed "to deprive her of her rights to equal treatment with members of the opposite sex. She is not required to allege that the . . . discriminatory treatment was classwide in its application by defendant."[46] A plaintiff may demonstrate that the employer and/or supervisors were aware of her grievance, discussed it among themselves, and either did nothing or themselves participated in the harassment.[47]

§ 4.13 —Title IX

Title IX of the 1964 Civil Rights Act prohibits sex discrimination in any educational program receiving federal financial assistance. Several courts have applied the standards governing Title VII to Title IX cases, at least when the action involved employment discrimination,[48] but few sexual harassment victims have sought relief under this statute. In *Alexander v. Yale University,*[49] a district court held that *quid pro quo* harassment was a justifiable claim under Title IX, but that a claim based only on allegations of a hostile environment was not viable. The Second Circuit affirmed without addressing the issue of hostile environment when it determined that the issue was moot. In *Moire v. Temple University,*[50] the court recognized the hostile environment claim but did not find such an environment in the case before it.

The First Circuit addressed the issue in *Lipsett v. University of Puerto Rico.*[51] Following the reasoning in *Meritor,* the court held that an educational institution is liable for hostile environment sexual harassment by its supervisors or coworkers upon employees if an institutional official knew, or should have known of the harassment, unless the official can show that he or she took appropriate steps to halt it. In this action by a female surgical

---

46 Skadegaard v. Farrell, 578 F. Supp. 1209, 1220 (D.N.J. 1984) (sexual harassment).

47 *See* Volk v. Coler, 845 F.2d 1422 (7th Cir. 1988) (sexual harassment).

48 Lipsett v. University of P.R., 864 F.2d 881 (1st Cir. 1988) (action involved plaintiff who was student and employee).

49 459 F. Supp. 1 (D. Conn. 1977), *aff'd,* 631 F.2d 178 (2d Cir. 1980).

50 800 F.2d 1136 (3d Cir. 1986).

51 864 F.2d 881 (1st Cir. 1988), *sustaining jury verdict after remand,* 759 F. Supp. 41 (D.P.R. 1991). The jury awarded the plaintiff $525,000 in damages.

resident, the constant attack by male residents on the capabilities of the plaintiff and other female residents and frequent sexual comments created a hostile environment so blatant that it put the defendants on constructive notice that sex discrimination permeated the residency program.

§ 4.14 —RICO Actions

The Racketeer Influenced and Corrupt Organizations Act (RICO)[52] provides a private civil action to recover treble damages for injury to a person in her or his business or property for a violation of § 1962. That section prohibits the use of income derived from a "pattern of racketeering activity" to acquire an interest in, establish, or operate an enterprise engaged in or affecting interstate commerce; the acquisition or maintenance of any interest in an enterprise through a pattern of racketeering activity; conducting or participating in the conduct of an enterprise through a pattern of racketeering activity; and conspiring to violate any of these provisions.[53] Allegations of a prolonged pattern and practice of sexual harassment may be sufficient to demonstrate a pattern of racketeering activity.[54] In *Hunt v. Weatherbee,*[55] allegations regarding the union shop steward's use of sexual harassment to coerce a female journeyman carpenter into purchasing raffle tickets for a union "political action fund," and of a pattern of sexual harassment against the plaintiff and other female union members, gave rise to a RICO claim when the union business agent allegedly condoned and ratified the harassing conduct.[56]

§ 4.15 —State Fair Employment Practice Laws

Most states have employment statutes that prohibit discrimination based on race, color, sex, religion, national origin, age, or handicap (see **Chapter 10**). Most of these statutes mirror the protections of Title VII, but many

---

[52] 18 U.S.C. §§ 1961–1968.

[53] *Id.* § 1962; Sedima, S.P.R.L. v. Imrex Co., 473 U.S. 479 (1985).

[54] Hunt v. Weatherbee, 626 F. Supp. 1097, 1104 (D. Mass. 1986). *Cf.* Fowler v. Burns Sec. Servs., 763 F. Supp. 862 (N.D. Miss. 1991) *aff'd,* 979 F.2d 1534 (5th Cir. 1992). RICO did not apply to a security guard company charged with sexual harassment when the company could not be both a person who allegedly conducted affairs of "enterprise" through a pattern of racketeering activity and the "enterprise" itself. Allegations that company officer forced her into a sexual relationship to keep her job does not relate to extortion as generally defined. Even if the plaintiff established the required racketeering activity, she did not show a pattern of such activity as required by the U.S. Supreme Court.

[55] 626 F. Supp. 1097, 1104 (D. Mass. 1986).

[56] *Id.* at 1108 (allegations were sufficient to withstand motion to dismiss).

include additional prohibitions involving discriminatory employment practices based on pregnancy, marital status, parenthood,[57] sexual preference, arrest record,[58] AIDS, sickle cell anemia,[59] family responsibility, matriculation, personal appearance, weight, political affiliation, sexual orientation,[60] receipt of public assistance,[61] or unfavorable discharge from the military.[62] Some states had distinct provisions related to sexual harassment, and such provisions may provide the exclusive statutory remedy. In *Bergeson v. Franchi,*[63] a former employee who was subjected to conduct by her employer including sexual advances, touching, threats, attempts to kiss her, discussion of rape and infidelity, begging her to fly to Florida with him and stay at his house there, and attempts to bribe her to accept his advances with a raise, a fur coat, money to finance her restaurant business, and medical expenses could not bring an independent cause of action under both the Massachusetts civil rights act and the Massachusetts discrimination statute based on a claim for sexual harassment.

> The plaintiff in the instant action followed the procedural, jurisdictional, and statute of limitations prerequisites to claim relief under Mass. Gen. L. ch. 151B, and this Court will not allow the plaintiff to allege a duplicative claim under the Act. To permit such duplication of remedies would allow claimants to bypass the procedural prerequisites defined by the legislature in Mass. Gen. L. ch. 151B, crippling the effectiveness of this specific statutory remedy for discrimination in employment.[64]

State antidiscrimination statutes generally are similar to Title VII, but differences in coverage, exhaustion of jurisdictional requirements, applicable statutes of limitation, the range of possible remedies, or the availability of attorneys' fees may render one or the other preferable in a particular situation. Counsel also should try to ascertain how sympathetic state courts are to employment discrimination plaintiffs generally and sexual harassment plaintiffs in particular if such a case has been litigated.

Although most statues cover public and private employers, some apply only to state workers. A number of statutes follow Title VII in requiring that the defendant employ at least 15 people before the antidiscrimination

---

57 *See, e.g.,* Alaska Stat. §§ 18.80.200(a)(e).

58 *See, e.g.,* Cal. Gov't Code § 12926(c).

59 *See, e.g.,* N.J. Rev. Stat. § 10:5-12(a).

60 *See, e.g.,* D.C. Code Ann. § 1-2512.

61 *See, e.g.,* Minn. Stat. § 363.03(1)(1).

62 *See, e.g.,* Ill. Rev. Stat. Ann. ch. 68, para. 1-102(A).

63 783 F. Supp. 713 (D. Mass. 1992) (Caffrey, J.).

64 *Id.* at 721.

statute applies.[65] However, many have no such minimum requirement,[66] and in others, the minimum number of employees ranges from 2 to 12.[67]

Exhaustion of state administrative requirements is required by almost half of the state antidiscrimination statutes. Like Title VII, some state antidiscrimination statutes also prohibit retaliation against people who have asserted their rights under the relevant law.

A jury trial is available under almost half the state statutes. A number of state antidiscrimination statutes provide for a range of relief beyond Title VII's provisions, including actual damages, incidental damages for pain and suffering, compensatory damages, treble damages, damages for pain, humiliation, mental anguish, and embarrassment, and punitive damages. Some limit damage awards to $1,000 to $8,500.[68]

More than half of the state antidiscrimination statutes provide for an award of attorneys' fees, at least to prevailing plaintiffs.[69] In some states, prevailing defendants are entitled to attorneys' fees if the action was brought in bad faith or if the complaint was frivolous (see **Chapter 10**). Attorneys' fee awards are available under Title VII. In the absence of a fee provision in the state statute, a contingent fee arrangement is possible if damages are available under the state statute.

§ 4.16 —State Equal Rights Amendments

"The equal protection guaranty and *a fortiori* an equal rights amendment condemn discrimination on grounds of sex."[70] In *O'Connell v. Chasdi,*[71] the Massachusetts Supreme Court construed the state equal rights amendment to prohibit sexual harassment in the workplace. State equal rights amendments seldom are asserted as grounds for a sexual harassment suit, perhaps because of the success of state and federal antidiscrimination laws and the availability of damages under state common law. Courts have also

---

65 *See, e.g.,* Ariz. Rev. Stat. Ann. § 41-1461(2); Fla. Stat. Ann. § 760.02(b).

66 *See, e.g.,* Alaska Stat. § 18.80.220; Colo. Rev. Stat. § 24-34-402.

67 *See, e.g.,* Conn. Gen. Stat. Ann. § 46a-51(10) (employers with fewer than three employees excluded); Ind. Code Ann. § 22-9-1-3(h) (fewer than six employees).

68 *See, e.g.,* Idaho Code Ann. § 67-5908(3)(e) (up to $1,000 per willful violation); Kan. Stat. Ann. § 44-1005(k) (up to $2,000 for incidental damages for pain, suffering, or humiliation); Minn. Stat. § 363.071(2) (punitive damages up to $8,500; compensatory damages up to three times actual damages).

69 *See, e.g.,* D.C. Code Ann. § 1-2553(a)(1)(E); Minn. Stat. §§ 363.071(2), 363.14(3), 181.956; Or. Rev. Stat. § 659.121(1).

70 Attorney Gen. v. Massachusetts Interscholastic Athletic Ass'n, 378 Mass. 343, 351, 393 N.E.2d 284, 289 (1979).

71 400 Mass. 686, 511 N.E.2d 349 (1987).

attempted to resolve state statutory and/or common law issues without addressing constitutional claims.

§ 4.17 —Pendent or Supplemental Jurisdiction

Pendent state claims often are included in Title VII sexual harassment complaints.[72] Courts may assert supplemental jurisdiction over pendent

---

72 First Circuit: Guzman Robles v. Cruz, 670 F. Supp. 54 (D.P.R. 1987).

Third Circuit: Owens v. Turnage, 681 F. Supp. 1095 (D.N.J. 1988); Cremen v. Harrah's Marina Hotel Casino, 680 F. Supp. 150 (D.N.J. 1988); Miller v. Aluminum Co. of Am., 679 F. Supp. 495 (W.D. Pa.), *aff'd,* 856 F.2d 184 (3d Cir. 1988); Bowersox v. P.H. Glatfelter Co., 677 F. Supp. 307 (M.D. Pa. 1988); Porta v. Rollins Envtl. Servs., Inc., 654 F. Supp. 1275 (D.N.J. 1987), *aff'd,* 845 F.2d 1014 (3d Cir. 1988); Polay v. West Co., 629 F. Supp. 899 (E.D. Pa. 1986); Stringer v. Pennsylvania Dep't of Community Affairs, 446 F. Supp. 704 (M.D. Pa. 1978).

Fourth Circuit: Swentek v. USAIR, Inc., 830 F.2d 552, 558 (4th Cir. 1987); Magnuson v. Peak Technical Servs., Inc., 808 F. Supp. 500 (E.D. Va. 1992) (court exercised supplemental jurisdiction); Keziah v. W.M. Brown & Son, 683 F. Supp. 542 (W.D.N.C. 1988), *modified,* 888 F.2d 322 (4th Cir. 1989); Glezos v. Amalfi Ristorante Italiano, Inc., 651 F. Supp. 1271 (D. Md. 1987) (sexual harassment); Thomas v. Trustees of Livingston College, 43 Fair Empl. Prac. Cas. (BNA) 885 (M.D.N.C. 1987).

Fifth Circuit: Waltman v. International Paper Co., 875 F.2d 468 (5th Cir. 1989); Valdez v. Church's Fried Chicken, Inc., 683 F. Supp. 596 (W.D. Tex. 1988); Saulsberry v. Atlantic Richfield Co., 673 F. Supp. 811 (N.D. Miss. 1987); Benton v. Kroger Co., 640 F. Supp. 1317 (S.D. Tex. 1986).

Sixth Circuit: Boyd v. James S. Hayes Living Health Care Agency, 671 F. Supp. 1155 (W.D. Tenn. 1987); Pease v. Alford Photo Indus., 667 F. Supp. 1188 (W.D. Tenn. 1987); Coley v. Consolidated Rail Corp., 561 F. Supp. 645 (E.D. Mich. 1982); Robson v. Eva's Mkt., 538 F. Supp. 857, 859 (N.D. Ohio 1982).

Seventh Circuit: Gilardi v. Schroeder, 833 F.2d 1226 (7th Cir. 1987); Dockter v. Rudolf Wolff Futures, Inc., 684 F. Supp. 532, 539 (N.D. Ill. 1988), *aff'd,* 913 F.2d 456 (7th Cir. 1990); Busse v. Gelco Express Corp., 678 F. Supp. 1398 (E.D. Wis. 1988); Clay v. Quartet Mfg. Co., 644 F. Supp. 56 (N.D. Ill. 1986); Horbaczewsky v. Spider Staging Sales Co., 621 F. Supp. 749 (N.D. Ill. 1985); Scott v. Sears Roebuck & Co., 605 F. Supp. 1047 (N.D. Ill. 1985), *aff'd,* 798 F.2d 210 (7th Cir. 1986); Zabkowicz v. West Bend Co., 589 F. Supp. 780 (E.D. Wis. 1984), *aff'd in part, rev'd in part,* 789 F.2d 540 (7th Cir. 1986).

Eighth Circuit: Phillips v. Smalley Maintenance Servs. Corp., 711 F.2d 1524 (8th Cir. 1983); Flowers v. Rego, 675 F. Supp. 1165, 1167 (E.D. Ark. 1988).

Ninth Circuit: Lapinad v. Pacific Oldsmobile-GMC, Inc., 679 F. Supp. 991 (D. Haw. 1988); Seib v. Elko Motor Inn, Inc., 648 F. Supp. 272 (D. Nev. 1986); Priest v. Rotary, 634 F. Supp. 571 (N.D. Cal. 1986).

Eleventh Circuit: Studstill v. Borg Warner Leasing, 806 F.2d 1005 (11th Cir. 1986); Bell v. Crackin Good Bakers, Inc., 777 F.2d 1497 (11th Cir. 1985); Brown v. City of Miami Beach, 684 F. Supp. 1081 (S.D. Fla. 1988); Guyette v. Stauffer Chem. Co., 518 F. Supp. 521 (D.N.J. 1981).

claims that arise out of "a common nucleus of operative fact" with the Title VII action.[73] Tort theories that have been asserted include intentional infliction of emotional distress,[74] assault and battery,[75] tortious interference with an employment contract,[76] false imprisonment,[77] and negligence.[78] An attorney must decide whether the facts of the case warrant the inclusion of state law claims (see **Chapter 9**).

In *United Mine Workers v. Gibbs,*[79] the U.S. Supreme Court established a two-pronged standard for pendent state claims. A court must first determine whether it has jurisdiction over the state law claims and then it must decide whether it should hear them. Jurisdiction may be asserted over state claims if (1) there exists a federal claim with "substance sufficient to confer subject matter jurisdiction on the court," (2) the state and federal claims "derive from a common nucleus of operative fact," and (3) the claims are such that the plaintiff would "ordinarily be expected to try them all in one proceeding."[80] *Gibbs* set out a number of factors that courts have considered in deciding whether to exercise jurisdiction over pendent state claims:

1. Judicial economy, convenience, and fairness to the litigants[81]

---

[73] United Mine Workers v. Gibbs, 383 U.S. 715, 725 (1966). *See also* Saulsberry v. Atlantic Richfield Co., 673 F. Supp. 811 (N.D. Miss. 1987) (repeated attempts by defendant to seduce plaintiff, which constituted the core of the intentional infliction of emotional distress claim, were essential to Title VII claim); Guzman Robles v. Cruz, 670 F. Supp. 54 (D.P.R. 1987); Thomas v. Trustees of Livingston College, 43 Fair Empl. Prac. Cas. (BNA) 885 (M.D.N.C. 1987); Frykberg v. State Farm Mut. Auto. Ins. Co., 557 F. Supp. 517 (W.D.N.C. 1983) (sexual harassment). *Cf.* Swanson v. Elmhurst Chrysler/Plymouth, Inc., 43 Fair Empl. Prac. Cas. (BNA) 399 (N.D. Ill. 1987) (sexual harassment) (federal and state claims presented entirely different facts and theories).

[74] Kalinauskas v. Wong, 808 F. Supp. 1469 (D. Nev. 1992) (supplemental jurisdiction could be exercised over state law tort claims).

[75] Campbell v. Kansas State Univ., 804 F. Supp. 1393 (D. Kan. 1992) (pendent jurisdiction exercised over state claims of assault and battery); Priest v. Rotary, 634 F. Supp. 571 (N.D. Cal. 1986).

[76] *See, e.g.,* Favors v. Alco Mfg. Co., 186 Ga. App. 480, 367 S.E.2d 328 (1988); Lewis v. Oregon Beauty Supply Co., 302 Or. 616, 733 P.2d 430 (1987).

[77] Favors v. Alco Mfg. Co., 186 Ga. App. 480, 367 S.E. 2d 328 (Ga. 1988); Lewis v. Oregon Beauty Supply Co., 302 Or. 616, 733 P.2d 430 (1987).

[78] Favors v. Alco Mfg. Co., 186 Ga. App. 480, 367 S.E.2d 328 (1988).

[79] 383 U.S. 715 (1966).

[80] *Id.* at 725. *See also* Moor v. County of Alameda, 411 U.S. 693 (1973).

[81] *See also* Flowers v. Rego, 675 F. Supp. 1165, 1167 (E.D. Ark. 1988) ("Because the plaintiff's Title VII and state law claims were premised on the same allegations of fact and would involve testimony by the same witnesses, . . . judicial economy, convenience and fairness to the litigants would best be served by trying both claims in one proceeding"); Saulsberry v. Atlantic Richfield Co., 673 F. Supp. 811 (N.D. Miss. 1987); Glezos

2. Whether the pendent state claims present unsettled questions of state law[82]
3. Whether state issues predominate in terms of proof, scope of issues raised, or comprehensiveness of remedies sought[83]
4. Whether the existence of divergent state and federal claims and theories would confuse a jury.[84]

Courts have declined to exercise pendent jurisdiction over related state claims when the only substantial federal claim arose under Title VII,[85] when state law claims invoke undecided issues of state law,[86] or when the defendant would be unduly prejudiced if the claims were tried in one proceeding.[87] Some courts also have held that the congressional mandates that Title VII actions be tried by a judge and that such actions be expedited support the finding of "a congressional negation of the exercise of pendent jurisdiction."[88]

Plaintiffs may also plead state civil rights claims. In *Bridges v. Eastman Kodak Co.*,[89] the court exercised pendent jurisidiction over the plaintiff's state human rights act claims despite the defendants' contention that both jury confusion and predomination of state issues were likely to result because of the disparity in damages awarded under state and federal laws and different standards of employer liability. The Civil Rights Act of 1991 (CRA) provides that the jury not be informed of damages limitations, and juries are instructed regularly on different theories of relief, even when only federal claims are present. "The mere existence of one difference in

---

v. Amalfi Ristorante Italiano, Inc., 651 F. Supp. 1271 (D. Md. 1987) (sexual harassment); Swanson v. Elmhurst Chrysler/Plymouth, Inc., 43 Fair Empl. Prac. Cas. (BNA) 399 (N.D. Ill. 1987) (sexual harassment); Bakken v. North Am. Coal Corp., 641 F. Supp. 1015 (D.N.D. 1986); Zamore v. Dyer, 597 F. Supp. 923 (D. Conn. 1984).

82 Flowers v. Rego, 675 F. Supp. 1165, 1167 (E.D. Ark. 1988).

83 *Id.*; Kritil v. Port E. Transfer, Inc., 661 F. Supp. 66 (D. Md. 1986); Glezos v. Amalfi Ristorante Italiano, Inc., 651 F. Supp. 1271 (D. Md. 1987) (sexual harassment).

84 Flowers v. Rego, 675 F. Supp. 1165, 1167 (E.D. Ark. 1988); Glezos v. Amalfi Ristorante Italiano, Inc., 651 F. Supp. 1271 (D. Md. 1987) (sexual harassment).

85 Bouchet v. National Urban League, Inc., 730 F.2d 799 (D.C. Cir. 1984) (collects cases).

86 Guzman Robles v. Cruz, 670 F. Supp. 54 (D.P.R. 1987) (sexual harassment) (The Supreme Court of Puerto Rico had not decided whether under a particular law compensatory damages for emotional distress were available to an employee who had been discharged.).

87 Swanson v. Elmhurst Chrysler/Plymouth, Inc., 43 Fair Empl. Prac. Cas. (BNA) 399 (N.D. Ill. 1987) (sexual harassment).

88 Guzman Robles v. Cruz, 670 F. Supp. 54, 57 (D.P.R. 1987). *See also* Kritil v. Port E. Transfer, Inc., 661 F. Supp. 66 (D. Md. 1986).

89 800 F. Supp. 1172 (S.D.N.Y. 1992).

legal theory does not create a sufficient likelihood of jury confusion to justify dismissing plaintiffs' HRL [state antidiscrimination law] claims."[90]

A court may refuse to hear state law claims if doing so would complicate the trial and result in the predominance of state issues.[91] Jury confusion may result if state law standards for proving sex discrimination are stricter or broader than under Title VII.[92] If the federal claims are dismissed before trial, state claims may be dismissed as well.[93] "The district court, of course, has the discretion to determine whether its investment of judicial energy justifies retention of jurisdiction. . . or if it should more properly dismiss the claims without prejudice."[94] Several courts have rejected arguments that the existence of a state antidiscrimination statute preempts common law tort remedies.[95]

§ 4.18 —State Common Law Claims

The inclusion of pendent state law claims may either enhance or hinder a Title VII sexual harassment action, depending on the facts surrounding the case. Counsel should carefully weigh the relative advantages of applicable legal theories to maximize potential recovery without compromising the client's financial and emotional needs.

Although compensatory and punitive damages are now available in Title VII actions under the Civil Rights Act of 1991, such damages are limited depending on the size of the employer, and so may be more appropriately sought under state common law.

---

90 *Id.* at 1179. *See also* Bonilla v. Liquilux Gas Corp., 812 F. Supp. 286 (D.P.R. 1993) (court would exercise jurisdiction over pendent Puerto Rico Civil rights claims, despite different standards of proof for sake of judicial economy and similarity of remedies).

91 Barbetta v. Chemlawn Servs. Corp., 669 F. Supp. 569 (W.D.N.Y. 1987) (sexual harassment). *See also* Kelsey v. Sheraton Corp., 662 F. Supp. 10 (D. Conn. 1986); Polay v. West Co., 629 F. Supp. 899 (E.D. Pa. 1986).

92 Barbetta v. Chemlawn Servs. Corp., 669 F. Supp. 569 (W.D.N.Y. 1987).

93 United Mine Workers v. Gibbs, 383 U.S. 715, 726 (1966); Otto v. Heckler, 802 F.2d 337 (9th Cir. 1986); Foster v. Township of Hillside, 780 F. Supp. 1026 (D.N.J. 1992) (Wolin, J.) (the court would not exercise pendent jurisdiction over state law claims when it granted summary judgment as to the plaintiff's federal law claims).

94 Otto v. Heckler, 802 F.2d 337, 338 (9th Cir. 1986). Fowler v. Burns Sec. Servs., 763 F. Supp. 862 (N.D. Miss. 1991) *aff'd,* 979 F.2d 1534 (5th Cir. 1992). The court refused to hear pendent state law claims of intentional infliction of emotional distress, assault, seduction and threat and extortion in a RICO action when after struggling with these novel and complex issues, the court concluded that resolution of those matters was best left to appropriate state tribunal.

95 *See* Rojo v. Kliger, 205 Cal. App. 3d 646, 252 Cal. Rptr. 605 (1988); Erickson v. Marsh & McLennan Co., 227 N.J. Super. 78, 545 A.2d 812 (1988); Palmer v. BiMart Co., 92 Or. App. 470, 758 P.2d 888 (1988).

A jury trial may be available under pendent common law claims,[96] as long as the defendant is not a government official.[97]

---

96 The Seventh Amendment to the Constitution provides an inviolate right to jury trial "in Suits at common law, where the value in controversy shall exceed twenty dollars."

97 Walters v. City of Atlanta, 803 F.2d 1135 (11th Cir. 1986); Cancellier v. Federated Dep't Stores, 672 F.2d 1312 (9th Cir.), *cert. denied,* 459 U.S. 859 (1982).

CHAPTER 5

ADMINISTRATIVE PROCEDURES

§ 5.1 Introduction

Most sexual harassment suits are brought under Title VII of the Civil Rights Act of 1964,[1] which prohibits a covered employer from discriminating against any employee or applicant on account of race, color, sex, religion, or national origin. Title VII suits may be brought by both private

[1] 42 U.S.C. §§ 2000e to 2000e-17.

individuals[2] and the Equal Employment Opportunity Commission (EEOC)[3] against a private employer, employment agency, union, or joint labor-management training committee. Federal employees also may bring an employment discrimination action under Title VII.[4] The EEOC may bring a pattern-or-practice action or a suit to enforce a conciliation agreement as well as individual actions.[5]

Title VII and EEOC regulations set forth the jurisdictional requirements for bringing a discrimination action. Administrative requirements generally must be satisfied before a Title VII action may be brought in federal court.[6] The purpose of these requirements is to provide an opportunity to settle disputes through conciliation and to encourage cooperation and voluntary compliance as the preferred means for eliminating discriminatory employment practices.[7] A private individual generally must file a charge with the EEOC before bringing suit in federal court (see **§ 5.7** for exceptions to this rule). Time limitations under Title VII have been held to be subject to equitable modification and thus are not jurisdictional requirements.[8]

§ 5.2 Employee Actions

Title VII covers all private employers with at least 15 employees on each working day during at least 20 weeks in the current or preceding calendar year and who are engaged in an industry affecting interstate commerce.[9] Title VII coverage extends to state and local governments, governmental agencies, and political subdivisions.[10] Also covered are labor organizations representing employees engaged in an industry affecting interstate commerce.[11]

---

2 *Id.* § 2000e-5.

3 *Id.* §§ 2000e-5 and -6.

4 *Id.* § 2000e-16.

5 *Id.* §§ 2000e-5(f)(3), 2000e-6(b).

6 Alexander v. Gardner-Denver Co., 415 U.S. 36 (1974); McDonnell Douglas Corp. v. Green, 411 U.S. 792, 798 (1973); Kerans v. Porter Paint Co., 656 F. Supp. 267, 269 (S.D. Ohio 1987) (sexual harassment). Failure to exhaust administrative remedies before bringing suit does not deprive the court of subject matter jurisdiction. Womble v. Bhangu, 864 F.2d 1212 (5th Cir. 1989).

7 Alexander v. Gardner-Denver Co., 415 U.S. 36, 44 (1974); Kerans v. Porter Paint Co., 656 F. Supp. 267, 269 (S.D. Ohio 1987).

8 Zipes v. Trans World Airlines, Inc., 455 U.S. 385 (1982); Love v. Pullman, 404 U.S. 522 (1972). *Cf.* Mohasco Corp. v. Silver, 447 U.S. 807 (1980) (in deferral states, an EEOC charge must be filed within 240 days of violation); EEOC v. Commercial Office Prods. Co., 486 U.S. 107 (1988).

9 42 U.S.C. §§ 2000e-2(b), (c).

10 *Id.* §§ 2000e(a), (b); 2000e-5(c).

11 *Id.* §§ 2000e-2(c), (e).

Title VII protects an individual, employee, or applicant who has been discriminated against in a work environment regardless of whether the parties have a current employment relationship.[12] Independent contractors usually do not fall within the parameters of the statute. Several recent cases have addressed the sexual harassment of independent contractors. Although as a general rule, independent contractors may not sue their employers for discrimination under Title VII, when an employer exerts significant control over the working conditions of its independent contractors and their emloyees, when it controls their access to office space, their receipt of substantial allowances for office supplies and secretarial help, and their remedies for resolving workplace grievances, a power to interfere with employment opportunities may exist.[13] In *Benavides v. Moore,*[14] evidence raised a fact issue as to whether the plaintiff female insurance agent alleging sexual harassment was an employee under the state human rights act, thus precluding summary judgment on her retaliatory discharge and sexual harassment claims. Her contract stated that she was an independent contractor, contract terms were not negotiable, agents were required to perform certain customer services, the agents may sell only defendant's insurance, the agents were required to keep office hours, and the company provided secretarial and support services for the agents. While her contract stated that she was an independent contractor, the facts established a dispute under the economic realities/rights of control test. But in *Barnes v. Colonial Life & Accident Insurance Co.,*[15] evidence did not establish that the plaintiff insurance agent was an employee of the company for purposes of Title VII. She was paid by commission only, the defendant did not withhold taxes from her commissions, she received no medical or vacation leave, she was not directly reimbursed for normal sales expenses, she had substantial independence in where she worked and how she dealt with her own employees, and she could establish her own schedule and business hours.

Noncivil-service state or local government elected officials and selected staff, policy-making appointees, and advisors also generally are exempt from Title VII.[16]

Title VII also prohibits discrimination by an employment agency in referrals[17] or by a labor organization that operates a hiring hall or has 15 or more members and is a certified or recognized representative or affiliate of a covered labor organization.[18]

---

[12] *Id.* § 2000e-2.

[13] Matthews v. New York Life Ins. Co., 780 F. Supp. 1019 (S.D.N.Y. 1992).

[14] 848 S.W.2d 190 (Tex. Ct. App. 1993).

[15] 818 F. Supp. 978 (N.D. Tex. 1993).

[16] 42 U.S.C. § 2000e(f).

[17] *Id.* § 2000e-2(b).

[18] *Id.* § 2000e-7.

Most aggrieved federal employees may file an action under § 717 of Title VII.[19] Federal employees excluded from Title VII coverage include congressional employees,[20] aliens,[21] or members of the armed forces.[22] Senate employees and executive branch policitical appointees are now covered by the Civil Rights Act of 1991.[23]

§ 5.3 EEOC Actions

The EEOC may bring either individual or pattern-or-practice suits. Title VII gives the EEOC discretion to determine which actions it will bring on behalf of private individuals.[24] In determining whether it will file an action, the commission looks at whether the case (1) has the potential to promote the development of law favorable to the purposes of Title VII, (2) promotes the integrity of the commission's investigative and conciliation processes, (3) involves violations of established antidiscrimination principles, (4) involves the provision of important enhanced services to protected groups and individuals, and (5) is of special concern to particular geographic regions.[25] Charges filed by a commission member must be deferred to a state or local fair employment practices agency (FEP) if the challenged conduct occurred in a deferral state. Deferral is accomplished by notifying the FEP agency that the charge has been filed and offering to refer the charge to that agency. If no request is made by the FEP agency within a 10-day period, the commission may process the charge.

The commission may not sue the government, one of its agencies, or political subdivisions. If attempts at conciliation with the employer fail, the EEOC must refer the case to the U.S. Attorney General for disposition.[26]

---

19 *Id.* § 2000e-16(c).

20 Davis v. Passman, 442 U.S. 228 (1979).

21 Jalil v. Campbell, 590 F.2d 1120 (D.C. Cir. 1978).

22 Roper v. Department of the Army, 832 F.2d 247 (2d Cir. 1987); Johnson v. Alexander, 572 F.2d 1219 (8th Cir.), *cert. denied,* 439 U.S. 986 (1978), *reh'g denied,* 439 U.S. 1135 (1979). A member of the state national guard is an exempted member of the military. Stinson v. Hornsby, 821 F.2d 1537 (11th Cir. 1987), *cert. denied,* 488 U.S. 959 (1988).

23 See **Ch. 2.**

24 United States v. Allegheny-Ludlum Indus., Inc., 517 F.2d 826 (5th Cir. 1975), *cert. denied,* 425 U.S. 944 (1976). *See also* EEOC v. Gurnee Inn Corp., 48 Fair Empl. Prac. Cas. (BNA) 871 (N.D. Ill. 1988) (sexual harassment).

25 National Litigation Plan adopted by EEOC (Nov. 22, 1983).

26 42 U.S.C. § 2000e-5(f)(1).

§ 5.4 Charging Process

In *McDonnell Douglas Corp. v. Green,*[27] the U.S. Supreme Court held that an individual satisfies the statutory requirement to exhaust administrative procedures by filing a timely charge with the EEOC, or a state administrative agency if appropriate, and acts pursuant to a right-to-sue letter issued by the EEOC. Broad interpretation has been given to the procedural requirements of Title VII to make the statute accessible to the unrepresented complainant. Although the courts have held that an attorney's representation does not preclude such liberal interpretation,[28] attorneys should not rely on the court's magnanimity to circumvent statutory requirements.[29]

The following checklist outlines the charging procedures for a Title VII claim. Each element will be discussed separately in §§ **5.5** through **5.16.**

__1. Individuals or persons representing them must file a charge with either the EEOC or the relevant state or local agency. A charge may be filed by an aggrieved person, a commissioner, or a person or organization on behalf of an aggrieved person, by mail or in person at any EEOC office.

__2. A charge is a written, sworn statement alleging one or more Title VII violations, against a charged person or organization (see § **5.10**).

__3. A charge must be timely filed (see § **5.5**).

__4. A charge must be filed with the EEOC within 180 days of the occurrence of the alleged discriminatory conduct unless the following occur:

  __a. A charge has been filed by the plaintiff with a state or local deferral agency or referred by the EEOC to the deferral agency, thus extending the filing period to 300 days, or

  __b. A state or local agency has sent final notice that the charge has been processed. A charge may then be filed within 30 days of receipt of notice or 300 days after the act of discrimination, whichever occurs first.

__5. A charge may not be filed with the EEOC until 60 days after the filing of the same charge with a state or local agency,

---

27 411 U.S. 792 (1973).

28 Bethel v. Jefferson, 589 F.2d 631 (D.C. Cir. 1978).

29 Marrero-Rivera v. Department of Justice, 800 F. Supp. 1024 (D.P.R. 1992). Most important among administrative prerequisites is the timely filing of a charge with the EEOC and the request of a right-to-sue letter (citing A. Conte, Sexual Harassment in the Workplace: Law and Practice (John Wiley & Sons, Inc. 1990)).

unless the state or local agency has waived its processing right, or the state law that created the state or local agency is in its first year of operation, in which case there is a 120-day waiting period.[30]

__6. The EEOC must notify the respondent that it has been named in a Title VII charge within 10 days of the receipt of the charge.[31]

__7. A discrimination charge will be processed through one of five administrative procedures or be dismissed.

__8. The EEOC should render a determination of whether there is reasonable cause within 120 days of receiving a charge from a complainant or a deferral agency.[32] After this period has expired and regardless of whether the EEOC has reached any determination, administrative remedies will have been deemed exhausted, subject to the complainant's receipt of an EEOC right-to-sue letter.

§ 5.5 Timely Filing

Under Title VII, one of two limitations periods applies to filing a discrimination charge with the EEOC, depending on whether the discrimination occurred in a jurisdiction with a state or local unfair employment practices agency (deferral agency). If no deferral agency exists, a plaintiff has 180 days from the date of the alleged unlawful practice to file a charge with the EEOC.[33] In jurisdictions that have such agencies, the charge must be filed within 300 days of the alleged violation or within 30 days of receiving notice that the state or local agency has terminated proceedings under state or local law, whichever is earlier.[34]

The U.S. Supreme Court has held that a complainant who files a discrimination charge that is untimely under state law is still entitled to the 300-day filing period.[35]

---

30 42 U.S.C. § 2000e-5(e).

31 *Id.* § 2000e-5(b).

32 *Id.*

33 *Id.* § 2000e-5(e); 29 C.F.R. § 1601.13(a) (1993).

34 42 U.S.C. § 2000(e); *see also* Peterson v. City of Wichita, 706 F. Supp. 766 (D. Kan.), *rev'd on other grounds,* 888 F.2d 1307 (10th Cir 1989), *cert. denied,* 495 U.S. 932 (1990); EEOC v. Metal Serv. Co., 706 F. Supp. 401 (W.D. Pa. 1989). *Cf.* Mohasco Corp. v. Silver, 447 U.S. 807 (1980).

35 EEOC v. Commercial Office Prods. Co., 486 U.S. 107 (1988). *Accord* Mennor v. Fort Hood Nat'l Bank, 829 F.2d 553 (5th Cir. 1987); Maurya v. Peabody Coal Co., 823 F.2d 933 (6th Cir. 1987), *cert. denied,* 484 U.S. 1067 (1988); EEOC v. Shamrock Optical Co., 788 F.2d 491 (8th Cir. 1986).

The limitations period begins when a victim of discrimination knew or reasonably should have known that the challenged conduct was performed,[36] not when the perpetrator decided to commit the act.[37] In *quid pro quo* sexual harassment cases, a violation of Title VII occurs when an employer or supervisor alters the job status of an employee because she resisted sexual advances. Hostile environment harassment usually is repetitive, so a violation occurs when the challenged conduct alters the plaintiff's work conditions and remains unremedied, despite the plaintiff's complaints. In a constructive discharge action, the statutory filing period begins on the date the complainant learns or realizes that the employer will not respond to her complaints.[38]

§ 5.6 Equitable Tolling, Waiver, and Estoppel

The requirement that a complainant file a timely charge with the EEOC is not jurisdictional.[39] The filing period may be subject to tolling, estoppel, and waiver,[40] and claims may relate back to allegations in an earlier timely charge.[41] The failure to file with the EEOC at all, however, may warrant dismissal.[42] The requirements of verification,[43] notice of charge by the EEOC to the charged party within 10 days,[44] a reasonable cause finding within 120 days,[45] conciliation by the EEOC,[46] or the issuance of a right-to-sue notice within 180 days are not jurisdictional prerequisites to filing a

---

36 Allen v. United States Steel Corp., 665 F.2d 689, 692 (5th Cir. 1982).

37 Merrill v. Southern Methodist Univ., 806 F.2d 600, 605 (5th Cir. 1986).

38 Llewellyn v. Celanese Corp., 693 F. Supp. 369, 381 (W.D.N.C. 1988) (sexual harassment).

39 Rasimas v. Michigan Dep't of Mental Health, 714 F.2d 614 (6th Cir. 1983), *cert. denied,* 466 U.S. 950 (1984); Peterson v. City of Wichita, 706 F. Supp. 766 (D. Kan.), *rev'd on other grounds,* 888 F.2d 1307 (10th Cir 1989), *cert. denied,* 110 S. Ct. 2173 (1990).

40 Zipes v. Trans World Airlines, Inc., 455 U.S. 385 (1982). *See also* Valenzuela v. Kraft, 801 F.2d 1170 (9th Cir. 1986), *modified,* 815 F.2d 570 (9th Cir. 1987).

41 Washington v. Kroger Co., 506 F. Supp. 1158, *amended,* 512 F. Supp. 67 (W.D. Mo. 1981), *vacated on other grounds,* 671 F.2d 1072 (8th Cir. 1982).

42 Worrell v. Uniforms To You & Co., 673 F. Supp. 1461 (N.D. Cal. 1987) (sexual harassment).

43 42 U.S.C. § 2000e-5(b); 29 C.F.R. § 1601.9. *See also* Price v. Southwestern Bell Tel. Co., 687 F.2d 74 (5th Cir. 1982).

44 42 U.S.C. § 2000e-5(b). *See also* EEOC v. Burlington N., Inc., 644 F.2d 717 (8th Cir. 1981).

45 Alexander v. Gardner-Denver Co., 415 U.S. 36 (1974); McDonnell Douglas Corp. v. Green, 411 U.S. 792 (1973).

46 Canavan v. Beneficial Fin. Corp., 553 F.2d 860 (3d Cir. 1977).

suit in court.[47] A complainant is not required to demand a right-to-sue letter after the 180-day period has expired. However, a long delay without any effort by the complainant to obtain a right-to-sue letter could unduly prejudice the defendant and preclude suit under the theory of laches (see **Chapter 6**).

An EEOC decision to process an untimely charge is not binding on the court in a subsequent judicial proceeding.[48]

In sexual harassment cases, a mental or emotional disability may warrant equitable tolling of the filing periods. Sexual harassment victims may be distraught and under medical or psychiatric care. In *Llewellyn v. Celanese Corp.,*[49] tolling was appropriate when an employee went on medical leave because of depression and anxiety and her illness combined with medication hindered her ability to perform everyday activities.[50] But in *Barnell v. Paine Webber Jackson & Curtis, Inc.,*[51] a psychiatrist's diagnosis of anxiety neurosis was insufficient to establish tolling as a matter of law when the complainant clearly had the ability to function in society and was thus able to protect her legal rights.[52]

Victims of sexual harassment also may be unrepresented by counsel at the time of dismissal or constructive discharge and unprepared to begin legal proceedings against the harasser or employer. Courts also have recognized equitable tolling when the defendant has actively misled the plaintiff regarding the cause of action and the plaintiff reasonably relied on the misrepresentations,[53] and when the defendant has failed to post a

---

47 42 U.S.C. § 2000e-5(f)(1). The time provision is not mandatory. Younger v. Glamorgan Pipe & Foundry Co., 310 F. Supp. 195 (W.D. Va. 1969).

48 Goldman v. Sears, Roebuck & Co., 607 F.2d 1014, 1017 (1st Cir. 1979), *cert. denied,* 445 U.S. 929 (1980); Corbin v. Pan Am. World Airways, 432 F. Supp. 939, 943–44 (N.D. Cal. 1977).

49 693 F. Supp. 369, 379 (W.D.N.C. 1988) (sexual harassment).

50 *See also* Moody v. Bayliner Marine Corp., 664 F. Supp. 232, 234 (E.D.N.C. 1987) (sexual harassment).

51 No. 82 Civ. 1988 (S.D.N.Y. Sept. 17, 1987).

52 *See also* Steward v. Holiday Inn (SIC), Inc., 609 F. Supp. 1468 (E.D. La. 1985) (physical and/or mental incapacity does not toll limitations period).

53 Miller v. Aluminum Co. of Am., 679 F. Supp. 495, 502 (W.D. Pa. 1988), *aff'd,* 856 F.2d 184 (3d Cir. 1988) (sexual harassment). *See also* Franco-Rivera v. Chairman of Bd. of Directors of Fed. Dep. Ins. Corp., 690 F. Supp. 118 (D.P.R. 1988) (tolling was proper when employer admitted it concealed that it paid lower salaries to plaintiffs than to comparable employees of other facilities); King v. Telesphere Int'l, Inc., 632 F. Supp. 981 (N.D. Ill. 1986) (tolling was proper when employer did not provide plaintiff with reasons for termination). Tolling was not appropriate in the following cases: Day v. Rourke, 813 F.2d 400 (4th Cir. 1987); Peterson v. City of Wichita, 706 F. Supp. 766 (D. Kan. 1989) (employer gave only mistaken advice to a represented complainant); Sharpe v. American Express Co., 689 F. Supp. 294 (S.D.N.Y. 1988) (offering an employee assistance in finding another position in company did not toll limitations

legally sufficient notice of charge-filing requirements.[54] Although the time limit for filing EEOC charges may be tolled if the EEOC inadvertently misleads the complainant about proper procedure,[55] administrative error by the EEOC may not toll the statutory time period when the complainant is represented by counsel.[56] Courts may be less likely to apply principles of equitable tolling if the plaintiff is represented by counsel throughout the proceedings.[57] Moreover, incorrect information from the EEOC may toll the limitations period only if the complainant actually follows the advice.[58] Tolling may not be asserted in a conclusory manner.[59]

There are several other exceptions to the timeliness requirement. A complainant who has not exhausted administrative requirements may intervene in an action by a similarly situated plaintiff who has exhausted administrative remedies.[60] A charge of continuing violation may affect the timeliness requirement (see **§ 5.9**). An employer also may waive or be estopped from asserting a timeliness defense.[61]

Like nonfederal employees, federal employees may toll the filing period by alleging continuing discrimination. When a federal complainant was not

---

period); Mauro v. Board of Higher Educ., 658 F. Supp. 322 (S.D.N.Y. 1986), *aff'd,* 819 F.2d 1130 (3d Cir.), *cert. denied,* 484 U.S. 865 (1987). *See also* Kocian v. Getty Ref. & Mktg. Co., 707 F.2d 748, 753 (3d Cir.), *cert. denied,* 464 U.S. 852 (1983).

54 Linquist v. AT&T Info. Sys., No. 86C 124 (June 10, 1987). *See also* Llewellyn v. Celanese Corp., 693 F. Supp. 369, 378 (W.D.N.C. 1988) (sexual harassment) (filing period was tolled when the posted notice required employees to communicate with company officials rather than with EEOC). *Cf.* DiMaggio v. United States Postal Serv., 643 F. Supp. 1 (D. Conn. 1984) (employer's failure to post EEO notices did not toll filing period when complainant had already successfully prosecuted another sex discrimination action).

55 Chappell v. Emco Mach. Works Co., 601 F.2d 1295 (5th Cir. 1979).

56 Hamel v. Prudential Ins. Co., 640 F. Supp. 103 (D. Mass. 1986) (sexual harassment).

57 Dixon v. Westinghouse Elec. Corp., 615 F. Supp. 538 (D. Md. 1985), *aff'd,* 787 F.2d 943 (4th Cir.), *reh'g denied,* 795 F.2d 368 (4th Cir. 1986).

58 Welty v. S.F.&G., Inc., 605 F. Supp. 1548 (N.D. Ala. 1985).

59 Dixon v. Westinghouse Elec. Corp., 615 F. Supp. 538 (D. Md. 1985), *aff'd,* 787 F.2d 943 (4th Cir.), *reh'g denied,* 795 F.2d 368 (4th Cir. 1986).

60 Cook v. Boorstin, 763 F.2d 1462 (D.C. Cir. 1985); Foster v. Gueory, 655 F.2d 1319 (D.C. Cir. 1981); Wheeler v. American Home Prods. Corp., 563 F.2d 1233 (5th Cir. 1977); Allen v. Amalgamated Transit Union Local 788, 554 F.2d 876 (8th Cir.), *cert. denied,* 434 U.S. 891 (1977).

61 Nordell v. Bowen, 42 Fair Empl. Prac. Cas. (BNA) 465, 468 (D.D.C. 1986). *See also* EEOC v. Mico Oil Co. LEXIS 13627 (D. Kan. 1988) (timeliness objections were waived when defendant admitted in his answer that all conditions precedent to filing lawsuit were fulfilled). *Cf.* Crandell v. New Jersey Transit Bus Operations, 42 Fair Empl. Prac. Cas. (BNA) 1888 (D.N.J. 1986) (conduct of employer did not suggest a waiver when employer raised timeliness issue in its answer to complaint and served relevant discovery materials).

notified of the time limitations and was not otherwise aware of them, or was prevented by circumstances beyond the complainant's control from meeting the filing deadline, EEOC Merit Systems Protection Board regulations require the employing agency to waive the 30-day time limit for filing the initial charge or complaint.[62] It is unclear whether the acceptance and processing of an untimely complaint without an express waiver by the agency estops the agency from asserting an untimeliness defense.[63]

The filing period for federal employees also may be tolled by the receipt of misleading information from the EEOC, even if the conduct was inadvertent.[64]

A federal employee who has not complied with exhaustion requirements may intervene in an action by a similarly situated employee who has fulfilled administrative requirements.[65]

§ 5.7 Deferral to State Agency

An aggrieved party must file discrimination charges with a state or local antidiscrimination agency, if one exists, before filing a complaint with the EEOC.[66] The EEOC has adopted a procedure whereby the complainant need not file with the state agency directly, but with the EEOC itself, which will refer the charge to the appropriate agency.[67] The relevant state agency must have the authority to handle the particular discriminatory practice in question.[68] If the complaint alleges a number of practices, state procedures must be followed if the agency has jurisdiction over most of the raised allegations.[69] State procedures must be utilized even if fewer remedies are available than under Title VII.[70]

---

62 29 C.F.R. § 1613.214(a)(4). *See* Ettinger v. Johnson, 556 F.2d 692, 697–98 (3d Cir. 1977).

63 *Compare* Sims v. Heckler, 725 F.2d 1143 (7th Cir. 1984) *and* Stockton v. Harris, 434 F. Supp. 276, 280 (D. Colo. 1977) (agency not estopped) *with* Jarrell v. United States Postal Serv., 753 F.2d 1088 (D.C. Cir. 1985) (agency estopped).

64 Miller v. Marsh, 766 F.2d 490 (11th Cir. 1985).

65 De Medina v. Reinhardt, 686 F.2d 997 (D.C. Cir. 1982).

66 42 U.S.C. § 2000e-5(c); Love v. Pullman, 404 U.S. 522 (1972).

67 29 C.F.R. § 1601.13(a)(3); Mohasco Corp. v. Silver, 447 U.S. 807, 816 (1980); Love v. Pullman, 404 U.S. 522 (1972); Urrutia v. Valero Energy Corp., 841 F.2d 123 (5th Cir.), *cert. denied,* 488 U.S. 829 (1988); Scott v. Sears Roebuck & Co., 605 F. Supp. 1047, 1053 (N.D. Ill. 1985), *aff'd,* 798 F.2d 210 (7th Cir. 1986); Wilson v. St. Louis-San Francisco Ry., 673 F.2d 1152 (10th Cir. 1982).

68 29 C.F.R. § 1601.13(a)(2); Cunningham v. Litton Indus., 413 F.2d 887 (9th Cir. 1969).

69 EEOC v. Union Bank, 408 F.2d 867 (9th Cir. 1968).

70 Crosslin v. Mountain States Tel. & Tel. Co., 422 F.2d 1028 (9th Cir. 1970), *vacated on other grounds,* 400 U.S. 1004 (1971).

State and local agencies have their own timing requirements for discrimination charges. Failure to timely file a charge with a state or local agency may affect a subsequent state action, but a timely state or local filing of a discrimination charge is not a jurisdictional prerequisite to a Title VII suit, as long as the state filing is made in sufficient time to allow an effective filing with the EEOC within 300 days.[71]

The complainant starts a state proceeding by filing a written and signed factual charge.[72] The state agency then has 60 days to respond to the discrimination charge.[73] A federal district court may stay an action for up to 60 days pending the termination of the state agency processing.[74] The court also may assume jurisdiction over the case pursuant to the filing of a Title VII charge as long as the state or local agency has had an opportunity to investigate the complainant's allegations[75] and the plaintiff has received a right-to-sue letter before trial.[76] State time limitations for filing discrimination charges govern state agency proceedings, but Title VII time limits apply for the purpose of bringing a Title VII suit.[77]

Worksharing agreements usually divide responsibilities for charges between the relevant state agency and the EEOC. The state agency contracts to investigate to conclusion a minimum number of charges at a fixed price per charge.[78] This process helps avoid duplication of effort and promotes the resolution of claims. Through these agreements, state agencies may waive their rights to first consideration of discrimination complaints. Complainant's failure to exhaust state agency procedures is not a bar to civil suit when these rights are waived.[79]

---

[71] EEOC v. Commercial Office Prods. Co., 486 U.S. 107 (1988).

Third Circuit: Stringer v. Pennsylvania Dep't of Community Affairs, 446 F. Supp. 704 (M.D. Pa. 1978) (sexual harassment).

Fourth Circuit: EEOC v. Hansa Prods., 844 F.2d 191 (4th Cir. 1988) (sexual harassment).

Seventh Circuit: Sere v. Board of Trustees, 628 F. Supp. 1543 (N.D. Ill. 1986), *aff'd,* 852 F.2d 285 (7th Cir. 1988).

Eighth Circuit: EEOC v. Shamrock Optical Co., 788 F.2d 491 (8th Cir. 1986); Owens v. Ramsey Corp., 656 F.2d 340 (8th Cir. 1981).

Tenth Circuit: Downum v. City of Wichita, 675 F. Supp. 1566 (D. Kan. 1986) (sexual harassment); Torriero v. Olin Corp., 684 F. Supp. 1165 (S.D.N.Y. 1988) (sexual harassment).

[72] 42 U.S.C. § 2000e-5(c).

[73] 29 C.F.R. § 1601.13(a)(3)(ii) (1988).

[74] 42 U.S.C. § 2000e-5(f)(1).

[75] Metcalf v. Omaha Steel Castings Co., 507 F. Supp. 679 (D. Neb. 1981).

[76] Wrighten v. Metropolitan Hosps., Inc., 726 F.2d 1346 (9th Cir. 1984).

[77] 42 U.S.C. § 2000e-5(c); Oscar Mayer & Co. v. Evans, 441 U.S. 750 (1979).

[78] EEOC Compliance Manual (CCH) § 5.2, ¶ 282 (1982 & Supp. 1988).

[79] Douglas v. Red Carpet Corp., 538 F. Supp. 1135 (E.D. Pa. 1982).

§ 5.8 Federal Employees and Exhaustion of Administrative Remedies

Under EEOC regulations, processing a discrimination charge against the government begins with a counseling period. A complainant must contact designated EEO counselors within 45 days of "the matter alleged to be discriminatory"[80] unless the complainant can show cause for failing to meet the deadline.[81] The counselor advises the complainant of her rights and responsibilities, and the counseling period ends 30 days after the complainant's first contact with the counselor, unless the complainant and the agency agree in writing to extend the period for up to 60 days.[82]

Federal employees must exhaust administrative remedies before filing suit in federal court unless they can demonstrate that exhaustion would be futile[83] or that good faith attempts were hindered by agency personnel.[84] A party must submit a charge to the relevant EEO counselor within 30 days of the alleged act of discrimination.[85] Most courts have held that this is not a jurisdictional requirement.[86] If practical, the EEO counselor shall complete the final interview within 21 days of the charge.[87] The party then has

---

80 29 C.F.R. § 1614.105(a)(1).

81 *Id.* § 1614.105(a)(2).

82 *Id.* § 1614.105(e).

83 Thornton v. Coffey, 618 F.2d 686 (10th Cir. 1980).

84 Allen v. Butz, 390 F. Supp. 836 (E.D. Pa. 1975); Ellis v. Naval Air Rework Facility, 404 F. Supp. 377 (N.D. Cal. 1975).

85 29 C.F.R. § 1613.214(a(1))(i).

86 Boddy v. Dean, 821 F.2d 346, 350 (6th Cir. 1987); Henderson v. United States Veterans Admin., 790 F.2d 436, 440 (5th Cir. 1986); Zografov v. Veterans Admin., 779 F.2d 967, 968 (4th Cir. 1985); Boyd v. United States Postal Serv., 752 F.2d 410, 414 (9th Cir. 1985); Saltz v. Lehman, 672 F.2d 207, 208 (D.C. Cir. 1982); Neves v. Kolaski, 602 F. Supp. 645 (D.R.I. 1985). *Cf.* Perel v. Health Care Fin. Admin., 804 F.2d 678 (4th Cir. 1986) (dismissal was appropriate when complainant did not notify EEO counselor until almost two years after alleged denial of promotion, even though complainant did go to his union representative within 30 days and representative filed timely charge on his behalf); Theard v. United States Army, 653 F. Supp. 536 (M.D.N.C. 1987) (letter to the EEO alleging discrimination did not constitute a timely contact with an EEO counselor); Andrzejewski v. United States Postal Serv., 636 F. Supp. 758 (E.D. Mo. 1986) (action was time-barred when even though complainant consulted her EEO officer within 30 days, she sought only information and did not indicate she had suffered discrimination or file complaint). *But see* Polisoto v. Weinberger, 638 F. Supp. 1353 (W.D. Tex. 1986) (requirement is jurisdictional). *Accord* Sims v. Heckler, 725 F.2d 1143 (7th Cir. 1984). However, the failure to exhaust administrative remedies is an affirmative defense the employer is required to prove. Young v. National Ctr. for Health Servs. Research, 828 F.2d 235 (4th Cir. 1987).

87 29 C.F.R. § 1613.213(a).

15 days from the date of the formal notice from the EEO counselor to file a formal complaint and seek a hearing.[88]

A party may appeal to the EEOC or file a civil action even if she does not file a formal complaint.[89] An appeal to the EEOC must be filed within 20 days of receiving notice of final agency action.[90] A federal employee may appeal to the district court if there has not been a final agency action on the claim six months after its filing. However, she is not required to do so and may instead wait for a final determination.[91]

§ 5.9 Continuing Violation

When discriminatory conduct persists over the course of employment, a sexual harassment claim may proceed as long as the final act of discrimination occurred during the charging period.[92] "Sexual innuendos and ongoing disparate treatment based on sex have been found to constitute a continuing violation."[93] A claim for sexual harassment is not time-barred when there are continuous acts of discrimination over a period of time as long as some of the acts fall within the limitations period. In *Accardi v. Superior Court (Simi Valley),*[94] a state sexual harassment suit, the former police officer plaintiff alleged that over the course of 11 years, she was subjected to numerous and continuing episodes of discrimination and harassment, including, among other things, spreading untrue rumors about her abilities, deliberately singling her out for unfavorable work assignments and work shifts, making unsubstantiated complaints about her performance, making statements that her baton was only useful to perform sex acts, stuffing her shotgun barrels with paper so that the weapon would explode if fired, spreading rumors that she had slept with superior officers to receive favorable assignments, making sexual advances towards her, admitting to her that there were double standards and that she must live with them, mimicking

---

88 *Id.* § 613.214(a)(1)(ii).

89 The decision to file an appeal of a Merit Systems Protection Board Final Order to the district court rather than the EEOC did not constitute a failure to exhaust administrative remedies. Wood v. Regan, 622 F. Supp. 399 (E.D. Pa. 1985).

90 29 C.F.R. § 1613.233(a).

91 Gomez v. Department of the Air Force, 869 F.2d 852 (5th Cir. 1989).

92 Held v. Gulf Oil Co., 684 F.2d 427 (6th Cir. 1982); Fuchilla v. Prockop, 682 F. Supp. 247, 258 (D.N.J. 1987) (sexual harassment); Clay v. Quartet Mfg. Co., 644 F. Supp. 56 (N.D. Ill. 1986) (sexual harassment and equal pay); Vermett v. Hough, 627 F. Supp. 587 (W.D. Mich. 1986) (sexual harassment).

93 Porta v. Rollins Envtl. Servs., Inc., 654 F. Supp. 1275, 1282 (D.N.J. 1987), *aff'd,* 845 F.2d 1014 (3d Cir. 1988); Held v. Gulf Oil Co., 684 F.2d 427 (6th Cir. 1982).

94 21 Cal. Rptr. 292 (Ct. App. 1993) (Gilbert, J.).

and making fun of her in front of a room filled with officers, and threatening to disrupt her wedding. Although acts that were alleged to have taken place in the last two years may not have been actionable viewed in isolation, a complaint for sexual harassment must not be read too narrowly:

> A single photograph of two sumo wrestlers engaged in combat may give the impression they are dancing a pas de deux. One must witness the entire match to appreciate its meaning and significance. . . .
>
> . . . A view of the events from beginning to end enables the trier of fact to see their relationship to one another, and consequently their meaning and significance. That there are gaps between specific incidents of sexual harassment does not preclude a finding of continuing violation.[95]

A hostile environment inherently may be a continuing violation, particularly when based on classwide harassment. In *Jenson v. Eveleth Taconite Co.,*[96] a class action, the court noted that:

> In the arena of sexual harassment, particularly that which is based on the existence of a hostile environment, it is reasonable to expect that violations are continuing in nature: a hostile environment results from acts of sexual harassment which are pervasive and continue over time, whereas isolated or single incidents of harassment are insufficient to constitute a hostile environment. Accordingly, claims based on sexual harassment often straddle both sides of an artificial statutory, cut-off date.
>
> Moreover, evidence of what occurred prior to the beginning of the statutory period is relevant evidence which may be considered in determining whether a hostile environment existed during the relevant period. This view is implied in *Meritor:* the Supreme Court considered acts of harassment that had occurred over a four year period. At no time did the court mention that some of those events occurred outside the relevant time period. Similarly, in *Robinson,* the court found that incidents of harassment which predated the beginning of the statutory period were a necessary part of its review of Robinson's claims.[97]

A discriminatory policy is not a continuing violation per se, but the application to the plaintiff of that policy during the limitations period will render the charge timely.[98] Even if only one adverse employment action has

---

95 *Id.* 297. *See also* Berry v. Board of Supervisors, 715 F.2d 971 (5th Cir. 1983), *cert. denied,* 479 U.S. 868 (1986).

96 824 F. Supp. 847 (D. Minn 1993).

97 *Id.* at 877.

98 Abrams v. Baylor College of Medicine, 805 F.2d 528 (5th Cir. 1986); Davis v. Richmond, Fredericksburg & Potomac R.R., 803 F.2d 1322 (4th Cir. 1986); Cobb v. Stringer, 660 F. Supp. 1133 (W.D. Ark. 1987), *modified,* 850 F.2d 356 (8th Cir. 1988).

occurred during the statutory filing period, a continuing violation may be found if the employment action is reasonably related to previous sexual harassment.[99] The complaint must allege present and ongoing discrimination for conduct occurring outside the limitations period to be actionable.[100] The repetitive nature of the challenged conduct and the relationship between the specific acts of discrimination should be clearly set out in the charge.

§ 5.10 Contents of the Charge

Title VII provides:

> a charge . . . filed by or on behalf of a person claiming to be aggrieved, or by a member of the Commission, alleging that an employer, employment agency, labor organization, or joint labor-management committee . . . has

---

[99] Porta v. Rollins Envtl. Servs., Inc., 654 F. Supp. 1275, 1282 (D.N.J. 1987), *aff'd,* 845 F.2d 1014 (3d Cir. 1988) (events that happened prior to discharge, within the statute of limitations, were reasonably related to termination).

[100] Delaware State College v. Ricks, 449 U.S. 250, 257 (1980); United Air Lines v. Evans, 431 U.S. 553 (1977); Porta v. Rollins Envtl. Servs., Inc., 654 F. Supp. 1275, 1281–82 (D.N.J. 1987), *aff'd,* 845 F.2d 1014 (3d Cir. 1988). The plaintiff's ultimate burden is to show by a preponderance of the evidence some form of intentional discrimination to be company policy or procedure. . . . For summary judgment purposes, she must at least identify the policy or practice upon which she bases the claim of continuing violation and show some support for her claim.

See also Stair v. Lehigh Valley Carpenters Local Union No. 600, 813 F. Supp. 1112 (E.D. Pa. 1993). In an action by a former union member against the international and local unions and the union's business agent, the court held that the plaintiff could introduce evidence concerning a remark made outside the statutes of limitations period when allegations of individual incidents of harassment, made up of a number of comments about the plaintiff's buttocks as well as the distribution by the union from 1987 to 1990 of calendars of women in various stages of nudity were sufficient to allow the plaintiff to proceed on a continuing violation theory and thus she could introduce the remark.

Cf. Purrington v. University of Utah, 966 F.2d 1025 (10th Cir. 1993). The observation by the plaintiff of two incidents of sexual harassment by her former supervisor after the supervisor was transferred to a different department did not meet the requirements necessary for a continuing violation to toll the charge-filing deadlines of a Title VII suit. Testimony that there had been a lot of complaints against the supervisor did not equitably toll the limitations period when the plaintiff failed to pursue formal action after knowing that the university investigations and remedies would be inadequate.

Cf. Miller v. Aluminum Co. of Am., 679 F. Supp. 495, 500 (W.D. Pa.), *aff'd,* 856 F.2d 184 (3d Cir. 1988). A plaintiff who was demoted and later terminated did not demonstrate the existence of a continuing violation by showing that her supervisor had had affairs with other female employees at the times of the employment decisions. "At best, Miller alleges two separate discriminatory acts against the same employee with the same general discriminatory motive. This does not make out a continuing violation."

> engaged in an unlawful employment practice, . . . shall be in writing under oath or affirmation and shall contain such information and be in such form as the Commission requires.[101]

Despite this language, the courts have liberally applied the Act and have required only that the charge be in writing.[102] The Ninth Circuit has held that an intake questionnaire, filled out by all complainants who visit an EEOC office, fulfills this requirement, even though the questions ordinarily are not answered under oath.[103] Defects in the charge, including the failure of the EEOC to verify the charge or to clarify or amplify its allegations, usually may be cured through amendment.[104] An unsigned charge even may survive initial scrutiny.[105]

Unlawful employment practices must be directly related to or grow out of the original filed charge for EEOC investigations[106] and federal lawsuits,[107] but courts have been reluctant to find that sexual harassment charges were related to or grew out of wage-based or other discrimination

---

101 42 U.S.C. § 2000e-5(b). *See also* EEOC Compliance Manual (CCH) § 2.2, ¶ 152 (1982 & Supp. 1989).

102 Cobb v. Stringer, 850 F.2d 356 (8th Cir. 1988).

103 *Cf.* Peterson v. City of Wichita, 706 F. Supp. 766 (D. Kan.), *rev'd on other grounds,* 888 F.2d 1307 (10th Cir 1989), *cert. denied,* 110 S. Ct. 2173 (1990) (oath requirement is mandatory and not subject to waiver); Buffington v. General Time Corp., 677 F. Supp. 1186 (M.D. Ga. 1988); Hamel v. Prudential Ins. Co., 640 F. Supp. 103 (D. Mass. 1986) (even if intake questionnaire were considered a charge, the complainant did not file until at least 348 days after the last alleged act of sexual harassment); Proffit v. Keycom Elec. Publishing, 625 F. Supp. 400 (N.D. Ill. 1985); Casavantes v. California State Univ., 732 F.2d 1441 (9th Cir. 1984). *See also* Gilardi v. Schroeder, 833 F.2d 1226, 1229–30 (7th Cir. 1987) (sexual harassment).

104 29 C.F.R. § 1601.12(b) (1988). *See also* Hall v. F.O. Thacker Contracting Co., 24 Fair Empl. Prac. Cas. (BNA) 1499, 1502 (N.D. Ga. 1980) (verification may be supplied later); Ludington v. Sambo's Restaurants, Inc., 474 F. Supp. 480, 483 (E.D. Wis. 1979). *See also* EEOC v. Calumet Photographic, Inc., 687 F. Supp. 1249 (N.D. Ill. 1988) (complainant cannot bring an action based on an unverified, unamended charge; compliance with statutory oath is required to perfect the charge).

105 Price v. Southwestern Bell Tel. Co., 687 F.2d 74 (5th Cir. 1982). *See also* Casavantes v. California State Univ., 732 F.2d 1441 (9th Cir. 1984) *Cf.* Peterson v. City of Wichita, 706 F. Supp. 766 (D. Kan. 1989) (unsworn and unverified "discrimination complaint form" transferred to the EEOC was not a charge under Title VII).

106 Bennett v. New York City Dep't of Corrections, 705 F. Supp. 979 (S.D.N.Y. 1989) (no jurisdiction over plaintiff's claim that she was discriminatorily denied computer training when such a claim was factually dissimilar from charges that she was harassed on the basis of race and sex).

107 Clay v. Quartet Mfg. Co., 644 F. Supp. 56 (N.D. Ill. 1986) (sexual harassment and equal pay). *Cf.* Anderson v. Lewis Rail Serv. Co., 868 F.2d 774 (5th Cir. 1989) (the court considered only those grounds raised during the administrative process).

claims without separate allegations of sexual harassment.[108] Complainants therefore should make sure to allege sexual harassment separately[109] from any other unlawful employment practice. In *Cruz v. Ecolab Pest Elimination Div., Ecolab, Inc.*,[110] the plaintiff's EEOC charge containing allegations of discriminatory discharge did not give the employer sufficient notice of intention to raise sexual harassment claims:

> The agency complaint was one of discriminatory discharge, no less but no more, a discrete claim, standing alone, and failing to suggest, explicitly or implicitly, any other form of conduct violative of Title VII. In short, Cruz' EEOC charge failed in its important public policy purpose of giving defendants sufficient notice of her intention to raise allegations pertaining to discrimination in areas other than a discriminatory discharge, thereby depriving defendants and the agency itself of the opportunity of reconciliation.[111]

In *Zakutansky v. Bionetics Corp.*,[112] a retaliation charge could be filed within 90 days after the issuance of the EEOC right-to-sue letter, even though the letter did not refer to retaliation when the plaintiff's EEOC charge asserted a belief that she had been retaliated against for resisting sexual harassment. An EEOC charge should, at the very least, identify the parties and describe generally the challenged practice.[113] In *Kinnally v. Bell of Pennsylvania*,[114] the failure by the plaintiff to name the president, manager, and direct supervisor of the defendant company in her EEOC charge did not warrant dismissal of the Title VII action when she referred to the president, fellow engineers, and supervisors in the charge, the parties communicated with the company EEO investigator regarding the sexual harassment allegations, and the manager and supervisor were present at the state FEP agency's fact-finding hearing. The court noted that jurisdictional

---

108 Carter v. Sedgwick County, 705 F. Supp. 1474 (D. Kan. 1988) (district court did not have jurisdiction to consider plaintiff's sexual harassment claims when the original charge alleged racial but not sex discrimination); Torriero v. Olin Corp., 684 F. Supp. 1165, 1170 (S.D.N.Y. 1988); Bartha v. Service Sys. Corp., 44 Fair Empl. Prac. Cas. (BNA) 1765, 1766 (W.D.N.Y. 1987); Clay v. Quartet Mfg. Co., 644 F. Supp. 56, 60 (N.D. Ill. 1986). *See also* Hornsby v. Conoco, Inc., 777 F.2d 243 (5th Cir. 1985).

109 *Cf.* Zalewski v. M.A.R.S. Enters., 561 F. Supp. 601, 605 (D. Del. 1982) (although complainant told intake clerk of her sexual harassment, she asked that it not be included in charge and thus could not later bring suit in federal court on that basis).

110 817 F. Supp. 388 (S.D.N.Y. 1993).

111 *Id.* at 391–92.

112 806 F. Supp. 1362 (N.D. Ill. 1992).

113 29 C.F.R. § 1604.12(b). Waiters v. Robert Bosch Corp., 683 F.2d 89 (4th Cir. 1982). *See also* Marrero-Rivera v. Department of Justice, 821 F. Supp. 65 (D.P.R. 1993). The plaintiff could not amend her complaint to add two defendants who were not named in the EEOC charge.

114 748 F. Supp. 1136 (E.D. Pa. 1990).

requirements should be liberally construed: "This is especially so where, as here, the preliminary pleadings were substantially crafted *pro se.* In such circumstances, courts not only considered the parties formally listed as respondents, but look to plaintiff's 'factual statement' as 'the crucial element' in determining whether the requirements of the pleading have been met."[115]

An employment discrimination charge may be filed in person or by mail either at the EEOC office in Washington D.C., at any of its district or area offices, or with any designated representative of the commission.[116]

§ 5.11 Charge Processing Procedures

The EEOC uses several charge processing procedures, depending on the type of charge and the stage of the investigation. Most disparate treatment charges go through the rapid charge processing system, the goal of which is settlement by the parties on mutually acceptable terms. In this system, the EEOC reviews a copy of every charge alleging retaliation or otherwise warranting preliminary relief. The EEOC compliance manual notes that sexual harassment cases often warrant priority.[117] The EEOC performs a detailed intake interview for screening and emergency relief for entitled complainants. Within 10 days, the EEOC serves the employer with a copy of the charge and a request for relevant information,[118] which may include a copy of the defendant's sexual harassment policy and implementation procedures, personnel files of the charging party, the alleged harasser and other employees who have complained of sexual harassment, and copies of previous complaints of sexual harassment. If the matter is not resolved at this point, the EEOC investigator conducts a fact-finding conference with the parties to further define the issues. The presence of attorneys at this conference is permitted but discouraged. Attendance is not mandatory, but it is important for all parties to be present. If these efforts at conciliation are not successful, the EEOC will either conduct a more extensive investigation or make a cause finding that the case has no merit.

The systemic case processing system targets employers whose policies and practices result in the low utilization of women and/or minorities. They employ a substantially smaller proportion of women and/or minorities than other employers in the same labor market or have fewer women

---

115 *Id.* at 1139–40.

116 29 C.F.R. § 1601.8.

117 EEOC Compliance Manual (CCH) § 2.8, ¶ 158 (1982 & Supp. 1989).

118 42 U.S.C. § 2000e-5(b).

and/or minorities in their higher-paid job categories than in their lower-paid job categories.[119]

Title VII charges that do not involve allegations of retaliation or do not otherwise warrant preliminary relief are channeled through the extended charge processing system.[120]

§ 5.12 EEOC Investigation

An EEOC investigation may encompass all employer practices "like or related" to the discriminatory conduct alleged in the charge.[121] The commission may obtain any information relevant to its investigation[122] and may use any relevant information that state or local agencies have already gathered.[123] The EEOC may require a fact-finding conference with the parties "to define the issues, to determine which elements are undisputed, to resolve those issues that can be resolved and to ascertain whether there is a basis for negotiated settlement of the charge."[124]

The complainant has a right to see the information in her file, including that obtained from employer records.[125]

During the intake process, the EEOC may interview witnesses who may provide crucial testimony regarding the alleged sexual harassment. The EEOC Policy Guidance Statement notes that investigators should question the charging party and the alleged harasser in detail, and that supervisory and managerial employees, as well as coworkers, should be asked about their knowledge of the alleged harassment.[126] The EEOC uses its broad power to subpoena documents and witnesses.[127] To uphold a challenged subpoena, a court need only find that the subpoena was valid and that the

---

119 EEOC Compliance Manual (Callaghan) pt. III, § 1.105 (1984).

120 EEOC Compliance Manual (CCH) § 2.8, ¶ 158 (1982 & Supp. 1989).

121 Jenkins v. Blue Cross Mut. Hosp. Ins. Co., 538 F.2d 164 (7th Cir.), *cert. denied,* 429 U.S. 986 (1976).

122 New Orleans Pub. Serv. v. Brown, 507 F.2d 160 (5th Cir. 1975); EEOC v. University of N.M., 504 F.2d 1296 (10th Cir. 1974); Motorola, Inc. v. McClain, 484 F.2d 1339 (7th Cir. 1973), *cert. denied,* 416 U.S. 936 (1974); Parliament House Motor Hotel v. EEOC, 444 F.2d 1335 (5th Cir. 1971); EEOC v. National Elec. Benefit Fund, 12 Fair Empl. Prac. Cas. (BNA) 1006 (D.D.C. 1976).

123 29 C.F.R. § 1601.15(a).

124 *Id.* § 1601.15(c).

125 EEOC v. Associated Dry Goods Corp., 449 U.S. 590 (1981), *on remand,* 720 F.2d 804 (4th Cir. 1983).

126 8 Fair Empl. Prac. Cas. (BNA) 405:6687 (Mar. 19, 1990).

127 42 U.S.C. § 2000e-9; 29 C.F.R. §§ 1601.16(a), 1601.17. *See also* EEOC Compliance Manual (Callaghan) pt. III, § 1.107 (1984).

requested material is relevant to the charge.[128] The court need not hold an evidentiary hearing or oral argument when the issues involve questions of law and no factual disputes need to be resolved.[129] The U.S. Supreme Court has stated that "any effort by the court to assess the likelihood that the Commission would be able to prove the claims made in the charge would be reversible error."[130] The employer does not have a right to ascertain through discovery the underlying basis for the subpoena.[131]

Courts have enforced subpoenas despite challenges that compliance would be burdensome[132] or that the information sought was confidential.[133] The Seventh Circuit has held that the alleged untimeliness of a discrimination claim does not negate the investigative authority of the EEOC and thus is not a proper defense to enforcement of a subpoena requesting information about an employer's hiring, layoff, and recall practices.[134] Other courts, however, have denied subpoenas based on untimely charges[135] unless the EEOC is investigating whether a continuing violation

---

128 EEOC v. Shell Oil Co., 466 U.S. 54 (1984).

129 EEOC v. Astronautics Corp. of Am., 660 F. Supp. 838 (E.D. Wis. 1987).

130 EEOC v. Shell Oil Co., 466 U.S. 54, 72 n.26 (1984).

131 EEOC v. K-Mart Corp., 694 F.2d 1055 (6th Cir. 1982). *Accord In re* EEOC, 709 F.2d 392 (5th Cir. 1983); Food Town Stores v. EEOC, 708 F.2d 920 (4th Cir. 1983), *cert. denied,* 465 U.S. 1005 (1984).

132 EEOC v. Maryland Cup Corp., 785 F.2d 471 (4th Cir.), *cert. denied,* 479 U.S. 815 (1986); EEOC v. Quick Shop Mkts., Inc., 526 F.2d 802 (8th Cir. 1975); New Orleans Pub. Serv. v. Brown, 507 F.2d 160 (5th Cir. 1975); Circle K Corp. v. EEOC, 501 F.2d 1052 (10th Cir. 1974); Local 104, Sheet Metal Workers Int'l Assoc. v. EEOC, 439 F.2d 237 (9th Cir. 1971); EEOC v. Astronautics Corp. of Am., 660 F. Supp. 838 (E.D. Wis. 1987); EEOC v. Kelly-Springfield Tire Co., 38 Fair Empl. Prac. Cas. (BNA) 194 (E.D.N.C. 1985). *Cf.* EEOC v. Bay Shipbuilding Corp., 668 F.2d 304 (7th Cir. 1981) (subpoena was not enforced when defendant demonstrated that compliance would threaten normal operation of the business); Valley Indus. Servs., Inc., v. EEOC, 570 F. Supp. 902 (N.D. Cal. 1983) (compiling information would be extremely expensive).

133 EEOC v. University of N.M., 504 F.2d 1296 (10th Cir. 1974).

134 EEOC v. Tempel Steel Co., 814 F.2d 482, 485 (7th Cir. 1987):

> As long as the investigation is within the agency's authority, the subpoena is not too indefinite, and the information sought is reasonably relevant, the district court must enforce an administrative subpoena. . . . While an exception might exist if the party under investigation were able to establish that there was clearly no factual or legal support for the agency's preliminary determination to investigate, . . . this is not such a case.

See also EEOC v. Bellemar Parts Indus., 865 F.2d 780 (6th Cir.), *modified on other grounds,* 868 F.2d 199 (6th Cir. 1989) (filing of charge is jurisdictional prerequisite to judicial enforcement of subpoena issued by EEOC); EEOC v. Roadway Express, 750 F.2d 40 (6th Cir. 1984); EEOC v. South Carolina Nat'l Bank, 562 F.2d 329 (4th Cir. 1977); EEOC v. General Tire & Rubber Co., 22 Fair Empl. Prac. Cas. (BNA) 574 (N.D. Ohio 1980).

135 *See, e.g.,* EEOC v. Air Prods. & Chems., Inc., 652 F. Supp. 113 (N.D. Fla. 1986).

has occurred.[136] Courts also have refused to enforce extremely vague or broad EEOC subpoenas.[137]

The EEOC may dismiss a discrimination charge that is not timely filed or otherwise fails to state a claim.[138] A charge also may be dismissed if the complainant fails to provide requested information, cannot be located, or refuses to accept a settlement offer that would afford full relief for the alleged harm.[139]

§ 5.13 Special Investigatory Issues in Sexual Harassment Charges

In a recent policy statement, the EEOC provided guidance regarding the investigation of a sexual harassment charge, noting that investigators should address the issues of welcomeness of the challenged conduct, whether the alleged harassment constituted a hostile environment, the complainant's relationship to the alleged harasser, and the response of the employer to complaints of harassment.

Welcomeness of the Challenged Conduct. The EEOC instructs its investigators to determine whether conduct was welcome from the perspective of a totality of circumstances.[140] Although conduct is generally not welcome when there is evidence of contemporaneous protest, such evidence is not determinative because there may be a number of reasons why an employee would not complain about harassment, such as fear of reprisal. When there is no evidence of complaints, an investigator must try to ascertain the reasons for silence.[141]

---

136 EEOC v. Western Publishing Co., 502 F.2d 599 (8th Cir. 1974); Pacific Maritime Ass'n v. Quinn, 491 F.2d 1294 (9th Cir. 1974).

137 General Ins. Co. v. EEOC, 491 F.2d 133 (9th Cir. 1974) (demand was unduly broad when it reached back almost eight years and sought evidence regarding forms of discrimination not charged); EEOC v. Packard Elec. Div., GM Corp., 569 F.2d 315 (5th Cir. 1978); Joslin Dry Goods Co. v. EEOC, 483 F.2d 178 (10th Cir. 1973); Manpower, Inc. v. EEOC, 346 F. Supp. 126 (E.D. Wis. 1972) (vagueness). *Cf.* EEOC v. MCI Telecommunications Corp., 45 Fair Empl. Prac. Cas. (BNA) 1650 (D.D.C. 1988) (subpoena that sought documents demonstrating or relating to reasons for employee's discharge and documents identifying relevant witnesses was specific enough).

138 29 C.F.R. § 1601.18(a). The EEOC requires that a person have standing to file a charge if it is to be investigated. EEOC Compliance Manual (CCH) § 4.3(c) ¶ 253 (1982 & Supp. 1992).

139 29 C.F.R. § 1601.18(b), (c), (d).

140 8 Fair Empl. Prac. Cas. (BNA) 405:6685 (Mar. 19, 1990).

141 *Id.*

Existence of a Hostile Environment. The EEOC has adopted a "reasonable person" standard for determining whether challenged conduct constitutes a hostile environment regarding Title VII.[142] A single incident may not suffice unless it is particularly egregious.[143] Touching a complainant's intimate body areas is sufficiently offensive to alter the conditions of her working environment,[144] but verbal harassment will be examined more closely to determine the nature, frequency, context, and intended target of the language, as well as the relationship between the complainant and the alleged harasser, whether the complainant participated in the conduct, and whether the language was hostile and derogatory.[145]

The Complainant's Relationship to the Alleged Harasser. To determine the employer's liability, the EEOC investigators must seek information regarding the relationship between the parties using agency principles. An employer will be liable for hostile environment sexual harassment by a coworker or a supervisor if the employer knew or should have known about the harassment. *Quid pro quo* sexual harassment in a supervisor relationship may result in strict liability for employers if the underlying harassment is proven.

Employer's Response to Complaints of Harassment. An investigator will try to determine whether an employer conducted a prompt and thorough investigation of the sexual harassment allegations and, if appropriate, whether an employer took prompt and corrective action. If the harassment is eliminated, the victims made whole, and preventive measures instituted, the commission generally will close the charge.[146]

§ 5.14 Predetermination Settlement

Before making a reasonable cause determination, the EEOC may ask the parties again to discuss the possibility of settlement.[147] The EEOC will not be a party to and thus cannot enforce a settlement that contains unlawful provisions or that appears to sanction or approve an uninvestigated policy or practice, or that contains a waiver of prospective rights.[148] At the respondent's request, the complainant may stipulate that she waives the right to sue

---

[142] *Id.* 405:6689.

[143] *Id.* 405:6690.

[144] *Id.* 405:6691.

[145] *Id.*

[146] *Id.* 405:6701.

[147] 29 C.F.R. § 1601.19(a).

[148] EEOC Compliance Manual (CCH) § 15.7, ¶ 547 (1982 & Supp. 1988).

under the relevant statutes in exchange for monetary relief, hiring, promotion, reinstatement, or other equitable relief. The respondent would thus be released from additional investigation and potentially greater liability.[149] The EEOC may not disclose any information during these settlement discussions.[150] If the matter is not resolved, the EEOC will issue a reasonable cause determination.

§ 5.15 Reasonable Cause Determination

At the end of its investigation, the EEOC will determine whether the charge has sufficient merit to warrant litigation if conciliation is unsuccessful. A reasonable cause finding is a determination that the charging party and/or class members probably suffered discrimination, based upon evidence that establishes a prima facie case and, if the respondent asserts a reasonable defense, whether the defense was pretextual.[151] Conciliation efforts are not required prior to a reasonable cause determination,[152] but once the EEOC finds reasonable cause, it must attempt to conciliate the matter[153] (see **§ 5.16**). If conciliation is unsuccessful, the commission may then file suit in federal court.[154]

Although under Title VII the commission should render a reasonable cause determination within 120 days after the charge is filed, compliance with this provision is not required.[155] A number of factors, including the cooperation of the parties and the complexity of the issues, determine the time period necessary for charge processing. If the EEOC has found reasonable cause, it will notify the complainant and invite participation in conciliation efforts. The complainant does not receive a right-to-sue notice with the determination letter when cause is found, but one may be requested if the 180 days have passed since the complainant filed the charge.

If the EEOC field office concludes there is no reasonable cause to believe that the alleged discrimination has occurred, the EEOC will issue a letter of determination to all parties.[156] The no cause determination letter informs the aggrieved party of the right to sue within 90 days of receipt of the letter of

---

149 *Id.* § 15.6, ¶ 546 (1982 & Supp. 1988).

150 Sears, Roebuck & Co. v. EEOC, 435 F. Supp. 751 (D.D.C. 1971), *aff'd in part & rev'd in part on other grounds,* 581 F.2d 941 (D.C. Cir. 1978).

151 EEOC Compliance Manual (CCH) § 40.2, ¶ 1062 (1982 & Supp. 1988).

152 EEOC v. St. Anne's Hosp., 664 F.2d 128 (7th Cir. 1981).

153 42 U.S.C. § 2000e-5(b).

154 *Id.* at § 2000e-5(f).

155 Stewart v. EEOC, 611 F.2d 679 (7th Cir. 1979); Kelly v. EEOC, 468 F. Supp. 417 (D. Md. 1979).

156 29 C.F.R. § 1601.19(a) (1988).

determination.[157] The Commission or an issuing director may on its own initiative reconsider a final determination of no reasonable cause.[158] If a notice of intent to reconsider is issued within 90 days of receipt of the final no cause determination, and the person claiming to be aggrieved or the person on whose behalf a charge was filed has not filed suit and has not requested or received a right-to-sue notice, the notice of intent to reconsider vacates the letter of determination and revokes the charging party's right to sue in 90 days.[159] After reconsideration, the Commission or issuing director will issue a new determination.[160] A no cause determination does not bar a Title VII suit, but it is admissible in court as evidence of lack of discrimination.[161]

§ 5.16 Conciliation

Upon a finding of reasonable cause that a violation has occurred, Title VII requires that the EEOC attempt to eliminate the alleged illegal employment practices through conference, conciliation, and persuasion.[162] After notifying all the parties, the conciliator will meet with the charging party to determine whether any events have occurred since the investigation was completed that would affect the complainant's original remedial objectives, such as employment history, interest in reinstatement, and loss of earnings computation.[163] If the complainant is represented by an attorney, the conciliator should meet with the charging party only with the attorney's agreement.[164] The conciliator will inform the charging party that the EEOC seeks the same remedy that a federal court would provide should the complainant prevail in litigation,[165] and that the complainant, upon receipt of a right-to-sue

---

157 *Id.*

158 *Id.* § 1601.19(b).

159 *Id.*

160 *Id.*

161 Barfield v. Orange County, 911 F.2d 644 (11th Cir. 1990); Smith v. Universal Servs., 454 F.2d 154 (5th Cir. 1972); Grant v. Morgan Guar. Trust Co., 638 F. Supp. 1528 (S.D.N.Y. 1986). *Cf.* Cortes v. Maxus Exploration Co., 977 F.2d 195 (5th Cir. 1992) (Title VII and state duress claim). A determination that the prejudicial effect of EEOC documents, concluding that no reasonable cause existed to believe that unlawful discrimination occurred, outweighed their probative value was not an abuse of discretion when these documents contained only conclusory determinations that were not based on detailed evidentiary statements.

162 42 U.S.C. § 2000e-5(b); 29 C.F.R. § 1601.24(a). Defendants do not have a right under statute to conciliation efforts by the EEOC. Sedlacek v. Hoch, 752 F.2d 333 (8th Cir. 1985).

163 EEOC Compliance Manual (CCH) § 62.4(a), ¶ 1264 (1982 & Supp. 1988).

164 *Id.* § 62.4(c), ¶ 1264.

165 *Id.* § 62.4(a), ¶ 1264.

letter (see **§ 5.17**), may file under the relevant statutes before the conciliatory process is completed.[166]

After meeting with the complainant and preparing conciliation proposals, the conciliator will schedule a conference with the respondent employer.[167] At the conference, the conciliator will explain to the respondent that the commission seeks a written agreement, containing a waiver of the charging party's right to sue, that remedies the violation and provides relief for the complainant and all other aggrieved persons.[168] The conciliator then will present the proposal.[169] If necessary, the respondent may submit modifications within 10 days.[170] The agreement is then presented to the charging party for review and signature. Minor changes may be submitted to the respondent for approval.[171] If the charging party refuses to accept the relief and other class members are affected, the EEOC may resolve matters other than those specifically relating to the charging party.[172]

If conciliation efforts are successful, the terms of the agreement are reduced to writing and copies are sent to the aggrieved party and the respondent.[173] However, if an employer refuses to participate in conciliation or if conciliation fails, the EEOC may send the complainant a right-to-sue notice (see **§ 5.17**) or may file suit on behalf of the complainant.[174] All matters relating to conciliation are confidential,[175] but this requirement does not preclude releasing the identities of complainants or the complaints themselves to the employer.[176] Proof of the employer's compliance with Title VII must be obtained by the commission before a case is closed.[177]

§ 5.17 EEOC Suits

Before the EEOC begins a discrimination action in federal court, it must file a written administrative charge that is signed and verified.[178] The failure

166 *Id.* § 62.4(b)(2), ¶ 1264.

167 *Id.* § 62.5, ¶ 1265.

168 *Id.* § 64.2, ¶ 1292.

169 *Id.* § 64.4, ¶ 1294.

170 *Id.* § 64.6(a), ¶ 1296.

171 *Id.* § 64.7, ¶ 1297.

172 *Id.* §§ 63.3, 64.7, ¶ 1283, 1297.

173 29 C.F.R. § 1601.24(a).

174 *Id.* § 1601.25.

175 42 U.S.C. § 2000e-5(b); 29 C.F.R. § 1601.26(a).

176 Whitaker v. Carney, 778 F.2d 216 (5th Cir. 1985), *cert. denied,* 479 U.S. 813 (1986).

177 29 C.F.R. § 1601.24(c).

178 *Id.* § 1601.11(a).

to verify a charge may be cured by subsequent verification[179] unless the employer has been prejudiced.[180] Nor will the EEOC's failure to notify an employer of a charge filed against it as required by Title VII necessarily bar a civil action unless the employer can show prejudice or bad faith.[181] Although not required by Title VII, courts have required an investigation by the EEOC before filing suit (see § **5.12**)[182] and before beginning conciliation efforts (see § **5.15**).[183] The EEOC also must make a reasonable cause determination (see § **5.14**) at the administrative level to bring a Title VII action in federal court.[184] This finding must provide sufficient notice of the allegations to the employer, because the scope of a subsequent court action will be limited by the reasonable cause finding.[185]

Conciliation efforts (see § **5.15**) also must precede the filing of a civil action.[186] The EEOC must conciliate with all parties charged in the action[187] and allow each a fair opportunity to address the asserted issues.[188] The commission need not conciliate all the relief it may seek later in federal court.[189]

---

179 Sears, Roebuck & Co. v. EEOC, 504 F. Supp. 241 (N.D. Ill.), *motion for reconsideration denied,* 24 Fair Empl. Prac. Cas. (BNA) 1202 (N.D. Ill. 1980).

180 EEOC v. Sears, Roebuck & Co., 490 F. Supp. 1245 (M.D. Ala. 1980).

181 EEOC v. Burlington N., Inc., 644 F.2d 717 (8th Cir. 1981); EEOC v. Sears, Roebuck & Co., 490 F. Supp. 1245 (M.D. Ala. 1980) (broad charge subsequently brought against only one of employer's 3000 facilities was dismissed without prejudice when employer did not have adequate notice of specific charge).

182 E.I. Du Pont de Nemours & Co. v. EEOC, 373 F. Supp. 1321 (D. Del. 1974), *aff'd on other grounds,* 516 F.2d 1297 (3d Cir. 1975); EEOC v. Container Corp. of Am., 352 F. Supp. 262 (M.D. Fla. 1972). *See also* EEOC v. Keco Indus., 748 F.2d 1097 (6th Cir. 1984) (inquiry into sufficiency of EEOC's investigation was not proper when commission merely broadened scope of employee's charge by adding more employees to number victimized by employer's allegedly discriminatory practices).

183 EEOC v. Bailey Co., 563 F.2d 439 (6th Cir. 1977), *cert. denied,* 435 U.S. 915 (1978).

184 E.I. Du Pont de Nemours & Co. v. EEOC, 373 F. Supp. 1321 (D. Del. 1974), *aff'd on other grounds,* 516 F.2d 1297 (3d Cir. 1975).

185 EEOC v. General Elec. Co., 532 F.2d 359 (4th Cir. 1976).

186 42 U.S.C. § 2000e-5(f)(1); EEOC v. Newtown Inn Assocs., 647 F. Supp. 957 (E.D. Va. 1986) (sexual harassment); EEOC v. One Bratenahl Place Condominium Ass'n, 644 F. Supp. 218 (N.D. Ohio 1986) (sexual harassment).

187 Raymond Metals Co. v. EEOC, 385 F. Supp. 907 (D. Md. 1974), *aff'd in part & rev'd in part on other grounds,* 530 F.2d 590 (4th Cir. 1976).

188 EEOC v. Sears, Roebuck & Co., 650 F.2d 14 (2d Cir. 1981); EEOC v. Zia Co., 582 F.2d 527 (10th Cir. 1978) (EEOC failed to allow enough time for negotiations); EEOC v. Sears, Roebuck & Co., 490 F. Supp. 1245 (M.D. Ala. 1980).

189 EEOC v. Massey-Ferguson, Inc., 622 F.2d 217 (7th Cir. 1980). *Cf.* EEOC v. American Express Publishing Corp., 681 F. Supp. 216 (S.D.N.Y. 1988) (class claims were dismissed when EEOC conciliated only individual complainant's claims, because defendant could not have fairly anticipated class claims, even though EEOC filed suit on behalf of complainant and others adversely affected by employer's practices).

However, it may make a sufficient initial effort "without undertaking exhaustive investigation or proving discrimination to the employer's satisfaction, . . . so long as it makes a sincere and reasonable effort to negotiate by providing the defendant a reasonable opportunity to respond to and negotiate all charges."[190] If an employer refuses to participate in conciliation or rejects the offer, the EEOC's obligation to pursue resolution is terminated.[191] The EEOC generally must notify an employer if it decides that it is unable to conciliate a discrimination charge and that further efforts to do so would be futile or nonproductive.[192]

An EEOC charge also must be processed by relevant state deferral agencies, unless worksharing agreements allow such agencies to waive jurisdiction for EEOC charges (see **§ 5.7**).

The EEOC may bring suit on an individual charge if it has been unable to obtain an acceptable conciliation agreement from the employer within 30 days after a charge was filed or within 30 days after any deferral period expired.[193] If, during its investigation, the EEOC uncovers other unlawful employment practices, it may bring suit even if it were to conclude that no reasonable cause exists to believe that the original charge was true.[194]

The EEOC has the authority to bring a pattern-or-practice suit in federal district court when it has reasonable cause to believe that any person or group has engaged in a pattern or practice hindering the enjoyment of rights protected by Title VII.[195]

The EEOC also may bring suit to enforce a conciliation agreement if it does not believe the employer has adequately complied with it.[196]

When an EEOC district director determines that attempts at conciliation have failed, the case file is referred to a regional attorney who decides whether to recommend or reject a case for litigation.[197] If the respondent is the government, a government agency, or a political subdivision, the commissioner will refer the case to the Attorney General, who may then bring

---

[190] Marshall v. Hartford Fire Ins. Co., 78 F.R.D. 97, 107 (D. Conn. 1978) (EEOC gave only lip service to conciliation).

[191] EEOC v. Newtown Inn Assocs., 647 F. Supp. 957 (E.D. Va. 1986); EEOC v. One Bratenahl Place Condominium Ass'n, 644 F. Supp. 218 (N.D. Ohio 1986).

[192] 29 C.F.R. § 1601.25; EEOC v. Hickey-Mitchell Co., 507 F.2d 944 (8th Cir. 1974). *Cf.* Kimberly-Clark Corp. v. EEOC, 511 F.2d 1352 (6th Cir.), *cert. denied,* 423 U.S. 994 (1975) (failure to give notice to employer was "harmless error" when respondent was not prejudiced).

[193] 42 U.S.C. § 2000e-(f)(1); 29 C.F.R. § 1601.27. *See also* EEOC v. Newtown Inn Assocs., 647 F. Supp. 957 (E.D. Va. 1986) (sexual harassment).

[194] EEOC v. Brookhaven Bank & Trust Co., 614 F.2d 1022 (5th Cir. 1980).

[195] 42 U.S.C. § 2000e-6(c).

[196] EEOC Compliance Manual (CCH) § 80.13(c), ¶ 1683 (1982 & Supp. 1988).

[197] 29 C.F.R. § 1601.25; EEOC Compliance Manual (CCH) § 66.5, ¶ 1315 (1982 & Supp. 1989).

a civil action.[198] A district director who is dissatisfied with a decision not to bring suit may refer the case to the executive director, who may review the case with the general counsel. The general counsel may recommend a case for litigation despite a rejection by the regional attorney.[199]

Although the regional attorney may file an approved action immediately, a presuit letter may be sent to the employer to expedite settlement efforts. If such efforts fail, the regional attorney will file suit. The commission may bring an action for temporary or preliminary relief pending the final disposition of the charge. The case must be assigned for hearing at the first practical date.[200]

§ 5.18 Right-to-Sue Letter

A private individual may bring an action in the district court 180 days after a charge was filed with the EEOC.[201] Once an aggrieved private party has received a right-to-sue notice from the EEOC, the party has 90 days to bring a civil action against the respondent named in the charge.[202] A right-to-sue letter includes authorization to bring a civil action within 90 days of receiving it, advice regarding instituting the civil suit, a copy of the charge, and the decision of the commission.[203] The charging party has a right to obtain a right-to-sue letter from the EEOC 180 days after having filed the charge, regardless of whether the commission's administrative procedures have been concluded by that time.[204]

Generally, a civil action under Title VII may not be started without the receipt of a right-to-sue letter or notice of charge dismissal from the EEOC.[205] However, the EEOC's failure to issue a right-to-sue notice is not a jurisdictional bar to a Title VII action,[206] in light of *Zipes v. Trans World*

---

198 42 U.S.C. § 2000e-5(f)(1).

199 EEOC Compliance Manual (CCH) § 66.5(e), ¶ 1315 (1982 & Supp. 1989).

200 42 U.S.C. § 2000e-5(f)(2).

201 42 U.S.C. § 2000e-5(f)(1).

202 *Id.* § 2000e-5(f).

203 29 C.F.R. § 1604.28(e)(1)–(4) (1988).

204 *Id.* § 1604.28(a).

205 There are exceptions to this rule. Courts have allowed complainants to bring suit seeking preliminary relief before receiving the right-to-sue letter (see **Chapter 6**). Issuance of the right-to-sue notice after the complaint was filed but before a motion to dismiss was decided has been held to cure the original defect. *See, e.g.,* Gooding v. Warner-Lambert Co., 744 F.2d 354 (3d Cir. 1984); Williams v. Washington Metro. Area Transit Auth., 721 F.2d 1412 (D.C. Cir. 1983).

206 Fouche v. Jekyll Island-State Park Auth., 713 F.2d 1518 (11th Cir. 1983).

Airlines, Inc.[207] Thus, a technical error by the EEOC or a mistake by the complainant[208] has not barred individuals from maintaining an action under Title VII.[209] The absence of a right-to-sue letter may be cured by issuing one prior to the dismissal of the claims.[210]

The EEOC may issue a right-to-sue letter before the 180-day period expires, if it determines that agency action will not occur within that time,[211] although some courts have stated that Congress intended the EEOC to retain jurisdiction over a charge for the full 180 days.[212] If the commission fails to make such a determination, the right-to-sue letter will not be effective until the end of the 180-day period.[213]

---

207 455 U.S. 385, 393 (1982) ("filing a timely charge of discrimination with the EEOC is not a jurisdictional prerequisite to suit in a federal court, but a requirement that, like a statute of limitations, is subject to waiver, estoppel, and equitable tolling").

208 Movement for Opportunity & Equality v. General Motors Corp., 622 F.2d 1235 (7th Cir. 1980) (misleading acts by the EEOC may prevent a complainant from seeking a right-to-sue letter); Black v. Brown Univ., 555 F. Supp. 880 (D.R.I. 1983) (complainant misunderstood EEOC instructions).

209 Kahn v. Pepsi-Cola Bottling Group, 526 F. Supp. 1268 (E.D.N.Y. 1981) (EEOC lost file); National Org. for Women v. Sperry Rand Corp., 457 F. Supp. 1338 (D. Conn. 1978) (EEOC erred in refusing to issue right-to-sue letter); EEOC v. Rinella & Rinella, 401 F. Supp. 175 (N.D. Ill. 1975) (right-to-sue letter sent to organization that had filed suit on individual's behalf).

210 Fourth Circuit: Henderson v. Eastern Freightways, Inc., 460 F.2d 258 (4th Cir. 1972), *cert. denied,* 410 U.S. 912 (1973).

Fifth Circuit: Pinkard v. Pullman-Standard, 678 F.2d 1211 (5th Cir.), *reh'g denied,* 685 F.2d 1383 (5th Cir. 1982), *cert. denied,* 459 U.S. 1105 (1983).

Seventh Circuit: *Cf.* Gibson v. Kroger Co., 506 F.2d 647 (7th Cir. 1974), *cert. denied,* 421 U.S. 914 (1975) (action dismissed when employee failed to obtain a right-to-sue letter before filing suit and failed to amend his complaint to assert that he had received notice after employer filed a motion to dismiss).

Ninth Circuit: Wrighten v. Metropolitan Hosps. 726 F.2d 1346 (9th Cir. 1984).

211 29 C.F.R. § 1601.28(a)(2).

Second Circuit: Weise v. Syracuse Univ., 522 F.2d 397 (2d Cir. 1975).

Fourth Circuit: Vanguard Justice Soc'y, Inc. v. Hughes, 471 F. Supp. 670 (D. Md. 1979).

Fifth Circuit: Wells v. Hutchinson, 499 F. Supp. 174 (E.D. Tex. 1980).

Sixth Circuit: Cattell v. Bob Frensley Ford, Inc., 505 F. Supp. 617 (M.D. Tenn. 1980).

Seventh Circuit: Rolark v. University of Chicago Hosps., 688 F. Supp. 401 (N.D. Ill. 1988).

Ninth Circuit: Bryant v. California Brewers Ass'n, 585 F.2d 421 (9th Cir. 1978), *vacated on other grounds,* 444 U.S. 598 (1980).

212 Second Circuit: Spencer v. Banco Real, S.A., 87 F.R.D. 739 (S.D.N.Y. 1980).

Fourth Circuit: Loney v. Carr-Lowery Glass Co., 458 F. Supp. 1080 (D. Md. 1978).

Fifth Circuit: Grimes v. Pitney-Bowes, Inc., 480 F. Supp. 1381 (N.D. Ga. 1979).

Tenth Circuit: Mills v. Jefferson Bank E., 559 F. Supp. 34 (D. Colo. 1983).

213 Allen v. Schwab Rehabilitation Hosp., 509 F. Supp. 151 (N.D. Ill. 1981).

A complaint may be considered timely filed even if it fails to comply with formal requirements in local rules.[214] Some courts have held that the EEOC's failure to issue a right-to-sue letter does not foreclose a Title VII action, as long as the plaintiff is entitled to receive the letter.[215] The filing period starts on the day the complainant receives the right-to-sue letter, not the day the EEOC issued it.[216] Although some courts have held that the plaintiff must personally receive the letter to trigger the 90-day filing period,[217] others have held that constructive receipt of the right-to-sue letter through delivery to and acceptance by a responsible person living with the claimant is adequate.[218] When a letter is sent to a previous address, the court will look at whether the complainant failed to furnish the EEOC with a current address or whether the circumstances of the address change were beyond the complainant's control. If the complainant failed to notify the EEOC of her whereabouts, the 90-day period may begin on the day the notice was delivered to the most recent address on file.[219] The Sixth Circuit has held that the period begins to run on the fifth day after the date the EEOC mailed the right-to-sue notice to the last known address when the complainant failed to notify the EEOC of a move,[220] but again, the filing period will not begin if the address change is beyond the complainant's

---

214 Gilardi v. Schroeder, 833 F.2d 1226, 1233 (7th Cir. 1987) (sexual harassment).

215 Cordes v. County of Yavapai, 17 Fair Empl. Prac. Cas. (BNA) 1224 (D. Ariz. 1978) (sexual harassment).

216 McDonnell Douglas Corp. v. Green, 411 U.S. 792 (1973).

217 Archie v. Chicago Truck Drivers, 585 F.2d 210 (7th Cir. 1978) (receipt by spouse did not trigger filing period); *Accord* Croffut v. United Parcel Serv., Inc., 575 F. Supp. 1264 (E.D. Mo. 1984); Killingham v. Board of Governors of State Colleges & Univs., 549 F. Supp. 225 (N.D. Ill. 1982) (mother received notice); Fletcher v. Royston, 30 Fair Empl. Prac. Cas. (BNA) 286 (D.D.C. 1982) (father-in-law received notice); Harris v. Warner-Lambert Co., 486 F. Supp. 125 (N.D. Ga. 1980) (Title VII action was not untimely when claimant was not home the day the right-to-sue notice was delivered and the suit was filed within 90 days after plaintiff actually received notice).

218 Harvey v. City of New Bern Police Dep't, 813 F.2d 652 (4th Cir. 1987) (when complainant's wife received right-to-sue notice only six days before complainant saw it, the failure to bring suit within 90 days of date that wife received letter barred suit); Law v. Hercules, Inc., 713 F.2d 691 (11th Cir. 1983); Bell v. Eagle Motor Lines, 693 F.2d 1086 (11th Cir. 1982); Sager v. Hunter Corp., 665 F. Supp. 575 (N.D. Ill. 1986) (90-day period started when employee's girlfriend picked up right-to-sue letter at employee's post office box); Mouriz v. Avondale Shipyards, Inc., 428 F. Supp. 1025 (E.D. La. 1977).

219 St. Louis v. Alverno College, 744 F.2d 1314 (7th Cir. 1984). *See also* Josiah-Faeduwor v. Communications Satellite Corp., 785 F.2d 344 (D.C. Cir. 1986) (receipt of right-to-sue notice by complainant's attorney started 90-day period even though complainant did not receive notice until some time later because she failed to file a change of address with the EEOC).

220 Hunter v. Stephenson Roofing, Inc., 790 F.2d 472 (6th Cir. 1986).

control.[221] Several circuit courts have held that when the right-to-sue notice is to be received by the complainant's attorney, the filing period starts the day the attorney receives it.[222] Other courts have measured the nature and extent of the attorney-client relationship to determine whether the client knew that the filing period had started. These factors include whether the client or attorney requested that notice be sent to the attorney,[223] whether the attorney was authorized to receive and open mail on behalf of the client,[224] and whether and when the complainant received a copy of the right-to-sue-notice.[225]

Because a determination about whether the delayed receipt of the right-to-sue notice was the complainant's fault is subject to the court's discretion,[226] and the law is somewhat ambiguous in this area, the EEOC should be notified promptly of any address changes, and suit should be filed promptly to avoid timeliness challenges.

A copy of the right-to-sue notice will suffice as long as the letter clearly indicates its purpose and the time when the 90-day filing period begins.[227]

Amended pleadings relate back to the original pleading when the allegations in the amendment arise from the conduct challenged in the original complaint. For example, a § 1983 sexual harassment claim may be amended to assert Title VII allegations when the § 1983 claim was filed within 90 days of the complainant's receipt of a right-to-sue letter and the claims are based on the same allegedly harassing conduct.

---

221 Lewis v. Conners Steel Co., 673 F.2d 1240 (11th Cir. 1982) (action was improperly dismissed when plaintiff had not been allowed to offer evidence that he notified EEOC of his current address).

222 Ringgold v. National Maintenance Corp., 796 F.2d 769 (5th Cir. 1986); Mosel v. Hills Dep't Store, Inc., 789 F.2d 251 (3d Cir. 1986); Josiah-Faeduwor v. Communications Satellite Corp., 785 F.2d 344 (D.C. Cir. 1986); Jones v. Madison Serv. Corp., 744 F.2d 1309, 1312 (7th Cir. 1984); Yourse v. Miller, 38 Fair Empl. Prac. Cas. (BNA) 287, 288 (M.D.N.C. 1982) (sexual harassment).

223 Harper v. Burgess, 701 F.2d 29 (4th Cir. 1983); Gonzalez v. Stanford Applied Eng'g, Inc., 597 F.2d 1298 (9th Cir. 1979).

224 Decker v. Anheuser-Busch, 670 F.2d 506 (5th Cir. 1982), *on remand,* 558 F. Supp. 445 (M.D. Fla. 1983).

225 *Id.* When both the complainant and counsel receive a copy of the right-to-sue notice, the date on which the first copy is received may trigger the filing period. Jones v. Madison Serv. Corp., 744 F.2d 1309 (7th Cir. 1984).

226 *See, e.g.,* Cook v. Providence Hosp., 820 F.2d 176 (6th Cir. 1987) (employment discrimination action was time-barred when employee had actual knowledge that EEOC had given her right to sue for one full year before she brought suit).

227 Missirlian v. Huntington Memorial Hosp., 662 F.2d 546 (9th Cir. 1981), *cert. denied,* 456 U.S. 906 (1982) (letter from EEOC merely stated that complainant could request a document entitled "90-day Notice of Right-to-Sue"). *Cf.* Vargas v. New York Univ. Medical Ctr., 26 Fair Empl. Prac. Cas. (BNA) 967 (S.D.N.Y. 1981) (incorrect date on EEOC letter did not render notice defective when complainant did not allege that he was in any way misled by the EEOC).

CHAPTER 6

TRYING THE SEXUAL HARASSMENT CASE

PRETRIAL MATTERS

TRIAL MATTERS

PROOF ISSUES

SETTLEMENT AND COSTS

§ 6.1 Introduction

After receiving a right-to-sue notice, a party may bring a Title VII action in federal court. This chapter examines the sexual harassment claim in the various stages of litigation from pretrial pleadings to appeals. Because of the unique character of the sexual harassment action, trial strategy diverges from that of traditional sex discrimination cases. The litigation structure depends on the type of harassment asserted. Discovery and evidentiary strategy are vital in sexual harassment cases, when the credibility of witnesses may decide the outcome of the litigation.

PROCEDURAL REQUIREMENTS

§ 6.2 Procedures in Private Actions

An aggrieved individual may assert Title VII protection in several ways, all of which except preliminary relief must be preceded by an Equal Employment Opportunity Commission (EEOC) right-to-sue notice (see **Chapter 5**). An individual may request a right-to-sue notice and bring suit in district court if 180 days have passed since the charge was filed with the EEOC, even if the EEOC's administrative process is pending.[1]

The dismissal of a charge by the EEOC does not strip a complainant of the right to bring suit in federal court, because a right-to-sue letter accompanies the dismissal notice. An individual may also bring suit when EEOC conciliation efforts have failed, and the commission has issued a right-to-sue letter.[2] If the EEOC decides to sue, however, the aggrieved party may not bring her own suit but may intervene in the EEOC's action.[3]

Title VII authorizes the EEOC, or the Attorney General in actions against a state or local government, to seek preliminary relief before the end of the administrative process when an investigation indicates that "prompt judicial action is necessary to carry out the purposes of the Act."[4] It is unclear whether an individual may seek preliminary relief without exhausting the EEOC's administrative procedures.[5] While a number of

---

[1] 42 U.S.C. § 2000e-5(f)(1).

[2] 42 U.S.C. § 2000e-5(f)(1).

[3] McClain v. Wagner Elec. Corp., 550 F.2d 1115 (8th Cir. 1977).

[4] 42 U.S.C. § 2000e-5(f)(2).

[5] Cases decided before the 1972 amendments to Title VII allowed individuals to seek preliminary relief. Culpepper v. Reynolds Metals Co., 421 F.2d 888 (5th Cir. 1970); Bowe v. Colgate-Palmolive Co., 272 F. Supp. 332 (S.D. Ind. 1967), *aff'd in part, rev'd in part on other grounds*, 416 F.2d 711 (7th Cir. 1969).

courts have permitted individuals to seek such relief pending commission action on a charge,[6] others have held that such relief is not available without the right-to-sue letter.[7]

§ 6.3 Venue and Jurisdiction

A Title VII action may be brought in any judicial district in which an unlawful employment practice allegedly has occurred,[8] relevant employment records are maintained and administered,[9] or in which the complainant would have worked but for the alleged discrimination. If the respondent cannot be found in any of these districts, the case may be brought in the district in which the respondent has its principal office.[10] Venue requirements apply to intervening as well as original plaintiffs.[11]

Federal courts may decline to entertain state claims when there is an adequate state forum for resolving the issues.[12] Federal courts may hear state statutory or common law claims under pendent jurisdiction (see **Chapter 4**).

In *Yellow Freight System v. Donnelly,*[13] the U.S. Supreme Court unanimously held that state courts have concurrent jurisdiction over Title VII actions, noting that Congress had not expressly limited jurisdiction to federal courts nor excluded state courts, and that even though a number of provisions in Title VII's legislative history indicated that Title VII cases

---

[6] Sheehan v. Purolator Courier Corp., 676 F.2d 877 (2d Cir. 1981), *cert. denied*, 488 U.S. 891 (1988); Berg v. Richmond Unified Sch. Dist., 528 F.2d 1208 (9th Cir. 1975), *vacated on other grounds,* 434 U.S. 158 (1977); Drew v. Liberty Mut. Ins. Co., 480 F.2d 69 (5th Cir.), *reh'g denied,* 480 F.2d 924 (5th Cir. 1973), *cert. denied*, 417 U.S. 935 (1974); Hochstadt v. Worcester Found. for Experimental Biology, Inc., 425 F. Supp. 318 (D. Mass.), *aff'd on other grounds,* 545 F.2d 222 (1st Cir. 1976); Mead v. United States Fidelity & Guar. Co., 442 F. Supp. 102 (D. Minn. 1977); Hyland v. Kenner Prods. Co., 10 Fair Empl. Prac. Cas. (BNA) 367 (S.D. Ohio 1974).

[7] Hunter v. Ward, 476 F. Supp. 913 (E.D. Ark. 1979); McGee v. Purolator Courier Corp., 430 F. Supp. 1285 (N.D. Ala. 1977); Nottelson v. A.O. Smith Corp., 397 F. Supp. 928 (E.D. Wis. 1975); Troy v. Shell Oil Co., 378 F. Supp. 1042 (E.D. Mich. 1974), *appeal dismissed,* 519 F.2d 403 (6th Cir. 1975); Collins v. Southwestern Bell Tel. Co., 376 F. Supp. 979 (E.D. Okla. 1974).

[8] Bartel v. Federal Aviation Admin., 617 F. Supp. 190 (D.D.C. 1985); Allen v. Bolger, 597 F. Supp. 482 (D. Kan. 1984); Kravec v. Chicago Pneumatic Tool Co., 579 F. Supp. 619 (N.D. Ga. 1983).

[9] Kravec v. Chicago Pneumatic Tool Co., 579 F. Supp. 619 (N.D. Ga. 1983).

[10] 42 U.S.C. § 2000e-5(f)(3). *See also* Arrocha v. Panama Canal Comm'n, 609 F. Supp. 231 (E.D.N.Y. 1985).

[11] Allen v. Isaac, 99 F.R.D. 45 (N.D. Ill.), *amended,* 100 F.R.D. 373 (N.D. Ill. 1983).

[12] Baker v. Durkee Foods, 33 Empl. Prac. Dec. (CCH) ¶ 34,035 (N.D. Ill. 1982).

[13] Yellow Freight System v. Donnelly, 494 U.S. 820 (1990).

would be heard in federal court, such an expectation was not sufficient to preclude state court jurisdiction.[14]

§ 6.4 Plaintiffs

A Title VII action may be brought by an aggrieved party, including persons alleged to be aggrieved in a charge filed by the EEOC.[15] "A person claiming to be aggrieved" has been defined broadly.[16] Sexual harassment complainants are aggrieved parties under Title VII in a number of situations. For example, a complainant may assert that a tangible job benefit was denied or altered as a result of sexually discriminating harassment aimed at the plaintiff personally or at a third party. She also may claim that harassment created a hostile work environment, or that she was a victim of retaliation for having objected to harassment upon her or upon another employee.[17]

A federal employee is an aggrieved person entitled to bring a Title VII action if the administrative proceeding did not afford complete relief.[18]

The EEOC may bring a Title VII suit on behalf of an aggrieved party or parties. It is unclear whether the commencement of a private action[19] or the issuance of a right-to-sue letter to the charging party[20] strips the EEOC

---

[14] *Id.* at 825.

[15] 42 U.S.C. § 2000e-5(f)(1).

[16] Third Circuit: Hackett v. McGuire Bros., 445 F.2d 442 (3d Cir. 1971) (although plaintiff had applied for and been granted pension benefits, he was an "aggrieved" person for seeking previously denied benefits).

Sixth Circuit: Senter v. General Motors Corp., 532 F.2d 511 (6th Cir.), *cert. denied,* 429 U.S. 870 (1976) (fact that plaintiff may have been offered a promotion did not strip him of standing to challenge promotional practices on behalf of a class).

Seventh Circuit: Retail, Wholesale & Dep't Store Union v. Standard Brands, Inc., 540 F.2d 864 (7th Cir. 1976) (labor union may represent individual members).

District of Columbia Circuit: Gray v. Greyhound Lines, E., 545 F.2d 169 (D.C. Cir. 1976) (hired employee could challenge hiring practices when he alleged that such practices affected his treatment at work and his psychological well-being).

[17] Nordell v. Bowen, 42 Fair Empl. Prac. Cas. (BNA) 465 (D.D.C. 1986).

[18] Fischer v. Adams, 572 F.2d 406 (1st Cir. 1978).

[19] *Cf. also* EEOC v. Contour Chair Lounge Co., 596 F.2d 809 (8th Cir. 1979) (once a charging party has filed an action, the EEOC retains only right of permissive intervention) with EEOC v. North Hills Passavant Hosp., 544 F.2d 664 (3d Cir. 1976) (EEOC has statutory authority to sue nongovernment party at any time).

[20] *Cf.* EEOC v. Cleveland Mills Co., 364 F. Supp. 1235 (W.D.N.C. 1973), *rev'd on other grounds,* 502 F.2d 153 (4th Cir. 1974), *cert. denied,* 420 U.S. 946 (1975) (following issuance of right-to-sue letter, aggrieved party alone may bring suit). *Accord* EEOC v. Missouri Pac. R.R., 493 F.2d 71 (8th Cir. 1974); EEOC v. C&D Sportswear Corp., 398 F. Supp. 300 (M.D. Ga. 1975). *Cf.* EEOC v. Duval Corp., 528 F.2d 945 (10th Cir. 1976) (if EEOC is first to file during 90-day period, aggrieved party should intervene);

of the right to sue. The EEOC may bring suit to challenge employment practices not alleged by the private complainant or to challenge a broader range of practices that grew out of the same charge.[21] The EEOC may not, however, bring an action on behalf of a federal employee.

§ 6.5 Defendants

Title VII covers an employer "engaged in an industry affecting commerce who has 15 or more employees for each working day in each of 20 or more calendar weeks in the current or preceding calendar year."[22] The number of employees is a jurisdictional requirement.[23] Enlisted armed forces personnel are not covered by Title VII. Religious institutions are exempt only to the extent that alleged discrimination is religion-based.

An employee also may bring a Title VII action against a union as well as the employer. Unions may be sued under the Title VII provision that controls the conduct of labor organizations.[24] Under Title VII, a union has an affirmative duty to alleviate sex discrimination in employment.[25] Thus, a union violates Title VII if it acquiesces in an employer's discriminatory policy and procedures.[26] The absence of notice to the union of discriminatory conduct by its members does not preclude a finding of liability.[27] The court must determine the agency relationship between the union and the offending member.[28] Unions may be joined under Federal Rule of Civil Procedure 20.

Courts are split on whether officers or officials of the defendant employer may themselves be subject to personal liability under Title VII.[29]

EEOC v. Rexall Drug Co., 10 Fair Empl. Prac. Cas. (BNA) 450 (E.D. Mo. 1974) (EEOC loses right to sue only if private suit is brought during 90-day filing period).

21 Kimberly-Clark Corp. v. EEOC, 511 F.2d 1352 (6th Cir.), *cert. denied,* 423 U.S. 994 (1975).

22 42 U.S.C. § 2000e(b).

23 Bonomo v. National Duckpin Bowling Congress, Inc., 469 F. Supp. 467, 470 (D. Md. 1979).

24 42 U.S.C. § 2000e-2(c) (1982); Jennings v. American Postal Workers Union, 672 F.2d 712 (8th Cir. 1982); Egger v. Local 276, Plumbers & Pipefitters Union, 644 F. Supp. 795 (D. Mass. 1986) (sexual harassment).

25 Chrapliwy v. Uniroyal, Inc., 458 F. Supp. 252, 283 (N.D. Ind. 1978). *See also* 29 C.F.R. § 1604.11(f).

26 *Cf.* Faris v. Henry Vogt Mach. Co., 813 F.2d 786 (6th Cir. 1987) (district court properly concluded that evidence did not establish that relevant decisions of union not to file grievances over certain of plaintiff's charges were arbitrary, discriminatory, or taken in bad faith).

27 Meritor Sav. Bank v. Vinson, 477 U.S. 57, 72 (1986).

28 Egger v. Local 276, Plumbers & Pipefitters Union, 644 F. Supp. 795 (D. Mass. 1986) (sexual harassment).

29 Bertoncini v. Schrimpf, 712 F. Supp. 1336 (N.D. Ill. 1989) (sexual harassment).

Some courts have held that individuals who participate in a Title VII violation may be held personally liable along with their employers if the individuals are supervisors or managers, and thus agents of the employer for personnel decisions.[30] Those courts holding that individuals are not subject to personal liability focused on the fact that only equitable relief was available for Title VII violations.[31]

The head of the relevant federal department, agency, or unit is the only proper defendant in a discrimination action filed by a federal employee.[32]

---

30 Third Circuit: Acampora v. Boise Cascade Corp., 635 F. Supp. 66 (D.N.J. 1986); Guyette v. Stauffer Chem. Co., 518 F. Supp. 521, 525–26 (D.N.J. 1981).

Fourth Circuit: Ponton v. Newport News Sch. Bd., 632 F. Supp. 1056, 1068 (E.D. Va. 1986); Jeter v. Boswell, 554 F. Supp. 946, 952–53 (N.D. W. Va. 1983).

Fifth Circuit: Hamilton v. Rogers, 791 F.2d 439, 442 (5th Cir. 1986); Anderson v. Phelps, 655 F. Supp. 560 (M.D. La. 1985).

Sixth Circuit: Romain v. Kurek, 772 F.2d 281 (6th Cir. 1985).

Seventh Circuit: Feng v. Sandrik, 636 F. Supp. 77 (N.D. Ill. 1986). *Cf.* Bertoncini v. Schrimpf, 712 F. Supp. 1336, 1339 (N.D. Ill. 1989) (sexual harassment) (fact that plaintiff named municipality in her EEOC charge but not her complaint strongly suggested that she sought liability against municipality through individual defendant trustees; thus, the court found that plaintiff sued defendants in their official capacities and that the only real defendant was the village).

Ninth Circuit: *Cf.* Canada v. Boyd Group, Inc., 809 F. Supp. 771 (D. Nev. 1992) (individual defendants cannot be held liable for back pay under Title VII or compensatory damages under the CRA of 1991).

Tenth Circuit: Tafoya v. Adams, 612 F. Supp. 1097 (D. Colo. 1985), *aff'd,* 816 F.2d 555 (10th Cir. 1987); Hendrix v. Fleming Cos., 650 F. Supp. 301, 303 (W.D. Okla. 1986).

Eleventh Circuit: Steele v. Offshore Shipbuilding, Inc., 867 F.2d 1311 (11th Cir. 1989). A supervisor who often engaged in sexually oriented joking with employees, requested sexual favors, commented on employees' attire in a suggestive manner, asked them to visit him on the couch in his office, and gave employees sexually explicit gifts created a hostile work environment and was ordered to pay plaintiff employees nominal damages and attorneys' fees. The corporate employer was not liable for the hostile environment because it took prompt remedial action after it learned of the supervisor's actions.

District of Columbia Circuit: Thompson v. International Ass'n of Machinists & Aerospace Workers, 580 F. Supp. 662 (D.D.C. 1984).

31 Bertoncini v. Schrimpf, 712 F. Supp. 1336, 1340 (N.D. Ill. 1989) (sexual harassment).

Second Circuit: Bradley v. Consolidated Edison Co., 657 F. Supp. 197, 207 (S.D.N.Y. 1987).

Fifth Circuit: Clanton v. Orleans Parish Sch. Bd., 649 F.2d 1084 (5th Cir. 1981).

Sixth Circuit: Williams v. Hevi-Duty Elec. Co., 668 F. Supp. 1062, 1070 (M.D. Tenn. 1986), *rev'd on other grounds*, 819 F.2d 620 (6th Cir. 1987).

Eleventh Circuit: Williams v. City of Montgomery, 742 F.2d 586, 589 (11th Cir. 1984), *cert. denied,* 470 U.S. 1053 (1985).

32 42 U.S.C. § 2000e-16(c).

An action by a federal employee may be dismissed for failing to name the appropriate party,[33] unless the filing papers clearly demonstrate that the plaintiff intended to name the particular party.[34] Parties lower in rank than the agency head need not be dismissed if ultimately they might be in the better position to provide the relief sought.[35] Although the United States is liable for any ultimate award,[36] it is not a proper party defendant.[37]

Although Title VII states that a civil action may be brought against a respondent named in the EEOC charge,[38] courts have been flexible in this area, finding that an uncharged party may be named as a defendant in a number of situations. In making such a determination, courts have considered whether:

1. The role of the uncharged party could have been reasonably ascertained at the time the charge was filed with the EEOC.[39]
2. An identity of interests exists between the charged and uncharged parties that would render unnecessary participation by the uncharged party in conciliation efforts.[40]
3. The uncharged party was prejudiced by its absence in the EEOC proceeding.[41]

---

33 Ellis v. United States Postal Serv., 784 F.2d 835 (7th Cir. 1986) (federal employee's complaint was properly dismissed when plaintiff was granted leave to amend the complaint to sue the proper party and had not done so); Svenson v. Thomas, 607 F. Supp. 1004 (D.D.C. 1985).

34 Rice v. Hamilton Air Force Base Commissary, 720 F.2d 1082 (9th Cir. 1983); Cupp v. Veterans Admin. Hosp., 677 F. Supp. 1018 (N.D. Cal. 1987). These were pro se cases, however, and court may hold represented parties to a higher standard.

35 I.M.A.G.E. v. Bailar, 78 F.R.D. 549 (N.D. Cal. 1978).

36 58 Op. Comp. Gen. 311 (1979).

37 Brooks v. Brinegar, 391 F. Supp. 710 (W.D. Okla. 1974); Jones v. United States, 376 F. Supp. 13 (D.D.C. 1974).

38 42 U.S.C. § 2000e-5(f)(1).

39 Eggleston v. Chicago Journeymen Plumbers' Local Union No. 130, U.A., 657 F.2d 890 (7th Cir. 1981), *cert. denied,* 455 U.S. 1017 (1982); Romero v. Union Pac. R.R., 615 F.2d 1303 (10th Cir. 1980); Thompson v. International Ass'n of Machinists & Aerospace Workers, 580 F. Supp. 662 (D.D.C. 1984).

40 Eggleston v. Chicago Journeymen Plumbers' Local Union No. 130, U.A., 657 F.2d 890 (7th Cir. 1981), *cert. denied,* 455 U.S. 1017 (1982); Romero v. Union Pac. R.R., 615 F.2d 1303 (10th Cir. 1980). *See also* Fuchilla v. Prockop, 682 F. Supp. 247, 256 (D.N.J. 1987) (sexual harassment); Yourse v. Miller, 38 Fair Empl. Prac. Cas. (BNA) 287 (M.D.N.C. 1982) (sexual harassment).

41 Eggleston v. Chicago Journeymen Plumbers' Local Union No. 130, U.A., 657 F.2d 890 (7th Cir. 1981), *cert. denied,* 455 U.S. 1017 (1982); Romero v. Union Pac. R.R., 615 F.2d 1303 (10th Cir. 1980); Davis v. University of Chicago Hosps. & Clinics, No. 83-C6803 (N.D. Ill. Sept. 20, 1984).

4. The uncharged party represented to the plaintiff that its relationship to the plaintiff was through a named party.[42]
5. Charged and uncharged parties were alleged to have engaged in a common discriminatory scheme.[43]
6. The uncharged party had adequate notice of the charge.[44]
7. Joinder is necessary to preserve a plaintiff's Title VII remedies.[45]

Despite this flexibility, the inclusion of all possible respondents in the initial charge is preferable, and counsel should move to amend and add any additional defendants as soon as possible.

The EEOC itself may not be sued for failing to enforce the provisions of Title VII.[46] EEOC employees also may not bring an action against the agency to contest the handling of a charge[47] or for failing to adequately defend the employee in a suit by a subordinate.[48]

§ 6.6 Intervention

Intervention in private Title VII actions may be appropriate to avoid duplication of effort by parties alleging discriminatory conduct identical to that suffered by the plaintiff.

Aggrieved persons may intervene in an EEOC action when the EEOC filed the action in response to a charge brought by either the person seeking the intervention or a party having a nearly identical discrimination claim.[49] Although individual members of an organization may intervene in a discrimination action, an organization as a separate entity is not an

---

42 Eggleston v. Chicago Journeymen Plumbers' Local Union No. 130, U.A., 657 F.2d 890 (7th Cir. 1981), *cert. denied,* 455 U.S. 1017 (1982); Romero v. Union Pac. R.R., 615 F.2d 1303 (10th Cir. 1980); Fuchilla v. Prockop, 682 F. Supp. 247 (D.N.J. 1987).

43 Mathews v. Houston Indep. Sch. Dist., 595 F. Supp. 445 (S.D. Tex. 1984).

44 Tuber v. Continental Grain Co., 36 Fair Empl. Prac. Cas. (BNA) 993 (S.D.N.Y. 1984); American Fed'n of State, County, & Mun. Employees v. New York, 599 F. Supp. 916 (S.D.N.Y. 1984); Koster v. Chase Manhattan Bank, 554 F. Supp. 285 (S.D.N.Y. 1983) (sexual harassment); EEOC v. Newtown Inn Assocs., 647 F. Supp. 957 (E.D. Va. 1986) (sexual harassment).

45 Kritil v. Port E. Transfer, Inc., 661 F. Supp. 66, 67 (D. Md. 1986) (sexual harassment).

46 Brown v. EEOC, No. 83 Civ. 6776 (S.D.N.Y. Oct. 26, 1984).

47 Sears, Roebuck & Co. v. EEOC, 42 Fair Empl. Prac. Cas. (BNA) 1890 (D.D.C. 1987).

48 Falkowski v. EEOC, 719 F.2d 470 (D.C. Cir. 1973).

49 Spirt v. Teachers Ins. & Annuity Ass'n, 93 F.R.D. 627 (S.D.N.Y.), *aff'd in part, rev'd in part on other grounds,* 691 F.2d 1054 (2d Cir. 1982), *vacated on other grounds,* 463 U.S. 1223 (1983).

aggrieved person entitled to intervene under Title VII. An organization can file its own charges with the EEOC and suits in federal court.[50]

A motion for intervention must be timely.[51] Timeliness is determined from the date the movant became aware that her interests would not be protected by the plaintiff, not the date on which she learned of the litigation.[52]

The EEOC may intervene in an individual action when it certifies that a sexual harassment action alleging a hostile environment is of general public importance.[53] In determining whether the EEOC met this requirement in *McElrea v. Volt Information Sciences, Inc.*,[54] the court considered the possible prejudice to the rights of other parties and the implications of potential delay.[55] The EEOC may intervene in a private Title VII action even when its complaint raises issues identical to those of the private party,[56] as such intervention may bolster representation. The Fifth Circuit further has held that the commission as intervenor may continue to litigate the action even after the party who brought the action has been dismissed.[57]

§ 6.7 Class Action Litigation

Class actions are complex and have a body of law all their own.[58] Sexual harassment allegations have been part of a number of broad-based class actions.[59] In *Jenson v. Eveleth Taconite Co.*,[60] a district court certified a class of:

> all women who have applied for, or have been employed in, hourly positions at Eveleth Mines at any time since December 30, 1983, and who have been, are being, or as a result of the operation of current practices, will be discriminated against with regard to the terms and conditions of their employment because of gender.

---

[50] United States v. Allegheny-Ludlum Indus., Inc., 517 F.2d 826 (5th Cir. 1975), *cert. denied*, 425 U.S. 944 (1976).

[51] Craighead v. Norfolk & W. Ry., No. 15-1321 (4th Cir. June 18, 1986); Nevilles v. EEOC, 511 F.2d 303 (8th Cir. 1975).

[52] Johnson v. North Carolina State Highway Patrol, 91 F.R.D. 406 (E.D.N.C. 1980).

[53] 42 U.S.C. §§ 2000e-4(g)(6), 2000e-5(f)(1).

[54] McElrea v. Volt Info. Sciences, Inc., 119 F.R.D. 630 (E.D. Pa. 1987) (intervention permitted in sexual harassment case).

[55] *Id.*

[56] Stuart v. Hewlett-Packard Co., 66 F.R.D. 73 (E.D. Mich. 1975).

[57] Harris v. Amoco Prod. Co., 768 F.2d 669 (5th Cir. 1985), *cert. denied*, 475 U.S. 1011 (1986).

[58] *See* H. Newberg & A. Conte, Newberg on Class Actions (3d ed. 1992).

[59] *See, e.g.*, Sheehan v. Purolator, Inc., 839 F.2d 99 (2d Cir.), *cert. denied*, 488 U.S. 891 (1988); Holden v. Burlington N., Inc., 665 F. Supp. 1398 (D. Minn. 1987).

[60] Jensen v. Eveleth Taconite Co., 139 F.R.D. 657, 667 (D. Minn. 1991).

Plaintiffs claimed that defendents allowed, and in some instances promoted, a hostile environment, submitting evidence concerning various incidents of sexual harassment ranging from open display of pictures of nude females to incidents of physical harassment. Though hailed as the first sexual harassment class action,[61] the action contains other sex discrimination allegations, and other certified class actions have asserted sexual harassment claims.[62] It was the first time, however, that a court articulated the application of all the class action requirements specifically to the sexual harassment claims, and that a sexual harassment class action was tried successfully to completion.

Class action treatment may not be viable in most *quid pro quo* sexual harassment cases. However, it may be appropriate in a continuing hostile environment case that involves either other potential complainants who might be reluctant to sue for fear of retaliation or other factors,[63] or so many other complainants that joinder would be impracticable.

A party seeking to bring a class action must meet the requirements of Federal Rule of Civil Procedure 23, which governs the maintenance of class actions. In *General Telephone Co. v. Falcon,*[64] a discrimination action, the U.S. Supreme Court held that conclusory presumptions regarding the fulfillment of Rule 23(a) requirements are improper. Thus, a named plaintiff must provide underlying facts supporting an assertion that Rule 23 criteria have been met.[65] In turn, the court must provide an adequate explanation of its analysis under Rule 23.[66] *General Telephone* does not require the introduction of evidence going to the merits of the litigation.[67] Plaintiffs are required only to provide enough factual information to allow the court to form a reasonable judgment of the class issues.[68]

---

[61] *See, e.g.*, E. Pollock, *Judge Approves First Sex-Bias Class Action*, Wall St. J., Dec. 18, 1991, at B1.

[62] *See, e.g.,* Meiresonne v. Marriott Corp., 124 F.R.D. 619 (N.D. Ill 1989); Frazier v. Southeastern Pa. Transp. Auth., Inc., 123 F.R.D. 195 (E.D. Pa. 1988).

[63] *See, e.g.,* Jenson v. Eveleth Taconite Co., 139 F.R.D. 657, 667 (D. Minn. 1991); Meiresonne v. Marriott Corp., 124 F.R.D. 619 (N.D. Ill. 1989) (class of all female management employees, management trainees, and supervisors employed by Marriott Corp. charged the existence of discriminatory evaluation system, training practices, and hostile environment).

[64] General Tel. Co. v. Falcon, 457 U.S. 147 (1982).

[65] *See, e.g.,* Roby v. St. Louis S.W. Ry., 775 F.2d 959 (8th Cir. 1985); Jaxon v. Circle K Corp., 773 F.2d 1138 (10th Cir. 1985); Price v. Cannon Mills, 113 F.R.D. 66 (M.D.N.C. 1986); Selzer v. Board of Educ., 112 F.R.D. 176 (S.D.N.Y. 1986).

[66] Lily v. Harris-Teeter Supermkt., 545 F. Supp. 686, 705 (W.D.N.C. 1982), *modified on other grounds,* 720 F.2d 326 (4th Cir. 1983).

[67] This is prohibited by the U.S. Supreme Court decision in Eisen v. Carlisle & Jacquelin, 417 U.S. 156 (1974). *See also* Hawkins v. Fulton County, 95 F.R.D. 88 (N.D. Ga. 1982).

[68] Blackie v. Barrack, 524 F.2d 891, 901, 901 n.17 (9th Cir. 1975), *cert. denied,* 429 U.S. 816 (1976).

§ 6.8 —Rule 23(a)

Rule 23(a) requires that (1) joinder be impracticable, (2) there be questions of law or fact in common with members of the putative class, (3) the claims or defenses of the named plaintiff be typical of those of class members, and (4) the named plaintiff be an adequate representative of the putative class.

An analysis of the joinder impracticability requirement takes into account the number of members in the proposed class,[69] the injunctive nature of the relief sought,[70] the geographic dispersement,[71] and identifiability of the class members.[72] In *Jenson,* the joinder impracticability requirement was satisfied by plaintiffs alleging a hostile work environment when they asserted that 65 women had been employed at the mine during the relevant period and at least 23 women had applied for employment. The court rejected the defendant's argument that a number of current female employees were disinclined to join the class, finding the defendants' position particularly problematic when, as in this case, an applicant class would be certified:

> The Court observes further that differing levels of interest will not, alone, defeat the requirements of Rule 23(a). . . . It is, of course, unlikely that potential class members would be unanimously supportive when most potential class members have an interest in maintaining amicable relationships at work. The Court is mindful that a principal purpose of class actions is "the efficiency and economy of litigation." *American Pipe & Construction Co. v. Utah,* 414 U.S. 538 . . . (1974). Here, the efficency and economy of resolving common issues in one lawsuit clearly outweigh any concerns about numbers of plaintiffs. Moreover, because all members of the proposed class will benefit by the relief sought, individual disinterest, alone, is insufficient to defeat class certification.[73]

Certified employment discrimination classes have numbered in the twenties[74] to the several thousands.[75]

---

69 The exact number is not necessary. Presseisen v. Swarthmore College, 71 F.R.D. 34 (E.D. Pa. 1976); Marshall v. Electric Hose & Rubber Co., 68 F.R.D. 287 (D. Del. 1975).

70 Neff v. Janitorial Aero-Div., 29 Fair Empl. Prac. Cas. (BNA) 629, 631 (S.D. Ohio 1980).

71 Garcia v. Gloor, 618 F.2d 264 (5th Cir. 1980), *cert. denied,* 449 U.S. 1113 (1981); Allen v. Isaac, 39 Fair Empl. Prac. Cas. (BNA) 1142 (N.D. Ill. 1986); Ivy v. Meridian Coca-Cola Bottling Co., 108 F.R.D. 118 (S.D. Miss. 1985); Avagliano v. Sumitomo Shoji Am., Inc., 103 F.R.D. 562 (S.D.N.Y. 1984).

72 Gilchrist v. Bolger, 89 F.R.D. 402 (S.D. Ga. 1981); Fewlass v. Allyn & Bacon, Inc., 83 F.R.D. 161 (D. Mass. 1979).

73 Jensen v. Eveleth Taconite Co.,139 F.R.D. 657, 665 (D. Minn. 1991) (footnote omitted).

74 Slanina v. William Penn Parking Corp., 106 F.R.D. 419 (M.D. Pa. 1984) (25 class members); Hoston v. United States Gypsum Co., 67 F.R.D. 650 (E.D. La. 1975) (23–33 members); Walls v. Bank of Greenwood, 20 Fed. R. Serv. 2d (Callaghan) 112 (N.D. Miss. 1975) (23 members); Sabala v. Western Gillette, Inc., 362 F. Supp. 1142 (S.D.

The common questions requirement of Rule 23(a)(2) is met when the plaintiff asserts with supporting facts that the defendant's employment practice affects all members of the putative class.[76] Factual differences will not bar certification when the plaintiff alleges a pervasive policy of discrimination.[77] The common questions requirement was satisfied in *Jenson* by plaintiffs alleging a hostile work environment despite defendants' contention that reactions to profanity, pornography, or other potentially offensive material were highly individualized and not susceptible to class treatment when the common question of law was not how an individual class member reacted to the challenged conduct, but whether a reasonable woman would find the work environment hostile.

Certification may be denied, however, if the plaintiff's claims are highly individualized.[78] In hostile environment sexual harassment actions, common questions include whether the employer discriminated against women employees by subjecting them to an abusive work environment, and whether the employer knew of the sexual harassment or did anything to remedy the situation once known.

Rule 23(a)(3) looks at whether the named plaintiff's factual circumstances and legal theories are typical of those of potential class members. Typicality is usually found when the named plaintiff shares the same grievances with class members.[79] However, allegations of a general policy of discrimination may be insufficient if no other evidence is offered that class members were victims of discrimination.[80] Although individual factual

---

Tex. 1973), *modified on other grounds,* 516 F.2d 1251 (5th Cir. 1975) (26 members). *Cf.* Rodriquez v. Department of Treasury, 108 F.R.D. 360 (D.D.C. 1985) (the numerosity requirement was not met when class would contain only 15 members at most).

75 *See, e.g.,* Kuenz v. Goodyear Tire & Rubber Co., 104 F.R.D. 474 (E.D. Mo. 1985); Briggs v. Brown & Williamson Tobacco Corp., 414 F. Supp. 371 (E.D. Va. 1976); Ellis v. Naval Air Rework Facility, 404 F. Supp. 391 (N.D. Cal. 1975).

76 Rossini v. Ogilvy & Mather, Inc., 798 F.2d 590 (2d Cir. 1986); Barefield v. Chevron, USA, 44 Fair Empl. Prac. Cas. (BNA) 1885 (N.D. Cal. 1987); American Fed'n of State, County, & Mun. Employees v. County of Nassau, 664 F. Supp. 64 (E.D.N.Y. 1987); Bullick v. City of Philadelphia, 110 F.R.D. 518 (E.D. Pa. 1986); Irvine v. American Nat'l Bank & Trust Co., 108 F.R.D. 12 (N.D. Ill. 1985).

77 Holsey v. Armour & Co., 743 F.2d 199 (4th Cir. 1984).

78 Frazier v. Conrail, 41 Fair Empl. Prac. Cas. (BNA) 665 (D.D.C. 1986).

79 Bullick v. City of Philadelphia, 110 F.R.D. 518 (E.D. Pa. 1986); Kuenz v. Goodyear Tire & Rubber Co., 104 F.R.D. 474 (E.D. Mo. 1985). *Cf.* Coon v. Georgia Pac. Corp., 829 F.2d 1563 (11th Cir. 1987) (typicality was not met when plaintiff's individual claim was for discriminatory denial of promotion while proposed class members included all women employees and applicants).

80 Berggren v. Sunbeam Corp., 108 F.R.D. 410 (N.D. Ill. 1985). Class members need only be described, not identified. Proof of others being similarly situated goes to the merits of the case and is often unknown until there has been an opportunity for discovery. *See* H. Newberg and A. Conte, 1 Newberg on Class Actions, § 2.04 (3d ed. 1992).

differences will not preclude a finding of typicality,[81] certification may be denied if discrimination claims require unique proof or defenses.[82]

A named plaintiff must show vigorous prosecution and the absence of antagonistic interests to meet the adequacy of representation requirement of Rule 23(a)(4). Vigorous prosecution usually is left to class counsel, but a named plaintiff must display a familiarity with the facts of the case, an active interest in the litigation, and integrity. In *Stone v. Pirelli Armstrong Tire Corp.,*[83] the Iowa Supreme Court found that the trial court properly determined that the named plaintiff would not fairly and adequately protect the interests of the class in an action against a tire manufacturer and the rubber workers' union for alleged sexual harassment by a coworker in the form of lewd, obscene, and suggestive gestures and comments, the distribution and display of lewd magazines, photographs, pin-ups, and drawings, and unwanted physical touching. The district court described why the plaintiff in this class was inadequate:

> Fifteen present Pirelli . . . women employees testified that they did not want to be a part of the lawsuit, nor have the plaintiff represent them in the event they became a part of the class. Further, some of the witnesses contradicted some of the testimony the plaintiff gave concerning complaints that they may have made. In addition, Mary Stone is not now employed by Pirelli . . . . Further, her residence now is in the state of Virginia. In addition, her finances seem limited by reason of the fact that while several thousand dollars of expenses have been incurred to the time of our hearing, she had only been able to pay the filing fee. More disturbing to the court, however, is the admission by the plaintiff that in a divorce action she obtained her medical records from her physician and destroyed them so that they could not be part of her dissolution of marriage action.[84]

The court of appeals found this evidence compelling:

> The stature of the purported class representative is a legitimate area of inquiry. . . . The fact that fifteen of the present forty-five women employees of Pirelli do not want Stone to represent them is indicative of a lack of confidence in Stone and a lack of community of interest.

---

[81] Meiresonne v. Marriott Corp., 124 F.R.D. 619 (N.D. Ill. 1989) (sexual harassment; "Most importantly for purposes of typicality, plaintiffs are not claiming damages for all class members based on individual incidents of sexual hostility. Instead they are alleging an atmosphere of sexual hostility that evidences discrimination. . . . [P]laintiffs are not now called upon to provide conclusive proof of such an atmosphere." *Id.* at 624–25).

[82] Sheehan v. Purolator, Inc., 103 F.R.D. 641 (S.D.N.Y. 1984), *aff'd,* 839 F.2d 99 (2d Cir.), *cert. denied,* 488 U.S. 891 (1988) (sexual harassment).

[83] Stone v. Pirelli Armstrong Tire Corp., 497 N.W.2d 843 (Iowa 1993) (Lavorto, J.).

[84] *Id.* at 847.

> Closely tied to stature is credibility, another important consideration on the issue of adequate representation. A class representative's lack of credibility can render him or her an inadequate class representative. . . . This can happen when evidence on such credibility is so damaging that a fact finder might reasonably focus on the representative's credibility to the detriment of the absent class members' claims.
>
> Stone admitted that, several years before this case, she destroyed evidence unfavorable to her in a divorce proceeding to which she was a party. The bizarre manner in which she did so compounded her deceit. She went to her doctor's office, asked to see her medical records, and while the office clerk was not looking, ripped two pages from her files. She then ran out of the office with the records.
>
> This is a form of deceit that is highly relevant on any litigant's ability to convince a fact finder that the litigant's claim or defense has merit. The district court here could rightfully be concerned that this evidence is so damaging that it might divert the fact finder's focus from the important issues.[85]

The court of appeals also noted that many of the women employees who testified contradicted Stone's allegations of plantwide public display of offensive sexually explicit material, and this conflict in testimony would stand in the way of class action certification.

The fact that a named plaintiff in a sexual harassment case may suffer stress-related symptoms as a result of the harassment does not render her an inadequate representative as long as the symptoms do not interfere with the plaintiff's ability to think logically or exercise judgment.[86] The possibility that putative class members may, in the future, compete with the named plaintiff for promotional opportunities does not create antagonism between the parties when they share an interest in enjoining the employer's discrimination.[87]

Although the ability of the named plaintiff to finance the litigation is relevant to a finding of adequate representation, certification is seldom denied on this basis alone.[88] Because attorney's fees usually are available in successful Title VII actions, class counsel may represent to the court that litigation costs will be advanced to the plaintiff. Under the new ABA Model Rules of Professional Conduct, an attorney may properly advance litigation costs on a contingency basis.[89] Under the former Code, the

---

[85] *Id.* at 847–48.

[86] Barefield v. Chevron, USA, 44 Fair Empl. Prac. Cas. (BNA) 1885 (N.D. Cal. 1987).

[87] Kuenz v. Goodyear Tire & Rubber Co., 104 F.R.D. 474 (E.D. Mo. 1985).

[88] Wilmington Firefighters Local 1590 v. City of Wilmington, 109 F.R.D. 89 (D. Del. 1985). *See also* Stone v. Pirelli Armstrong Tire Corp., 497 N.W.2d 843 (Iowa 1993) (Lavorto, J.) ("[o]ther than a bare promise", plaintiff had made no showing as to how she would reimburse her attorneys for litigation expense advancement if she lost. *Id.* at 848).

[89] Model Rule of Professional Conduct 1.8(e)(1), (2) (Aug. 1983).

plaintiff need only assert an understanding that she is ultimately responsible for litigation costs.[90]

Generally, the courts do not scrutinize the competence of class counsel unless the defendant asserts a serious challenge to representation. If counsel were to file a class certification motion late, it could lead to a finding of inadequate representation, particularly if other litigation errors or inappropriate conduct[91] were present.

§ 6.9 —Rule 23(b)

A proposed class action also must fall under one of the three categories in Rule 23(b). Rule 23(b)(1) classes were designed to avoid prejudice to the defendant or absent class members that would have resulted from the prosecution of individual actions. A Rule 23(b)(2) class action is appropriate when injunctive relief is sought for conduct based on grounds generally applicable to the class. Rule 23(b)(3) is the most comprehensive category of the class action rule. It applies when a class action is superior to other available methods for adjudicating the controversy and when common questions predominate over individual ones. This provision usually applies to actions in which damages are sought.

Employment discrimination suits usually are brought under Rule 23(b)(2). Rather than compensatory damages, back pay has been deemed equitable relief or incidental to primary injunctive relief, and therefore usually is available in Rule 23(b)(2) employment discrimination class actions.[92] The availability of compensatory and punitive damages under

---

[90] Merrill v. Southern Methodist Univ., 806 F.2d 600 (5th Cir. 1986) (adequacy of representation requirement was not met when, among other things, plaintiff appeared unable or unwilling to finance class action).

[91] Wrighten v. Metropolitan Hosps., Inc., 726 F.2d 1346 (9th Cir. 1984) (counsel was an inadequate representative due to an untimely class certification motion, failure to respond to discovery requests, disruption of depositions with inappropriate comments, failure to associate local counsel as required by local rule, and "assembly line" quality of pleadings and interrogatories); Armstrong v. Chicago Park Dist., 117 F.R.D. 623 (N.D. Ill. 1987); Key v. Gillette Co., 104 F.R.D. 139 (D. Mass. 1985), *aff'd,* 782 F.2d 5 (1st Cir. 1986). *Cf.* Calloway v. Westinghouse Elec. Corp., 642 F. Supp. 663 (M.D. Ga. 1986), *dismissed without opinion,* 831 F.2d 1069 (11th Cir. 1987) (although class counsel could have been more aggressive in discovery during early stages of litigation, a lengthy delay in prosecution of an employment discrimination action did not render counsel's representation inadequate when EEOC had retained jurisdiction over the case for eight years before making a reasonable cause determination, and the subsequent delay was caused by a number of factors including complexity of action, large number of personnel files that had to be reviewed, and heavy caseload of court).

[92] Probe v. State Teachers' Retirement Sys., 780 F.2d 776 (9th Cir.), *cert. denied,* 476 U.S. 1170 (1986); Kuenz v. Goodyear Tire & Rubber Co., 104 F.R.D. 474 (E.D. Mo. 1985); Avagliano v. Sumitomo Shoji Am., Inc., 103 F.R.D. 562 (S.D.N.Y. 1984).

the new Civil Rights Act of 1991 may result in the certification of hybrid Rule 23(b)(3)/(b)(2) classes.[93]

§ 6.10 Prima Facie Sexual Harassment Case in Class Action

In *Jenson,* the plaintiffs later prevailed on their classwide claims of sexual harassment,[94] and the court addressed the unique aspects of the sexual harassment class action:

> In the usual "pattern or practice" case—for example, an alleged pattern or practice of discrimination in hiring on the basis of sex—a determination in the liability phase that the employer engaged in a pattern or practice of discrimination entitled the *plaintiff class* to appropriate prospective relief and entitled each *member* of the class to a presumption that the employer unlawfully discriminated against her. . . . Thus, in the recovery phase the burden of persuasion shifts to the employer to show that it did not discriminate against individual members of the class who show that they are potential victims of the proved discrimination, e.g., they applied for a job and were not hired. . . .
>
> Where, however, a plaintiff *class* brings a claim of *sexual harassment* based upon hostile environment, the determination made after the liability phase, and hence the allocations of burdens in the recovery phase, is different. The liability phase is limited to determining whether the plaintiff class has established that the employer engaged in pattern or practice of exposing women to a sexually hostile environment. This determination is the focus of the liability phase because at issue therein is the common question of law which makes a class action an appropriate vehicle for prosecuting claims of sexual harassment: "whether a reasonable woman would find the work environment hostile." . . . 139 F.R.D. at 665.
>
> Should the employer be found to have engaged in a pattern or practice of discriminating against women by maintaining a hostile environment, the plaintiff class will be eligible for appropriate prospective relief and other remedies consistent with a finding of liability in other pattern or practice cases. However, the nature of a hostile environment claim mandates that the nature of the recovery phase differ from traditional pattern and practice cases. Specifically, a determination that the employer engaged in a pattern or practice of discrimination by maintaining a hostile environment does not entitle every member of the plaintiff class to a presumption that they were sexually harassed—the burden of persuasion does not shift to the employer. . . . Instead, the burden of persuasion remains on the individual class members; each must show by a preponderance of the evidence that she was as affected as the reasonable woman. If this showing is made, the individual

---

93 *See* H. Newberg & A. Conte, 5 Newberg on Class Actions § 24.122 (3d ed. 1992).

94 Jenson v. Eveleth Taconite Co., 824 F. Supp. 847 (D. Minn 1993).

> member is entitled to all the remedies available under Title VII and MHRA. In a hostile environment action, therefore, every member of the plaintiff class remains a "potential victim" in the true sense of the term.
>
> This result is dictated by the fact that the proof introduced during the liability phase cannot resolve a disparate issue of fact essential to claims alleging hostile environment: whether individual members of the plaintiff class were as affected as the reasonable woman would have been. . . . Because the *employee's* subjective response to acts of sexual harassment is an essential part of proving a claim of hostile environment sexual harassment, a presumption that the employer discriminated against individual class members may not arise from a determination that the reasonable woman would have been affected by the acts of sexual harassment. Individual employees should not be allowed to circumvent an essential element of a hostile environment claim merely because they are permitted to pursue their claims as a class; Fed.R.Civ.P. 23 involves issues other than the merits of the case.
>
> Nevertheless, . . . liability to the class is established by a determination that the employer engaged in a pattern or practice of exposing women to acts of sexual harassment sufficient to alter the terms or conditions of the reasonable woman's employment. Accordingly, individual class members need only show that they were at least as affected as the reasonable woman. The other elements of a hostile claim are established by the court's determination in the liability phase of the proceeding.[95]

§ 6.11 Welcomeness of Conduct in Sexual Harassment Class Actions

To demonstrate that sexual harassment is unwelcome when a class action claim is at issue, the plaintiff class must show by a preponderance of the evidence that women, by their conduct, indicated that the acts of sexual harassment were unsolicited and regarded as undesirable or offensive.[96] Women's actions and use of language are relevant evidence in determining whether women found particular conduct unwelcome, but although women cursed at the mines, there was no evidence here that the women used language and epithets that were intensely degrading to women such as "bitch," "whore," and "cunt," which were extremely powerful words. In addition, women did not discuss their sex lives at work in front of men, nor did they, with the exception of one woman on one occasion, engage in questioning men about their sex lives or interest in sexual activities. Moreover, the fact that "women say 'fuck' at work does not imply that they are inviting any and every form of sexual harassment."[97]

---

[95] *Id.* at 875–76 (footnotes omitted).

[96] *Id.* at 847.

[97] *Id.* at 883.

Women employees who testified at trial expressed different perspectives on the acts of sexual harassment occurring at Eveleth Mines; some were offended and affected a great deal by almost everything, whereas others were offended or affected only to a limited extent. All of this testimony was credible. However, the Court finds that the effect, and possibly the intent, of the sexualized environment that existed at Eveleth Mines was to inform women that they were perceived primarily as sexual objects and inferior to men, rather than as co-workers, and that these perceptions were an integral part of working at Eveleth Mines.

There was also testimony by men who work at Eveleth Mines that Eveleth Mines was not a sexually-charged work environment and that women did not complain of sexual harassment, at least not to them. As with many gender-related issues however, men, when they are in the majority and when they control the avenues of power, and thus are generally immune to unwelcome conduct, may fail to observe what a reasonable women perceives on a continual basis. Differences in perception, therefore, are attributable to the fact of gender; that women were offended when men were not does not alter the possibility that a woman's negative reactions to offensive conduct were reasonable.

As it is used in a hostile environment case, "employment" relates to the entire context in which an individual or group of people work. It includes not only the activities comprising the specific tasks for which employees are compensated, but also the overall ability of an employee or group of employees to spend their work hours focused on concerns relating to work and themselves as workers. A work environment affects a term or condition of employment, that is, it is "hostile" to women, when a woman or women must spend their day running a "gauntlet of sexual abuse in return for the privilege of being allowed to work and make a living." *Meritor,* 477 U.S. at 67 . . . In other words, where women are presented with constant and pervasive references to women, perhaps even themselves, as sexual objects and are subjected to acts in which their sexuality and sex role is elevated over their status as an employee, —that is, they are subject to pervasive sexual harassment on account of their sex—the reasonable woman would find the terms, conditions, and privileges of her employment affected by that sexual harassment.[98]

§ 6.12 Timeliness of Filing the Complaint

Upon receipt of a right-to-sue letter, a complainant has 90 days to file suit against the defendant named in the charge (see **Chapter 5**). Untimeliness is an affirmative defense that must be expressly pleaded.[99] State statutes of limitation do not apply to Title VII actions, but analogous state statutes

---

[98] *Id.* at 885–86 (footnotes omitted).

[99] Fed. R. Civ. P. 8(c); Mohasco Corp. v. Silver, 447 U.S. 807 (1980).

are used to determine time limitations for § 1983 actions (see **Chapter 8**). Title VII contains no statute of limitations for pattern-or-practice suits brought by either an individual party[100] or the EEOC.[101] Although pattern-or-practice suits have been rare for sexual harassment, the principle is compatible with the hostile environment theory of harassment. Under the continuing violations doctrine, discriminatory acts performed before the limitations period may be challenged if the complainant demonstrates that the offending conduct is ongoing,[102] and that at least one such act has occurred during the limitations period.[103]

§ 6.13 —Federal Employers

A federal employee charging discrimination may bring a civil action 180 days after a complaint has been filed with the employer agency, if there has been no decision by that agency, or 180 days after an appeal was filed with the EEOC, if the EEOC has made no decision.[104] After receiving the final decision of the relevant agency, a federal employee has 30 days to file a Title VII civil action.[105] An agency decision is final when determinations have been made on all issues in the complaint, including attorney's fees.[106] If the decision was appealed to the EEOC, the employee has 30 days after receiving the EEOC decision to file suit.[107] The District of Columbia Circuit has held that when a complainant has filed a request for reconsideration of an EEOC decision, the initial decision is not a final decision for the filing period requirement.[108]

Notices regarding final action by a federal agency or an EEOC decision must inform the complainant of the right to file an action in federal court.[109] Recent cases have held that the limitations period may begin

---

[100] United States v. Masonry Contractors Ass'n, 497 F.2d 871 (6th Cir. 1974).

[101] 42 U.S.C. § 2000e-6.

[102] Brown v. Brown, 528 F. Supp. 686 (D.N.J. 1981).

[103] See **Ch. 5.**

[104] 42 U.S.C. § 2000e-16(c); 29 C.F.R. §§ 1613.281, 1613.641(a).

[105] 42 U.S.C. § 2000e-16(c). *See also* Hernandez v. Aldridge, 866 F. 2d 800 (5th Cir. 1989) (30-day period is jurisdictional; court could not hear discrimination claim that was marked "received" but was not actually filed within 30-day period).

[106] 29 C.F.R. §§ 1613.281, 1613.641(a).

[107] 42 U.S.C. § 2000e-16(c).

[108] Nordell v. Heckler, 749 F.2d 47 (D.C. Cir. 1984).

[109] First Circuit: Fischer v. United States Dep't of Transp., 430 F. Supp. 1349 (D. Mass. 1977), *aff'd in part, rev'd in part,* 572 F.2d 406 (1st Cir. 1978).

Third Circuit: Allen v. United States, 542 F.2d 176 (3d Cir. 1976).

Fifth Circuit: *Cf.* Eastland v. Tennessee Valley Auth., 553 F.2d 364 (5th Cir.), *cert. denied,* 434 U.S. 985 (1977).

when the complainant's counsel has received the right-to-sue notice on the client's behalf, provided there is an ongoing attorney-client relationship with the complainant when the notice is received, and the attorney personally acknowledges receipt of the notice.[110] However, many earlier courts held that the complainant personally must receive notice of the action or decision to start the 30-day filing period.[111]

The disposition of a prematurely filed federal employment complaint is subject to the discretion of the court.[112]

§ 6.14 —EEOC Actions

The commission may bring a civil action against a private respondent named in the charge if, within 30 days after a charge is filed, the commission has been unable to obtain an appropriate conciliation agreement[113] (see **Chapter 5**). Although the commission may bring suit after 30 days, it also may continue its attempts at conciliation. The EEOC's right to bring suit under Title VII on behalf of an aggrieved individual is not limited by either state statutes of limitation or the 180-day period during which the EEOC may attempt conciliation. A lengthy delay, however, might severely prejudice a defendant and give rise to the defense of laches.[114] The EEOC may bring a civil action despite the issuance of a right-to-sue letter or the failure of the complainant to bring suit within the 90-day statutory period.[115]

Ninth Circuit: Mahroom v. Hook, 563 F.2d 1369 (9th Cir. 1977), *cert. denied,* 436 U.S. 904 (1978).

District of Columbia Circuit: Williams v. Hidalgo, 663 F.2d 183 (D.C. Cir. 1980).

[110] Fizer-Bullock v. United States Dep't of Hous. & Urban Dev., 37 Fair Empl. Prac. Cas. (BNA) 1601 (D.D.C. 1985); Craig v. Department of Health, Educ. & Welfare, 581 F.2d 189 (8th Cir. 1978).

[111] Sixth Circuit: Rea v. Middendorf, 587 F.2d 4 (6th Cir. 1978).

Eighth Circuit: Craig v. Department of Health, Educ. & Welfare, 581 F.2d 189 (8th Cir. 1978).

District of Columbia Circuit: Bell v. Brown, 557 F.2d 849 (D.C. Cir. 1977).

[112] Johnson v. United States Postal Serv., 364 F. Supp. 37 (N.D. Fla. 1973), *aff'd,* 497 F.2d 128 (11th Cir. 1974).

[113] 42 U.S.C. § 2000e-5(f)(1).

[114] Occidental Life Ins. Co. v. EEOC, 432 U.S. 355 (1977).

[115] EEOC v. Appleton Elec. Co., 487 F. Supp. 1207 (N.D. Ill. 1980).

§ 6.15 Tolling the Statute of Limitations

The tolling doctrine may apply to otherwise time-barred discrimination complaints.[116] Title VII's 90-day filing period may be tolled when errors by the EEOC,[117] plaintiff's counsel,[118] or the court,[119] or misrepresentations by the defendant,[120] have caused the plaintiff to file an untimely charge. Tolling also may apply if a timely initial complaint was defective and the corrected complaint is filed after the filing period ends,[121] or the plaintiff files a right-to-sue letter and requests counsel,[122] or elects to proceed *in*

---

116 *Cf.* Mitchell v. Los Angeles Community College Dist., 861 F.2d 198 (9th Cir. 1988) (90-day limitations period for filing suit after receiving right-to-sue letter is jurisdictional and mandatory).

117 Feng v. Sandrik, 636 F. Supp. 77 (N.D. Ill. 1986) (federal employment); Whitehead v. Reliance Ins. Co., 632 F.2d 452 (5th Cir. 1980); Ramos v. Port Auth., 20 Fair Empl. Prac. Cas. (BNA) 174 (S.D.N.Y. 1976). *Cf.* Brown v. Mead Corp., 646 F.2d 1163 (6th Cir. 1981); (EEOC erroneously issued a right-to-sue letter and four years passed between date of initial charge and filing of lawsuit).

118 *Cf.* Simpson v. City of Chicago Fire Dep't, No. 86-C840 (N.D. Ill. April 24, 1986) (filing period was not tolled when although plaintiff's attorney failed to notify plaintiff of receipt of right-to-sue letter or bring suit within time limit, noncommunication or reliance on attorney's advice in not filing timely complaint was not ground for tolling, particularly when three years had passed since period had expired); Lancaster v. Holt, Rienhart & Winston, Inc., 31 Fair Empl. Prac. Cas. (BNA) 1390 (N.D. Fla. 1983) (filing period was not tolled when plaintiff's attorney failed to tell plaintiff of filing requirement before end of 90-day period).

119 Suarez v. Little Havana Activities, 721 F.2d 338 (11th Cir. 1983) (complaint was mailed two days before end of filing period but for unknown reasons was not filed in court clerk's office until four days later); Gonzalez-Aller Balseyro v. GTE Lenkurt, Inc., 702 F.2d 857 (10th Cir. 1983) (plaintiff was advised by court clerk that filing right-to-sue notice tolled filing period until plaintiff could obtain counsel and defendants did not allege prejudice). *Cf.* Aljadir v. University of Pa., 547 F. Supp. 667 (E.D. Pa. 1982), *aff'd without opinion,* 709 F.2d 1490 (3d Cir. 1983) (plaintiff did not attempt to file until 90th day and did not file successfully until 91st day because of allegedly incorrect information given to him by court clerk).

120 *Cf.* Williams v. Army & Air Force Exch. Serv., 830 F.2d 27 (3d Cir. 1987) (filing period was not tolled when federal employee improperly named agency as defendant in her Title VII action pursuant to statements by defendant that might have led her counsel to believe the agency should be named when statements were accurate and did not involve "active" misrepresentation); Hinton v. CPC Int'l, Inc., 520 F.2d 1312 (8th Cir. 1975) (reliance by plaintiff on defendant counsel's offer not to raise statute of limitations defense was no justification for failing to comply with filing requirement).

121 Nielsen v. Flower Hosp., 639 F. Supp. 738 (S.D.N.Y. 1986); Loya v. Desert Sands Unified Sch. Dist., 721 F.2d 279 (9th Cir. 1983); Cox v. Consol. Rail, 557 F. Supp. 1261 (D.D.C. 1983).

122 Baldwin County Welcome Ctr. v. Brown, 466 U.S. 147 (1984).

Fifth Circuit: Wrenn v. American Cast Iron Pipe Co., 575 F.2d 544 (5th Cir. 1978). *Cf.* Antoine v. United States Postal Serv., 781 F.2d 433 (5th Cir. 1986) (filing period

forma pauperis.[123] Although a right-to-sue letter alone is not a proper form of complaint,[124] a right-to-sue letter filed within the statutory filing period may toll the limitations period,[125] particularly when a formal complaint is filed within a reasonable amount of time.[126]

Courts have refused to apply the tolling doctrine in situations in which the plaintiff[127] or another similarly situated person[128] has filed an administrative charge with the EEOC[129] or a motion to intervene in another action.[130] Other reasons for refusal include plaintiff's mistake,[131]

---

was not tolled in federal employment action when counsel was appointed a week before end of 30-day period and counsel did not request additional time for filing complaint).

Sixth Circuit: Harris v. Walgreen's Distrib. Ctr., 456 F.2d 588 (6th Cir. 1972); Salins v. Dayton, 624 F. Supp. 632 (S.D. Ohio 1985).

Seventh Circuit: Brown v. J.I. Case Co., 756 F.2d 48 (7th Cir. 1985). *Cf.* Hale v. United States Postal Serv., 663 F. Supp. 7 (N.D. Ill. 1986), *aff'd,* 826 F.2d 1067 (7th Cir. 1987) (filing period was not tolled when plaintiff submitted incomplete forms and failed to include merits of his claim on his complaint).

Eighth Circuit: Wingfield v. Goodwill Indus., 666 F.2d 1177 (8th Cir. 1981).

123 Salins v. Dayton, 624 F. Supp. 632 (S.D. Ohio 1985); Quiles v. O'Hare Hilton, 572 F. Supp. 866 (N.D. Ill. 1983); Yelverton v. Blue Bell, Inc., 530 F. Supp. 701 (E.D.N.C. 1982). *Cf.* Daniel v. S.E.S. Dev. Co., 703 F. Supp. 601 (N.D. Tex. 1988) (90-day period was not tolled when no appointment of counsel was sought until after 90-day period had expired, plaintiff actually received a right-to-sue letter, and record did not indicate that employer actively misled plaintiff or that court led plaintiff to believe he had done everything required).

124 Baldwin County Welcome Ctr. v. Brown, 446 U.S. 147 (1984) (Filing period starts again if petition is denied, but may toll again if plaintiff files a motion for reconsideration of denial); Ortiz v. Clarence H. Hackett, Inc., 581 F. Supp. 1258 (N.D. Ind. 1984).

125 Metcalf v. Omaha Steel Castings Co., 476 F. Supp. 870 (D. Neb. 1979); Beckum v. Tennessee Hotel, 341 F. Supp. 991 (W.D. Tenn. 1971); Reyes v. Missouri-Kan.-Tex. R.R., 53 F.R.D. 293 (D. Kan. 1971); Austin v. Reynolds Metal Co., 327 F. Supp. 1145 (E.D. Va. 1970).

126 Trader v. Fiat Distribs., Inc., 476 F. Supp. 1194 (D. Del. 1979); Hawkins v. International Harvester, 461 F. Supp. 588 (W.D. Tenn. 1978).

127 Vuksta v. Bethlehem Steel Corp., 540 F. Supp. 1276 (E.D. Pa. 1982), *aff'd without opinion,* 707 F.2d 1405 (3d Cir.), *cert. denied,* 464 U.S. 835 (1983).

128 Watson v. Carpenter Tech. Corp., No. 82-1800 (E.D. Pa. Dec. 2, 1985).

129 Hill v. John Chezik Imports, 869 F.2d 1122 (8th Cir. 1989) (complainant's failure to notify EEOC of change in address, which caused her right-to-sue letter to be sent and accepted at her previous address, did not warrant tolling, especially when there was ample time to bring suit after complainant found out that letter had been sent); Vuksta v. Bethlehem Steel Corp., 540 F. Supp. 1276 (E.D. Pa. 1982), *aff'd without opinion,* 707 F.2d 1405 (3d Cir.), *cert. denied,* 464 U.S. 835 (1983).

130 Banks v. Teletype Corp., 563 F. Supp. 1358 (E.D. Ark. 1983). *Cf.* Braxton v. Virginia Folding Box Co., 72 F.R.D. 124 (E.D. Va. 1976).

131 Christopher v. General Motors Parts Div., 525 F. Supp. 634 (E.D. Mich. 1981), *aff'd without opinion,* 703 F.2d 559 (6th Cir. 1982); Ivy v. Meridian Coca-Cola Bottling Co., 108 F.R.D. 118 (S.D. Miss. 1985) (plaintiff mistakenly believed he could not file suit until he received a right-to-sue notice on all three EEOC charges to which he was a party).

illness,[132] or other personal problems,[133] causing the filing of an untimely complaint, an action mistakenly filed in state court,[134] an action dismissed without prejudice,[135] and others.[136]

Federal Rule of Civil Procedure 6(a) governs all time periods in federal civil actions.

§ 6.16 Defense of Laches

The equitable doctrine of laches may be raised as a defense to an untimely Title VII complaint. For a Title VII defendant to prevail on such a claim, the court must find that there was an inexcusable delay in bringing suit[137] and that the delay unduly prejudiced the defendant.[138] The doctrine of laches has been applied in private suits[139] and in actions by the EEOC.[140]

---

132 Lopez v. Citibank, 808 F.2d 905 (1st Cir. 1987); Dumas v. Agency for Child Dev., N.Y., 569 F. Supp. 831 (S.D.N.Y. 1983).

133 Scott v. St. Paul Postal Serv., 720 F.2d 524 (8th Cir. 1983), *cert. denied,* 465 U.S. 1083 (1984) (plaintiff could not take time off from work to file a complaint and had trouble finding an attorney).

134 Sager v. Hunter Corp., 665 F. Supp. 575 (N.D. Ill. 1986). *Cf.* Valenzuela v. Kraft, 801 F.2d 1170 (9th Cir. 1976), *modified,* 815 F.2d 570 (9th Cir. 1987); Brown v. Commonwealth Edison Co., 647 F. Supp. 1456 (N.D. Ill. 1986), *aff'd,* 852 F.2d 932 (7th Cir. 1988); Dickinson v. Chrysler Corp., 456 F. Supp. 43 (E.D. Mich. 1978).

135 Wilson v. Grumman Ohio Corp., 815 F.2d 26 (6th Cir. 1987); Scoggins v. Douglas, 760 F.2d 535 (4th Cir. 1985); Moore v. St. Louis Music Supply Co., 539 F.2d 1191 (8th Cir. 1976); Cleveland v. Douglas Aircraft Co., 509 F.2d 1027 (9th Cir. 1975); Hewlett v. Russo, 649 F. Supp. 457 (E.D. Va. 1986); Harris v. Brock, 642 F. Supp. 1134 (N.D. Ill. 1984); Braxton v. Virginia Folding Box Co., 72 F.R.D. 124 (E.D. Va. 1976), *aff'd,* 835 F.2d 1190 (7th Cir. 1987).

136 Froneberger v. Yadkin County Sch., 630 F. Supp. 291 (M.D.N.C.), *aff'd,* 804 F.2d 677 (4th Cir. 1986) (plaintiff was convicted of felony and was in prison almost two months into 90-day period); Hibbard v. Don Love, Inc., 584 F. Supp. 2 (S.D. Tex. 1984) (plaintiff moved from one state to another during 90-day filing period).

137 EEOC v. Star Tool & Die Works, Inc., 699 F. Supp. 120 (E.D. Mich. 1987) (EEOC backlog, staff shortage, or attorney turnover will not justify an unreasonable delay in bringing a Title VII action).

138 *Id.* (a seven-and-a-half-year delay between filing of charges and filing of discrimination complaint by EEOC warranted dismissal when 21-month delay between failure of conciliation and preparation of presentation memorandum by EEOC was unexplained; EEOC then took another year and a half to revise memorandum and file complaint, and many records were lost or destroyed during this time). *See also* Costello v. United States, 365 U.S. 265 (1961); Gardner v. Panama R.R., 342 U.S. 29 (1951).

139 Whitfield v. Anheuser-Busch, Inc., 820 F.2d 243 (8th Cir. 1987); Jeffries v. Chicago Transit Auth., 770 F.2d 676 (7th Cir. 1985).

140 EEOC v. CW Transp., Inc., 658 F. Supp. 1278 (W.D. Wis. 1987); EEOC v. Indiana Bell Tel. Co., 641 F. Supp. 115 (S.D. Ind. 1986); EEOC v. Firestone Tire & Rubber Co., 626 F. Supp. 90 (M.D. Ga. 1985).

PREPARING THE PLEADINGS

§ 6.17 Pleadings and Motions

Because the defendant most likely will attempt to shorten litigation by moving for summary judgment or to dismiss for failure to state a claim or jurisdictional deficiencies, pleadings must be timely and specific. Anticipating procedural challenges and rectifying deficiencies early allows the litigation to proceed more efficiently, prevents the procedural issues from diluting the case's merits, and keeps the parties from testing the court's patience. **Appendix A** contains sample complaints that illustrate effective ways of pleading sexual harassment claims.

§ 6.18 Drafting the Complaint

A plaintiff begins a civil discrimination action in federal court by timely filing a complaint with the clerk of the federal district court.[141] The complaint must contain:

1. A short, plain statement of the grounds upon which the court's jurisdiction depends[142]
2. A short, plain statement of the claim showing that the pleader is entitled to relief
3. A demand for relief

Under Federal Rule of Civil Procedure 8, each factual averment must be simple, concise, and direct,[143] and must be made in numbered paragraphs, each of which should be limited as far as practicable to a statement of a single set of circumstances.[144] Despite the simple "notice pleading" requirements, the complaint should not merely reiterate the language of Title VII.[145]

---

[141] Fed R. Civ. P. 3.5(e).

[142] Kerans v. Porter Paint Co., 656 F. Supp. 267 (S.D. Ohio 1987) (failure to allege compliance with jurisdictional requirements warranted dismissal of action); Collins v. Pfizer, Inc., 39 Fair Empl. Prac. Cas. (BNA) 1316 (D. Conn. 1985) (failure to allege that plaintiff filed charges with deferral agency did not warrant dismissal when employer introduced into evidence agency decisions implying that plaintiff filed charges upon which agency acted). *Accord* Brown v. Miami Beach, 684 F.2d 1081 (S.D. Fla. 1988).

[143] Fed. R. Civ. P. 8(e)(1). *See* Acampora v. Boise Cascade Corp., 635 F. Supp. 66, 68 (D.N.J. 1986) (sexual harassment).

[144] Fed. R. Civ. P. 10(b).

[145] Edwards v. Amoco Oil Co., No. 86-2366 (D. Kan. Jan. 26, 1987).

Each statement must be made in such a way that the opposing party is given fair notice of the nature of and grounds for the claim.[146] Attorneys should plead with specificity when possible, particularly with respect to the challenged acts.[147] Pendent state common law claims need only satisfy federal notice pleading requirements, not state law rules.[148]

The scope of the allegations asserted in Title VII complaints may be much broader than the allegations in the administrative charge. The allegations "may encompass any kind of discrimination like or related to allegations contained in the charge and growing out of such allegations during the pendency of the case before the commission."[149] The complaint may include allegations of any discriminatory employment practice for which the EEOC has conducted an investigation, attempted conciliation, and made a reasonable cause determination, as well as the allegations in the original EEOC charge.[150] But in *Sandom v. Travelers Mortgage Services,*[151] claims of sexual harassment were dismissed in a sex discrimination action when the plaintiff failed to allege sexual harassment in her EEOC charges, the claims apparently were not investigated by the EEOC, and arose from

---

146 Marshall v. Electric Hose & Rubber Co., 65 F.R.D. 599 (D. Del. 1974); Otto v. Sterling Elecs. Corp., 5 Fair Empl. Prac. Cas. (BNA) 1176 (S.D. Tex. 1973).

147 Trader v. Fiat Distribs., Inc., 476 F. Supp. 1194 (D. Del. 1979).

148 Moffett v. Gene B. Glick, Co., 604 F. Supp. 229 (N.D. Ind. 1984).

149 King v. Georgia Power Co., 295 F. Supp. 943, 947 (N.D. Ga. 1968).

See also Fourth Circuit: EEOC v. Newtown Inn Assocs., 647 F. Supp. 957 (E.D. Va. 1986) (sexual harassment) (allegations of retaliatory reassignment in EEOC charge filed by two waitresses properly encompassed constructive discharge claims of five other waitresses).

Fifth Circuit: Gupta v. East Tex. State Univ., 654 F.2d 411 (5th Cir. 1981); Sanchez v. Standard Brands, Inc., 431 F.2d 455 (5th Cir. 1970).

Sixth Circuit: Tipler v. E.I. Du Pont de Nemours & Co., 443 F.2d 125 (6th Cir. 1971).

Seventh Circuit: Babrocky v. Jewel Food Co., 773 F.2d 857 (7th Cir. 1985); Jenkins v. Blue Cross Mut. Hosp. Ins. Co., 538 F.2d 164 (7th Cir. 1976).

Eighth Circuit: Satz v. ITT Fin. Corp., 619 F.2d 738 (8th Cir. 1980).

Ninth Circuit: Brown v. Continental Can Co., 765 F.2d 810 (9th Cir. 1985); Waters v. Hueblein, Inc., 547 F.2d 466 (9th Cir. 1976), *cert. denied,* 433 U.S. 915 (1977); Oubichon v. North Am. Rockwell Corp., 482 F.2d 569 (9th Cir. 1973).

Tenth Circuit: *Cf.* Archuleta v. Colorado Dept. of Insts., 936 F.2d 483 (10th Cir. 1991) (claims of nonretaliatory sexual harassment were properly dismissed when plaintiff's EEOC charge was based on retaliation).

Eleventh Circuit: Evans v. United States Pipe & Foundry Co., 696 F.2d 925 (11th Cir. 1983).

150 *See, e.g.,* Ray v. Freeman, 626 F.2d 439 (5th Cir. 1980), *cert. denied,* 450 U.S. 997 (1981); EEOC v. General Elec. Co., 532 F.2d 359 (4th Cir. 1976).

151 Sandom v. Travellers Mortgage Servs., 752 F. Supp. 1240 (D.N.J. 1990).

a set of facts wholly distinct from a contention of sexual discrimination with respect to salaries or job responsibilities:

> The sexual harassment claim would, most likely, not have arisen out of a reasonable EEOC investigation of the filed claim absent a specific allegation in the charge. Furthermore, the sexual harassment claim is not a claim of retaliation for the earlier filing of an EEOC charge, nor assists in clarifying the earlier complaint.[152]

Similarly, in *Cruz v. Ecolab Pest Elimination Div., Ecolab, Inc.,*[153] the plaintiff's EEOC charge containing allegations of discriminatory discharge did not give the employer sufficient notice of intention to raise sexual harassment claims:

> The agency complaint was one of discriminatory discharge, no less but no more, a discrete claim, standing alone, and failing to suggest, explicitly or implicitly, any other form of conduct violative of Title VII. In short, Cruz' EEOC charge failed in its important public policy purpose of giving defendants sufficient notice of her intention to raise allegations pertaining to discrimination in areas other than a discriminatory discharge, thereby depriving defendants and the agency itself of the opportunity of reconciliation.[154]

Sexual harassment claims are discrete claims that probably would not be deemed to grow out of a nonsexual harassment sex discrimination charge, but some courts have allowed plaintiffs to include in the complaint all claims pertaining to sexually discriminatory practices, including sexual harassment, even if the original EEOC charge and investigation involved only discriminatory wage allegations.[155] A constructive discharge claim may grow out of allegations of sex discrimination.[156]

The complaint also must contain a demand for relief. Under Title VII, the court may award such relief as it deems appropriate,[157] and thus the failure to request a particular form of relief does not preclude consideration of such relief by the court.[158] The demand for relief also should include a request for attorney's fees.[159]

---

[152] *Id.* at 1248.

[153] Cruz v. Ecolab Pest Elim. Div., Ecolab, Inc., 817 F. Supp. 388 (S.D.N.Y. 1993).

[154] *Id.* at 391–92.

[155] *See* Polay v. West Co., 629 F. Supp. 899 (E.D. Pa. 1986).

[156] EEOC v. Newtown Inn Assocs., 647 F. Supp. 957 (E.D. Va. 1986).

[157] 42 U.S.C. § 2000e-5(g).

[158] Sias v. City Demonstration Agency, 588 F.2d 692 (9th Cir. 1978). *See also* Doss v. South Cent. Bell Tel. Co., 834 F.2d 421 (5th Cir. 1987), *reh'g denied,* 837 F.2d 1090 (5th Cir. 1988).

[159] 42 U.S.C. § 2000e-5(k).

The right-to-sue letter should be attached to the complaint. Courts have expressed different views about the importance of including the letter,[160] so filing it with the complaint will avoid unneccessary challenge by the defendant.

Two sample complaints of sexual harassment can be found in **Appendix A.**

§ 6.19 Pleading *Quid Pro Quo* Harassment

A *quid pro quo* sexual harassment complaint must include specific pleadings about the manner in which the challenged conduct affected the terms and conditions of employment. The complaint must allege, with supporting facts, that:

1. The jurisdictional requirements of Title VII have been satisfied.
2. The employer or agent made advances or demands of a sexual nature upon the plaintiff.
3. The plaintiff's continued employment, promotion, or other job-related benefit was conditioned upon compliance with the sexual advances or demands.
4. The sexual advances or demands were made on the plaintiff because she is a woman.
5. Negative job consequences resulted from the failure by the plaintiff to comply with the advances or demands.
6. The employer knew or should have known of the harassment.[161]

The first sample complaint in **Appendix A** contains allegations of a *quid pro quo* harassment action.

If the plaintiff was constructively discharged, she should allege that as a result of her noncompliance with the sexual demands or advances, her working conditions were made so intolerable that she was forced to quit.

Retaliation claims should be alleged with a statement describing the protected conduct and the adverse employment consequences and that the two are causally connected (see **Chapter 3**).

---

160 Burwell v. Eastern Air Lines, Inc., 394 F. Supp. 1361 (E.D. Va. 1975); Stanley v. Indiana Civil Rights Comm'n, 557 F. Supp. 330 (N.D. Ind. 1983), *aff'd,* 740 F.2d 972 (7th Cir. 1984) (action would not be dismissed for failure to allege receipt of right-to-sue letter as long as plaintiff filed letter with court later).

161 Employers may be strictly liable for *quid pro quo* harassment (see **Chs. 2** and **3**), but evidence of knowledge will bolster the claim.

§ 6.20 Pleading Hostile Environment Harassment

Allegations of a hostile environment should stress the frequency and repetitive nature of offensive acts, the unwelcome nature of those acts, and the effect this conduct had on the plaintiff's ability to perform her work. The complaint should allege that:

1. The jurisdictional requirements of Title VII have been met.
2. The plaintiff is a member of the protected class.[162]
3. The plaintiff was subjected (repeatedly, for the best case) to unwelcome sexual or otherwise abusive conduct directed at her as a woman.
4. The plaintiff was subjected to and/or offended by this harassment because of her gender.
5. The sexual harassment affected a "term, condition or privilege" of employment by creating an abusive work environment that affected her psychological and/or physical well-being.
6. The plaintiff gave notice of the sexual harassment to the employer or its agents.
7. The employer failed to take prompt or adequate remedial action in response to actual or constructive notice of the sexual harassment.

For examples of hostile environment sexual harassment complaints, see **Appendix A.**

If possible, the plaintiff should allege specifically the ways that the offensive conduct has affected her work productivity and her mental and physical health. These allegations will solidify the cause of action for summary judgment purposes and establish for the court the chronology of events. When a plaintiff has been fired from her job, these allegations help establish from the beginning that the plaintiff was not terminated because of alleged poor work performance but because of the sexual harassment that led to poor work performance. Under *Harris v. Forklift Systems, Inc.,*[163] a plaintiff need not demonstrate psychological injury in order to prove a hostile environment, but need only show that the environment could reasonably be perceived as hostile or abusive.[164]

Allegations of constructive discharge often are included in complaints alleging a hostile work environment because quitting to escape the abuse is a natural consequence of such an atmosphere. A plaintiff need not allege

[162] Henson v. City of Dundee, 682 F.2d 897 (11th Cir. 1982) (this requires only a stipulation that the employee is a woman or man).

[163] Harris v. Forklift Systems, Inc., 114 S. Ct. 367 (1993).

[164] *Id.* at 371.

conduct more severe than that to establish a hostile environment generally, but allegations regarding the mounting abuse or tension resulting from the abuse may be helpful to show that the plaintiff had no choice but to quit.

Allegations of retaliation also may be included in a hostile environment complaint when abuse has escalated because of sexual harassment complaints by employees or when an employment situation was otherwise altered (see **Appendix A**).

Charges of race and sex discrimination may be appropriate. Racial discrimination allegations may be either independent or woven into a hostile environment charge. Courts have recognized the cumulative burden of racial and sexual harassment (see **Chapter 3**).

§ 6.21 —Allegations of Harassment by Coworkers

Coworker harassment is a common element of the hostile work environment. A finding of liability often turns on whether the employer or supervisor had or should have had knowledge of the harassment. Thus, specific allegations regarding notice or constructive notice should accompany the complaint. A complaint containing allegations of coworker harassment should contain statements regarding:

1. The nature and context of the offensive conduct
2. The impact of the offensive conduct on the plaintiff's work or physical or emotional health
3. Notice or constructive notice to the employer or supervisor
4. The failure of the employer promptly or effectively to remedy the situation despite receipt of notice

If a supervisor was among those employees participating in the offensive conduct, the inclusion of that fact will bolster the claim of hostile environment harassment. A subordinate employee also may create a hostile environment, despite the hierarchal imbalance.

§ 6.22 —Allegations of Harassment by Nonemployees

Allegations of sexual harassment by a nonemployee or client must focus on the actions of the employer or supervisor that encouraged such conduct. This type of harassment usually is brought on by employer requirements that employees wear revealing uniforms or engage in provocative behavior. Once again, the employer must have had notice of the offensive conduct, despite the fact that the effect of the costume or behavior requirements is predictable and should eliminate the need for notice. A complaint alleging this type of harassment should contain statements regarding:

1. Employer requirements, such as the type of revealing uniforms or provocative conduct that result in sexual harassment by nonemployees or clients
2. The type of offensive conduct that such employer requirements encouraged, such as unsolicited leering, touching, or propositions by customers
3. The fact that men have not been required to engage in similar conduct or wear comparable clothes
4. Actual or constructive notice to the employer of the harassment
5. The failure by the employer to take prompt or effective action in response to such notice

§ 6.23 Parties Named in the Complaint

In a Title VII action, the plaintiff must name the parties unless she can demonstrate a compelling need to protect privacy.[165] In *Doe v. Roster,*[166] a district court observed that:

> a plaintiff should be permitted to proceed anonymously in cases where a substantial privacy interest is involved. The most compelling situations involve matters which are highly sensitive, such as social stigmatization, real danger of physical harm, or where the injury litigated against would occur as a result of the disclosure of the plaintiff's identity. That the plaintiff may suffer some embarrassment or economic harm is not enough. There must be strong social interest in concealing the identity of the plaintiff.[167]

The district court refused to allow a plaintiff to maintain her action under a pseudonym in *Doe v. Hallock,*[168] despite allegations that she had been subjected to retaliatory incidents since filing the suit. The plaintiff's claim was directed at a limited number of individuals and it was unlikely that she could expect harassment from the community in general. The court stated that "the source of any harassment apparently is already aware of plaintiff's identity, and there is little reason to believe that disclosure of

165 Southern Methodist Univ. Ass'n of Women Law Students v. Wynne & Jaffe, 599 F.2d 707 (5th Cir. 1979).

166 Doe v. Roster, 89 F.R.D. 158, 162 (N.D. Cal. 1981).

167 *Id.* at 162.

168 Doe v. Hallock, 119 F.R.D. 640 (S.D. Miss. 1987).

her identity in this lawsuit would serve to increase the number of such incidents."[169]

Employees who have been harassed by coworkers should name the employer as well as the coworkers.[170] The failure to name certain employees in the EEOC charge may not preclude a Title VII action against those employees if it can be inferred from the charges that violated Title VII.[171]

§ 6.24 Federal Employment Action Allegations

In addition to the subjective and jurisdictional facts required in the complaint, a federal employee must allege that her claims were brought to the federal agency employer and that the claims are cognizable under Title VII.[172] If administrative requirements are not fulfilled, the plaintiff must plead equitable reasons for failing to meet them.[173] Discrepancies between the administrative charge and the judicial complaint do not bar the civil action as long as the complaint encompasses discrimination similar to, or reasonably related to, that alleged in the administrative charge.[174] Retaliation is a common addition to complaints because it often occurs after the charge has been filed.[175]

§ 6.25 Amendments to Pleadings

Before a responsive pleading is served, a party may amend that pleading as a matter of right.[176] (A motion for summary judgment by the defendant

---

169 *Id.* at 644.

170 Flowers v. Rego, 691 F. Supp. 177 (E.D. Ark. 1988).

171 Wangler v. Hawaiian Elec. Co., 742 F. Supp. 1458 (D. Haw. 1990) (failure to name two employees in EEOC charges did not preclude a Title VII action against those employees when it could be inferred from charges that employees violated Title VII, as one employee was responsible for hiring plaintiff and the other for training her, the parties clearly could have been involved in acts that gave rise to the charges; both individual defendants worked in the same department with plaintiff, and allegedly had considerable contact with her at various times during her employment).

172 42 U.S.C. § 2000e-16.

173 Saltz v. Lehman, 672 F.2d 207 (D.C. Cir. 1982).

174 Chisholm v. United States Postal Serv., 665 F.2d 482 (4th Cir. 1981); Ong v. Cleland, 642 F.2d 316 (9th Cir. 1981); Haynes v. Mark, 520 F. Supp. 1183 (D. Colo. 1981); Beasley v. Griffin, 427 F. Supp. 801 (D. Mass. 1977).

175 Haynes v. Mark, 520 F. Supp. 1183 (D. Colo. 1981).

176 Fed. R. Civ. P. 15(a); Washington v. New York City Bd. of Estimate, 709 F.2d 792 (2d Cir.), *cert. denied,* 464 U.S. 1013 (1983); Zaidi v. Ehrlich, 732 F.2d 1218 (5th Cir. 1984).

is not a responsive pleading under the Federal Rules of Civil Procedure.[177]) After a responsive pleading is served, a party must obtain leave of the court or the opposing party's consent to amend a pleading. Requests for leave to amend the complaint usually will be granted unless prejudice to the defendant would warrant an amendment unjust.[178] The nonmoving party must demonstrate that it was either deprived of the opportunity to present evidence it would have offered had the pleading been made before a responsive pleading or that it was unfairly disadvantaged.[179]

A claim asserted in the amended pleading that arose out of the conduct, transaction, or occurrence set forth or attempted to be set forth in the original pleading relates back to the date of the original pleading[180] for timeliness.[181] A plaintiff may add otherwise time-barred parties only, however, if the new party had sufficient notice to prevent prejudice and if the failure to name the party was a mistake.[182]

Courts often will grant leave for the plaintiff to amend a complaint in response to a motion to dismiss by the defendant.[183]

PRETRIAL MATTERS

§ 6.26 Motions

A number of preliminary motions are available under Federal Rule of Civil Procedure 12. Plaintiffs may move for a more definite statement, to strike, or for judgment on the pleadings. A defendant waives defenses regarding personal jurisdiction, venue, and sufficiency of process and service of process unless they are raised in a motion prior to or in the answer.[184] Other

---

177 Mikucki v. United States Postal Serv., 41 Fair Empl. Prac. Cas. (BNA) 1503 (D. Mass. 1986).

178 Bernstein v. National Liberty Int'l Corp., 407 F. Supp. 709 (E.D. Pa. 1976); Dozier v. Chupka, 395 F. Supp. 836 (S.D. Ohio 1975).

179 Cuffy v. Getty Ref. & Mktg. Co., No. 84-761 MMS (D. Del. Nov. 12, 1986).

180 Fed. R. Civ. P. 15(c).

181 Cooper v. United States Postal Serv., 740 F.2d 714 (9th Cir. 1984), *cert. denied,* 471 U.S. 1022 (1985); Grattan v. Burnett, 710 F.2d 160 (4th Cir. 1983), *aff'd sub nom.,* Burnett v. Grattan, 468 U.S. 42 (1984); Ramirez v. Burr, 36 Fair Empl. Prac. Cas. (BNA) 545 (S.D. Tex. 1984); St. Cyr v. Merrill Lynch, Pierce, Fenner & Smith, 540 F. Supp. 889 (S.D. Tex. 1982); Bates v. Western Elec., 420 F. Supp. 521 (E.D. Pa. 1976).

182 Fed. R. Civ. P. 15(c).

183 Maxey v. Thompson, 680 F.2d 524 (7th Cir. 1982); Bethel v. Jendoco Const. Corp., 570 F.2d 1168 (3d Cir. 1978); Hiduchenko v. Minneapolis Medical & Diagnostic Center, 475 F. Supp. 1175 (D. Minn. 1979).

184 Fed. R. Civ. P. 12(h)(1).

defenses, such as failure to state a claim on which relief can be granted, failure to join a necessary party, or failure to object if a legal defense to a claim has not been stated, may be raised later.[185]

Before responding to a pleading, a plaintiff may move to strike any insufficient defense or any redundant, immaterial, impertinent, or scandalous matter from any pleading,[186] but this is not a common practice.[187]

Either party may move for judgment on the pleadings after the pleadings are closed, but without delaying trial.[188] If the court subsequently is presented with information outside the pleadings, the court will treat the motion as one for summary judgment, and the parties will be able to submit all relevant information. Because the Federal Rules of Civil Procedure require only notice of the pleading, these motions are not often granted in Title VII actions.[189]

A summary judgment can be granted upon the motion of either party if the pleadings, deposition, answers to interrogatories, admissions, and affidavits demonstrate that there is no genuine issue of any material fact and that the movant is entitled to a judgment as a matter of law.[190] Summary

---

185 Fed. R. Civ. P. 12(h)(2).

186 Fed. R. Civ. P. 12(f).

187 Torres v. Wisconsin Dep't of Health & Social Servs., 35 Fair Empl. Prac. Cas. (BNA) 1037 (E.D. Wis. 1983).

188 Fed. R. Civ. P. 12(c).

189 Marcarelli v. Delaware County Memorial Hosp., No. 86-1630 (E.D. Pa. Sept. 25, 1986).

190 Fed. R. Civ. P. 56(c). *See also* Simmons v. Lyons, 746 F.2d 265 (5th Cir. 1984) (sexual harassment).

For examples of cases that survived motions for summary judgment, see Kauffman v. Allied Signal, 970 F.2d 178 (6th Cir. 1992). See § **6.43.**

Gomez v. Metro Dade County, Fla., 801 F. Supp. 674 (S.D. Fla. 1992) (Title VII and 1983). An employer may avoid liability when there is an explicit policy against sexual harassment and effective grievance procedures calculated to encourage victims of harassment to come forward but which plaintiff did not employ. In this action by a demoted county employee charging sexual harassment by the county personnel director and demotion in alleged retaliation for filing a sexual harassment complaint, a material question of fact existed as to effectiveness of such procedures and thus precluded entry of summary judgment against plaintiffs when four complaints of sexual harassment had been filed against a supervisor but no discipline was imposed.

Summerlin v. Morrison, 59 Fair Empl. Prac. Cas. (BNA) 1530 (D. Kan. 1992). Summary judgment is not appropriate when questions of fact exist as to whether an alleged harasser's conduct was sufficiently severe or pervasive as to create a hostile work environment.

Halasi-Schmick v. City of Shawnee, 759 F. Supp. 747 (D. Kan. 1991). A female fire inspector/code enforcement officer who alleged that the fire chief referred to her as a dumb blonde, a supervisor told another employee that she was having an affair with a coworker, the city manager told another employee that she was a bitter woman, and that she was subjected to different treatment on account of her gender were insufficient to

judgment is not favored in Title VII actions generally. It is seldom granted in sexual harassment cases because factual disputes almost always exist, and the credibility of the parties often plays a critical role in the litigation. Pleadings and documentary evidence are to be construed liberally in favor

---

show a hostile environment. The court found that plaintiff could not rely on hearsay about incidents involving the nine other female employees of the city in opposing the defendants' motion for summary judgment.

Potts v. BE&K Constr. Co., 59 Fair Empl. Prac. Cas. (BNA) 1381, 604 So. 2d 398 (Ala. 1992). The state supreme court reversed a ruling of summary judgment in favor of defendant employer in a sexual harassment action when a genuine factual issue existed as to whether an employer ratified one employee's alleged sexual harassment of another employee when the employer knew of conduct before complaint was made but took no disciplinary action at time of complaint and did not monitor situation afterwards.

Campbell v. Board of Regents, 770 F. Supp. 1479 (D. Kan. 1991). The summary judgment motion is rarely an appropriate vehicle for assessing reasonableness of an employer's response to complaints of sexual harassment.

Wallace v. Dunn Constr., 59 Fair Empl. Prac. Cas. (BNA) 994 (N.D. Ala. 1991), *rev'd & rem. on other grounds,* 968 F.2d 1174 (11th Cir. 1992). Upon defendant's motion for summary judgment, court found that a factual issue existed regarding whether employer's response to claims of grabbing, pinching and "lurid sexual comments" by coworkers and supervisors action was prompt enough. The court rejected defendant's contention that the court should not second-guess a company's investigation, which in this case involved asking the harassers if they did the harassment, when cases cited by defense involved situations in which harassment stopped after the company took remedial action:

> In the present case, plaintiffs claim that the harassment did not stop. This brings into question whether the remedial action was prompt enough. In addition, it seems [that] if no second-guessing is allowed, employers could easily take advantage of the situations by shoddy "investigations", as may have been the case here. Dunn also argues that it had a formal sexual harassment policy (only after 1989, though), which plaintiffs should have followed every time an act of harassment occurred. Under this policy, plaintiffs could have bypassed complaints to their supervisor and gone to a person with higher authority. This is relevant because, according to plaintiffs, almost every supervisor plaintiffs complained to sexually harassed them. However, such a fact may help plaintiffs more than it hurts them, because it arguably constituted a situation where the harassment was so pervasive that an inference of constructive knowledge by Dunn is possible.

Id. at 996.

Reynolds v. Atlantic City Convention Ctr., 53 Fair Emp. Prac. Cas. (BNA) 1852 (D.N.J. 1990) Consideration of the effect of alleged sexual harassment on a reasonable person is a threshold matter to finding alleged incidents actionable for a summary judgment motion, rejecting reasoning in Blesedell v. Mobil Oil Co., 708 F. Supp. 1408, 1418–19 (S.D.N.Y. 1989).

Cf. Taylor v. National Group, 729 F. Supp. 575 (N.D. Ohio 1989). Summary judgment in favor of defendants was not warranted in sexual harassment case when although defendants set forth facts that tended to indicate that "any office horseplay was harmless and in a spirit of jocularity," plaintiffs did point to portions of the record that could indicate "a more offensive atmosphere which could fall within the realm of sexually hostile environment", *Id.* at 834.

of the party opposing summary judgment.[191] Retaliation claims, a common component of the sexual harassment action, are not amenable to summary judgment because the primary issue is one of intent and motive, and thus genuine issues of fact usually exist.[192]

§ 6.27 Discovery

Several procedures take place during the pretrial stage of a Title VII action, including discovery, class action proceedings when applicable, intervention, preliminary motions, and pretrial conferences. Counsel should pay close attention to local court rules that may differ from the Federal Rules of Civil Procedure (Federal Rules).

Rules 26 through 37 of the Federal Rules govern discovery matters. The scope of discovery is limited not only by the scope of the administrative discovery, but also by the Federal Rules. Under them, information is discoverable if it is reasonably calculated to lead to the discovery of admissible evidence.[193] Counsel thus must try to ascertain and refute every possible theory on which the defendant might base the relevancy of the evidence. A determination of the relevant time period for conducting discovery usually is subject to the discretion of the court. The court may issue protective orders to prevent parties from annoyance, embarrassment, oppression, or undue burden or expense.[194]

Because the credibility of witnesses plays a critical role in sexual harassment cases, deposition testimony of defendants establishes a factual foundation against which subsequent statements will be compared as the case develops. Discovery efforts should focus on the sexual harassment theory asserted and information necessary to rebut the defendant's explanation for the challenged conduct. Plaintiff's attorney should be prepared to depose the harasser, supervisors who knew or should have known of

---

191 Scott v. City of Overland Park, 595 F. Supp. 520, 522 (D. Kan. 1984) (sexual harassment).

192 Romero v. Union Pac. R.R., 615 F.2d 1303 (10th Cir. 1980).

193 Fed. R. Civ. P. 26(b); Cook v. Yellow Freight Sys., 132 F.R.D. 548 (E.D. Cal. 1990). Plaintiff female former employees alleging that their employer was negligent in retaining a supervisor who sexually harassed them when he had a history of such harassment could obtain addresses and phone numbers of previous victims of harassment when their testimony was highly relevant to the plaintiffs' case, but the scope of disclosure was circumscribed: The court directed plaintiffs' attorneys to draft a letter subject to approval of the court to be sent to all former female employees during the relevant time period, for requesting their consent to be contacted for this lawsuit. Further discovery of employees and their files was subject to their individual consent and was to be used solely for this lawsuit.

194 Fed. R. Civ. P. 26(c).

the harassment from actual or constructive notice, and those supervisors who did investigate or should have investigated plaintiff's complaints.

The defendant in a sexual harassment case may attempt to discover or introduce evidence regarding the plaintiff's psychological state and sexual history. These matters are discussed as evidentiary issues in **§ 6.31.**

A private party generally has access to the same information that is available to the EEOC in its investigation.[195] A plaintiff who has suffered an adverse employment action as a result of noncompliance with sexual demands or compliance by another employee, or who has been subjected to a hostile work environment may want to discover, through a request to produce:

1. Personnel files of other employees containing documents regarding qualifications and work performance
2. Records regarding the disposition of employee grievances
3. All data regarding sex discrimination complaints, suits, investigations made against the employer, and the complainants' employment records
4. Data regarding employee discharges and disciplinary proceedings
5. The employment records of the alleged harasser

Appendix E contains a sample plaintiff's request for production of documents.

The plaintiff also may review the information contained in EEOC case files.[196] However, no information stemming from the EEOC's informal attempts at conciliation may be made public by the EEOC or offered as evidence in a subsequent proceeding without the consent of the concerned parties.[197]

The scope of EEOC discovery is limited by the charge and the facts developed in the course of the commission's investigation.[198]

A party may move to compel discovery if the opposing party refuses to cooperate with requests for discovery,[199] although communications between an employer and an alleged harasser may be protected. In *Cook v. Yellow Freight System,*[200] plaintiff female former employees alleging that their supervisor sexually harassed them were not entitled to obtain written communications between the employer and supervisor regarding his termination

---

[195] Burns v. Thiokol Chem. Corp., 483 F.2d 300 (5th Cir. 1973).

[196] *See* EEOC v. Associated Dry Goods Corp., 499 U.S. 590 (1981).

[197] 42 U.S.C. § 2000e-5(b).

[198] EEOC v. Honeywell, Inc., 73 F.R.D. 496 (N.D. Ill. 1977).

[199] Fed. R. Civ. P. 37(a)(2).

[200] Cook v. Yellow Freight Sys., 132 F.R.D. 548 (E.D. Cal. 1990).

and possible settlement when such communications were privileged and protected by the right of privacy:

> [O]ne consideration in precluding the discovery of documents generated in the course of settlement discussions lies in the fact that such discussions are frequently not the product of truth seeking. Settlement negotiations are typically punctuated with numerous instances of puffing and posturing. . . . What is stated as fact on the record could very well not be the sort of evidence which the parties would otherwise actually contend to be wholly true. That is, the parties may assume disputed facts to be true for the unique purpose of settlement negotiations. The discovery of these sort of "facts" would be highly misleading if allowed to be used for purposes other than settlement. . . .
>
> Moreover, . . . the fact that the documents requested pertain to settlement discussions and not to any finalized settlement belies the plaintiffs' assertion that the documents are relevant to the existence of bias on the part of Fawcett as a possible key witness. If the defendant and Fawcett had come to terms, the plaintiff could argue that the settlement itself was conditioned on the Fawcett's cooperation at trial or that Fawcett was promised future employment or compensation. However, the existence of unaccepted proposals alone do very little to establish bias and, at any rate, any marginal relevance is outweighed by the privileged nature of settlement discussions.[201]

A court may find that the plaintiff is entitled to an inference establishing the relevant point if a defendant refuses to allow discovery, even if the plaintiff has not moved to compel.[202] A matter also may be deemed admitted if a party fails to respond to a request for admissions.[203] If a party does move successfully to compel discovery, attorneys' fees and expenses incurred in seeking the order may be obtained. Fees and expenses are available unless the court finds that the opposition was substantially justified or that other circumstances would make an award unjust. This award also is available to defendants who successfully defend motions to compel discovery and may be apportioned should the court grant the motion in part and deny the motion in part.[204]

§ 6.28 Protective Orders

Federal or state discovery rules may be used to protect the sexual harassment plaintiff from potentially abusive litigation practices. Federal Rule

---

201 *Id.* at 554–55.

202 Donnell v. General Motors Corp., 576 F.2d 1292 (8th Cir. 1978).

203 Fed. R. Civ. P. 37(c).

204 Fed. R. Civ. P. 37(a)(4).

of Civil Procedure 26(c) allows the court to deny or limit even relevant discovery to the extent that its admission is outweighed by its potential to oppress, embarrass, annoy, unduly burden, or cause expense to a party. In *Priest v. Rotary,*[205] the district court noted that the discovery of intimate details of persons' lives discourages the prosecution of sexual harassment cases, is a serious invasion of privacy, and thus should not be permitted in the absence of extraordinary circumstances. Protective orders also may be sought if the defendant seeks an order permitting a psychological or physical examination of the plaintiff.

Either party in a sexual harassment lawsuit may seek a protective order to prevent opposing counsel from communicating with the plaintiff or other employees without the moving party's counsel's consent.[206] Courts have not favored attempts to limit communication with potential witnesses.[207] In *Cram v. Lamson & Sessions Co., Carlon Div.,*[208] plaintiff's counsel in an action alleging sexual harassment and retaliation could engage in *ex parte* communications with former employees of defendant without violating the state code of professional responsibility proscription on attorney communications with represented parties when the underlying policies of the rule were not served by extending its application to former employees. Former employees are not agents of an employer, and a formal opinion by a relevant ABA committee supported such a conclusion. To determine whether good cause exists, courts have considered whether opposing counsel's inquiries produce statements likely to be admissible under Federal Rule of Evidence 801(d)(2)(D) and whether a protective order is necessary to ensure effective representation by opposing counsel.[209]

§ 6.29 Interrogatories

Interrogatories are an inexpensive means to much information. They may relate to any matters that are discoverable under Federal Rule of Civil Procedure 26(b), and the answers may be used if they are admissible under the rules of evidence. Questions should be clear, concise, and limited to the conduct alleged in the complaint. **Appendix C** contains sample interrogatories for the sexual harassment case. **Appendix D** is a sample brief opposing a defendant's motion to compel answers to interrogatories.

---

205 Priest v. Rotary, 98 F.R.D. 755, 762 (N.D. Cal. 1983).

206 Mompoint v. Lotus Dev. Corp., 110 F.R.D. 414 (D. Mass. 1986).

207 *See, e.g.,* IBM Corp. v. Edelstein, 526 F.2d 37, 41–42 (2d Cir. 1975).

208 Cram v. Lamson & Sessions Co., Carlon Div., 148 F.R.D. 259 (S.D. Iowa 1993).

209 Mompoint v. Lotus Dev. Corp., 110 F.R.D. 414 (D. Mass. 1986).

TRIAL MATTERS

§ 6.30 The Trial

Trial procedure is set forth in the Federal Rules of Civil Procedure. Private Title VII plaintiffs receive a trial de novo in which every claim is litigated independent of EEOC findings.[210]

Federal employee Title VII plaintiffs are entitled to a trial de novo.[211] However, a final EEOC order in favor of the plaintiff is binding upon a district court, and the merits of the discrimination action should not be reconsidered absent a request by the employee. The employee has the option of adjudicating the discrimination matter in the administrative forum or in the district court.[212] Should the plaintiff request a trial de novo, administrative findings may be admitted into evidence.[213]

Appendix B contains a sample of a plaintiff's questions for *voir dire.*

§ 6.31 Evidentiary Issues

The admissibility and weight of evidence in employment discrimination actions are governed by the Federal Rules of Evidence and the court's discretion.[214] Testimonial evidence plays a critical role in sexual harassment actions in which the credibility of the various players may be determinative. Evidence may be excluded if its probative value is substantially outweighed by considerations of undue delay, waste of time, confusion of the issues, or needless presentation of cumulative evidence.[215]

Although the Federal Rules of Evidence generally prohibit introducing evidence regarding a person's character or prior behavior as proof of a particular action, such evidence may be admissible if it is offered for another purpose[216] or if the plaintiff's character is an essential element in the litigation.[217] The character trait cannot be used circumstantially, and a

---

210 Alexander v. Gardner-Denver Co., 415 U.S. 36 (1974). *See also* Long v. Laramie County Community College Dist., 840 F.2d 743 (10th Cir.), *cert. denied,* 488 U.S. 825 (1988) (court was not bound by findings of college's grievance committee, its board of trustees, or EEOC).

211 Chandler v. Roudebush, 425 U.S. 840 (1976).

212 Moore v. Devine, 780 F.2d 1559 (11th Cir. 1985).

213 Prewitt v. United States Postal Serv., 662 F.2d 292 (5th Cir. 1981).

214 Baylor v. Jefferson County Bd. of Educ., 733 F.2d 1527 (11th Cir. 1984).

215 Fed. R. Evid. 403.

216 Fed. R. Evid. 404(a).

217 Fed. R. Evid. 405(b).

plaintiff's sexual history or aggressiveness is not an essential element of a defense in a sexual harassment case. There have been very few situations in which a character trait has been found to be an essential element of a claim or defense, and none has been in the sexual harassment context. Such evidence possibly would be relevant only if the plaintiff's sexuality were affected by the challenged conduct. For example, the plaintiff might allege that she had been a virgin until the harasser coerced her into having sexual relations, or that her ability to perform sexually had been altered by the harassment.

§ 6.32 Ordering Examinations

Federal Rule of Civil Procedure 35(a) permits the ordering of a mental examination under certain circumstances, namely "when the mental or physical condition . . . of a party . . . is in controversy. . . . The order may be made only on motion for good cause shown and . . . shall specify the time, place, manner, conditions, and scope of the examination and the person or persons by whom it is to be made."[218] The U.S. Supreme Court has held that the "in controversy" and "good cause" requirements:

> are not met by mere conclusory allegations of the pleadings—nor by mere relevance to the case—but require an affirmative showing by the movant that each condition as to which the examination is sought is really and genuinely in controversy and that good cause exists for ordering each particular examination.[219]

In *Robinson v. Jacksonville Shipyards, Inc.*,[220] the district court for the Middle District of Florida held that allegations of hostile environment sexual harassment did not place the mental condition of the plaintiff "in controversy" within the meaning of the Federal Rule, even though the plaintiff alleged that a hostile work environment seriously affected her psychological well-being and sought back pay for lost work time.

In *Harris v. Forklift Systems, Inc.*,[221] the U.S. Supreme Court held that a plaintiff need not prove psychological injury to win a Title VII action. Most cases in which the plaintiff's mental condition is at issue involve tort claims for emotional distress damages (see **Chapter 9**). Title VII, however,

---

218 Fed. R. Civ. P. 35(a).

219 Schlagenhauf v. Holder, 379 U.S. 104, 118 (1964). *See also, In re* Mitchell, 563 F.2d 143 (5th Cir. 1977) (Rule 35 order requires a greater showing than general Rule 26 discovery).

220 Robinson v. Jacksonville Shipyards, Inc., 118 F.R.D. 525 (M.D. Fla. 1988).

221 114 S. Ct. 367 (1993).

involves the application of an objective standard that "is not informed by evidence which may be obtained in a mental examination."

> The hostile work environment sexual harassment plaintiff must show that she is at least as affected as the reasonable person under like circumstances. . . . Title VII liability attaches when the case is proved as to the reasonable person, and it does not extend further based on any hypersensitivity of a particular plaintiff. . . .
>
> When claims have successfully alleged that the harassing behavior constituted a Title VII violation, . . . the court evaluated the totality of circumstances and determined that the alleged harassing behavior could be objectively classed as the kind that would seriously affect the psychological well-being of a reasonable individual.
>
> * * *
>
> Framed as an objective standard, it becomes clear that plaintiff has not put her mental condition in controversy, not even by claiming backpay for days lost to the stress of the hostile work environment. A backpay award is not compensatory damages for harm suffered; it is a "make whole" equitable remedy for discriminatory practices. . . . The Court perceives that plaintiff bears an additional burden beyond proof of a hostile work environment in order to establish eligibility for a backpay award. Plaintiff would have to demonstrate the functional equivalent of an intermittent constructive discharge, that is, she proves that working conditions were so difficult and unpleasant that a reasonable person in her shoes would have felt compelled to resign or take time off, in order to cope with the working conditions. . . . Plaintiff does not place her mental condition in controversy by alleging that her psychological well being, as well as the psychological well being of all reasonable individuals exposed to like circumstances, is seriously affected by defendants' behavior.
>
> . . . Because claims in this area are measured against an objective standard, a ruling in favor of a mental examination in this case would endorse mental examinations in every Title VII hostile environment sexual harassment case. This result is unacceptable, . . . and the price would be too high. Plaintiffs in these cases would face sexual denigration in order to secure their statutory right to be free from sexual denigration. . . . Reporting of sexual harassment claims would certainly be discouraged, . . . thereby undercutting the remedial effect intended by Congress in enacting Title VII. . . .[222]

Even in cases claiming compensatory damages for emotional distress, the plaintiff needs to submit to a psychological examination only upon a showing of good cause[223] and if the trial court is satisfied that the mental

---

222 Robinson v. Jacksonville Shipyards, Inc., 118 F.R.D. 525, 530–31 (M.D. Fla. 1988).

223 Fed. R. Civ P. 35 and state rules.

condition of the plaintiff is at issue. If the defendant does not demonstrate that the discovery sought cannot be obtained by less intrusive means, plaintiff's counsel should oppose the motion on the basis that the onerous nature of the psychological examination outweighs its probative value to the defendant.

The court also may order the plaintiff to produce the psychiatric or medical records upon which a plaintiff is basing claims of mental and emotional distress[224] or may allow the defendant to depose the plaintiff's psychologist or psychiatrist.[225] When pendent state tort claims accompany the Title VII claim, the plaintiff must be prepared to submit to a psychological or physical examination or produce relevant records. Medical records may be protected by a Constitutional right of privacy.[226] A psychologist's or psychiatrist's expert opinion relating to the extent of the plaintiff's emotional trauma is relevant to the issue of damages. If the opinion is based on evidence that may otherwise be irrelevant, it still may be admissible because it is part of the reasoning process.[227]

Courts have consistently held that the right to privacy is waived when a party places her mental or physical condition at issue.[228] Before filing the complaint, therefore, counsel must weigh with the client the advantages of such pendent claims against the implications of their inclusion. Under Federal Rule of Evidence 403, a court may exclude evidence if "its probative value is substantially outweighed by the danger of unfair prejudice, confusion of the issues, or misleading the jury." *Robinson* offers a compelling argument for the exclusion of this type of evidence when no pendent state tort claims are alleged. In cases with pendent claims, the parties may agree to refer this question to an independent forensic expert.[229]

§ 6.33 Plaintiff's Sexual History

A defendant may attempt to discover or introduce evidence of the plaintiff's sexual history to try to show that the plaintiff's promiscuous nature invited the alleged sexual advances or conduct.[230] He may try to show that it was unlikely for a woman with a sexual past to be offended or affected

---

224 Zises v. Department of Social Servs., 112 F.R.D. 223 (E.D.N.Y. 1986).

225 Mitchell v. Hutchings, 116 F.R.D. 481 (D. Utah 1987).

226 Mann v. University of Cincinnati, 824 F. Supp. 1190 (S.D. Ohio 1993) (plaintiff's medical records were protected by a constitutional right to privacy and could not be disclosed by defendant in sexual harassment action without a release by the patient or valid court order).

227 Mitchell v. Hutchings, 116 F.R.D. 481, 485 (D. Utah 1987).

228 Ferrell v. Brick, 678 F. Supp. 111, 112–13 (E.D. Pa. 1987) (citing cases).

229 *Id.* at 113.

230 Priest v. Rotary, 98 F.R.D. 755 (N.D. Cal. 1983).

by the challenged behavior, that the plaintiff would readily participate in such conduct, or that the plaintiff's credibility is questionable. While such an approach and the underlying message that promiscuity is unique to women is unpalatable and ultimately may be unsuccessful legally, the coercive effect on the plaintiff is powerful. The prospect of public humiliation can deter the most adamant of plaintiffs, and thus counsel must be prepared to protect clients from improper discovery and introduction of evidence.

In *Mitchell v. Hutchings,*[231] the district court held that while evidence of sexual conduct in the workplace is relevant in analyses of both Title VII sexual harassment and state emotional distress claims, sexual conduct that is remote in time or place from the plaintiff's working environment is irrelevant:

> [The defendant] cannot possibly use evidence of sexual activity of which he was unaware or which is unrelated to the alleged incidents of sexual harassment as evidence to support his defense. . . . Given the annoying and embarrassing nature of this discovery, the court holds, as a matter of law, that Rule 26 of the Federal Rules of Civil Procedure preponderates against its discoverability.[232]

Evidence regarding the plaintiff's alleged tendency to be sexually aggressive or promiscuous is not admissible to show that her interaction with the alleged harasser conformed with these tendencies.[233] On the other hand, evidence may be admissible as proof of motive, opportunity, intent, preparation, plan, knowledge, identity, or absence of mistake or accident.[234] A defendant thus may try to demonstrate that sexual history is relevant to show that the plaintiff intended to seduce the alleged harasser for economic benefit, and that the sexual harassment suit was brought in retaliation for having failed at her plan. However, the defendant may not discover past conduct to show a propensity to seduce.[235] Sexual history also is irrelevant to a showing of intent to retaliate.

For evidence of past conduct to constitute habit under Federal Rule of Evidence 406, as distinguished from character evidence, the conduct must occur with almost invariable regularity in response to a particular situation.[236]

---

231 Mitchell v. Hutchings, 116 F.R.D. 481 (D. Utah 1987).

232 *Id.* at 484.

233 United States v. Kasto, 584 F.2d 268 (8th Cir. 1978), *cert. denied,* 440 U.S. 930 (1979); Priest v. Rotary, 98 F.R.D. 755, 758 (N.D. Cal. 1983).

234 Fed. R. Evid. 404(b). *Cf.* Burns v. McGregor Electronic Ind., 989 F.2d 959 (8th Cir. 1993), discussed in § 3.13.

235 Priest v. Rotary, 98 F.R.D. 755, 760 (N.D. Cal. 1983).

236 J. Wigmore, Evidence § 92 (1940); Priest v. Rotary, 98 F.R.D. 755, 758 (N.D. Cal. 1983). *See also* United States v. Sampol, 636 F.2d 621 (D.C. Cir. 1980); Frase v. Henry, 444 F.2d 1228 (10th Cir. 1971).

Under most circumstances, habitual behavior would not include past sexual conduct.[237] Such an approach also is inconsistent with the notion that a victim of harassment schemes to encourage the challenged sexual conduct. "The discovery of such evidence cannot possibly lead to admissible evidence and would only serve to embarrass and annoy the plaintiffs."[238]

In response to allegations that the plaintiff was injured by the challenged conduct, the defendant may try to introduce evidence of plaintiff's sexual history to show that such injury was unlikely.[239] In particular, the defendant may want to show that the plaintiff participated in workplace conduct before alleging that she was offended by her coworkers' behavior.

Alternatively, the defendant also may try to show that the plaintiff was oversensitive to sexually oriented conduct and caused her own injuries through the discovery of psychological records.[240] In an action under Title VII alone, the plaintiff's psychological state should not be at issue. Counsel should argue that the focus should be on the defendant's conduct and a reasonable woman's response thereto. If the action contains state common-law charges of emotional distress, however, the plaintiff's psychological state is discoverable.[241]

A plaintiff's past sexual conduct does not have a bearing on psychological and emotional damages caused by sexual harassment:

> Past sexual conduct does not, as defendants would argue, create emotional calluses that lessen the impact of unwelcomed sexual harassment. The fact that the plaintiffs may welcome sexual advances from certain individuals has absolutely no bearing on the emotional trauma they may feel from sexual harassment that is unwelcome. . . . This court cannot condone a wholesale inquiry into the past sexual conduct of the plaintiffs under such a theory.[242]

§ 6.34 Evidence of Sexual Harassment of Other Employees

A plaintiff may introduce testimony by other employees regarding the discriminatory conduct of the defendant to demonstrate a predisposition toward discrimination against women.[243] Evidence of the sexual harassment

---

237 Mitchell v. Hutchings, 116 F.R.D. 481, 485 (D. Utah 1987); Priest v. Rotary, 98 F.R.D. 755 (N.D. Cal. 1983).

238 Mitchell v. Hutchings, 116 F.R.D. 481, 485 (D. Utah 1987).

239 *Id.*

240 Jennings v. D.H.L. Airlines, 101 F.R.D. 549 (N.D. Ill. 1984).

241 *Id.* at 551.

242 Mitchell v. Hutchings, 116 F.R.D. 481, 485 (D. Utah 1987).

243 Thompson v. McDonnell Douglas Corp., 416 F. Supp. 972, 981 (E.D. Mo. 1976), *aff'd,* 552 F.2d 220 (8th Cir. 1977); Pettit v. United States, 488 F.2d 1026, 1033 (Ct. Cl. 1973).

of other employees is not necessary to a finding of either *quid pro quo* or hostile environment harassment, but may bolster a claim that would otherwise turn on credibility determinations of the plaintiff and her alleged harasser.[244] For example, although testimony regarding an alleged harasser's sexual harassment of a former secretary could not have contributed to the hostility the plaintiff received in her office, the district court in *Campbell v. Board of Regents*[245] allowed such allegations because they were relevant to the credibility of the defendant's denial of the plaintiff's allegations. A showing that the defendant has acted in a sexually offensive way toward other employees will undercut any contention by the defendant that the plaintiff welcomed or solicited sexual advances and will help establish the frequency most courts require in hostile environment cases. Although a defendant may argue that evidence of past conduct is not admissible for the same reasons that evidence of the plaintiff's sexual history should be inadmissible (see **§ 6.31**), the two types of behavior are not legally analogous.

In *Kay v. Peter Motor Co.*,[246] a Minnesota sexual harassment action by a terminated employee of a car dealership, the trial court properly admitted testimony of former employees to demonstrate the alleged harasser's intent to make harassing comments to the plaintiff, his knowledge of the offensive nature of his comments, and the hostile working environment he created by making such remarks, as well as his motive to make the remarks. The trial court determined that the offered testimony of other employees was not received to use past wrongs to prove current conduct.

Watts v. New York City Police Dept., 724 F. Supp. 99 (S.D.N.Y. 1989) (evidence supporting an assertion that other women in the workplace were harassed may be probative of a general work atmosphere hostile toward women, including plaintiff). *Accord*, Lehtiene v. Bill Communications, 1989 U.S. Dist. LEXIS 3707 (S.D.N.Y. 1989).

Cf. Halasi-Schmick v. City of Shawnee, 759 F.Supp. 747 (D. Kan. 1991). A female fire inspector/code enforcement officer alleged that the fire chief referred to her as a dumb blonde, a supervisor told another employee that she was having an affair with a coworker, the city manager told another employee that she was a bitter woman, and that she was subjected to different treatment because of her gender. These claims were insufficient to show a hostile environment. The court found that plaintiff could not rely on hearsay about incidents involving the nine other female employees of the city in opposing defendants' motion for summary judgment.

244 *See, e.g.*, Delgado v. Lehman, 665 F. Supp. 460, 468 (E.D. Va. 1987). *Cf.* Campbell v. Board of Regents, 770 F. Supp. 1479 (D. Kan. 1991) (although testimony regarding alleged harasser's sexual harassment of former secretary could not have contributed to hostility plaintiff received in her office, such allegations were relevant to the credibility of defendant's denial of plaintiff's allegations).

245 Campbell v. Board of Regents, 770 F. Supp. 1479 (D. Kan. 1991).

246 Kay v. Peter Motor Co., 483 N.W.2d 481 (Minn. Ct. App. 1992) (Crippen, J.).

In *State ex rel. Tinsman v. Hott,*[247] evidence of the employer's earlier sexual harassment of other employees was properly excluded on the issue of liability, but was admissible on the issue of punitive damages:

> Although we agree with Mrs. Tinsman that events occurring before her employment could be evidence of a hostile working environment, for these events to be relevant, and therefore admissible, they must have helped to create her work environment. The evidence that the Tinsmans seek to introduce would not show any impact on Mrs. Tinsman's work environment. [The alleged harasser's] former wife's testimony would concern events that allegedly occurred four years before Mrs. Tinsman's employment in a different employment agency in a different state. The court reporter's testimony would concern commissions based on an unrelated employment contract.[248]

Evidence regarding the employer's previous responses to sexual harassment complaints that are unrelated to the present action may be admitted to determine whether the employer's sexual harassment policy is effective.[249] The plaintiff also may be able to inquire as to whether the employer was aware of any other allegations against the alleged harasser.

In *Jones v. Commander, Kansas Army Ammunitions Plant,*[250] an action by a female employee alleging that she was sexually harassed by her female supervisor, complaints regarding the supervisor's sexual conduct were not discoverable, but the plaintiff would be allowed to inquire into whether the employer was aware of any other allegations of sexual harassment against the supervisor. The court noted that in hostile environment action, incidents of sexual harassment directed at employees other than the plaintiff can be used as proof of the plaintiff's claims, but incidents too remote in time or too attenuated from the plaintiff's situation are not relevant:

> Plaintiff's request for production number three seeks any and all complaints, memoranda, notes or other documents memorializing or evidencing any formal or informal complaint or report of sexual harassment or other sexual conduct by Captain Blanton against any employee or member of the United States Army. First, plaintiff fails to establish the relevance of any complaint regarding the Captain's sexual conduct. Furthermore, plaintiff fails to define what she means by complaints of sexual conduct. The term is thus vague and ambiguous, making an adequate response very difficult. Furthermore, this case involves allegations of sexual harassment. Thus, discovery should be focused on that issue. While the court acknowledges the

---

247 State *ex rel.* Tinsman v. Hott, 188 W.Va. 349, 424 S.E.2d 584 (Sup. Ct. App. 1992) (per curiam).

248 *Id.* at 588.

249 EEOC v. General Motors Corp., 48 Fair Empl. Prac. Cas. (BNA) 1285 (D. Kan. 1988).

250 Jones v. Commander, Kan. Army Ammunitions Plant, 147 F.R.D. 248 (D. Kan. 1993).

> potential difficulty in obtaining this material on the Captain, as the government has set forth in its brief, the court finds the information potentially relevant and a reasonable request. Plaintiff is entitled to inquire into whether or not the U.S. Army was aware of other allegations of sexual harassment against Captain Blanton.[251]

The court also held that the supervisor's sexual preference, habits, history, or behavior other than the extent to which she was alleged to have engaged in sexual harassment in the past, was irrelevant.

Evidence that the alleged harasser sexually harassed other employees also may be introduced to demonstrate the effect of the conduct on the plaintiff's working conditions and that the incidents of harassment were pervasive rather than sporadic or isolated.[252]

When possible, complaints should include allegations of hostile environment harassment as a separate cause of action to ensure admissibility of evidence of the harassment of other employees. A hostile environment plaintiff should show that the challenged conduct created a psychologically damaging work atmosphere. An essential element of the hostile environment claim is a showing that the harassment was "sufficiently pervasive so as to alter the conditions of employment and create an abusive working environment."[253] The plaintiff should testify that she was aware that the defendant was harassing other female employees and was psychologically affected by the conduct. This testimony is evidence of an essential element of the plaintiff's case and is thus admissible. Several courts have admitted such evidence.[254]

Under Rule 404(b) of the Federal Rules of Evidence, evidence of the harasser's prior conduct may be admitted to show intent or motive. Therefore, evidence that the defendant harassed other employees and retaliated against those who rejected his advances may be admitted to show that the plaintiff's job status was altered in response to noncompliance with sexual demands.

Prior acts also may be admissible on rebuttal to demonstrate that the employer's proffered reason for the employment decision was pretextual.

---

251 *Id.* at 251.

252 Waltman v. International Paper Co., 875 F.2d 468, 477 (5th Cir. 1989).

253 Henson v. City of Dundee, 682 F.2d 897 (11th Cir. 1982).

254 Bundy v. Jackson, 641 F.2d 934, 940 n. 3 (D.C. Cir. 1981); Morgan v. Hertz Corp., 542 F. Supp. 123 (W.D. Tenn. 1981), *aff'd,* 725 F.2d 1070 (6th Cir. 1984). *See also* Vinson v. Taylor, 753 F.2d 141 (D.C. Cir. 1985), *aff'd in part, rev'd in part sub nom.* Meritor Sav. Bank v. Vinson, 477 U.S. 57 (1986).

§ 6.35 Testimony

Testimonial evidence plays a significant role in sexual harassment actions. Many cases turn on the credibility of the parties. Most courts in sexual harassment cases have permitted the introduction of testimony by other employees in support of the plaintiff's claims, although the plaintiff's inability to produce eyewitnesses to the harassment does not defeat her claim.[255] Testimony regarding the plaintiff's reaction to alleged harassment is particularly useful to establish that the conduct was unwelcome.[256]

---

[255] EEOC Policy Guidance on Current Issues of Sexual Harassment, N-915.035 (Oct. 25, 1988) D at 11–12 [hereinafter EEOC Policy Guidance]. (see Appendix G).

Sixth Circuit: Kirkland v. Brinias, 741 F. Supp. 692 (E.D. Tenn. 1989), *aff'd without opinion,* 944 F.2d 905 (6th Cir. 1991). Plaintiff waitresses alleged that a busboy created a hostile environment by offering money for sex, threats, pats on the rear end, hugs, arm grabbing, hostile pranks, and other conduct. Sexual harassment was not found despite corroboration by other former employees of plaintiffs' accounts and other evidence of coworker misconduct that would create a hostile and intimidating working environment when the court determined that there was no showing that the conduct had any harmful psychological effect on waitresses, the waitresses were well able to handle the alleged harassment and would not have hesitated to ask management for help if needed, and there was no preponderance of evidence regarding whether management recognized or should have recognized that any of their employees were offended by the conduct.

Seventh Circuit: *Cf.* Juarez v. Ameritech Mobile Communications, 746 F. Supp. 798 (N.D. Ill. 1990), *aff'd,* 957 F.2d 317 (7th Cir. 1992). Testimony by employee that she had heard of four other instances of conduct by alleged harasser that she considered to be sexual harassment was insufficient to raise a genuine issue of material fact as to whether the employer knew or should have known about alleged harassment when the witness had no idea whether those incidents had been reported to management.

Ninth Circuit: Dias v. Sky Chefs, 919 F.2d 1370 (9th Cir. 1990), *vacated on other grounds,* 111 S. Ct. 2791, *on remand,* 948 F.2d 532 (9th Cir. 1991), *cert. denied,* 112 S. Ct. 1294 (1992). Admitted testimony on discussions of sexual harassment not directly protested by plaintiff was relevant both to show defendant's awareness of and failure to rectify harassment, and to show the basis for and significance of protests that the plaintiff did in fact make. The lower court did not abuse its discretion in admitting such testimony without first establishing that she knew of incidents, when the court did permit her attorney on some occasions to establish her knowledge of specific incidents of harassment after witnesses were questioned about them rather than before, by way of a foundation. *Cf.* Hanson v. American Express, 53 Fair Emp. Prac. Cas. (BNA) 1193 (D. Utah 1986). Although plaintiff alleged that several other female employees had been sexually harassed by a supervisor, this allegation carried little weight when she introduced no evidence other than her own affidavit to support her assertion and in fact the record demonstrated that two of those women testified that they had not been sexually harassed.

[256] EEOC Policy Guidance at 11–12.

§ 6.36 Credibility of Witnesses

Sexual harassment cases often are considered to be *swearing contests*[257] and the credibility of the parties and witnesses is critical. In weighing the testimony of witnesses, courts consider:

1. The relationship of each witness to the parties
2. The witness's interest in the outcome of the proceedings
3. The witness's prejudice or bias
4. The witness's demeanor as it reflects candor, fairness, and intelligence
5. The witness's opportunity to observe or acquire knowledge regarding the subject matter of the testimony
6. The extent to which the testimony is supported or contradicted by other credible evidence.[258]

The demeanor of the parties on the witness stand may be telling. Hostility or theatrical behavior before the court may imply that the plaintiff is difficult at work or overreactive towards unoffensive conduct.[259] Testimony of nonmanagement employees that corroborates the plaintiff's position may be deemed more credible than that of other witnesses because they have no personal stake in testifying, and, in fact, "giving testimony unfavorable to their employer is not in their best interests."[260]

Courts have found that the failure to report harassment dilutes a plaintiff's credibility.[261]

---

257 Shrout v. Black Clawson Co., 689 F. Supp. 774, 1340 (S.D. Ohio 1988). *See also* Hall v. F.O. Thacker Contracting Co., 24 Fair Empl. Prac. Cas. (BNA) 1499, 1503 (N.D. Ga. 1980).

258 *See, e.g.*, Shrout v. Black Clawson Co., 689 F. Supp. 774, 1340 (S.D. Ohio 1988); Jackson-Colley v. Army Corp. of Eng'rs, 655 F. Supp. 122, 124 (E.D. Mich. 1987).

259 *See, e.g.*, Norton v. Vartanian, 31 Fair Empl. Prac. Cas. (BNA) 1259, 1260 n.1 (D. Mass. 1983):

> The actions of the parties themselves in the courtroom and on the witness stand assisted measurably in understanding the events in the stormy months leading up to the plaintiff's discharge. Norton was theatrical and emotional, leaving the courtroom more than once in tears. On the other hand, Connelly, the supervisor who was the target of her accusations, appeared stubborn and inflexible. He interrupted questions, and during cross-examination banged his fist on the witness stand. These were not easy personalities.

260 EEOC v. Judson Steel Co., 33 Fair Empl. Prac. Cas. (BNA) 1286, 1293 (N.D. Cal. 1982).

261 Neville v. Taft Broadcasting Co., 42 Fair Empl. Prac. Cas. (BNA) 1314 (W.D.N.Y. 1987) (although the court found that testimony regarding a kiss was credible, failure by plaintiff to fully report other alleged instances of physical contact led court to conclude

Evidence regarding a witness's character[262] or specific conduct[263] may be admitted only to determine truthfulness.

§ 6.37 Testimony of Coworkers

The defendant may introduce testimony by the plaintiff's coworkers in support of its reasons for terminating the plaintiff. Plaintiff's counsel may attempt to discredit this testimony by showing:

1. Any financial or other business interests in the defendant company
2. Familial or interpersonal ties between the defendant and the witness
3. Unfamiliarity of the witness with the plaintiff's work habits, such as from working different shifts or having noninterdependent tasks[264]
4. Coercion of witnesses by the defendant
5. Evidence of previous complaints of harassment by the witness

§ 6.38 Expert Witnesses

An expert witness may testify to help the trier of fact understand the evidence or to determine a fact in issue.[265] An expert in women's studies or psychology may be useful in a sexual harassment case, especially if there are pendent state claims and the case is tried before a jury, to explain the psychological impact of sexual harassment on women and to offer an opinion based on the facts before the court.

In *Stockett v. Tolin,*[266] a female employee in a film industry training program was subjected to a hostile environment when a managing agent harassed her physically and verbally for over a year. Among other things,

---

that the events did not occur, or if they did, plaintiff did not find them significant enough to bring up until after the suit was filed).

262 Fed. R. Evid. 608(a).

263 Fed. R. Evid. 608(b).

264 Priest v. Rotary, 634 F. Supp. 571 (N.D. Cal. 1986).

265 Fed. R. Evid. 701.

Robinson v. Jacksonville Shipyards, Inc., 706 F. Supp. 1486 (M.D. Fla. 1991) (court relied on testimony of an expert on sexual stereotyping and one on sexual harassment to determine that pinups of nude and partially nude women, demeaning sexual remarks, and other harassment created a hostile working environment).

Syndex Corp. v. Dean, 57 Fair Empl. Prac. Cas. (BNA) 547, 820 S.W. 2d 869 (Tex. Ct. App. 1991) (trial court properly admitted testimony of a certified social worker and psychotherapist who had counselled a sexually harassed employee under medical treatment exception of the hearsay rule).

266 Stockett v. Tolin, 791 F. Supp. 1536 (S.D. Fla. 1992).

the defendant put his arms around the plaintiff from behind, pressed his body up against her and said that he'd love to eat her all up, repeatedly pressed down on her shoulders while she sat in a chair so that she couldn't get up, squeezed her breasts, walked into the women's room while the plaintiff was changing her clothes, twice stuck his tongue in her ear and told her that he wanted to have sex with her, repeatedly cornered her and ran his hands over her nipples, saying "You like that, don't you?", constantly grabbed her buttocks and finally told the plaintiff: "Fuck me or you're fired." The plaintiff subsequently resigned. The court found that the plaintiff did not in any way encourage the advances; on the contrary, she repeatedly pushed the defendant away and told him to stop, avoided him, and tried to never be alone with him. The plaintiff's account of a pervasively hostile work environment was corroborated by the testimony of many other female employees at the defendant companies. The plaintiff had been warned that the defendant liked "young girls," and she warned others. The plaintiff suffered severe emotional distress as a result of the harassment, including sleep disturbances, depression, loss of energy, general anxiety, a sense of uncertainty, anger, and an inability to trust men. The plaintiff presented expert testimony by a clinical psychologist regarding both the psychological effects of her experience and why she tolerated the sexual advances. The expert testified that:

> sexual harassment is an example of a process known as victimization that ranges from the consequences of rape to family violence to spouse abuse to sexist slurs and low grade mistreatment of others. In less violent, more chronic situations, such as those that he opined occurred in this case, a person slowly evolves a sense of helplessness in coping with the situation. This results in anxiety, depression, feelings of personal incompetence, loss of a sense of self confidence and worth, and the inability to develop strategies for handling the treatment.[267]

An expert may also be used to testify on the subject of sexual stereotyping and its relationship to sexual harassment. In *Jenson,*[268] an expert witness appeared to testify both at proceedings in 1991 and at trial in 1992:

> Dr. Borgid concluded that the major effect of sex stereotyping was "sexual spillover," which is the idea that "the sexual dimension that characterizes male-female relationships outside of a work environment, spills over, . . . into the work environment, and . . . becomes part of the working environment." . . . Sexual spillover creates a sexualized work environment, which Dr. Borgida found to be represented by sexual photographs, cartoons, and jokes, as well as sexual language directed at women.

---

267 *Id.* at 1549.

268 Jensen v. Eveleth Taconite Co., 824 F. Supp. 847 (D. Minn 1993).

Dr. Borgida identified three preconditions that enhance the presence of stereotyping in the work place: (1) rarity, (2) sexualized work environment, and (3) ambiguous criteria for evaluating employee performance. On cross-examination, Dr. Borgida was asked about a fourth precondition which he had identified in a scholarly article published in 1981. This fourth condition, "paucity of information," is the lack of "individuating" information, that is subjective information about a particular individual. . . . Dr. Borgida testified that he had not relied on the paucity of information precondition; the relevance of that precondition had been qualified in subsequent research. . . .

In 1992, Dr. Borgida repeated much of his testimony concerning the three preconditions. He also presented testimony concerning two other areas. First, he elaborated on the "paucity of information" precondition, stating that three separate aspects of this precondition can be associated with stereotypic thinking: (1) lack of information; (2) a mixture of relevant and irrelevant information, resulting in ambiguous information; and (3) the presence of irrelevant information. . . . Dr. Borgida testified that as a result of subsequent research, he had decided to afford the paucity of information factor less weight to sexual stereotyping at Eveleth Mines.

Second, Dr. Borgida related the results of a research study conducted subsequent to the 1991 hearing. The study focused on the "priming" effect that a sexualized work environment can have on stereotypic thinking and whether that effect is linked to sexually harassing behavior. . . . Dr. Borgida's research showed that men exposed to priming materials—advertisements that were rated as "sexist"—thought of, evaluated, and acted toward women in sexual terms more than men who were not primed.

Eveleth Mines failed to provide a basis for questioning the sexual stereotyping theory and its relationship to the work place. Although Eveleth Mines focused on questioning Dr. Borgida's conclusions about (1) the effect that sexual stereotyping could have at Eveleth Mines, and (2) the sources of priming materials, the Court failed to provide any bases on which to discredit Dr. Borgida's testimony concerning sex stereotyping.

It is true that sexual stereotyping has only rarely been applied to claims of sexual harassment and that applying sexual stereotyping to hostile environment claims is an extension of the theory. . . . Nevertheless, sexual stereotyping is relevant to the question whether women were sexually harassed at Eveleth Mines because all three preconditions exist at Eveleth Mines. First, the number of women at Eveleth Mines is far below the 15% figure which Dr. Borgida testified was a baseline for rarity. Second, as has been previously discussed, the work place contained sexually-focused materials and behavior, thereby supporting a conclusion that the work place was sexualized. Third, although seniority governs movement into hourly jobs, criteria for evaluating performance, if any, are subjective and ambiguous.

The court has already found that women at Eveleth Mines were exposed to sexually-focused materials as well as verbal and physical conduct that was sexually-focused. The Court has further concluded that said materials and conduct constitute acts of sexual harassment. Although the Court's findings and conclusions would remain the same absent Dr. Borgida's testimony, his

> testimony on sexual stereotyping provides a sound, credible framework that confirms the Court's conclusion that the presence of the visual materials as well as verbal and physical behaviors previously described constitute acts of sexual harassment. In addition, sexual stereotyping generally, and "priming" research specifically, provide a framework for understanding why consistent and pervasive acts of sexual harassment occur in work environments similar to Eveleth Mines. . . .[269]

§ 6.39 Agency Records

Federal Rule of Evidence 803(8), an exception to the hearsay rule, governs the admission into evidence of the reports and records of the EEOC and other public agencies. This rule covers evidence regarding the activities of the agency, matters observed and reported under a duty imposed by law, or factual findings made pursuant to an investigation, unless there is evidence of lack of trustworthiness.[270] Counsel should be aware that the demonstration of lack of trustworthiness can dilute the weight accorded to an EEOC determination. The admission of such evidence is subject to the discretion of the court,[271] and an adverse ruling can only be reversed for an abuse of discretion.[272] The weight accorded to administrative findings also is subject to the discretion of the court, which must consider the degree of procedural fairness in the administrative process, the thoroughness of the agency's review of the claims, and the adequacy of the plaintiff's representative.[273]

The admissibility of EEOC investigative files has been subject to dispute.[274] Most courts, however, leave the issue to the trial court's discretion.[275]

---

[269] *Id. at* 881–83 (footnotes omitted).

[270] Chandler v. Roudebush, 425 U.S. 840, 864 n.39 (1976).

[271] Walton v. Eaton Corp., 563 F.2d 66 (3d Cir. 1977) (en banc).

[272] McClure v. Mexia Indep. Sch. Dist., 750 F.2d 396 (5th Cir. 1985).

[273] Alexander v. Gardner-Denver Co., 415 U.S. 36 (1974).

[274] *See, e.g.,* Tulloss v. Near N. Montessori Sch., Inc., 776 F.2d 150 (7th Cir. 1985) (court criticized a *per se* admissibility standard for investigative materials that can be a "mish-mash of self-serving and hearsay statements and records"); Fowler v. Blue Bell, Inc., 737 F.2d 1007 (11th Cir. 1984) (affidavits gathered by EEOC during its investigation were admissible in court); Nieves v. Metropolitan Dade County, 598 F. Supp. 955 (S.D. Fla. 1984) (gave evidence very little weight in finding for defendant employer when investigator's testimony contained assumptions that were unsupported or contradicted; investigator discounted evidence supporting defendant's position and failed to interview witnesses who testified on behalf of employer at trial); Peters v. Jefferson Chem. Co., 516 F.2d 447 (5th Cir. 1975) (investigative files may be highly probative).

[275] Second Circuit: Gillin v. Federal Paper Bd. Co., 52 F.R.D. 383 (D. Conn. 1970).

Fourth Circuit: Georator Corp. v. EEOC, 592 F.2d 765 (4th Cir. 1979).

Fifth Circuit: *Cf.* Peters v. Jefferson Chem. Co., 516 F.2d 447 (5th Cir. 1975) (admissibility requirement).

§ 6.40 Administrative Decisions

The U.S. Supreme Court has held that under Federal Rule of Evidence 803(8)(C), prior administrative decisions may be admitted as evidence in federal district court,[276] and thus most courts have held that such admission is subject to the trial court's discretion.[277] However, the Ninth Circuit has ruled that an EEOC probable cause determination must be admitted into evidence.[278]

Federal courts are not bound by the findings of state fair employment practices agencies.[279] The trial court must conduct its own inquiry into the matter.[280] The admissibility of state agency findings is within the discretion of the trial court.[281]

Despite the fact that EEOC guidelines are not formally promulgated administrative regulations, courts in sexual harassment cases have afforded the guidelines considerable weight to the extent that they do not contradict the U.S. Supreme Court findings in *Meritor Savings Bank v. Vinson*[282] (see **Chapter 2**).

§ 6.41 Conciliation and Settlement Discussions

Under Title VII, no part of EEOC conciliation efforts may be used as evidence in a subsequent proceeding without the written consent of the parties concerned.[283] It is unlikely that a defendant would agree to admit this kind of evidence. Information ascertained during conciliation may be helpful as a frame of reference for future discovery requests.

Seventh Circuit: Tulloss v. Near N. Montessori Sch., Inc., 776 F.2d 150 (7th Cir. 1985).

Eleventh Circuit: Fowler v. Blue Bell, Inc., 737 F.2d 1007 (11th Cir. 1984); Watford v. Birmingham Stove & Range Co., 14 Fair Empl. Prac. Cas. (BNA) 626 (N.D. Ala. 1976).

District of Columbia Circuit: Kinsey v. Legg, Mason & Co., 10 Fair Empl. Prac. Cas. (BNA) 1013 (D.D.C. 1974), *rev'd,* 557 F.2d 830 (D.C. Cir. 1977).

276 Chandler v. Roudebush, 425 U.S. 840 (1976).

277 Whatley v. Skaggs Cos., 707 F.2d 1129 (10th Cir.), *cert. denied,* 464 U.S. 938 (1983); Strickland v. American Can Co., 575 F. Supp. 1111 (N.D. Ga. 1983).

278 Bradshaw v. Zoological Soc'y, 569 F.2d 1066 (9th Cir. 1978).

279 Kuck v. Berkey Photo, Inc., 81 F.R.D. 736 (S.D.N.Y. 1979).

280 Bastiste v. Furnco Constr. Corp., 503 F.2d 447 (7th Cir. 1974), *cert. denied,* 420 U.S. 928 (1975).

281 Jordan v. Clark, 847 F.2d 1368 (9th Cir. 1988), *cert. denied,* 488 U.S. 1006 (1989) (sexual harassment; administrative record admitted).

282 Meritor Sav. Bank v. Vinson, 477 U.S. 57 (1986).

283 42 U.S.C. § 2000e-5(b).

The Federal Rules of Evidence prohibit the introduction of evidence of settlement offers to demonstrate liability. Exclusion is not required if the evidence is offered for other purposes, such as to show bias or prejudice of a witness.[284]

The U.S. Supreme Court has held that a prior unsuccessful arbitral decision may not bar a subsequent Title VII action, but may be admitted as evidence.[285] If an arbitral determination fully considers an employee's Title VII rights, a court may accord it great weight.

PROOF ISSUES

§ 6.42 Proof

Proof of sexual harassment depends on the type of harassment asserted. *Quid pro quo* harassment turns on a showing that an employment benefit or job status was conditioned upon compliance with sexual advances. This type of proof often is reduced to a factual inquiry regarding the respective parties' credibility because *quid pro quo* harassment usually occurs without witnesses. Hostile environment claims require proof that verbal and/or physical conduct in the workplace was offensive enough to alter the terms or conditions of the plaintiff's work environment. Courts have required a higher showing in hostile environment cases that the conduct "was pervasive and destructive of the working environment."[286]

Sexual harassment may be proven with direct or circumstantial evidence. Because employers rarely offer direct evidence of discriminatory motivation, many sexual harassment cases, especially those alleging a hostile environment, are built on circumstantial evidence. Some courts, however, have applied a direct evidence standard in cases charging retaliation when plaintiffs have proven the existence of sexual harassment. The elements of a prima facie sexual harassment case generally are adapted from those established in *McDonnell Douglas Corp. v. Green*[287] and *Texas Department of Community Affairs v. Burdine*.[288]

---

284 Fed. R. Evid. 408.

285 Alexander v. Gardner-Denver Co., 415 U.S. 36 (1974).

286 Jones v. Flagship Int'l, 793 F.2d 714, 720 (5th Cir. 1986), *cert. denied*, 479 U.S. 1065 (1987) (sexual harassment).

287 McDonnell Douglas Corp. v. Green, 411 U.S. 792 (1973).

288 Texas Dep't of Community Affairs v. Burdine, 450 U.S. 248 (1981).

§ 6.43 Prima Facie *Quid Pro Quo* Case

Courts generally treat sexual harassment actions as disparate treatment cases. The employee bears the burden of establishing a prima facie case of discrimination.[289] "The burden of making out a prima facie case under Title VII is not an arduous one."[290] A district court may not require direct evidence of intentional discrimination.[291] Eyewitness testimony seldom is available in *quid pro quo* sexual harassment cases.[292] The plaintiff only must produce evidence that might indicate that improper sexual considerations were a major factor in an adverse employment decision.[293] In *quid pro quo* sexual harassment cases, the point in time at which the tangible

---

[289] *Cf.* Dockter v. Rudolf Wolff Futures, Inc., 684 F. Supp. 532, 534 (N.D. Ill. 1988), *aff'd,* 913 F.2d 456 (7th Cir. 1990) (sexual harassment).

[290] Christoforou v. Ryder Truck Rental, Inc., 668 F. Supp. 294, 302 (S.D.N.Y. 1987) (sexual harassment). *See also* Sumner v. San Diego Urban League, 681 F.2d 1140, 1142 (9th Cir. 1982).

[291] United States Postal Serv. Bd. of Governors v. Aikens, 460 U.S. 711, 714 n.3 (1983); Texas Dep't of Community Affairs v. Burdine, 450 U.S. 248 (1981).

[292] United States Postal Serv. Bd. of Governors v. Aikens, 460 U.S. 711, 716 (1983).

[293] Christoforou v. Ryder Truck Rental, Inc., 668 F. Supp. 294, 302 (S.D.N.Y. 1987) (sexual harassment).

First Circuit: Showalter v. Allison Reed Group, Inc., 767 F. Supp. 1205 (D.R.I. 1991). Male employees were subjected to sexual harassment when their supervisor forced them to engage in various sexual activities with his secretary by threatening them with discharge if they did not acquiesce. Though neither employee complained to anyone, both participated because they feared losing their jobs and employer did not have a formal grievance procedure. The fact that both plaintiffs contributed to sexual innuendo prevalent at the workplace did not vitiate their claims of sexual harassment.

Second Circuit: Bridges v. Eastman Kodak Co., 822 F. Supp. 1020 (S.D.N.Y. 1993). Female employees stated a claim of *quid pro quo* sexual harassment when they asserted that one alleged harasser, their supervisor, had the authority to alter terms, conditions, and privileges of their employment. Allegations that supervisor threatened plaintiffs with termination, discipline, or economic loss if they were to complain to upper management were sufficient at this state of litigation to demonstrate that supervisor had power to make personnel decisions regarding the plaintiffs' employment.

Seventh Circuit: Perkins v. Silverstein, 939 F.2d 463 (7th Cir. 1991). A discharged employee did not state claim for *quid pro quo* or hostile environment sexual harassment when she did not identify any specific incidents of harassment, when they occurred, or how the terms of her employment were affected by them.

Saxton v. American Tel. & Tel. Co., 785 F. Supp. 760 (N.D. Ill. 1992). An employee failed to state a claim for *quid pro quo* sexual harassment when she did not allege that her supervisor's conduct was more than inappropriate advances, and although supervisor boasted about transferring her to his department in a higher level position, plaintiff knew that she was not qualified for the job.

Silverberg v. Baxter Healthcare Corp., 52 Fair Emp. Prac. Cas. (BNA) 1848 (N.D. Ill. 1990). Conjecture regarding whether a supervisor who discharged plaintiff, and who reported to a manager who had previously made sexual advances toward her, did not

aspect of the plaintiff's employment was affected is the point at which the period for bringing suit begins to run. In *Marrero-Rivera v. Department of Justice,*[294] the period began when the plaintiff's supervisor told her that he no longer wished to work with her and that she was being transferred to a less desirable job, rather than the earlier date on which the last sexual "incident" occurred between the plaintiff and her supervisor.

Once such a case is established, the burden shifts to the employer to articulate a legitimate nondiscriminatory reason for the challenged employment decision. If this burden is met, the employee must demonstrate that the employer's explanation was a pretext for discrimination. This last requirement goes to the intent of the employer to discriminate.

In *McDonnell Douglas,*[295] the U.S. Supreme Court set forth the elements of a prima facie case in a disparate treatment action. Although the prima facie case might vary to accommodate the facts of the case, it generally is applicable in *quid pro quo* cases. The employee plaintiff must demonstrate by a preponderance of the evidence that:

1. She is a member of the protected class.
2. She applied for and was qualified for the position for which the defendant was seeking applicants.
3. Despite her qualifications, she was rejected for the position.
4. After the rejection, the position remained open and the employer continued to seek applicants from persons of complainant's qualifications.[296]

---

support a claim that her discharge stemmed from rejection of those advances. Moreover, the fact that alleged sexual harassment occurred approximately two years before plaintiff's discharge "further diminishes any appearance of a connection between the alleged discriminatory acts and the discharge." *Id.* at 1854.

Eleventh Circuit: Sparks v. Regional Medical Center Bd., 792 F. Supp. 735 (N.D. Ala. 1992). An employee did not prove *quid pro quo* sexual harassment when her supervisor's alleged misconduct consisted "only" of sexual comments and jokes directed at plaintiff, offensive language, and instances of rough contact.

Stockett v. Tolin, 791 F. Supp. 1536 (S.D. Fla. 1992). A female employee in film industry training program was subjected to *quid pro quo* sexual harassment when a managing agent harassed her physically and verbally for over a year and then told her that she would be fired if she did not submit to his advances.

District of Columbia Circuit: Diggs v. Campbell, 54 Fair Emp. Prac. Cas. (BNA) 773 (D.D.C. 1990). The employer was entitled to summary judgment when *pro se* plaintiff offered nothing to support allegations that she was terminated because she refused employer official's sexual advances and made no effort to challenge defendant's assertion that she was terminated because of "erratic" performance and unexplained absences and because she improperly removed certain corporate materials.

[294] Marrero-Riviera v. Department of Justice, 821 F. Supp. 65 (D.P.R. 1993).

[295] McDonnell Douglas Corp. v. Green, 411 U.S. 792 (1973).

[296] *Id.* at 802.

In *Henson v. City of Dundee,*[297] the Eleventh Circuit summarized the prima facie elements of a *quid pro quo* sexual harassment claim:

> In order to establish a violation of Title VII on grounds of sexual harassment of this kind, an employee must prove a number of elements, many of which are similar to the proof required to establish the existence of a hostile or offensive work environment:
>
> 1. The employee belongs to a protected group.
> 2. The employee was subject to sexual harassment.
> 3. The harassment complained of was based on sex.
> 4. The employee's reaction to harassment complained of affected tangible aspects of the employee's compensation, terms, conditions, or privileges of employment. The acceptance or rejection of the harassment by an employee must be an express or implied condition to the receipt of a job benefit or the cause of a tangible job detriment in order to create liability under this theory of sexual harassment. As in the typical disparate treatment case, the employee must prove that she was deprived of a job benefit which she was otherwise qualified to receive because of the employer's use of a prohibited criterion in making the employment decision.
> 5. Respondeat superior.[298]

A showing that the challenged conduct was unwelcome is particularly important in both *quid pro quo* and hostile environment harassment cases.[299] Although notice is not required to establish employer liability for supervisor conduct in *quid pro quo* sexual harassment cases, evidence of such notice does support allegations that the conduct was not welcome. The plaintiff also should demonstrate that the offending supervisor had the authority to carry out the relevant employment decision.[300] In *Kauffman v.*

---

297 Henson v. City of Dundee, 682 F.2d 897 (11th Cir. 1982).

298 *Id.* at 909. The court noted that in holding that an employer was strictly liable for actions of its supervisors in *quid pro quo* cases, it was requiring "differing treatment of respondeat superior claims in the two types of sexual harassment cases." *Id.* at 911. *See also* Heelan v. Johns-Manville Corp., 451 F. Supp. 1382, 1389 (D. Colo. 1978) (sexual harassment). *See also* Neville v. Taft Broadcasting Co., 42 Fair Empl. Prac. Cas. (BNA) 1314 (W.D.N.Y. 1987) (sexual harassment).

299 Meritor Sav. Bank v. Vinson, 477 U.S. 57 (1986). *See also* Koster v. Chase Manhattan Bank, 46 Fair Empl. Prac. Cas. (BNA) 1436 (S.D.N.Y. 1988) (sexual harassment).

300 Koster v. Chase Manhattan Bank, 46 Fair Empl. Prac. Cas. (BNA) 1436 (S.D.N.Y. 1988) (sexual harassment) (plaintiff employee did not show that defendant participated in decision not to allow plaintiff to interview for position or that he had authority to prevent her transfer or terminate her).

Cf. Watts v. New York City Police Dep't, 724 F. Supp. 99 (S.D.N.Y. 1989) Plaintiff former probationary officer alleged that one of her instructors grabbed her breast during practice and in reaction to her protestations, the instructor told her she would fail her test, threatened to "kick the shit out of her" if she did not bend down further while she

Allied Signal,[301] a female employee who had had a breast enlargement brought an action charging that her supervisor sexually harassed her by touching her breast and retaliating against her for objecting to his conduct by assigning her to a manual press that was disliked within the department, throwing a spark plug insulator at her, and ordering other employees to make comments to the plaintiff about her breasts. When the plaintiff went to her union representative, who brought her complaint to the director of employee relations, the harasser was fired. The plaintiff claimed that she was subjected to harassment and hostility even after the supervisor was fired, and ultimately suffered a nervous breakdown and was unable to return to work. The district court found that the employer had no knowledge of the supervisor's actions and when he found out, he took immediate and effective remedial action by discharging the harasser, and that because the supervisor did not have the authority to hire, fire, promote, or discipline the plaintiff on his own, and because the company sexual harassment policy worked, the employer was not liable as a matter of law. The court of appeals disagreed with the district court's conclusion that the company was not liable because the harasser did not qualify as its agent under "scope of employment" standards, noting that the supervising employee need not have ultimate authority to hire or fire to qualify as an employer, so long as there is significant input into such personnel decisions. At the very least, there existed a question of fact as to whether the supervisor had enough authority to qualify as an agent and therefore as an employer under Title VII. The court thus reversed an order of summary judgment in favor of an employer on a *quid pro quo* claim of sexual harassment but affirmed summary judgment on the hostile environment claim.

An employer may try to show that his temper manifested itself indiscriminately against men and women.[302] Although courts have found

was loading and unloading her gun, and refused to have her gun serviced, even though it was later found to be broken, claiming that the problem was that plaintiff couldn't shoot. The next day, a coworker twice pulled plaintiff up against his body, and told her he wanted to feel her body and that her body felt good; during the second incident, plaintiff had to strike the coworker with a box of ammunition to get away. As a result of this conduct, plaintiff suffered severe and persistent headaches and stomach aches and took sick leave for one week. Upon her return, she filed a sexual harassment complaint and was subsequently subjected to further harassment by verbal attacks and ostracization by her coworkers and supervisors until her resignation a week later. The court held that plaintiff did not state a claim for *quid pro quo* sexual harassment with respect to her supervisor's refusal to send her gun to be repaired and his threat to fail her on her upcoming skill test, which he had responsibility to grade, when plaintiff did not assert that any repercussions ever arose from the threats.

301 Kauffman v. Allied Signal, 970 F.2d 178 (6th Cir. 1992), *cert denied,* 113 S. Ct. 831 (1993).

302 Sheehan v. Purolator, Inc., 839 F.2d 99 (2d Cir.), *cert. denied*, 488 U.S. 891 (1988); Halasi-Schmick v. City of Shawnee, 759 F. Supp. 747 (D. Kan. 1991).

indiscriminate treatment in some cases, others have found the disparity between the adverse treatment of men and that of women sufficient to render the conduct sexual harassment.[303] Nor does the fact that a male was offended by certain conduct mean that the harassment was not based on sex.[304]

One incident of *quid pro quo* sexual harassment may be sufficient to establish a prima facie case of sex discrimination.[305] Unlike hostile environment discrimination, for which most courts have required a pattern of offensive sexual activity, a single episode of *quid pro quo* harassment contains a clear element of blackmail that the courts have found easier to deem harassment.[306]

An employer or supervisor need not actually ask a female employee to have sex or to go on a date to be liable for this type of sexual harassment. In *Pease v. Alford Photo Indus., Inc.,*[307] a defendant supervisor who constantly touched female employees in a sexual manner and who terminated the plaintiff employee who complained of his conduct was liable for *quid pro quo* as well as hostile environment harassment:

> While this conduct may have been a source of fantasy and amusement to Mr. Alford, it was unwelcomed and humiliating to his female employees. Apparently, Mr. Alford thought he was at liberty to sexually harass female employees with impunity so long as, he testified, he did not ask them to go to bed or go out with him. The whole body of evidence in this case shows

---

303 Delgado v. Lehman, 665 F. Supp. 460, 465 (E.D. Va. 1987); EEOC v. FLC & Bros. Rebel, 663 F. Supp. 864 (W.D. Va. 1987), *aff'd,* 846 F.2d 70 (4th Cir. 1988).

304 Spencer v. General Elec. Co., 697 F. Supp. 204 (E.D. Va. 1988), *aff'd,* 894 F.2d 651 (4th Cir. 1990).

305 Second Circuit: Neville v. Taft Broadcasting Co., 42 Fair Empl. Prac. Cas. (BNA) 1314 (W.D.N.Y. 1987) (discharged plaintiff made a prima facie showing of *quid pro quo* harassment when her supervisor grabbed her, kissed her against her will, and told her that if she did everything right with the company she would go a long way).

Sixth Circuit: Boyd v. James S. Hayes Living Health Care Agency, 671 F. Supp. 1155 (W.D. Tenn. 1987) (conduct during one business trip was sufficient to find sexual harassment).

Ninth Circuit: Miller v. Bank of Am., 600 F.2d 211 (9th Cir. 1979).

District of Columbia Circuit: Barnes v. Costle, 561 F.2d 983 (D.C. Cir. 1977).

306 Ninth Circuit: Nichols v. Frank, 732 F. Supp. 1085 (D. Or. 1990) (employer may be liable for *quid pro quo* sexual harassment in situations that would not support claim for hostile environment harassment).

Cf. Morley v. New Eng. Tel. Co., 47 Fair Empl. Prac. Cas. (BNA) 917, 924 (D. Mass. 1987) (employee who had personality conflict with supervisor and demonstrated that she was discriminatorily denied promotion was not sexually harassed when only two statements by supervisor could be considered to have sexual overtones: "I don't want a reluctant bride" and "You couldn't look good if you tried").

307 Pease v. Alford Photo Indus., 667 F. Supp. 1188, 1202 (W.D. Tenn. 1987).

> that Mr. Alford never crossed the threshold, set in his mind, of asking any female employee to go to bed or go out with him. This circumstance, the Court finds, indicates that Mr. Alford acted intentionally and deliberately.[308]

Courts also have accepted straight disparate treatment analyses to find sexual harassment-based sex discrimination without reference to *quid pro quo* harassment. A prima facie case can be established by presenting evidence creating an inference that the plaintiff was subjected to an adverse employment decision for reasons prohibited by Title VII.[309] In *Cortes v. Maxus Exploration Co.,*[310] acts of harassment that occurred outside the limitations period could be considered in determining whether an employer's action in transferring an employee to the alleged harasser's department constituted sexual harassment and constructive discharge.

§ 6.44 Prima Facie Hostile Environment Case

The prima facie elements of *McDonnell Douglas* do not easily apply to hostile environment situations that do not necessarily involve job status or economic discrimination. A disparate treatment analysis is not quite appropriate because hostile environment claims do not deal with the employer's intent. In *Henson,*[311] the Eleventh Circuit outlined the elements of a prima facie hostile environment case:

> 1. The employee belongs to a protected group. As in other cases of sexual discrimination, this requires a simple stipulation that the employee is a man or woman. . . .

---

308 *Id.* at 1202; Boyd v. James S. Hayes Living Health Care Agency, 671 F. Supp. 1155, 1165 (W.D. Tenn. 1987) (supervisor's conduct during business trip was sexual harassment despite the fact that he did not explicitly invite or force plaintiff to have sex. "[T]he insistence on plaintiff's coming to his hotel room, the wine, the [pornographic] movie and the magazines, the effort to restrain plaintiff's departure, the slammed door and other factors" demonstrated that the defendant's conduct was of a sexual nature). *Cf.* Lipsett v. Rive-Mora, 669 F. Supp. 1188, 1200 (D.P.R. 1987), *rev'd on other grounds,* 864 F.2d 881 (1st Cir. 1988) ("Plaintiff never established that [the defendant] demanded, explicitly or implicitly, that she submit to sexual acts.").

309 Delgado v. Lehman, 665 F. Supp. 460, 466 (E.D. Va. 1987); Showalter v. Allison Reed Group, Inc., 767 F. Supp. 1205 (D.R.I. 1991). Male employees were subjected to sexual harassment when their supervisor forced them to engage in various sexual activities with his secretary by threatening them with discharge if they did not acquiesce. Though neither employee complained to anyone, both participated becaused they feared losing their jobs and employer did not have a formal grievance procedure. The fact that both plaintiffs contributed to sexual innuendo prevalent at workplace did not vitiate their claims of sexual harassment.

310 Cortes v. Maxus Exploration Co., 977 F.2d 195 (5th Cir. 1992).

311 Henson v. City of Dundee, 682 F.2d 897 (11th Cir. 1982).

2. The employee was subject to unwelcome sexual harassment. The E.E.O.C. regulations helpfully define the type of conduct that may constitute sexual harassment: "sexual advances, requests for sexual favors, and other verbal or physical conduct of a sexual nature. . ." In order to constitute harassment, this conduct must be unwelcome in the sense that the employee did not solicit or invite it, and in the sense that the employee regarded the conduct as undesirable or offensive. . . .
3. The harassment complained of was based upon sex. . . . [T]he employee must show that but for the fact of her sex, she would not have been the object of harassment. . . .
4. The harassment complained of affected a "term, condition, or privilege of employment." For sexual harassment to state a claim under Title VII, it must be sufficiently pervasive so as to alter the conditions of employment and create an abusive working environment. . . .
5. Respondeat superior. Where . . . the plaintiff seeks to hold the employer responsible for the hostile environment created by the plaintiff's supervisor or coworker, she must show that the employer knew of or should have known of the harassment in question and failed to take prompt remedial action.[312]

In *Andrews v. Philadelphia,*[313] the Third Circuit held that five constituents must converge to bring a successful claim for a sexually hostile work environment under Title VII:

> (1) the employees suffered intentional discrimination because of their sex; (2) the discrimination was pervasive and regular; (3) the discrimination detrimentally affected the plaintiff; (4) the discrimination would detrimentally affect a reasonable person of the same sex in that position; and (5) the existence of respondeat superior liability. . . .
>
> It is particularly important to note that these factors include both a subjective standard (No.3) and an objective standard (No.4). The subjective factor is crucial because it demonstrates that the alleged conduct injured this particular plaintiff giving her a claim for judicial relief. The objective factor, however, is the more crucial for it is here that the finder of fact must actually determine whether the work environment is sexually hostile. Congress designed Title VII to prevent the perpetuation of stereotypes and a sense of degradation which serve to close or discourage employment opportunities for women. . . . Congress expected that Title VII would result in the "removal of artificial, arbitrary, and unnecessary barriers to employment when the barriers operate invidiously to discriminate on the basis of racial or other impermissible classification." *Griggs v. Duke Power Co.,* 401 U.S. 424, 431 . . . (1971). Such an objective can only be achieved if women are allowed to work without being harassed. Women who know that they will

---

312 *Id.* at 903–05 (footnote omitted). *See also* Meritor Sav. Bank v. Vinson, 477 U.S. 57 (1986).

313 Andrews v. Philadelphia, 895 F.2d 1469 (3d Cir. 1990).

be subject to harassment will be deterred from joining the work force or accepting certain jobs. The objective standard protects the employer from the "hypersensitive" employee, but still serves the goal of equal opportunity by removing the walls of discrimination that deprive women of self-respecting employment.[314]

A showing that the challenged conduct was not welcome is critical in hostile environment cases. This may be demonstrated with evidence that:

1. The plaintiff complained to supervisors or coworkers. Courts may give less weight to coworkers' testimony when the plaintiff had an effective means to complain to higher management.[315] Each complaint and the response to it by management, if relevant, should be documented. The likelihood of a finding of hostile environment increases with the number of complaints made.
2. The plaintiff unsuccessfully attempted to use a formal in-house grievance procedure. Under *Meritor,* the existence of a grievance procedure or a policy against sex discrimination does not preclude a finding of employer liability when the system is not effective.[316] These efforts also should be fully documented.

---

314 *Id.* 1482–83.

315 Slate v. Kingsdown, 46 Fair Empl. Prac. Cas. (BNA) 1495 (M.D.N.C. 1987).

316 Meritor Sav. Bank v. Vinson, 477 U.S. 57, 72 (1986). *See also* EEOC v. Hacienda Hotel, 881 F.2d 1504 (9th Cir.1989) Female housekeepers were subjected to severe and pervasive sexual harassment when chief of engineering and executive housekeeper (a woman) repeatedly subjected employees to sexual harassment, including crude and disparaging remarks to a pregnant women, such as saying "that's what you get for sleeping without your underwear", asking why she was pregnant by another man and making comments about her "ass." The executive housekeeper told one pregnant employee that she did not like "stupid women who have kids" and on many occasions called her "dog", "whore," or "slut." *Id.* at 1507. The chief of engineering told another pregnant employee that women "get pregnant because they like to suck men's dicks", threatened to have her fired if she did not submit to his sexual advances, and stated that the employee had "such a fine ass. It's a nice ass to stick a nice dick into. How many dicks have you eaten?" *Id.* at 1508. There was no dispute that the challenged acts occurred, and that they were unwelcome. The district court found that defendant could be held liable for supervisors' actions because the general manager of the Hacienda had actual knowledge of allegations of harassment and defendant should have known of harassment because it was severe and pervasive and "seriously tainted" the complainants' working environment. The court rejected defendant's contention that complainants failed to pursue internal remedies under appellant's general nondiscrimination policy when employer's policy did not specifically proscribe sexual harassment, and its internal procedures required initial resort to a supervisor who was accused of engaging in or condoning the harassment of which the employees complained.

EEOC v. Gurnee Inn Corp., 48 Fair Empl. Prac. Cas. (BNA) 871 (N.D. Ill. 1988) ("policy" was handed out to employees only sporadically and grievance procedure was not effective when employees were forced to complain to immediate supervisor).

3. The plaintiff was forced to seek medical or psychiatric assistance as a result of the harassment.[317] This evidence may be important, but counsel should be prepared for the defense's attempt to use psychiatric testimony, particularly if the plaintiff had undergone any treatment before the harassment, to establish that the plaintiff is either a troublemaker or has an emotional problem with men that precludes "normal" interaction with them. Medical testimony regarding injuries suffered as a result of sexual or other assault by the alleged harasser will be more credible if the plaintiff has witnesses or circumstantial evidence tying the injury to the assault at the workplace.
4. The plaintiff sought a transfer as a result of the abusive work atmosphere. The plaintiff should show that she informed the relevant officials that the harassment forced her to seek a transfer.
5. The plaintiff's work performance suffered as a result of the harassment. This element is difficult in situations in which the plaintiff was terminated or otherwise had her employment status changed because the defendant will try to demonstrate that the plaintiff's work performance was the basis for her discharge. Most courts have avoided this factor from the plaintiff's perspective when there has been a strong showing of the pervasiveness of the harassment and the futility of complaints. Plaintiff may want to tie her inability to work to the hostile environment by introducing medical evidence supporting her increased use of sick time or sluggish performance.
6. The plaintiff underwent personality changes over the course of the harassment. Courts have accepted the testimony of spouses who have witnessed personality changes in their wives over the course of the sexual harassment. Because of the marital relationship, the weight given to such testimony may be minimal, but the testimony is worth introducing.

A court may find that challenged conduct was not unwelcome if:

1. The plaintiff did not complain to supervisors. This appears to be the most important factor in a judicial determination of hostile environment harassment. The failure to complain is discounted only by a grievance scheme in which a plaintiff may only complain through the harassing supervisor.[318] Complaints to coworkers may not be sufficient. Verbal complaints to management may be inadequate as well if there were no witnesses to the grievances.

---

[317] Llewellyn v. Celanese Corp., 693 F. Supp. 369 (W.D.N.C. 1988), *aff'd,* 914 F.2d 815 (7th Cir. 1990).

[318] EEOC v. Gurnee Inn Corp., 48 Fair Empl. Prac. Cas. (BNA) 871 (N.D. Ill. 1988), *aff'd,* 914 F.2d 815 (7th Cir 1990).

2. The plaintiff participated in the conduct. Despite the many reasons that employees join in workplace banter or conduct they find offensive, courts have not looked upon such conduct with favor in the hostile environment context. If the plaintiff did participate in sexually oriented conduct such as the use of language, touching, or provocative behavior, counsel must be prepared to demonstrate the basis for the plaintiff's conduct was fear of reprisal, intimidation, or socialization. If the plaintiff complained of the atmosphere, her participation should not be too damaging, but the absence of such complaints may be determinative. Conduct indicating that the plaintiff welcomed the challenged behavior may be rectified by a showing that the plaintiff made it clear that she no longer found the conduct welcome.

Whether the challenged conduct rises to an actionable level is a fact-specific question that depends upon the totality of the circumstances.[319] Although one or two offensive acts usually will not establish a violation of Title VII,[320] particularly when employers take prompt remedial steps in

---

319 Harris v. Forklift Systems, Inc., 114 S. Ct. 367, 371 (1993); Campbell v. Board of Regents, 770 F. Supp. 1479 (D. Kan. 1991).

320 Meritor Sav. Bank v. Vinson, 477 U.S. 57, 67 (1986).

First Circuit: Seligson v. Massachusetts Inst. of Technology, 677 F. Supp. 648, 656 (D. Mass. 1987) (supervisor's comments regarding plaintiff's scheduled work-related trips, deadlines, and problems with other employees did not alter plaintiff's conditions of employment); Del Valle Fontanez v. Aponte, 660 F. Supp. 145, 148–49 (D.P.R. 1987) (Plaintiff's contradicted testimony alleging only one incident in which her supervisor summoned her to his office, behind locked doors, and allegedly forced his body upon hers did not prove harassment so severe as to constitute a hostile environment in light of credible testimony that defendant called plaintiff into his office to discuss her poor work performance and plaintiff never mentioned the incident to a psychiatrist she was seeing until he asked her about it because he had been asked to testify in the case. "[T]his is not to say that a single sexual advance could not constitute sexual harassment.").

Second Circuit: Sheehan v. Purolator, Inc., 839 F.2d 99 (2d Cir. 1988), *cert. denied* 488 U.S. 891 (1988) (incidents alleged too isolated); Babcock v. Frank, 59 Fair Empl. Prac. Cas. (BNA) 410 (S.D.N.Y. 1992). "Occasional or isolated utterances of offensive epithets, although repugnant, are not so pervasive as to affect the conditions of employment to a degree which violates Title VII." *Id.* at 417; Christoforou v. Ryder Truck Rental, Inc., 668 F. Supp. 294, 301 (S.D.N.Y. 1987).

Third Circuit: Miller v. Aluminum Co. of Am., 679 F. Supp. 495 (W.D. Pa. 1988), *aff'd,* 856 F.2d 184 (3d Cir. 1988) (single comment about plaintiff's breasts inadequate).

Fourth Circuit: Keziah v. W.M. Brown & Son, 683 F. Supp. 542 (W.D.N.C. 1988), *modified,* 888 F.2d 322 (4th Cir. 1989) (two sexually oriented comments insufficient); Slate v. Kingsdown, 46 Fair Empl. Prac. Cas. (BNA) 1495 (M.D.N.C. 1987) (two incidents of grabbing plaintiff by shoulders and neck did not create hostile environment); Strickland v. Sears, Roebuck & Co., 46 Fair Empl. Prac. Cas. (BNA) 1024 (E.D. Va. 1987), *aff'd,* 846 F.2d 74 (4th Cir. 1988) (supervisor touched plaintiff once and made comment about 15 minutes later suggesting they should date).

Fifth Circuit: Bennett v. Corroon & Black Corp., 845 F.2d 104 (5th Cir. 1988), *cert. denied*, 489 U.S. 1020 (1989) (evidence that obscene cartoons depicting plaintiff were posted in the employer's men's room presented "meager proof" of conditions required by *Meritor*).

Sixth Circuit: Vermett v. Hough, 627 F. Supp. 587, 605–06 (W.D. Mich. 1986) (court found that only one of alleged incidents occurred).

Seventh Circuit: Hinton v. Methodist Hosps., 779 F. Supp. 956 (N.D. Ind. 1991) (plaintiff's hostile work environment claim failed when, among other things, her proof failed to establish any unwelcome sexual attention beyond one remark about "wild hair", which was not part of any wider pattern of abuse); Scott v. Sears, Roebuck & Co., 605 F. Supp. 1047 (N.D. Ill. 1985), *aff'd,* 798 F.2d 210, 214 (7th Cir. 1986) (plaintiff gave only one concrete example of being propositioned; comments and conduct of coworkers were "too isolated and lacking the repetitive and debilitating effect necessary to maintain a hostile environment claim"); Sardigal v. St. Louis Nat'l Stockyards Co., 42 Fair Empl. Prac. Cas. (BNA) 497 (S.D. Ill. 1986) (single request for waitress to work in her leotard without her skirt could not support sexual harassment claim). *Cf.* Dockter v. Rudolf Wolff Futures, Inc., 684 F. Supp. 532, 539 (N.D. Ill. 1988) (although plaintiff rejected defendant's sexual overtures, the court stated that "her initial rejections were neither unpleasant nor unambiguous, and gave [the defendant] no reason to believe that his moves were unwelcome;" thus, with the single exception of a breast-fondling incident, the court found defendant's conduct to be "essentially unoffensive and not even clearly unwelcome"), *aff'd,* 913 F.2d 456 (7th Cir. 1990). With respect to the district court determination that plaintiff did not establish a hostile environment, the court noted that although it agreed with the district court's conclusion, evidence indicated existence of a hostile environment:

> Based on this intimidating and offensive conduct which the district court inferentially adopted as fact, it would appear that Ms. Dockter's work environment during these initial two weeks was "hostile" such as to be actionable under Title VII. However, regardless of our view that Gannon's offensive conduct created a hostile work environment, Ms. Dockter has not alleged or proven an injury resulting from this conduct which can be remedied under the equitable provision of Title VII.
>
> The record reveals (and Ms. Dockter does not dispute) that Gannon's "preening, primping and posturing" ended after he was reprimanded on the evening that he fondled her breast. Further, Ms. Dockter does not allege that she was subjected to similar offensive conduct after that date by other male employees at Rudolf Wolff. As such, even if her initial two weeks were "hostile" such as to be actionable under Title VII, in the absence of any continuing sexual harassment or discharge based on that sexual harassment, Ms. Dockter cannot obtain relief under Title VII . . . . Because the sexual harassment about which Ms. Dockter complains had long-since ceased at the time of her termination and because her termination was not the result of sexually discriminatory motives, the decision in favor of Rudolf Wolff on Ms. Dockter's "hostile environment" claim was correct, albeit for reasons other than those stated by the district court.

Id. at 460–61 (footnotes omitted).

Eighth Circuit: Moylan v. Maries County, 792 F.2d 746, 749–50 (8th Cir. 1986); EEOC v. Murphy Motor Freight Lines, Inc., 488 F. Supp. 381 (D. Minn. 1980).

Eleventh Circuit: Henson v. City of Dundee, 682 F.2d 897 (11th Cir. 1982); Sapp v. City of Warner Robins, 655 F. Supp. 1043, 1049 (M.D. Ga. 1987) (court's finding of a single effort by defendant to get plaintiff police officer to go out with him "was not of a

response to employee complaints,[321] a single incident of sufficient severity may create a hostile environment in appropriate circumstances.[322] In some cases, however, the mere presence of a harasser may create a hostile environment. In *Radtke v. Everett,*[323] the constructive discharge claim of a female veterinary technician who was caressed and kissed by her supervisor during a break and who subsequently ended her employment and sought counseling should have survived summary judgment. The proper perspective to view the offensive conduct from was that of a reasonable woman:

---

repeated or continuous nature to be sufficiently pervasive enough to affect plaintiff's psychological well-being").

Federal Circuit: Downes v. Federal Aviation Admin., 775 F.2d 288, 293 (Fed. Cir. 1985).

Iowa: Edmunds v. Mercy Hospital, 62 Fair Empl. Prac. Cas. (BNA) 463 (Iowa Ct. App. 1993). The trial court properly determined that a supervisor never made any sexual overtures to nurse plaintiff and did not discuss sexual matters or his family with her; he admitted hugging plaintiff twice, but claimed that it was at plaintiff's request, and witnesses testified that hugging was common in the unit.

321 Strickland v. Sears, Roebuck & Co., 46 Fair Empl. Prac. Cas. (BNA) 1024 (E.D. Va. 1987), *aff'd,* 846 F.2d 74 (4th Cir. 1988). *See also* Dornhecker v. Malibu Grand Prix Corp., 828 F.2d 307 (5th Cir. 1987) (plaintiff was told 12 hours after she complained about coworker's conduct that she would not have to work with offending coworker when current project ended in one-and-a-half days).

322 Henson v. City of Dundee, 682 F.2d 897, 904 n.8 (11th Cir. 1982); Radtke v. Everett, 442 Mich 368, 501 N.W.2d 155 (Mich. 1993) (Riley, J.); Lehmann v. Toys 'R' Us, Inc., 133 N.J. 587, 626 A.2d 445, 455 (N.J. 1993) (Garibaldi, J.) ("Although it will be a rare and extreme case in which a single incident will be so severe that it would, from the perspective of a reasonable woman, make the working environment hostile, such a case is certainly possible").

Barbour v. Department of Social Servs., 198 Mich. App. 183, 497 N.W.2d 216 (Ct. App. 1993) (per curiam). A claim of hostile environment sexual harassment may be based on a single incident.

Huitt v. Marher St. Hotel Corp., 62 Fair Empl. Prac. Cas. (BNA) 538 (D. Kan. 1993). The court had no difficulty concluding that even a single incident of rape, if proven, constitutes sexual harassment of a type sufficiently severe to support a claim of hostile environment sexual harassment. The court rejected defendant's contention that plaintiff was not subjected to any harassment while "at work" thus suggesting that the actionable harassment must occur at the place of business. The question rather is whether there are sufficient facts from which to infer a nexus between the sexual conduct and the work environment. In this case, the supervisor allegedly raped plaintiff while driving her home immediately after work; moreover, the supervisor was able to place himself in a position to drive plaintiff home by using his authority to make it more difficult for plaintiff to make other arrangements.

Del Valle Fontanez v. Aponte, 660 F. Supp. 145, 149 (D.P.R. 1987) ("Under *Meritor* and the EEOC Guidelines, it is conceivable that a single incidence of sexual aggression could, on the whole, constitute a case of sexual harassment actionable under Title VII"). EEOC Policy Guidance, N-915.035 (Oct. 25, 1988) C(2) at 16. "a single unwelcome physical advance can seriously poison the victim's working environment."

323 Radtke v. Everett, 56 Fair Emp. Prac. Cas. (BNA) 923 (Mich. Ct. App. 1991).

> We believe that a standard which views harassing conduct from the "reasonable person" perspective has the tendency to be male-biased and runs the risk of reinforcing the prevailing level of discrimination which the state Civil Rights Act and title VII were designed to eliminate. In such a case, harassers could continue to discriminate merely because such harassment was the norm at the workplace. . . . We believe that the adoption of the reasonable person standard, coupled with the consideration of the level of "obscenity" that pervaded the workplace before and after plaintiff's arrival, strips the provisions of the state Civil Rights Act of their effect. In essence, the principles in *Rabidue* prevent the state Civil Rights Act from achieving its purpose of eliminating sexual harassment from the workplace and ensuring employees the right to work in an environment free from discriminatory intimidation, ridicule, and insult.
>
> Accordingly, we adopt the "reasonable woman" perspective. This standard, which ensures a gender-conscious review of sexual harassment, will help enable women to participate in the work force on an equal footing with men, and prevent the trivializing of the effects of sexual harassment that has previously occurred under the gender-neutral "reasonable person" standard. . . .
>
> By adopting a gender-conscious standard that views the harassment from the victim's perspective, it is important to analyze and understand the different perspectives of men and women. . . . For example, because of their historical vulnerability in the work force, women are more likely to regard a verbal or physical sexual encounter as a coercive and degrading reminder that the woman involved is viewed more as an object of sexual desire than as a credible coworker deserving of respect. Such treatment can prevent women from feeling, and others from perceiving them, as equal in the workplace.[324]

In *Harris v. Forklift Systems, Inc.*,[325] the U.S. Supreme Court held that challenged conduct need not affect an employee's psychological well-being to be actionable under Title VII. A court should consider the totality of the circumstances in determining whether an environment is sufficiently hostile or abusive.[326] In *Canada v. Boyd Group, Inc.*,[327] a female employee alleged that over a two or three week period, her supervisor engaged in conduct including: two incidents of telling "off-color" jokes from which the plaintiff walked away, comments on how good the plaintiff looked in her uniform, smiling and looking at the plaintiff a great deal, one incident in which the supervisor leaned or rubbed the front of his body on the back of the plaintiff's body and placed his hand on her shoulder, another incident in which he placed his hand on her shoulder, and one incident when he made a phone call to her home. Soon after these incidents, the plaintiff requested a shift change, and over the next five weeks,

---

324 *Id.* at 926–27.

325 114 S. Ct. 367 (1993).

326 *Id.* at 370–71.

327 Canada v. Boyd Group, Inc., 809 F. Supp. 771 (D. Nev. 1992).

their relationship was strained and she was eventually fired. The court held that the plaintiff stated a claim for hostile environment sexual harassment when the answer to the question of whether a reasonable women who had worked with the supervisor would consider his conduct severe and/or frequent enough to create an abusive working environment was not sufficiently clear to warrant a grant of summary judgment to the defendant. "[W]hile frequency and severity of conduct are important factors to consider when assessing whether a hostile environment was created, ultimately it is the effect or consequences of conduct on the working environment that must be evaluated."[328]

But in *Graham v. American Airlines,*[329] the plaintiff failed to show that the alleged harassment, which included instances of touching by coworkers, was sufficiently severe or persistent as to affect seriously her psychological well-being. The court also noted that there was conflicting evidence regarding the "plaintiff's wearing of 'suggestive' T-shirts, and engaging in 'shop talk' (i.e., using profanity)",[330] and thus failed to sustain her burden of proof on the issue:

> The Court wishes to make clear that it is viewing the totality of the circumstances. The wearing of a T-shirt with a "suggestive" phrase or picture on it or the use of profanity is not an invitation to sexual harassment. In the face of conflicting testimony, even assuming arguendo that certain instances of touching by co-workers may well have occurred and been unwelcome, plaintiff has not shown that the sexual harassment was sufficiently severe or persistent to affect seriously her psychological well-being.[331]

In addition, when the plaintiff made her claims of sexual harassment, her allegations were thoroughly investigated, and appropriate action was taken.

Although sexual harassment need not exist over a long period of time for it to be considered pervasive,[332] courts consider the frequency and/or intensity of the offensive encounters.[333] In *Waltman v. International Paper*

---

328 *Id.* at 776.

329 Graham v. American Airlines, 731 F. Supp. 1494 (N.D. Okla. 1989).

330 *Id.* at 1500.

331 *Id.* at 1502.

332 Stockly v. AT&T Info. Sys., 678 F. Supp. 764, 774 (E.D.N.Y. 1988) (a pattern of incidents occuring within a very short time—including stroking a female employee's hair, analogizing telephone sales to picking up women in bars, using the phrase "oh, baby," inviting women employees out for a drink, and shooting rubber bands at women—"could certainly fall within the definition of sexual harassment and Title VII, EEOC and case law").

See also Hirschfield v. New Mexico Corrections Dep't, 916 F.2d 572 (10th Cir. 1990). A female corrections employee alleged harassment by an inmate who observed her surreptitiously and wrote her an anonymous letter, and a high-level security guard who allegedly hugged and kissed her over the course of several days. The inmate was placed in administrative detention, and the guard was subsequently demoted from Captain to Lieutenant, but the New Mexico State Personnel Board ruled that the demotion was invalid and he was reinstated to the position of Captain. After filing a formal grievance, plaintiff became the subject of rumors and received several obscene phone calls. About four months after the original incident, she left work and was diagnosed as having tonsillitis and a bladder infection and started seeing a psychiatrist, who diagnosed her as clinically depressed. Six months later, she spent a brief period in a psychiatric hospital and subsequently filed a Title VII action. The trial court found that although the Captain's conduct in combination with the incident by the inmate constituted sexual harassment that gave rise to an intimidating and offensive work environment, the state corrections department was not liable for the harassment. The court of appeals affirmed, finding that liability was not appropriate when the alleged harasser was not acting within the scope of his employment in harassing the plaintiff, and the department took prompt, effective remedial action upon receiving complaints from the plaintiff. Nor were agency principles possible bases for a finding of liability when plaintiff presented no evidence suggesting that the alleged harasser had any supervisory authority over plaintiff's position whatsoever, or that he ever invoked the authority he had over his subordinate security guards to facilitate his harassment of the plaintiff.

Ross v. Double Diamond, Inc., 672 F. Supp. 261 (N.D. Tex. 1987) (offensive conduct over a two-day period of employment constituted a hostile environment).

333 Rabidue v. Osceola Refining Co., 805 F.2d 611, 620 (6th Cir. 1986), *cert. denied,* 481 U.S. 1041 (1987) ("Sexually hostile or intimidating environments are characterized by multiple and varied combinations and frequencies of offensive exposures").

Fifth Circuit: Ross v. Double Diamond, Inc., 672 F. Supp. 261 (N.D. Tex. 1987) (plaintiff was asked during her first hour of work whether she "fooled around," was told to pull up her dress for a photograph, was unknowingly photographed underneath her dress, and was repeatedly touched during a two-day period).

Seventh Circuit: Dombeck v. Milwaukee Valve Co., 823 F. Supp. 1475 (W.D. Wis. 1993). The jury could reasonably find that alleged sexual harassment, including allegations that the alleged harasser used sexual language, forcefully placed his foot in plaintiff's crotch and wiggled it, pulled the waistband on her pants and exposed her underpants on at least two occasions, and slapped her buttocks, created a hostile environment and that the employer knew or should have known of the harassment but did nothing to rectify the problem. An award of $25,000 in compensatory damages was proper but punitive damages in the amount of $75,000 were vacated as there was no basis for any such award. There was no evidence that the failure by the employer to adequately respond to complaints of harassment was due to callous disregard of the employee's rights; the employee generally was on good terms with her supervisors, including the alleged harasser, and there was no evidence of any ill will by the employer towards the plaintiff or women in general. Compensatory damages could be awarded retroactively under the Civil Rights Act of 1991 if this action commenced after the enactment of the Act based on conduct prior to its effective date, but an award of punitive damages could not retroactively apply to conduct committed prior to enactment, even when the action was commenced after the effective date of the Act.

Eighth Circuit: Schiele v. Charles Vogel Mfg. Co., 787 F. Supp. 1541 (D. Minn. 1992). A former employee established a *prima facie* case of hostile environment sexual harassment under Title VII, alleging that her employer repeatedly subjected her to unwelcome physical contact and verbal communications of an intimidating, abusive, and sexual nature, such as delivering her a note that read "chocolate chip cookies are great but my favorite is Pussy—I don't mean cats either." *Id.* at 1545 n.1. When she

Co.,[334] the Fifth Circuit found that a female employee's "evidence of individual acts of harassment coupled with evidence of sexual graffiti throughout the workplace could support a finding that the acts of harassment were sufficiently recurrent to create a continuously hostile environment," despite contentions that not all the incidents involved the same people and that too much time elapsed between the specific incidents of harassment to support a finding of a continuing violation. The court noted that the focus should be on whether the plaintiff was subjected to recurring acts of discrimination, not whether a given individual harassed the plaintiff, and that other courts, including the U.S. Supreme Court in *Meritor,* have heard sexual harassment claims involving separate incidents spanning many years without even mentioning the timeliness issue.

Sexual harassment will not be actionable for "every sexual innuendo or flirtation,"[335] every crude joke or sexually explicit remark made on the

---

complained about the conduct, her immediate supervisor suggested that she look for another job.

Caleshu v. Merrill Lynch, Pierce, Fenner & Smith, Inc., 737 F. Supp. 1070 (E.D. Mo. 1990), *aff'd without opinion,* 985 F.2d 564 (8th Cir. 1991). Plaintiff who alleged that over a five month span her supervisor kissed her on two occasions and touched her thigh twice, all outside defendant's offices, told plaintiff two off-color jokes, invited plaintiff to dinner once, required plaintiff to pick him up at the airport once, showed up at a bar while she was there and gave her a birthday card and gift, did not establish a hostile environment. Moreover, plaintiff did not complain of the conduct until almost five months after the harassment apparently commenced, and when she did complain, management took immediate action.

Ninth Circuit: Kalinauskas v. Wong, 808 F. Supp. 1469 (D. Nev. 1992). Plaintiff stated a claim of hostile environment sexual harassment when she alleged that beginning in 1987 and through 1989 she was sexually harassed by coworkers when they asked her out on dates and often made sexually offensive remarks, and when she rejected them, the coworkers retaliated by making several false and conflicting statements to the supervisors, that such retaliation resulted in the plaintiff being banned from working in the more prestigious high-roller pits, that she received an anonymous letter that stated that the employer was trying to make her job so miserable that she would quit, and as a result of the letter, she was constructively discharged and suffered an emotional breakdown. She also complained to several supervisors of the inappropriate behavior.

Tenth Circuit: Williams v. Kansas Gas & Elec. Co., 805 F. Supp. 890 (D. Kan. 1992). A female employee did not state a claim of hostile environment sexual harassment when she alleged that she found sexist and racist cartoons in her supervisor's desk drawer while performing work-related duties when she was not forced to view the cartoons.

334 Waltham v. International Paper Co., 875 F.2d 468 (5th Cir. 1989).

335 Ferguson v. E.I. du Pont de Nemours & Co., 560 F. Supp. 1172, 1197 (D. Del. 1983); Sand v. Johnson, 33 Fair Empl. Prac. Cas. (BNA) 716, 719 (E.D. Mich. 1982); Heelan v. Johns-Manville Corp., 451 F. Supp. 1382, 1388 (D. Colo. 1978) ("A cause of action does not arise from an isolated incident or mere flirtation").

job,[336] "trivial and merely annoying vulgarity,"[337] isolated incidents, and occasional use of offensive language as part of casual conversation,[338] sporadic conduct,[339] or "petty slights of the hypersensitive."[340] The presence

---

336 Downes v. Federal Aviation Admin., 775 F.2d 288, 293 (Fed. Cir. 1985). *See also* Moylan v. Maries County, 792 F.2d 746, 750 (8th Cir. 1986) (plaintiff must generally show that harassment was "sustained and nontrivial"); Keziah v. W.M. Brown & Son, 683 F. Supp. 542 (W.D.N.C. 1988), *modified,* 888 F.2d 322 (4th Cir. 1989) (two "boorish" comments about plaintiff's breast surgery scars and a sexual position in the course of two years and nine months did not overcome defendant's showing that the incidents were isolated or genuinely trivial).

337 Rabidue v. Osceola Refining Co., 584 F. Supp. 419, 433 (E.D. Mich. 1984), *aff'd,* 805 F.2d 611 (6th Cir. 1986), *cert. denied,* 481 U.S.1041 (1987).

338 Second Circuit: Snell v. Suffolk County, 782 F.2d 1094, 1103 (2d Cir. 1986); Barbetta v. Chemlawn Servs. Corp., 669 F. Supp. 569, 572 (W.D.N.Y. 1987); Christoforou v. Ryder Truck Rental, Inc., 668 F. Supp. 294, 301 (S.D.N.Y. 1987) (plaintiff had trouble coming up with more than three incidents over one-and-a-half years); Neville v. Taft Broadcasting Co., 42 Fair Empl. Prac. Cas. (BNA) 1314, 1317 (W.D.N.Y. 1987) ("Plaintiff was not subject to repeated sexual demands, unwanted sexual contact, or insulting sexual comments" after an incident involving one kiss and a comment that plaintiff would go far in the company if she did everything right; the kiss and comment did establish a *prima facie* case of *quid pro quo* harassment.).

Third Circuit: Petrosky v. Washington-Greene County Ass'n for the Blind, 663 F. Supp. 821 (W.D. Pa. 1987) (one kissing incident alone with inappropriate use of endearing terms did not automatically establish sexual harassment).

Seventh Circuit: Scott v. Sears, Roebuck & Co., 605 F. Supp. 1047 (N.D. Ill. 1985), *aff'd,* 798 F.2d 210, 213 n.2 (7th Cir. 1986) ("Title VII is not a clean language act, and it does not require employers to extirpate all signs of centuries-old prejudices," quoting Katz v. Dole, 709 F.2d 251, 256 (4th Cir. 1983)); Saxton v. American Tel. & Tel. Co., 785 F. Supp. 760 (N.D. Ill. 1992). An employee failed to state a claim for hostile environment sexual harassment when alleged conduct consisted of sexual advances by a supervisor at a jazz club after work one evening, and on another day, after having lunch together, the supervisor drove to a park and lurched at plaintiff from behind some bushes. After that incident, the supervisor did not harass her sexually, but undermined her ability to get work done by not speaking with her, cancelling meetings, and teasing her about her relationship with another coworker. The plaintiff admitted that the supervisor was very busy and cancelled meetings with other employees also. The court deemed it significant that the two parties were at one time friends.

Volk v. Coler, 638 F. Supp. 1555, 1558–59 (C.D. Ill. 1986), *aff'd in part, rev'd in part,* 845 F.2d 1422 (7th Cir. 1988).

339 Trotta v. Mobile Oil Corp., 788 F. Supp. 1336 (S.D.N.Y. 1992). A former employee who alleged that defendant corporation allowed sexually offensive conduct at mandatory business meetings and related social functions and that such conduct included the presence of female strippers and women clad in leather astride motorcycles, sexually suggestive gifts, and the projection of a slide of her backside at a company outing and that such conduct caused her to leave the company, failed to show that conditions of her employment were altered, that she was subjected to a hostile work environment, or that the alleged incidents were sufficiently severe or pervasive to create a hostile work environment.

340 Zabkowicz v. West Bend Co., 589 F. Supp. 780, 784 (E.D. Wis. 1984).

of sexual tension alone will not suffice without a showing of its severity.[341] Evidence must demonstrate that hostility is sex-based and does not stem from competitiveness.[342] Evidence of the harassment of other women employees may, on the other hand, bolster a finding of pervasiveness.[343]

Unless the harassment is so pervasive that the employer's awareness may be inferred, notice to the employer is required.[344] Although *Meritor* held that the absence of notice "does not necessarily insulate the employer from liability,"[345] failure to report incidents of abuse for a significant

---

Pacheco v. Hercules, Inc., 61 Fair Empl. Prac. Cas. (BNA) 825 (D. Utah 1993) (Greene, J.). A male former employee could not pursue a claim for intentional infliction of emotional distress against the employer despite the supervisor's alleged reckless and wanton conduct in failing to control a female coworker's allegedly offensive sexual language and conduct when plaintiff's response to the conduct was, according to one of plaintiff's treating psychiatrists, "excessive and unusual . . . to a situation which generally would be handled by most individuals without such an intense reaction." *Id.* at 827–28. Moreover, undisputed facts supported the conclusion that plaintiff's injuries were not reasonably foreseeable and that defendant employer had no knowledge of plaintiff's propensity for such an injury.

Hanson v. American Express, 53 Fair Emp. Prac. Cas. (BNA) 1193 (D. Utah 1986). While sexual invitations may be made subtly, social invitation cannot serve as the sole basis for finding that sexual harassment occurred.

341 Christoforou v. Ryder Truck Rental, Inc., 668 F. Supp. 294, 300 (S.D.N.Y. 1987).

342 Murray v. Wal-Mart Stores, 61 Fair Empl. Prac. Cas. (BNA) 850 (D. Kan. 1993). A female former employee did not state claim for hostile environment sexual harassment when she was replaced by another woman. "If the males at Hypermart were determined to drive plaintiff out so that [a woman] could take her position, they were motivated by a bias against plaintiff personally, not against plaintiff as a woman." *Id.* at 854. Moreover, evidence did not demonstrate that conditions were so severe or pervasive that they created an abusive working environment. The environment was competitive, but not sexually hostile; there were no incidents of physical touching, sexual innuendo, sexual pressure, or sexually derogatory language.

343 Katz v. Dole, 709 F.2d 251 (4th Cir. 1983); Broderick v. Ruder, 685 F. Supp. 1269 (D.D.C. 1988); Delgado v. Lehman, 665 F. Supp. 460, 468 (E.D. Va. 1987) (plaintiff established that harassment was not isolated or trivial by showing, among other things, that employer harassed other individuals).

Cf. Grier v. Casey, 643 F. Supp. 298 (W.D.N.C. 1986) (allegations that other women were harassed were unsupported); Hanson v. American Express, 53 Fair Emp. Prac. Cas. (BNA) 1193 (D. Utah 1986). Although plaintiff alleged that several other female employees had been sexually harassed by a supervisor, this allegation carried little weight when she introduced no evidence other than her own affidavit to support her assertion and in fact the record demonstrated that two of those women testified that they had not been sexually harassed.

344 Bohen v. City of E. Chicago, 799 F.2d 1180, 1187 (7th Cir. 1986) (no response to notice of harassment by employee); Busse v. Gelco Express Corp., 678 F. Supp. 1398, 1399 (E.D. Wis. 1988).

345 Meritor Sav. Bank v. Vinson, 477 U.S. 57, 72 (1986).

Ninth Circuit: Nichols v. Frank, 732 F. Supp. 1085 (D. Or. 1990). Hearing-impaired postal worker employee who alleged that her supervisor repeatedly required her to go

period of time may support a finding that the alleged harassment was not offensive to the plaintiff.[346] Even when harassment is deemed pervasive enough to give constructive notice to the employer, courts have examined

---

from the work floor to a private locked office where he forced her to perform sexual acts stated claims for *quid pro quo* and hostile environment sexual harassment. The court rejected defendant's contention that the action should be dismissed because plaintiff failed to allege that the Postal Service knew or should have known of alleged harassment when in her complaint, plaintiff alleged that her supervisor had authority to give her permission to take leave and he generally directed her work:

> The cases regarding hostile environment harassment generally treat the issue of employer liability as a question of fact and emphasize that various circumstances may be considered in determining employer liability, such as the duties and authority of the supervisor, and the existence and efficacy of anti-discrimination policies and grievance procedures. . . .

Id. at 1090. Moreover, plaintiff's allegations supported a claim for *quid pro quo* harassment as well so that even if the Ninth Circuit would not impose strict liability in context of hostile environment harassment, the action would stand.

346 Second Circuit: Christoforou v. Ryder Truck Rental, Inc., 668 F. Supp. 294, 300 (S.D.N.Y. 1987) (plaintiff told no one of alleged harassment and one woman testified that she had previously agreed to fabricate testimony about defendant's misconduct, and plaintiff never told her about the alleged incidents); Neville v. Taft Broadcasting Co., 42 Fair Empl. Prac. Cas. (BNA) 1314 (W.D.N.Y. 1987) (female employee's failure to report alleged sexual advances, apart from one kiss, to management or to include them in her EEOC charge indicated either that the incidents did not occur or that plaintiff did not consider them to be significant enough to mention until after the lawsuit was filed).

Third Circuit: Raley v. Board of St. Mary's County Comm'rs, 752 F. Supp. 1272 (D. Md. 1990) (plaintiff alleged only two isolated incidents of touching and two incidents of sexual innuendos during relevant time period); Monroe-Lord v. Hytche, 668 F. Supp. 979, 986 (D. Md. 1987), *aff'd,* 854 F.2d 1317 (4th Cir. 1988) Plaintiff who had never complained about sexual harassment during seven years of employment, never filed a grievance, offered apparently altered handwritten copies of her charge with the Commission on Human Relations, and continued to meet with the alleged harasser alone, could not bring an untimely claim of sexual harassment. The failure to raise the allegation of sexual harassment in either her administrative charge or civil complaint negated "her self-serving testimony that she did not complain of the harassment because she feared reprisal."

Fourth Circuit: Slate v. Kingsdown, 46 Fair Empl. Prac. Cas. (BNA) 1495 (M.D.N.C. 1987) (although plaintiff did complain to coworker, she never lodged a complaint concerning two incidents in which her immediate supervisor grabbed her by the shoulders and neck; the alleged harassment was not so pervasive that defendant's awareness could be inferred).

Sixth Circuit: Highlander v. K.F.C. Nat'l Mgmt. Co., 805 F.2d 644, 650 (6th Cir. 1986) (plaintiff's failure to report alleged episode of sexual harassment for three months, coupled with her husband's characterization of the incident as having been made in jest, indicated that she was not offended in any significant way by asserted incidents); Hollis v. Fleetguard, Inc., 668 F. Supp. 631, 635 (M.D. Tenn. 1987) (plaintiff who only informed management of alleged sexual harassment after a work counseling session regarding her poor job performance did not demonstrate the existence of a hostile work environment).

whether the plaintiff complained about the offensive conduct.[347] Such complaints serve to reinforce even the strong hostile environment claim.

Eighth Circuit: Parton v. GTE N., Inc., 971 F.2d 150 (8th Cir. 1992). A female who worked in the installation and repair department of GTE brought an action charging discriminatory discharge and sexual harassment, alleging that her department was hostile to women employees. Evidence of such harassment included sexually suggestive gestures and comments, posting and distributing lewd cartoons, and assigning undesirable work to plaintiff and other women when available male employees were not so assigned. The incidents occurred over the course of years, but plaintiff never filed a sexual harassment complaint while she was an employee or made such allegations to union officials or at the union grievance hearing preceding her discharge. Evidence also showed that plaintiff had a record of poor performance, and the lower court concluded that the employer's legitimate reasons for Parton's discharge were not proven to be pretextual by a preponderance of the evidence. The court of appeals rejected plaintiff's contention that this was a mixed motive case and that the trial court could not find that she was subjected to a sexually hostile environment, as it did, without also concluding that Parton's gender was a factor in her termination. There was no direct evidence that GTE was motivated to terminate the plaintiff for gender-based reasons, and thus this was not a mixed-motive case.

Eighth Circuit: Caleshu v. Merrill Lynch, Pierce, Fenner & Smith, Inc., 737 F. Supp. 1070 (E.D. Mo. 1990), *aff'd without opinion,* 985 F.2d 564 (8th Cir. 1991); Walter v. KFGO Radio, 518 F. Supp. 1309 (D.N.D. 1981).

347 Ross v. Double Diamond, Inc., 672 F. Supp. 261 (N.D. Tex. 1987).

Fourth Circuit: Llewellyn v. Celanese Corp., 693 F. Supp. 369 (W.D.N.C. 1988).

Sixth Circuit: Kirkland v. Brinias,741 F. Supp. 692 (E.D. Tenn. 1989), *aff'd without opinion,* 944 F.2d 905 (6th Cir. 1991). Plaintiff waitresses alleged that a busboy created a hostile environment by offering money for sex, threats, pats on the rear end, hugs, arm grabbing, hostile pranks, and other conduct. Sexual harassment was not found despite corroboration by other former employees of plaintiffs' accounts and other evidence of coworker misconduct that would create a hostile and intimidating working environment when the court determined that there was no showing that the conduct had any harmful psychological effect on waitresses, the waitresses were well able to handle alleged harassment and would not have hesitated to ask management for help if needed, and there was no preponderance of evidence regarding whether management recognized or should have recognized that any of their employees were offended by the conduct. Although the court acknowledged that plaintiffs failed to expressly complain of sexual harassment because neither believed that defendants would be sympathetic, the court gave weight to testimony of an assistant manager establishing that "much of the difficulty experienced by the waitresses . . . was a matter of cultural misunderstandings," *id.* at 695 and of the busboy defendant himself, who "emphatically and emotionally denied ever improperly touching any woman." *Id.* The court concluded that plaintiffs quit their jobs because they felt that their employers were unwilling to listen to their side of an issue when they felt unjustly accused of something, rather than because of any overtly sexual conduct:

> In fact, plaintiff Kirkland wrote defendant Brinias a twelve-page letter after her resignation in which she catalogued her many grievances against her former employers. These included lack of vacation pay, lack of maternity leave, false accusations, etc., but did not mention sexual harassment. In fact, the evidence was overwhelming that both plaintiffs were well able to handle the situation; that they were both capable, outspoken women; and that, if they had needed help from the management, they would not have hesitated to ask for it.

Whether the alleged harassment is adequately pervasive or severe is a circumstantial assessment made according to an objective standard involving a reasonable woman's reaction to a similar environment, rather than the feelings of a given plaintiff.[348] Most situations in which courts have found a hostile environment in violation of Title VII have involved repeated abuse and clear hostility toward women.[349] This conduct "need not take the form of overt sexual advances or suggestions, but may consist of such things as verbal abuse of women if it is sufficiently patterned to compose a condition and is apparently caused by the sex of the harassed

---

Id. at 698.

Eighth Circuit: Morris v. American Nat'l Can Corp., 730 F. Supp. 1489 (E.D. Mo. 1989), *modified,* 941 F.2d 710 (8th Cir. 1991). Although plaintiff reported almost each incident of harassment to her supervisor, and asked him to do something to stop their occurrence, the supervisor characterized some of the materials received by plaintiff as "sickening", but did not consider any of the incidents as sexual harassment or as anything more than "horseplay" and "pranks" to which a number of employees were subjected. Occasionally during his weekly staff meetings, he would mention that horseplay would not be tolerated. Once or twice he mentioned to his supervisor, who also allegedly harassed plaintiff, that there was conflict among department employees, and on occasion, he would advise the manager of the human relations department of problems with pranks in the department.

348 Vermett v. Hough, 627 F. Supp. 587, 605 (W.D. Mich. 1986).

Ninth Circuit: Ellison v. Brady, 924 F.2d 872 (9th Cir. 1991) (applying the reasonable woman standard).

Eleventh Circuit: Robinson v. Jacksonville Shipyards, Inc., 760 F. Supp. 1486 (M.D. Fla. 1991); Scheider v. NBC News Bureaus, 56 Fair Emp. Prac. Cas. (BNA) 1602 (S.D. Fla. 1991). A reasonable woman would not find offensive two tourism posters of women in bikinis and wet T-shirts, one hanging in a supervisor's office and the other outside a female employee's office. "The display of female anatomy is far more revealing and suggestive in advertisements in the media than in either of these posters." *Id.* at 1609.

See § **3.17.**

349 Supreme Court: Meritor Sav. Bank v. Vinson, 477 U.S. 57 (1986) (repeated sexual demands, intercourse 40–50 times, indecent exposure).

First Circuit: Egger v. Local 276, Plumbers & Pipefitters Union, 644 F. Supp. 795, 797 (D. Mass. 1986) (threats, comments about plaintiff's chest size and sex life, demeaning pranks, graphic descriptions of male employees' sex lives to plaintiff, showing plaintiff pornographic books, and asking her to participate in a sexually explicit home video).

Second Circuit: Kotcher v. Rosa & Sullivan Appliance, 957 F.2d 59 (2d Cir. 1992) (manager who regularly commented that his sales would be more substantial if he had the same bodily "equipment" as the female employee plaintiff and who often pretended to masturbate and ejaculate at her behind her back created a hostile work environment); Danna v. New York Tel. Co., 752 F. Supp. 594 (S.D.N.Y. 1990). Plaintiff telephone company employee proved that she was subjected to a hostile work environment in violation of Title VII. The plaintiff, a service technician in a male-dominated realm, complained of "incidents that were overtly sexual in nature at the Telco work place" *Id.* at

608: (1) in response to a question regarding where she could find a certain key, a supervisor allegedly informed her that what she needed was "a good fuck in the ass". *Id.* (2) lewd graffiti directed specifically at Danna were scribbled on the walls of the terminal rooms in JFK airport used by Telco's employees, including "Fran Danna you ungrateful cunt you suck", "Sit on Danna's face", depicting a picture of a face with a penis in the mouth, and "Just when you thought it was safe to go into the airport again . . . Fran Danna II", showing an act of anal sex. *Id.* at 608. This graffiti was on the terminal walls for at least two years. Although plaintiff admitted that she also had written graffiti on the terminal walls, she only did so in response to graffiti written about her and never wrote derogatory remarks or used profanity. Although plaintiff's supervisors were aware of the graffiti, and with the exception of one incident when an employee was authorized to spray paint over certain graffiti directed at Danna, they did nothing to have it removed. The plaintiff was allegedly told that the supervisor did not think he could do very much about it, and she would be better off not making a stink about it because coworkers would do it even more.

Berkman v. City of N.Y., 580 F. Supp. 226, 230–32, 240 (E.D.N.Y. 1983), *aff'd,* 755 F.2d 913 (2d Cir. 1985) (constant hazing of women firefighters by other male employees, graffiti and cartoons sexually mocking plaintiffs, placing sexual devices in plaintiff's bed, stealing plaintiffs' work instruments, breaking their equipment, touching of breasts, waist, buttocks and hair, and exclusion of women from meals).

Third Circuit: Atwood v. Biondi Mitsubishi, 61 Fair Empl. Prac. Cas. (BNA) 1357 (W.D. Pa. 1993). The plaintiff stated a claim for sexual harassment when she alleged that she had been subjected to almost daily harassment during her six weeks of employment. It was apparent by the record that significant questions of fact existed with respect to the five elements necessary for a hostile environment claim.

Fourth Circuit: Llewellyn v. Celanese Corp., 693 F. Supp. 369 (W.D.N.C. 1988); Delgado v. Lehman, 665 F. Supp. 460 (E.D. Va. 1987).

Fifth Circuit: Ross v. Double Diamond, Inc., 672 F. Supp. 261 (N.D. Tex. 1987).

Seventh Circuit: Bohen v. City of E. Chicago, 799 F.2d 1180, 1183 (7th Cir. 1986) (supervisors subjected plaintiff to lewd language, forced her to listen to their sexual fantasies of which she was the object, rubbed themselves against her rear when she stood, forced her to leave the bathroom door open when she used it, and responded to her "cool reception to their constant invitations to engage in deviate sexual conduct" as "evidence of lesbian tendencies"); Moffett v. Gene B. Glick Co., 621 F. Supp. 244, 270 (N.D. Ind. 1985) ("Regular, almost daily exposure to terms such as 'stupid cunt,' 'whore,' 'bitch' and 'nigger lover' over the course of six to seven months").

Eighth Circuit: Morris v. American Nat. Can Corp., 730 F. Supp. 1489 (E.D. Mo. 1989), *modified,* 941 F.2d 710 (8th Cir. 1991). The sexual harassment of a machinist by her manager and his supervisor included the following unwelcome conduct: asking whether she "got any", did she "spit or swallow", moving plaintiff's head while stating that she "might as well sit underneath his desk since that's where everybody says you do your best work", touching plaintiff's buttocks, leaving objects at or near her work station such as a sausage with a note stating "bite me baby", a clay replica of a penis with steel wool testicles and a semen-like substance on it, a welded figure of a man with a penis, a pair of women's underwear with a sanitary napkin having a reddish substance on it and a note saying "Jackie you lost this", a pile of substance described as semen-like, a picture of an erect penis, and "Playboy" type pictures. Harassment conducted after filing an administrative charge included the words "bitch" and "slut" written on her desk, a large replica of an erect penis and a note saying "Hey Jake [sic]— Heard ya got one in your pants the same size. I never knew, think we could get together. Your Lesbian

Friend", the words "Jackie blows heads" written on a shelf, a picture of a nude woman sitting on the edge of a bathtub and touching her breasts with a note stating "You should be doing this instead of a man's job," a sign on the department bulletin board reading "Jackie—Attention! Because of the outbreak of A.I.D.S. you are no longer required to kiss the boss's ass", and a cartoon on a bulletin board of five men with handwritten words "Jackie," "suck me asshole," and "full of shit". In addition, plaintiff's equipment was sabotaged: the wires to her radio were cut, black grease was placed in her welding helmet, the fan at her work station was damaged, her roller cabinet was "locktighted", which required breaking and replacing the cabinet's lock to fix it, the cabinet was subsequently dented, someone put a substance smelling like urine in her air line, a semen-like substance was placed in her toolbox, some tools were stolen, and subsequently plaintiff found a note at her work station stating "Mold shop missing tool relief fund & tax deduction (1986 only)" and a tin can having only one cent in it. *Id.* at 1491.

Hall v. Gus Constr. Co., 842 F.2d 1010 (8th Cir. 1988); Jones v. Wesco, 846 F.2d 1154 (8th Cir. 1988); Moylan v. Maries County, 792 F.2d 746 (8th Cir. 1986) (rape).

Ninth Circuit: Dias v. Sky Chefs, 919 F.2d 1370 (9th Cir. 1990), *vacated on other grounds,* 111 S. Ct. 2791, *on remand,* 948 F.2d 532 (9th Cir. 1991), *cert. denied,* 112 S. Ct. 1294 (1992). Sexual harassment by the general manager of defendant corporation allegedly took the form of daily comments about the breasts, buttocks, and physical appearance of individual female employees, suggestions to women that they show him a good time and treat him as well as the women employees in the office from which he had been transferred, and staff meetings at which he established job standards for women that included wearing dresses or skirts, and nylons and heels specifically so that he could admire women employees' legs.

EEOC v. Hacienda Hotel, 881 F.2d 1504 (9th Cir.1989) Female housekeepers were subjected to severe and pervasive sexual harassment when the chief of engineering and the executive housekeeper (a woman) repeatedly subjected employees to sexual harassment, including crude and disparaging remarks to a pregnant women, such as saying "that's what you get for sleeping without your underwear", asking why she was pregnant by another man and making comments about her "ass." The executive housekeeper told one pregnant employee that she did not like "stupid women who have kids" and on many occasions called her "dog", "whore", or "slut." *Id.* at 1507. The chief of engineering told another pregnant employee that women "get pregnant because they like to suck men's dicks", threatened to have her fired if she did not submit to his sexual advances, and stated that the employee had "such a fine ass. It's a nice ass to stick a nice dick into. How many dicks have you eaten?" *Id.* at 1508. There was no dispute that the challenged acts occurred, and that they were unwelcome. The district court found that defendant could be held liable for the supervisors' actions; the general manager of the Hacienda had actual knowledge of allegations of harassment and that defendant should have known of the harassment because it was severe, pervasive, and "seriously tainted" the complainants' working environment. The court rejected defendant's contention that complainants failed to pursue internal remedies under appellant's general nondiscrimination policy when employer's policy did not specifically proscribe sexual harassment, and its internal procedures required initial resort to a supervisor who was accused of engaging in or condoning the harassment of which the employees complained.

Tenth Circuit: Hansel v. Public Service Co., 778 F. Supp. 1126 (D. Colo. 1991). Merely discussing the matter of sexual harassment with four of the perpetrators was insufficient to halt sexual harassment of female machine operators by male coworkers at a power plant over an eight year period. The alleged harassment included fondling genitals, grabbing breasts and buttocks, filling workgloves with bathroom cleaner, male employees entering the women's room while plaintiff was using it, degrading comments, and sexually explicit graffiti throughout the plant, some of it explicitly directed at plaintiff. Although the physical harassment ceased, other forms continued:

> [N]ot every response by an employer will be sufficient to discharge its legal duty. The response must be reasonable under the totality of the circumstances. What is appropriate remedial action necessarily depends on the particular facts of each case with focus upon the severity and persistence of the harassment and the effectiveness of any initial remedial steps. . . .
>
> Here, because the overt, physical harassment stopped, PSC argues it took appropriate remedial action in 1983 when it merely discussed Hansel's allegations with four of her co-workers. PSC misconstrues the nature of the remedial action required of it by Title VII under the circumstances of this case.
>
> A hostile environment is like a disease. It can have many symptoms, some of which change over time, but all of which stem from the same root. The etiology in this case is pure gender bias.
>
> PSC may have attempted treatment of one symptom of the hostile environment, the physical abuse, but it failed completely to remedy the disease of hostile work environment. Moreover, the sexual harassment here was so egregious that merely "discussing" the matter with four of the perpetrators cannot reasonably be calculated to halt the harassment. Indeed, the hostile environment continued unabated after 1983.

Id. at 1132.

Eleventh Circuit: Huddleston v. Roger Dean Chevrolet, Inc., 845 F.2d 900 (11th Cir. 1988); Henson v. City of Dundee, 682 F.2d 897 (11th Cir. 1982).

District of Columbia Circuit: Bundy v. Jackson, 641 F.2d 934 (D.C. Cir. 1981).

A hostile environment was not found in the following cases, despite the existence of repeated advances or other sexual conduct:

First Circuit: Hallquist v. Max Fish Plumbing & Heating Co., 46 Fair Empl. Prac. Cas. (BNA) 1855, 1860 (D. Mass. 1987) (fact that plaintiff plumber was the subject of gender-related jokes and occasional teasing was relevant to the question of whether defendant's explanation for her termination was credible, but it alone was insufficient to establish a hostile environment claim; in addition to the jokes, plaintiff was closely supervised and "babied" "in a manner that demeaned her demonstrable plumbing skills," and after she was laid off, the employer "continued to maintain, and add to, his plumbing force.").

Sixth Circuit: Kirkland v. Brinias, 741 F. Supp. 692 (E.D. Tenn. 1989), *aff'd without opinion,* 944 F.2d 905 (6th Cir. 1991). Although the court concluded that there was "no question that the plaintiffs . . . were subjected to sexual harassment on the job", *Id.* at 698, the owners of a restaurant were not liable for the harassment of two waitresses by a busboy, when despite the court's acknowledgment that some of the misconduct, which included offering money for sex, touching of the buttocks, whispering desire to have sex, snapping of bras and assaultive behavior, "would create a hostile and intimidating working environment for a reasonable person under those circumstances," there was "no hint that it had any harmful psychological effect on the plaintiffs." *Id.*, both plaintiffs quit their jobs because they felt that their employers were unwilling to listen to their side of an issue when they felt unjustly accused of something rather than as a direct result of any overtly sexual conduct. The court noted that the evidence was "overwhelming" that both plaintiffs "were well able to handle the situations; that they were both capable, outspoken women; and that, if they had needed help from the management, they would have not have hesitated to ask for it." *Id.* Evidence that defendant employers recognized, or should have recognized, that any of their employees found the busboy's conduct sexually offensive did not preponderate in favor of plaintiffs.

Seventh Circuit: Scott v. Sears, Roebuck & Co., 605 F. Supp. 1047 (N.D. Ill. 1985), *aff'd,* 798 F.2d 210 (7th Cir. 1986) (requests for rubdowns, invitations to go for drinks after job hours, sexual propositions, obscene comments, winking, and being slapped on the buttocks did not constitute illegal harassment).

Eighth Circuit: Morris v. American Nat'l Can Corp., 730 F. Supp. 1489 (E.D. Mo. 1989), *modified on other grounds*, 941 F.2d 710 (8th Cir. 1991). A supervisor was not liable for sexual harassment for making several comments about plaintiff's "nice ass" and saying that "he'd like to have a piece of that" and for touching plaintiff's buttocks on occasion, even though defendant's denials were not clearly credible because other employees testified to seeing such conduct. *Id.* at 1490.

Ninth Circuit: Intlekofer v. Turnage, 973 F.2d 773 (9th Cir. 1992). The United States Veterans Administration (VA) did not take prompt and appropriate remedial action in response to continued complaints by a female employee of sexual harassment by a coworker when it failed to take more severe disciplinary action against the alleged harasser after learning that the harassment had not stopped. Although the VA had investigated plaintiff's complaints regarding inappropriate touching, suggestions, threats, and drawing of a dildo on plaintiff's locker, and held continuous counseling sessions with the alleged harasser, it was apparent that these measures were ineffective. Under *Ellison v. Brady,* 924 F.2d 872 (9th Cir. 1991), an employer must take some form of disciplinary action if it knows or should know of the harassment:

> Of course, I acknowledge that "discipline" can take many forms, and I do not attempt to confine the employer to options specifically mentioned in this opinion. The important point is that the appropriateness of the remedy depends on the seriousness of the offense, the employer's ability to stop the harassment, the likelihood that the remedy will end the harassment, and "the remedy's ability to persuade potential harassers to refrain from unlawful conduct." [*Ellison,* 924 F.2d at 882]
>
> Intlekofer argues that counseling can never be considered "disciplinary," and that therefore the VA failed to satisfy its duty under *Ellison.* Although *Ellison* stated that "Title VII requires more than a mere request to refrain from the discriminatory conduct," counseling sessions are not necessarily insufficient. [Id.] Indeed, an oral rebuke may be very effective in stopping the unlawful conduct. At the first sign of sexual harassment, an oral warning in the context of a counseling session may be an appropriate disciplinary measure if the employer expresses strong disapproval, demands that the unwelcome conduct cease, and threatens more severe disciplinary action in the event that the conduct does not cease. I approve of the remedy in a case such as this where the harassing conduct is not extremely serious and the employer cannot elicit a detailed description concerning the occurrence from the victim. I stress, however, that counseling is sufficient only as a first resort. If the harassment continues, limiting discipline to further counseling is inappropriate. Instead, the employer must impose more severe measures in order to ensure that the behavior terminates. Again, the extent of the discipline depends on the seriousness of the conduct.

Id. at 779.

employee."[350] In *Robinson v. Jacksonville Shipyards, Inc.*,[351] the court concluded that the posting of pinups of nude and partially nude women, sexually demeaning remarks, and general harassment created a hostile working environment. The court noted that the causation requirement—that a plaintiff must show that but for the fact of her sex, she would not have been the object of harassment—encompasses several types of claims: (1) harassing behavior lacking a sexually explicit content but directed at women and motivated by animus against women, (2) sexual behavior directed at women, and (3) behavior that is not directed at a particular individual or group of individuals, but is disproportionately more offensive or demeaning to one sex. In this case, a female welder experienced all three types of behavior from coworkers; she was subjected to nonsexual verbal abuse and to harassment such as the posting of a "Men Only" sign, she suffered incidents of directed sexual behavior both before and after she lodged her complaints about the pinups, and the pinups themselves constituted behavior that did not originate with the intent of offending women in the workplace, as there were no women in this workplace when the behavior began, but clearly had a disproportionate demeaning impact on the women now working at the shipyard.

§ 6.45 Prima Facie Retaliation Case

Similar to whistle-blowing statutes, Title VII protects persons from retaliation by employers because they attempted to or did exercise their rights to obtain redress for an alleged violation of Title VII. Retaliation claims are prevalent in Title VII sexual harassment actions. It may be asserted by sexual harassment victims and by employees who were offended by the sexual harassment of others and complained or advised those harassed to

---

[350] Delgado v. Lehman, 665 F. Supp. 460, 468 (E.D. Va. 1987). *See also* McKinney v. Dole, 765 F.2d 1129, 1138 (D.C. Cir. 1985).

Cf. Pagana-Fay v. Washington Suburban Sanitary Comm'n, 797 F. Supp. 462 (D. Md. 1992). A discharged female employee failed to prove by a preponderance of the evidence that she was subjected to sexual harassment by one or more of her supervisors when several incidents of offensive language and one incident during which a coworker fondled his own genitals in plaintiff's presence did not constitute sexual harassment as defined by *Meritor*. "Rather than being intimidated, [the plaintiff] was the one who sought to gain her way with male coworkers and superiors by constant threats that she would file internal complaints, charges of discrimination with the EEOC, or lawsuits if the others crossed her in any significant way." *Id.* at 470. A jury verdict for plaintiff and damages in the amount of $50,000 for sexual harassment were vacated upon defendant's motion for judgment notwithstanding the verdict.

[351] Robinson v. Jacksonville Shipyards, Inc., 760 F. Supp. 1486 (M.D. Fla. 1991).

assert their legal rights.[352] Title VII protects two general types of activities: opposition and participation. Opposition is protected by the clause that prohibits employers from discriminating against an employee who opposed an employment practice made unlawful by Title VII. The participation clause prohibits discrimination against the employee who has made a charge, testified, assisted, or participated in any manner in an investigation, proceeding, or hearing under Title VII.

Termination is the most common type of retaliatory conduct, but it also can include employment practices such as demotion, transfer, or increased harassment. A lateral transfer may constitute retaliatory conduct even if it was not accompanied by a pay reduction or loss of benefits.[353]

---

352 Kotcher v. Rosa & Sullivan Appliance, 957 F.2d 59 (2d Cir. 1992). A sexual harassment case was remanded to consider whether plaintiff had been subjected to retaliation after complaining to management. Although plaintiff never used the word "retaliation", she alleged that she was fired soon after she complained about harassment by her supervisor:

> It might be argued that Kotcher's allegations do not establish a conventional retaliation claim, where the protected activity usually takes the form of filing a formal complaint with an agency or filing a lawsuit . . . .
>
> In this case, Kotcher had not filed a formal agency complaint before she was fired, but did make an internal complaint to company management, protesting the sexually harassing actions of their supervisor. Surely this opposition to the unlawful practice of sexual harassment is protected activity within the policies of Title VII . . . .

Id. at 65.

Wilson v. UT Health Ctr., 973 F.2d 1263 (5th Cir. 1992), *cert. denied,* 113 S. Ct. 1644 (1993) (§ 1983). The district court improperly dismissed a female former campus police officer's First Amendment claim, charging that her right to free speech was violated in retaliation for her speech about sexual harassment by fellow police officers, on the grounds that her speech concerned a matter of insufficient public concern to merit constitutional protection when the content of her speech was of great public concern. The court rejected the lower court's conclusion that plaintiff made the written reports as an employee rather than as a citizen because she acknowledged some duty as a police officer to report sexual harassment, when she made the reports as a citizen and a police officer, started them after personally experiencing considerable harassment at work, and had a stake as a citizen in stopping the conduct. If a jury found that plaintiff acted in good faith in reporting sexual harassment, the university's interest in maintaining a police force free of sexual intimidation would outweigh any interest in departmental efficiency and harmony.

Castillo Morales v. Best Fin. Co., 652 F. Supp. 412 (D.P.R.), *aff'd,* 831 F.2d 280 (1st Cir. 1987) (no prima facie case established when pleadings did not state how, when, or if employer gained knowledge that the victim of sexual harassment complained because of her coworker's advice); Jenkins v. Orkin Exterminating Co., 646 F. Supp. 1274 (E.D. Tex. 1986).

353 Collins v. State of Ill., 830 F.2d 692 (7th Cir. 1987).

Warren v. K Mart Corp., 61 Fair Empl. Prac. Cas. (BNA) 1364 (D. Kan. 1993). An employee's transfer after she filed a sexual harassment charge against her former manager was not retaliation when the transfer was not a demotion, did not involve loss of

To establish a prima facie case of retaliation, an employee must demonstrate that:

1. The plaintiff engaged in an activity protected by Title VII.
2. The exercise of civil rights was known by the defendant.
3. The defendant took an employment action adverse to the plaintiff.
4. There was a causal connection between the protected activity and the adverse employment action.[354]

As in the case of disparate treatment, the plaintiff meets her initial burden by establishing facts sufficient to permit an inference of retaliatory motive. Circumstantial evidence may be offered to prove such a motive.[355]

---

income, and was intended to get plaintiff off a career track because she did not want to relocate or advance. A reduction in a performance rating reflected a change in evaluation methods, not poor performance. There was no persuasive evidence that the manager called her a troublemaker and that the way to get her to quit was to "piss her off." *Id.* at 1365.

354 Hollis v. Fleetguard, Inc., 668 F. Supp. 631, 637–38 (M.D. Tenn. 1987). *See also* Haehn v. City of Hoisington, 702 F. Supp. 1526 (D. Kan. 1988) (plaintiff presented a prima facie case of retaliation for summary judgment proceedings when the temporal proximity between plaintiff's discharge and her sexual harassment complaints sustained an inference of a retaliatory motive); Wrenn v. Gould, 808 F.2d 493, 500 (6th Cir. 1987); Jenkins v. Orkin Exterminating Co., 646 F. Supp. 1274, 1277 (E.D. Tex. 1986).

355 Sahs v. Amarillo Equity Investors, 702 F. Supp. 256 (D. Colo. 1988) (sexual harassment).

Hawkins v. Hennepin Tech. Ctr., 900 F.2d 153 (8th Cir. 1990), *cert. denied,* 111 S. Ct. 150 (1990). The trial court unfairly prevented plaintiff from proving her case in an action charging sex discrimination and retaliation for plaintiff's complaints of sexual harassment when it excluded evidence of sexual harassment of plaintiff and others on the basis that such evidence was not relevant because plaintiff made no formal allegation of sexual harassment against any individual defendant and evidence of sexual harassment was irrelevant beyond the bare fact that a complaint was made:

> Because an employer's past discriminatory policy and practice may well illustrate that the employer's asserted reasons for disparate treatment are a pretext for intentional discrimination, this evidence should normally be freely admitted at trial. . . . Thus, it is not sufficient that the Magistrate allowed testimony that complaints of sexual harassment were made while disallowing testimony concerning the activities complained of and the Center's disposition of the complaints. Hawkin's claim is unlawful retaliation. But an atmosphere of condoned sexual harassment in a workplace increases the likelihood of retaliation for complaints in individual cases. Hawkins is entitled to present evidence of such an atmosphere.

Id. at 155–56. Improperly excluded evidence to be admitted on remand was grouped into three categories: "(1) some details of the nature of the alleged harassment, (2) all complaints made to Center supervisors, and (3) disposition of the complaints by the administration, particularly evidence of retaliation or inaction." *Id.* at 156. The court directed the judge on remand to consider the discussion in *Parklane Hosiery* concerning the offensive use of collateral estoppel with respect to findings of fact in a previous sexual harassment suit brought by students.

Once this burden is met, the employer must articulate the legitimate, nondiscriminatory reason for the personnel action. The employer may cite reasons similar to those stated in *quid pro quo* or hostile environment cases, such as poor work performance or personality clashes.[356] The plaintiff will prevail if she proves, by a preponderance of the evidence, that the proffered reason was but a pretext for retaliation or if she persuades the court that the desire to retaliate more likely motivated the employer.[357] The plaintiff may submit evidence that a favorable performance rating preceded her complaints of sexual harassment and a poor rating followed,[358] or evidence tending to show that if the defendant's proffered reasons for termination were true, more people would have been fired.[359]

Some courts have altered the standard in situations in which the plaintiff already has proven that she was a victim of discrimination.[360] "Discriminatory actions by the defendant having already been proved, uncertainty as to the motive underlying [the employment action] should be resolved against the defendant-employer."[361] A plaintiff may state a claim for retaliation for opposing sexual harassment even if the harassment occurred several years before the filing of the charge when she claimed that she was given less substantive assignments after she complained about the harassment and was eventually discharged.[362] The series of acts may have triggered her awareness of the injury only when they were considered cumulatively.[363]

---

356 Morley v. New Eng. Tel. Co., 47 Fair Empl. Prac. Cas. (BNA) 917, 924 (D. Mass. 1987); Jenkins v. Orkin Exterminating Co., 646 F. Supp. 1274, 1277 (E.D. Tex. 1986).

357 McKenna v. Weinberger, 729 F.2d 783 (D.C. Cir. 1984); Morley v. New Eng. Tel. Co., 47 Fair Empl. Prac. Cas. (BNA) 917, 924 (D. Mass. 1987).

358 Morley v. New Eng. Tel. Co., 47 Fair Empl. Prac. Cas. (BNA) 917, 924 (D. Mass. 1987).

359 Rogers v. Illinois Dep't of Children & Family Servs., 43 Fair Empl. Prac. Cas. (BNA) 1134, 1136 (N.D. Ill. 1987).

360 Bundy v. Jackson, 641 F.2d 934, 953 (D.C. Cir. 1981) (once a *prima facie* case is proven, "the employer must then bear the burden of showing, by clear and convincing evidence that he had legitimate and nondiscriminatory reasons" for the employment action). *See also* Fields v. Clark Univ., 817 F.2d 931 (1st Cir. 1987) (when plaintiff has proven by direct evidence that unlawful discrimination was a motivating factor in an employment decision, defendant must prove by preponderance of the evidence that the same decision would have been made absent the discrimination); Harrison v. Reed Rubber Co., 603 F. Supp. 1457 (E.D. Mo. 1985) (clear and convincing evidence required).

361 Harrison v. Reed Rubber Co., 603 F. Supp. 1457, 1462 (E.D. Mo. 1985).

362 Isaacson v. Keck, Mahin & Cate, 61 Fair Empl. Prac. Cas. (BNA) 1145 (N.D. Ill. 1993). *See also* Warren v. K Mart Corp., 61 Fair Empl. Prac. Cas. (BNA) 1364 (D. Kan. 1993) (evidence of sexual harassment was relevant to a claim of retaliation for pursuing a harassment claim, even though the sexual harassment claim was time-barred).

363 Isaacson v. Keck, Mahin & Cate, 61 Fair Empl. Prac. Cas. (BNA) 1145 (N.D. Ill. 1993).

§ 6.46 Prima Facie Constructive Discharge Case

A constructive discharge can result when the employer deliberately makes an employee's working conditions so intolerable that the employee is forced to resign.[364] A constructive discharge violates Title VII when the intolerable working conditions are caused by sexual harassment.[365] In determining whether constructive discharge took place, the court may look at the employee's objective feelings[366] and the employer's intent.[367]

---

364 Second Circuit: Maturo v. National Graphics, Inc., 722 F. Supp. 916 (D. Conn. 1989). Former bindery employee who was subjected to both oral and physical sexual harassment over a period of two years and which culminated in two physical attacks was constructively discharged when management refused to take corrective action after plaintiff's initial complaints.

Fourth Circuit: Hopkins v. Shoe Show, Inc., 678 F. Supp. 1241, 1245 (S.D. W. Va. 1988); Llewellyn v. Celanese Corp., 693 F. Supp. 369, 381 (W.D.N.C. 1988).

Fifth Circuit: Cortes v. Maxus Exploration Co., 977 F. 2d 195 (5th Cir. 1992) (Title VII and state duress claim). An employee was constructively discharged when she was transferred to the department in which she was to be supervised by her alleged harasser. Previous complaints of harassment were answered with unfulfilled promises of investigation, a demotion, advice that a slander suit could follow her complaints, and an observation that the harassment was like a "pink elephant—both would vanish with the snap of a finger." *Id.* at 201. The plaintiff was also told that it was not management's problem when she expressed fear about returning to the abusive environment.

Sixth Circuit: Yates v. Avco Corp., 819 F.2d 630, 636 (6th Cir. 1987); Pease v. Alford Photo Indus., Inc., 667 F. Supp. 1188, 1201 (W.D. Tenn. 1987).

Tenth Circuit: *Cf.* Hirschfield v. New Mexico Corrections Dep't, 916 F.2d 572 (10th Cir. 1990). The district court properly dismissed plaintiff corrections employee's constructive discharge claim when the alleged harasser never again confronted her after she complained to the warden, and plaintiff left work physically ill with tonsillitis, a bladder infection, and was mentally depressed four months after the last incident with the alleged harasser. The evidence linking her depressed state to the sexual harassment months prior was not convincing. The court properly concluded that while the plaintiff was disturbed by rumors about her, a reasonable person in the plaintiff's position would not have felt compelled to resign under the circumstances. The plaintiff had alleged harassment by an inmate who observed her surreptitiously and wrote her an anonymous letter, and a high-level security guard who allegedly hugged and kissed her over the course of several days.

Eleventh Circuit: Huddleston v. Roger Dean Chevrolet, Inc., 845 F.2d 900, 905 (11th Cir. 1988); Stockett v. Tolin, 791 F. Supp. 1536 (S.D. Fla. 1992) (see § 6.38); Ross v. Twenty-Four Collection, Inc., 681 F. Supp. 1547, 1552 (S.D. Fla. 1988), *aff'd,* 875 F.2d 873 (11th Cir. 1989).

A medical leave without pay also has been determined to be a constructive discharge. Llewellyn v. Celanese Corp., 693 F. Supp. 369, 381 (W.D.N.C. 1988).

365 Henson v. City of Dundee, 682 F.2d 897, 907 (11th Cir. 1982).

366 Courts have applied a reasonable woman or person standard. Lipsett v. Rive-Mora, 864 F.2d 881 (1st Cir. 1988) (reasonable person); Yates v. Avco Corp., 819 F.2d 630, 637 (6th Cir. 1987) (reasonable woman); Radtke v. Everett, 56 Fair Emp. Prac. Cas. (BNA) 923 (Mich. Ct. App. 1991) (reasonable woman); Ross v. Twenty-Four Collection, Inc.,

To prove constructive discharge, the plaintiff should show, if possible, that:

1. Resignation occurred following a sexual advance, during which it was made clear that an employment decision turned on her compliance.
2. After resisting such a sexual advance, the defendant started a campaign to force her to resign.
3. Resignation followed a series of incidents that constituted a hostile work environment.
4. She reported the incidents of harassment.[368]
5. She warned management personnel that she would have to resign if the harassment persisted.[369]
6. Her resignation letter indicated that the sexual harassment forced her to leave her job.[370]
7. The defendant did not attempt to remedy and rehire the plaintiff after her resignation.[371]

§ 6.47 Defendant's Reasons for Employment Decisions

If a plaintiff succeeds in proving her prima facie case with circumstantial evidence, the burden shifts to the defendant "to articulate some legitimate, nondiscriminatory reason for the employee's rejection,"[372] or in direct evidence, mixed-motive cases, to prove by a preponderance of the evidence that the employer would have made the same employment decision absent the discrimination. Defendants often assert that the plaintiff was fired for

---

681 F. Supp. 1547, 1552 (S.D. Fla. 1988), *aff'd,* 875 F.2d 873 (11th Cir. 1989). A medical leave without pay also has been determined to be a constructive discharge. Llewellyn v. Celanese Corp., 693 F. Supp. 369, 381 (W.D.N.C. 1988) (reasonable person).

[367] Yates v. Avco Corp., 819 F.2d 630, 636 (6th Cir. 1987).

[368] Pease v. Alford Photo Indus., Inc., 667 F. Supp. 1188, 1201 (W.D. Tenn. 1987).

[369] *Id.* at 1201.

[370] *Cf.* Huddleston v. Roger Dean Chevrolet, Inc., 845 F.2d 900 (11th Cir. 1988) (letter to employer gave other reasons for resignation).

[371] *Cf.* Yates v. Avco Corp., 819 F.2d 630, 637 (6th Cir. 1987) (plaintiff who inadvertently encountered her alleged harasser and then quit was not constructively discharged when employer called her to apologize and explain the mix-up).

[372] Texas Dep't of Community Affairs v. Burdine, 450 U.S. 248, 252 (1981).

poor work performance,[373] excessive absenteeism,[374] lack of credentials,[375] refusal to work at certain times or for certain people,[376] tardiness,[377]

---

373 Second Circuit: Tunis v. Corning Glass Works, 698 F. Supp. 452 (S.D.N.Y. 1988) (inadequate job performance was not a legitimate reason for discharge when the employee had worked for only a fraction of the time that the employer admitted was necessary to become proficient in the position and supervisors were unwilling to help plaintiff); Koster v. Chase Manhattan Bank, 46 Fair Empl. Prac. Cas. (BNA) 1436 (S.D.N.Y. 1988) (plaintiff was fired because she overstated experience and potential, refused to accept management's contrary assessment, and declined the only position available at the time for which she was qualified); Christoforou v. Ryder Truck Rental, Inc., 668 F. Supp. 294 (S.D.N.Y. 1987); Neville v. Taft Broadcasting Co., 42 Fair Empl. Prac. Cas. (BNA) 1314 (W.D.N.Y. 1987) (dismissal of account executive was shown to be due to failure to meet budget, excessive chargebacks, and poor servicing of accounts).

Fourth Circuit: Delgado v. Lehman, 665 F. Supp. 460 (E.D. Va. 1987).

Fifth Circuit: Lamb v. Drilco, 32 Fair Empl. Prac. Cas. (BNA) 105 (S.D. Tex. 1983).

Sixth Circuit: Hill v. BASF Wyandotte Corp., 27 Fair Empl. Prac. Cas. (BNA) 66 (E.D. Mich. 1981).

Eighth Circuit: McLean v. Satellite Tech. Servs., Inc., 673 F. Supp. 1458 (E.D. Mo. 1987); Mays v. Williamson & Sons, 591 F. Supp. 1518 (E.D. Ark. 1984), *aff'd,* 775 F.2d 258 (8th Cir. 1985).

Ninth Circuit: Priest v. Rotary, 634 F. Supp. 571 (N.D. Cal. 1986) (waitress allegedly failed to do "sidework," used "bad language," violated company policy by socializing in the lounge, and did not get along with other waitresses); Ambrose v. United States Steel Corp., 39 Fair Empl. Prac. Cas. (BNA) 30 (N.D. Cal. 1985).

Tenth Circuit: Bohen v. Valley Camp of Utah, Inc., 639 F. Supp. 1199 (D. Utah 1986); Davis v. Bristol Lab., 26 Fair Empl. Prac. Cas. (BNA) 1351 (W.D. Okla. 1981).

Eleventh Circuit: Hall v. F.O. Thacker Contracting Co., 24 Fair Empl. Prac. Cas. (BNA) 1499 (N.D. Ga. 1980).

District of Columbia Circuit: Broderick v. Ruder, 685 F. Supp. 1269 (D.D.C. 1988).

374 Hinton v. Methodist Hospitals, 779 F. Supp. 956 (N.D. Ind. 1991) (plaintiff did not prove *quid pro quo* sexual harassment when it was far more likely than not that she missed work for her own health reasons rather than the alleged harassment, and her termination resulted from her attempt to steal property and carry a weapon at work rather than the alleged rejection of her male coworker); Ambrose v. United States Steel Corp., 39 Fair Empl. Prac. Cas. (BNA) 30 (N.D. Cal. 1985); Sheekey v. Nelson, 40 Fair Empl. Prac. Cas. (BNA) 1216 (D.N.J. 1986); Macey v. World Airways, Inc., 14 Fair Empl. Prac. Cas. (BNA) 1426 (N.D. Cal. 1977).

375 Porta v. Rollins Envtl. Servs., Inc., 654 F. Supp. 1275 (D.N.J. 1987), *aff'd,* 845 F.2d 1014 (3d Cir. 1988).

376 Christoforou v. Ryder Truck Rental, Inc., 668 F. Supp. 294 (S.D.N.Y. 1987); Hosemann v. Technical Materials, Inc., 554 F. Supp. 659 (D.R.I. 1982); Meyers v. I.T.T. Diversified Credit Corp., 527 F. Supp. 1064 (E.D. Mo. 1981).

377 Mays v. Williamson & Sons, 591 F. Supp. 1518 (E.D. Ark. 1984), *aff'd,* 775 F.2d 258 (8th Cir. 1985); Broderick v. Ruder, 685 F. Supp. 1269 (D.D.C. 1988); Tunis v. Corning Glass Works, 698 F. Supp. 452 (S.D.N.Y. 1988) (tardiness was not a legitimate reason for plaintiff's discharge in light of the fact that defendant had long acquiesced to plaintiff's practice of arriving at work after 8:00 a.m.).

insubordination,[378] dishonesty,[379] personality conflicts,[380] "unladylike" conduct,[381] violation of company policy,[382] bad attitude,[383] or lack of work[384] (see **Chapter 7**). If the defendant adequately supports its assertions, the plaintiff must demonstrate that the proffered explanation was not the true reason for defendant's employment decision.[385]

§ 6.48 Plaintiff's Rebuttal

The ultimate burden of showing that the defendant's reason for an adverse employment decision is a pretext rests with the plaintiff. In *St. Mary's Honor Center v. Hicks,*[386] the U.S. Supreme Court recently held that a Title VII plaintiff must prove not only that the asserted reason for an adverse employment action was pretextual, but also that unlawful discrimination was the real reason for the challenged decision. Although defendant employers may assert legally sufficient justifications for their employment decisions, the employer's explanations may be rebutted in a number of ways. The plaintiff may point to the defendant's failure to (1) follow company procedure in making the employment decision,[387] (2) warn the plaintiff

---

378 Christoforou v. Ryder Truck Rental, Inc., 668 F. Supp. 294 (S.D.N.Y. 1987); McLean v. Satellite Tech. Servs., Inc., 673 F. Supp. 1458 (E.D. Mo. 1987); Petrosky v. Washington-Greene County Ass'n for the Blind, 663 F. Supp. 821 (W.D. Pa. 1987); Kramer-Navarro v. Postal Serv., 586 F. Supp. 677 (S.D.N.Y. 1984).

379 Sensibello v. Globe Sec. Sys. Co., 34 Fair Empl. Prac. Cas. (BNA) 1357 (E.D. Pa. 1984); Hinton v. Methodist Hospitals, 779 F. Supp. 956 (N.D. Ind. 1991).

380 Christoforou v. Ryder Truck Rental, Inc., 668 F. Supp. 294 (S.D.N.Y. 1987); Williams-Hill v. Donovan, 43 Fair Empl. Prac. Cas. (BNA) 253 (M.D. Fla. 1987).

381 EEOC v. FLC & Bros. Rebel, 663 F. Supp. 864 (W.D. Va. 1987), *aff'd,* 846 F.2d 70 (4th Cir. 1988).

382 Sparks v. Pilot Freight Carriers, Inc., 830 F.2d 1554 (11th Cir. 1987); Priest v. Rotary, 634 F. Supp. 571 (N.D. Cal. 1986); Sheekey v. Nelson, 40 Fair Empl. Prac. Cas. (BNA) 1216 (D.N.J. 1986); Kramer-Navarro v. Postal Serv., 586 F. Supp. 677 (S.D.N.Y. 1984); Sapp v. City of Warner Robins, 655 F. Supp. 1043 (M.D. Ga. 1987).

383 Tunis v. Corning Glass Works, 698 F. Supp. 452 (S.D.N.Y. 1988) (plaintiff's alleged disruptiveness in attempting to enforce company policy stemmed from failure by employer to take responsibility for and eliminate an offensive working environment, which it all but conceded existed); McLean v. Satellite Tech. Servs., Inc., 673 F. Supp. 1458 (E.D. Mo. 1987); Kramer-Navarro v. Postal Serv., 586 F. Supp. 677 (S.D.N.Y. 1984); Hill v. BASF Wyandotte Corp., 27 Fair Empl. Prac. Cas. (BNA) 66 (E.D. Mich. 1981).

384 Hallquist v. Max Fish Plumbing & Heating Co., 46 Fair Empl. Prac. Cas. (BNA) 1855 (D. Mass. 1987).

385 Texas Dep't of Community Affairs v. Burdine, 450 U.S. 248, 256 (1981).

386 St. Mary's Honor Ctr. v. Hicks, 113 S. Ct. 2742 (1993).

387 *See* Craig v. Y&Y Snacks, Inc., 721 F.2d 77 (3d Cir. 1983).

of poor performance, (3) uncover the basis for the deterioration of work performance or work-related habits, or (4) help the plaintiff improve her performance.[388] The court also will look at the time frame in which the adverse employment action and the alleged sexual harassment occurred. Evidence of a history of sex discrimination complaints also may prove pretext.

In response to assertions of excessive absences, the plaintiff may show that during the period before her termination she was absent fewer times than during the previous appraisal year, when her attendance was rated satisfactory.[389]

To rebut the defendant's assertion that dismissal was due to lack of work, a plaintiff may show that the employer continued to maintain and add to the work force after her termination, and that she was treated in a sexually harassing manner.[390]

If the defendant presents evidence that the plaintiff's work performance was substandard, the plaintiff must attempt to show that the decline in performance started as a result of the sexual harassment.[391] "Plaintiff's diminished performance cannot be asserted as a legitimate basis for her removal when that diminution is the direct result of the employer's discriminatory behavior."[392]

The defendant may show that the plaintiff was discharged because she could not get along with the other employees. In response, the plaintiff may demonstrate that other employees did not find her difficult, and that before the sexual harassment, the defendant responded favorably to her. Evidence of the harassment of other female employees is useful when the defendant is pointing to a character flaw to justify the employment decision.

If the defendant makes a showing of insubordination by the plaintiff, the plaintiff should try to show that she became recalcitrant only in response to the alleged harassment. She may show that up to the time of the harassment, her demeanor was acceptable to the defendant, or that she acted no differently than other employees who suffered no adverse employment action.

---

388 Barnes v. Callaghan & Co., 559 F.2d 1102 (7th Cir. 1977).

389 Ambrose v. United States Steel Corp., 39 Fair Empl. Prac. Cas. (BNA) 30, 34 (N.D. Cal. 1985).

390 Hallquist v. Max Fish Plumbing & Heating Co., 46 Fair Empl. Prac. Cas. (BNA) 1855 (D. Mass. 1987).

391 Delgado v. Lehman, 665 F. Supp. 460, 467 (E.D. Va. 1987).

392 Broderick v. Ruder, 685 F. Supp. 1269, 1280 (D.D.C. 1988); Delgado v. Lehman, 665 F. Supp. 460, 467 (E.D. Va. 1987); Moffett v. Gene B. Glick Co., 621 F. Supp. 244, 281 (N.D. Ind. 1985); Weiss v. United States, 595 F. Supp. 1050, 1057 (E.D. Va. 1984); Lamb v. Drilco, 32 Fair Empl. Prac. Cas. (BNA) 105, 107 (S.D. Tex. 1983). *See also* Henson v. City of Dundee, 682 F.2d 897, 910 (11th Cir. 1982).

The trauma of sexual harassment understandably may foster bad work habits. Pretext will be more difficult to show if the plaintiff had a record of tardiness or absences. If this is the case, the focus should be the employer's response. How was tardiness handled before the alleged harassment? Was the plaintiff advised that her conduct was unacceptable? Were other employees treated similarly?

Employers may hold women to a higher standard of conduct than men. For example, the use of sexual language on the job may be tolerated in men but discouraged in women. The defendant's use of the phrase "unladylike conduct" as a reason for discharge may constitute direct evidence of sex discrimination.[393]

Decisions regarding pretext often boil down to credibility determinations. Even if the plaintiff demonstrates that her performance was not consistently worse than that of other similarly situated employees, the court may find that the employer's reasons for dismissal were within its business discretion.[394]

SETTLEMENT AND COSTS

§ 6.49 Settlements

"It is a well-settled principle that the law generally favors the encouragement of settlements."[395] The U.S. Supreme Court has noted that in enacting Title VII, "Congress expressed a strong preference for encouraging voluntary settlements."[396] Sexual harassment actions are particularly conducive to settlement because of the sensitive nature of the facts and the ramifications of publicity. At the same time, most settlements in sexual

---

[393] EEOC v. FLC & Bros. Rebel, 663 F. Supp. 864, 869 (W.D. Va. 1987), *aff'd,* 846 F.2d 70 (4th Cir. 1988):

> Upon an express indication that an improper motive influenced an employment decision, proof of the employer's motive through circumstantial evidence is unnecessary. Rather, the burden of persuasion in this case shifts to the defendant, who must prove that absent discriminatory reason, [the plaintiff] would nevertheless have been fired.

[394] Neville v. Taft Broadcasting Co., 42 Fair Empl. Prac. Cas. (BNA) 1314, 1317 (W.D.N.Y. 1987); Jones v. Flagship Int'l, 793 F.2d 714 (5th Cir. 1986), *cert. denied,* 479 U.S. 1065 (1987).

[395] Airline Stewards & Stewardesses Ass'n Local 550 v. American Airlines, 573 F.2d 960, 963 (7th Cir.), *cert. denied,* 439 U.S. 876 (1978).

[396] Carson v. American Brands, Inc., 450 U.S. 79, 88 n.14 (1981). *See also* Carey v. United States Postal Serv., 812 F.2d 621, 624 (10th Cir. 1987).

harassment cases involve the release or waiver of claims by the plaintiff. Waivers of past claims repeatedly have been upheld,[397] while prospective waivers have been deemed invalid.[398] In determining whether to approve a proposed settlement, the court must find that the settlement is fair, adequate, reasonable, and not the product of collusion between the parties.[399]

A settlement by an individual of a Title VII action brought by the EEOC does not bar the EEOC from seeking injunctive relief against the same discrimination for other affected individuals.[400]

§ 6.50 Remedies

The basic purpose of Title VII relief is to "make whole" victims of unlawful discrimination.[401] Once the plaintiff proves a violation of Title VII, the court may award a range of relief, including reinstatement and/or back or "front" pay and compensatory and/or punitive damages.[402] Courts may fashion relief to suit the particular circumstances of the case.[403] Because a goal of Title VII is to make the aggrieved party whole again, relief is denied only in rare cases after liability has been demonstrated.[404] Courts

---

397 Alexander v. Gardner-Denver Co., 415 U.S. 36, 52 (1974).

398 *Id.* at 51.

399 Cotton v. Hinton, 559 F.2d 1326 (5th Cir. 1977); Young v. Katz, 447 F.2d 431 (5th Cir. 1971).

400 EEOC v. Goodyear Aerospace Corp., 813 F.2d 1539 (9th Cir. 1987).

401 Albemarle v. Moody, 422 U.S. 405, 418 (1975); Sowers v. Kemira, Inc., 46 Fair Empl. Prac. Cas. (BNA) 1825, 1837 (S.D. Ga. 1988) (sexual harassment).

402 See § **2.21.**

403 EEOC v. FLC & Bros. Rebel, 663 F. Supp. 864 (W.D. Va. 1987), *aff'd,* 846 F.2d 70 (4th Cir. 1988). The court concluded that plaintiff in a sexual harassment action was entitled to the equity interest in her car, which was repossessed after her discharge because she was unable to make the monthly payment. The court also awarded to plaintiff the amount of medical expenses she incurred while unemployed. *See also* Sowers v. Kemira, Inc., 46 Fair Empl. Prac. Cas. (BNA) 1825, 1837 (S.D. Ga. 1988) (sexual harassment).

Landgraf v. USI Film Prods., 968 F.2d 427 (5th Cir. 1992) (no nominal damages may be awarded under Title VII).

404 Franks v. Bowman Transp. Co., 424 U.S. 747 (1976); Albemarle Paper Co. v. Moody, 422 U.S. 405 (1975). *See also* Arnold v. City of Seminole, 614 F. Supp. 853, 871 (E.D. Okla. 1985) (sexual harassment) ("Plaintiff should be awarded back pay and retroactive reinstatement unless the defendant can prove by clear and convincing evidence that the plaintiff would not have been retained, even if there had been no discrimination").

Cf. Walker v. Anderson Electrical Connectors, 944 F.2d 841 (11th Cir. 1991), *cert. denied,* 113 S. Ct. 1043 (1993). A jury finding of sexual harassment did not mandate an award of nominal damages in an action against an employer and union when the employee had abandoned her request for declaratory relief and injunction at a pretrial

also may issue injunctions against discrimination by the defendant[405] and order the defendant employer to implement a comprehensive system to safeguard against all kinds of discriminatory conduct.[406] Attorneys' fees also are available to prevailing parties under Title VII (see **§ 6.47**).

Title VII authorizes courts to award compensatory and punitive damages, back pay, reinstatement, and "any equitable relief as the court deems appropriate."[407] Successful plaintiffs in sexual harassment actions have

---

conference in favor of a monetary award, and the jury awarded no damages. Moreover, the district court did not instruct the jury on the possibility of awarding nominal damages in the event of a finding of sexual harassment and plaintiff did not request a charge on nominal damages, nor did she object to the court's failure to make such a charge. The award of nominal damages is not required for statutory violations.

405 Ross v. Double Diamond, Inc., 672 F. Supp. 261, 267 (N.D. Tex. 1987) (sexual harassment); EEOC v. Hacienda Hotel, 881 F.2d 1504 (9th Cir.1989). The district court did not abuse its discretion by awarding permanent injunctive relief in a sexual harassment case when although defendant's recent efforts to train managerial employees regarding discrimination problems and absence of further EEOC charges in recent times was encouraging and laudable, the district court had found that multiple violations of Title VII warranted a permanent injunction and that defendant did not take prompt remedial action upon notification of the sexual harassment allegations against it. Victims of employment discrimination are entitled to an injunction against future discrimination unless the employer proves it is unlikely to repeat the practice.

Jenson v. Eveleth Taconite Co., 824 F. Supp. 847 (D. Minn. 1993); Boyd v. James S. Hayes Living Health Care Agency, 671 F. Supp. 1155, 1169 (W.D. Tenn. 1987); EEOC v. FLC & Bros. Rebel, 663 F. Supp. 864, 870–71 (W.D. Va. 1987), *aff'd,* 846 F.2d 70 (4th Cir. 1988); Morgan v. Hertz Corp., 542 F. Supp. 123 (W.D. Tenn. 1981), *aff'd,* 725 F.2d 1070 (6th Cir. 1984).

406 *See* Ross v. Double Diamond, Inc., 672 F. Supp. 261, 277 (N.D. Tex. 1987):

> Defendants should be particularly mindful of incorporating within the preventive system a means of educating employees as to their right to work in an environment free of discriminatory conduct; a means for employees to make an intracompany complaint regarding violations of Title VII; and a means for promptly and effectively dealing with these complaints.

See also Jones v. Wesco, 846 F.2d 1154, 1156 (8th Cir. 1988) (sexual harassment; notice to employees ordered); Boyd v. James S. Hayes Living Health Care Agency, 671 F. Supp. 1155, 1169 (W.D. Tenn. 1987); Arnold v. City of Seminole, 614 F. Supp. 853, 872 (E.D. Okla. 1985).

407 42 U.S.C. § 2000e-5(g). The Civil Rights Act of 1991 provides for compensatory and punitive damages under Title VII (see **§ 2.21**).

Second Circuit: Danna v. New York Tel. Co., 752 F. Supp. 594 (S.D.N.Y. 1990) (back pay award of $58,499; with prejudgment interest $76,971).

Fourth Circuit: Spencer v. General Elec. Co., 697 F. Supp. 204 (E.D. Va. 1988) (although plaintiff demonstrated the existence of a hostile work environment, she did not show any tangible loss as a result of her supervisor's conduct, and thus was only entitled to nominal damages of one dollar and attorneys' fees for prosecution of the hostile environment claims).

Fifth Circuit: Cortes v. Maxus Exploration Co., 977 F. 2d 195 (5th Cir. 1992) (Title VII and state duress claim; back pay damages of $97,857.70, $20,000 actual damages

been awarded several types of affirmative relief. Reinstatement usually is not appropriate unless the harasser has been transferred or terminated. Even then, antagonism between the parties may call for a different remedy.[408]

§ 6.51 —Front Pay

Instead of reinstatement, some courts have awarded "front" pay to compensate the plaintiff during the time it took to obtain comparable employment.[409] "Front pay is simply compensation for the post judgment effects

---

and $30,000 punitive damages for the tort of duress). Ross v. Double Diamond, Inc., 672 F. Supp. 216, 276 (N.D. Tex. 1987). *Cf.* Bennett v. Corroon & Black Corp., 845 F.2d 104 (5th Cir. 1988), *cert. denied,* 489 U.S. 1020 (1989) (sexual harassment; no equitable relief was available when employer promptly changed management and continued to pay plaintiff in full until she obtained employment elsewhere).

Eighth Circuit: Morris v. American Nat'l Can Corp., 730 F. Supp. 1489 (E.D. Mo. 1989), *modified,* 941 F.2d 710 (8th Cir. 1991). Plaintiff's entitlement to a full measure of relief included, but was not limited to, a seniority date retroactive to her initial date of hire, back pay from the date of discharge, any increases she would have received within that period, any fringe benefits she would have received, and appropriate injunctive relief. The court awarded $12,212 in back pay plus prejudgment interest of $2,503, $1,500 for work missed for the 11.5 days of pretrial preparation and trial, retroactive seniority, and attorney fees. The court also ordered the defendant corporation to develop a staff training program and establish a grievance procedure for sexual harassment occurring in the workplace.

Eleventh Circuit: Stockett v. Tolin, 791 F. Supp. 1536 (S.D. Fla. 1992). A female employee in a film industry training program was subjected to *quid pro quo* and hostile environment sexual harassment when a managing agent harassed her physically and verbally for over a year, and then told her that she would be fired if she did not submit to his advances. She was entitled to back pay in the amount of $46,305, less $4,401 that she earned from other employment, and front pay in the amount of $16,380.

408 Sowers v. Kemira, Inc., 46 Fair Empl. Prac. Cas. (BNA) 1825, 1838 (S.D. Ga. 1988) ("ill-feelings engendered on both sides by the circumstances of this somewhat bitterly contested lawsuit are likely irremediable"; plaintiff's psychiatrist advised her not to return to work for defendant); Meyers v. I.T.T. Diversified Credit Corp., 527 F. Supp. 1064 (E.D. Mo. 1981) (court awarded plaintiff $3,000 in lieu of reinstatement and in addition to back pay).

409 Snider v. Consolidated Coal Co., 973 F.2d 555 (7th Cir. 1992) (a jury award of front and back pay affirmed); Hansel v. Public Serv. Co., 778 F. Supp. 1126 (D. Colo. 1991); Sowers v. Kemira, Inc., 46 Fair Empl. Prac. Cas. (BNA) 1825 (S.D. Ga. 1988); Pease v. Alford Photo Indus., Inc., 667 F. Supp. 1188, 1203 (W.D. Tenn. 1987); Arnold v. City of Seminole, 614 F. Supp. 853, 873 (E.D. Okla. 1985) (front pay awarded in the amount of the salary, all benefits, and seniority to which plaintiff would be entitled were she reinstated until she could find equivalent employment or return to employment as a police officer with defendant city; plaintiff's physical and psychological readiness would have to be certified by her psychologist or psychiatrist and her physician).

of past discrimination."[410] Front pay is the difference between what the plaintiff would have earned at her job in the absence of the unlawful conduct, and what she will earn at a new job during the period until she reaches a level equivalent to the former position. In *Hansel v. Public Service Co.,*[411] a plaintiff employee who had suffered a nervous breakdown as a result of sexual harassment was awarded front pay to compensate her for the continuing effects of the defendant's hostile work environment when she was not receiving a salary and could not return to her employment at the defendant power plant. Similarly, in *Sowers v. Kemira, Inc.,*[412] the court held that a nine-month lump sum front pay would allow the plaintiff sufficient time to obtain additional psychiatric treatment and recover from her disability and find equivalent alternative employment.

§ 6.52 —Reinstatement

In cases in which reinstatement is appropriate,[413] it may be accompanied by retroactive seniority and benefits. An employee may be reinstated to a higher position than originally sought when a promotion should have been granted.[414] In cases in which the employee never left her position but was denied certain employment benefits such as advancement because of sexual harassment, the defendant may be ordered to promote the employee or raise her salary.[415] The choice of remedy is left to the discretion of the trial court.[416]

---

410 Pease v. Alford Photo Indus., Inc., 667 F. Supp. 1188, 1203 (W.D. Tenn. 1987).

411 Hansel v. Public Serv. Co., 778 F. Supp. 1126 (D. Colo. 1991).

412 Sowers v. Kemina, Inc., 46 Fair Empl. Prac. Cas. (BNA) 1825 (S.D. Ga. 1988).

413 Boyd v. James S. Hayes Living Health Care Agency, 671 F. Supp. 1155 (W.D. Tenn. 1987) (sexual harassment); EEOC v. FLC & Bros. Rebel, 663 F. Supp. 864 (W.D. Va. 1987), *aff'd,* 846 F.2d 70 (4th Cir. 1988) (sexual harassment); Joyner v. AAA Cooper Transp., 597 F. Supp. 537, 544 (M.D. Ala. 1983), *aff'd,* 749 F.2d 732 (11th Cir. 1984) (sexual harassment). *Cf.* Lamb v. Drilco, 32 Fair Empl. Prac. Cas. (BNA) 105 (S.D. Tex. 1983) (sexual harassment) (reinstatement was not appropriate when plaintiff eventually would have been laid off even if discrimination had not occurred).

414 Pecker v. Heckler, 801 F.2d 709 (4th Cir. 1986).

415 Shrout v. Black Clawson Co., 689 F. Supp. 774 (S.D. Ohio 1988).

416 Goss v. Exxon Office Sys. Co., 747 F.2d 885 (3d Cir. 1984). *See also* Fadhl v. City & County of S.F., 741 F.2d 1163 (9th Cir. 1984).

§ 6.53 —Back Pay

Back pay has been awarded consistently by courts when an employee has been terminated because of noncompliance with sexual demands,[417] or in retaliation for complaining of sexual harassment,[418] or for constructive discharge.[419] Back pay awards include the salary that the successful Title VII plaintiff would have received but for the discriminatory practices of the defendant[420] as well as other benefits such as pension contributions,[421] tips,[422] profit-sharing,[423] medical benefits,[424] overtime pay,[425]

---

417 Ross v. Twenty-Four Collection, Inc., 681 F. Supp. 1547, 1552 (S.D. Fla. 1988), *aff'd,* 875 F.2d 873 (11th Cir 1989) (sexual harassment); Jones v. Wesco, 846 F.2d 1154, 1155 (8th Cir. 1988) (sexual harassment).

418 Sahs v. Amarillo Equity Investors, 702 F. Supp. 256 (D. Colo. 1988) ($30,719 awarded).

419 EEOC v. Gurnee Inn Corp., 914 F.2d 815 (7th Cir. 1990). The district court properly awarded back pay damages to four sexual harassment claimants who were constructively discharged more than two years before the EEOC charge was filed, when defendant conceded that the EEOC established Title VII violations with respect to the four claimants and damages were awarded for periods of unemployment after the date the charge was filed.

Cortes v. Maxus Exploration Co., 977 F. 2d 195 (5th Cir. 1992) (Title VII and state duress claim). An award of back pay is proper when an employee is constructively discharged. The fact that the employer eliminated the employee's former position as part of its reorganization plan or whether others were laid off as a result of the plan was not relevant.

420 Ross v. Twenty-Four Collection, Inc., 681 F. Supp. 1547, 1555 (S.D. Fla. 1988), *aff'd,* 875 F.2d 873 (11th Cir 1989); Danna v. New York Tel. Co., 752 F. Supp. 594 (S.D.N.Y. 1990). In a successful sexual harassment action brought by a telephone company installation service technician, back pay was computed on the basis of the average salary of all service technicians during the applicable period, including those in repair as well as in installation, when the positions were generally interchangeable. The plaintiff sought out overtime work, she had been loaned to different units in the company when a need arose, and thus it was reasonable for the court in its discretionary capacity to determine damages based on a broader array of salaries.

Boyd v. James S. Hayes Living Health Care Agency, 671 F. Supp. 1155, 1169 (W.D. Tenn. 1987); Ambrose v. United States Steel Corp., 39 Fair Empl. Prac. Cas. (BNA) 30, 34 (N.D. Cal. 1985).

421 Meyers v. I.T.T. Diversified Credit Corp., 527 F. Supp. 1064 (E.D. Mo. 1981); Macey v. World Airways, Inc., 14 Fair Empl. Prac. Cas. (BNA) 1426, 1430 (N.D. Cal. 1977).

422 Priest v. Rotary, 634 F. Supp. 571, 579–80, 585 (N.D. Cal. 1986) (cocktail waitresses).

423 EEOC v. Kallir, Philips, Ross, Inc., 401 F. Supp. 66, 74 (S.D.N.Y. 1975), *cert denied,* 434 U.S. 920 (1977).

424 Meyers v. I.T.T. Diversified Credit Corp., 527 F. Supp. 1064 (E.D. Mo. 1981).

425 Arnold v. City of Seminole, 614 F. Supp. 853, 871 (E.D. Okla. 1985); Lamb v. Drilco, 32 Fair Empl. Prac. Cas. (BNA) 105 (S.D. Tex. 1983); Meyers v. I.T.T. Diversified Credit Corp., 527 F. Supp. 1064 (E.D. Mo. 1981). *Cf.* Macey v. World Airways, Inc., 14 Fair Empl. Prac. Cas. (BNA) 1426, 1430 (N.D. Cal. 1977) (plaintiff did not show that health and pension plans had a cash value to her).

bonuses,[426] sick pay,[427] shift differential,[428] vacation pay,[429] and employment-related publications.[430] Prejudgment and postjudgment interest also may be added to the award,[431] subject to the court's discretion. Back pay interest is available in suits against the federal government as a result of amendments to the Back Pay Act.[432] Back pay liability accrues no more than two years prior to the filing of the EEOC charge in actions against local governments.[433]

The tax implications of a large lump sum back pay award should be considered. In such a case, the court may adjust for tax liability.[434]

"In calculating a back pay award, it is appropriate to resolve uncertainties against the discriminating employer, and not the victim."[435] Unrealistic

---

426 Cox v. American Cast Iron Pipe Co., 784 F.2d 1546, 1562 (11th Cir.), *cert denied,* 479 U.S. 883 (1986).

427 Yates v. Avco Corp., 819 F.2d 630, 638 (6th Cir. 1987) (a successful sexual harassment plaintiff was entitled to recover back pay for the time she was on extensive sick leave, for which she was paid at a lower level than she would have been had she remained at work).

428 Ross v. Twenty-Four Collection, Inc., 681 F. Supp. 1547, 1552 (S.D. Fla. 1988), *aff'd,* 875 F.2d 873 (11th Cir 1989) (sexual harassment); Arnold v. City of Seminole, 614 F. Supp. 853, 871 (E.D. Okla. 1985).

429 Meyers v. I.T.T. Diversified Credit Corp., 527 F. Supp. 1064 (E.D. Mo. 1981).

430 Ross v. Twenty-Four Collection, Inc., 681 F. Supp. 1547, 1556 (S.D. Fla. 1988), *aff'd,* 875 F.2d 873 (11th Cir 1989).

431 Loeffler v. Frank, 486 U.S. 549 (1988); EEOC v. Gurnee Inn Corp., 914 F.2d 815 (7th Cir. 1990) (district court properly awarded prejudgment interest); Danna v. New York Tel. Co., 752 F. Supp. 594 (S.D.N.Y. 1990); Sowers v. Kemira, Inc., 46 Fair Empl. Prac. Cas. (BNA) 1825, 1838 (S.D. Ga. 1988) (sexual harassment); Jones v. Wesco, 846 F.2d 1154, 1155 (8th Cir. 1988); Shrout v. Black Clawson Co., 486 U.S. 549 (S.D. Ohio 1988) (sexual harassment); Pease v. Alford Photo Indus., Inc., 667 F. Supp. 1188, 1203 (W.D. Tenn. 1987) (sexual harassment); EEOC v. FLC & Bros. Rebel, 663 F. Supp. 864 (W.D. Va. 1987), *aff'd,* 846 F.2d 70 (4th Cir. 1988) (sexual harassment); Ambrose v. United States Steel Corp., 39 Fair Empl. Prac. Cas. (BNA) 30 (N.D. Cal. 1985) (sexual harassment); Lamb v. Drilco, 32 Fair Empl. Prac. Cas. (BNA) 105 (S.D. Tex. 1983) (sexual harassment); Meyers v. I.T.T. Diversified Credit Corp., 527 F. Supp. 1064 (E.D. Mo. 1981) (sexual harassment). *Cf.* Proulx v. Citibank, 659 F. Supp. 972 (S.D.N.Y. 1987) (prejudgment interest was not awarded when, among other things, plaintiff's credibility was questionable); Boyd v. James S. Hayes Living Health Care Agency, 671 F. Supp. 1155 (W.D. Tenn. 1987) (award of interest was not appropriate); Macey v. World Airways, Inc., 14 Fair Empl. Prac. Cas. (BNA) 1426 (N.D. Cal. 1977) (interest award was not appropriate when it would be speculative).

432 5 U.S.C. § 5596(b)(2)(A)(1988).

433 42 U.S.C. § 2000e-5(g); Shrout v. Black Clawson Co., 689 F. Supp. 774 (S.D. Ohio 1988); Arnold v. City of Seminole, 614 F. Supp. 853, 871 (E.D. Okla. 1985).

434 Sears v. Atchison, Topeka & Santa Fe Ry., 749 F.2d 1451, 1456 (10th Cir. 1984), *cert. denied,* 471 U.S. 1099 (1985).

435 Sowers v. Kemira, Inc., 46 Fair Empl. Prac. Cas. (BNA) 1825, 1837 (S.D. Ga. 1988) (sexual harassment), *citing* Horn v. Duke Homes, Inc., 755 F.2d 599, 607 (7th Cir. 1985) (sexual harassment); Goss v. Exxon Office Sys. Co., 747 F.2d 885, 889 (3d Cir. 1984).

exactitude is not required.[436] In determining the termination date for back pay, courts often use the date upon which all matters affecting the plaintiff's relief have been resolved.[437]

Although back pay liability can be substantial,[438] Title VII states that back pay awards must be reduced by interim earnings or by amounts that the plaintiff could have earned with reasonable diligence.[439] A plaintiff must try to mitigate damages by seeking comparable employment.[440] The burden is on the defendant to prove a lack of diligence in mitigating damages.[441] If the plaintiff takes a lower paying job, the court may subtract the

---

436 Stewart v. General Motors Co., 542 F.2d 445, 452 (7th Cir. 1976), *cert. denied,* 433 U.S. 919, *reh'g denied,* 434 U.S. 881 (1977); Arnold v. City of Seminole, 614 F. Supp. 853, 871 (E.D. Okla. 1985) (sexual harassment; "The wrongdoer bears the risk of the uncertainty it has created").

437 Arnold v. City of Seminole, 614 F. Supp. 853, 871 (E.D. Okla. 1985).

438 *See, e.g.,* Ambrose v. United States Steel Corp., 39 Fair Empl. Prac. Cas. (BNA) 30, 34 (N.D. Cal. 1985) (sexual harassment plaintiff awarded $90,016).

439 42 U.S.C. § 2000e-5(g). *See also* EEOC v. FLC & Bros. Rebel, 663 F. Supp. 864 (W.D. Va. 1987), *aff'd,* 846 F.2d 70 (4th Cir. 1988) (sexual harassment); Joyner v. AAA Cooper Transp., 597 F. Supp. 537, 544 (M.D. Ala. 1983), *aff'd,* 749 F.2d 732 (11th Cir. 1984) (sexual harassment).

440 Jurinko v. Edwin L. Wiegand Co., 477 U.S. 1038 (3d Cir.), *vacated & remanded,* 414 U.S. 970 (1973), *on remand,* 497 F.2d 403 (3d Cir. 1974) (per curiam); Maturo v. National Graphics, Inc., 722 F. Supp. 916 (D. Conn. 1989) (plaintiff's efforts to secure alternative employment constituted reasonable diligence to mitigate her damages when her inability to work during her unemployment periods was the direct result of emotional injuries caused by the sexual harassment); Proulx v. Citibank, 659 F. Supp. 972 (S.D.N.Y. 1987) (sexual harassment); Hopkins v. Shoe Show, Inc., 678 F. Supp. 1241, 1246 (S.D. W. Va. 1988) (sexual harassment); Coley v. Conso. Rail Corp., 561 F. Supp. 645, 651–52 (E.D. Mich. 1982) (sexual harassment; plaintiff failed to mitigate damages when her own testimony established that she did not attempt to find work because of her defensive attitudes toward middle-aged men, but there was no evidence that she was psychologically disabled from employment); Meyers v. I.T.T. Diversified Credit Corp., 527 F. Supp. 1064 (E.D. Mo. 1981).

See also Sowers v. Kemira, Inc., 46 Fair Empl. Prac. Cas. (BNA) 1825 (S.D. Ga. 1988) (plaintiff was not required to take a position in another city to mitigate damages).

Cf. Ross v. Twenty-Four Collection, Inc., 681 F. Supp. 1547, 1554 (S.D. Fla. 1988), *aff'd,* 875 F.2d 873 (11th Cir 1989) (plaintiff failed to seek alternative employment not because she did not desire a different position, but because she was legally barred through a noncompetition agreement from accepting comparable employment, and other employment in her field was unavailable).

441 Sowers v. Kemira, Inc., 46 Fair Empl. Prac. Cas. (BNA) 1825, 1838 (S.D. Ga. 1988).

EEOC v. Gurnee Inn Corp., 914 F.2d 815 (7th Cir. 1990). The district court properly awarded back pay to sexual harassment claimants despite defendant's contention that claimants failed to mitigate their damages when they did not seek employment after being constructively discharged when defendant failed to establish that there was a reasonable chance that the claimants could have found comparable employment and thus failed to sustain its burden of proof. Moreover, the record supported the district court's

amounts earned from the amount the plaintiff would have earned but for the discrimination.[442] It is unclear whether a back pay award may be reduced by unemployment compensation received during the relevant period[443] (see **Chapter 11**).

A back pay award may include periods of disability when the disability can be attributed to the sexual harassment.[444] In *Brooms v. Regal Tube Co.*,[445] the Seventh Circuit upheld the trial court's determination that the plaintiff could not maintain a position until she completed therapy, and therefore included that time within the back pay award. In *EEOC v. Gurnee Inn Corp.*,[446] the court held that the plaintiff had not failed to mitigate damages when she could not work because she feared "she would run into the same situation again," noting that "it would not be unreasonable

---

conclusion that six of the eight claimants searched for work after leaving defendant's employment and the other two claimants had adequate reasons for not looking for work.

Proulx v. Citibank, 659 F. Supp. 972 (S.D.N.Y. 1987).

442 The court also may subtract earned income from the amount the plaintiff earned during the last year at the company. *See, e.g.*, Jenkins v. Orkin Exterminating Co., 646 F. Supp. 1274, 1279 (E.D. Tex. 1986) (sexual harassment) ($21,907 awarded); Joyner v. AAA Cooper Transp., 597 F. Supp. 537, 544 (M.D. Ala. 1983), *aff'd*, 749 F.2d 732 (11th Cir. 1984) (sexual harassment) ($4,947 awarded).

443 *See, e.g.*, Craig v. Y&Y Snacks, Inc., 721 F.2d 77 (3d Cir. 1983) (sexual harassment) (award should not be reduced). *Accord* Brown v. A.J. Gerrard Mfg. Co., 715 F.2d 1549 (11th Cir. 1983) (en banc); Kauffman v. Sidereal Corp., 695 F.2d 343 (9th Cir. 1982); Boyd v. James S. Hayes Living Health Care Agency, 671 F. Supp. 1155, 1169 (W.D. Tenn. 1987) (sexual harassment); EEOC v. Sandia Corp., 23 Fair Empl. Prac. Cas. (BNA) 799 (10th Cir. 1980); Mabin v. Lear Siegler, Inc., 4 Fair Empl. Prac. Cas. (BNA) 679 (W.D. Mich. 1971), *aff'd*, 457 F.2d 806 (6th Cir. 1972); Tidwell v. American Oil Co., 332 F. Supp. 424 (D. Utah 1971).

Grant v. Bethlehem Steel Corp., 22 Fair Empl. Prac. Cas. (BNA) 1596 (2d Cir. 1980) (reduction permitted). *Accord* Satty v. Nashville Gas Co., 522 F.2d 850 (6th Cir. 1975), *aff'd in part, rev'd in part*, 434 U.S. 136 (1977); Bowe v. Colgate-Palmolive Co., 416 F.2d 711 (7th Cir. 1969); Diaz v. Pan Am. World Airways, Inc., 442 F.2d 385 (5th Cir.), *cert. denied*, 404 U.S. 950 (1971); Gilardi v. Schroeder, 672 F. Supp. 1043, 1047 (N.D. Ill. 1986), *aff'd*, 833 F.2d 1226 (7th Cir. 1987); Lamb v. Drilco, 32 Fair Empl. Prac. Cas. (BNA) 105 (S.D. Tex. 1983) (sexual harassment); Meyers v. I.T.T. Diversified Credit Corp., 527 F. Supp. 1064 (E.D. Mo. 1981) (sexual harassment); Helbling v. Unclaimed Salvage & Freight Co., 489 F. Supp. 956 (E.D. Pa. 1980); Taylor v. Teletype Corp., 478 F. Supp. 1227 (E.D. Ark. 1979), *modified on other grounds*, 648 F.2d 1129 (11th Cir. 1981), *cert. denied*, 454 U.S. 969 (1981); Macey v. World Airways, Inc., 14 Fair Empl. Prac. Cas. (BNA) 1426 (N.D. Cal. 1977) (sexual harassment).

444 Sowers v. Kemira, Inc., 46 Fair Empl. Prac. Cas. (BNA) 1825, 1838 (S.D. Ga. 1988); Arnold v. City of Seminole, 614 F. Supp. 853 (E.D. Okla. 1985).

445 Brooms v. Regal Tube Co., 881 F.2d 412, 423–24 n.8 (7th Cir. 1989).

446 EEOC v. Gurnee Inn Corp., 48 Fair Empl. Prac. Cas. (BNA) 871, 882 (N.D. Ill.1988), *aff'd*, 914 F. 2d 815 (7th Cir. 1990).

for a young woman having gone through the experience of these women to feel 'gun shy' about looking for a similar position."[447]

An appropriate and unconditional job offer by the defendant to the plaintiff may toll the accrual of back pay liability.[448] In *Morris v. American National Can Corp.*,[449] evidence indicated that the defendant employer was sincere in its claim that it was prepared to protect the plaintiff from any further sexual harassment and thus the back pay award was properly terminated at the time the employer made his offer of reinstatement:

> In light of the egregious conduct that occurred here, we sympathize with Morris' statement that she reasonably refused to accept American Can's offer of reinstatement. Nevertheless, a plaintiff's refusal of a reinstatement offer is measured by an objective standard: "Generally, it is the duty of the trier of fact to weigh the evidence to determine whether a reasonable person would refuse the offer of reinstatement." *Fiedler [v. Indianhead Truck Line, Inc.]*, 670 F.2d [806] at 808 [(8th Cir. 1982)]. We have reviewed the correspondence between American Can and Morris regarding the terms of her reinstatement, as well as the testimony of company representatives and we are satisfied that this evidence shows that American Can was sincere in its claim that it was prepared to protect Morris from any further sexual harassment. We also view Morris's ultimate return to her position as evidence that the company was prepared to protect Morris from any further sexual harassment. Although we may have viewed the evidence differently, we cannot conclude that the district court clearly erred in tolling American Can's offer of backpay on September 8, 1987.[450]

---

447 *Id.*

448 Ford Motor Co. v. EEOC, 458 U.S. 219 (1982). *See also* Hopkins v. Shoe Show, Inc., 678 F. Supp. 1241 (S.D. W. Va. 1988) (sexual harassment; plaintiff could not refute defendant's position that she rejected an unconditional offer made by defendant); Davis v. Western-Southern Life Ins. Co., 34 Fair Empl. Prac. Cas. (BNA) 97 (N.D. Ohio 1984) (sexual harassment; plaintiff who had resigned because of alleged harassment waived her right to reinstatement, back pay, or other relief when she turned down an offer to return to the same job at a different location). *Cf.* Harrison v. Reed Rubber Co., 603 F. Supp. 1457, 1462 (E.D. Mo. 1985) (sexual harassment; court rejected plaintiff's contention that defendant was liable for a 50-cent-per-hour loss suffered upon her demotion when plaintiff was offered but refused position of assistant "foreman" at only 25 cents per hour less).

449 Morris v. American Nat'l Can Corp., 941 F.2d 710 (8th Cir. 1991).

450 *Id.* at 714.

§ 6.54 —Compensatory and Punitive Damages

Sexual harassment often occurs without the loss of pay or other employment-related benefits that characterize typical sex discrimination suits. The Civil Rights Act of 1991 gave sexual harassment victims new recourse by providing for compensatory and punitive damages to victims of employment discrimination. Compensatory damages may be awarded for intentional discrimination even when there has been no economic loss and are available from private employers and federal, state, and local governments. Punitive damages, however, may only be recovered from private employers when the employer acted "with malice or with reckless indifference to" the rights of the victim. The total amount of damages will be capped at $50,000 for companies of 15–100 workers and at $100,000 for companies with 101 to 200 employees, $200,000 for employers with 201 to 500 employees, and $300,000 for employers of over 500 employees. Compensatory damages include "future pecuniary losses, emotional pain, suffering, inconvenience, mental anguish, loss of enjoyment of life, and other nonpecuniary losses."[451] Punitive damages may be recovered when the plaintiff can demonstrate that the employer acted "with malice or with reckless indifference" to the individual's federally protected rights.[452] In jury trials the court may not inform the jury of the damages cap.[453]

§ 6.55 Awards of Attorneys' Fees

Title VII authorizes an award of reasonable attorneys' fees to prevailing parties.[454] The fee provision was enacted to encourage private litigants to

---

451 Civil Rights Act of 1991, Pub. L. No. 102-166 § 102(b)(3), 105 Stat. 1071, 1073 (1991).

452 Civil Rights Act of 1991, Pub. L. No. 102-166 § 102(b)(1), 105 Stat. 1071, 1073 (1991).

453 Civil Rights Act of 1991, Pub L. No. 102-166 § 102(a)(3), 105 Stat. 1071, 1072–73 (1991).

454 42 U.S.C. § 2000e-5(k). *See also* A. Conte, *Attorney Fee Awards,* Ch. 11 (2d ed. 1993).

Cases in which attorneys' fees have been awarded to successful sexual harassment plaintiffs include:

First Circuit: Lipsett v. Blanco, 975 F.2d 934 (1st Cir. 1992) (attorney fees of $545,281 awarded).

Fourth Circuit: Spencer v. General Elec. Co., 894 F.2d 651 (4th Cir. 1990). The district court properly concluded that although the plaintiff failed on charges of *quid pro quo* sexual harassment and state law claims, she prevailed on her claim of hostile environment sexual harassment, and the lawsuit served as a catalyst for the prompt development and promulgation of a revised anti-harassment policy and thus was a prevailing party for attorney fees.

enforce their civil rights laws and provide a remedy for those who otherwise would have no recourse against discrimination.[455] Courts have construed Title VII's fee provision broadly, finding that parties have prevailed when their actions have "arguably advanced the purposes of Title VII unless special circumstances would render such an award unjust."[456]

A plaintiff need not be awarded monetary damages to recover attorneys' fees under Title VII.[457] A sexual harassment plaintiff is a prevailing party if she has proven discrimination, even if the only relief available is injunctive. In *Farrar v. Hobby,*[458] the U.S. Supreme Court confirmed that a

---

Fifth Circuit: Jenkins v. Orkin Exterminating Co., 646 F. Supp. 1274, 1277 (E.D. Tex. 1986).

Sixth Circuit: Boyd v. James S. Hayes Living Health Care Agency, 671 F. Supp. 1155 (W.D. Tenn. 1987); Coley v. Conso. Rail Corp., 561 F. Supp. 645 (E.D. Mich. 1982).

Eighth Circuit: Jones v. Wesco, 846 F.2d 1154, 1155 (8th Cir. 1988); Jenson v. Eveleth Taconite Co., 824 F. Supp. 847 (D. Minn. 1993); Davis v. Tri-State Mack Distribs., 57 Fair Empl. Prac. Cas. (BNA) 1025 (E.D. Ark. 1991) ($64,540 in attorneys' fees and $8,748 in expenses); Harrison v. Reed Rubber Co., 603 F. Supp. 1457 (E.D. Mo. 1985); Wright v. Missouri Dep't of Consumer Affairs, 512 F. Supp. 729 (E.D. Mo. 1981).

Ninth Circuit: Stewart v. County of Sonoma, 634 F. Supp. 773 (N.D. Cal. 1986); Macey v. World Airways, Inc., 14 Fair Empl. Prac. Cas. (BNA) 1426 (N.D. Cal. 1977).

Tenth Circuit: Arnold v. City of Seminole, 614 F. Supp. 853 (E.D. Okla. 1985).

Eleventh Circuit: McKenzie v. Cooper, Levins & Pastko, Inc., 990 F.2d 1183 (11th Cir. 1993) (attorney fees of $102,912 plus interest awarded); Ross v. Twenty-Four Collection, Inc., 681 F. Supp. 1547, 1551 (S.D. Fla. 1988), *aff'd,* 875 F.2d 873 (11th Cir 1989); Sowers v. Kemira, Inc., 46 Fair Empl. Prac. Cas. (BNA) 1825 (S.D. Ga. 1988).

455 *See* Christiansburg Garment Co. v. EEOC, 434 U.S. 412 (1978).

456 Kulkarni v. Alexander, 662 F.2d 758, 766 n.18 (D.C. Cir. 1978).

457 City of Riverside v. Rivera, 477 U.S. 561 (1986); Spencer v. General Elec. Co., 706 F. Supp. 1234 (E.D. Va. 1989), *aff'd,* 894 F.2d 651 (4th Cir. 1990). A female employee was entitled to attorneys' fees when she proved that her employer maintained a sexually hostile work environment in violation of Title VII, despite the fact that she obtained only one dollar in nominal damages. The court determined that injunctive relief was unnecessary; the litigation was a catalyst for the prompt development and promulgation of comprehensive antisexual harassment policy by employer, and a statement to that effect in the employees' handbook, and resulted in demotion and ultimate firing of harassing supervisor.

See also Walker v. Anderson Elec. Connectors, 944 F.2d 841 (11th Cir. 1991), *cert. denied,* 113 S. Ct. 1043 (1993). A jury finding of sexual harassment alone was not sufficient in itself to render an employee a prevailing party for attorney fees when plaintiff did not obtain even a declaratory judgment. The jury had found that plaintiff had sustained no monetary damage as a proximate result of violations of Title VII and the state common law right to privacy.

458 Farrar v. Hobby, 113 S. Ct. 566 (1992).

person who wins nominal damages is a prevailing party under § 1988, but held that to recover attorney fees, a civil rights plaintiff must obtain an enforceable judgment or comparable relief through a consent decree or settlement against defendants from whom fees are sought, and that the relief secured must directly benefit the plaintiff at the time of judgment or settlement. "In short, a plaintiff 'prevails' when actual relief on the merits of his claim materially alters the legal relationship between the parties by modifying the defendant's behavior in a way that directly benefits the plaintiff."[459] In this case, the plaintiff alleged due process violations and malicious prosecution in connection with the closing of his school for delinquent, disabled, and disturbed teens by the state following a murder indictment charging the plaintiff with willful failure to administer proper medical treatment and failure to provide timely hospitalization. The plaintiff sought $17 million in damages but was awarded only nominal damages. The district court awarded the plaintiff $280,000 in fees plus expenses and interest. On appeal, a divided Fifth Circuit panel reversed the fee award,[460] and held that the plaintiffs were not prevailing parties, and thus were not entitled to fees under § 1988. The U.S. Supreme Court held that although the court of appeals erred in failing to recognize that the plaintiffs were prevailing parties, it properly reversed the district court's fee award when plaintiffs could not prove actual, compensable injury:

> Although the "technical" nature of a nominal damages award or any other judgment does not affect the prevailing party inquiry, it does bear on the propriety of fees awarded under § 1988. Once civil rights litigation materially alters the legal relationship between the parties, "the degree of the plantiff's overall success goes to the reasonableness" of a fee award under *Hensley v. Eckerhart,* 461 U.S. 424 (1983). . . . Indeed, "the most critical factor" in determining the reasonableness of a fee award "is the degree of success obtained." *Hensley, supra,* at 436. . . . In this case, petitioners received nominal damages instead of the $17 million in compensatory damages that they sought. This litigation accomplished little beyond giving petitioners "the moral satisfaction of knowing that a federal court concluded that [their] rights had been violated" in some unspecified way. *Hewitt [v. Helms,* 482 U.S. 755 (1987)] at 762. We have already observed that if "a plaintiff has achieved only partial or limited success, the product of hours reasonably expended on the litigation as a whole times a reasonable hourly rate may be an excessive amount." *Hensley, supra,* at 436. Yet the District Court calculated petitioners' fee award in precisely this fashion, without engaging in any measured exercise of discretion. . . . Having considered the amount and nature of damages awarded, the court may lawfully award low

---

[459] *Id.* at 573.

[460] Estate of Farrar v. Cain, 941 F2d 1311 (5th Cir 1991).

> fees or no fees without reciting the 12 factors bearing on reasonbleness, see *Hensley,* 461 U.S. at 430, n. 3, or multiplying "the number of hours reasonably expended . . . by a reasonable hourly rate," *Id.,* at 433.
>
> In some circumstances, even a plaintiff who formally "prevails" under § 1988 should receive no attorney's fees at all. A plaintiff who seeks compensatory damages but receives no more than nominal damages is often such a prevailing party. As we have held, a nominal damages award does render a plaintiff a prevailing party by allowing [her or] him to vindicate [her or] his absolute right to procedural due process through enforcement of a judgment against the defendant. . . . In a civil rights suit for damages, however, the awarding of nominal damages also highlights the plaintiff's failure to prove actual, compensable injury. . . . When a plaintiff recovers only nominal damages because of [the] failure to prove an essential element of [her or] his claim for monetary relief, . . . the only reasonable fee is usually no fee at all.[461]

Attorneys' fees also may be awarded following the negotiation of a favorable settlement[462] and for work performed in state or local proceedings pursuant to exhaustion of remedies requirements.[463] If a plaintiff prevails on the administrative level in a Title VII action against a federal agency, the agency has the discretion to award fees.[464] However, a grievance procedure is not a proceeding for which attorneys' fees may be awarded under Title VII.[465]

Section 113(a) of the Civil Rights Act of 1991 amends the Civil Rights Attorney's Fees Awards Act and Title VII to provide for reimbursement to prevailing parties for expert witness fees.[466]

---

461 Farrar v. Hobby, 113 S. Ct. 574–75(1992).

See also Parton v. GTE N., Inc., 971 F.2d 150 (8th Cir. 1992). A finding by the court that the employee's termination was not gender-based did not bar an award of nominal damages on her sexual harassment claim. It is the law of the circuit that nominal damages are appropriately awarded when a Title VII violation is proven even though no actual damages are awarded.

462 Liverman-Melton v. British Aerospace, Inc., 628 F. Supp. 102 (D.D.C. 1986); Wright v. Department of Agric., 41 Fair Empl. Prac. Cas. (BNA) 1391 (D. Md. 1986).

463 New York Gaslight Club v. Carey, 447 U.S. 54 (1980). *Cf.* Haskins v. United States Dep't of the Navy, 808 F.2d 1192 (6th Cir.), *cert. denied,* 484 U.S. 815 (1987) (an employee who received favorable liability determination at the administrative level was not a prevailing party even though defendant employer admitted that he had discriminated against her when the employee would not have been promoted even in the absence of discrimination).

464 Smith v. Califano, 446 F. Supp. 530 (D.D.C. 1978).

465 Mertz v. Marsh, 786 F.2d 1578 (11th Cir.), *cert. denied,* 479 U.S. 1008 (1986). *See also* Cooper v. Williamson County Bd. of Educ., 820 F.2d 180 (6th Cir. 1987), *cert. denied,* 484 U.S. 1006 (1988) (dismissal proceedings were not useful or necessary to protect Title VII rights even though plaintiff had to participate in the proceedings to keep his job).

466 Title VII, § 703(k)(1)(A)(ii).

Rule 68 of the Federal Rules of Civil Procedure permits a defendant to make a timely offer of judgment before trial and provides that if the judgment obtained by the offeree is not more favorable than the offer, the offeree must pay the costs incurred after the making of the offer. In *Spencer v. General Elec. Co.,*[467] a sexual harassment action, the district court properly limited attorney fees to those incurred before an offer of judgment. Guided by the U.S. Supreme Court decision in *Pavelic & Leflore v. Marvel Entertainment Group,*[468] in which the Court admonished that the Federal Rules of Civil Procedure must be given their plain meaning, the court of appeals considered whether a trial court is constrained by the plain language of Rule 68 and must compare only the terms of the actual judgment entered, as opposed to the actual result entered with the terms of the offer, and whether the plaintiff was not a prevailing party in this litigation because she was primarily seeking monetary damages, which she did not receive, rather than the implemented sexual harassment policy. Although on different reasoning, the Court affirmed the trial court's holding that the Rule 68 offer precluded the award of postoffer fees and costs:

> We begin our discussion of the Rule 68 issues by disposing of Spencer's contention that the Rule's application to Title VII cases in some way undercuts the policy goals of the Act. In *Mark v. Chesny*, 473 U.S. 1, 10–12 . . . (1985), . . . the Supreme Court . . . simply found nothing incompatible between the policies of protecting civil rights and promptly settling litigation. . . .
>
> Further, the fact that a civil rights defendant can voluntary comply with Title VII and negate the basis for a plaintiff's request for injunctive relief after a Rule 68 offer has been rejected does not make the Rule hostile to Title VII. In all litigation, after a plaintiff rejects a settlement offer, a defendant can always change its conduct to comply with a plaintiff's demands, thereby reducing the plaintiff's chances for victory and reducing her claims and fees. This is one of the inherent risks of litigation that falls no more heavily on a Title VII litigant than it does on any other civil complainant. Rule 68 must apply with full force to this claim as it does to all other civil actions brought in the federal courts.
>
> [With respect to the construction of Rule 68, t]he language of the Rule could not be more plain. A court's task under the Rule is to compare the offer of "judgment" to the "judgment finally obtained" by the offeree and determine if the latter is more favorable than the former. In making this comparison, the court below strayed from this plain mandate, seeing fit to include the non-judgment relief Spencer acquired as part of her "judgment finally obtained." . . . This was in error.

* * *

---

467 Spencer v. General Elec. Co., 894 F.2d 651 (4th Cir. 1990).

468 Pavelic & Leflone v. Marvel Entertainment Group, 493 U.S. 120 (1989).

> Spencer's and EEOC's arguments . . . seem to assume that "judgment finally obtained" really means "relief finally obtained." Overlooking the fact that this assumption ignores the plain working of the Rule, we note that common sense informs that often the relief a plaintiff obtains from a lawsuit is quite different from the judgment obtained from that lawsuit. In fact, many lawsuits are voluntarily dismissed before ever reaching the judgment stage because the mere filing of the suits enabled the aggrieved parties to obtain all the relief they sought. Thus "judgment" and "relief" are commonly understood to be two very different concepts and to treat the two interchangeably is an interpretation of the Rule we cannot adopt.
>
> We find implicit in Spencer's and EEOC's arguments the suggestion that Rule 68 should be given an expansive interpretation to effectuate the strong public polices behind Title VII. We reject this temptation. Rule 68 is a rule of procedure, not substance. Its purpose is to provide an efficient and neutral means to settle litigation, irrespective of the nature of the underlying disputes.[469]

Attorneys' fees also may be assessed against an unsuccessful plaintiff, including the EEOC, under Title VII if the defendant shows that the plaintiff's action was "frivolous, unreasonable, or without foundation, even though not brought in subjective bad faith."[470] Plaintiffs who file frivolous pleadings also may be assessed with sanctions under Rule 11 of the Federal Rules of Civil Procedure.[471]

In deciding the amount of fees to be awarded, the court determines the lodestar, the number of hours reasonably expended times a reasonable hourly rate, and the extent to which the plaintiff has prevailed. The court may reduce the lodestar for time spent on unsuccessful claims or may enhance the lodestar in certain circumstances on the basis of risk,[472] the contingent nature of the action, or exceptional results. The burden is on the fee petitioner to demonstrate that the rates and hours requested are reasonable.[473]

A fee award entered after a final disposition on the merits is a final, appealable decision under 28 U.S.C. § 1291, and generally the decision may be reviewed only for abuse of discretion.[474] Factual findings are subject to a clearly erroneous standard of review.[475]

---

469 Spencer v. General Elec. Co., 894 F.2d 651, 662–64 (4th Cir. 1990) (footnote omitted).

470 Christiansburg Garment Co. v. EEOC, 434 U.S. 412 (1978). *See* A. Conte, Attorney Fee Awards, § 5.01 (2d ed. 1993).

471 A. Conte, Attorney Fee Awards, Ch. 7 (2d ed. 1993).

472 Pennsylvania v. Delaware Valley Citizens' Council for Clean Air, 483 U.S. 711 (1987).

473 Blum v. Stenson, 465 U.S. 886 (1984).

474 *Id.*; Hensley v. Eckerhart, 461 U.S. 424 (1983).

475 Blum v. Stenson, 465 U.S. 886 (1984); Hensley v. Eckerhart, 461 U.S. 424 (1983); Institutionalized Juveniles v. Secretary of Pub. Welfare, 758 F.2d 897, 909 n.21 (3d Cir. 1985).

A sample brief in support of a plaintiff's application for attorneys' fees is in **Appendix F.**

§ 6.56 Awards of Costs

Costs may be assessed against the losing party in a Title VII action pursuant to Federal Rule of Civil Procedure 54(d) and 28 U.S.C. § 1920. A party's attorney may be liable for costs for bringing multiplicitous proceedings under 42 U.S.C. § 1927. A frivolous appeal may warrant the assessment of costs under Federal Rule of Appellate Procedure 38.

Under Federal Rule of Civil Procedure 68, which governs offers of judgment, if the outcome of the litigation is less favorable than the settlement offer, the assessment of costs, including attorneys' fees, shifts to the plaintiff as of the time the offer of judgment was made.[476]

§ 6.57 Appeals

Title VII determinations may be appealed to federal courts of appeal in a timely manner, pursuant to 28 U.S.C. §§ 1291 and 1292. A district court decision cannot be set aside unless the factual findings are clearly erroneous.[477] A decision is clearly erroneous when the appellate court "is left with the definite and firm conviction that a mistake has been committed," not when the evidence could have been interpreted differently.[478] Credibility determinations generally are reviewed under the clearly erroneous standard.[479] A district court need not make specific findings of fact regarding every piece of evidence,[480] but its findings cannot be conclusory.

Findings of fact include whether a sexual harassment plaintiff was subjected to unwelcome sexual advances or other sexual conduct,[481] determinations of continuing violations to govern calculation of the filing period,[482] and diligence in mitigating damages.[483] However, the decision of

---

476 Delta Air Lines, Inc. v. August, 450 U.S. 346 (1981) (the Rule does not apply to situations when plaintiff loses the action completely).

477 Cortes v. Maxus Exploration Co., 977 F.2d 195 (5th Cir. 1992); Barrett v. Omaha Nat'l Bank, 726 F.2d 424 (8th Cir. 1984).

478 United States v. United States Gypsum Co., 333 U.S. 364, 395 (1948); Anderson v. City of Bessemer City, 470 U.S. 564 (1985).

479 Anderson v. City of Bessemer City, 470 U.S. 564 (1985).

480 Smith v. Honeywell, Inc., 735 F.2d 1067 (8th Cir.), *cert. denied,* 460 U.S. 1077 (1984).

481 Meritor Sav. Bank v. Vinson, 477 U.S. 57, 68 (1986).

482 Abrams v. Baylor College of Medicine, 805 F.2d 528 (5th Cir. 1986).

483 Walters v. City of Atlanta, 803 F.2d 1135 (11th Cir. 1986).

whether the conduct was so severe or pervasive that it altered the plaintiff's employment by creating an abusive work environment requires the court to consider "legal concepts in the mix of fact and law and to exercise judgment about the values that animate legal principles."[484] An appellate court generally defers to a credibility determination made by the trial court.[485]

---

484 United States v. McConney, 728 F.2d 1195, 1202 (9th Cir.), *cert. denied,* 469 U.S. 824 (1984); Jordan v. Clark, 847 F.2d 1368, 1375 (9th Cir. 1988), *cert. denied,* 488 U.S. 1006 (1989) (sexual harassment).

485 Lee v. Russell County Bd. of Educ., 744 F.2d 768 (11th Cir. 1984).

CHAPTER 7

EMPLOYER DEFENSES

§ 7.1 Introduction

An employer may act within the bounds of its legitimate business discretion in making employment decisions, as long as the action is not discriminatory.[1] To rebut circumstantial evidence of discrimination, the defendant employer generally need produce only a permissible nondiscriminatory reason for altering the plaintiff's employment status.[2] When there is "direct testimony that the defendant acted with a discriminatory motive,

[1] Neville v. Taft Broadcasting Co., 42 Fair Empl. Prac. Cas. (BNA) 1314, 1324 (W.D.N.Y. 1987).

[2] Texas Dep't of Community Affairs v. Burdine, 450 U.S. 248, 254–55 (1981).

and the trier of fact accepts this testimony, the ultimate issue of discrimination is proved."[3]

The employer must present some objective evidence of its probable decision without the presence of an impermissible motive. Proving "that the same decision would have been justified . . . is not the same as proving that the same decision would have been made,"[4] however:

> An employer may not, in other words, prevail in a mixed-motives case by offering a legitimate and sufficient reason for its decision if that reason did not motivate it at the time of the decision. . . . [A]n employer may not meet its burden in such a case by merely showing that at the time of the decision, it was motivated only in part by a legitimate reason. The very premise of a mixed-motives case is that a legitimate reason was present. . . . The employer instead must show that its legitimate reason, standing alone, would have induced it to make the same decision.[5]

In cases based on circumstantial evidence, it is sufficient that the employer's evidence raises a genuine issue of fact as to whether it discriminated against the plaintiff.[6] The standard Title VII order of proof is appropriate when the challenged conduct resulted in a change of employment status[7] (see **Chapter 6**) or a constructive discharge. (see **§ 7.17**). However, when the plaintiff alleges a hostile work environment and no change in employment status, it becomes difficult to assert a "legitimate business justification" for the harassing conduct. Some courts have required defendants in hostile environment cases to show by clear and convincing evidence that the plaintiff would not have been treated differently if she had not opposed the harassment.[8] This higher standard is

---

3 Bell v. Birmingham Linen Serv., 715 F.2d 1552, 1557 (11th Cir. 1983), *cert. denied,* 467 U.S. 1204 (1984). *See also* Sowers v. Kemira, Inc., 46 Fair Empl. Prac. Cas. (BNA) 1825, 1835 (S.D. Ga. 1988) (plaintiff presented direct evidence of discriminatory motive when she testified that her supervisor made a number of sexual advances to her, many of them in the context of discussions regarding plaintiff's possible promotion, and when plaintiff later inquired about the promotion, the supervisor told her that she would get what she wanted if she played his game).

4 Texas Dep't of Community Affairs at 252, *quoting* Givhan v. Western Line Consol. Sch. Dist., 439 U.S. 410, 416 (1979).

5 *Id.* at 252.

6 *Id.* at 256 (1981). *See also* EEOC v. Judson Steel Co., 33 Fair Empl. Prac. Cas. (BNA) 1286 (N.D. Cal. 1982) (burden one of persuasion, not proof).

7 See **Ch. 6.**

8 Bundy v. Jackson, 641 F.2d 934, 952–53 (D.C. Cir. 1981); Day v. Mathews, 530 F.2d 1083, 1085 (D.C. Cir. 1976); Baxter v. Savannah Sugar Ref. Corp., 495 F.2d 437, 444–45 (5th Cir.), *cert. denied,* 419 U.S. 1033 (1974); Broderick v. Ruder, 685 F. Supp. 1269, 1279–80 (D.D.C. 1988).

based on the notion that "once a plaintiff establishes that she was harassed . . . it is hard to see how an employer can justify [the] harassment."[9] Some courts apply a two-step analysis:

> First, the plaintiff must make a prima facie showing that sexually harassing conduct took place, and if this is done, the employer may rebut the showing either directly by proving that the events did not take place, or indirectly, by showing that they were isolated or genuinely trivial. Second, the plaintiff must show that the employer knew or should have known of the harassment, and took no effectual action to correct the situation. This showing can also be rebutted by the employer directly, or by pointing to prompt remedial action reasonably calculated to end the harassment.[10]

Most courts use a five-part analysis for hostile environment claims. It requires the plaintiff to allege and prove that she belongs to a protected group, she was subjected to unwelcome sexual harassment, the harassment was based on sex, the harassment affected a term, condition, or privilege of employment, and the employer knew or should have known of the harassment.[11] An employer can rebut any of those elements or show that it made a prompt and appropriate response to the allegations of harassment. (see § **7.6**).

The ultimate burden remains with the plaintiff throughout to prove the existence and intentional nature of the sexual harassment.[12]

Thorough documentation of complaints, misconduct, work-related conversations between management and nonmanagement employees, and remedial action taken will strengthen a valid defense. Supporting testimony by coworkers also will enhance defendant's rebuttal.[13]

§ 7.2 Conduct Was Nondiscriminatory

Acts of harassment generally are deemed discriminatory only if they are aimed toward a member of a specific class.[14] Situations involving *quid pro*

---

9 Moffett v. Gene B. Glick Co., 621 F. Supp. 244, 266 (N.D. Ind. 1985). *See also* Bundy v. Jackson, 641 F.2d 934, 953 (D.C. Cir. 1981).

10 Katz v. Dole, 709 F.2d 251, 255–56 (4th Cir. 1983).

11 Vermett v. Hough, 627 F. Supp. 587 (W.D. Mich. 1986).

12 *Id.* at 604.

13 Del Valle Fontanez v. Aponte, 660 F. Supp. 145 (D.P.R. 1987).

14 *Cf.* De Cintio v. Westchester County Medical Ctr., 807 F.2d 304, 306–07 (2d Cir. 1986), *cert. denied,* 484 U.S. 825 (1987). "The proscribed differentiation under Title VII . . . must be a distinction based on a person's sex, not on his or her sexual affiliations." Male plaintiffs were not prejudiced because of their status as males but because their superior preferred his paramour for a promotion.

quo harassment usually are clearly based on sex and may involve either heterosexual or homosexual advances. The question of whether particular conduct was aimed at one sex arises more often in hostile environment cases. An employer may argue that a supervisor treated all employees equally with disdain or in a vulgar manner.[15] However, a court may determine that sexual slurs, for example, are far more oppressive to women than to men, and thus find sexual harassment. Moreover, a plaintiff would argue that an environment contaminated by sexual slurs negatively affects both sexes with respect to their perception of women's roles in the workplace, and thus cannot be condoned on the basis that all employees are subjected to the conduct.

Conduct need not be explicitly sexual to constitute sexual harassment. However, the less sexual the conduct, the less likely a court may conclude that the challenged behavior was based on sex.[16]

§ 7.3 Conduct Was Welcome

Liability for sexual harassment will not attach if the employer can demonstrate that the plaintiff welcomed the challenged conduct. The employer need not actually show that the plaintiff invited the alleged harassment. Evidence of plaintiff's participation in the conduct is not determinative, but it may suggest that the conduct was welcome.[17] However, participation may be viewed as a response linked to the plaintiff's fear of losing her

---

15 *See, e.g.,* Sheehan v. Purolator, Inc., 839 F.2d 99 (2d Cir.), *cert. denied,* 488 U.S. 891 (1988); Jackson–Colley v. Army Corps of Engr's, 655 F. Supp. 122, 127 (E.D. Mich. 1987) (testimony elicited numerous responses indicating that supervisor had habit of swearing and cursing "at the sky").

16 *See, e.g.,* Seligson v. Massachusetts Inst. of Tech., 677 F. Supp. 648 (D. Mass. 1987).

17 Smith v. Acme Spinning Co., 40 Fair Empl. Prac. Cas. (BNA) 1104 (W.D.N.C. 1986) (court's view of the alleged incidents was "influenced significantly" by the undisputed fact that plaintiff frequently participated in on-the-job horseplay that included a good deal of rubbing and touching of male employees, including her supervisor); Evans v. Mail Handlers, 32 Fair Empl. Prac. Cas. (BNA) 634 (D.D.C. 1983) (when plaintiff carried on an open, sexual relationship with the alleged harasser for several years and did not consider the challenged conduct to be offensive or intimidating until the relationship began to deteriorate, the alleged harassing conduct was substantially welcomed); Ukarish v. Magnesium Elektron, 31 Fair Empl. Prac. Cas. (BNA) 1315 (D.N.J. 1983) (although plaintiff made entries in her diary that sexual banter was unwelcome, she joined in on the banter at work and seemed to accept the atmosphere and never expressed her concerns to coworkers or supervisors); Reichman v. Bureau of Affirmative Action, 536 F. Supp. 1149 (M.D. Pa. 1982) (plaintiff acted in "very flirtatious and provocative" manner around defendant and invited him to her home for dinner on several occasions; the alleged harassment consisted of one attempt to kiss plaintiff).

job. Nor can evidence of past participation be used to support a finding of welcomeness when the plaintiff shows that at some point she changed her mind and found the conduct offensive.[18] Courts generally look at whether the plaintiff complained about the challenged behavior in determining whether the conduct was welcome.[19] This issue usually comes up in hostile environment cases.[20] Although fear of termination or recrimination also may make the harassed employee reluctant to speak out about her treatment, she may express her anxiety through conversations with coworkers, doctors, psychologists, or family members. Still, an employer may argue that it had no knowledge of the harassment, separate from the welcomeness issue.

§ 7.4 Conditions or Terms of Employment Not Affected

A *quid pro quo* claim turns on evidence that the receipt or retention of an employment benefit was conditioned upon compliance with sexual advances. An employer may try to demonstrate that threats were never made,[21] that the relevant supervisor did not have authority to make the asserted employment decision,[22] or that the plaintiff's success and advancement could not have been affected by alleged sexual demands because there was no change in employment status or denial of job benefit.[23]

If an employment change or discipline did occur, an employer may argue that it happened as a result of the plaintiff's conduct rather than that of the alleged harasser.[24]

---

18 Swentek v. USAIR, Inc., 830 F.2d 552 (4th Cir. 1987).

19 Koster v. Chase Manhattan Bank, 46 Fair Empl. Prac. Cas. (BNA) 1436, 1447 (S.D.N.Y. 1988) ("not a scintilla of evidence was proffered that even hinted the affair with defendant Ross was unwelcome").

20 *See, e.g.*, Gan v. Kepro Circuit Sys., Inc., 28 Fair Empl. Prac. Cas. (BNA) 639 (E.D. Mo. 1982).

21 Hill v. BASF Wyandotte Corp., 27 Fair Empl. Prac. Cas. (BNA) 66 (E.D. Mich. 1981).

22 Koster v. Chase Manhattan Bank, 46 Fair Empl. Prac. Cas. (BNA) 1436, 1447 (S.D.N.Y. 1988); Sheekey v. Nelson, 40 Fair Empl. Prac. Cas. (BNA) 1216 (D.N.J. 1986) (manager who had allegedly harassed plaintiff had not handed in her termination and at least on one occasion saved her job); Kwiatkowski v. Postal Serv., 39 Fair Empl. Prac. Cas. (BNA) 1740 (N.D. Ill. 1985).

23 Jones v. Flagship Int'l, 793 F.2d 714 (5th Cir. 1986), *cert. denied*, 479 U.S. 1065 (1987) (record failed to establish that plaintiff was required to accept sexual harassment as condition of a job benefit because plaintiff could not prove that sexual harassment affected her pay, promotion, or responsibilities).

24 *See, e.g.*, Wimberly v. Shoney's, Inc., 39 Fair Empl. Prac. Cas. (BNA) 444 (S.D. Ga. 1985) (disciplinary notice was due to plaintiff's irritability; it was reasonable to discipline an employee who might thwart the morale of other employees).

In the hostile environment context, the plaintiff's most difficult job is to demonstrate that the sexually abusive environment was severe enough to affect a term or condition of her employment, particularly when she participated in the conduct[25] or did not complain about the harassment.[26] An employer can suggest that had the conduct been intolerable, the plaintiff would have quit or at least reported the harassment to someone who could have remedied the situation. One or two incidents of harassment seldom are found to create a hostile environment.[27] Evidence that the plaintiff did not take the challenged conduct seriously also may overcome an inference that the acts were unwelcome.[28] Even if the employer knew or should have known of the harassment because of its pervasive nature, a showing that the conduct was welcome and encouraged may be fatal to a prima facie case of sexual harassment.[29]

§ 7.5 Employer Had No Notice of Harassment

Lack of notice because of an employee's failure to invoke an internal grievance procedure is not determinative in a sexual harassment action.

---

25 Gan v. Kepro Circuit Sys., Inc., 28 Fair Empl. Prac. Cas. (BNA) 639, 641 (E.D. Mo. 1982).

26 *See also* Highlander v. K.F.C. Nat'l Mgmt. Co., 805 F.2d 644 (6th Cir. 1986) (plaintiff waited three months before complaining about harassment).

27 Petrosky v. Washington-Greene County Ass'n for the Blind, 663 F. Supp. 821 (W.D. Pa. 1987) (plaintiff who had been kissed once by supervisor did not establish sexual harassment); Sapp v. City of Warner Robins, 655 F. Supp. 1043 (M.D. Ga. 1987); Strickland v. Sears, Roebuck & Co., 46 Fair Empl. Prac. Cas. (BNA) 1024 (E.D. Va. 1987), *aff'd,* 846 F.2d 74 (4th Cir. 1988) (no sexual harassment was found when supervisor touched plaintiff only once, a comment about dating plaintiff occurred only 15 minutes after alleged touching incident, it was uncontested that this was the only incident, and manager took prompt remedial action to ensure such events would not happen again); Vermett v. Hough, 627 F. Supp. 587, 607 (W.D. Mich. 1986) (one act involving the shining of a flashlight between the plaintiff's legs at knee level was "[c]hildish, yes; sexual harassment, no"); *See also* Smith v. Acme Spinning Co., 40 Fair Empl. Prac. Cas. (BNA) 1104 (W.D.N.C. 1986) (three isolated incidents of harassment by supervisor extending over three years did not result in liability).

28 Highlander v. K.F.C. Nat'l Mgmt. Co., 805 F.2d 644, 650 (6th Cir. 1986) (plaintiff had stated she did not think asserted incident was "that big a deal"); Smith v. Acme Spinning Co., 40 Fair Empl. Prac. Cas. (BNA) 1104 (W.D.N.C. 1986) (from plaintiff's own testimony it was clear that even if touching incident occurred, plaintiff neither regarded it as serious nor did it influence her decision to leave her job); Collins v. Pfizer, Inc., 39 Fair Empl. Prac. Cas. (BNA) 1316, 1330 (D. Conn. 1985) ("As recently as the trial itself plaintiff swore she was very happy in the job and would like to come back—hardly the attribute of a woman who was subjected to such demeaning conduct").

29 Gan v. Kepro Circuit Sys., Inc., 28 Fair Empl. Prac. Cas. (BNA) 639, 641 (E.D. Mo. 1982).

Nor may an employer avoid liability in the absence of such procedures merely because he or she personally was not aware of the harassment.[30] Employers are strictly liable for the conduct of supervisors when the alleged harassment involves tangible employment benefits (see **Chapter 3**). When an employee charges that supervisors or coworkers created a hostile work environment, an employer is liable if he knew or should have known of the challenged conduct.[31] For example, in *Canada v. Boyd Group, Inc.*,[32] a female employee alleged that over a two or three week period her supervisor engaged in conduct including: two incidents of telling "off-color" jokes from which the plaintiff walked away, comments on how good the plaintiff looked in her uniform, smiling and looking at the plaintiff a great deal, one incident in which the supervisor leaned or rubbed the front of his body on the back of the plaintiff's body and placed his hand on her shoulder, another incident in which he placed his hand on her shoulder, and made one phone call to her home. Soon after these incidents, the plaintiff requested a shift change, and over the next five weeks,

---

30 Meritor Sav. Bank v. Vinson, 477 U.S. 57, 72 (1986); *See also* Kirkland v. Brinias, 741 F. Supp. 692 (E.D. Tenn. 1989), *aff'd without opinion,* 944 F.2d 905 (5th Cir. 1991). Although the court concluded that there was "no question that the plaintiffs. . . were subjected to sexual harassment on the job", *id. at 588,* owners of a restaurant were not liable for the sexual harassment of two waitresses by a busboy when the unwelcome behavior came from a subordinate, not a supervisor, and there was no hint that plaintiffs were psychologically harmed by the conduct. Neither plaintiff expressly complained to their employers when neither believed defendants would be sympathetic; Hopkins v. Shoe Show of Va., Inc., 678 F. Supp. 1241 (S.D. W. Va. 1988) (genuine issue of material fact regarding reasonableness of plaintiff's failure to make employer aware of supervisor's conduct precluded summary judgment on issue of employer liability).

31 Hrabak v. Marquip, Inc., 798 F. Supp. 550 (W.D. Wis. 1992). In a sexual harassment suit by a female sales administrative assistant against her employer, its president, one of its supervisor employees and its insurer, a material issue of fact existed as to whether an employer knew or should have known of alleged harassment by a coworker of plaintiff, which included verbal and written requests that plaintiff wear revealing clothing, and compliments on her legs, figure and body. Even though the coworker was not the direct supervisor of plaintiff, he virtually had complete control over the conditions of the employee's work environment. He controlled all of her work, was the principal force of any evaluation of her performance, and could summon her to his office at any time. Also at issue was the effectiveness of the remedial measures taken by the employer after plaintiff complained of the harassment.

Silverstein v. Metroplex Communications, Inc., 678 F. Supp. 863 (S.D. Fla. 1988) (alleged harassment was not so pervasive as to put defendant on constructive notice of conduct); Smith v. Acme Spinning Co., 40 Fair Empl. Prac. Cas. (BNA) 1104 (W.D.N.C. 1986) (evidence of three isolated incidents of harassment extending over three years did not provide a sufficient basis to impute constructive knowledge to defendant); Kwiatkowski v. Postal Serv., 39 Fair Empl. Prac. Cas. (BNA) 1740 (N.D. Ill. 1985).

32 809 F. Supp. 771 (D. Nev. 1992).

their relationship was strained and she was eventually fired. The court held that there was a genuine issue of material fact as to whether the defendants had actual knowledge of the harassment when the plaintiff alleged that she had met with higher management and expressed her concerns about the supervisor, and a defendant admitted in deposition that there was a series of concern regarding the supervisor's professional conduct. The supervisor had been instructed to "take a course at the community college on how to get along with people as far as body language and as far as stuff like this right here."[33] Courts often base findings of liability at least in part on whether the plaintiff complained of the harassment.[34] If the plaintiff employee did complain, the court will examine the quality

---

33 *Id.* at 778.

34 Second Circuit: Collins v. Pfizer, Inc., 39 Fair Empl. Prac. Cas. (BNA) 1316 (D. Conn. 1985) (plaintiff never complained of alleged hostile environment).

Third Circuit: Reynolds v. Atlantic City Convention Ctr., 53 Fair Empl. Prac. Cas. (BNA) 1852 (D.N.J. 1990) (plaintiff did not complain of harassment).

Fourth Circuit: Dwyer v. Smith, 867 F.2d 184 (4th Cir. 1989) (plaintiff female officer was on police force for years before she complained of harassment); Slate v. Kingsdown, 46 Fair Empl. Prac. Cas. (BNA) 1495 (M.D.N.C. 1987) (plaintiff never lodged complaint of sexual harassment and defendant's awareness could not be inferred when record disclosed only two unwitnessed incidents of alleged harassment that occurred in a very short period of time).

Sixth Circuit: Rose v. Figgie Int'l, 56 Fair Empl. Prac. Cas. (BNA) 41 (W.D. Mich. 1990). An employee who alleged that her supervisor sexually harassed her for over 15 years until her resignation was not subjected to a hostile environment when she testified that no challenged conduct had occurred for at least a year or two before her resignation, she never complained to her supervisor about his conduct, there was no evidence that his alleged hostility affected her career, and she could not allege any direct sexual advances; Kirkland v. Brinias, 741 F. Supp. 692 (E.D. Tenn. 1989), *aff'd without opinion*, 944 F.2d 905 (6th Cir. 1991). Plaintiff waitresses alleged that a busboy created a hostile environment in the form of offering money for sex, threats, pats on the rear end, hugs, arm grabbing, hostile pranks, and other conduct. Sexual harassment was not found despite corroboration by other former employees of the plaintiffs' accounts and other evidence of coworker misconduct that would create a hostile and intimidating working environment when the court determined that there was no showing that the conduct had any harmful psychological effect on waitresses, the waitresses were well able to handle the alleged harassment and would not have hesitated to ask management for help if needed and there was no preponderance of evidence regarding whether management recognized or should have recognized that any of their employees were offended by the conduct. Although the court acknowledged that plaintiffs failed to expressly complain of sexual harassment because neither believed that defendants would be sympathetic, the court gave weight to testimony of an assistant manager establishing that "much of the difficulty experienced by the waitresses . . . was a matter of cultural misunderstandings." *Id.* at 695, and of the busboy defendant himself, who "emphatically and emotionally denied ever improperly touching any woman." *Id.* at 697. The court concluded that plaintiffs quit their jobs because they felt that their employers were unwilling to listen to their side of an issue when they felt unjustly accused of something, rather than the result of any overtly sexual conduct:

and timing[35] of the complaints to determine whether the employer was reasonably informed of the alleged harassment. Occasional, informal remonstrances may not be sufficient to establish liability in some cases,[36] but the level of objection required may turn on the severity of the conduct. If the plaintiff did not complain, the court may evaluate the basis for her reticence to determine whether the employer should have known about the harassment anyway.

Documentation of plaintiff's complaints may be used to discredit later testimony regarding the nature of the harassment.

§ 7.6 Employer Took Prompt and Appropriate Remedial Action

An employer may avoid liability if he or she took prompt and appropriate action in response to employee complaints of harassment or after otherwise learning of the harassing conduct. How prompt the response must be depends on the severity of the challenged conduct. The action taken by the employer must be "reasonably calculated" to put an end to the sexual harassment.[37] For example, in *Dornhecker v. Malibu Grand Prix*

> In fact, plaintiff Kirkland wrote defendant Brinias a twelve-page letter after her resignation in which she catalogued her many grievances against her former employers. These included lack of vacation pay, lack of maternity leave, false accusations, *etc.*, but did not mention sexual harassment. In fact, the evidence was overwhelming that both plaintiffs were well able to handle the situation; that they were both capable, outspoken women; and that, if they had needed help from the management, they would not have hesitated to ask for it.

Id. at 698; Davis v. Western-Southern Life Ins. Co., 34 Fair Empl. Prac. Cas. (BNA) 97 (N.D. Ohio 1984) (plaintiff never brought alleged harassment to attention of appropriate supervisors).

Tenth Circuit: Brown v. City of Guthrie, 22 Fair Empl. Prac. Cas. (BNA) 1627 (W.D. Okla. 1980) (employer ignored complaints of sexual harassment).

Eleventh Circuit: Silverstein v. Metroplex Communications, Inc., 678 F. Supp. 863 (S.D. Fla. 1988) (plaintiff failed to complain about alleged harassment even though she had opportunity to do so); Wimberly v. Shoney's, Inc., 39 Fair Empl. Prac. Cas. (BNA) 444 (S.D. Ga. 1985).

35 Highlander v. K.F.C. Nat'l Mgmt. Co., 805 F.2d 644, 650 (6th Cir. 1986) (plaintiff failed to report episode of harassment for three months).

36 Lake v. Baker, 662 F. Supp. 392 (D.D.C. 1987) (complaints to coworkers may be insufficient); Slate v. Kingsdown, 46 Fair Empl. Prac. Cas. (BNA) 1495 (M.D.N.C. 1987).

37 Katz v. Dole, 709 F.2d 251, 256 (4th Cir. 1983).

Second Circuit: Babcock v. Frank, 59 Fair Empl. Prac. Cas. (BNA) 410 (S.D.N.Y. 1992). The court dismissed a sexual harassment complaint, finding that plaintiff did not suffer a tangible job detriment as a result of her rejection of Musso's sexual advances. "Moreover, the postal service acted promptly and appropriately when it learned of

Corp.,[38] the plaintiff advised management of several incidents of harassment that occurred while the plaintiff was on an out-of-town business trip. The president of the company told the plaintiff that she would not have to work with the alleged harasser after the end of the trip, which was to last another one-and-a-half days. The plaintiff resigned that day and brought suit alleging, among other things, that the employer was not appropriately responsive to her claims of harassment. The court rejected this contention:

Musso's threat to harm plaintiff's career for refusing his advances, which it completely and unambiguously repudiated." *Id.* at 415.

Fifth Circuit: Landgraf v. USI Film Prods., 968 F.2d 427 (5th Cir. 1992). Although it was uncontested that plaintiff suffered significant sexual harassment by her coworker in the form of continuous and repeated inappropriate verbal comments and physical contact, the lower court did not clearly err when it concluded that the employer tooks steps reasonably calculated to end coworker's sexual harassment of plaintiff by giving the alleged harasser its most serious form of reprimand and acting to reduce workplace contact between the parties.

Sixth Circuit: Kauffman v. Allied Signal, 970 F.2d 178 (6th Cir. 1992), *cert. denied,* 113 S. Ct. 831 (1993). A female employee who had had breast enlargement brought an action charging that her supervisor sexually harassed her by touching her breast and retaliating against her for objecting to his conduct by assigning her to a manual press that was disliked within the department, throwing a spark plug insulator at her, and ordering other employees to make comments to plaintiff about her breasts. When plaintiff went to her union representative, who brought her complaint to the director of employee relations, the harasser was fired. Plaintiff claimed that she was subjected to harassment and hostility even after the supervisor was fired, and ultimately suffered a nervous breakdown and was unable to return to work. The district court found that the employer had no knowledge of the supervisor's actions and when they found out, they took immediate and effective remedial action by discharging the harasser, and that because the supervisor did not have the authority to hire, fire, promote, or discipline plaintiff on his own, and because the company sexual harassment policy worked, the employer was not liable as a matter of law. The court of appeals disagreed with the district court's conclusion that the company was not liable because the harasser did not qualify as its agent under "scope of employment" standards, noting that the supervising employee need not have ultimate authority to hire or fire to qualify as an employer, so long as there is significant input into such personnel decisions. At the very least, there existed a question of fact as to whether the supervisor had enough authority to qualify as an agent and therefore as an employer under Title VII. The court thus reversed an order of summary judgment in favor of an employer on a *quid pro quo* claim of sexual harassment, but affirmed summary judgment on the hostile environment claim.

Seventh Circuit: Juarez v. Ameritech Mobile Communications, 746 F. Supp. 798 (N.D. Ill. 1990), *aff'd,* 957 F. 2d 317 (7th Cir. 1992). An employer's response to complaints of sexual harassment was reasonably calculated to prevent further harassment: Management investigated the complaint on the very day plaintiff lodged her formal complaint. Two days later, the alleged harasser was confronted, and within five days, the alleged harasser was suspended without pay for one week. The alleged harasser ultimately quit his job and moved, and plaintiff was never again harassed by him or any other employee.

[38] 828 F.2d 307 (5th Cir. 1987).

> Since the demise of the institution of duelling, society has seldom provided instantaneous redress for dishonorable conduct. In this case, the district court found that Malibu's president personally reassured Mrs. Dornhecker that Rockefeller would not be working with her after the Florida trip. This assurance occurred approximately 12 hours after Mrs. Dornhecker had tearfully confronted Kyrsia Swift in the ladies room and first acquainted her with Rockefeller's behavior. Considered in terms of the speed with which the company addressed Mrs. Dornhecker's complaint or the length of time it proposed to resolve that complaint, Malibu's remedial action was unusually prompt.[39]

In *Foster v. Township of Hillside*,[40] plaintiff civilian police dispatcher did not state a claim of hostile environment sexual harassment or retaliation when the defendants responded promptly to complaints that the alleged harasser had exposed himself and masturbated in front of the plaintiff as well as wear women's lingerie, and when the plaintiff had a long history of tardiness and absenteeism. The day that the plaintiff reported the harassment to a sergeant, the sergeant met individually with each woman that the alleged harasser supervised and took statements, and later management interviewed the plaintiff, the alleged harasser, and 18 coworkers and supervisors. The court rejected the plaintiff's contention that management dragged its feet by allowing the investigator seven months to complete her investigation when the hold up had to do with the fact that the plaintiff had pressed criminal charges against the alleged harasser, and he refused to speak with the investigator until the plaintiff withdrew the charges because it would have violated his Fifth Amendment rights.

In *Sparks v. Regional Medical Center Bd.*,[41] a hospital employer's response to complaints of sexual harassment was both appropriate and prompt when it quickly investigated, discussed its findings with the plaintiff and the alleged harasser, instructed the alleged harasser to stop the harassment, and made adjustments in the plaintiff's work schedule so as to avoid future harassment. After another complaint two months later, the employer again promptly investigated, took steps to prevent retaliation by the alleged harasser, and warned him that any future retaliation or harassment would result in the termination of his assocation with the hospital. The court rejected the plaintiff's argument that the hospital's failure to transfer her to another floor in effect constructively discharged her when she was given the choice of either remaining in her current job or returning to her former job, at the same pay, and on the same shift, and she rejected these choices.

---

[39] *Id.* at 309; Graham v. American Airlines, 731 F. Supp. 1494 (N.D. Okla. 1989) (employer took immediate and appropriate action).

[40] 780 F. Supp. 1026 (D.N.J. 1992).

[41] 792 F. Supp. 735 (N.D. Ala. 1992).

A defendant should show that it promptly investigated allegations of harassment. In *Saxton v. American Tel. & Tel. Co.,*[42] the employer took appropriate corrective action when it became aware of alleged sexual harassment when the department head promptly began a thorough investigation of the employee's charges, interviewing principals as well as witnesses, recommended the separation of the parties, began the process of transferring the supervisor after learning that the employee did not want a transfer, and allowed the employee to work at home during the entire process. The fact that the plaintiff saw the supervisor in her department two or three times after his transfer for about two seconds each time did not diminish the employer's effort. "We agree with AT&T's assessment that what Saxton perceives to be the 'desired effect' is not the proper inquiry."[43] The question was whether the course of action taken by the employer was reasonably likely to prevent the misconduct from recurring. Failure to demonstrate prompt investigation may constitute tacit approval of sexual harassment.[44] The depth and scope of investigation required may depend on the circumstances. Allegations of harassment that are investigated only to the extent that the alleged harasser denies the charges may be insufficient.[45]

---

[42] 785 F. Supp. 760 (N.D. Ill. 1992).

[43] *Id.* at 767.

[44] Llewellyn v. Celanese Corp., 693 F. Supp. 369, 380 (W.D.N.C. 1988). Although plaintiff repeatedly inquired about the resolution of her complaints of sexual harassment, it took management weeks to talk to the alleged harasser, despite a threat of bodily harm by the supervisor. "This inaction is evidence of defendants' callous disregard for plaintiff's claim of harassment and the threat to her safety".

See also Potts v. BE&K Constr. Co., 59 Fair Empl. Prac. Cas. (BNA) 1381, 604 So. 2d 398 (Ala. 1992). The state supreme court reversed a ruling of summary judgment in favor of the defendant employer in a sexual harassment action when a genuine factual issue existed as to whether an employer ratified one employee's alleged sexual harassment of another employee when the employer knew of the conduct before the complaint was made but took no disciplinary action at the time of the complaint and did not monitor the situation afterwards.

Kinnally v. Bell of Pa., 748 F. Supp. 1136 (E.D. Pa. 1990). The fact that management and executive personnel allegedly failed to adequately respond to allegations of sexual harassment may serve as a basis for Title VII liability even when they played no direct role in the alleged discrimination.

Robson v. Eva's Mkt., 538 F. Supp. 857, 859 (N.D. Ohio 1982); Munford v. James T. Barnes & Co., 441 F. Supp. 459 (E.D. Mich. 1977). Some approval is not so tacit. When plaintiff in *Bundy v. Jackson,* 641 F.2d 934, 940 (D.C. Cir. 1981) complained to the superior of the two supervisors who were harassing her, he "casually dismissed Bundy's complaints, telling her that 'any man in his right mind would want to rape you,'. . . and then proceeding to request that she begin a sexual relationship with him in his apartment."

[45] Mays v. Williamson & Sons, Janitorial Servs., 591 F. Supp. 1518 (E.D. Ark. 1984), *aff'd,* 775 F.2d 258 (8th Cir. 1985) (investigation was inadequate when company president only asked his brother, the alleged harasser, if charges made by plaintiff and other employees were true); Heelan v. Johns-Manville Corp., 451 F. Supp. 1382 (D. Colo. 1978).

Upon defendant's motion for summary judgment, the court in *Wallace v. Dunn Construction,*[46] found that a factual issue existed regarding whether the employer's response to claims of grabbing, pinching and "lurid sexual comments" by coworkers and supervisors was prompt enough. The court rejected the defendant's contention that the court should not second-guess a company's investigation, which in this case involved asking the harassers if they did the harassment, when the cases cited by the defense involved situations in which the harassment stopped after the company took remedial action:

> In the present case, plaintiffs claim that the harassment did not stop. This brings into question whether the remedial action was prompt enough. In addition, it seems [that] if no second-guessing is allowed, employers could easily take advantage of the situations by shoddy "investigations", as may have been the case here. Dunn also argues that it had a formal sexual harassment policy (only after 1989, though), which plaintiffs should have followed every time an act of harassment occurred. Under this policy, plaintiffs could have bypassed complaints to their supervisor and gone to a person with higher authority. This is relevant because, according to plaintiffs, almost every supervisor plaintiffs complained to sexually harassed them. However, such a fact may help plaintiffs more than it hurts them, because it arguably constituted a situation where the harassment was so pervasive that an inference of constructive knowledge by Dunn is possible.[47]

In *Heelan v. Johns-Manville Corp.*,[48] management's response to an employee's complaints of sexual harassment by a supervisor consisted of nothing more than calling the accused harasser on the telephone for verification or denial and "hardly" satisfied the company's obligation under Title VII. An employer should be able to prove that it attempted to resolve the matter by confronting the alleged harasser, interviewing witnesses, and meeting with the complainant and/or monitoring the alleged harasser's behavior to assess whether the conduct has ceased.[49] The United States Veterans Administration did not take prompt and appropriate remedial action in response to continued complaints by a female employee of sexual harassment by a coworker in *Intlekofer v. Turnage,*[50] when it failed to take more severe disciplinary action against the alleged harasser after learning that the harassment had not stopped. Although the VA had investigated the

---

46 59 Fair Empl. Prac. Cas. (BNA) 994 (N.D. Ala. 1991), *rev'd and remanded on other grounds,* 968 F.2d 1174 (11th Cir. 1992).

47 59 Fair Empl. Prac. Cas. (BNA) at 996.

48 451 F. Supp. 1382 (D. Colo. 1978).

49 Harrison v. Reed Rubber Co., 603 F. Supp. 1457 (E.D. Mo. 1985) (employer failed to monitor behavior).

50 973 F.2d 773 (9th Cir. 1992).

plaintiff's complaints regarding inappropriate touching, suggestions, threats, the drawing of a dildo on plaintiff's locker, and held continuous counseling sessions with the alleged harasser, it was apparent that these measures were ineffective.[51] Under *Ellison v. Brady*,[52] an employer must take some form of disciplinary action if it knows or should have known of the harassment:

> Of course, I acknowledge that "discipline" can take many forms, and I do not attempt to confine the employer to options specifically mentioned in this opinion. The important point is that the appropriateness of the remedy depends on the seriousness of the offense, the employer's ability to stop the harassment, the likelihood that the remedy will end the harassment, and "the remedy's ability to persuade potential harassers to refrain from unlawful conduct." [*Ellison,* 924 F.2d at 882]
>
> Intlekofer argues that counseling can never be considered "disciplinary," and that therefore the VA failed to satisfy its duty under *Ellison.* Although *Ellison* stated that "Title VII requires more than a mere request to refrain from the discriminatory conduct," counseling sessions are not necessarily insufficient. [*Id.*] Indeed, an oral rebuke may be very effective in stopping the unlawful conduct. At the first sign of sexual harassment, an oral warning in the context of a counseling session may be an appropriate disciplinary measure if the employer expresses strong disapproval, demands that the unwelcome conduct cease, and threatens more severe disciplinary action in the event that the conduct does not cease. I approve of the remedy in a case such as this where the harassing conduct is not extremely serious and the employer cannot elicit a detailed description concerning the occurrence from the victim. I stress, however, that counseling is sufficient only as a first resort. If the harassment continues, limiting discipline to further counseling is inappropriate. Instead, the employer must impose more severe measures in order to ensure that the behavior terminates. Again, the extent of the discipline depends on the seriousness of the conduct.[53]

In *Neidhart v. D.H. Holmes,*[54] the court found that the employer conducted a fair, unbiased, and complete investigation of the plaintiff's initial allegation

---

[51] *See also* Jenson v. Eveleth Taconite Co., 824 F. Supp. 847 (D. Minn 1993). Although the defendant employer responded to some specific incidents of sexual harassment, it never took any steps to determine whether the incidents were indicative of a larger problem requiring a company-wide response, and never established a system for either creating or processing records of complaints, even though such records could have facilitated the monitoring of the work environment. The defendant did not, on an official and companywide basis, seek to prevent offensive materials from remaining on or in the desks of supervisors, little or no effort was made to identify or discipline the persons responsible for displaying offending material, and no effort was made to communicate to male employees the need to respect female coworkers.

[52] Ellison v. Brady, 924 F.2d 872 (9th Cir. 1991).

[53] Intlekofer v. Turnage, 973 F.2d 773, 779–80 (9th Cir. 1992).

[54] 21 Fair Empl. Prac. Cas. (BNA) 452 (E.D. La. 1979).

of sexual harassment, came to the conclusion that the allegation was not substantiated, and then indicated to the plaintiff that she would be terminated for making a false accusation against her superior. When the plaintiff subsequently proffered corroborating testimony, however, the company immediately withdrew her termination and commenced further investigation. Only after thoroughly interviewing the plaintiff did the employer determine from the totality of the evidence that the allegations were unfounded and reactivated the plaintiff's termination.

The employer may show that the complainant's lack of cooperation hindered the investigation of harassment charges.[55] An employer also may show that although changes were implemented to prevent further harassment, the plaintiff refused to give them an opportunity to work.[56] The employer may strengthen its case by showing that it reissued a policy statement regarding sexual harassment to its employees, held office meetings to discuss the issue,[57] or otherwise demonstrated its disapproval of sexual harassment.

An employer may take appropriate remedial action in response to complaints of sexual harassment without terminating the alleged harasser.[58] In

---

[55] Hill v. BASF Wyandotte Corp., 27 Fair Empl. Prac. Cas. (BNA) 66 (E.D. Mich. 1981) (plaintiff refused to discuss her claims with employee responsible for ascertaining merits of her charges). *Cf.* Hansel v. Public Serv. Co., 778 F. Supp. 1126 (D. Colo. 1991).

[56] Ross v. Communications Satellite Corp., 34 Fair Empl. Prac. Cas. (BNA) 260, 265 (D. Md. 1984).

[57] Taylor v. Faculty-Student Ass'n of State Univ. College, 40 Fair Empl. Prac. Cas. (BNA) 1292 (W.D.N.Y. 1986) (summary judgment motion by defendant was denied, when it was uncertain when defendant became aware of plaintiff's allegations of sexual harassment, leaving question as to whether defendant took immediate and appropriate action). *Cf.* Delgado v. Lehman, 665 F. Supp. 460 (E.D. Va. 1987) (supervisors did not monitor hostile environment after office meeting in which employees discussed the issue).

[58] Second Circuit: Kotcher v. Rosa & Sullivan Appliance, 957 F.2d 59 (2d Cir. 1992). A manager who regularly commented that his sales would be more substantial if he had the same bodily "equipment" as the female employee plaintiff and who often pretended to masturbate and ejaculate at her behind her back created a hostile work environment. The company took appropriate action by giving the alleged harasser a written warning. Not every response to a sexual harassment complaint should take the form of discharge; the district court could reasonably have found that the employer had responded appropriately to complaints of harassment because a written warning was sufficient to make the alleged harasser aware that the harassment would not be tolerated on its premises.

Fifth Circuit: Landgraf v. USI Film Prods., 968 F.2d 427 (5th Cir. 1992). Although it was uncontested that plaintiff suffered significant sexual harassment by her coworker in the form of continuous and repeated inappropriate verbal comments and physical contact, the lower court did not clearly err when it concluded that the employer took steps reasonably calculated to end coworker's sexual harassment of plaintiff by giving the alleged harasser its most serious form of reprimand and acting to reduce workplace contact between the parties.

Barrett v. Omaha National Bank,[59] for example, the court rejected the plaintiff's contention that her employer's investigation of sexual harassment at a bank conference by a coworker was "totally superficial." The employer had talked to the parties involved as well as to other bank employees who attended the conference and, within four days of the complaint, reprimanded the coworker, placed him on 90 days of probation, and warned him that further misconduct would result in termination. A supervisor also was reprimanded for his failure to intervene on behalf of the plaintiff. The court found that the employer's response to the complaint of harassment was "prompt remedial action reasonably calculated to end the harassment."[60] This was not the case, however, in *Harrison v. Reed Rubber Co.,*[61] in which the plaintiff alleged that her supervisor frequently asked her about her home life, suggested that she divorce her husband for him, initiated physical contact, placed himself unnecessarily close to her, remained in her work area more often than necessary, and repeatedly called her away from her work station both for personal and work-related reasons. In response to the plaintiff's complaint, the supervisor was instructed not

---

Seventh Circuit: Guess v. Bethlehem Steel, 913 F.2d 463 (7th Cir. 1990). An employer properly transferred plaintiff into another unit, rather than discharging or transferring the alleged harasser, when plaintiff was on temporary assignment to the unit in which she encountered the offensive conduct and was merely returned to her regular employment when her assignment ended.

Eighth Circuit: Barrett v. Omaha Nat'l Bank, 726 F.2d 424 (8th Cir. 1984);

Ninth Circuit: Bigoni v. Pay 'n Pak Stores, 746 F. Supp. 1 (D. Or. 1990) A warning written to an alleged harasser after a sexual harassment action was filed could not be used to prove that the actions of the alleged harasser were forseeable by the employer. Nor did the fact that the alleged harasser had admitted acting inappropriately toward plaintiff upon investigation by management raise the inference that the employer could have foreseen that the alleged harasser would threaten her to withdraw her earlier action. Management had indicated to the alleged harasser that his behavior was inappropriate and that he would be terminated if it happened again.

Penk v. Oregon State Bd. of Higher Educ., 48 Fair Empl. Prac. Cas. (BNA) 1724 (D. Or. 1985) (alleged harasser told to modify his behavior).

59 726 F.2d 424 (8th Cir. 1984).

60 *Id.* at 427. *See also* Strickland v. Sears, Roebuck & Co., 46 Fair Empl. Prac. Cas. (BNA) 1024 (E.D. Va. 1987), *aff'd,* 846 F.2d 74 (4th Cir. 1988). Plaintiff complained that her supervisor approached her at her desk, rubbed his hands all over her shoulders and neck, ran his fingers through her hair, and made other unwelcome sexual advances toward her, and that 15 minutes later he made a false statement in front of coworkers about the two of them going out and having a good time together. Afterward, the manager announced to the supervisor that there was to be no touching of employees in any manner or form, reassured plaintiff that there would be no more touching, and later held a meeting with the supervisor when he again explained the seriousness of plaintiff's accusations and reiterated that there would be no more touching. No further touching took place.

61 603 F. Supp. 1457 (E.D. Mo. 1985).

to be in plaintiff's work area for more than 10 minutes in the morning and 10 minutes in the afternoon. When the supervisor failed to heed these instructions, the plaintiff again complained. The supervisor then was relieved of his duties as plant superintendent and reinstated to his previous clerking position, but he suffered no loss of wages or fringe benefits, and no one replaced him. The supervisor continued to attempt to make contact with the plaintiff, calling her at her mother's home and sending her a note at work. To avoid him, the plaintiff requested a transfer to the night shift at 15 cents per hour less than she was making. The supervisor occasionally stood in the doorway and watched the plaintiff work. Several months later, she was hospitalized for depression and subsequently resigned her position. The court concluded that although the supervisor would stay away from the plaintiff for several days at a time after her complaints, the harassment never finally ceased. The employers' instructions to stay away from the plaintiff apparently were based on productivity considerations and did not include directives to cease all sexual harassment:

> Nor did the Reeds monitor [the supervisor's] behavior to ascertain whether all harassment ceased. Consequently, plaintiff was eventually forced to switch departments in an effort to avoid [the supervisor], at a monetary loss to herself. Thus, defendant has failed to rebut plaintiff's evidence proving an offensive work environment in violation of Title VII.[62]

In *Hansel v. Public Service Co.,*[63] merely "discussing" the matter of sexual harassment with four of the perpetrators was insufficient to halt sexual harassment of female machine operators by male coworkers at a power plant over an eight year period. The alleged harassment included fondling genitals, grabbing breasts and buttocks, filling workgloves with bathroom cleaner, male employees making degrading comments, male employees entering the women's room while the plaintiff was using it, and sexually explicit graffiti throughout the plant, some of it explicitly directed at the plaintiff. Although the physical harassment ceased, other forms continued:

> [N]ot every response by an employer will be sufficient to discharge its legal duty. The response must be reasonable under the totality of the circumstances. What is appropriate remedial action necessarily depends on

---

[62] *Id.* at 1461. *See also* Cortes v. Maxus Exploration Co., 977 F.2d 195 (5th Cir. 1992) (Title VII and state duress claim). An employer was liable for sexual harassment when he placed an employee under the supervision of a supervisor who had previously sexually harassed her and refused to take any remedial measures to protect her when she expressed her fears about being transferred.

Broom v. Regal Tube Co., 44 Fair Empl. Prac. Cas. (BNA) 1119 (N.D. Ill. 1987).

[63] 778 F. Supp. 1126 (D. Colo. 1991).

> the particular facts of each case with focus upon the severity and persistence of the harassment and the effectiveness of any initial remedial steps. . . .
>
> Here, because the overt, physical harassment stopped, PSC argues it took appropriate remedial action in 1983 when it merely discussed Hansel's allegations with four of her co-workers. PSC misconstrues the nature of the remedial action required of it by Title VII under the circumstances of this case.
>
> A hostile environment is like a disease. It can have many symptoms, some of which change over time, but all of which stem from the same root. The etiology in this case is pure gender bias.
>
> PSC may have attempted treatment of one symptom of the hostile environment, the physical abuse, but it failed completely to remedy the disease of hostile work environment. Moreover, the sexual harassment here was so egregious that merely "discussing" the matter with four of the perpetrators cannot reasonably be calculated to halt the harassment. Indeed, the hostile environment continued unabated after 1983.[64]

If the employer finds alleged incidents to be completely unsupported, it may be sufficient to reiterate to the employees the employer's disapproval of sexual harassment. If there is evidence of harassment, proper discipline in the form of a reprimand, probation, warning that further misconduct would warrant dismissal, or a transfer of the alleged harasser to a different or less preferable job may suffice.

The complainant's transfer or a change of supervisor[65] also may constitute an appropriate remedy if it is acceptable to the complainant and does not penalize her for coming forward. The employer should be prepared to justify choosing the employee rather than the alleged harasser for transfer.

When the alleged harassers are nonemployees, an employer should show that it attempted to remove the complainant from the harassing situation or, in the case of offensive customers, expelled the alleged harasser or threatened him with expulsion for further misconduct.

Although a prompt investigation and appropriate corrective action may prevent a finding of liability against the employer,[66] *Henson v. City of*

---

64 *Id.* at 1132.

65 Long v. First Family Fin. Servs., Inc., 677 F. Supp. 1226 (S.D. Ga. 1987).

66 *See, e.g.,* Kotcher v. Rosa & Sullivan Appliance, 53 Fair Empl. Prac. Cas. (BNA) 1148 (N.D.N.Y. 1990). Plaintiff former employee was subjected to "continuous episodes of distasteful and abrasive comments and gestures" by a store manager who often would pretend to masturbate and ejaculate at her behind her back when he was angry at her and who said that his sales would be more substantial if he had plaintiff's bodily "equipment" established that the conduct was unwelcome but did not report the conduct in a timely manner. When the procedure to make complaints was finally utilized by plaintiff, the employer conducted an investigation within twenty-four hours and subsequently transferred and demoted the manager.

Sapp v. City of Warner Robins, 655 F. Supp. 1043 (M.D. Ga. 1987); Ferguson v. E.I. Du Pont de Nemours & Co., 560 F. Supp. 419 (D. Del. 1983).

Dundee[67] suggests that in some cases, remedial action only may serve to mitigate damages.

Finally, some courts have held that employers have an affirmative duty to seek out and eradicate a hostile environment. In *Hansel*,[68] the defendant power plant could not escape liability for sexual harassment of female machine operators by male coworkers by blaming the victim for not coming forward with more detailed information; Title VII imposes on employers an affirmative duty to seek out and eradicate a hostile work environment. "An employer simply cannot sit back and wait for complaints. The very nature of sexual harassment inhibits its victims from coming forward because of fear of retaliation."[69] The defendant's "blame the victim" attitude was also evidenced by its list of responsive actions following the plaintiff's complaints, which included requiring her to carry a knife, form a support group with "other gals," or to develop a thicker skin. "This employer cannot discharge its legal duty by requiring the victim of the sexual harassment to remedy the situation herself. Rather, it was PSC's duty to provide Hansel a workplace free from sexual harassment."[70]

§ 7.7 Company Policy and Grievance Procedures

The existence of a policy against sexual harassment is not a complete defense to a claim of sexual harassment, but it is relevant to whether the plaintiff took advantage of such procedures and whether the mechanisms available encouraged complaint resolution.[71] In *Meritor Savings Bank v.*

---

67 682 F.2d 897, 910 n.19 (11th Cir. 1982) (an employer may not escape responsibility "merely by taking subsequent remedial action").

68 Hansel v. Public Serv. Co., 778 F. Supp. 1126 (D. Colo. 1991).

69 *Id.* at 1133.

70 *Id.*

71 Katz v. Dole, 709 F.2d 251 (4th Cir. 1983) (FAA did have an articulated policy against sexual harassment that involved seminars on the issue for its supervisors, but the policy was not effective and was known not to be effective by FAA supervisors).

EEOC v. Gurnee Inn Corp., 914 F.2d 815 (7th Cir. 1990). The district court properly issued an injunction against an employer who had tolerated a manager's sexual harassment despite the employer's contention that only one employee was responsible for the harassment when the district court had determined that the discrimination resulted from the manager's behavior and the employer's continued toleration of that behavior, the employer had neither an antidiscrimination policy nor a grievance procedure through which employees could complain of sexual harassment, and the manager was still employed by the employer when the injunction was issued.

Hansel v. Public Serv. Co., 778 F. Supp. 1126 (D. Colo. 1991) (there was no persuasive evidence that defendant had an effective EEO mechanism in place to monitor the state of its work environment); Neidhardt v. D.H. Holmes, 21 Fair Empl. Prac. Cas. (BNA) 452, 469 (E.D. La. 1979).

Vinson,[72] the U.S. Supreme Court rejected the defendant employer's contention that "the mere existence of a grievance procedure and a policy against discrimination, coupled with [the plaintiff's] failure to invoke that procedure, must insulate [the employer] from liability."[73] The Court noted that the employer's general policy of nondiscrimination did not address sexual harassment specifically. The employer's policy also required employees to complain first to their supervisor, often an obstacle in sexual harassment cases when the supervisor is the harasser or is friendly with coworker harassers. A defendant should demonstrate that it had a specific policy against discrimination and an effective internal procedure for grievances that allowed employees to by-pass their supervisors when necessary.[74] Plaintiffs may try to introduce evidence of the employer's failure to respond to previous unrelated sexual harassment complaints to prove that the company sexual harassment policy is not effective.[75]

In *Jenson v. Eveleth Taconite Co.*,[76] the court rejected the defendant company and union's contention that they could not be liable for sexual harassment because of the plaintiffs' failure to grieve such incidents when the grievance procedure at the time was insufficient to create a mandatory or effective system for raising and resolving claims of sexual harassment.

---

72 477 U.S. 57 (1986).

73 *Id.* at 72. *See also* Cummings v. Walsh Const. Co., 561 F. Supp. 872, 878 (S.D. Ga. 1983):

> The fact that the plaintiff did not employ the defendant's or her union's grievance system before filing her EEOC charges is irrelevant and immaterial to the viability of her claim. *Henson* does not indicate that exhaustion of non-judicial remedies is a necessary prerequisite for the filing of a Title VII action. . . . The Supreme Court has clearly stated that Title VII rights are independent of any contractual rights. A plaintiff is not required to submit to contractually provided arbitration before resorting to federal court. *Alexander v. Gardner-Denver Co.*, 415 U.S. 36, 47–48 (1974).

74 *Cf.* Monroe-Lord v. Hytche, 668 F. Supp. 979 (D. Md. 1987), *aff'd*, 854 F.2d 1317 (4th Cir. 1988) (university defendant had no written policy regarding sexual harassment, but a faculty member could report a grievance to the department head or the director of human relations).

75 EEOC v. General Motors Corp., 48 Fair Empl. Prac. Cas. (BNA) 1285 (D. Kan. 1988); Gomez v. Metro Dade County, Florida, 801 F. Supp. 674 (S.D. Fla. 1992) (Title VII and 1983). An employer may avoid liability when there is an explicit policy against sexual harassment and effective grievance procedures calculated to encourage victims of harassment to come forward but which the plaintiff did not employ. In this action by a demoted county employee charging sexual harassment by the county personnel director and demotion in alleged retaliation for filing a sexual harassment complaint, a material question of fact existed as to the effectiveness of such procedures, and thus precluded entry of summary judgment against plaintiffs when four complaints of sexual harassment had been filed against a supervisor but no discipline was imposed.

76 824 F. Supp. 847 (D. Minn 1993).

Until 1987, the collective bargaining agreement contained no provision on sexual harassment, and thus the addition of such a statement was completely ineffective in establishing the mines' position on sexual harassment prior to its creation. Nor did the defendants make any effort to communicate to the work force that the stated policy could and would be enforced through the grievance process. The fact that a few women used the grievance process was not sufficient to make the system an effective and therefore obligatory means to press sexual harassment claims:

> Under the existing grievance process, were a female employee to bring a charge against a fellow bargaining unit employee, the Union would be required to simultaneously press the woman's claim and seek to avoid punishment for the alleged male perpetrator. The need to stand on both sides of a charge of sexual harassment presents a potential conflict of interest which reasonably renders the CBA's grievance procedure ineffective as the primary mechanism for addressing complaints of sexual harassment brought by one bargaining unit member against another.[77]

Despite the U.S. Supreme Court's admonition against finding liability solely on the basis of the plaintiff's failure to invoke an existing grievance procedure, courts repeatedly have pointed to the existence of such procedures and the plaintiff's failure to take advantage of them to deny claims of sexual harassment.[78]

§ 7.8 Business Reasons for Employment Decisions

Employers charged with sexual harassment successfully have asserted a number of reasons to dispel an inference of disparate treatment. These include poor work performance, chronic absenteeism or tardiness, lack of qualifications, failure to adhere to company policy, attitude problems, and misconduct. The viability of a particular defense may turn on the strength of a plaintiff's prima facie case.

§ 7.9 —Poor Work Performance

Poor work performance is a legitimate basis for termination or demotion.[79] However, to successfully rebut a claim that the plaintiff was terminated

---

[77] *Id.* at 879 (footnotes omitted).

[78] Monroe-Lord v. Hytche, 668 F. Supp. 979 (D. Md. 1987), *aff'd,* 854 F.2d 1317 (4th Cir. 1988).

[79] Second Circuit: Christoforou v. Ryder Truck Rental, Inc., 668 F. Supp. 294 (S.D.N.Y. 1987); Ramsey v. Olin Corp., 39 Fair Empl. Prac. Cas. (BNA) 959 (S.D.N.Y. 1984)

because of her failure to acquiesce to sexual advances, an employer should detail the deficiencies in work performance and prove that the plaintiff was given notice of these shortcomings.[80] In *Strickland v. Sears, Roebuck & Co.,*[81] the court rejected the plaintiff's claim that the defendant Sears retaliated against her for filing a sexual harassment charge involving her supervisor by singling her out for poor work performance, telling her that her job was in jeopardy if her sales did not improve, and withholding a raise she was due to receive. Despite the fact that the plaintiff had previously received several merit certifications for sales performance while she was at Sears, her sales did drop drastically for two months in a row. She was called into the office of the supervisor responsible for sales personnel, a woman, and was told that failure to improve her sales could result in her termination. The plaintiff's sales increased dramatically the next month and she was congratulated by letter by her supervisor, who emphasized that her performance would have to remain consistent for her to keep her job. She received her raise as soon as her sales improved. On the basis of these facts, and testimony that other employees were similarly reprimanded for poor sales, the court concluded that the defendant demonstrated legitimate business management practices rather than discriminatory intent. It should be noted, however, that the court also found that the alleged conduct, involving only one incident of touching followed by one

---

(defendant presented unchallenged evidence of errors and failure to keep up with orders as well as plaintiff's own deposition testimony relating to her poor attitude and her desire to be transferred).

Ninth Circuit: *Cf.* Ambrose v. United States Steel Corp., 39 Fair Empl. Prac. Cas. (BNA) 30, 34 (N.D. Cal. 1985) (defendant offered no credible evidence as to plaintiff's poor job performance; "Indeed, the evidence established that plaintiff was a competent guard supervisor, who was highly regarded by her peers").

Eleventh Circuit: Hall v. F.O. Thacker Contracting Co., 24 Fair Empl. Prac. Cas. (BNA) 1499 (N.D. Ga. 1980) (plaintiff was frequently absent from her work area, forcing others to answer her phone, her secretarial skills were inadequate, and she failed to appear at an important meeting).

District of Columbia Circuit: Diggs v. Campbell, 54 Fair Empl. Prac. Cas. (BNA) 773 (D.D.C. 1990) (employer was entitled to summary judgment when pro se plaintiff offered nothing to support allegations that she was terminated because she refused employer official's sexual advances and made no effort to challenge the defendant's assertion that she was terminated because of "erratic" performance, unexplained absences, and that she improperly removed certain corporate materials).

80 Mays v. Williamson & Sons, Janitorial Servs., 591 F. Supp. 1518 (E.D. Ark. 1984), *aff'd,* 775 F.2d 258 (8th Cir. 1985). *See also* Neville v. Taft Broadcasting Co., 42 Fair Empl. Prac. Cas. (BNA) 1314 (W.D.N.Y. 1987) (termination was justified when evidence showed errors by plaintiff, poor servicing of accounts, and complaints by clients).

81 46 Fair Empl. Prac. Cas. (BNA) 1024 (E.D. Va. 1987), *aff'd,* 846 F.2d 74 (4th Cir. 1988).

comment about dating, did not constitute harassment. Under different circumstances, a swift drop in sales performance could have reflected plaintiff's response to an abusive environment.[82]

In *Lamb v. Drilco*,[83] the plaintiff was unable to eat, sleep, or concentrate, and began to drink more alcohol than usual because of verbal and physical sexual advances by her supervisor, which included disturbing telephone calls to her home. She began making mistakes in measurements and paperwork on the job and was discharged. The court found that plaintiff's termination for poor work performance was pretextual when her decline in productivity could be attributed to the existence of unlawful sexual harassment. Similarly, in *Broderick v. Ruder*,[84] the evidence established that sexual harassment was so pervasive at the plaintiff's workplace that it "affected the motivation and work performance of those who found such conduct repugnant and offensive."[85] The plaintiff "amply demonstrated, through both lay and expert witnesses, that any alleged deficiencies in her work performance, which rested largely on her failure to interact with her supervisors, were directly attributable to the atmosphere in which she worked."[86]

A court will be suspicious of notes placed in personnel files that have not been reviewed by targeted employees[87] or terminations based on one incident when the employee previously had a good work record.[88] A file inflated with reports of trivial events may itself be evidence of harassment, and the fact that the petty matters were given no weight in an adverse employment decision does not lessen their impact as harassment to the plaintiff.[89]

Even if an employer establishes a legitimate reason for terminating the employee, the plaintiff may be able to show pretext by proving that other

---

[82] Henson v. City of Dundee, 682 F.2d 897, 910 (11th Cir. 1982) ("An employer cannot use an employee's diminished work performance as a legitimate basis for removal where the diminution is the direct result of the employer's discriminatory behavior").

[83] 32 Fair Empl. Prac. Cas. (BNA) 105 (S.D. Tex. 1983).

[84] 685 F. Supp. 1269, 1278 (D.D.C. 1988).

[85] *Id.* at 1278.

[86] *Id.* at 1280. *See also* Delgado v. Lehman, 665 F. Supp. 460 (E.D. Va. 1987) (inability of plaintiff to adequately perform her job was due to sex discrimination; her supervisor deliberately interfered with execution of her duties by refusing her access to necessary mail and materials, by refusing to give her supervisory guidance on completion of various tasks, and by undermining whatever progress she managed to make); Grier v. Casey, 643 F. Supp. 298, 309 (W.D.N.C. 1986).

[87] Mays v. Williamson & Sons, Janitorial Servs., 591 F. Supp. 1518 (E.D. Ark. 1984), *aff'd*, 775 F.2d 258 (8th Cir. 1985).

[88] Harrison v. Reed Rubber Co., 603 F. Supp. 1457 (E.D. Mo. 1985).

[89] Capaci v. Katz & Besthoff, Inc., 525 F. Supp. 317, 347 (N.D. La. 1981), *modified on other grounds*, 711 F.2d 647 (5th Cir. 1983).

employees with comparable work records were not treated similarly, or that the employer failed to follow standard company discipline procedures.[90] An employer should be able to demonstrate that the plaintiff was not singled out for her work habits.[91]

---

90 Jenkins v. Orkin Exterminating Co., 646 F. Supp. 1274, 1277 (E.D. Tex. 1986) (corporate policy required a verbal warning, a written warning, and a three-day suspension before discharging an employee, but plaintiff was given only one corrective interview notice before his termination).

91 Strickland v. Sears, Roebuck & Co., 46 Fair Empl. Prac. Cas. (BNA) 1024, 1027 (E.D. Va. 1987), *aff'd,* 846 F.2d 74 (4th Cir. 1988).

Discharge on the basis of poor work performance was found to be pretextual in the following cases:

Fourth Circuit: Delgado v. Lehman, 665 F. Supp. 460 (E.D. Va. 1987).

Fifth Circuit: Jenkins v. Orkin Exterminating Co., 646 F. Supp. 1274 (E.D. Tex. 1986) (in an action by male employee alleging he had been terminated for reporting a female coworker's sexual harassment complaints, employer's reasons for discharging plaintiff, including failure to make his draw, disruption of sales meetings, failure to complete paperwork, lack of creativity, and use of provocative and abusive language were pretextual because a salesperson of plaintiff's caliber would not have been terminated for said grounds absent some other motivation); Lamb v. Drilco, 32 Fair Empl. Prac. Cas. (BNA) 105 (S.D. Tex. 1983).

Seventh Circuit: Juarez v. Ameritech Mobile Communications, 746 F. Supp. 798 (N.D. Ill. 1990) *aff'd,* 957 F.2d 317 (7th Cir. 1992). A plaintiff who was terminated six months after she filed a sexual harassment complaint was properly discharged for poor work performance despite the fact that employees documented her poor work performance only after she filed her complaint when the plaintiff presented no evidence that the employees who evaluated her had a discriminatory motive to retaliate against her for her discrimination complaints and at least four employees complained; "although reprehensible, sexual harassment does not entitle the victim to lifetime tenure at her place of employment." *Id.* at 805.

Eighth Circuit: Harrison v. Reed Rubber Co., 603 F. Supp. 1457 (E.D. Mo. 1985); Mays v. Williamson & Sons, Janitorial Servs., 591 F. Supp. 1518 (E.D. Ark. 1984), *aff'd*, 775 F.2d 258 (8th Cir. 1985).

Ninth Circuit: Priest v. Rotary, 634 F. Supp. 571 (N.D. Cal. 1986) (defendant's reasons for plaintiff's termination, that she failed to do "sidework," was a poor waitress, did not get along with other waitresses, used "bad language," and violated defendant's policy forbidding employees from socializing in restaurant lounge were pretextual because evidence showed adverse treatment was because of plaintiff's negative reaction to defendant's requests for sexual favors).

Tenth Circuit: Heelan v. Johns-Manville Corp., 451 F. Supp. 1382 (D. Colo. 1978).

Eleventh Circuit: Phillips v. Smalley Maintenance Servs., Inc., 711 F.2d 1524 (11th Cir. 1983).

District of Columbia Circuit: Williams v. Civiletti, 487 F. Supp. 1387 (D.D.C. 1980).

§ 7.10 —Tardiness or Absenteeism

Evidence of the complainant's excessive lateness or unexcused absences also may overcome a prima facie case of termination based on sexual harassment.[92] The defendant should show that the charges were documented,[93] plaintiff was reprimanded for or warned about excessive tardiness or absenteeism before termination,[94] and other employees with similar records of lateness or absences also were disciplined or discharged.[95]

---

[92] First Circuit: Hosemann v. Technical Materials, Inc., 554 F. Supp. 659 (D.R.I. 1982) (when employer repeatedly attempted to no avail to ascertain when female employee would return from disability leave and held her position open for her for five weeks, termination was reasonable).

Second Circuit: Torriero v. Olin Corp., 684 F. Supp. 1165 (S.D.N.Y. 1988); Collins v. Pfizer, Inc., 39 Fair Empl. Prac. Cas. (BNA) 1316 (D. Conn. 1985) (plaintiff's gross absences unduly burdening her coworkers gave defendant legitimate reason to discharge her).

Third Circuit: Foster v. Township of Hillside, 780 F. Supp. 1026 (D.N.J. 1992); Sheekey v. Nelson, 40 Fair Empl. Prac. Cas. (BNA) 1216, 1219 (D.N.J. 1986) (record disclosed plaintiff's "horrendous record of absences, tardiness and improper procedures in shift-switching").

Sixth Circuit: Sand v. Johnson, 33 Fair Empl. Prac. Cas. (BNA) 716 (E.D. Mich. 1982) (discharge was proper for "habitual tardiness").

Seventh Circuit: Swanson v. Elmhurst Chrysler Plymouth, 47 Fair Empl. Prac. Cas. (BNA) 1694 (N.D. Ill. 1988). Plaintiff was discharged when after taking several days off for illness, she took day off for personal reasons, going over her supervisor's head to the very person she claimed harassed her. Although plaintiff also proved that she had been sexually harassed, she failed to prove that she was fired because of that harassment.

Eighth Circuit: McLean v. Satellite Tech. Servs., Inc., 673 F. Supp. 1458 (E.D. Mo. 1987).

District of Columbia Circuit: Diggs v. Campbell, 54 Fair Empl. Prac. Cas. (BNA) 773 (D.D.C. 1990).

[93] Meyers v. ITT Diversified Credit Corp., 527 F. Supp. 1064 (E.D. Mo. 1981) (charges of excessive absenteeism and disregard of duties were not documented).

[94] Collins v. Pfizer, Inc., 39 Fair Empl. Prac. Cas. (BNA) 1316 (D. Conn. 1985) (employer sent plaintiff warning letters regarding absenteeism). *Cf.* Craig v. Y&Y Snacks, Inc. 721 F.2d 77, 80 (3d Cir. 1983) (district court properly found that defendant's assertion that plaintiff was terminated because of her record of absenteeism and tardiness was pretextual when employer failed to give plaintiff a three-day suspension before firing her, a "mandatory predicate for the ultimate sanction of discharge"); Ambrose v. United States Steel Corp., 39 Fair Empl. Prac. Cas. (BNA) 30 (N.D. Cal. 1985) (although defendant introduced much evidence regarding plaintiff's excessive absenteeism, plaintiff showed that when her supervisor recommended that she be fired, plaintiff had been absent far fewer times than she had during previous appraisal year when supervisor had rated her attendance as satisfactory); Mays v. Williamson & Sons, Janitorial Servs., 591 F. Supp. 1518 (E.D. Ark. 1984), *aff'd,* 775 F.2d 258 (8th Cir. 1985) (plaintiff never received reprimand for excessive absenteeism during tenure with defendant).

[95] Halpert v. Wertheim & Co., 27 Fair Empl. Prac. Cas. (BNA) 21 (S.D.N.Y. 1980). *See also* Sheekey v. Nelson, 40 Fair Empl. Prac. Cas. (BNA) 1216 (D.N.J. 1986) (evidence

§ 7.11 —Lack of Qualifications

Discharge properly may be based on an employee's failure to meet ongoing standards or misrepresentation of qualifications.[96] An employer should be prepared to demonstrate that other employees in similar positions did meet those standards and that the plaintiff's qualifications were not at issue before her complaints of sexual harassment.

§ 7.12 —Failure to Follow Company Policy

An employer may dispel an adverse inference of discrimination by showing that the plaintiff did not follow company policy with respect to dress,[97]

---

clearly showed that plaintiff had worst attendance record of any employee whose personnel file she put into evidence for comparison); Collins v. Pfizer, Inc., 39 Fair Empl. Prac. Cas. (BNA) 1316 (D. Conn. 1985) (plaintiff's "meager" proof that 14-year-old male employee also was absent and not discharged was not applicable when coworker's total absence over a period of prior years could not compare with plaintiff's total absenteeism in a much shorter period). *Cf.* Macey v. World Airways, Inc., 14 Fair Empl. Prac. Cas. (BNA) 1426 (N.D. Cal. 1977) (management employee admitted that several male probationary employees had as many or more absences as plaintiff and were not discharged).

The court found that discharge for tardiness or absenteeism was pretextual in the following cases:

Third Circuit: Craig v. Y&Y Snacks, Inc. 721 F.2d 77 (3d Cir. 1983); Macey v. World Airways, Inc., 14 Fair Empl. Prac. Cas. (BNA) 1426 (N.D. Cal. 1977).

Eighth Circuit: Meyers v. ITT Diversified Credit Corp., 527 F. Supp. 1064 (E.D. Mo. 1981).

Ninth Circuit: Ambrose v. United States Steel Corp., 39 Fair Empl. Prac. Cas. (BNA) 30 (N.D. Cal. 1985).

Eleventh Circuit: Sowers v. Kemira, Inc., 46 Fair Empl. Prac. Cas. (BNA) 1825 (S.D. Ga. 1988).

District of Columbia Circuit: Broderick v. Ruder, 685 F. Supp. 1269, 1280 (D.D.C. 1988).

[96] Second Circuit: Koster v. Chase Manhattan Bank, 46 Fair Empl. Prac. Cas. (BNA) 1436 (S.D.N.Y. 1988) (plaintiff overstated her experience and potential).

Third Circuit: Freedman v. American Standard, 41 Fair Empl. Prac. Cas. (BNA) 471 (D.N.J. 1986) (plaintiff pilot was discharged not because of alleged sexual harassment, but because she had three times failed to pass the basic flight checks on which her employment depended).

Eleventh Circuit: Hall v. F.O. Thacker Contracting Co., 24 Fair Empl. Prac. Cas. (BNA) 1499 (N.D. Ga. 1980) (plaintiff's secretarial skills were inadequate).

District of Columbia Circuit: Bouchet v. National Urban League, Inc., 730 F.2d 799 (D.C. Cir. 1984) (plaintiff was terminated properly when she lacked qualifications and experience necessary for position).

[97] Bellissimo v. Westinghouse Elec. Corp., 764 F.2d 175 (3d Cir. 1985), *cert. denied,* 475 U.S. 1035 (1986). *See also* Kramer-Navarro v. Postal Serv., 586 F. Supp. 677 (S.D.N.Y. 1984) (open-toed shoes violated safety regulation).

workload,[98] use of facilities,[99] working on weekends,[100] use of sick leave,[101] and socializing with coworkers[102] or customers.[103]

§ 7.13 —Employee's Misconduct

Courts have considered the employee's defiant or belligerent attitude in determining whether the employer was justified in its adverse employment decision.[104] However, the defendant should show that the plaintiff

---

98 Bellissimo v. Westinghouse Elec. Corp., 764 F.2d 175 (3d Cir. 1985), *cert. denied,* 475 U.S. 1035 (1986).

99 Lynch v. Dean, 39 Fair Empl. Prac. Cas. (BNA) 338 (M.D. Tenn. 1985).

100 Christoforou v. Ryder Truck Rental, Inc., 668 F. Supp. 294, 302 (S.D.N.Y. 1987).

101 Kramer-Navarro v. Postal Serv., 586 F. Supp. 677 (S.D.N.Y. 1984).

102 Del Valle Fontanez v. Aponte, 660 F. Supp. 145 (D.P.R. 1987).

103 Bellissimo v. Westinghouse Elec. Corp., 764 F.2d 175 (3d Cir. 1985), *cert. denied,* 475 U.S. 1035 (1986); McLean v. Satellite Tech. Servs., Inc., 673 F. Supp. 1458 (E.D. Mo. 1987).

104 Second Circuit: Christoforou v. Ryder Truck Rental, Inc., 668 F. Supp. 294 (S.D.N.Y. 1987); Kramer-Navarro v. Postal Serv., 586 F. Supp. 677 (S.D.N.Y. 1984) (plaintiff's insubordination and failure to report to work were legitimate, nondiscriminatory reasons for discharge).

Third Circuit: Petrosky v. Washington-Greene County Ass'n for the Blind, 663 F. Supp. 821, 825 (W.D. Pa. 1987) (defendant established the fact that board members "felt plaintiff acted in an abrasive and disrespectful manner toward them through a litany of incidents which elicited their anger and made them distrustful of plaintiff in general and apart from her charge" of sexual harassment against the board chair); Burns v. Terre Haute Regional Hosp., 581 F. Supp. 1301 (S.D. Ind. 1983) (plaintiff was terminated properly for poor attitude).

Sixth Circuit: Rabidue v. Osceola Ref. Co., 805 F.2d 611 (6th Cir. 1986), *cert. denied*, 481 U.S. 1041 (1987) (plaintiff was discharged properly when she was rude and failed to follow employer's policies); Lynch v. Dean, 39 Fair Empl. Prac. Cas. (BNA) 338 (M.D. Tenn. 1985) (plaintiff deliberately violated written job rules and was insubordinate).

Eighth Circuit: McLean v. Satellite Tech. Servs., Inc., 673 F. Supp. 1458 (E.D. Mo. 1987).

Eleventh Circuit: Williams-Hill v. Donovan, 43 Fair Empl. Prac. Cas. (BNA) 253 (M.D. Fla. 1987) (personality conflicts led to transfer).

District of Columbia Circuit: Jones v. Lyng, 669 F. Supp. 1108 (D.D.C. 1986) (in an action by a federal employee who charged he was transferred for disclosing alleged sexual harassment of female employees, record clearly showed that plaintiff had a long history of performance inadequacies, that he frequently challenged major decisions of his superiors, and was insubordinate and disloyal); Greater Wash. Business Ctr. v. District of Columbia Comm'n on Human Rights, 30 Fair Empl. Prac. Cas. (BNA) 975 (D.C. Ct. App. 1982) (plaintiff was discharged properly for insubordination because she refused to write a memorandum summarizing her conversation with a client, even

was difficult before the onset of the alleged harassment,[105] because the plaintiff may demonstrate that her work behavior changed as a result of the sexual harassment. Personality conflicts between the plaintiff and her superior also may justify termination or transfer,[106] but these conflicts cannot be based on notions of how women should behave. For example, in *EEOC v. FLC & Bros. Rebel,*[107] the defendant's use of the phrase "unladylike" language as a reason for plaintiff's discharge constituted some direct evidence of discrimination when it was apparent from his testimony that women were held to a somewhat higher standard than men.

Misconduct, including the falsification of reports,[108] the personal use of phones at office expense,[109] and lying,[110] clearly are legitimate reasons for termination in the absence of discrimination.

---

though the memorandum had been requested by the harassing supervisor after a complaint against the plaintiff's rude behavior to the client by a vice president).

New Jersey: Erickson v. Marsh & McLennan Co., 53 Fair Empl. Prac. Cas. (BNA) 3 (N.J. Sup. Ct. 1988), *modified on other grounds,* 117 N.J. 539, 569 A.2d 793 (1990) (employer's dissatisfaction with an employee's contentiousness over disputed sex harassment charges that led to that employee's discharge is not discrimination based upon sex but simply a nondiscriminatory employer decision for handling a contentious employee as part of the management of its business).

105 Hill v. BASF Wyandotte Corp., 27 Fair Empl. Prac. Cas. (BNA) 66, 72 (E.D. Mich. 1981) ("The evidence shows and plaintiff's demeanor during the trial confirms that she was an uncooperative, often hostile employee").

106 Jordan v. Clark, 847 F.2d 1368, 1377 (9th Cir. 1988), *cert. denied*, 488 U.S. 1006 (1989) ("The conduct which Plaintiff asserts to be retaliatory appears to the Court to be more a reaction to a problem of clashing personalities than acts in retaliation for the filing of a discriminatory complaint"); Norton v. Vartanian, 31 Fair Empl. Prac. Cas. (BNA) 1259 (D. Mass. 1983); Robinson v. E.I. Du Pont de Nemours and Co., 33 Fair Empl. Prac. Cas. (BNA) 880 (D. Del. 1979) (personality problems affected job performance).

107 663 F. Supp. 864 (W.D. Va. 1987), *aff'd,* 846 F.2d 70 (4th Cir. 1988).

108 Davis v. Bristol Lab., 26 Fair Empl. Prac. Cas. (BNA) 1351 (W.D. Okla. 1981).

109 Ramsey v. Olin Corp., 39 Fair Empl. Prac. Cas. (BNA) 959 (S.D.N.Y. 1984); Davis v. Bristol Lab., 26 Fair Empl. Prac. Cas. (BNA) 1351 (W.D. Okla. 1981).

110 Grier v. Casey, 643 F. Supp. 298, 309 (W.D.N.C. 1986) ("The plaintiff has from the time she falsified her application not been honest with her employer"); Robinson v. Thornburgh, 54 Fair Emp. Prac. Cas. (BNA) 324 (D.D.C. 1990). The defendant articulated a legitimate nondiscriminatory reason for plaintiff's discharge when it introduced unchallenged evidence that plaintiff may have leaked sensitive information to prison inmates which, if true, endangered the safety of other marshals and convicted felons who were secretly cooperating with the government. The plaintiff did not introduce any evidence that such basis was a pretext for masking a discriminatory motive.

Cobb v. Dufresne-Henry, Inc., 603 F. Supp. 1048 (D. Vt. 1985).

See also Vasconcelos v. Meese, 907 F.2d 111 (9th Cir. 1990) The district court properly found that the plaintiff's discharge was due to lying during an internal affairs investigation involving whether she had invited the complained of sexual advances. The

§ 7.14 —Lack of Work

If an employee alleged that she was fired or not rehired because of sexual harassment, an employer should assert a lack of work defense only if it can show a decline in business during the relevant period coupled with a company policy supporting the propriety of laying off or failing to rehire the plaintiff. The employer also must show that no other comparable or less qualified employee was hired during that period.[111]

§ 7.15 —Customary Business Practice

Customary business practice has, in the past, been used to justify certain types of sexual harassment, such as the use of vulgar language on the job.[112] Over the years, however, courts have acknowledged the unique effect of such language on the morale and self-esteem of women workers and generally have declined to accept this justification[113] (see **Chapter 3**).

§ 7.16 Retaliation

Retaliation claims often accompany charges of sexual harassment. Although the facts of a case may support a separate charge of retaliation,

---

ban on retaliation under Title VII is limited to the EEOC investigation, and thus did not apply. "Accusations made in the context of charges before the Commission are protected by statute; charges made outside of that context are made at the accuser's peril." *Id.* at 113.

Defendant's assertion that plaintiff was discharged for misconduct was found to be pretextual in the following cases:

Third Circuit: Sensibello v. Globe Sec. Sys. Co., 34 Fair Empl. Prac. Cas. (BNA) 1357, 1363 (E.D. Pa. 1984) (allegations that plaintiff was fired because of dishonesty was pretextual when evidence as a whole left little doubt that many persons in positions of authority did not want a woman in such a position. It was apparent that "the defendant had decided to discharge plaintiff, and that it went to extreme lengths in trying, without notable success, to build a case against her.").

Ninth Circuit: EEOC v. Judson Steel Co., 33 Fair Empl. Prac. Cas. (BNA) 1286 (N.D. Cal. 1982).

[111] Joyner v. AAA Cooper Transp., 597 F. Supp. 537, 544 (M.D. Ala. 1983), *aff'd,* 749 F.2d 732 (11th Cir. 1984) (lack of work defense was pretextual when defendant demonstrated decline in business but hired a part-time employee to fill plaintiff's position, even though plaintiff was an experienced employee whose work had always been satisfactory and who had made it very clear that he desired reemployment).

[112] Halpert V. Wertheim & Co., 27 Fair Empl. Prac. Cas. (BNA) 21 (S.D.N.Y. 1980).

[113] *Cf.* Rabidue v. Osceola Ref. Co., 805 F.2d 611 (6th Cir. 1986), *cert. denied,* 481 U.S. 1041 (1987).

the retaliatory conduct sometimes is asserted only as part of the sexual harassment claim. A plaintiff may allege that in response to a complaint of sexual harassment, a superior threatened to or actually altered her employment status or increased the level of hostility in the workplace. An employer may successfully rebut a prima facie showing of retaliation by proving that:

1. There was no adverse action[114]
2. It was not aware of the plaintiff's complaints, so the employment decision could not have been made in response thereto
3. The decision to change the plaintiff's employment status was made before the employee complained of sexual harassment[115]
4. The plaintiff requested the employment change[116]
5. The employment decision was made after the plaintiff complained of sexual harassment but for reasons other than retaliation.[117]

A defendant also may challenge causation either by introducing evidence of no causal connection between the participation in the protected activity and the adverse employment action or of other cause.[118]

---

[114] Jordan v. Clark, 847 F.2d 1368, 1377 (9th Cir. 1988), *cert. denied*, 488 U.S. 1006 (1989).

[115] Seligson v. Massachusetts Inst. of Tech., 677 F. Supp. 648, 656 (D. Mass. 1987). *See also* Petrosky v. Washington-Greene County Ass'n for the Blind, 663 F. Supp. 821 (W.D. Pa. 1987) (board of directors felt that plaintiff was abrasive and disrespectful even before she filed sexual harassment charge against board chair).

[116] McKinney v. Dole, 765 F.2d 1129 (D.C. Cir. 1985) (plaintiff requested reassignment).

[117] Jones v. Flagship Int'l, 793 F.2d 714, 720 n.5 (5th Cir. 1986), *cert. denied,* 479 U.S. 1065 (1987) (plaintiff EEO officer was suspended after filing her discrimination charge to avoid the conflict of interest inherent in her representation of defendant before the agency to whom she had made the complaint). *See also* Hollis v. Fleetguard, Inc., 668 F. Supp. 631, 638 (M.D. Tenn. 1987) (plaintiff was fired more than three months after she expressed concern about the attention of her supervisor and almost four months after she was warned to "clean up her act"); Ross v. Communications Satellite Corp., 34 Fair Empl. Prac. Cas. (BNA) 260 (D. Md. 1984) (plaintiff's responsibilities were reduced, his salary and benefit increases were denied, and he was terminated eventually because he became involved in his own causes during working hours, he badgered and interfered with coworkers, and he told two other employees that he would "blow away" someone if he failed to win his EEOC case); Evans v. Mail Handlers, 32 Fair Empl. Prac. Cas. (BNA) 634 (D.D.C. 1983) (plaintiff's job was abolished when department was restructured but she was advised that she could "bump" anyone junior in the bargaining unit). *Cf.* Sowers v. Kemira, Inc., 46 Fair Empl. Prac. Cas. (BNA) 1825 (S.D. Ga. 1988). Plaintiff showed that timing of reprimands for attendance problems followed closely on the heels of the protected activity and did not make any sense in relation to her actual attendance record. Discipline in the form of a final warning memo referring to plaintiff's talking too much violated defendant's progressive discipline policy.

[118] Cobb v. Dufresne-Henry, Inc., 603 F. Supp. 1048 (D. Vt. 1985).

If discriminatory actions already have been proven, uncertainty about the motive underlying the adverse employment action should be resolved against the defendant-employer.[119]

§ 7.17 Constructive Discharge

Constructive discharge claims may be defended with evidence that the plaintiff resigned for reasons other than the alleged harassment.[120] Evidence that the employer attempted to correct the asserted problem before the plaintiff left her position may be offered to rebut a claim of constructive discharge.[121] An employer also may try to show lack of knowledge of the harassment or that, once it became aware of the conduct as a result of the plaintiff's resignation, it attempted to contact the plaintiff and work things out.[122] If possible, the employer should demonstrate that the employee did not allow the employer a fair opportunity to curb the offensive conduct.[123]

Failure by plaintiff to prove charges of sexual harassment or retaliation may cause a charge of constructive discharge to fail as well.[124]

---

[119] Harrison v. Reed Rubber Co., 603 F. Supp. 1457, 1462 (E.D. Mo. 1985).

[120] Huddleston v. Roger Dean Chevrolet, Inc., 845 F.2d 900 (11th Cir. 1988) (plaintiff's letter of resignation did not mention alleged harassment, but stated that she was quitting because of dispute with coworker about an ice cream truck she had bought for her daughter).

[121] Toscano v. Nimmo, 32 Fair Empl. Prac. Cas. (BNA) 1401 (D. Del. 1983) (alleged harasser had left defendant's employment one or two months before plaintiff quit her position). *Cf.* Llewellyn v. Celanese Corp., 693 F. Supp. 369 (W.D.N.C. 1988) (the failure of supervisors to take adequate remedial action in response to repeated complaints of sexual harassment evidenced an intent to force plaintiff to resign).

[122] Dornhecker v. Malibu Grand Prix Corp., 828 F.2d 307, 309 (5th Cir. 1987); Smith v. Acme Spinning Co., 40 Fair Empl. Prac. Cas. (BNA) 1104 (W.D.N.C. 1986) (plaintiff's refusal to come back to work despite her employer's prompt efforts to secure her return stemmed from her anger over the denial of a job transfer request rather than three isolated incidents of harassment over three years).

[123] Dornhecker v. Malibu Grand Prix Corp., 828 F.2d 307, 310 (5th Cir. 1987).

[124] Barrett v. Omaha Nat'l Bank, 726 F.2d 424 (8th Cir. 1984); Smith v. Acme Spinning Co., 40 Fair Empl. Prac. Cas. (BNA) 1104 (W.D.N.C. 1986).

CHAPTER 8

SEXUAL HARASSMENT CLAIMS UNDER OTHER CIVIL RIGHTS LAWS

SECTION 1983 CLAIMS

§ 8.1 Section 1983

Individuals whose federal rights are violated by a state or local official[1] are protected by 42 U.S.C. § 1983.[2] This statute states in its entirety:

> Every person who, under color of any statute, ordinance, regulation, custom, or usage, of any State or Territory or the District of Columbia, subjects, or causes to be subjected, any citizen of the United States or other person within the jurisdiction thereof to the deprivation of any rights, privileges, or immunities secured by the Constitution and laws, shall be liable to the party injured in an action at law, suit in equity, or other proper proceeding for redress. For the purposes of this section, any Act of Congress applicable exclusively to the District of Columbia shall be considered to be a statute for the District of Columbia.

Section 1983 has no substantive content but rather is a conduit through which relief is available for these violations.[3] Section 1983 claims stemming from sexual harassment typically are asserted by state or local government employees alleging equal protection or other constitutional violations. A plaintiff must establish that the alleged violator "was acting under color of law, with adequate state action, and that there was sufficient injury to a constitutionally protected right, as well as a causal relationship between the alleged wrongful act and the injury suffered."[4]

---

1 The Fourteenth Amendment sets out standards of conduct for state and local governments, but does not provide for redress.

2 As amended Pub. L. No. 96-170, § 1, 93 Stat. 1284 (1979).

3 Lipsett v. Rive-Mora, 669 F. Supp. 1188, 1195 (D.P.R. 1987), *rev'd on other grounds,* 864 F.2d 881 (1st Cir. 1988) (sexual harassment); Gobla v. Crestwood Sch. Dist., 609 F. Supp. 972 (M.D. Pa. 1985) (sexual harassment).

4 Lipsett v. Rive-Mora, 669 F. Supp. at 1195, *citing generally* Martinez v. California, 444 U.S. 277 (1980); Baker v. McCollan, 443 U.S. 137 (1979); Estelle v. Gamble, 429 U.S. 97 (1976); Moose Lodge No. 107 v. Irvis, 407 U.S. 163 (1972); Landrigan v. City of Warwick, 628 F.2d 736 (1st Cir. 1980).

Section 1983 covers alleged violations of federal statutory as well as constitutional rights.[5]

A number of sexual harassment actions have been brought under § 1983, alone or in combination with Title VII[6] and/or pendent state claims. Most courts agree that relief under § 1983 is available for a claim based on alleged constitutional rights violations notwithstanding the assertion of Title VII claims.[7] However, a "right created solely under Title VII cannot serve as the basis for an independent remedy under § 1983, lest Congress' prescribed remedies under Title VII be undermined."[8] Nor may § 1983 be used to circumvent the administrative requirements of Title VII.[9]

---

[5] Statutory laws include binding federal regulations. Samuels v. District of Columbia, 770 F.2d 184 (D.C. Cir. 1985); Alexander v. Polk, 750 F.2d 250 (3d Cir. 1984).

[6] Second Circuit: Taylor v. Faculty-Student Ass'n of State Univ. College, 40 Fair Empl. Prac. Cas. (BNA) 1292 (W.D.N.Y. 1986).

Third Circuit: Fuchilla v. Prockop, 682 F. Supp. 247 (D.N.J. 1987) (sexual harassment); Blessing v. Lancaster County, 609 F. Supp. 485 (E.D. Pa. 1985).

Fifth Circuit: Simmons v. Lyons, 746 F.2d 265 ((5th Cir. 1984).

Sixth Circuit: Kerans v. Porter Paint Co., 656 F. Supp. 267 (S.D. Ohio 1987).

Seventh Circuit: Volk v. Coler, 845 F.2d 1422 (7th Cir. 1988); Gray v. County of Dane, 854 F.2d 179 (7th Cir. 1988); Bohen v. City of E. Chicago, 799 F.2d 1180 (7th Cir. 1986).

Eighth Circuit: Minteer v. Auger, 844 F.2d 569 (8th Cir. 1988).

Ninth Circuit: Collins v. City of San Diego, 841 F.2d 337 (9th Cir. 1988).

Tenth Circuit: Scott v. City of Overland Park, 595 F. Supp. 520 (D. Kan. 1984).

Actions also have been brought with other civil rights statutes such as § 1985 (see **§ 8.15**), and Title IX. Lipsett v. University of Puerto Rico, 864 F.2d 881 (1st Cir. 1988) (see **Chapter 4**).

[7] Starrett v. Wadley, 876 F.2d 808 (10th Cir. 1989) (sexual harassment); Fuchilla v. Prockop, 682 F. Supp. 247, 259 (D.N.J. 1987) (sexual harassment); Skadegaard v. Farrell, 578 F. Supp. 1209 (D.N.J. 1984) (sexual harassment). *See also* Keller v. Prince George's County, 827 F.2d 952 (4th Cir. 1987); Ratliff v. Milwaukee, 795 F.2d 612 (7th Cir. 1986); Alexander v. Chicago Park Dist., 773 F.2d 850, 856 (7th Cir. 1985), *cert. denied,* 475 U.S. 1095 (1986); Trigg v. Fort Wayne Community Sch., 766 F.2d 299 (7th Cir. 1985). Some courts have held that a plaintiff may assert a claim under § 1983 only if the claim is based on different grounds from those available under Title VII. *See, e.g.,* Parker v. Department of Social Welfare, 811 F.2d 925, 927 n.3 (5th Cir. 1987).

[8] Starrett v. Wadley, 876 F.2d 808, 813 (10th Cir. 1989); Long v. Laramie County Community College Dist., 840 F.2d 743, 752 (10th Cir.) (right to be free from retaliation for filing sexual harassment charge, created by Title VII, cannot form sole basis of § 1983 action), *cert. denied*, 488 U.S. 827 (1988); Poulsen v. City of North Tonawanda, N.Y., 811 F. Supp. 884, 893 (W.D.N.Y. 1993); Carrero v. New York Hous. Auth., 890 F.2d 569 (2d Cir. 1989); Tafoya v. Adams, 816 F.2d 555, 558 (10th Cir.), *cert. denied,* 484 U.S. 851 (1987).

[9] Lipsett v. Rive-Mora, 669 F. Supp. 1188 (D.P.R. 1987), *rev'd on other grounds,* 864 F.2d 881 (1st Cir. 1988) (sexual harassment). *See also* Foster v. Wyrick, 823 F.2d 218 (8th Cir. 1987).

One court has held that amended Title VII, which provides for compensatory and punitive damages under certain circumstances, precluded an action under §1983.[10] Although the Civil Rights Act of 1991 now provides for compensatory and punitive damages under certain circumstances, at least one court has held that §1983 is not preempted as a federal discrimination statute by the Act because Title VII still does not provide all the relief available under §1983, which provides for a longer statute of limitations period and lacks the exhaustion requirements of Title VII.[11]

Sexual harassment suits brought under § 1983 usually assert violations of the equal protection clause of the Constitution but also may seek recovery for violations of due process, invasion of privacy, and first amendment rights. There are several reasons for a government employee who claims sexual harassment under Title VII to assert a constitutional claim under § 1983 as well. For instance, the remedies a plaintiff may seek under § 1983 are broader than those available under Title VII and include damages (see **§ 8.13**). The plaintiff also has a right to a jury trial under § 1983, and need not comply with exhaustion requirements.

Section 1983 does not contain a fee award provision, but attorneys' fees are available to prevailing plaintiffs, and under certain circumstances to prevailing defendants, under the Civil Rights Attorney's Fees Awards Act (see **§ 8.14**).

Section 1983 does not itself require intentional conduct, so the employer may be charged with negligence in certain circumstances, such as when the employer negligently deprives an employee of due process. However, most § 1983 sexual harassment claims are brought under the equal protection clause of the Fourteenth Amendment. The U.S. Supreme Court has held that plaintiffs alleging such violations are required to show discriminatory intent.[12]

DEFENDANTS IN § 1983 CLAIMS

§ 8.2 States or State Officials

In *Will v. Michigan Department of State Police*,[13] the U.S. Supreme Court held that neither states nor state officials acting in their official capacities are "persons" within the meaning of § 1983. However, a state official in her or his official capacity may be sued for injunctive relief under § 1983,

---

10 Marrero-Rivera v. Department of Justice, 800 F. Supp. 1024 (D.P.R. 1992).

11 Beardsley v. Isom, 61 Fair Empl. Prac. Cas. (BNA) 847, 849 (E.D. Va. 1993).

12 Personnel Admin'r v. Feeney, 442 U.S. 256 (1979).

13 491 U.S. 58 (1989).

because "official-capacity actions for prospective relief are not treated as actions against the state."[14] Moreover, a state official may be sued in her or his individual capacity under § 1983 (see **§ 8.3**).

§ 8.3 Local Government Entities

A party may sue any "person" who acts under color of state law under § 1983, including cities, counties, and other local government entities.[15] Municipalities may be held liable under § 1983 "only for acts for which the municipality itself is actually responsible, that is, acts which the municipality sanctioned or ordered."[16] In *Monell v. Department of Social Services,*[17] the U.S. Supreme Court held that a municipality cannot be held liable under a respondeat superior theory.[18] Thus, the isolated, intentional acts of an officer without authority to set municipal policy do not establish municipal liability under § 1983,[19] but the actions of a municipal officer with final policymaking authority might.[20] In addition, a pattern or series

---

14 State of Kentucky v. Graham, 473 U.S. 159, 167 n.14 (1985).

15 Lake County Estates v. Tahoe Regional Planning Agency, 440 U.S. 391, 405 n.29 (1979); Monell v. Department of Social Servs., 436 U.S. 658 (1978).

16 City of St. Louis v. Praprotnik, 485 U.S. 112, 123 (1988).

17 436 U.S. 658 (1978).

18 *See also* Collins v. Harker Heights, 112 S. Ct. 1061, 1063 (1992); Kelsey-Andrews v. City of Philadelphia, 713 F. Supp. 760 (E.D. Pa. 1989), *aff'd sub. nom.,* Andrews v. Philadelphia, 895 F.2d 1469 (3d Cir. 1990) (sexual harassment); Fuchilla v. Prockop, 682 F. Supp. 247 (D.N.J. 1987) (sexual harassment). Although Fuchilla involved municipal liability, it has been applied to all types of § 1983 cases. *See, e.g.,* Collins v. City of San Diego, 841 F.2d 337 (9th Cir. 1988) (sexual harassment); Lipsett v. Rive-Mora, 669 F. Supp. 1188 (D.P.R. 1987), *rev'd on other grounds,* 864 F.2d 881 (1st Cir. 1988) (sexual harassment).

19 Gray v. County of Dane, 854 F.2d 179 (7th Cir. 1988); Gomez v. Metropolitan Dade County, Fla., 801 F. Supp. 674 (S.D. Fla. 1992) (Title VII and 1983). An employer may avoid liability when there is an explicit policy against sexual harassment and effective grievance procedures calculated to encourage victims of harassment to come forward, but that the plaintiff did not employ. In this action by a demoted county employee charging sexual harassment by the county personnel director and demotion in alleged retaliation for filing a sexual harassment complaint, a material question of fact existed as to the effectiveness of such procedures, and thus precluded entry of summary judgment against plaintiffs when four complaints of sexual harassment had been filed against a supervisor, but no discipline was imposed.

20 *See* Kelsey-Andrews v. City of Philadelphia, 713 F. Supp. 760, 765–66 (E.D. Pa. 1989) (as police captain and sergeant, the alleged harassers could not be considered policymakers in the city police department; only the commissioner could by his acts and omission subject the city to liability. But even if the commissioner "failed to investigate the basis of his subordinates' discretionary decisions, such failure would not amount to a delegation of policymaking authority, especially when the wrongfulness of the subordinates'

of incidents of unconstitutional conduct may constitute "custom or usage" in violation of § 1983,[21] even though the practice was not approved officially. In *Reynolds v. Borough of Avalon,*[22] a female borough employee alleging that a coworker made comments to her of a sexual nature and on a few occasions touched her in a sexually offensive manner could hold the borough liable under § 1983 for sexual harassment on the theory that the failure of policymaking officials to prevent or stop the harassment constituted deliberate indifference to whether a constitutional violation occurred when she may be able to show that the risk of sexual harassment was obvious, the failure to inform employees of a policy against sexual harassment, and to institute reporting and investigation procedures created an extremely high risk that constitutional violations involving sexual harassment would occur:

> The availability of this constructive notice prong of the deliberate indifference standard . . . is of particular importance in sexual harassment cases because such incidents are by their very nature far less likely to be reported than other types of constitutional violations . . . . There are a number of disincentives to reporting peculiar to this type of violation, which stem from the social taboos surrounding sexual matters in general, the tendency of victims to feel embarrassment and guilt regarding such incidents, as well as fears that complaints will be ill-received by supervisors and thus impact negatively on the victim's work status. Thus, it is reasonable to suppose that in the absence of affirmative steps to encourage the reporting of sexual harassment in the workplace, the likelihood that higher level officials in policymaking positions will have knowledge of such incidents in time to make meaningful corrective action is particularly small.[23]

Sexual harassment is conduct that would constitute a "persistent, widespread"[24] practice actionable against local governments. Acts of sexual harassment engaged in by supervisors in the course of their duties may be attributed to the relevant entity when management knew of and tolerated or participated in the conduct.[25] Moreover, a policy or custom may be

---

decision might arise from a retaliatory motive or other unstated rationale"), *aff'd,* Andrews v. Philadelphia, 895 F.2d 1469 (3d Cir. 1990). The city was not liable under § 1983 for the sexual harassment of female police officers when the police commissioner, who was the official policymaker for the police deparment, did not delegate his authority to the offending supervisor and did not observe or acquiesce in the harassment.

21 *Id.*

22 799 F. Supp. 442 (D.N.J. 1992).

23 *Id.* at 447.

24 Bennett v. City of Slidell, 735 F.2d 861 (5th Cir. 1984), *cert. denied,* 472 U.S. 1016 (1985).

25 Bohen v. City of E. Chicago, 799 F.2d 1180, 1189 (7th Cir. 1986). *Cf.* Volk v. Coler, 845 F.2d 1422 (7th Cir. 1988). Although plaintiff introduced evidence that two management-level defendants knew of the alleged harassment and of plaintiff's grievances,

inferred if the acts or omissions of a municipality's supervisory officials are serious enough to amount to "deliberate indifference" to the constitutional rights of a plaintiff.[26] The U.S. Supreme Court has held that the mere lack of responsiveness, failure to supervise employees, or nonfeasance is insufficient to establish a causal link between a municipal custom or practice and a constitutional violation.[27]

As in a number of sexual harassment cases, the analysis may turn on whether the court believes that harassment can occur in the course of employment or is a purely personal action.[28]

In the absence of a formal policymaking activity, an official policy may be inferred from informal acts or omissions of supervisory municipal officials, although not from the conduct of single, low-level officers.[29] For example, in *Bohen v. City of East Chicago,*[30] the plaintiff dispatcher claimed she was a continual target for obscene comments by firefighters and other male employees and was subjected to unwelcome touching and other abusive conduct. The court concluded that management's response supported a finding that the alleged harassment reflected a custom or usage:

> The district court found that individual acts of harassment were engaged in by supervisory personnel in the course of their supervisory duties. Other

---

but approved decisions with respect to those grievances and agreed not to promote her, they were not liable under § 1983 when the alleged harassment did not occur at defendants' direction or with their knowledge and consent. One defendant was director of the department, the other was absent because of illness during most of the relevant time period, and both ensured that plaintiff's grievances were investigated:

> We do not suggest that any employee in a supervisory capacity equal to that assumed by Coler or Hairston is, by virtue of that capacity, necessarily removed from liability for acts similar to those which occurred here. Indeed, three supervisors were found liable for Volk's first amendment claims. Hairston's personal involvement was affected by her absence. Coler's capacity as DCFS Director by its nature distanced him from the actions about which Volk complains. He did not act to diminish this distance. Viewing the evidence in a light most favorable to Volk, Coler's and Hairston's actions, although very close to the line at which liability attaches, are not sufficient to establish their liability.

Id. at 1432.

26 Villante v. Department of Corrections, 786 F.2d 516, 519 (2d Cir. 1986).

27 Canton, Ohio v. Harris, 489 U.S. 378, 381 (1989).

28 This is an unsettled issue in the state workers' compensation context (see **Chapter 9**) and also emerges sometimes in the context of liability generally. *Cf.* Volk v. Coler, 845 F.2d 1422 (7th Cir. 1988) (sexual harassment) (the fact that defendant supervisors were acting under color of state law was not disputed).

29 Kelsey-Andrews v. City of Philadelphia, 713 F. Supp. 760 (E.D. Pa. 1989), *aff'd sub nom.,* Andrews v. Philadelphia, 895 F.2d 1469 (3rd Cir. 1990).

30 799 F.2d 1180 (7th Cir. 1986).

> management officials responsible for working conditions at the fire department "knew the general picture if not the details" of the pattern of sexual harassment. . . . Complaints by the victims of sexual harassment were addressed superficially if at all, and the department had no policy against sexual harassment. In sum, sexual harassment was the general, on-going, and accepted practice at the East Chicago Fire Department, and high-ranking, supervisory, and management officials responsible for working conditions at the department knew of, tolerated, and participated in the harassment. This satisfies § 1983's requirement that the actions complained of be the policy or custom of the state entity.[31]

The existence of "workable review procedures" at the local level may undermine a claim that there was a "custom or practice of discrimination . . . so well-established as to embody unwritten municipal policy."[32]

Under certain circumstances, a municipality may be found liable for a single decision or action by a municipal policymaker.[33] This liability attaches only when the decisionmaker has final authority to establish municipal policy with respect to the action ordered.[34] The local government unit must have actual or constructive notice of a challenged practice.[35]

Some degree of specificity is required in the pleading of a custom or policy on the part of a municipality.[36]

---

31 *Id.* at 1189. *See also* Handley v. Phillips, 715 F. Supp. 757 (M.D. Pa. 1989). The plaintiff, a former prison guard, could sue county officials under § 1983 for violations of plaintiff's constitutional rights to free speech, due process, and equal protection arising from the warden's alleged sexual discrimination when she alleged that the officials knew of the discrimination, failed to act to prohibit the conduct, and furthered the constitutional violations by discharging her, thus establishing a pattern or practice of discrimination. The court noted that it is well established that a claim under § 1983 is insufficient if it is based merely on a showing that the defendant is the supervisor of the person or persons who allegedly committed an illegal or unconstitutional act.

32 Gray v. County of Dane, 854 F.2d 179, 184 (7th Cir. 1988) (allegations regarding attribution of alleged discrimination to policy or established practice of county fell short, given that in response to her complaints of harassment, plaintiff was transferred to another supervisor and job slot).

33 Pembaur v. City of Cincinnati, 475 U.S. 469 (1986).

34 *Id.* at 481. *See also* Collins v. City of San Diego, 841 F.2d 337, 341 (9th Cir. 1988) (sexual harassment) (although police sergeant supervised actions of patrol officers in his squad, he was not a policymaker with respect to city employment relations between sergeants and subordinate police officers and was not acting as an official policymaker for city when he allegedly made sexual demands and caused plaintiff to be fired for refusing to comply).

35 Spell v. McDaniel, 824 F.2d 1380, 1387 (4th Cir. 1987), *cert. denied,* 484 U.S. 1027 (1988); Garza v. City of Omaha, 814 F.2d 553 (8th Cir. 1987).

36 Downum v. City of Wichita, 675 F. Supp. 1566, 1573 (D. Kan. 1986) (sexual harassment) (allegation that plaintiff was first female firefighter hired did not show a discriminatory policy toward females).

§ 8.4 Supervisors

Generally, supervisors may be held liable under § 1983 only for their own illegal conduct. A finding of the supervisor's liability does not necessarily extend to the state or local entity. The U.S. Supreme Court has stated that to establish that the supervisor was liable for the conduct of subordinates, the plaintiff must show an "affirmative link" between the occurrence of the conduct and "the adoption of any plan or policy" by the defendants, "express or otherwise—showing their authorization or approval of such misconduct."[37] Supervisors may be liable for the conduct of their subordinates when the supervisor knew or should have known of the conduct and failed to prevent future harm.[38] A court also may impose liability on a supervisor for failure to supervise when the challenged conduct constitutes "gross negligence" or "deliberate indifference."[39]

Thus, a sexual harassment plaintiff should show that the supervisor was responsible for supervising the wrongdoer and, depending on the facts, that the supervisor participated in the wrongdoing,[40] was grossly negligent in supervising the alleged harasser, and/or failed to remedy the situation after learning of the harassment. By these actions, the supervisor created a policy or custom under which unconstitutional practices occurred or allowed such a policy or custom to continue.[41]

In *Murphy v. Chicago Transit Authority*,[42] a supervisor was not liable for recklessly disregarding the sexually harassing conduct of transit authority staff attorneys. The conduct was not found to violate constitutional rights because it was not performed under color of state law, and thus did not form a basis for supervisor liability. However, the court stated

---

37 Rizzo v. Goode, 423 U.S. 362, 371 (1976). *See also* Oklahoma City v. Tuttle, 471 U.S. 808, 823 (1985).

38 *See, e.g.,* McClelland v. Facteau, 610 F.2d 693, 697 (10th Cir. 1979); Estate of Scott v. deLeon, 603 F. Supp. 1328 (E.D. Mich. 1985) (sexual harassment) (collecting cases); Wulf v. City of Wichita, 644 F. Supp. 1211, 1226 (D. Kan. 1986).

Cf. Carrillo v. Ward, 770 F. Supp. 815 (S.D.N.Y. 1991). A police captain was not liable for sexual harassment under § 1983 allegedly committed against a female officer when he took action to cure the harassment every time she brought it to his attention.

39 Languirand v. Hayden, 717 F.2d 220 (5th Cir. 1983), *cert. denied,* 467 U.S. 1215 (1984); Hays v. Jefferson County, 668 F.2d 869 (6th Cir. 1982), *cert. denied,* 459 U.S. 833 (1983).

See also Williams v. Smith, 781 F.2d 319, 323–24 (2d Cir. 1986) (more than mere negligence must be shown under the Rizzo v. Goode "affirmative link" requirement); Haynesworth v. Miller, 820 F.2d 1245, 1262 (D.C. Cir. 1987).

40 A supervisor's liability also may be based on "actual knowledge and acquiescence." Rode v. Dellarciprete, 845 F.2d 1195, 1207 (3d Cir. 1988).

41 Williams v. Smith, 781 F.2d 319, 323–24 (2d Cir. 1986).

42 638 F. Supp. 464 (N.D. Ill. 1986).

that the supervisors could be held liable if the plaintiff demonstrated that they "intended plaintiff to be the victim of discrimination through the medium of the staff attorneys."[43]

§ 8.5 Coworkers

Sexual harassment by coworkers may constitute sexual harassment under color of state law within the meaning of §1983 when the harasser has some authority over his female victim and uses that authority to treat her differently from her male workers. In *Poulsen v. City of North Tonawanda, N.Y.*,[44] the degree and nature of a coworker's authority over the plaintiff's daily assignments and performance evaluations as well as the degree of influence with those in higher authority within the department was a factual question surviving summary judgment. Although a lieutenant's responsibility appeared limited according to the table of command, the plaintiff offered evidence that her coworker's actual authority exceeded his status on paper.[45] Several cases have refused to find liability under §1983 when the harassment did not involve the use of state authority of position.[46] The mere fact that all the participants were state employees or that the offending acts occurred during working hours is not enough to render a coworker's act under color of state law.

§ 8.6 Private Individuals

Private individuals may be liable under § 1983 if the plaintiff shows that the connection between the challenged conduct and the state meets the Fourteenth Amendment's state action requirement.[47] "This may be because [she or] he has acted together with or has obtained significant aid from state officials or because [her or] his conduct is otherwise chargeable to the state."[48]

---

43 *Id.* at 469 (emphasis by the court).

44 811 F. Supp. 884 (W.D.N.Y. 1993).

45 *Id.* at 895.

46 Woodward v. City of Worland, 977 F.2d 1392 (10th Cir. 1992); Hughes v. Halifax County Sch. Bd., 855 F.2d 183, 186–87 (4th Cir. 1988), *cert denied,* 488 U.S. 1042 (1989); Murphy v. Chicago Transit Auth., 638 F. Supp. 464, 467–68 (N.D. Ill. 1986).

47 Adickes v. S.H. Kress & Co., 398 U.S. 144, 152 (1970).

48 Lugar v. Edmundson Oil Co., 457 U.S. 922, 937 (1982). *Cf.* Kerans v. Porter Paint Co., 656 F. Supp. 267 (S.D. Ohio 1987) (sexual harassment). The fact that defendant was licensed by the state does not create an action "under color of state law" for § 1983:

§ 8.7 Federal Officials

Actions of federal officials under color of state law may be covered by § 1983,[49] but actions under color of federal law are not,[50] although plaintiffs may be able to seek redress directly from the Constitution in such cases (see § **8.20**).

§ 8.8 Immunities

The Eleventh Amendment bars suits against the state. It does not apply to claims involving municipalities or personal liability. The eleventh amendment also does not apply to § 1983 actions brought in state court. Government officials may be protected by absolute or qualified immunity. Absolute immunity applies to the conduct of legislators within the "sphere of legitimate legislative activity."[51] Absolute immunity also has been accorded to judges[52] and executive officials engaging in "judicial acts."[53]

> That something more than the mere fact of state licensing must be shown in order to support an assertion that a private entity has acted under color of state law is fatal to Kerans' § 1983 claim. Kerans has alleged only that Porter Paint is licensed to do business in Ohio and that both it and [the store manager] are engaging in business in the state. She has not asserted (nor could she) that the state of Ohio, through its business-licensing function, has somehow coerced or encouraged Porter Paint to engage in the sexual harassment and deprivation of rights which form the basis of her claim.

Id. at 270.

[49] Francis-Sobel v. University of Me., 597 F.2d 15 (1st Cir.), *cert. denied,* 444 U.S. 949 (1979); Hampton v. Hanrahan, 600 F.2d 600 (7th Cir. 1979), *rev'd in part on other grounds,* 446 U.S. 754 (1980).

Cf. Rose v. Figgie Int'l, 56 Fair Empl. Prac. Cas. (BNA) 41 (W.D. Mich. 1990). Sexual harassment action by a contractor of the U.S. government could not be maintained under § 1983 against a federal entity or its agents when the employer merely contracts with the government or receives government funds, but the government is not a partner or joint venturer, does not own the facility, or does not supervise work or maintain an on-site presence.

[50] *See, e.g.*, Stonecipher v. Bray, 653 F.2d 398 (9th Cir. 1981), *cert. denied*, 454 U.S. 1145 (1982); Gillespie v. Civiletti, 629 F.2d 637 (9th Cir. 1980); Hubbert v. United States Parole Comm'n, 585 F.2d 857 (7th Cir. 1978) (per curiam); Smith v. United States Civil Serv. Comm'n, 520 F.2d 731 (7th Cir. 1975).

[51] Eastland v. United States Servicemen's Fund, 421 U.S. 491 (1975); Doe v. McMillan, 412 U.S. 306, 312 (1973). This type of immunity also applied to a number of nonemployment discrimination-related situations. *See* Nixon v. Fitzgerald, 457 U.S. 731 (1982).

[52] Stump v. Sparkman, 435 U.S. 349 (1978).

[53] Butz v. Economou, 438 U.S. 478, 508 (1978).

Issues of qualified immunity come up more frequently in employment discrimination suits. The doctrine states generally that public officials who carry out their duties in good faith are immune from monetary liability in their personal capacities. In *Scheuer v. Rhodes,*[54] the U.S. Supreme Court held that a state official is not liable under § 1983 unless she or he knows or should have known that the action taken within the sphere of official responsibility would violate the plaintiff's constitutional rights or if the action was taken with the malicious intention to deprive constitutional rights. In *Harlow v. Fitzgerald,*[55] the U.S. Supreme Court stated that "government officials performing discretionary functions generally are shielded from liability for civil damages insofar as their conduct does not violate clearly established statutory or constitutional rights of which a reasonable person would have known." Recovery under § 1983 thus would be allowed only if the official's conduct is unlawful in light of the preexisting law.[56] Courts have looked to case law, usually from the relevant circuit or federal courts, to determine whether rights are "clearly established" under *Harlow*.[57] In *Woodward v. City of Worland,*[58] an action by three police dispatchers alleging sexual harassment by police officers, the court of appeals held that the officers and supervisors were entitled to qualified immunity with respect to plantiffs' equal protection claims when the alleged conduct occurred before the date that it became clearly established in the Circuit that sexual harassment under color of state law violated equal protection.

The contours of the right must be sufficiently clear that a reasonable official would understand that his or her conduct violates that right.[59] A court must use a reasonable person standard to determine whether the defendant knew or should have known that the right at stake was "clearly established."[60] The particular conduct need not have been held unlawful previously,[61] nor must there be a strict factual correspondence between the

---

54 416 U.S. 232 (1974).

55 457 U.S. 800, 818 (1982).

56 Anderson v. Creighton, 483 U.S. 635, 639–40 (1987); Eastwood v. Department of Corrections, 846 F.2d 627, 629 (10th Cir. 1988) (sexual harassment).

57 Jones v. Preuit & Maudlin, 822 F.2d 998 (11th Cir. 1987). *Accord* People of Three Mile Island v. Nuclear Regulatory Comm'rs, 747 F.2d 139, 144 (3d Cir. 1984); Foster v. Township of Hillside, 780 F. Supp. 1026 (D.N.J. 1992); Ortega v. City of Kansas City, 659 F. Supp. 1201, 1208 (D. Kan. 1987).

58 977 F.2d 1392 (10th Cir. 1992).

59 Anderson v. Creighton, 483 U.S. 635, 640 (1987).

60 Harlow v. Fitzgerald, 457 U.S. 800, 818–19 (1982).

61 Anderson v. Creighton, 483 U.S. 635, 640 (1987).

cases establishing the law and the case at hand.[62] In *Poulsen*,[63] an action by a female police officer against the city, police chief and police lieutenant for *quid pro quo* and hostile environment sexual harassment, the court noted that while it was well established by 1989 that sexual harassment violated Title VII, neither the U.S. Supreme Court nor the Second Circuit had decided that sexual harassment constituted a violation of equal protection. But in 1987, a district court in the Second Circuit held that when defendants knowingly allowed an offensive and hostile work environment to exist and failed to protect plaintiffs from harassment and retaliation, they violated the plaintiffs' constitutional rights, and thus the police chief should reasonably have known when the plaintiff filed her complaint alleging sexual harassment that intentionally permitting a hostile environment, including continuing harassment and retaliatory behavior againt the plaintiff and another female officer on the force, deprived the plaintiff of her right to free speech and equal protection under the law.

In *Eastwood v. Department of Corrections,*[64] the plaintiff alleged that a fellow employee enticed her to his room after a training session and put a drug in her drink that rendered her unconscious. She awoke to find the coworker assaulting and molesting her. When she complained to a departmental supervisor, she was threatened with termination unless she signed a statement promising to forget the incident if the alleged harasser resigned. She then was forced to reveal facts about her sexual history. The investigator and other management-level employees allegedly also published offensive and insulting drawings within the facility, and insulted her repeatedly. The court rejected the defendants' contention that the questions regarding the plaintiff's sexual history were designed to test the validity of her complaint,[65] and upheld the district court's finding that the investigator should not be protected by qualified immunity:

> [P]laintiff in the instant case was forced to answer a number of irrelevant and embarrassing questions. To justify this invasion of plaintiff's privacy, the defendants argue that these questions were designed to test the validity of her complaint. A court certainly could find instead that the defendants sought to harass plaintiff into dismissing her complaint and quitting her job. The alleged subsequent behavior of defendants, including the publication of

---

62 Garcia v. Miera, 817 F.2d 650, 657 (10th Cir. 1987), *cert. denied,* 485 U.S. 959 (1988); Eastwood v. Department of Corrections, 846 F.2d 627, 629 (10th Cir. 1988) (sexual harassment).

63 Poulsen v. City of N. Tonawanda, N.Y., 811 F. Supp. 884 (W.D.N.Y. 1993).

64 Eastwood v. Department of Corrections, 846 F.2d 627 (10th Cir. 1988).

65 *Id.* at 631. The court noted that "[u]nstated in defendants' justification, but obviously present, is the implication that plaintiff's complaint is unworthy if she is less than sexually innocent. This antiquated notion overlooks the fact that everyone has the right to refuse a sexual advance." *Id.* at 631 n.2 (emphasis by the court).

> offensive drawings within the DOC facility, suggests such a motive. Furthermore, even if we were to believe that defendants sought this information to determine the validity of plaintiff's complaint, there exists little correlation between plaintiff's sexual history and whether she fabricated the story of being sexually molested. Indications of a victim's promiscuity are not probative of either credibility or consent to sexual advances. . . . Nor should such an inquiry be sanctioned in this case.[66]

The fact that a defendant's conduct may have clearly violated Title VII does not strip the defendant of immunity in a suit that is based on a constitutional violation.[67]

"In § 1983 actions that raise the issue of qualified immunity, plaintiff must plead facts with sufficient particularity to establish the foundation for recovery."[68] In the sexual harassment context, a plaintiff should date and explain the incidents of harassment in detail.[69]

§ 8.9 Venue

There are no special venue requirements under § 1983; the general venue statute for district courts applies.[70] In suits combining Title VII and § 1983 claims, the Title VII venue requirement controls.

§ 8.10 Statutes of Limitations

Because there is no specific federal statute of limitations for a job discrimination cause of action under § 1983, analogous state statutes of limitation, usually personal injury tort statutes, control.[71] In *Owens v. Okure,*[72] the U.S. Supreme Court held that the residual or general personal injury statute of limitations applied in those states with one or more statutes of limitations for certain enumerated torts, and a residual statute for all other personal injury actions.

---

66 *Id.* at 631 (footnote omitted).

67 Estate of Scott v. deLeon, 603 F. Supp. 1328, 1331 (E.D. Mich. 1985).

68 Eastwood v. Department of Corrections, 846 F.2d 627, 629 (10th Cir. 1988) (sexual harassment); Brown v. Texas A&M Univ., 804 F.2d 327, 333 (5th Cir. 1986).

69 Eastwood v. Department of Corrections, 846 F.2d 627, 629 (10th Cir. 1988).

70 Kohl Indus. Park Co. v. County of Rockland, 710 F.2d 895 (2d Cir. 1983).

71 Johnson v. Railway Express Agency, Inc., 421 U.S. 454 (1975). *See also* Wilson v. Garcia, 471 U.S. 261 (1985).

72 488 U.S. 235 (1989).

§ 8.11 Exhaustion Requirements

There are no exhaustion requirements under § 1983, and thus a claim under this section may be broader than a Title VII administrative charge. Nor is a plaintiff required to pursue state judicial[73] or administrative[74] remedies prior to commencing an action under this section.

ELEMENTS OF § 1983 CLAIMS

§ 8.12 Pleading § 1983 Claims

As noted in **§ 8.1,** § 1983 is a procedural device.[75] A party may not assert an independent claim under § 1983 without demonstrating a violation of a right protected by federal statutory or constitutional rights.[76] The plaintiff must establish that the offender, who may not be the state, was acting under color of law, with adequate state action, and that there was sufficient injury to a constitutionally protected right, as well as a causal relationship between the alleged wrongful act and the injury suffered.[77] Section 1983 claims based on the equal protection clause must demonstrate that the defendant intentionally discriminated against the plaintiff because the plaintiff was a member of a protected class.[78]

---

[73] Board of Regents v. Tomanio, 446 U.S. 478, 491 (1980).

[74] Patsy v. Board of Regents, 457 U.S. 496, 515 (1982). *Cf.* Patel v. Thomas, 793 P.2d 632 (Colo. Ct. App. 1990). A female state employee secretary who alleged that one of her supervisors grabbed her breasts, ran his hand up her legs, rubbed against her, followed her around the office, restricted her freedom of movement, and made lewd, suggestive, and aggressive comments, and that she was demoted as a result of her resistance to this conduct, could pursue a § 1983 action despite her failure to pursue her grievance with the state personnel board. Although the personnel board could have investigated whether sexual harassment occurred and ordered limited remedies, it had neither the expertise to handle all of the plaintiff's claims nor the power to provide an appropriate remedy for plaintiff's damages such as compensation for her mental anguish. Thus, the procedure was one that plaintiff could by-pass without forfeiting her judicial remedy in tort.

[75] Lipsett v. Rive-Mora, 669 F. Supp. 1188 (D.P.R. 1987), *rev'd on other grounds,* 864 F.2d 881 (1st Cir. 1988), *sustaining jury verdict after remand,* 759 F. Supp. 41 (D.P.R. 1991); Chapman v. Houston Welfare Rights Org., 441 U.S. 600, 616–18 (1979).

[76] West v. Atkins, 487 U.S. 42 (1988).

[77] Lipsett v. Rive-Mora, 669 F. Supp. 1188 (D.P.R. 1987), *rev'd on other grounds,* 864 F.2d 881 (1st Cir. 1988), *sustaining jury verdict after remand,* 759 F. Supp. 41 (D.P.R. 1991).

[78] Davis v. Passman, 442 U.S. 228 (1979); Personnel Admin'r v. Feeney, 442 U.S. 256 (1979).

A plaintiff asserting a claim under § 1983 must plead specific facts regarding the conduct that gave rise to a violation of federal rights.[79]

Although courts will consider § 1983 and Title VII claims together if the facts alleged give rise to violations of both causes of action, Title VII claims may not proceed through § 1983 actions to evade the required exhaustion of Title VII administrative remedies.[80]

§ 8.13 —Actions under Color of State Law

In *Blum v. Yaretsky*,[81] the U.S. Supreme Court set out the standard for determining whether particular conduct is state action for purposes of § 1983:

1. There must be "a sufficiently close nexus between the State and the challenged action of the regulated entity so that the action of the latter may be fairly treated as that of the State itself"[82]
2. The state may be liable for a private decision only when it has "exercised coercive power or has provided such significant encouragement, either overt or covert, that the choice must in law be deemed to be that of the state"[83]
3. The entity must have exercised powers "that are 'traditionally the exclusive prerogatives of the state.'"[84]

Whether conduct constituting sexual harassment is found to be under color of state law depends on whether the abusive behavior is deemed related to the duties and powers incidental to the job.[85] A finding of harassment should satisfy this inquiry per se by virtue of the fact that it is the harasser's position, a government position, that creates the dynamics necessary for a finding of sexual harassment.

---

79 Colburn v. Upper Darby Township, 838 F.2d 663 (3d Cir. 1988); Alfaro Motors v. Ward, 814 F.2d 883 (2d Cir. 1987); Barr v. Abrams, 810 F.2d 358 (2d Cir. 1987); Pace Resources v. Shrewsbury Township, 808 F.2d 1023 (3d Cir.), *cert. denied,* 482 U.S. 906 (1987); Chapman v. Detroit, 808 F.2d 459 (6th Cir. 1986); Jacquez v. Procunier, 801 F.2d 789 (5th Cir. 1986); Downum v. City of Wichita, 675 F. Supp. 1566, 1573 (D. Kan. 1986) (sexual harassment).

80 Day v. Wayne County Bd. of Auditors, 749 F.2d 1199 (6th Cir. 1984); Lipsett v. Rive-Mora, 669 F. Supp. 1188 (D.P.R. 1987), *rev'd on other grounds,* 864 F.2d 881 (1st Cir. 1988).

81 457 U.S. 991 (1982).

82 *Id.* at 1004, *quoting* Jackson v. Metropolitan Edison Co., 419 U.S. 345, 351 (1974).

83 *Id.*

84 *Id.* at 1005.

85 Murphy v. Chicago Transit Auth., 638 F. Supp. 464 (N.D. Ill. 1986).

§ 8.14 —Deprivation of Federal Rights

Violations of the Constitution as well as federal statutory law may give rise to actions under § 1983. In determining whether the section applies to a particular statute, the U.S. Supreme Court requires an examination of whether the statute indicates congressional intent not to preclude an action under § 1983 and creates rights, privileges, or immunities.[86]

A party also may bring an action under § 1983 when otherwise routine administrative decisions are made in retaliation for exercising a constitutionally protected right,[87] or if the party had a "legitimate claim of entitlement" to procedural safeguards before an adverse employment action or to ongoing employment.[88]

§ 8.15 —Equal Protection

Sexual harassment constitutes actionable sex discrimination under the equal protection clause of the Fourteenth Amendment to the Constitution.[89] The U.S. Supreme Court has held that the equal protection clause contains a "federal constitutional right to be free from gender discrimination" that does not "serve important governmental objectives" and is not "substantially related to those objectives."[90] Courts have interpreted this language to apply to sexual harassment.[91] "Forcing women and not men to work in an environment of sexual harassment is no different than forcing women to work in a dirtier or more hazardous environment than men simply

---

86 Pennhurst State Sch. v. Halderman, 451 U.S. 1, 15–27 (1981).

87 Gill v. Mooney, 824 F.2d 192, 194 (2d Cir. 1987).

88 San Bernardino Physicians' Servs. Medical Group, Inc. v. County of San Bernardino, 825 F.2d 1404, 1407–09 (9th Cir. 1987).

89 Bohen v. City of E. Chicago, 799 F.2d 1180 (7th Cir. 1986); Gobla v. Crestwood Sch. Dist., 609 F. Supp. 972 (M.D. Pa. 1985); Estate of Scott v. deLeon, 603 F. Supp. 1328 (E.D. Mich. 1985); Skadegaard v. Farrell, 578 F. Supp. 1209 (D.N.J. 1984); Woerner v. Brzeczek, 519 F. Supp. 517 (N.D. Ill. 1981).

90 Davis v. Passman, 442 U.S. 228, 234–35 (1979); Huebschen v. Department of Health & Social Servs., 716 F.2d 1167, 1171 (7th Cir. 1983).

91 First Circuit: Pontarelli v. Stone, 930 F.2d 104 (1st Cir. 1991).

Second Circuit: Bohen v. City of E. Chicago, 799 F.2d 1180 (7th Cir. 1986); Huebschen v. Department of Health & Social Servs., 716 F.2d 1167, 1171 (7th Cir. 1983); Poulsen v. City of N. Tonawanda, N.Y., 811 F. Supp. 884 (W.D.N.Y. 1993).

Third Circuit: Moire v. Temple Univ., 613 F. Supp. 1360, 1366 (E.D. Pa. 1983), *aff'd*, 800 F.2d 1136 (3d Cir. 1986); Gobla v. Crestwood Sch. Dist., 609 F. Supp. 972, 978–79 (M.D. Pa. 1985); Skadegaard v. Farrell, 578 F. Supp. 1209, 1216–17 (D.N.J. 1984).

Sixth Circuit: Estate of Scott v. deLeon, 603 F. Supp. 1328, 1332 (E.D. Mich. 1985) ("common sense as well as relevant Title VII case law indicated that harassment was

because they are women."[92] In *King v. Board of Regents,*[93] an assistant dean who sexually harassed a female assistant professor by repeatedly leering at her, rubbing up against her, placing objects between her legs, making suggestive remarks, commenting upon various parts of her body, and finally following her into a bathroom and forcibly kissing and fondling her violated the Equal Protection Clause, and was liable for damages in the amount of $60,000 for pain and suffering and $30,000 in punitive damages. The court rejected the defendant's contention that his actions were merely the result of his desire for the plaintiff and therefore not sex-based:

> Sonstein's argument, therefore, comes down to the assertion that harassment (Sonstein's argument does not address whether the conduct is harassing) based on sexual desire is not based on gender. One argument that Sonstein might advance to this end is that his sexual desire indicates that he did not have a policy of discrimination against womanhood as a whole; it was just King's particular sexual characteristics. We rejected this argument in *Bowen* where we stated "an equal protection plaintiff therefore need not prove a discriminatory policy against an entire class; discrimination against the plaintiff because of her membership in the class is by itself enough." 799 F.2d at 1187 (citations omitted). . . .
>
> Another argument to support Sonstein's position might be that his desire for a sexual affair was based on her characteristics other then sex, similar to the defendant in *Huebschen* who disliked the plaintiff as a person. To this end, Sonstein claims it was King as an individual to whom he was attracted,

---

the sort of invidious gender discrimination that the equal protection clause forbade: that is, intentional discrimination against a woman because of her sex by a person acting under color of law").

Seventh Circuit: Volk v. Coler, 845 F.2d 1422 (7th Cir. 1988); Woerner v. Brzeczek, 519 F. Supp. 517 (N.D. Ill. 1981).

Eighth Circuit: Headley v. Bacon, 828 F.2d 1272 (8th Cir. 1987).

Ninth Circuit: Candelore v. Clark County Sanitation Dist., 752 F. Supp. 956 (D. Nev. 1990), *aff'd,* 975 F.2d 588 (9th Cir. 1992).

Tenth Circuit: Starrett v. Wadley, 876 F.2d 808 (10th Cir. 1989); Downum v. City of Wichita, 675 F. Supp. 1566 (D. Kan. 1986); Scott v. City of Overland Park, 595 F. Supp. 520, 529 (D. Kan. 1984).

92 Bohen v. City of E. Chicago, 799 F.2d 1180, 1185 (7th Cir. 1986). *See also* Starrett v. Wadley, 876 F.2d 808 (10th Cir. 1989) (supervisor had made various sexual advances toward plaintiff, repeatedly asked her to meet him during business hours at his house or at other secluded locations, once asked her to go with him to a motel, at a business reception pinched plaintiff's buttocks with his full hand, later put his arm on plaintiff's leg and invited her to his hotel room, often made obscene gestures to plaintiff during work, and sexually harassed other female employees at the office, all of which conduct was sufficient to conclude supervisor had deprived plaintiff of right to equal protection of the law).

93 898 F.2d 533 (7th Cir 1990).

> not King as a woman. This argument, however, also misses the point. Sonstein wanted to have an affair, a liaison, illicit sex, a forbidden relationship. His actions are not consistent with platonic love. His actions were based on her gender and motivated by his libido.
>
> We have, in fact, previously rejected this very argument in the context of *quid pro quo* harassment. In *quid pro quo* cases, a supervisor demands sexual favors from an employee as a condition of employment. This is exactly the situation where a supervisor's only motivation is to have a conjugal relationship with the employee. In *Horn v. Duke* we considered the argument that the *quid pro quo* demands based on sexual desire were not based on sex. 755 F.2d 599, 604 (7th Cir. 1985). We found that "[b]ut for Horn's womanhood, Haas would not have demanded sex as a condition of employment. Because of her sex, therefore, Horn was disadvantaged by the pressure to submit to an additional, humiliating condition of employment that served no legitimate purpose of the employer." *Id.* In other words, treatment of individual based on sexual desire is sexually motivated. Sonstein's sexual desire does not negate his intent; rather it affirmatively establishes it.
>
> Yet a final argument that Sonstein might advance is that because his actions were motivated by her sex, he did not intend to harass her. It is clear, however, that the advances were unwelcome and that Sonstein knew they were unwelcome. This is not the case of a single, innocent, sexual query. Instead, we have repeated, unwelcome advances, fondling and a physical attack. The jury was justified in inferring intent to harass from these facts, and we affirm the verdict of sexual harassment against Sonstein.[94]

The core of an equal protection claim is a showing of intentional discrimination,[95] and a single discriminatory act generally can constitute intentional discrimination for the equal protection clause.[96] The plaintiff need not prove a discriminatory policy against an entire class, but only against the plaintiff because of her membership in the class.[97] Thus, in sexual

---

94 *Id.* at 539–40.

See also Barcume v. City of Flint, 819 F. Supp. 631 (E.D. Mich. 1993) (Newblatt, J.). Allegations by female police officers who brought an action under §§ 1983 and 1985 and the state civil rights act against the city, alleging violation of the duty of fair representation against their union that all male police officers engaged in harassment, made sexually explicit remarks and comments to female officers on a continual basis, and that sexually explicit pictures demeaning to women were constantly present throughout the police department, were sufficient to plead a prima facie case of sexual harassment.

95 Batson v. Kentucky, 476 U.S. 79, 90–93 (1986); Washington v. Davis, 426 U.S. 229 (1976); Kelsey-Andrews v. City of Philadelphia, 713 F. Supp. 760 (E.D. Pa. 1989).

96 Batson v. Kentucky, 476 U.S. 79, 90–93 (1986); Bohen v. City of E. Chicago, 799 F.2d 1180, 1186–87 (7th Cir. 1986).

97 Adickes v. Kress & Co., 398 U.S. 144, 152 (1970). Volk v. Coler, 845 F.2d 1422, 1433 (7th Cir. 1988). The court rejected defendant's argument that gender was merely coincidental to defendant's alleged conduct:

harassment cases alleging violations of the equal protection clause, "several broad outlines . . . become discernible":

> First, the ultimate inquiry is whether the sexual harassment constitutes intentional discrimination. This differs from the inquiry under Title VII as to whether or not the sexual harassment altered the conditions of the victim's employment. That standard comes from the regulations promulgated under Title VII . . . . Second, a plaintiff can make an ultimate showing of sex discrimination either by showing that sexual harassment that is attributable to the employer under § 1983 amounted to intentional discrimination or by showing that the conscious failure of the employer to protect the plaintiff from the abusive conditions created by fellow employees amounted to intentional discrimination. . . . To make this showing, it is not necessary to show that all women employees are sexually harassed. Harassment of the plaintiff alone because of her sex is enough. It is a good defense, however, if the employer can show that the harassment suffered by the plaintiff was directed at the plaintiff because of factors personal to her and not because she is a woman. . . . Finally, we find it most unlikely that a defendant can defeat a claim of sexual harassment by showing that the harassment was justified or had a legitimate business purpose. The nature of the harm is such that there is virtually no scenario imaginable where sexual harassment is a necessary business practice or is substantially related to important governmental objectives.[98]

The scope of the constitutional right to be free from sexual harassment has been interpreted similarly to Title VII. The equal protection clause is not violated for "every passing overture" made to a female employee.[99] On the contrary, liability under the equal protection clause has been found for "repeated crude sexual advances and suggestive comments" that "persisted despite plaintiff's explicit and consistent rejection" of a supervisor's advances,[100] and when the plaintiff repeatedly complained of her treatment to no avail.[101]

> The defendants' argument misconstrues the protection afforded by the equal protection clause and incorrectly suggests that the law recognizes two classes of women: those women who are sexually offended by improper overtures and those who are either not offended or not subjected to them. Discrimination and harassment against an individual woman because of her sex is a violation of the equal protection clause. . . . Volk's sex is an immutable characteristic. Even if Tapen did not choose to offend all women with whom he had contact, the law does not require such uniform treatment. Moreover, Volk offered evidence of Tapen's allegedly abusive and discriminatory conduct towards other female employees. . . .

Id. See also Gobla v. Crestwood Sch. Dist., 609 F. Supp. 972 (M.D. Pa. 1985) (sexual harassment).

[98] Bohen v. City of E. Chicago, 799 F.2d 1180, 1187 (7th Cir. 1986) (citations and footnote omitted).

[99] Skadegaard v. Farrell, 578 F. Supp. 1209, 1216 (D.N.J. 1984).

[100] *Id.* at 1212. *See also* Woerner v. Brzeczek, 519 F. Supp. 517, 518 (N.D. Ill. 1981).

[101] Bohen v. City of E. Chicago, 799 F.2d 1180, 1187 (7th Cir. 1986). *See also* Downum v. City of Wichita, 675 F. Supp. 1566, 1573 (D. Kan. 1986) (sexual harassment).

Once the plaintiff has made a prima facie showing of intentional discrimination, the burden shifts to the employer to demonstrate by a preponderance of the evidence that it would have reached the same adverse employment decision even in the absence of intentional discrimination.[102] If the defendants do articulate such a justification, the burden shifts back to the plaintiff to demonstrate that the proffered reason was a pretext for discrimination.

§ 8.16 —Due Process

When bringing a § 1983 action charging violations of due process, the plaintiff must show that she possesses a property or liberty interest in her employment to trigger the due process protections of the Fourteenth Amendment.[103] Whether the plaintiff has a property interest under state law sufficient to give rise to these protections is determined by whether the terms of employment create a legitimate claim of entitlement to her job rather than a mere unilateral expectation of continuing in her position.[104] At-will employees generally may not state claims for deprivation of due process. In *Beardsley v. Isom,*[105] a female police officer's claim that the sheriff violated her due process rights by failing to adequately investigate her sexual harassment complaint could not stand when neither the Virginia constitution nor the state code created a property interest in the plaintiff's employment.

Allegation that plaintiff was first female firefighter hired did not show a discriminatory policy toward females:

> The fact that plaintiff was the city's first female firefighter is not sufficient to show the existence of a discriminatory policy toward females. Plaintiff has not specified other acts as a basis for the city's custom or policy. Plaintiff admits she did not complain through official channels of any treatment she received, and it is uncontested that [the defendant] did not know of any sexually oppressive working conditions or of any specific instances of sexual harassment toward the plaintiff. Accordingly, no equal protection claim has been supported by the facts.

Id. at 1573–74.

102 Mt. Healthy City Sch. Dist. Bd. of Educ. v. Doyle, 429 U.S. 274 (1977).

103 Board of Regents v. Roth.; 408 U.S. 564 (1972); Handley v. Phillips, 715 F. Supp. 757 (M.D. Pa. 1989). Plaintiff's allegations of denial of due process were without merit when all of the process that was due to protect plaintiff's property and liberty interests were provided for in the terms of collective bargaining agreement, including adequate notice prior to and after suspension and/or termination; Downum v. City of Wichita, 675 F. Supp. 1566 (D. Kan. 1986) (sexual harassment).

104 Board of Regents v. Roth, 408 U.S. 564, 577 (1972); Downum v. City of Wichita, 675 F. Supp. 1566, 1571 (D. Kan. 1986) (sexual harassment).

105 61 Fair Empl. Prac. Cas. (BNA) 847 (E.D. Va. 1993).

In *Downum v. City of Wichita,*[106] the plaintiff was a probationary employee when she was transferred from firefighter to dispatcher as well as when she was terminated from the dispatcher job. She alleged that fellow recruits created a hostile environment by making belittling or offensive comments to her and that her supervisor drew her aside on five or six occasions for special instruction. The court found that she had no constitutionally protected property interest in continued employment. Nor did the plaintiff's transfer implicate a liberty interest based on false and defamatory information allegedly publicized by the defendants, suggesting that she was not competent to perform as a firefighter. The reason for the plaintiff's transfer, her scoliosis, was not sufficiently stigmatizing to create a liberty interest.

§ 8.17 —Right to Privacy

The constitutional right to privacy protects an individual from disclosing personal matters and protects the ability to make certain kinds of decisions independently.[107] This right is implicated when a person is forced to disclose information regarding sexual matters.[108] This is not an uncommon element of sexual harassment. A supervisor may ask an employee questions regarding her sexual practices or history or may make implications about the employee's sexual orientation in an effort to elicit a response. This type of harassment is usually of the environmental variety, but also may affect a tangible benefit. In *Eastwood,*[109] the plaintiff alleged that a fellow employee enticed her to his room after a training session, put a drug in her drink that rendered her unconscious, and then assaulted and molested her. Her departmental supervisor threatened her with termination unless she signed a statement promising to forget the incident if the alleged harasser resigned, and forced her to reveal facts about her sexual history. The court rejected the employer's contention that the questions were designed to test the validity of her complaint. "Unstated in defendants' justification, but obviously present, is the implication that plaintiff's complaint is unworthy if she is less than sexually innocent. This antiquated notion overlooks the fact that everyone has the right to refuse a sexual advance."[110]

---

[106] 675 F. Supp. 1566 (D. Kan. 1986) (sexual harassment).

[107] Whalen v. Roe, 429 U.S. 589, 599 (1977).

[108] Eastwood v. Department of Corrections, 846 F.2d 627 (10th Cir. 1988) (sexual harassment).

[109] *Id.*

[110] *Id.* at 631.

§ 8.18 —First Amendment

A First Amendment retaliation suit by a public employee generally is available whenever the employee's speech is on a matter of "public concern" and the employee's interests as a citizen outweigh the efficiency interests of the public employer.[111] A court must look at the speaker's motive in analyzing whether it qualifies as a matter of public concern. "Speech which discloses any evidence of corruption, impropriety, or other malfeasance on the part of city officials, in terms of content, clearly concerns matters of public import."[112] In *Poulsen,*[113] a plaintiff employee alleged that she was subjected to sexually harassing comments, jokes, offensive touching, ridicule, and retaliation in violation of her First Amendment rights to freedom of speech and freedom of association.

Although Poulsen's primary motivation for filing her EEOC complaint was to stop the harassment against her personally, she raised an issue of public concern in criticizing the treatment of women in the Police Department. After filing her complaint, the hostile work environment to which she was subjected intensified. She alleged that she was isolated in the Department, ridiculed and humiliated by Sedlacek and others, and that chief Graves did nothing to prevent this retaliatory behavior, but continued to challenge her to provide more evidence. . . .

> Sexual harassment within the Police Department is a matter of public concern, more so when the complaint involves a local police force and the ability of its officers to function. In weighing this public concern against the need for efficiency of the police force, it would appear that preventing or abating sexual harassment could only improve the efficiency of the Department. Poulsen's allegations that her First Amendment rights to freedom of speech and freedom of assocation were violated are sufficiently supported by the record to establish a §1983 claim.[114]

---

[111] Connick v. Myers, 461 U.S. 138 (1983).

[112] Conaway v. Smith, 853 F.2d 789, 796 (10th Cir. 1988).

[113] Poulsen v. City of N. Tonawanda, N.Y., 811 F. Supp. 884 (W.D.N.Y. 1993).

[114] *Id.* at 894.

REMEDIES

§ 8.19 Remedies for § 1983 Claims

A range of remedies is available to redress § 1983 violations, including injunctive relief,[115] and compensatory, punitive,[116] and nominal[117] damages. Compensatory damages may be awarded for emotional distress[118] as well as impaired reputation or humiliation.[119] Punitive damages are available to penalize particularly egregious conduct.[120] Nominal damages may be used to compensate a person whose rights have been violated, but who was unable to demonstrate a pecuniary loss.[121] In addition, back pay awarded under § 1983 is not subject to the statutory limitations of Title VII.

A plaintiff must demonstrate her entitlement to relief under § 1983 as well as overcome various immunity-related defenses. A claim for damages against the state or a state official in her or his official capacity is barred by the Eleventh Amendment.

§ 8.20 Attorneys' Fees

A prevailing plaintiff may recover attorneys' fees for violations of § 1983 under the Civil Rights Attorney's Fees Awards Act.[122] The language of the Act is similar to that of Title VII's fee provision, and the two have been similarly construed (see **Chapter 6**). Courts ordinarily award attorneys' fees to prevailing plaintiffs under the Act unless special circumstances would render such an award unjust.[123] The issues surrounding who is entitled to fees and how a fee award should be computed have generated an immense body of case law.

---

[115] Martinez v. Procunier, 354 F. Supp. 1092 (N.D. Cal. 1973) (three-judge court) (per curiam), *aff'd,* 416 U.S. 396 (1974).

[116] Smith v. Wade, 461 U.S. 30 (1983); Lipsett v. University of P.R., 759 F. Supp. 401 (D.P.R. 1991).

[117] Carey v. Piphus, 435 U.S. 247 (1978).

[118] Harris v. Harvey, 605 F.2d 330 (7th Cir. 1979), *cert. denied,* 445 U.S. 938 (1980); Simineo v. School Dist. No. 16, 594 F.2d 1353 (10th Cir. 1979).

[119] Memphis Community Sch. Dist. v. Stachura, 477 U.S. 299, 307 (1986), *quoting* Gertz v. Robert Welch, Inc., 418 U.S. 323, 350 (1974).

[120] Smith v. Wade, 461 U.S. 30 (1983).

[121] Carey v. Piphus, 435 U.S. 247, 266 (1978).

[122] 42 U.S.C. § 1988.

[123] Hensley v. Eckerhart, 461 U.S. 424, 429 (1983), *quoting* S. Rep. No. 94–1011 p.4 (1976), *quoting* Newman v. Piggie Park Enters., 390 U.S. 400, 402 (1968); Lipsett v. University of P.R., 759 F. Supp. 401 (D.P.R. 1991).

In *Hensley v. Eckerhart,*[124] the U.S. Supreme Court held that plaintiffs are prevailing parties if they succeed on any significant issue in the litigation that achieves some of the benefit sought in bringing the lawsuit. After determining whether the plaintiff is a prevailing party, the court must decide the amount of a reasonable fee. This analysis should consider the results obtained compared to the time expended. A party who has prevailed substantially may be compensated fully for the time put into the case, while a reduced fee may be awarded to parties who have obtained limited success. A fee may be increased in limited circumstances.[125]

To be a prevailing party, a plaintiff need not obtain a formal judgment. A party to a settlement may prevail for purposes of attorneys' fees if the lawsuit was a catalyst in obtaining the sought relief.[126] A plaintiff also may prevail when the lawsuit is mooted by changes motivated by the action.

Reasonable attorneys' fees must be calculated according to the prevailing market rates in the relevant community, regardless of whether the prevailing party is represented by private counsel or nonprofit legal service organizations.[127]

Prevailing defendants may be entitled to a fee award when the plaintiff's action was frivolous, vexatious, or meritless.[128] A defendant need not demonstrate subjective bad faith on the part of the plaintiff to recover fees under the Act.[129] Sanctions may be assessed against either party for frivolous filings under Federal Rule of Civil Procedure 11 or other federal rules.[130]

OTHER POSSIBLE BASES FOR CLAIMS

§ 8.21 Section 1985(3)

Section 1985(3) authorizes damages for injuries resulting from a conspiracy to deprive a party of the equal protection and equal privileges under the law. A victim of sexual harassment may allege that resistance to harassment gave rise to a conspiracy to force her discharge or otherwise

---

124 461 U.S. 424, 433 (1983).

125 *See* A. Conte, Attorney Fee Awards Ch. 10 (2d ed. 1993).

126 Hanrahan v. Hampton, 446 U.S. 754 (1980); Maher v. Gagne, 448 U.S. 122 (1980).

127 Blum v. Stenson, 465 U.S. 886 (1984).

128 Hensley v. Eckerhart, 461 U.S. 424, 429 n.2 (1983); Christiansburg Garment Co. v. EEOC, 434 U.S. 412, 421 (1978); United States Steel Corp. v. United States, 519 F.2d 359 (3d Cir. 1975).

129 Christiansburg Garment Co. v. EEOC, 434 U.S. 412, 421 (1978).

130 A. Conte, Attorney Fee Awards Ch. 7 (2d ed. 1993).

retaliate against her.[131] Like § 1983, this provision does not create substantive rights but is a remedial statute. To successfully bring a claim of conspiracy under this section, a plaintiff must show that a conspiracy existed "to deprive her of her rights to equal treatment with members of the opposite sex"[132] and that she was injured by this conspiracy. It is not necessary for the plaintiff to allege that all women were discriminated against; she need only show that she is a member of a discernible class within the framework of § 1985(3).[133]

§ 8.22 —Defendants in § 1985(3) Claims

The immunity doctrines of § 1983 have been applied to actions under § 1985(3).[134] The statute may be used to reach state and local officials, municipalities, and private individuals.[135] Because § 1985(3) does not require state action, some courts have allowed federal officials to be sued under this section. However, under *Brown v. GSA*,[136] employment discrimination actions against federal officials in their official capacities most likely would be brought under Title VII.

§ 8.23 —Intraentity Conspiracies

Section 1985(3) may apply to conspiracies between a company and its employees[137] unless the challenged conduct is essentially a single act of discrimination by a single business entity.[138] An intracorporate exception

---

131 Volk v. Coler, 845 F.2d 1422 (7th Cir. 1988); Gobla v. Crestwood Sch. Dist., 609 F. Supp. 972 (M.D. Pa. 1985).

132 Skadegaard v. Farrell, 578 F. Supp. 1209 (D.N.J. 1984) (sexual harassment). *See also* Great Am. Fed. Sav. & Loan Ass'n v. Novotny, 442 U.S. 366, 372 (1979); Volk v. Coler, 845 F.2d 1422 (7th Cir. 1988) (sexual harassment).

133 Volk v. Coler, 845 F.2d 1422 (7th Cir. 1988); Gobla v. Crestwood Sch. Dist., 609 F. Supp. 972 (M.D. Pa. 1985).

134 *See, e.g.,* An-Ti Chai v. Michigan Tech. Univ., 493 F. Supp. 1137, 1162 (W.D. Mich. 1980) (sovereign immunity); Lawrence v. Acree, 665 F.2d 1319 (D.C. Cir. 1981) (qualified immunity).

135 Private individuals may be found liable under this section when conspiracies stem from "some racial, or perhaps otherwise class-based, invidiously discriminatory animus." Griffin v. Breckenridge, 403 U.S. 88, 105 (1971).

136 425 U.S. 820 (1976).

137 Volk v. Coler, 845 F.2d 1422, 1434–35 (7th Cir. 1988) (sexual harassment). *But see* Kerans v. Porter Paint Co., 656 F. Supp. 267, 271 (S.D. Ohio 1987) (in a civil conspiracy, a corporation cannot conspire with its agents or employees).

138 Dombrowski v. Dowling, 459 F.2d 190, 196 (7th Cir. 1972).

to proof of a conspiracy reflects a notion that a company cannot conspire with its own employees because those employees are acting to further the interests of the corporation.[139] Sexual harassment, however, often involves a number of discrete actions by several corporate players. For example, an employee may complain of coworker harassment to a supervisor who responds to her complaints by participating in the harassment. The employee goes over the head of the supervisor to upper management who chooses to ignore the grievance. The supervisor subsequently retaliates against the employee by harassing her further or advising upper management that the employee should be terminated for a fabricated work performance reason. Or, more simply, an employee may state a claim for conspiracy if her employer fires her for complaining of supervisor harassment. "It makes no sense to immunize illegal discriminatory activity merely because the activity arose in a corporate setting. Where two or more corporate officers by agreement commit different discriminatory acts against plaintiff, . . . a § 1985(3) violation has occurred."[140]

§ 8.24 —Pleading the § 1985(3) Claims

To state a claim of conspiracy under § 1985(3), a plaintiff must allege:

1. The existence of a conspiracy
2. That the conspiracy was conducted for the purpose of depriving the plaintiff, directly or indirectly, of equal protection under the law or of equal privileges and immunities under the law
3. That the conspirators acted to further the conspiracy
4. That the plaintiff suffered an injury[141]

Plaintiff's alleging violations of § 1985(3) must plead facts with specificity. General allegations of sex discrimination or sexual harassment generally will not support a cause of action under this section. Although a plaintiff may not be able to allege that the defendants agreed beforehand to discriminate against her, she should specify the time, place, and manner of the defendant's actions and the effects of the conduct.[142]

---

[139] Lattimore v. Loews Theatres, Inc., 410 F. Supp. 1397 (M.D.N.C. 1975).

[140] An-Ti Chai v. Michigan Tech. Univ., 493 F. Supp. 1137, 1166–67 (W.D. Mich. 1980).

[141] Griffin v. Breckenridge, 403 U.S. 88, 103–04 (1971).

[142] Hunt v. Weatherbee, 626 F. Supp. 1097, 1107 (D. Mass. 1986).

§ 8.25 —Remedies for § 1985(3) Claims

The range of damages available under § 1983 also may be awarded for a successful claim of conspiracy under § 1985(3). A successful plaintiff in a § 1985(3) action may not recover damages for the conspiracy if she already has been awarded damages for claims arising from the same conduct.[143]

§ 8.26 Claims under the Constitution

A person whose constitutional rights have been violated by a government official may sue directly under the United States Constitution if she has no alternative avenue of relief.[144] In *Brown*[145] the U.S. Supreme Court held that Title VII is the exclusive avenue of redress for federal employment discrimination, and thus most courts have barred these types of constitutional claims.[146] Courts also have refused to allow actions directly under the Constitution when relief is available under § 1983.[147] Because most sexual harassment claims may be brought under these remedial statutes, direct constitutional claims are rare.[148]

---

143 Volk v. Coler, 845 F.2d 1422 (7th Cir. 1988).

144 Bivens v. Six Unknown Fed. Narcotics Agents, 403 U.S. 388 (1971).

145 Brown v. GSA, 425 U.S. 820 (1976).

146 Gissen v. Tackman, 537 F.2d 784, 786–87 (3d Cir. 1976) (en banc); Carter v. Marshall, 457 F. Supp. 38, 42–43 (D.D.C. 1978); Berio v. EEOC, 446 F. Supp. 171, 173–74 (D.D.C. 1978). *Cf.* Neely v. Blumenthal, 458 F. Supp. 945, 955 (D.D.C. 1978) (constitutional action may be available because Title VII does not allow damages).

147 Thomas v. Shipka, 818 F.2d 496 (6th Cir.), *reh'g in part on other grounds,* 829 F.2d 570 (6th Cir. 1987), *vacated on other grounds,* 488 U.S. 1036 (1989); Williams v. Bennett, 689 F.2d 1370 (11th Cir. 1982), *cert. denied,* 464 U.S. 932 (1983); Ward v. Caulk, 650 F.2d 1144, 1148 (9th Cir. 1981); Hearth, Inc. v. Department of Pub. Welfare, 617 F.2d 381 (5th Cir. 1980); Turpin v. Mailet, 591 F.2d 426 (2d Cir. 1979) (en banc); Cale v. City of Covington, 586 F.2d 311 (4th Cir. 1978); Molina v. Richardson, 578 F.2d 846 (9th Cir.), *cert. denied,* 439 U.S. 1048 (1978); Mahone v. Waddle, 564 F.2d 1018 (3d Cir. 1977), *cert. denied,* 438 U.S. 904 (1978); Kostka v. Hogg, 560 F.2d 37 (1st Cir. 1977).

148 Otto v. Heckler, 781 F.2d 754, 757 (9th Cir.), *modified on other grounds,* 802 F.2d 337 (9th Cir. 1986) (claims of constitutional violations were defeated by the fact the injuries alleged were "precisely the injuries cognizable and remediable under Title VII").

CHAPTER 9

COMMON LAW LIABILITY

§ 9.1 Introduction

Although state and federal antidiscrimination laws provide a comprehensive remedy for those who have suffered employment discrimination, Title VII of the 1964 Civil Rights Act seldom may not fully compensate victims of sexual harassment for the emotional and physical harm they sustain. Damages are now available for Title VII violations under the Civil Rights Act of 1991, but such damages are limited by the size of the employer's company and may not quite address the specific nature of the plaintiff's injury.

The employee who loses a position or job status for failure to comply with sexual demands suffers much more than the loss of money. The shame, embarrassment, loss of self-esteem, and other psychological and physical manifestations are not addressed by an injunction or back pay.

The degradation engendered by a hostile work environment claim can also be addressed by tort law. Moreover, a relatively small back pay award and an injunction against sexual harassment often amount to little more than a slap on the employer's wrist. On the other hand, the punitive and compensatory damages available under common law theories may act as deterrents and reaffirm the severity of the problem. At the same time, however, the common law claim seeks an individual remedy and may fail to address the overall scope of the problem. Catherine MacKinnon notes:

> The tort remedy attempts to monetize physical and psychic damage to the person, sometimes including punitive damages representing outrage, rather than to formulate redress in terms of hiring, seniority, or promotion, although these remedies are not precluded. To the extent that tort theory fails to capture the broadly social sexuality/employment nexus that comprises the injury of sexual harassment, by treating the incidents as if they are outrages particular to an individual woman rather than integral to her social status as a woman worker, the personal approach on the legal level fails to analyze the relative dimensions of the problem.[1]

The injury to the plaintiff may be such that no employment-specific remedy will suffice. An injunction, for example, will duly protect the interests of the employees left behind, but will do little to compensate the person who took on the inherent risks of litigation and endured the process. Such a victory may have cathartic value, but it does not pick up all the pieces. Thus, the goals of social retribution and personal loss may best be served by a lawsuit containing federal and pendent state law claims. For example, some acts of sexual harassment may be prosecuted in the criminal courts under rape, assault, battery, or harassment statutes. *Quid pro quo* sexual harassment also may constitute bribery or blackmail. Although a jury trial is now available under Title VII for sexual harassment suits seeking compensatory or punitive damages, plaintiffs should still seek the sympathetic jurisdictions. Courts have already granted motions for verdicts notwithstanding the judgment for what they may believe to be overreactions by juries. For example, in *Pagana-Fay v. Washington Suburban Sanitary Com'n.,*[2] a jury verdict for the plaintiff and damages in the amount of $50,000 for sexual harassment were vacated upon defendant's motion for judgment notwithstanding the verdict when the court concluded that a discharged female employee failed to prove by a preponderance of the evidence that she was subjected to sexual harassment by one or more of her supervisors when several incidents of offensive language and one incident during which a coworker fondled his own genitals in the plaintiff's presence did not

---

[1] C. MacKinnon, Sexual Harassment of Working Women 88 (1979) (footnote omitted).

[2] 797 F. Supp. 462 (D. Md. 1992).

constitute sexual harassment as defined by *Meritor Sav. Bank v. Vinson.* "Rather than being intimidated, [the plaintiff] was the one who sought to gain her way with male coworkers and superiors by constant threats that she would file internal complaints, charges of discrimination with the EEOC, or lawsuits if the others crossed her in any significant way."[3]

Victims of sexual harassment have brought common law actions based on both tort and contract theories, although tort actions are far more prevalent. Important differences between contract and tort claims include the availability of punitive damages, statutes of limitations, and immunity issues. Although punitive damages may be awarded in tort actions, they usually are not recoverable in contract actions even when the breach was willful,[4] although some courts have awarded punitive damages when the challenged contractual conduct also was a tort.[5] The statute of limitations for contract claims may be longer than that for tort actions.[6] Absolute or qualified immunity may bar tort actions against government defendants,[7] but a government or government officials may be liable for breach or other contract claims.[8] Using common law claims, a plaintiff may seek damages against the harassers themselves, rather than the employer.

This chapter reviews the various common law theories under which sexual harassment actions may be brought. Although different state common law doctrines often share common elements, the following discussion cannot apply to any particular jurisdiction. Nor are the theories

---

3 *Id.* at 470.

4 White v. Benkowski, 37 Wis. 2d 285, 155 N.W.2d 74 (1967); Den v. Den 222 A.2d 647 (D.C. 1966).

5 Restatement (Second) of Contracts § 355 (1981). *See also* Farnsworth, Contracts § 12.8 at 842–43 (1982); Kahal v. J.W. Wilson & Assocs., 673 F.2d 547, 548 (D.C. Cir. 1982) (per curiam).

6 Prosser & Keeton on the Law of Torts § 92 at 655 (W. Keeton, 5th ed. 1984). *See also* Staggs v. Wang, 185 Ga. App. 310, 363 S.E.2d 808 (1987) (plaintiff's sexual harassment claims sounded in tort and not in contract and thus were subject to a two-year statute of limitations); Brockmeyer v. Dun & Bradstreet, 113 Wis. 2d 561, 335 N.W.2d 834 (1983).

7 Federal officials have absolute immunity for torts committed while performing discretionary acts within the "outer perimeter of her or his line of duty." Butz v. Economou, 438 U.S. 564 (1959). Legislative and judicial officers enjoy absolute immunity from torts stemming from "judicial" or "legislative" acts. Stump v. Sparkman, 435 U.S. 349 (1978) (judicial); Hutchinson v. Proxmire, 443 U.S. 111 (1979) (legislative). Executive officials and employees are not immune to tort actions for conduct arising out of ministerial acts that involve the execution of policy, but have qualified immunity for discretionary acts that involve the formulation of policy. Scheuer v. Rhodes, 416 U.S. 232, 247 (1974); Harlow v. Fitzgerald, 457 U.S. 800, 807 (1982).

8 S. Williston, A Treatise on the Law of Contracts § 1751 at 156–58 (3d ed. 1967 & Supp. 1979).

presented exhaustive. A creative attorney may be able to fit the facts of a case into a number of other legal doctrines.[9]

Chapter 10 contains a state-by-state analysis of the construction of sexual harassment law under the state antidiscrimination statutes and common law. All cases cited in this chapter are discussed at length in **Chapter 10.**

§ 9.2 Effect of State Antidiscrimination Laws

Most courts that have addressed the issue have held that the state antidiscrimination law does not bar common law tort claims,[10] but several courts have concluded that state human rights or fair employment acts may provide the exclusive remedies for sexual harassment. In *Harrison v. Chance,*[11] the exclusive remedy provision of the state Human Rights Act applied to an employee's tort action against her employer for sexual harassment. The court rejected the plaintiff's argument that her claim did not fall under the act because the alleged conduct was sexual harassment

---

9 Other possible actions include:

1. Common law claims of negligence, Favors v. Alco Mfg. Co., 186 Ga. App. 480, 367 S.E.2d 328 (1988); Newsome v. Cooper-Wiss, Inc., 179 Ga. App. 670, 347 S.E.2d 619 (1986); Cox v. Brazo, 165 Ga. App. 888, 303 S.E.2d 71, *aff'd,* 251 Ga. 491, 307 S.E.2d 474 (1983).

2. Intentional and negligent misrepresentation, Fawcett v. IDS Servs., 41 Fair Empl. Prac. Cas. (BNA) 589 (W.D. Pa. 1988).

3. Constructive discharge, Glezos v. Amalfi Ristorante Italiano, Inc., 651 F. Supp. 1271 (D. Md. 1987); Board of Directors, Green Hills Country Club v. Illinois Human Rights Comm'n, 162 Ill. App. 3d 216, 514 N.E.2d 1227 (1987); Lui v. Intercontinental Hotels Corp., 634 F. Supp. 684 (D. Haw. 1986); Continental Can Co., v. State, 297 N.W.2d 241, 22 Fair Empl. Prac. Cas. (BNA) 1808 (Minn. 1980).

4. Retaliation, Polk v. Yellow Freight Sys., Inc., 801 F.2d 190 (6th Cir. 1986); College-Town, Div. of Interco, Inc. v. Massachusetts Comm'n Against Discrimination, 400 Mass. 156, 508 N.E.2d 587 (1987).

10 District of Columbia: Coleman v. American Broadcasting Co., 38 Fair Empl. Prac. Cas. (BNA) 65 (D.D.C. 1985).

Hawaii: Lui v. Intercontinental Hotels Corp., 634 F. Supp. 684 (D. Haw. 1986).

Illinois: Zakutansky v. Bionetics Corp., 806 F. Supp. 1362 (N.D. Ill. 1992) (Illinois Human Rights Act did not preempt employee's intentional infliction of emotional distress claim against her employer and individual defendants arising from sexual harassment); Clay v. Quartet Mfg. Co., 644 F. Supp. 56 (N.D. Ill. 1986).

Massachusetts: Egger Plumbers & Pipefitters Union, 644 F. Supp. 795 (D. Mass. 1986).

Montana: Drinkwater v. Shipton Supply Co., 732 P.2d 1335 (Mont. 1987).

Pennsylvania: Fawcett v. IDS Servs., 41 Fair Empl. Prac. Cas. (BNA) 589 (W.D. Pa.1988).

11 797 P.2d 200 (Mont. 1990).

rather than sex discrimination, relying on dicta in *Drinkwater v. Shipton Supply Co.,* when the Human Rights Commission had defined sexual harassment as sexual discrimination, and every state court considering the issue has reached the conclusion that sexual harassment is sex discrimination: "The reason behind this rule is apparent. When sexual harassment is directed at an employee solely because of gender, the employee is faced with a working environment fundamentally different from that faced by an employee of the opposite gender. . . . That difference constitutes sexual discrimination in employment."[12] The court also rejected the plaintiff's contention that her supervisor's acts fell under the "bisexual" exception to the general rule that sexual harassment is sexual discrimination because the supervisor made sexual advances to both her and her son. The bisexual harassment issue was not raised until after the trial court had issued its order granting summary judgment, and thus the district court properly failed to consider the issue. Finally, the Human Rights Act was the exclusive vehicle for relief in this case, even though the alleged acts provided grounds for a number of tort claims when the gravamen of the plaintiff's claim was sexual harassment, and to "allow such re-characterization of what is at heart a sexual discrimination claim, would be to eviscerate the mandate of the Human Rights Commission."[13] The exclusive remedy provision was properly applied even though the acts complained of predated the passage of the provision when the plaintiff filed her action six months after the Act's effective date and the exclusive remedy provision applied to all cases not settled before the time of the enactment. In *Greenland v. Fairtron Corp.,*[14] an employee who brought a sexual harassment suit could proceed with claims of assault and battery, but her emotional distress claim was preempted by the state antidiscrimination law when success on the emotional distress claim turned on proof of discrimination:

> Greenland's alternative claims are thus preempted if she must prove discrimination to be successful in them. The test is whether, in light of the pleadings, discrimination is made an element of the alternative claims.
>
> We think the answer with regard to the emotional distress claim is yes, resulting in preemption. Discrimination through sexual harassment is the "outrageous conduct" Greenland specifically alleges in her claim for intentional infliction of emotional distress. So under the facts she alleges, if she were to fail in her claim of discrimination, Greenland would necessarily fail

---

[12] *Id.* at 204.

[13] *Id.* at 205.

See also Royal v. City of Albuquerque, 653 F. Supp. 102 (D.N.M. 1986) (district court refused to exercise pendent jurisdiction over a claim for intentional infliction of emotional distress when such a claim had been brought in conjunction with a claim under the State Human Rights Act).

[14] 500 N.W.2d 36 (Iowa 1993).

in her claim of intentional infliction of emotional distress. Stated otherwise, it is impossible for Greenland to establish the emotional distress she alleges without first proving discrimination.

* * *

Under the same test both the assault and the battery claims are not preempted. Unlike the claim for intentional infliction of emotional distress, Greenland's claims for assault and for battery are not bound up in her discrimination complaints. On the facts alleged, discrimination becomes a part and parcel of a showing of intentional infliction of emotional distress. The assault and battery claims, on the other hand, are completely without any reference to discrimination.[15]

§ 9.3 Liability under Common Law Theories

Under common law theories applicable to sexual harassment, an employer may be directly or indirectly liable for its own conduct or that of its employees. The doctrine of respondeat superior extends liability to the employer for acts of its agent when the agent's act is expressly authorized by the principal, when the act is committed within the scope of employment and in furtherance of the principal's business, or when the act is ratified by the principal.[16] Obviously, sexual harassment is seldom officially authorized by the employer or committed in furtherance of the principal's business, except perhaps in cases involving revealing dress requirements. Conduct is implicitly ratified when it involves *quid pro quo* sexual harassment. In *Lehmann v. Toys 'R' Us, Inc.,*[17] the New Jersey Supreme Court noted that in cases of *quid pro quo* sexual harassment, the employer is strictly liable for all equitable damages and relief, including hiring or reinstating the victim, disciplining, transferring or firing the harasser, proving back or front pay, and taking preventative and remedial measures at work. In cases of hostile environment sexual harassment, employers are vicariously liable if the supervisor acted within the scope of his or her employment. If the supervisor acted outside the scope of employment, the employer will be vicariously liable if the employer contributed to the harm through its negligence, intent, or apparent authorization of the harassing conduct, or if the supervisor was aided in the commission of the harassment by the agency relationship. The employer may be vicariously liable for compensatory damages stemming from a supervisor's creation of a hostile

---

15 *Id.* at 38–39 (footnotes omitted).

16 Restatement (Second) of Agency §§ 215–267 (1958). *See* **Ch. 3.**

17 133 N.J. 587, 626 A.2d 445 (1993).

work environment if the employer grants the supervisor the authority to control the working environment and the supervisor abuses that authority to create a hostile environment.[18] An employer also may be held vicariously liable for compensatory damages for supervisory sexual harassment occurring outside the scope of the supervisor's authority if the employer had actual or constructive notice of the harassment, or even if the employer did not have actual or constructive notice, if the employer negligently or recklessly failed to have an explicit policy that bans sexual harassment and that provides an effective procedure for the prompt investigation and remediation of such claims.[19]

The employer may be liable for punitive damages only in the event of actual participation or willful indifference.[20] In *Monge v. Superior Court,*[21] the plaintiff pleaded facts sufficient to demonstrate oppression and malice for purposes of punitive damages when she alleged that corporate officers conspired to display the message "How about a little head?" on her computer terminal, then retaliated against her when she complained.

§ 9.4 Tort Claims Based on Sexual Harassment

Tort law has been recognized repeatedly as a proper remedy for the sexual harassment victim. Actions have been brought under the theories of assault and battery, intentional infliction of emotional distress, invasion of privacy, tortious interference with contractual relations, and others. However, because sexual harassment does not fit neatly into the traditional grounds for relief, and because the courts are unclear about what sexual harassment is, the application of these theories has been inconsistent. Although it is clear that the standards for tortious conduct are connected to the relative authority of the parties,[22] courts are sometimes

---

18 *Id.*

19 *Id.*

20 California: Priest v. Rotary, 634 F. Supp. 571, 582–85 (N.D. Cal. 1986).

New Jersey: Lehmann v. Toys 'R' Us, Inc., 133 N.J. 587, 626 A.2d 445 (1993).

Ohio: Shrout v. Black Clawson Co., 689 F. Supp. 774, 780 (S.D. Ohio 1988).

Oregon: Dias v. Sky Chefs, 919 F.2d 1370 (9th Cir. 1990), *vacated on other grounds,* 111 S. Ct. 2791 (1991), on remand, 948 F.2d 532 (9th Cir. 1991), *cert. denied,* 112 S. Ct. 1294 (1992).

Pennsylvania: Clemens v. Gerber Scientific, 1989 U.S. Dist. LEXIS 376 (E.D. Pa. 1989).

Tennessee: Pease v. Alford Photo Indus., 667 F. Supp. 1188, 1192 (W.D. Tenn. 1987).

21 176 Cal. App. 3d 503, 222 Cal. Rptr. 842, 860 (1989).

22 Regarding the tort of intentional infliction of emotional distress, the Restatement (Second) of Torts, § 46 comment e (1965) states that the "extreme and outrageous

unwilling to find liability for the abuse of authority if there is no physical injury or loss of a tangible work benefit. Others acknowledge the unique economic coercion inherent in workplace sexual harassment in sustaining claims for intentional infliction of emotional distress.[23] Conceptual distinctions based on the unique character of the relationship between superior and subordinate are proper and necessary. Economic considerations affect coworker relationships as well. Although the coworker harasser may not possess the means to alter the victim's work status, her economic dependence on her job limits her options.

§ 9.5 Workers' Compensation Statutes

A significant obstacle to finding employer liability in tort actions by employees is workers' compensation law. State workers' compensation statutes generally provide an exclusive remedy for workplace injuries. Many states, however, have developed exceptions to the exclusivity provision of these laws. In *Gantt v. Sentry Insurance,*[24] the court declined the invitation to retreat from its long-held view that employees discharged in violation of fundamental public policy may bring an action against their employers sounding in tort, and held that the exclusive remedy provisions of the state workers' compensation act did not preempt the plaintiff's wrongful discharge claim in an action charging that the plaintiff was constructively discharged in retaliation for supporting a coworker's claim of sexual harassment. The court rejected the defendant's contention that there was something anomalous in restricting the recovery of an employee who incurs a standard industrial injury, while extending a tort remedy to one who suffers similar injuries from sexual or racial discrimination:

---

character of the conduct may arise from an abuse by the actor of a position, or a relation with the other, which gives [her or] him actual or apparent authority over the other, or power to affect [her or] his interests."

23 Alabama: Rice v. United Ins. Co. of Am., 465 So. 2d 1100 (Ala. 1984).

California: Hart v. National Mortgage & Land Co., 189 Cal. App. 3d 1420, 235 Cal. Rptr. 68 (1987).

District of Columbia: Rogers v. Loews L'Enfant Plaza Hotel, 526 F. Supp. 523 (D.D.C. 1981).

Pennsylvania: Shaffer v. National Can Corp., 565 F. Supp. 909 (E.D. Pa. 1983); Vegh v. General Elec. Co., 34 Fair Empl. Prac. Cas. (BNA) 135 (E.D. Pa. 1983).

The workplace, of course, is not the only coercive environment. For example, sexual harassment in education, medicine, and housing also involve unequal power relationships that invite a similar analysis.

24 1 Cal. 4th 1083, 4 Cal. Rptr. 2d 874, 824 P.2d 680 (Cal. 1992).

> The answer is that the two employees are *not* similarly situated. We emphasized the difference in *Tameny [v. Atlantic Richfield Co.,* 27 Cal. 3d 167, 164 Cal. Rptr. 839, 610 P.2d 1330 (1980)], when we recognized that "'public policy and sound morality'" set the latter apart: "'It would be obnoxious to the interests of the state and contrary to public policy and sound morality to allow an employer to discharge any employee . . . on the ground that the employee declined to commit perjury, an act specifically enjoined by statute. . . .'" (27 Cal. 3d at p. 173 . . ., quoting *Petermann v. International Brotherhood of Teamsters,* 174 Cal. App. [184,] 188–189 [(1959)] . . .) . . . .
>
> The same core values that underlay our holding in *Tameny* explain why such misconduct cannot be deemed "a risk reasonably encompassed within the compensation bargain." . . . Just as the individual employment agreement may not include terms which violate fundamental public policy . . ., so the more general "compensation bargain" cannot encompass conduct, such as sexual or racial discrimination, obnoxious to the interests of the state and contrary to public policy and sound morality."[25]

Although the scope of injuries covered by state workers' compensation laws varies, most courts have held that common law tort claims arising from sexual harassment are not barred by the statutes.[26] Some courts have

---

[25] *Id.* at 691–92.

[26] Alabama: Wallace v. Dunn Constr., 59 Fair Empl. Prac. Cas. (BNA) 994 (N.D. Ala. 1991) *rev'd and remanded on other grounds,* 968 F.2d 1174 (11th Cir. 1992) (claims of assault and battery in sexual harassment suit were not barred by the exclusivity provision of the state workers' compensation act when such a tort was not interwoven with compensation and therefore does not come within the exclusivity provision).

Arizona: Ford v. Revlon, Inc., 153 Ariz. 38, 734 P.2d 580 (1987) (assault and battery and intentional infliction of emotional distress).

California: Accardi v. Superior Court (Simi Valley), 21 Cal. Rptr. 292 (Ct. App. 1993). Sexual harassment claim by female former police officer was not preempted by the state workers' compensation law.

Hart v. National Mortgage & Land Co., 189 Cal. App. 3d 1420, 235 Cal. Rptr. 68 (1987).

Colorado: *Cf.* Stamper v. Hiteshew, 797 P.2d 784 (Colo. Ct. App. 1990).

District of Columbia: Coleman v. American Broadcasting Co., 38 Fair Empl. Prac. Cas. (BNA) 65 (D.D.C. 1985).

Cf. Underwood v. Washington Post Credit Union, 59 Fair Empl. Prac. Cas. (BNA) 952 (D.C. Sup. Ct. 1992). In an action alleging sexual harassment and intentional infliction of emotional distress by female credit union employee who had broken off an affair with the chair of the board of the credit union and was subsequently subjected to hostile treatment, the claim for intentional infliction of emotional distress against the credit union was barred by the workers' compensation act. While general mental distress was not a covered injury, where the emotional distress has as its consequence physical disability the administrative agency and the courts have both ruled that the injury is a covered one.

Florida: Gomez v. Metro Dade County, 801 F. Supp. 674 (S.D. Fla. 1992) (Title VII and §1983) (county employee's state law claims against the county for alleged negligent retention and supervision of supervisor who allegedly sexually harassed her were not barred by the exclusivity provision of the state workers' compensation act as a matter of public policy).

Byrd v. Richardson-Greenshields Secs., Inc., 552 So. 2d 1099 (Fla. 1989).

Georgia: Cummings v. Walsh Constr. Co., 561 F. Supp. 872 (S.D. Ga. 1983).

Hawaii: Lapinad v. Pacific Oldsmobile-GMC, Inc., 679 F. Supp. 991 (D. Haw. 1988).

Illinois: Pommier v. James L. Edelstein Enterprises, 816 F. Supp. 476 (N.D. Ill. 1993) (claim for intentional infliction of emotional distress was not preempted by the state workers' compensation act).

Zakutansky v. Bionetics Corp., 806 F. Supp. 1362 (N.D. Ill. 1992) (state workers' compensation act did not preempt an employee's intentional infliction of emotional distress claim against her employer and individual defendants arising from sexual harassment).

Indiana: Eskridge v. Coates, 57 Fair Empl. Prac. Cas. (BNA) 589 (N.D. Ind. 1991). Female former employee's claims of assault and battery, intentional infliction of emotional distress, invasion of privacy and interference with advantageous business relationships stemming from alleged sexual harassment were barred by the Indiana Workers' Compensation Act; a supervisor could be liable for these torts when the challenged conduct could not be for the benefit of the employer, and thus did not arise out of the supervisor's employment.

Louisiana: Waltman v. International Paper Co., 47 Fair Empl. Prac. Cas. (BNA) 671 (W.D. La. 1988), *rev'd on other grounds*, 875 F.2d 468 (5th Cir. 1989).

Massachusetts: Bergeson v. Franchi, 783 F. Supp. 713 (D. Mass. 1992) (Caffrey, J.) (intentional infliction of emotional distress); O'Connell v. Chasdi, 400 Mass. 686, 511 N.E.2d 349 (1987) (assault and battery and intentional infliction of emotional distress); College-Town, Div. of Interco, Inc. v. Massachusetts Comm'n Against Discrimination, 400 Mass. 156, 508 N.E.2d 587 (1987); Egger v. Plumbers & Pipefitters Union, 644 F. Supp. 795 (D. Mass. 1986).

Minnesota: Johnson v. Ramsey County, 424 N.W.2d 800 (Minn. Ct. App. 1988) (battery and intentional infliction of emotional distress).

Missouri: Pryor v. United States Gypsum Co., 47 Fair Empl. Prac. Cas. (BNA) 159 (W.D. Mo. 1984) ("The court is simply not prepared to say that a female who goes to work in what is apparently a predominately male workplace should reasonably expect sexual harassment as part of her job." *Id.* at 316); Hollrah v. Freidrich, 634 S.W.2d 221, 223 (Mo. Ct. App. 1982).

Cf. Yount v. Davis, 846 S.W.2d 780 (Mo. Ct. App. 1993) (lower court properly ruled that it did not have jurisdiction to determine whether alleged acts of sexual harassment and assault and battery arose out of and in the course of employment as the workers' compensation law provided the exclusive remedy).

New Jersey: Cremen v. Harrah's Marina Hotel Casino, 680 F. Supp. 150 (D.N.J. 1988).

New York: Hart v. National Mortgage & Land Co., 189 Cal. App. 3d 1420, 235 Cal. Rptr. 68 (1987).

North Carolina: Hogan v. Forsyth Country Club Co., 340 S.E.2d 116 (N.C. Ct. App. 1986).

Pennsylvania: Fawcett v. IDS Servs., 41 Fair Empl. Prac. Cas. (BNA) 589 (W.D. Pa. 1988).

found sexual harassment to fall within the willful physical assault[27] or intentional wrong[28] exceptions to exclusivity provisions. Under the doctrine of ratification, an employee who was harassed by a supervisor or

---

Texas: Mitchell v. Aetna Casualty & Sur. Co., 722 S.W.2d 522 (Tex. Ct. App. 1986), *reh'g denied,* (Jan. 7, 1987).

Virginia: Beardsley v. Isom, 61 Fair Empl. Prac. Cas. (BNA) 847 (E.D. Va. 1993) (claim of intentional infliction of emotional distress was not barred by the exclusivity provision of the state workers' compensation act).

Haddon v. Metropolitan Life Ins. Co., 52 Fair Empl. Prac. Cas. (BNA) 478 389 S.E.2d 712 (Va. 1990) (Virginia Workers' Compensation Act was the exclusive remedy for an employee who alleged severe emotional distress and permanent disability as a result of sexual harassment by a supervisor when the injury resulting from an intentional tort is "injury by accident" under the Act).

Wisconsin: Hrabak v. Marquip, Inc., 798 F. Supp. 550 (W.D. Wis. 1992) (employee's state claims of battery and intentional infliction of emotional distress were barred by the exclusivity provisions of the state workers' compensation act when plaintiff did not indicate that touching by her coworker was intended to cause or caused bodily harm).

Busse v. Gelco Express Corp., 678 F. Supp. 1398 (E.D. Wis. 1988) (assault and battery).

Cf.: Florida: Studstill v. Borg Warner Leasing, 806 F.2d 1005 (11th Cir. 1986) (assault and battery action barred against employer, but could be brought against supervisor harasser). *Accord* Schwartz v. Zippy Mart, 470 So. 2d 720 (Fla. Dist. Ct. App. 1985).

Hawaii: Wangler v. Hawaiian Elec. Co., 742 F. Supp. 1465 (D. Haw. 1990). Although plaintiff made a persuasive argument that her sexual harassment claims against her employer corporation should stand under law prevailing in other jurisdictions, claims of intentional and negligent infliction of emotional distress and for assault and battery were precluded by the exclusivity provision of the Hawaii workers' compensation statute. There is no exception for fraudulent concealment under Hawaii law. Common law claims could be asserted against the individual defendants when although the workers' compensation law extends immunity to coemployees acting within the scope of their employment, it does not relieve coemployees of liability to the extent that a fellow employee's personal injury is caused by their willful and wanton misconduct. Plaintiff's affidavit raised several questions as to the willful and wanton nature of individual defendants' alleged conduct, and therefore the court would not find that as a matter of law that the state law claims against the defendant were barred.

Lui v. Intercontinental Hotels Corp., 634 F. Supp. 684 (D. Haw. 1986) (assault and battery).

Michigan: Eide v. Kelsey-Hayes Co., 154 Mich. App. 142, 397 N.W.2d 532 (1986), *modified on other grounds,* 431 Mich. 58, 427 N.W.2d 488 (1988).

Missouri: Harrison v. Reed Rubber Co., 603 F. Supp. 1457 (E.D. Mo. 1985).

Wisconsin: Zabkowicz v. West Bend Co., 789 F.2d 540 (7th Cir. 1986).

27 California: Hart v. National Mortgage & Land Co., 189 Cal. App. 3d 1420, 235 Cal. Rptr. 68 (1987).

Cf. Michigan: Eide v. Kelsey-Hayes Co., 154 Mich. App. 142, 397 NW.2d 532 (1986), *modified on other grounds,* 431 Mich. 58, 427 NW.2d 488 (1988).

28 Arizona: *Cf.* Irvin Investors v. Superior Court, 54 Fair Empl. Prac. Cas. (BNA) 954 (Ariz. App. Ct. 1990). Female former employee's claims against her employer for negligently

coworker may state a sexual harassment claim against an employer by alleging that the employer knew of the conduct but did nothing to discipline the offender.[29] In *Dickert v. Metropolitan Life Ins. Co.,*[30] the state workers' compensation act provided the exclusive remedy in a sexual harassment claim against an employer, but a coworker could be held individually liable for an intentional tort committed while acting within the scope of employment.

One point of contention in these cases is whether sexual harassment arises out of employment for workers' compensation statutes,[31] as illustrated by cases under Missouri law. In *Pryor v. United States Gypsum*

---

hiring, supervising, and retaining supervisor who allegedly sexually molested her were barred by the Arizona workers' compensation statute when plaintiff was not subjected to intentional misconduct by the employer, her alleged injuries fell within the parameters of the statute, and she was injured while she was within the course and scope of her employment; "Just because the person who injured her was not within the course and scope of his employment does not mean that she is barred from recovering workers' compensation." *Id.* at 955.

Illinois: Fitzgerald v. Pratt, 223 Ill. App. 3d 785, 166 Ill. Dec. 200, 585 N.E.2d 1222 (Ill. Ct. App. 1992) (intentional tort claims against coworker for sexual harassment were not barred by the exclusive remedy provisions of the workers' compensation law).

Louisiana: Waltman v. International Paper Co., 47 Fair Empl. Prac. Cas. (BNA) 671 (W.D. La. 1988), *rev'd on other grounds*, 875 F.2d 468 (5th Cir. 1989).

Michigan: *Cf.* Eide v. Kelsey-Hayes Co., 154 Mich. App. 142, 397 N.W.2d 532 (1986), *modified on other grounds,* 431 Mich. 58, 427 NW.2d 488 (1988).

Montana: Vainio v. Brookshire, 852 P.2d 596 (Mont. 1993) (district court properly held that the state workers' compensation act does not provide the exclusive remedy for sexual harassment; sexual harassment is an intentional act not arising from an accident).

New Jersey: Cremen v. Harrah's Marina Hotel Casino, 680 F. Supp. 150 (D.N.J. 1988).

New York: Hart v. Sullivan, 84 A.D.2d 865, 445 N.Y.S.2d 40 (1981).

29 Stingley v. State, 796 F. Supp. 424 (D. Ariz. 1992) (claim that coworker poked plaintiff twice in the buttocks with a plastic fork and explained his action as checking to see if "the meat" was done was sufficiently egregious to preclude summary judgment on a claim of intentional infliction of emotional distress against coworker, but not against superiors who did not know about the incident).

Hart v. National Mortgage & Land Co., 189 Cal. App. 3d 1420, 235 Cal. Rptr. 68, 75 (1987).

30 428 S.E.2d 700 (S.C. 1993).

31 *See, e.g.,* Wangler v. Hawaiian Elec. Co., 53 Fair Empl. Prac. Cas. (BNA) 949 (D. Haw. May 9, 1990) (exclusivity provision of the Hawaii workers' compensation statute barred a female employee from suing her employer for intentional infliction of emotional distress and for assault and battery when the act complained of occurred at her place of employment while she was working as a chemist); Bennett v. Furr's, 549 F. Supp. 887 (D. Colo. 1982) (summary judgment was not warranted on the basis of the state workers' compensation law when there was a substantial question regarding whether the alleged injuries in an assault and battery and outrageous conduct action were related to her job).

Co.,[32] an assault and battery action, the District Court for the Western District of Missouri could not conclude that as a matter of law the plaintiff's injuries from sexual harassment arose out of her employment, even though the alleged incidents occurred in the workplace during normal working hours:

> [T]he first amended complaint alleged a campaign of assault and harassment against Susan Lawson Pryor based primarily on her sex and only incidentally on her status as an employee. The mere fact that the alleged perpetrators were her supervisors and employer does not necessarily mean that any resulting injuries arise out of employment so as to bring them within the Workers' Compensation Law. . . . On the pleadings now presented, the court cannot say that what allegedly happened to Susan Lawson Pryor was "a rational consequence of some hazard connected" with her employment. . . . Certainly it is rational to expect that an employee may not perform to the satisfaction of an employer and may be subject to reprimand or other discipline. It is also apparently rational to expect that such encounters may become quite hostile and yet remain covered under Workers' Compensation Law. . . . However, the facts alleged in the first amended complaint, construed favorably to plaintiffs, go well beyond this. The court is simply not prepared to say that a female who goes to work in what is apparently a predominately male workplace should reasonably expect sexual harassment as part of her job, so as to bring any such injuries under the Workers' Compensation Law.[33]

However, in *Miller v. Lindenwood Female College*,[34] an action charging intentional infliction of emotional distress, the District Court for the Eastern District of Missouri noted that it would be inconsistent to deem sexual harassment by a supervisor as outside the course of employment for purposes of the workers' compensation law, but within the course of employment when establishing vicarious liability against the employer for the wrongful acts of its agent.[35] The Eastern District also held that the

---

32 47 Fair Empl. Prac. Cas. (BNA) 159 (W.D. Mo. 1984).

33 *Id.* at 163. *See also* O'Connell v. Chasdi, 400 Mass. 686, 511 N.E.2d 349, 352 (1987) ("Such intentional torts are not an accepted risk of doing business").

34 616 F. Supp. 860 (E.D. Mo. 1985).

35 Vallerey Stylianoudis v. Westinghouse Credit Corp., 785 F. Supp. 530 (W.D. Pa. 1992). A state law claim for intentional infliction of emotional distress was barred by the exclusivity provision of the state workers' compensation law:

> That the sexually harassing behavior claimed in this litigation is work-related cannot be challenged by a plaintiff who chose to sue her employer for it. Indeed, if plaintiff desires to hold the corporate defendants responsible for the alleged behavior of their employees at count I of her amended complaint, she must accept that this same behavior arose in an employment context for purposes of defining a compensable "injury" under § 411 of the WCA.

workers' compensation law barred an action for assault and battery and intentional infliction of emotional distress arising from sexual harassment in *Harrison v. Reed Rubber Co.,*[36] when the alleged injuries occurred at the place of employment and arose out of and in the scope of the plaintiff's employment.[37] The Missouri State Court of Appeals held in *Hollrah v. Freidrich*[38] that an employee could properly assert tort claims against her employer and a coworker when the record did not indicate that the conduct arose in the course of and out of the employment.[39]

The facts underlying these cases do not vary significantly. Workers' compensation law was not designed to protect employers from intentional torts like sexual harassment and should not protect conduct that violates public policy. "[W]hen employers step out of their roles . . . and commit acts which do not fall within the reasonably anticipated conditions of work, they may not hide behind the shield of workers' compensation."[40]

> Further, Pennsylvania's courts have held that psychological or emotional harm, such as that alleged in a plaintiff's proposed tort claim, is a compensable "within the meaning of the WCA."

Id. at 532.

36 603 F. Supp. 1457 (E.D. Mo. 1985).

37 *See also* Lui v. Intercontinental Hotels Corp., 634 F. Supp. 684 (D. Haw. 1986) (assault and battery claim stemming from sexual harassment that occurred during working hours was barred by state workers' compensation law).

38 634 S.W.2d 221, 223 (Mo. Ct. App. 1982).

39 *See also* Johnson v. International Minerals & Chem. Corp., 40 Fair Empl. Prac. Cas. (BNA) 1651 (D.S.D. 1986) (battery claim based on a kiss was not barred by the state workers' compensation statute when although the kiss occurred at work, it has no association with the job itself).

Indiana: Eskridge v. Coates, 57 Fair Empl. Prac. Cas. (BNA) 589 (N.D. Ind. 1991). Female former employee's claims of assault and battery, intentional infliction of emotional distress, invasion of privacy, and interference with advantageous business relationships stemming from alleged sexual harassment were barred by the Indiana Workers' Compensation Act. A supervisor could be liable for these torts when the challenged conduct could not be for the benefit of the employer, and thus did not arise out of the supervisor's employment.

Courts have allowed claims against parties individually. Radtke v. Everett, 56 Fair Empl. Prac. Cas. (BNA) 923 (Mich. Ct. App. 1991) (exclusive remedy provision of the state Workers' Disability Compensation Act did not bar claims for assault and battery against supervisor who allegedly sexually harassed a veterinary technician when the action was brought against the veterinarian individually and not the hospital that employed plaintiff).

40 Hart v. National Mortgage & Land Co., 189 Cal. App. 3d 1420, 235 Cal. Rptr. 68, 75 (1987). On the other hand, some employees may want to avoid a tort action and would prefer to resolve their sexual harassment claims through the workers' compensation system. One district court has held that recovery of workers' compensation benefits does not bar a Title VII action arising from the same facts. Jeppsen v. Wunnicke, 611 F. Supp. 78 (D. Alaska 1985).

Some courts frame the issue in terms of whether the conduct was employment related or "personal." In *Fernandez v. Ramsey County,*[41] an action by a county employee against supervisors and the county alleging sexually motivated assault and battery stemming from acts including touching breasts, massaging shoulders and neck, dropping paper clips down her blouse, fluffing her hair, and standing so close as to touch her body, the court of appeals held that whether such a common law action arising from employment was barred by the exclusivity provisions of the workers' compensation statute turned on whether the alleged intent to injure was for personal reasons or directed against the employee as an employee.

Employees who seek to recover workers' compensation benefits for injuries due to sexual harassment have tried to prove that the challenged conduct arose out of employment. In *Cox v. Chino Mines/Phelps Dodge,*[42] an employee's injury from three instances of sexual harassment in the workplace did not arise out of employment for workers' compensation. The incidents included being accosted on the job twice by a coworker who attempted to hug and kiss her and stated that he wanted to take her to bed, and hearing a comment by a coworker to several other coworkers that another employee had obtained a job "because he sucked cock."[43] All three incidents were reported and the coworker who accosted her was threatened with discharge after the second incident. The claimant subsequently saw a psychiatrist and complained of anxiety, gastric pain, depression, sleeplessness, lack of energy, crying spells, and feelings of despair, all due to the incidents of sexual harassment. Her subsequent workers' compensation claim was dismissed, and the court of appeal affirmed:

> Here, the incidents involving Claimant were isolated and were not part of the conditions of employment. While we do not believe that the rules concerning horseplay should be superimposed onto sexual harassment situations, . . . sexual harassment was not a regular incident of the employment and Employer had specific policies in place prohibiting sexual harassment. In this regard, Feeley, the employee who accosted Claimant, was warned to stop his conduct or he would be discharged. Thereafter, the sexual harassment incidents stopped. Thus, sexual harassment was not a peculiar risk at this workplace. In fact, Claimant admits in her testimony that she had experienced no incidents of sexual harassment in approximately nine years of previous employment with Employer and that she was unaware of any other female employee who had previously been sexually harassed at this workplace.[44]

---

41 495 N.W.2d 859 (Minn. App. 1993).

42 850 P.2d 1038 (N.M. Ct. App. 1993).

43 *Id.* at 1039.

44 *Id.* at 1041.

§ 9.6 Intentional Infliction of Emotional Distress

Intentional infliction of emotional distress is the most widely asserted tort claim in sexual harassment acts and is recognized in most jurisdictions. In most states, a plaintiff must demonstrate that:

1. The defendant acted outrageously
2. The defendant intentionally caused or should have known that his conduct would cause plaintiff's emotional distress
3. The defendant actually and proximately caused plaintiff's severe or extreme emotional distress
4. The plaintiff suffered severe or extreme emotional distress[45]

The tort of intentional infliction of emotional distress clearly applies to sexual harassment cases:

> The extreme and outrageous nature of the conduct may arise not so much from what is done as from abuse by the defendant of some relation or position which gives the defendant actual or apparent power to damage the plaintiff's interests. The result is something very like extortion.
>
> * * *
>
> The social context as well as the relationship between the parties also appears to be an important factor. The work environment, for example, is one in which employees must expect to be evaluated, not always favorably; thus questioning, criticism, and discharge of an employee do not necessarily constitute outrageous conduct. And the work culture in some situations may contemplate a degree of teasing and taunting that in other circumstances might be considered cruel and outrageous. But though the social context may make some questionable conduct tolerable, the same social context may make other acts especially outrageous. Sexual harassment on the job is undoubtedly an intentional infliction of emotional distress, for example, and harassment is probably more readily found in the acts of a supervisor than in the acts of acquaintances at a dinner party.[46]

A District of Columbia court held that a finding by the jury that the plaintiff had not been sexually harassed did not mean that the employer and its chair could not be found liable for intentional infliction of emotional distress, despite the defendants' argument that sexual harassment

---

[45] Restatement (Second) of Torts § 46 (1965). *See also* Fletcher v. Western Nat'l Life Ins. Co., 10 Cal. App. 3d 376, 89 Cal. Rptr. 78 (1970).

[46] Prosser & Keeton on the Law of Torts, § 12 at 61 (W. Keeton, 5th ed. 1984) & § 12 at 18 (Supp. 1988).

has a lower threshold than intentional infliction of emotional distress. In *Underwood v. Washington Post Credit Union,*[47] an action alleging sexual harassment and intentional infliction of emotional distress by a female credit union employee who had broken off an affair with the chair of the credit union board and was subsequently subjected to hostile treatment, the court noted that jury verdicts may be inconsistent, and because the elements of sexual harassment and intentional infliction of emotional distress differ somewhat, it was at least theoretically possible on the facts of this case for the jury to have reached different verdicts on the two claims. The claim for intentional infliction of emotional distress against the credit union was barred by the workers' compensation act. While general mental distress was not a covered injury, "where the emotional distress has as its consequence physical disability the administrative agency and the courts have both ruled that the injury is a covered one."

Because employment status entitles a person to greater protection from insult and outrage,[48] sexual harassment in employment, as defined under Title VII and state antidiscrimination statutes, should be deemed outrageous per se. In *Retherford v. AT&T Communications,*[49] a sexual harassment and retaliation action by a former employee against her employer, supervisors, and coworkers, allegations that after she complained about sexual harassment, coworkers followed her around and intimidated her with threatening comments and looks, and manipulated circumstances at her work in ways that made her job markedly more stressful were sufficient to satisfy the objective conduct requirement of the tort of intentional infliction of emotional distress:

> It is worth stating that any other conclusion would amount to an intolerable refusal to recognize that our society has ceased seeing sexual harassment in the work place as a playful inevitability that should be taken in good spirits and has awakened to the fact that sexual harassment has a corrosive effect on those who engage in it as well as those who are subjected to it and that such harassment has far more to do with the abusive exercise of one person's power over another than it does with sex.[50]

Like racial slurs, the impact of such conduct, however "mild," is invidious. Although many states have heard claims for intentional inflictions of

---

47 59 Fair Empl. Prac. Cas. (BNA) 952 (D.C. Sup. Ct. 1992).

48 Alcorn v. Anbro Eng'g, 2 Cal. 3d 493, 498 n.2, 86 Cal. Rptr. 88, 90 n.2, 468 P.2d 216, 218 n.2 (1970) (racial harassment) (some courts have not found the employment relationship to be special, however). *See, e.g.,* Bowersox v. P.H. Glatfelter Co., 677 F. Supp. 307 (M.D. Pa. 1988).

49 844 P.2d 949 (Utah 1992).

50 *Id.* at 978.

emotional distress,[51] the standard for "outrageous" conduct is unclear. The Restatement (Second) of Torts offers this circular explanation:

> Liability has been found only where the conduct has been so outrageous in nature, and so extreme in degree, as to go beyond all possible bounds of decency and to be regarded as atrocious, and utterly intolerable in a civilized

---

[51] Arizona: Ford v. Revlon, Inc., 153 Ariz. 38, 734 P.2d 580 (1987).

Arkansas: Flowers v. Rego, 691 F. Supp. 177 (E.D. Ark. 1988).

California: Seritis v. Lane, 30 Fair Empl. Prac. Cas. (BNA) 423 (Cal. App. Dep't Super. Ct. 1980).

District of Columbia: Coleman v. American Broadcasting Co., 38 Fair Empl. Prac. Cas. (BNA) 65 (D.D.C. 1985); Howard Univ. v. Best, 484 A.2d 958, 36 Fair Empl. Prac. Cas. (BNA) 482 (D.C. 1984); Stewart v. Thomas, 538 F. Supp. 891 (D.D.C. 1982); Epps v. Ripley, 30 Fair Empl. Prac. Cas. (BNA) 1632 (D.D.C. 1982).

Florida: Studstill v. Borg Warner Leasing, 806 F.2d 1005 (11th Cir. 1986); Ponton v. Scarfone, 468 So. 2d 1009 (Fla. Dist. Ct. App. 1985); Forde v. Royal's, Inc. 537 F. Supp. 1173 (S.D. Fla. 1982).

Hawaii: Lapinad v. Pacific Oldsmobile-GMC, Inc., 679 F. Supp. 991 (D. Haw. 1988).

Illinois: Gilardi v. Schroeder, 672 F. Supp. 1043 (N.D. Ill. 1986), *aff'd,* 833 F.2d 1226 (7th Cir. 1987); Clay v. Quartet Mfg. Co., 644 F. Supp. 56 (N.D. Ill. 1986).

Louisiana: Waltman v. International Paper Co., 47 Fair Empl. Prac. Cas. (BNA) 671 (W.D. La. 1988), *rev'd on other grounds,* 875 F.2d 468 (5th Cir. 1989).

Massachusetts: College-Town, Div. of Interco, Inc. v. Massachusetts Comm'n Against Discrimination, 400 Mass. 156, 508 N.E.2d 587 (1987); Egger v. Local 276, Plumbers & Pipefitters Union, 644 F. Supp. 795 (D. Mass. 1986).

Michigan: Polk v. Yellow Freight Sys., Inc., 801 F.2d 190 (6th Cir. 1986); Eide v. Kelsey-Hayes Co., 154 Mich. App. 142, 397 N.W.2d 532 (1986), *modified on other grounds,* 431 Mich. 58, 427 N.W.2d 488 (1988).

Minnesota: Thorkildson v. Insurance Co. of N. Am., 631 F. Supp. 372 (D. Minn. 1986); Pilkop v. Burlington N. R.R., 42 Fair Empl. Prac. Cas. (BNA) 1822 (Minn. 1985), *cert. denied,* 480 U.S. 951 (1987).

New Jersey: Porta v. Rollins Envtl. Servs. Inc., 654 F. Supp. 1275 (D.N.J. 1987), *aff'd,* 845 F.2d 1014 (3d Cir. 1988); NPS Corp. v. Insurance Co. of N. Am., 213 N.J. Super. 547, 517 A.2d 1211 (1986).

New York: O'Reilly v. Executone of Albany, Inc., 121 A.D.2d 772, 503 N.Y.S.2d 185 (1986); Kersul v. Skulls Angels, Inc., 130 Misc. 2d 345, 495 N.Y.S.2d 886 (Sup. Ct. 1985).

Pennsylvania: Clay v. Advanced Computer Applications, Inc., 370 Pa. Super. 477, 536 A.2d 1375 (1988); Miller v. Aluminum Co. of Am., 679 F. Supp. 495 (W.D. Pa.), *aff'd,* 856 F.2d 184 (3d Cir. 1988); Bowersox v. P.H. Glatfelter Co., 677 F. Supp. 307 (M.D. Pa. 1988); Fawcett v. IDS Servs., 41 Fair Empl. Prac. Cas. (BNA) 589 (W.D. Pa. 1988); Aquino v. Sommer Maid Creamery, Inc., 657 F. Supp. 208 (E.D. Pa. 1987); Shaffer v. National Can Corp., 565 F. Sup. 909 (E.D. Pa. 1983); Vegh v. General Elec. Co., 34 Fair Empl. Prac. Cas. (BNA) 135 (E.D. Pa. 1983).

Tennessee: Pease v. Alford Photo Indus., Inc., 667 F. Supp. 1188 (W.D. Tenn. 1987).

> community. Generally, the case is one in which the recitation of the facts to an average member of the community would arouse [her or] his resentment against the actor, and lead [her or] him to exclaim, "Outrageous!"[52]

What is considered outrageous may work in the plaintiff's favor but may be based on an antiquated notion of women's roles. Although the plaintiff failed to show that a cartoon drawn by a coworker in which she was depicted in a "sexually compromising" position with a male coworker was gender oriented or that the posting of the cartoon created a hostile environment, in *Linebaugh v. Sheraton Michigan Corp.,*[53] the trial court erred in granting summary disposition to the defendant coworker regarding the claim of intentional infliction of emotional distress:

> Once having viewed the cartoon at issue, a reasonable factfinder could conclude that the depiction of plaintiff engaged in a sexual act with a co-worker constitutes conduct so outrageous in character and so extreme in degree that it goes beyond all bounds of common decency in a civilized society. We note that a number of plaintiffs' co-workers testified that the cartoon was offensive. Furthermore, Herring's creation of the cartoon and his delivery of it to Shorkey may well constitute reckless behavior.[54]

The Restatement also notes that the distress must be "so severe that no reasonable man could be expected to endure it. The intensity and the duration of the distress are factors to be considered in determining its severity,"[55] as well as the response by management to complaints of harassment.[56] In

---

52 Restatement (Second) of Torts § 46 comment d (1965).

Baker v. Weyerhaeuser Co., 903 F.2d 1342 (10th Cir. 1990). The jury properly determined that plaintiff had been subjected to intentional infliction of emotional distress based on defendant employer's failure to curb coworker sexual harassment in the form of repeated offensive sexual flirtations, advances, propositions, and continued and sexually suggestive conduct. The court rejected defendant's contention that "by no stretch of anyone's imagination could its 'conduct' equate with 'outrageous conduct,' and therefore Baker's pendent claim must fail in its entirety, which would include her claim for both actual and punitive damages." *Id.* at 1877; that when defendant learned of coworker's conduct, it promptly took the ultimate disciplinary action by firing him. The plaintiff asserted that coworker should have been fired long before he was and that in the interim between the time he should have been fired and was fired, the defendant did nothing, and by its inaction "permitted a known sex maniac to run amok in the workplace, inflicting extreme emotional distress on a twenty-five year mother of two who desperately needed to keep her job." *Id.*

53 198 Mich. App. 335, 49 N.W.2d 585 (Mich. App. 1993).

54 *Id.* at 588–89.

55 *Id.* at § 46 comment j (1965).

56 Baab v. AMR Servs. Corp., 811 F. Supp. 1246 (N.D. Ohio 1993). In an action for constructive discharge for sexual harassment, intentional infliction of emotional distress, and discriminatory discharge based on handicapped status, alleged harassing conduct,

Laughinghouse v. Risser,[57] the plaintiff proved that her supervisor's conduct was extreme and outrageous for her outrage claim when during the 18 months following the plaintiff's refusal of her supervisor's sexual advance, he was constantly critical, cursed, called the plaintiff "stupid," attacked her personal life, threatened to fire her, screamed, threw things, constantly engaged in sexual overtones, and that he tried to "squeeze" employees until they "popped" if he wanted employees to leave. In *Bustamento v. Tucker*,[58] a female employee was harassed almost daily over a two year period by a coworker who cursed at her; made sexual comments, innuendos, and advances; invaded her privacy by asking her about her marital affairs and sexual relationship with her husband; and threatened her with physical violence, including rape, running her out of the plant, and running her over with his forklift. He also used his forklift to terrorize her by driving it at her, attempting to run her over and pinning her against the walls of the plant. The U.S. Supreme Court held that in an action for intentional infliction of emotional distress resulting from sexual harassment, when the acts or conduct are continuous on an almost daily basis, by the same action, of the same nature, and the conduct becomes tortious and actionable because of its continuous, cumulative, synergistic nature, a one-year prescription does not commence until the last act occurs or the conduct is abated. But in *Hendrix v. Phillips*,[59] the state court properly held that conduct by an employee, including showing the plaintiff a hole in the crotch of his pants and asking her in the presence of coworkers if she would like to staple the hole closed, showing her a drawing he made depicting fecal matter moving through a colon, a lewd gesture referring to sexual activity he supposed she engaged in with her husband on a vacation trip, a verbal confrontation during which he cursed her, and a series of complaints he filed against her with her supervisor, was "tasteless and rude social conduct" but did not rise to the level necessary to inflict emotional distress.[60] The trial court could grant

---

including the continuous receipt of pornographic pictures in her personal locker, despite her attempts to seal the air vents, and the display of pornographic and sexually explicit pictures on walls and bulletin boards in common areas for a period of seven months until plaintiff's active employment was discontinued, did not rise to the level of tortious conduct sufficient to support plaintiff's claims of intentional infliction of emotional distress. The employer was not negligent as required for the claim of intentional infliction of emotional distress when there was no evidence establishing the identity of the harasser, evidence of past history of sexually harassing conduct about which the employer knew or should have known, and the employee's supervisors took and recommended corrective action.

57 786 F. Supp. 920 (D. Kan. 1992).

58 607 So. 2d 532 (La. 1992).

See also Brown v. Vaughn, 589 So. 2d 63 (La. Ct. App. 1991).

59 207 Ga. App. 394, 428 S.E.2d 91 (Ga. Ct. App. 1993).

60 *See also* Anspach v. Tomkins Indus., Inc., 817 F. Supp. 1499 (D. Kan. 1993). Female employee brought a sexual harassment, constructive discharge, and retaliation action

summary judgment without first ruling on the sufficiency of affidavits from the plaintiff's treating psychiatrist and psychologist tending to show that she suffered severe depression and anxiety as a result of the harassment when the plaintiff failed to establish a prima facie case of liability.

The court should consider the context in which the acts were committed as well as the severity of the acts themselves. In *Dias v. Sky Chefs,*[61] the jury properly found for the plaintiff on her intentional infliction of emotional distress claim. Oregon courts have held that rude or tyrannical behavior by supervisors, or excessive supervision and unjustified reprimands, when occurring in the context of discharges not invoking any significant public interest could not in themselves give rise to an intentional tort claim. At the same time, the outrageousness of the conduct is measured not merely by the severity of the acts themselves, but also by the context in which the acts were committed. In this case, the injury suffered by the plaintiff was distinguishable from ordinary employment abuses because it was carried out in the context of an allegedly sexually abusive work environment intentionally established by Sky Chef's local general

---

under Title VII and the state antidiscrimination law, as well as claims of intentional infliction of emotional distress and negligence, and her husband, a coworker, charged retaliation, intentional infliction of emotional distress, and negligence. The district court held that neither plaintiff's nor her husband's claims of intentional infliction of emotional distress could stand when, although there was evidence of harassment by coworkers, the only evidence indicating direct sexual harassment by a named defendant was when while putting eyedrops in plaintiff's eye, the personnel manager told her he did not want it to turn into a wet T-shirt contest, and under Kansas law, the employer and its management were not vicariously liable for the outrageous treatment of employees by nonmanagement employees.

Jenkins v. City of Grenada, 813 F. Supp. 443 (N.D. Miss. 1993) (former employee did not state a claim for intentional infliction of emotional distress when although the supervisor's conduct, which included conversations about how much she sexually aroused him, and subsequent criticism of her work, poor evaluations, and demands that she quit or face the threat of defendant fabricating a case against her to justify termination, may have been "nervewracking, upsetting, and even improper," no reasonable juror could conclude that it rose to the heightened level of extreme and outrageous).

Beardsley v. Isom, 61 Fair Empl. Prac. Cas. (BNA) 847 (E.D. Va. 1993). A female former lieutenant did not state a claim for intentional infliction of emotional distress for her supervisor's conduct, including calling her "honey" and "dear," touching her shoulder and massaging it for 10–20 seconds on two occasions, accusing her of "making out" with other officers, and asking intimate questions about her underwear and her methods of birth control. She also alleged that she learned from her husband that her supervisor wanted to "borrow" her and take her to a bar all dolled up in tight clothes" and that he wanted her to drive him to his car and that it was "his turn" to "make out" with her in the parking lot.

61 919 F.2d 1370 (9th Cir. 1990), *vacated on other grounds,* 111 S. Ct. 2791 (1991), *on remand,* 948 F.2d 532 (9th Cir. 1991), *cert. denied,* 112 S. Ct. 1294 (1992).

manager; the jury was entitled to consider that context and look behind the manager's specific acts in its determination of outrageousness.[62]

Testimony of treating physicians or psychiatrists may weigh heavily. In *Benavides v. Moore,*[63] a plaintiff did not state a claim for intentional infliction of emotional distress when although the plaintiff testified that she felt stress and anguish from her termination because her income decreased and she did not know why she was fired, she admitted that she consulted no psychologists or psychiatrists and had no plans to do so, and offered no evidence that directly showed the severity of her distress.[64] The severity of the distress is an element of a cause of action for intentional infliction of emotional distress, not only of damages. But in *Hackney v. Woodring,*[65] an action by a female employee against her employer alleging assault, battery, false imprisonment, and intentional infliction of emotional distress stemming from acts including touching, fondling, spanking, holding her down in his lap, threatening her life while ripping off her clothes, and exposing himself, the court of common pleas improperly granted the employer's motion for judgment notwithstanding the verdict in favor of the plaintiff for the intentional infliction of emotional distress claim and for $15,000 in compensatory damages on the ground that the plaintiff, by failing to introduce expert medical testimony, had not sustained her burden of proof as to damages:

> Here, we are confronted with the sexual harassment, intimidating, abuse, and retaliatory discharge of a young woman, just eighteen years of age, in her first job, by her employer, a man in a position of authority. Hackney's testimony, which was supported by the testimony of two of her fellow workers, was compelling. After describing numerous incidents of unwanted touching and fondling by Woodring during school hours, Hackney described one incident which happened when she accompanied Woodring, at his request, to the school "home office":

---

[62] Dias was *vacated,* 111 S. Ct. 2791 (1991) in light of Edmonson v. Leesville, 111 S. Ct. 2077 (1991), which held that a private litigant in a civil case may not use preemptory challenges to exclude jurors on the basis of race. *On remand,* 948 F.2d 532 (9th Cir. 1991) (court of appeals declined to decide whether jurors were improperly excluded on the basis of sex because employer failed to make a proper and timely objection to employee's use of preemptory challenges to strike males from jury venire), *cert. denied,* 112 S. Ct. 1294 (1992).

[63] 848 S.W.2d 190 (Tex. Ct. App. 1993).

[64] *Cf.* Hendrix v. Phillips, 207 Ga. App. 394, 428 S.E.2d 91 (Ga. Ct. App. 1993) (trial court could grant summary judgment without first ruling on the sufficiency of affidavits from plaintiff's treating psychiatrist and psychologist tending to show that she suffered severe depression and anxiety as a result of the harassment when plaintiff failed to establish a prima facie case of liability).

[65] 622 A.2d 286 (Pa. Super. Ct. 1993).

> And he was holding me down and he was threatening me and told me that if I didn't do what he said, that he would kill me and that nobody would believe me anyway and that my job depended on it, and he tried—kept telling me this was for my self-esteem.
>
> And he put his hands all over me, and I kept trying to tell him to stop and push away and to leave, and he kept telling me, This is for your self esteem, you'll feel better.
>
> * * *
>
> At one point when I stood up, he stood up and pulled the top of my pants where they unsnap and kind of zip down. Then I sat back—he pulled me back down. I stood back up, and he pulled my pants down not all the way to the floor but down close to my knees, and he kept telling me that I had to do it . . .
>
> At one point when he had me pushed up against the desk, we heard a noise out in the hall. And he looked at me and said, that must be the janitor. So he told me to get behind the door and not say anything or he would kill me, and I was—I was scared.
>
> * * *
>
> He told me nobody would believe me, and he told me that he would kill me. And he had told me on other occasions that he had a gun in the office.
>
> * * *
>
> Here, Hackney's testimony, supported by that of her co-workers, revealed the severe emotional trauma which Woodring caused her to suffer. The suffering . . . is within the understanding of the average juror. While the average juror may not have personally experienced the extreme fright, humiliation, embarrassment and loss of self-esteem to which Hackney testified, these feelings are within the realm of common understanding which all jurors bring with them to the jury box. Expert testimony was not necessary to explain the issues in this case, and would have only served the purpose of buttressing Hackney's credibility, thus usurping the province of the jury.[66]

In the sexual harassment context, the court should analyze the facts from the perspective of a reasonable woman in an employment situation because only this standard can capture the essence of sexual harassment. Once a finding of sexual harassment renders the challenged conduct outrageous per se, the disparity among injuries can be addressed through the amount or type of damages awarded.

---

66 *Id.* at 289–90.

The per se approach has found acceptance in some state courts.[67] In *Howard University v. Best,*[68] the District of Columbia Court of Appeals rejected the notion that appears to form the basis for much of the disparity in sexual harassment decisions:

> Recognizing that women suffer sexual harassment in the workplace, based on outmoded sexual stereotypes and male domination of subordinate female employees, we reject the view, articulated by the trial court, that, as a matter of law, the degrading and humiliating behavior herein detailed was at worse a "social impropriety" which did not amount to the intentional infliction of emotional distress.[69]

Some courts seem to distinguish between verbal harassment and conduct that includes physical contact,[70] despite the fact that in most states, a plaintiff need not have suffered a physical injury to recover for intentional infliction of emotional distress.[71] In *Class v. New Jersey Life Insurance*

---

67 Howard Univ. v. Best, 484 A.2d 958, 36 Fair Empl. Prac. Cas. (BNA) 482 (D.C. 1984). *See also* Porta v. Rollins Envtl. Servs. Inc., 654 F. Supp. 1275 (D.N.J. 1987), *aff'd,* 845 F.2d 1014 (3d Cir. 1988); NPS Corp. v. Insurance Co. of N. Am., 213 N.J. Super. 547, 517 A.2d 1211 (1986) (no touching involved).

68 484 A.2d 958, 36 Fair Empl. Prac. Cas. (BNA) 482 (D.C. 1984).

69 *Id.* at 986.

70 Florida: Studstill v. Borg Warner Leasing, 806 F.2d 1005 (11th Cir. 1986); Ponton v. Scarfone, 468 So. 2d 1009 (Fla. Dist. Ct. App. 1985); Forde v. Royal's, Inc., 537 F. Supp. 1173 (S.D. Fla. 1982).

Michigan: Polk v. Yellow Freight Sys., Inc., 801 F.2d 190 (6th Cir. 1986).

Missouri: Beeman v. Safeway Stores, 724 F. Supp. 674 (W.D. Mo. 1989) (implying that sexual advances and leering sexual comments alone were insufficient to prove outrageousness).

North Carolina: Keziah v. W.M. Brown & Son, 683 F. Supp. 542 (W.D.N.C. 1988); Hogan v. Forsyth Country Club Co., 79 N.C. App. 483, 340 S.E.2d 116 (Ct. App. 1986).

Pennsylvania: Miller v. Aluminum Co. of Am., 679 F. Supp. 495 (W.D. Pa. 1988); Bowersox v. P.H. Glatfelter Co., 677 F. Supp. 307 (M.D. Pa. 1988); Aquino v. Sommer Maid Creamery, Inc., 657 F. Supp. 208 (E.D. Pa. 1987); Clay v. Advanced Computer Applications, Inc., 536 A.2d 1375 (Pa. Super. 1988); Hooten v. Pennsylvania College of Optometry, 601 F. Supp. 1151 (E.D. Pa. 1984).

Virginia: Swentek v. USAIR, Inc., 830 F.2d 552 (4th Cir. 1987).

Wisconsin: Hrabak v. Marquip, Inc., 798 F. Supp. 550 (W.D. Wis. 1992) (employee's state claims of battery and intentional infliction of emotional distress were barred by the exclusivity provisions of the state workers' compensation act when plaintiff did not indicate that touching by her coworker was intended to cause or caused bodily harm).

71 *See, e.g.,* Arkansas: Mumphrey v. James River Paper Co., 777 F. Supp. 1458 (W.D. Ark. 1991) (plaintiff, a female African-American employee, stated a claim for outrage under Arkansas law when she presented evidence that her supervisor commented on her clothing and physical appearance, accused her of taking breaks without permission, refused to

Co.,[72] the court held that the conduct of a male supervisor would not have been sufficiently outrageous had it remained verbal, even though he subjected the plaintiff to an eight-week period consisting of daily sexual jokes, personal stories of group sex, invitations to visit his home, asking if she swallowed during oral sex, describing the size of his penis, and commenting that he enjoyed anal sex with women. What made the difference for the court was that the alleged harasser *retaliated* against the plaintiff for complaining about his conduct. The Restatement supports a distinction between verbal and physical conduct.[73] One court has held that verbal harassment alone is not outrageous conduct unless tangible work benefits are at stake.[74] Another deemed the absence of overt propositions determinative. In *Kinnally v. Bell of Pennsylvania,*[75] a phone company engineer was subjected to a "regime of misogynous comments"; one defendant made "vulgar and suggestive comments in her presence, some of which were directed toward plaintiff, and showed a videotape of rabbits mating at a meeting where she was the only female present."[76] Another defendant unnecessarily singled her out as a woman on a memorandum recording attendance rates and repeated to plaintiff comments made by the defendant and others regarding the ability of women to work as engineers. After

---

allow her to take certain breaks, sent her to certain areas of the plant and then accused her of being in those areas without permission, required her to do work that she was not authorized to do, used scrutiny so intensive as to make her nervous and to cause her to suffer extreme anxiety, and treated her differently from Caucasians and men).

Smith v. Southern Starr of Arkansas, Inc., 700 F. Supp. 1026 (E.D. Ark. 1988). The plaintiff stated a claim for outrage when she alleged that she was fired because she would not agree to her supervisor's demands for sexual favors. Her employer then represented in relation to her unemployment compensation claim that she had been fired for misconduct.

California: Alcorn v. Anbro Eng'g, 2 Cal. 3d 493, 468 P.2d 216, 86 Cal. Rptr. 88 (1970); Perati v. Atkinson, 213 Cal. App. 2d 472, 28 Cal. Rptr. 898 (1963).

Massachusetts: Agis v. Howard Johnson Co., 371 Mass. 140, 355 N.E.2d 315 (1976).

Minnesota: Pikop v. Burlington N. R.R., 390 N.W.2d 743 (Minn. 1985), *cert. denied,* 480 U.S. 951 (1987).

New Jersey: Porta v. Rollins Envtl. Servs., Inc., 654 F. Supp. 1275 (D.N.J. 1987), *aff'd,* 845 F.2d 1014 (3d Cir. 1988); NPS Corp. v. Insurance Co. of N. Am., 213 N.J. Super. 547, 517 A.2d 1211 (1986).

72 53 Fair Empl. Prac. Cas. (BNA) 1583 (N.D. Ill. 1990).

73 Restatement (Second) of Torts § 46(1) (1965): "One who by extreme and outrageous conduct intentionally or recklessly causes severe emotional distress to another is subject to liability for such emotional distress, and if bodily harm to the other results from it, for such bodily harm".

74 Seritis v. Lane, 30 Fair Empl. Prac. Cas. (BNA) 423 (Cal. App. Dep't Super. Ct. 1980).

75 748 F. Supp. 1136 (E.D. Pa. 1990).

76 *Id.* at 1138.

a history of superior work performance, the plaintiff received an unjustifiably poor work evaluation from one defendant. Plaintiff subsequently suffered a mental breakdown. "However disturbing" the allegations were, "the regime of derision and intimidation" fell short of the state prescription for intentional infliction of emotional distress. "Plaintiff does not claim to be either the recipient or the victim of any overt propositions. Accordingly, her claim of intentional infliction of emotional distress must be dismissed."[77] Several courts have found at least a stated claim for intentional infliction of emotional distress when the challenged conduct included unwelcome touching.[78] When appropriate, an accompanying claim for assault and battery may bolster an emotional distress claim. Allegations of retaliation also may support such a claim.[79] In *Pommier v. James L. Edelstein Enterprises,*[80] a female former employee stated a claim for intentional infliction of emotional distress when the plaintiff alleged

---

[77] *Id.* at 1145.

[78] Illinois: Gilardi v. Schroeder, 672 F. Supp. 1043 (N.D. Ill. 1986), *aff'd,* 833 F.2d 1226 (7th Cir. 1987).

Class v. New Jersey Life Ins. Co., 746 F. Supp. 776 (N.D. Ill. 1990). Although alleged salacious comments by male supervisor to female employee in the form of daily sex-related jokes, discussions regarding his sexual exploits and his invitations to plaintiff to come to his home for the implied purpose of sexual activity did not support a claim for intentional infliction of emotional distress, alleged threats to "get even" with plaintiff for making a sexual harassment complaint and the undermining of her authority until she was fired by her employer, if proven, would support such a claim.

Louisiana: Waltman v. International Paper Co., 47 Fair Empl. Prac. Cas. (BNA) 671 (W.D. La. 1988), *rev'd on other grounds*, 875 F.2d 468 (5th Cir. 1989).

New York: O'Reilly v. Executone of Albany, Inc., 121 A.D.2d 772, 503 N.Y.S.2d 185 (1986).

North Carolina: Hogan v. Forsyth Country Club Co., 79 N.C. App. 483, 340 S.E.2d 116 (1986).

Oregon: *Cf.* Carlson v. Crater Lake Lumber Co., 103 Or. App. 190, 796 P.2d 1216 (Ct. App. 1990) *on reconsideration,* 105 Or. App. 314, 804 P.2d 511 (1991) (discharged family members (mother, father, and two daughters), who alleged that they were discharged in retaliation for one daughter's resistance to sexual harassment, did not have a claim for intentional infliction of emotional distress based on their firing when as a matter of law, their discharge, even if motivated by malice towards one of the daughters, was not conduct that exceeded the bounds of social toleration).

Pennsylvania: Fawcett v. IDS Servs., 41 Fair Empl. Prac. Cas. (BNA) 589 (W.D. Pa. 1988); Vegh v. General Elec. Co., 34 Fair Empl. Prac. Cas. (BNA) 135 (E.D. Pa. 1983).

Tennessee: Pease v. Alford Photo Indus., Inc., 667 F. Supp. 1188 (W.D. Tenn. 1987).

[79] District of Columbia: Coleman v. American Broadcasting Co., 38 Fair Empl. Prac. Cas. (BNA) 65 (D.D.C. 1985).

Pennsylvania: Fawcett v. IDS Servs., 41 Fair Empl. Prac. Cas. (BNA) 589 (W.D. Pa. 1988); Shaffer v. National Can Corp., 565 F. Supp. 909 (E.D. Pa. 1983).

[80] 816 F. Supp. 476 (N.D. Ill. 1993) (Aspen, J.).

repeated acts of sexual harassment and a pattern of retaliation in response to her internal complaint of sexual harassment—defendants allegedly withheld information necessary to perform her job, sabotaged programs she had implemented to ensure she would fail, and interfered with her customer contacts to ruin her professional reputation and credibility.

Employment has been considered a property right,[81] and both tangible and hostile environment harassment interfere with the enjoyment of that right. The notion that in the absence of accompanying trespass or assault there was "no harm in asking"[82] has given way to a heightened societal sensitivity regarding the "bounds of decency." Fueled by the activism of the 1960s, the parameters of tort law have expanded as we challenge what was once the norm. We have recognized, for example, that racial epithets, "once part of common usage," are more than "merely insulting language."[83] From the body of law regarding racial harassment emerged a recognition of both the sexually hostile environment under Title VII and a cause of action for sexual harassment under tort law. Although the injuries generated by a threat to job security or retaliatory conduct may appear to present a clearer case of intentional infliction of emotional distress, harassment engendered by words, looks, and gestures may in fact be more emotionally debilitating. In the tangible harassment situation, an employee may feel wronged and angry because the nature of the injury is straightforward. An employee who is subjected to a hostile work environment and whose job is not directly threatened, however, may be more likely to live with the degradation longer and suffer more far-reaching consequences. Physical complications are not uncommon. Sexual harassment victims experience a range of stress-related ailments including high blood pressure, nausea, chest pains, nervous tics, weakness, insomnia, and headaches.[84]

A claim for intentional infliction of emotional distress may be a useful addition or viable alternative to a federal Title VII claim. An emotional distress claimant seeks damages for injuries incurred to herself, not her job status. This means that intentional infliction of emotional distress can be proven based on facts that might not support a finding of sex discrimination under Title VII. Moreover, the plaintiff need not show that the challenged

---

81 Perry v. Sindermann, 408 U.S. 593, 601 (1972).

82 C. Magruder, *Mental and Emotional Disturbance in the Law of Torts,* 49 Harv. L. Rev. 1033, 1055 (1936).

83 Alcorn v. Anbro Eng'g, 2 Cal. 3d 493, 499, 468 P.2d 216, 219, 86 Cal. Rptr. 88, 91 (1970).

84 *See, e.g.,* Arizona: Ford v. Revlon, Inc., 153 Ariz. 38, 734 P.2d 580 (1987).

California: Vinson v. Superior Ct. (Peralta Community College Dist.), 43 Cal. 3d 833, 740 P.2d 404, 239 Cal. Rptr. 292, (1987); Monge v. Superior Ct. (Crown Gibralter Graphic Ctr., Inc.), 176 Cal. App. 3d 503, 222 Cal. Rptr. 64 (1986).

Pennsylvania: Bowersox v. P.H. Glatfelter Co., 677 F. Supp. 307 (M.D. Pa. 1988).

conduct was based on sex, so a defendant cannot argue that the particular conduct was directed equally to women and men.

As discussed in **Chapter 6,** a claim for intentional infliction of emotional distress brings into question the plaintiff's mental state, so the plaintiff must be prepared for discovery requests for psychiatric and medical records and/or submission to physical or psychological examinations.

A claim of intentional infliction of emotional distress may be brought against an employer, a supervisor, or a coworker. An employer may be responsible for failing to respond to complaints of sexual harassment by a supervisor or coworker.[85] A showing of intent may not be necessary in this situation; a reckless disregard of the harassing conduct may be sufficient. Generally, the more attenuated the employment relationship between the parties, the greater the injury must be to establish a claim.

A full range of tort remedies, including punitive damages, is available for successful claims of intentional infliction of emotional distress.[86]

Appendix A contains a sexual harassment complaint alleging, among other things, intentional infliction of emotional distress.

§ 9.7 Assault and Battery

The torts of assault and battery provided remedies for early victims of sexual harassment. A number of cases dating back to the turn of the century allowed recovery in tort for "taking indecent liberties with a woman

---

[85] Arizona: Ford v. Revlon, Inc., 153 Ariz. 38, 734 P.2d 580 (1987).

Hawaii: Lapinad v. Pacific Oldsmobile-GMC, Inc., 679 F. Supp. 991 (D. Haw. 1988).

Illinois: *Cf.* Juarez v. Ameritech Mobile Communications, 746 F. Supp. 798 (N.D. Ill. 1990), *aff'd,* 957 F.2d 317 (7th Cir. 1992) (female former employee could not hold her employer liable for intentional infliction of emotional distress caused by her supervisor in the form of "sexually suggestive" comments made directly to her face and over the phone when plaintiff proffered no evidence of the fact that the employer itself directed, encouraged, or committed extreme and outrageous conduct against her).

Oregon: *Cf.* Lewis v. Oregon Beauty Supply Co., 302 Or. 616, 733 P.2d 430 (1987).

[86] *See, e.g.,* Illinois: Gilardi v. Schroeder, 672 F. Supp. 1043 (N.D. Ill. 1986), *aff'd,* 833 F.2d 1226 (7th Cir. 1987) ($50,000 compensatory, $50,000 punitive damages for battery and intentional infliction of emotional distress).

Massachusetts: O'Connell v. Chasdi, 400 Mass. 686, 511 N.E.2d 349 (1987) ($100,000 for assault and battery and intentional infliction of emotional distress).

Oregon: Lewis v. Oregon Beauty Supply Co., 302 Or. 616, 733 P.2d 430 (1987) ($75,000 punitive damages).

Tennessee: Pease v. Alford Photo Indus., Inc., 667 F. Supp. 1188 (W.D. Tenn. 1987) ($2,500 compensatory, $1,000 punitive damages).

without her consent,"[87] including assault by a coworker.[88] Although assault and battery are separate civil actions, they often are brought in tandem. Assault occurs when a person "acts intending to cause a harmful or offensive contact with the person of the other or a third person or an imminent apprehension of such conduct and . . . the other is thereby put in such imminent apprehension."[89] Verbal harassment alone without a threat of physical harm thus may not constitute assault.[90] This threat may be in the form of a gesture or movement toward the plaintiff. Liability for battery results from intentional unwelcome physical contact, which may include touching, kissing, embracing, or rubbing up against the body of the plaintiff.[91] In *Waltman v. International Paper Co.,*[92] an employee stated claim for battery when she alleged subjection to unwelcome touching and pinching of breasts and thighs and placing of air hose between her legs. Damages have been awarded for assault and battery based on sexual advances and unwelcome touching.[93] Touching need not be of sexual areas

---

[87] Prosser & Keeton on the Law of Torts 36 (W. Keeton, 5th ed. 1984). *See also* Martin v. Jansen, 113 Wash. 290, 193 P. 674 (1920) (damages awarded to woman who claimed that she had been fondled in a lewd and lascivious manner without her consent); Hatchett v. Blacketer, 162 Ky. 266, 172 S.W. 533 (1915); Hough v. Iderhoff, 69 Or. 568, 139 P. 931, 932 (1914) (a man put his hands upon a woman "with a view to violate her person"); Kline v. Kline, 158 Ind. 602, 64 N.E. 9, 10 (1902); Ragsdale v. Ezell, 20 Ky. 1567, 49 S.W. 775, 776 (1899) (assault and battery found when a man squeezed the breast and touched the face of a woman).

[88] Wisconsin: Craker v. Chicago & N.W. R.R., 35 Wis. 657 (1895) (compensatory damages awarded for both mental suffering and sense of having been wronged).

[89] Restatement (Second) of Torts § 21 (1965). *See also* Rogers v. Loews L'Enfant Plaza Hotel, 526 F. Supp. 523 (D.D.C. 1981).

[90] Restatement (Second) of Torts § 31 (1965).

[91] *See, e.g.,* Newsome v. Cooper-Wiss, Inc., 179 Ga. App. 670, 347 S.E.2d 619 (1986). Prosser notes that contact with a plaintiff's clothing has been held sufficient to constitute battery, Prosser & Keeton on the Law of Torts § 9 (W. Keeton, 5th ed. 1984), *citing* United States v. Ortega, 4 Wash. C.C. 531, Fed. Cas. No. 15,971 (3d Cir. 1925); Piggly-Wiggly Ala. Co. v. Rickles, 212 Ala. 585, 103 So. 860 (1925); Geraty v. Stern, 30 Hun. 426 (N.Y. 1883). "The defendant may be liable when intending only a joke, or even a compliment, as where an unappreciated kiss is bestowed without consent, or a misguided effort is made to render assistance." *Prosser & Keeton* at 41–42.

[92] 47 Fair Empl. Prac. Cas. (BNA) 671 (W.D. La. 1988), *rev'd on other grounds,* 875 F.2d 468 (5th Cir. 1989).

[93] Arizona: Skousen v. Nidy, 90 Ariz. 215, 367 P.2d 248 (1961), *reh'g denied,* (1962) (assaults included placing hands on plaintiff's "private parts" and attempting to seduce her; $3,500 in actual and $1,500 in punitive damages awarded).

District of Columbia: Clark v. World Airways, 24 Fair Empl. Prac. Cas. (BNA) 305 (D.D.C. 1980) ($52,000 awarded for offensive touching, explicit sexual touching, and "off-color" remarks).

Illinois: Gilardi v. Schroeder, 672 F. Supp. 1043 (N.D. Ill. 1986), *aff'd,* 833 F.2d 1226 (7th Cir. 1987) (drugging and raping female employee by supervisor constituted civil battery).

to be actionable,[94] but the plaintiff usually must demonstrate that the touching incident itself, apart from previous harassment, caused an injury.[95] Mental suffering is an injury for which damages may be awarded.[96] Evidence of repeated physical contact, however, is more likely to sustain a claim of battery.[97]

Damages available for assault and battery include those for humiliation and fright.

§ 9.8 Tortious Interference with Contracts

A plaintiff may recover compensatory and punitive damages from a defendant who "intentionally acts to deprive another of an economic benefit."[98] Under this theory, a victim of sexual harassment may recover damages directly from the person who harassed her. To state a claim for tortious interference with an employment contract, a plaintiff must prove that:

1. A valid contract existed at the time of the harassment
2. The defendant, who was not a party to the contract, had knowledge of the contractual relationship

---

Tennessee: Pease v. Alford Photo Indus., Inc., 667 F. Supp. 1188 (W.D. Tenn. 1987) ($2,500 in compensatory and $10,000 in punitive damages awarded).

Texas: Valdez v. Church's Fried Chicken, Inc., 683 F. Supp. 596 (W.D. Tex. 1988) (punitive damages awarded for attempted rape).

94 Georgia: Newsome v. Cooper-Wiss, Inc., 179 Ga. App. 670, 347 S.E.2d 619 (1986).

95 Tennessee: Boyd v. James S. Hayes Living Health Care Agency, 671 F. Supp. 1155 (W.D. Tenn. 1987).

96 Arizona: Skousen v. Nidy, 90 Ariz. 215, 367 P.2d 248 (1961), *reh'g denied,* (Jan. 3, 1962).

97 Georgia: Newsome v. Cooper-Wiss, Inc., 179 Ga. App. 670, 347 S.E.2d 619 (1986).

Louisiana: Waltman v. International Paper Co., 47 Fair Empl. Prac. Cas. (BNA) 671 (W.D. La. 1988), *rev'd on other grounds*, 875 F.2d 468 (5th Cir. 1989).

New York: O'Reilly v. Executone of Albany, Inc., 121 A.D.2d 772, 503 N.Y.S.2d 185 (1986).

Tennessee: Pease v. Alford Photo Indus., Inc., 667 F. Supp. 1188 (W.D. Tenn. 1987).

Cf. Illinois: Dockter v. Rudolf Wolff Futures, Inc., 684 F. Supp. 532 (N.D. Ill. 1988), *aff'd,* 913 F.2d 456 (7th Cir. 1990).

98 Kyriazi v. Western Elec. Co., 461 F. Supp. 894, 950 (D.N.J. 1978), *modified,* 473 F. Supp. 786 (D.N.J. 1979), *aff'd,* 647 F.2d 388 (3d Cir. 1981).

3. The defendant intentionally interfered with the contract for an improper purpose or by an improper means
4. The plaintiff suffered damages as a result of the interference.[99]

Many state courts have recognized actions brought under this theory even when the employment involved is at will.[100] Because the action may not be brought against a party to the employment contract[101] and the plaintiff must demonstrate the loss of an economic benefit, this theory may have limited value. However, it may be useful when supervisors or coworkers force an employee to quit by making her work environment intolerable,[102] or when a supervisor or coworker retaliates against an employee who has rejected his advances by maligning that employee to his superior, who discharges the harassed employee or otherwise alters her employment status.[103] For example, in *Favors v. Alco Mfg. Co.*,[104] the plaintiff alleged that her supervisor tortiously interfered with her employment contract when he facilitated her discharge after she rejected his sexual advances. In *Lewis v. Oregon Beauty Supply Co.*,[105] punitive damages were warranted when a male coworker's threats, insults and intimidation forced the plaintiff to leave her job. In *Fisher v. San Pedro Peninsula Hospital,*[106] however, a plaintiff nurse did not prove that a doctor's sexual harassment of other nurses negatively affected her employment relationship with the hospital when the court found no evidence that the doctor intended to disrupt the plaintiff's employment relationship through the sexual harassment of others.

When the employer is the alleged harasser, a breach of contract action may be appropriate. A supervisor cannot be liable for intentional interference with an employment contract if he is acting within the legitimate

---

99 Restatement (Second) of Torts §§ 766–67 (1979).

100 Lewis v. Oregon Beauty Supply Co., 302 Or. 616, 733 P.2d 430, 433 (1987) ("The parties to an at-will employment relationship have no less of an interest in the integrity and security of their contract than do any other contracting parties").

101 *Id.;* Restatement (Second) of Torts § 766 (1977).

102 *See, e.g.,* Kyriazi v. Western Elec. Co., 461 F. Supp. 894 (D.N.J. 1978), *modified,* 473 F. Supp. 786 (D.N.J. 1979), *aff'd,* 647 F.2d 388 (3d Cir. 1981).

103 Georgia: Favors v. Alco Mfg. Co., 186 Ga. App. 480, 367 S.E.2d 328 (1988).

Oregon: Lewis v. Oregon Beauty Supply Co., 302 Or. 616, 733 P.2d 430 (1987).

Cf. Illinois: Woerner v. Brzeczek, 519 F. Supp. 517 (N.D. Ill. 1981) (female police officers who alleged that defendants intentionally and maliciously interfered with the pursuit of their profession by harassing male officers who attempted to work with one plaintiff and harassed plaintiffs in the performance of their duties did not state claims for either interference with contractual relationships or interference with prospective economic advantage).

104 186 Ga. App. 480, 367 S.E.2d 328 (1988).

105 302 Or. 616, 733 P.2d 430 (1987).

106 214 Cal. App. 3d 590, 262 Cal. Rptr. 842 (1989).

scope of authority, so a plaintiff must argue that the defendant acted out of improper personal reasons.[107]

To establish a claim for intentional interference with an employment contract, the plaintiff must show that the alleged harasser acted intentionally,[108] but a finding of malice is not required for liability.[109] Proof of an interference claim also may require that "the interference either be in pursuit of an improper or wrongful motive or involve the use of an improper or wrongful means."[110] The motives or means may be defined as improper in a statute or other regulation or a recognized rule of common law, but it is unnecessary to prove all the elements of another tort.[111]

A range of remedies, including punitive damages, is available for intentional interference with an employment relationship.[112]

§ 9.9 Defamation, Libel, and Slander

A sexual harassment plaintiff may sue for defamation when the employer makes false statements about the employee to coworkers or to a prospective employer.[113] A plaintiff must establish that:

1. The defendant made a false or defamatory statement
2. The defendant made that statement in an unprivileged communication to a third party
3. The defendant was at least negligent in communicating the statement
4. The communication either proximately caused plaintiff special harm or was actionable irrespective of special harm.[114]

---

107 Favors v. Alco Mfg. Co., 186 Ga. App. 480, 367 S.E.2d 328 (1988).

108 Restatement (Second) of Torts § 766 comment j states that interference is intentional even if defendant "does not act for the purpose of interfering with the contract or desire it but knows that the interference is certain or substantially certain to occur as a result of [her or] his action."

109 Prosser & Keeton on the Law of Torts § 129 at 983 (W. Keeton, 5th ed. 1984).

110 Lewis v. Oregon Beauty Supply Co., 302 Or. 616, 733 P.2d 430 (1987).

111 *Id.* at 434.

112 *Id.*

113 District of Columbia: Coleman v. American Broadcasting Co., 38 Fair Empl. Prac. Cas. (BNA) 65 (D.D.C. 1985).

New York: Carpenter v. County of Chenango, 135 A.D.2d 936, 522 N.Y.S.2d 339 (1987); Kersul v. Skulls Angels, Inc., 130 Misc. 2d 345, 495 N.Y.S.2d 886 (Sup. Ct. 1985).

114 Restatement (Second) of Torts § 558 (1977).

Written defamatory matter has traditionally been considered libel, while oral defamation constitutes slander. An individual may prove libel without any proof of special harm. In *Linebaugh*,[115] although the plaintiff failed to show that a cartoon drawn by a coworker in which she was depicted in a "sexually compromising" position with a male coworker was gender oriented or that the posting of the cartoon created a hostile environment, the drawing of the cartoon was actionable as libel irrespective of special harm because the cartoon could be interpreted as depicting the plaintiff in a sexual act with a man other than her husband that thus imputed want of chastity to the plaintiff. Proof of actual damage is required in slander cases unless the slander involves the plaintiff's business, trade, or profession, the commission of a crime by the plaintiff, the contraction of a "loathsome" disease, or the unchasteness of a female plaintiff.[116] In *Garcia v. Williams,*[117] the plaintiff sustained a slander claim when she alleged that her former employer, a judge, had told other people that she was romantically interested in him. In *Chamberlin v. 101 Realty,*[118] the plaintiff who was discharged for allegedly resisting her employer's sexual advances stated a claim for defamation when the employer made statements implying that the plaintiff had improperly removed property from the employer's office.

Although defaming communications made in the context of sexual harassment may seem blatantly offensive, the plaintiff must be careful to plead special damages when the facts do not allege defamation per se and must specifically set forth the exact words used and the time, manner, and persons to whom the communication was made.[119]

§ 9.10 Invasion of Privacy

There are several different types of torts under the general heading of invasion of privacy. Applicable to sexual harassment are intrusion, public disclosure of private facts, and false light publicity.

Intrusion

Sexual harassment may constitute the tortious invasion of privacy called intrusion when, for example, an alleged harasser badgers an employee by

---

[115] Linebaugh v. Sheraton Mich. Corp., 198 Mich. App. 335, 49 N.W.2d 585 (Mich. App. 1993).

[116] W. Prosser & P. Keeton §112 at 788–93.

[117] 704 F. Supp. 984, 1001 (N.D. Cal. 1988).

[118] 626 F. Supp. 865 (D.N.H. 1985).

[119] Kersul v. Skulls Angels, Inc., 130 Misc. 2d 345, 495 N.Y.S.2d 886 (Sup. Ct. 1985).

following her into her office, telephoning her in her office or at home, making sexually related inquiries, or putting her in fear of sexual contact.[120] Under the Restatement (Second) of Torts, a plaintiff usually can establish intrusion by showing that:

1. The defendant committed an intentional intrusion, physical or otherwise, upon the solitude or seclusion of the employee's private affairs or concerns
2. This intrusion would be highly offensive to a reasonable person
3. The plaintiff suffered damages as a result of this intrusion.[121]

In the employment context, intrusion usually involves an invasion by the employer or supervisor into an area in which the employee had a reasonable expectation of privacy, to elicit personal information from the employee.[122] This tort protects the sanctity of physical areas a person would consider private and off limits to uninvited persons. Although in some instances physical location may be a factor in determining whether the alleged intrusion is actionable, the challenged conduct may be so offensive that it would be actionable no matter where it occurred.[123] The actions of the defendant must be unwanted, uninvited and unwarranted.[124] Sexual touching and advances may support a claim of intrusion. In *Waltman,*[125] the plaintiff stated a claim for invasion of privacy when the plaintiff alleged that a coworker placed a high-pressure air hose between her legs.

The right to privacy may be waived by discussing the relevant issues in the work place. In *Moffett v. Gene B. Glick Co.,*[126] the plaintiff's open

---

120 Otto v. Heckler, 781 F.2d 754 (9th Cir.), *modified on other grounds,* 802 F.2d 337 (9th Cir. 1986); Rogers v. Loews L'Enfant Plaza Hotel, 526 F. Supp. 523 (D.D.C. 1981) (employee plaintiff stated claim for invasion of privacy when defendant phoned her at work and at home and the conversations included comments about plaintiff's personal and sex life). *See also* Pease v. Alford Photo Indus., Inc., 667 F. Supp. 1188 (W.D. Tenn. 1987) (invasion of privacy found when employer subjected female employee to touching, fondling, and stroking of her breast, thigh, hair, neck, shoulders, and buttocks).

121 Restatement (Second) of Torts § 652B (1977).

122 Phillips v. Smalley Maintenance Servs. Corp., 435 So. 2d 705 (Ala. 1983).

123 Phillips v. Smalley Maintenance Servs. Corp., 435 So. 2d 705, 711 (Ala. 1983). *See also* Keehr v. Consolidated Freightways, 825 F.2d 133 (7th Cir. 1987) (statements made regarding sexual conduct of employee's spouse); Waltman v. International Paper Co., 47 Fair Empl. Prac. Cas. (BNA) 671 (W.D. La. 1988), *rev'd on other grounds,* 875 F.2d 468 (5th Cir. 1989) (employee stated claim for invasion of privacy when she alleged that coworkers placed an air hose between her legs).

124 Cummings v. Walsh Constr. Co., 561 F. Supp. 872 (S.D. Ga. 1983).

125 Waltman v. International Paper Co., 47 Fair Empl. Prac. Cas. (BNA) 671 (W.D. La. 1988), *rev'd on other grounds,* 875 F.2d 468 (5th Cir. 1989).

126 621 F. Supp. 244 (N.D. 1985).

discussions about her interracial relationship waived a privacy claim based on racial comments and threats by supervisory personnel. Privacy rights may also be waived by acquiescing to the challenged conduct. In *Cummings v. Walsh Construction*,[127] the court held that a plaintiff waived her right to privacy when she yielded to her supervisor's sexual advances.

A plaintiff may recover general and special damages for the tort of intrusion.[128]

Public Disclosure of Private Facts

Generally, there are four elements to a claim of unauthorized disclosure of private facts:

1. The defendant publicized a private matter about the plaintiff
2. The publicity would be highly offensive to a reasonable person
3. The disclosed matter was not of legitimate concern to the public
4. The plaintiff suffered injury from the publicity.[129]

A plaintiff may negate the effect of a challenged publication by communicating the events herself to third persons.[130]

False Light Publicity

A plaintiff may recover for publicity that places her in a false light in the public eye. Publicity requires "communicati[on] to the public at large, or to so many persons that the matter must be regarded as substantially certain to become one of public knowledge."[131] The false light must be objectionable to a reasonable person, but need not be defamatory. For example, in *Tomson v. Stephan*,[132] a federal district court held that a female employee could seek damages for the tort of false light publicity for injuries arising from her employer's failure to keep the terms of a sexual harassment settlement confidential by discussing it at a news conference and declaring the lawsuit "without merit" and "totally unfounded."

---

127 561 F. Supp. 872 (S.D. Ga. 1983).

128 Phillips v. Smalley Maintenance Servs. Corp., 435 So. 2d 705 (Ala. 1983).

129 Restatement (Second) of Torts § 652D (1977).

130 Cummings v. Walsh Constr. Co., 561 F. Supp. 872, 885 (S.D. Ga. 1983).

131 Restatement (Second) of Torts § 652D comment a (1977).

132 696 F. Supp. 1407 (D. Kan. 1988).

§ 9.11 False Imprisonment

The tort of false imprisonment involves an act by a person who intends to confine another person "within the boundaries fixed by the act" that results in a confinement of which the confined person is aware. Acts of sexual harassment often include conduct that falls within the parameters of this tort. A cause of action for false imprisonment may be stated when a person restrains another's freedom of movement, such as when a supervisor calls an employee into an office and subsequently blocks the entrance or locks the door. In *Priest v. Rotary,*[133] a restaurant owner was guilty of false imprisonment when he picked up a waitress and carried her across the room and later trapped her while he fondled her. Employees who have been forced to remain in supervisors' hotel rooms while on business also may claim false imprisonment. Physical force is not necessary as long as the plaintiff demonstrates unwelcome restraint. Despite the physical nature of the tort, the injury is in large part a mental one, and a successful plaintiff may recover damages for injuries including mental suffering and humiliation.[134]

§ 9.12 Loss of Consortium by Partner of Victim

A person whose spouse has brought a common law claim for damages stemming from sexual harassment may bring an accompanying claim for loss of consortium.[135] In several reported opinions, courts have heard loss of consortium claims from husbands whose wives became nervous, depressed, and withdrawn, and suffered physical symptoms as a result of sexual harassment at work.[136] Although an injury need not be physically disabling to form the basis of a loss of consortium claim,[137] plaintiffs in the reported opinions either suffered physical injuries that gave rise to assault and battery charges[138] or physical symptoms of emotional stress, such as

---

133 634 F. Supp. 571 (N.D. Cal 1986).

134 Prosser & Keeton on the Law of Torts § 11 at 48 (W. Keeton, 5th ed. 1984).

135 Despite this doctrine's unpalatable origin, which involved the protection of a man's right to his wife's sexual services, it has properly evolved to remedy harms to the partnership of marriage.

136 *See, e.g.,* Missouri: Pryor v. United States Gypsum Co., 47 Fair Empl. Prac. Cas. (BNA) 159 (W.D. Mo. 1984).

Pennsylvania: Bowersox v. P.H. Glatfelter Co., 677 F. Supp. 307 (M.D. Pa. 1988).

West Virginia: State ex rel. Tinsman v. Hott, 188 W.Va. 349, 424 S.E.2d 584 (Sup. Ct. App. 1992) (per curiam) (husband brought loss of consortium claim).

137 Bowersox v. P.H. Glatfelter Co., 677 F. Supp. 307 (M.D. Pa. 1988).

138 Pryor v. United States Gypsum Co., 47 Fair Empl. Prac. Cas. (BNA) 159 (W.D. Mo. 1984).

headaches and nausea.[139] In *Bowersox v. P.H. Glatfelter Co.,*[140] the court noted that the manifestations of sexual harassment, including depression, severe emotional distress, headaches, and nausea clearly may result in the deprivation of society and companionship.

Damages for loss of consortium also have been awarded under state antidiscrimination laws.[141]

Appendix A contains a sexual harassment complaint alleging, among other things, loss of consortium.

§ 9.13 Wrongful Discharge

Historically, courts generally considered employment contracts to be "at will" unless otherwise specified, making them terminable with or without cause by either party at any time. Over the years, however, construction of this doctrine has narrowed, and employees have enjoyed an increasing number of implied rights notwithstanding the absence of a formal contract.[142] In a wrongful discharge action, a victim of sex discrimination may argue that she has an implied right to be free from conduct that violates public policy, or that the employer has an implied good faith duty to refrain from acting in a malicious or arbitrary manner when discharging employees. In *Monge v. Beebe Rubber Co.,*[143] for example, the New Hampshire Supreme Court ruled in favor of a female employee who was given different duties and ultimately discharged when she refused to submit to her supervisor's sexual advances. The court noted that "a termination by the employer of a contract of employment at will which is motivated by bad faith or malice or based on retaliation is not in the best interest of the economic system or the public good and constitutes a breach of the employment contract."[144] In *Chamberlin,*[145] the district court of New Hampshire noted that the state supreme court had narrowed the scope of *Monge* somewhat by requiring the plaintiff in a wrongful discharge action to show that the defendant was motivated by bad faith, malice, or retaliation, and that he or she was discharged for performing an act that public policy would encourage or for refusing to do something that

---

139 Bowersox v. P.H. Glatfelter Co., 677 F. Supp. 307 (M.D. Pa. 1988).

140 *Id.*

141 *See* Eide v. Kelsey-Hayes Co., 154 Mich. App. 142, 397 N.W.2d 532 (1986), *modified on other grounds,* 431 Mich. 58, 427 N.W.2d 488 (1988).

142 Some states, including California, Georgia, Montana, and South Dakota, have codified the employment-at-will doctrine.

143 114 N.H. 130, 316 A.2d 549 (1974).

144 Monge v. Beebe Rugger Co., 316 A.2d at 551.

145 Chamberlin v. 101 Realty, 626 F. Supp. 865 (D.N.H. 1985).

public policy would condemn.[146] However, the court was satisfied that public policy would condemn the endurance of sexual harassment as a means of retaining employment.[147] Evidence that conduct violates Title VII or state antidiscrimination law supports a finding that the conduct was in contravention of an express public policy.[148]

A wrongful discharge action must stem from conduct by a party who has authority to participate in personnel actions against the plaintiff.[149]

In states recognizing a cause of action for wrongful discharge, such actions may sound in either tort or contract, depending on the jurisdiction. Actions brought under a public policy exception to the at-will rule usually are characterized as tort claims.

---

146 *Id.* at 867, *citing* Cloutier v. Great Atl. & Pac. Tea Co., 121 N.H. 915, 436 A.2d 1140 (1981). *Cf.* Crosier v. United Parcel Serv., Inc., 150 Cal. App. 3d 1132, 198 Cal. Rptr. 361 (1983) (discharged male employee failed to make a colorable claim that his employer did not act in good faith in discharging him because of his romantic relationship with a nonmanagement employee when the employer was legitimately concerned with possible claims of sexual harassment and claims of favoritism). *See also* Hallquist v. Max Fish Plumbing & Heating Co., 46 Fair Empl. Prac. Cas. (BNA) 1855 (D. Mass. 1987). *Contra* Kersul v. Skulls Angels, Inc., 130 Misc. 2d 345, 495 N.Y.S.2d 886 (Sup. Ct. 1985) (discharged at-will employee could not bring an action for wrongful discharge).

147 Chamberlin v. 101 Realty, Inc., 626 F. Supp. 865, 867 (D. N.H. 1985), *aff'd,* 915 F.2d 777 (1st Cir. 1990).

See also Dias v. Sky Chefs, 919 F.2d 1370 (9th Cir. 1990) (wrongful discharge). The jury properly found that plaintiff was wrongfully discharged in a sexual harassment action when evidence demonstrated that the alleged sexual harassment occurred and that plaintiff actively resisted it. "A jury could have concluded that her firing was caused by her actions involving this 'important public interest'". *Id.* at 1374. The Supreme Court *vacated,* 111 S. Ct. 2791 (1991) in light of Edmonson v. Leesville, 111 S. Ct. 2077 (1991), which held that a private litigant in a civil case may not use preemptory challenges to exclude jurors on the basis of race. *On remand,* 948 F.2d 532 (9th Cir. 1991) (court of appeals declined to decide whether jurors were improperly excluded on the basis of sex because the employer failed to make a proper and timely objection to the employee's use of preemptory challenges to strike males from jury venire); *cert. denied,* 112 S. Ct. 1294 (1992).

Hallquist v. Max Fish Plumbing & Heating Co., 46 Fair Empl. Prac. Cas. (BNA) 1855 (D. Mass. 1987). *Cf.* Scott v. Sears, Roebuck & Co., 605 F. Supp. 1047 (N.D. Ill. 1985), *aff'd,* 798 F.2d 210 (7th Cir. 1986) (an at-will employee could not claim that her termination violated an implied covenant of good faith and fair dealing pursuant to state law).

148 Hallquist v. Max Fish Plumbing & Heating Co., 46 Fair Empl. Prac. Cas. (BNA) 1855 (D. Mass. 1987).

149 Hogan v. Forsyth Country Club Co., 79 N.C. App. 483, 340 S.E.2d 116 (Ct. App. 1986) (sexual harassment charge against coworker could not give rise to wrongful discharge action against employer).

Carlson v. Crater Lake Lumber Co., 103 Or. App. 190, 796 P.2d 1216 (1990) *on reconsideration,* 105 Or. App. 314, 804 P.2d 511 (1991) (summary judgment on

A wrongful discharge claim may not be viable in states whose courts have held that the state employment discrimination statute is the exclusive remedy for those claims predicated on the policies or provisions of the state law.[150]

§ 9.14 Negligent Hiring, Retention, and Supervision

Several recent sexual harassment cases have asserted, among others, claims of negligent hiring, retention, and/or supervision.[151] To find negligent hiring or retention, the court generally must find that the employer knew or should have known of the employee's offensive conduct.[152] In *Geise v. Phoenix Company of Chicago, Inc.,*[153] the district court improperly dismissed the plaintiff's claims for the negligent hiring and retention of a manager who was sexually harassing her by attempting to kiss and touch her body, placing his hands on her body, and putting objects down the front of her dress. The court recognized a duty on the part of the employer to make a prehiring inquiry into an applicant's history of workplace harassment:

---

employee's claim for wrongful discharge for resistance to sexual harassment was precluded by questions of fact regarding whether the supervisor slapped the employee and harassed her after she told him never to touch her again, and whether he urged the mill manager to deny the bonus on the supervisor's advice).

150 Hawaii: Lapinad v. Pacific Oldsmobile-GMC, Inc., 679 F. Supp. 991 (D. Haw. 1988); Lui v. Intercontinental Hotels Corp., 634 F. Supp. 684 (D. Haw. 1986).

Illinois: Clay v. Quartet Mfg. Co., 644 F. Supp. 56 (N.D. Ill. 1986); Horbaczewsky v. Spider Staging Sales Co., 621 F. Supp. 749 (N.D. Ill. 1985).

Pennsylvania: Aquino v. Sommer Maid Creamery, Inc., 657 F. Supp. 208 (E.D. Pa. 1987); Wolk v. Saks Fifth Ave., Inc., 728 F.2d 221 (3d Cir. 1984).

Wisconsin: Zywicki v. Versa Technology, 31 Fair Empl. Prac. Cas. (BNA) 1348 (E.D. Wis. 1983).

Cf. Hallquist v. Max Fish Plumbing & Heating Co., 46 Fair Empl. Prac. Cas. (BNA) 1855 (D. Mass. 1987) (evidence of sexual harassment that established a Title VII violation proved that defendant's action was in contravention of express public policy, and thus was sufficient to warrant judgment in favor of plaintiff on wrongful termination claim).

151 Fourth Circuit: Paroline v. Unisys Corp., 879 F.2d 100 (4th Cir. 1989) (remanded for determination as to whether plaintiff had a cause of action under Virginia law); Harrison v. Edison Bros. Apparel Stores, 724 F. Supp. 1185 (M.D.N.C. 1989); Byrd v. Richardson Greenshields Sec., Inc., 552 So. 2d 1099 (Fla. 1989).

152 Phillips v. J.P. Stevens, 61 Fair Empl. Prac. Cas. (BNA) 1568 (M.D.N.C. 1993) (female employee alleging that she was sexually harassed by several supervisors did not state a claim of negligent hiring under North Carolina law when she did not allege that her employer knew or had reason to know that it hired managers who possessed any tortious propensities).

153 615 N.E.2d 1179 (Ill. App. Ct. 1993).

The declaration of a duty in a negligence case reflects the foreseeability of the harm, but emphasizes considerations of public policy and social requirements related to the magnitude of the burden of guarding against the harm and the consequences of placing that burden on the defendant; the determination of whether there exists a duty is inevitably the product of policy considerations related to which plaintiffs should be afforded protection by the tort law. . . . Furthermore, an analysis of whether a duty exists is specific to the historical circumstances when it is made; duty is not a static concept, but one that changes with societal changes—a reflection of the needs, wishes, and tolerances of society as determined by the court facing a current duty issue. . . .

* * *

Given the serious harm that sexual harassment has been legislatively deemed to constitute, the foreseeable hazard of that harm's occurring upon hiring a new manager of a staff comprised primarily of persons not of the manager's gender, the plaintiff's allegation that the employer could have but failed to learn through investigation that the manager had a predisposition to female co-workers, and the plaintiff's allegation of her proximate injuries from the employer's failure to act, we find that the plaintiff adequately pleaded a cause of action in tort. . .

Our judgment falls short of a declaration of a specific duty to investigate and fully learn potential management employees' sexual harassment history and, thus, it is short of the duty declared by the plaintiff. Rather, our conclusion is merely that the plaintiff's pleadings support her cause of action, considering the Illinois' courts' long-held view that an employer has a duty to exercise ordinary and reasonable case in the employment and selection of careful and skillful co-employees . . . and to discharge that duty with care commensurate with the perils and hazards likely to be encountered in the employee's performance of [her or] his job. . . .

With reference to the serious concern now afforded to the issue of sexual harassment in the workplace, we find that the plaintiff sufficiently pleaded a cause of action based on whether the company negligently breached its duty of diligent and cautious hiring in consideration of co-workers. . . . In our judgment, that duty can comprise a need to make the sort of investigation urged by the plaintiff here, and even with that inclusion, it imposes no inappropriate administrative or economic burden for employers. . . . We also find that in being sufficiently broad to address the harm of sexual harassment, that duty serves a prophylactic role in the interest of today's ethical or moral thinking and in the general interest of justice. . . .[154]

The court rejected the defendant's contention that such a duty could not be recognized because no precisely analogous duty had been recognized in Illinois:

[154] *Id.* at 1183–84, 1185.

> It is clear that the concept of duty is an ever-evolving one. . . . Furthermore, in our mere recognition that an employer can violate its duty of nonnegligent hiring by a failure to make a "reasonable examination" of management candidates' history of sexual harassment, we do not, contrary to the company's assertion, begin a slippery slope of judicial involvement in the quality and breath of the investigation requirement; courts have long relied on the feasibility of a rule of "reasonableness."[155]

With respect to the negligent retention claim, the plaintiff properly stated a claim when she alleged that she suffered proximate injury after she repeatedly informed the company of the manager's sexually harassing conduct towards her and that the company took no action. The court did not find that the plaintiff's complaint was rendered insufficient by her acknowledgment that the manager's sexual harassment ended after the company verified her complaints; the complaint alleged that before the harassing conduct ended, she complained of it to the company and that despite her claim that the company knew or should have known of the conduct, the company took no responsive action. "The plaintiff has, thus, alleged claims based on the company's failure to act when on notice of its employee's sexual harassment of a co-worker."[156]

Some courts have held that the tort of negligent supervision or retention requires a showing of bodily injury.[157] In *Laughinghouse,*[158] the physical harm requirement for emotional distress damages in a negligent retention suit against the employer was satisfied by evidence that the employee suffered life-threatening hives, high blood pressure, angina, fatigue, depression, and posttraumatic stress disorder as a result of her supervisor's harassment.

An assumption of risk defense is not an appropriate response to a claim of negligent retention.[159]

Negligent hiring, supervisor, or retention claims may be barred by the exclusivity provisions of state workers' compensation laws.[160] In *Byrd v. Richardson-Greenshields Securities,*[161] however, the Florida Supreme

---

155 *Id.* at 1185–86.

156 *Id.* at 1186.

157 Spencer v. General Elec. Co., 894 F.2d 651 (4th Cir. 1990).

See also Perkins v. Spivey, 911 F.2d 22 (8th Cir 1990), *cert denied,* 499 U.S. 920 (1991).

158 Laughinghouse v. Risser, 786 F. Supp. 920 (D. Kan. 1992).

159 Perkins v. Spivey, 911 F.2d 22 (8th Cir. 1990).

160 Brooms v. Regal Tube Co., 881 F.2d 412 (7th Cir. 1989); Fields v. Cummins Employees Fed. Credit Union, 540 N.E.2d 631 (Ind. Ct. App. 1989).

161 552 So. 2d 1099 (Fla. 1989).

Court held that workers' compensation laws were never intended to address acts of sexual harassment, and thus declined to apply the exclusivity provisions to claims of negligent hiring and retention, noting that state and federal policies are strongly committed to eliminating sex discrimination in employment.[162]

§ 9.15 The Common Law Tort of Sexual Harassment

In *Kerans v. Porter Paint Co.,*[163] the Ohio Supreme Court created a common law tort remedy for sexual harassment, holding that workplace sexual harassment could be a tort in and of itself for which the victim could file suit not only against the offending employee, but also against the employer. To hold the employer liable, the victim must demonstrate that the offending employee had a past of sexually harassing behavior and the employer knew or should have known about it.[164] In *Kerans,* a store employee was molested by a supervisor five separate times in one day; the manager touched her breasts without her consent, put his hand up her dress and rubbed her buttocks without her consent, forced her to touch his penis, exposed himself to her, appeared naked before her and asked her to watch him masturbate, and asked her repeatedly if his penis was as large as her husband's. The plaintiff suffered severe emotional injury as a result of this conduct, including nightmares, flashbacks, and stomach cramps, and was in psychiatric care for at least a couple of years. No immediate action was taken when she finally complained even though the alleged harasser had engaged in similar conduct on at least eight other occasions with five other female employees, and the employer knew or should have known about these incidents.[165] The company responded to other complaints with a "boys will be boys" attitude.[166]

The state Supreme Court concluded that at least a genuine issue of fact existed for a jury as to whether employer respondeat superior liability could be imposed in this case when the employer had put the alleged harasser in a supervisory position where he could exert control over the victim and cause her to believe that she would have to endure the harassment to keep her position. The court went on to find that liability could be

---

162 *See also* Hogan v. Forsyth Country Club Co., 79 N.C. App. 483, 340 S.E.2d 116, 124 (Ct. App. 1986) (plaintiff's negligent retention claim not barred by state workers' compensation law).

163 575 N.E.2d 428 (Ohio 1991).

164 *Id.* at 434–35.

165 *Id.* at 434.

166 *Id.*

imposed on an employer for sexual harassment under the Restatement (Second) of Torts section 317 that provides that an employer can be liable for failing to take appropriate action against an offending employee when the employer knows or has reason to know that the alleged harasser poses an unreasonable risk of harm to other employees.